SHEVCHENKO AND THE CRITICS 1861-1980

Taras Shevchenko, self-portrait, oil, 1840-1

Edited by George S.N. Luckyj

Translations by Dolly Ferguson and Sophia Yurkevich

Introduction by Bohdan Rubchak

Shevchenko and the Critics 1861-1980

Published in association with
the Canadian Institute of Ukrainian Studies
by University of Toronto Press
Toronto   Buffalo   London

© University of Toronto Press 1980
Toronto Buffalo London
Printed in Canada
ISBN 0-8020-2346-0 cloth
0-8020-6377-2 paper

Canadian Cataloguing in Publication Data

Main entry under title:
Shevchenko and the critics 1861-1980

Includes index.
ISBN 0-8020-2346-0 bd. ISBN 0-8020-6377-2 pa.

1. Shevchenko, Taras Hryhorovych, 1814–1861 –
Criticism and interpretation – Addresses, essays,
lectures. I. Luckyj, George, 1919– II. Canadian
Institute of Ukrainian Studies.

PG3948.S51S53   891.7′91′2   C80-094541-7

Contents

vii Contents

Editor's Note

Taras Shevchenko (1814-61), the greatest poet of Ukraine, has exercised an enormous influence upon the literary and intellectual life of his country, an influence which is still felt. It is sometimes argued, with some justification, that modern Ukraine as an identifiable society with a culture of its own owes its very existence to Shevchenko. He was the first to formulate its *raison d'être*. No wonder, therefore, that a critical appraisal of Shevchenko is of paramount importance for any understanding of Ukrainian intellectual history. Although the significance of Shevchenko's work has never been in doubt, its interpretation has varied a great deal. He has been acclaimed as a prophet of national liberation, a rebel in the cause of social justice, a peasant seeker for God's truth, an atheist, and many other things, so that often his significance as a poet has been lost in the ideological struggle about him. The confusion grew worse after 1930, when a particular political interpretation was foisted upon Shevchenko by Soviet scholars, opposed by both Ukrainian and non-Ukrainian critics in the West. The 'battle for Shevchenko' (to use an early Soviet title) is far from over. The 1976 Kiev edition of his works omits several of his anti-Russian poems.

Shevchenko's background was conditioned on the one hand by the tsarist cultural policy proclaimed in 1833 and based on 'orthodoxy, autocracy, nationality,' and, on the other, by the impact of Western European romanticism. The former tended, within the government-sponsored doctrine of 'official nationality,' to allow considerable scope for study of and interest in the language, customs, and history of the Ukrainians, who had lost their autonomous Cossack hetman state in 1764 and their famous Zaporozhian Sich, a Cossack fortress on the Dnieper, in 1775. Memories of Cossack

glory and also of the bloody peasant rebellion against the Poles in 1768
haunted Shevchenko as well as other contemporary poets and scholars. The
literary significance of romanticism, which came to Ukraine chiefly through
Russia and Poland, was far stronger. It legitimized the literary use of the
language spoken by the people and offered new and rich material for the
poetic imagination – folklore and native history. By turning to folk culture,
Ukrainian writers and intellectuals also became aware of the social conditions of the peasant-serfs, who were now considered by them as part of the
Ukrainian nation. Thus, literary and scholarly interests led to populist
sentiments and even to political programs, such as the one put forward in
1846-7 by the Brotherhood of Saints Cyril and Methodius, to which Shevchenko and many of his Kievan friends belonged. With the arrest of all the
Brotherhood members in the spring of 1847, a relatively liberal era in the
life of Russian Ukraine came to an end. Shevchenko, who was exiled to
serve as a private soldier in distant provinces, received the severest punishment. Born a serf, liberated at the age of twenty-four, he lost his freedom
once more and remained in exile for ten years. Pardoned in 1857, he lived
four more years and died, unmarried, in 1861. His life, though tragic, was
also very creative. His first publication, *Kobzar* (The Minstrel, 1840), was
well received, but his later poems from the 1843-5 period, and those written during and after exile, confirmed the greatness of his work when they
were published posthumously.

This volume aims at a selection of the most significant Shevchenko
criticism from the time of his death until the present. It therefore includes
both pre- and post-revolutionary criticism written by Ukrainians and non-
Ukrainians, those living in Ukraine and in other parts of the world. The
selection, naturally, cannot be representative of all the criticism; it remains
a *selection*. The reader is offered a wide spectrum of interpretations (Marxist – Richytsky; nationalist – Hrinchenko; socialist – Drahomanov). Some
vital aspects of Shevchenko's biography and activities have also been taken
into account (Miiakovsky on the Brotherhood of Sts Cyril and Methodius,
Swoboda on Shevchenko and Belinsky, Mohyliansky on Shevchenko and
Kulish, and Hudzii on Shevchenko and the Russian radicals). Much attention has been devoted to Shevchenko's poems, in the belief that any university study of literature must concentrate on the texts themselves (hence
there are detailed analyses of poems in the articles by Franko, Drai-
Khmara, Rylsky, Smal-Stotsky, and Shevelov). Two articles attempt to place

Shevchenko within the framework of romanticism (Fylypovych, Schneider), while four others view him through well-known critical approaches (Rubchak, Chyzhevsky, Pliushch, Luckyj). A not particularly scholarly but incisive approach to Shevchenko is represented by the work of Kulish, Ievshan, and Chukovsky. Articles on Shevchenko's language and his place in the history of Ukrainian language were omitted from the volume because of their rather specialized interest, which is difficult to treat adequately in English translation.

The main purpose of the volume is to provide a critical textbook primarily for university students. The scholarly apparatus has been retained, but trimmed in some articles, while explanatory notes have been added to others. Some articles have been abbreviated. There is some lack of uniformity in Ukrainian quotations from Shevchenko. Many articles were written before the definitive text of Shevchenko's works was established. It was decided to keep different versions as the authors of the articles knew them. Translations of all quotations have been provided. An overall view of the problems of modern Shevchenko scholarship has been provided in Professor Rubchak's extensive introduction. As in all selections, it has been impossible to satisfy every taste and predilection, but it is hoped that the volume will enhance appreciation of Shevchenko by viewing him and his work from many different perspectives.

Several people have assisted me in the preparation of this volume. Invaluable advice was given to me by professors Rubchak, Shevelov, I.L. Rudnytsky, and P. Odarchenko. Articles 2-19 and article 26 were translated by Dolly Ferguson and Sophia Yurkevich; the others were already available in English. My wife read and commented on the entire manuscript, while Jean Wilson was responsible for the final editing. The index was prepared by Mr Roman Senkus. I wish to thank all of them. A modified Library of Congress transliteration of Ukrainian and Russian has been used. The assistance provided for the publication of the volume by the Ontario Ministry of Culture and Recreation is gratefully acknowledged.

GSNL

SHEVCHENKO AND THE CRITICS 1861-1980

I

Introduction

BOHDAN RUBCHAK

In 1925 the émigré poet Evhen Malaniuk characterized the stature of Taras Shevchenko as follows:

Ne poet – bo tse do boliu malo,
Ne trybun – bo tse lysh rupor mas,
I vzhe mensh za vse – 'kobzar Taras,'
Vin, kym zainialos i zapalalo.

He is not a poet, for that is painfully insufficient; / He is not a tribune, for that means a megaphone of the masses; / And least of all is he 'minstrel Taras,' / He, who became the spark and the conflagration.

Malaniuk's stanza synthesizes many problems affecting Shevchenko criticism and scholarship; more important, it reflects the 'cult of Shevchenko' among Ukrainians, since criticism too frequently depends on and develops cult. Malaniuk discards the image of the poet as a bull horn – an image cultivated by various socialists and communists. He negates even more vehemently the 'ikon' of Shevchenko as 'minstrel Taras,' an image promoted by the populists and their supporters in the second half of the nineteenth century. Malaniuk considers Shevchenko's significance as a poet and even as a central figure in the history of Ukrainian literature 'painfully insufficient,' regarding him as a symbol of national awakening and of the ensuing struggle of Ukrainians for independence. Malaniuk embodies this sentiment in the 'spark and conflagration' image.

The contemporary Polish poet and literary historian Czesław Miłosz makes the following perceptive comment on the role of Polish romantic poets in shaping Polish national consciousness:

Though Shelley called the poet a lawgiver of humanity, few people in England, we may suspect, took that claim seriously. As a consequence of national misfortunes, the reading public in Poland gave literal acceptance to a similar claim on the part of their own poets. The poet was hailed as a charismatic leader, the incarnation of the collective strivings of the people; thus, his biography, not only his work, entered the legend.[1]

When we consider the tragic history of the Ukrainian people as compared to the far easier lot of the Poles, we realize why among Ukrainians such honouring of their national poet as supporter of the right to personal and national freedom increases a hundredfold. Apart from literature, Shevchenko figures in many major works on philosophy, intellectual and social history, ethnopsychology, and in thousands of journalistic items and political propaganda.

This is not the place to describe the 'cult' of Shevchenko among Ukrainians or to speculate on its interesting psychosociological reverberations. Probably every Ukrainian who speaks the language has committed at least some lines from *Kobzar* to memory (there are many who know all of it by heart); in every Ukrainian community throughout the world his birthday is celebrated by solemn assemblies that become, particularly for emigrants, ceremonies of re-dedication to the national cause; there is hardly another poet in world literature with more monuments to his honour (in every major city of Ukraine, in Moscow, Leningrad, Paris, Rome, Washington, Cleveland, Winnipeg, Toronto, Buenos Aires, two in the state of New York) or with more towns, streets, city squares, schools, and museums named after him. Doubtless all this is crucial for the maintenance of the high level of Ukrainian national consciousness: the poet's name has become not only a symbol of the national rebirth that took place in the nineteenth century but also the incarnation of the continuity of the Ukrainian cause. However, such fame, bordering as it does on religious adulation and bearing awesome responsibility for Shevchenko's heritage, tends to overshadow his being a poet by implying the 'painful insufficiency' of such an occupation.

The 'cult of Shevchenko' tends not only to diminish but to distort his art. Indeed, his posthumous roles as 'minstrel Taras' and as the rallying point for all sorts of revolutionaries have contributed frequently to a simplistic treatment of his best work. And since the poet's name has become synonymous with the national consciousness of his people, such distortions are by no means limited to more or less incidental well-intentioned educational or even ideological uses of his poems. Often the text of *Kobzar* has been flagrantly violated. Most such violations occur in Soviet editions of Shevchenko's works: for example, in the lines 'Za shcho skorodyly spysamy / moskovski rebra' (Why did we rake with our spears / the ribs of Muscovites), the adjective 'moskovski' is frequently changed to 'tatarski' (of the Tatars). During the Nazi occupation of Ukraine, the publishing of Shevchenko was predicated upon the soft-pedaling of his numerous unkind references to the Germans; and so, *nimota* (a pejorative word for Germans) had to be changed to *holota* (the rabble). Less frequently, such censorship has been imposed from within. As a result of clerical pressure, for instance, the line 'Ia ne znaiu Boha' (I do not know God) was changed in an 1870s popular edition of *Kobzar* to 'Ia vzhe znaiu Boha' (I already know God).

The most glaring distortions of Shevchenko's heritage have resulted from the tragic division of the Ukrainians into Soviet and western 'camps,' which Soviets characteristically call 'the struggle for Shevchenko.' Such a 'struggle' over the work of a man whose most cherished dream was to see a united and strong Ukrainian nation is both grotesque and profoundly sad; it is made sadder still by its historical inevitability. Although it began in the first years of the Soviet rule in Ukraine, since the early 1930s Soviet ideologues have been intensifying it by thoroughly 'remodeling' the poet. In their hands he has turned into a grateful house guest of Russian culture, a servile imitator of Russian poetry, and particularly a 'megaphone' for the political ideas of the 'revolutionary democrats' Chernyshevsky, Dobroliubov, and even the chauvinist Belinsky, who repeatedly attempted to undercut the poet's greatness. Needless to say, the mental acrobatics required for such a feat are spectacular indeed; they are more intricate than recent attempts to turn Dostoevsky into a 'revolutionary democrat,' since the question of Ukraine's independence obviously becomes central in Shevchenko's case. In their zeal to defend the poet's heritage, some critics from the Western camp have also been guilty of oversimplification and even distortion. It is, of course, Shevchenko's art that suffers most: *Kobzar* frequently ceases to be a living text and becomes an object of prejudiced commentary or fanciful political improvisation, palmed off as literary interpretation.

It is becoming increasingly difficult for the Ukrainian-born commentator to 'see Shevchenko whole': the various 'uses' of the poet's work, layer upon layer of misreading, and also the veneration in which the nation holds it, inhibit him not only intellectually but also emotionally. The freedom with which some early critics treated Shevchenko is enviable, since he has now become a gilded idol, discouraging easy familiarity. Although every line of his poetry is closer than ever to the Ukrainian mentality, the totality of his life and work recedes. An alarming symptom of this is that in our time it has become a national duty to revere Shevchenko: to my knowledge, only the controversial émigré critic Ihor Kostetsky dares to express reservations about his art. As I will show later, such dissenting opinions were by no means so rare in the past.

This volume, therefore, becomes particularly important, and not only for the obvious reason of promoting the significance of Shevchenko in the Western world. The individual selections afford the reader various aspects of Shevchenko criticism: the biographical, sociological, historical, comparative, archetypal, philological, formalist, thematic structural, and phenomenological. Responsible examples of the 'ideological' approach have not been ignored, and both sides of the 'struggle' are represented. Some articles, moreover, provide an imaginatively illuminated background for Shevchenko's person and *persona*. The chronological arrangement of the pieces by itself demonstrates the continuity of Shevchenko criticism from one decade to the next, together with the various triumphs and pitfalls of its career. What is perhaps most interesting in the editor's catholic selection are the metamorphoses Shevchenko's image has undergone in the Ukrainian consciousness from one generation to the next. And since Shevchenko is not only historically linked with the Ukrainian consciousness but becomes its externalized, embodied symbol, this volume may also be read as an informal history of the progress of modern Ukrainian consciousness itself, of which literature has always been a vital part.

The 'struggle for Shevchenko' seems to have begun during the poet's own lifetime, its main outlines occasionally emerging in the earliest reviews of his poetry. The difficulties reviewers experienced with the startling phenomenon of the first *Kobzar*, published in 1840, and the publication of *Hamaliia* and *Haidamaky*, appear to have stemmed from the dichotomy between the national and the social significance of his poetry: was Shevchenko a defender of the oppressed across national borders, or was he a champion of Ukrainian interests across the social strata of his nation? For Russian reviewers, *Kobzar* and the early poems often involved the question of the very existence of the Ukrainian language and the Ukrainian people as an ethnic entity. Even if some of them recognized the existence of Ukraine, they asked whether or not the 'peasant dialect' in which the poet wrote was suitable as a vehicle of literature. The ugly implication here was that it should never be allowed to become such a vehicle, since the political potential of any linguistic entity is incalculable. That implication became overt by 1876, when, largely as a result of Shevchenko's tremendous posthumous influence, Ukrainian culture became so threatening to the Empire that all public expressions of it had to be banned by imperial decree. Finally, even if Ukrainian were admitted to the status of a literary language, the next question was to what degree the nascent Ukrainian literature was dependent upon the Russian. There was no doubt about the answer in the minds of most Russian reviewers: in their chauvinistic blindness to Shevchenko's genius, even the friendliest among them thought that they paid him a high compliment by comparing him with the minor Russian 'folk poets' Koltsov and Nikitin.

The Russian attitude to the Ukrainian language and literature, catalysed by the appearance of Shevchenko's early work, cannot be charted according to political affiliation. The conservative journal *Maiak*, for instance, defended the maturity of the language as a vehicle for serious literature, while in this volume Viktor Swoboda reports on the proto-fascist stand of the radical Belinsky on that issue. The conservative journals *Biblioteka dlia chteniia* and *Syn otechestva* sneered at Shevchenko and the idea of Ukrainian literature, while Chernyshevsky, citing the example of Shevchenko, defended it and even went so far as to claim that it was now ready to wean itself from Russian tutelage. True, Chernyshevsky was writing in 1861, when Shevchenko's message became clearer than it had been in the 1840s and 1850s. Soviet critics attempt to convince us that at that time, had he been alive, Belinsky, too, would have supported the poet's legacy. This is doubtful, however: the clever Belinsky simply saw earlier than his cohorts that Shevchenko would be useless for any Russian revolutionary cause.

It was Shevchenko's Russian friend and translator, the poet Aleksei Pleshcheev, who was the first to recognize his true stature. In the following comment of 1860, Pleshcheev incidentally throws light on the Russian attitude toward Ukrainian culture of earlier decades:

The high degree of excellence of Shevchenko's poetical works serves as a plain negation of the opinion, prevalent in our literature ten or twenty years ago, that the Little Russian [Ukrainian] language is not capable of further development and that the Little Russian environment cannot yield themes for literary works. Notice how this language, which was then regarded as provincial, has fully developed under Shevchenko's pen and how the Little Russian poet, remaining a part of his people and accessible to the common folk, could nevertheless incorporate in his poetry elements of universal human concerns.[2]

We see in this quotation how the specific question of Shevchenko's *narodnist* still blinded the vision of the well-disposed Pleshcheev: as Hrinchenko and others were to insist towards the end of the century, it is quite doubtful that Shevchenko's greatest poems are so easily accessible to the common folk. But the image of 'minstrel Taras' already loomed large in Shevchenko's own lifetime. The history of that image, even in its origins, is extremely complex, since it was used by various groups for quite different purposes. Some unfriendly Russians, together with reactionary Ukrainians, insisted that Ukrainian literature, including that by Shevchenko, is too weak to transcend the geographical and spiritual borders of the 'Little Russian provinces' and therefore is fated, like the folk song or the proverb, to remain an instrument 'of household use.' Some Russian reactionaries simply laughed at Shevchenko's work as the babbling of a slightly demented peasant. Slavophile conservatives, on the other hand, did not look upon Shevchenko's *narodnist* as a drawback. Treating the poet like some 'primitive' or *fauve* artist, they saw him as an intuitive bard of the mystical Slavic ethos. The more extreme among them began to believe that he was something of a *iurodyvyi*, a 'holy fool,' whose 'folk poems' were inspired by the mystical energy of the Slavic spirit or even of the Slavic Christ.

Most westernizing radicals and liberals, such as Dobroliubov or Pypin, shared the view that Shevchenko was far from ready for Petersburg fame. What appealed to them in his work, however, was his passionate concern for social justice. Even when the friendly critic Chernyshevsky in passing compares Shevchenko to Pushkin and Mickiewicz, he does so only on the basis of the revolutionary fervour of their poetry. Some of the Russian radicals realized that the conservatives' minstrel Taras image deliberately diminishes Shevchenko's significance as a protestant against the throne; it was, therefore, in their political interest to demolish that image. This, of course, implied its neutralization as a symbol of Ukrainian patriotism. Thus the image of Shevchenko as a 'tribune' or 'megaphone of the masses' slowly took shape.

The prevalent attitude of Ukrainians towards Shevchenko, from the beginning, was unabashed adulation: after all, he miraculously concretized their most daring dreams of cultural, if not political, rebirth. It was the intellectuals Panteleimon Kulish and Mykola Kostomarov who initially shaped Shevchenko's image as a *Ukrainian* poet. Included in this volume is an excellent article by Mykhailo Mohyliansky, dealing with Kulish's difficult emotional attitude to the poet's person and heritage; Mohyliansky, Iefremov, and Miiakovsky, moreover, give us an interesting composite portrait of Kostomarov.

It was in the interest of early Ukrainian critics to preserve and cultivate the image of minstrel Taras. To begin with, Kulish, Kostomarov, and other Ukrainian intellectuals of the time were not eager to join the Russian radical movement. They saw their primary task as the 'education' of the Ukrainian masses and the raising of the national consciousness of illiterate serfs and the demoralized gentry, without which calls to revolution would be nothing but noise. Moreover, even the most innocent signs of a national movement within the Empire would have been stopped immediately by the tsarist police (note the fate of the fairly meek Brotherhood of Sts Cyril and Methodius, described by Miiakovsky). Finally, neither Kulish nor Kostomarov were revolutionaries by temperament or conviction: both Mohyliansky's and Miiakovsky's articles elucidate their political views. Hence the minstrel Taras image, together with its would-be accessibility and simplicity, had the double advantage of being good strategic camouflage and an excellent educational tool. It goes without saying that the Russian version of that image had to be drastically altered.

The 'peasant class,' of which some Russians regarded Shevchenko as the bard, was limited by Ukrainian critics to Ukrainian villagers: intimations of 'all-Russian' peasant messianism were gently pushed out. While thus defined horizontally, the 'peasant stratum' was expanded vertically both upwards and downwards. By 'upwards' I mean that all Ukrainian social strata were implicitly included in it: Ukraine was an agricultural country, the great majority of its people were tied, more or less directly, to the soil, and to be a man of the land was a matter of pride, rather than cause for embarrassment. Kulish made a point of putting the Ukrainian country gentry at the centre of Ukrainian culture, while Kostomarov claimed that urban culture and an 'intelligentsia' are foreign to the spirit of Ukraine. By 'downwards' I mean that the idea of 'folk culture' was implanted as it had never been before. Borrowing from the theories of nationality developed by the German romantics, Kulish and Kostomarov insisted that within the words of Ukrainian folk songs, folk tales, and other collective literature were the seeds of a noble, peace-loving, and idealistic national ethos, as opposed to its dark, gloomy, and basically immoral Russian counterpart. Kulish bluntly stated that contacts between Russian and Ukrainian culture were detrimental to the latter. Thus, the image of minstrel Taras acquired in its Ukrainian interpretation the stature of an incarnation of the Ukrainian spirit. Although Ukrainian critics of that time were still psychologically unprepared to confront Malaniuk's image of Shevchenko as 'the spark and the conflagration,' the subtle implications of such a possibility exist in their work.

Kulish and Kostomarov knew and respected Western art and thought. Hence in their view Shevchenko's minstrel Taras image did not preclude his participation in the highest activities of the human spirit, including Western culture. In purely romantic, proto-Hegelian terms Kulish claimed that the poet's genius reached the highest cultural plateaus common to all mankind through his unique and ineffable national soul, as interpreted by his unique personality. It is, indeed, possible to claim that Shevchenko himself 'transformed' Western romantic themes into Ukrainian 'peasant' terms (as Franko, Fylypovych, Schneider, and Pliushch show in this volume), in order to restore them to the common spiritual treasury of humanity. Kulish insisted that since Shevchenko had shown how Ukrainian literature was fed by folk poetry, which incarnates the Ukrainian spirit, and conveyed its energies into his own poetry, Ukrainian literature would henceforth have no need for foreign literary models: although Ukrainians would continue to read and respect Pushkin, Mickiewicz, Byron, and Schiller, they would find it unnecessary to imitate them. Even more important, Ukrainian literature would rid itself of its direct dependence upon the Russian, which had been more harmful than beneficial.

Kulish's seemingly anti-intellectual attack on bookish 'academism,' echoing Shevchenko's own 'Epistle,' implies criticism of Ukrainian intellectuals' slavish devotion to everything foreign, especially Russian, at the expense of their own national roots. Only in the villages and country estates, unsullied by imperialistic cultural influences, could one enjoy direct contact with the healthful national currents of energy that produced people 'noble in spirit, pure of heart, dignified, of high repute.' Kulish is not so just, however, when he inveighs against the Ukrainian literature of the baroque, which he despised for lacking the inspiration of the nation's collective genius, and for being expressed in antiquated, bookish language: he fails to see the tremendous influence of folk literature upon these works. Furthermore, Kulish's attack on Kotliarevsky for 'having made our simple life and wise customs seem like a refuse heap outside the door of the gentry' has been challenged by most twentieth-century literary historians. What Kulish and Shevchenko himself found lacking in the ironic Kotliarevsky is precisely that idealistic transmutation and elevation of folk material by individual genius which is so important for any romantic poet, particularly for a Ukrainian romantic poet. Moreover, Kotliarevsky seems even now a rather supercilious mocker of Ukrainian village ways.[3]

If Shevchenko did not yet symbolize the 'conflagration' of the Ukrainian spirit in the decades following his death, he certainly was its 'spark.' His life and work raised many Ukrainians' awareness of their place in their nation and their responsibilities towards it: the old-fashioned patronizing attitude towards Ukrainian culture among older Ukrainian writers like Kotliarevsky – writers who, as it were, experimented with the 'alternative possibilities' of Ukrainian – was no longer morally viable. Although the way towards the rebirth of Ukrainian consciousness had been indicated vaguely by the early romantics, Shevchenko's own radical choices forced many of his compatriots into crucial decisions about their own lives.

Russian reaction sharpened correspondingly. What a few years before had seemed to the government like a more or less interesting ethnic experiment now became something considerably more threatening, more difficult to understand and therefore to control. Thus, the question of the existence, let alone the efficacy, of Ukrainian as a language was taken out of the hands of contributors to the Russian 'thick journals' and was turned over to the police. In 1863 the Minister of the Interior, Piotr Valuev, assured the throne in a secret circular that the Ukrainian language had never existed, did not exist, and would never exist; in 1876 Tsar Alexander II himself signed a decree in which he pronounced the publishing of Ukrainian books a state crime (with the exception of some *belles-lettres*), the production of plays and concerts in Ukrainian, any form of instruction in the language, and related activities. Much Ukrainian intellectual life, as a consequence, shifted to Western Ukraine (then part of the Austro-Hungarian Empire) where the attitude towards 'ethnic groups' was much more civilized than in the Russian Empire, and also to various émigré centres in Western Europe. Writers who remained in Russian-occupied Ukrainian territories clandestinely sent their manuscripts beyond the western border, and printed books found their way, illegally, into Ukraine.

Encouraged by such harsh administrative measures, reactionary Russian intellectuals increased their vitriolic attacks on Shevchenko. Important people in the literary establishment such as Katkov and Miliukov denied any possible value of *Kobzar* or of Ukrainian literature in general. Hacks drew caricatures of the poet in their would-be novels, and someone called Veinberg even dared to besmirch his illness and death with malicious lies. The Russians were assisted in such smear campaigns by the assorted Sokovenkos, Khanenkos, and other 'Little Russian' servants of the Empire. The Russian poet and critic Apollon Grigoriev rather weakly defended Shevchenko's heritage, writing that at times his talent equalled and even surpassed that of Pushkin and Mickiewicz, but that in its totality his work belonged in the category of folk art, rather than with the great poetry in the 'European' sense. Shevchenko's sometime friend Nikolai Leskov admitted the poet's great talent but attacked his 'disloyal' anti-Russian sentiments. In the 1880s the literary historian Aleksandr Pypin, who earlier had doubted the importance of Ukrainian literature, defended Shevchenko, claiming that he combined the sentiments and the language of his people with the highest humanistic ideals. S. Shashkov unreservedly compared Shevchenko with great Russian poets like Pushkin and Lermontov, and towards the end of the century the scholar D. Ovsianiko-Kulikovsky compared some of Shevchenko's lyrical poetry with that of Goethe, Schiller, and Heine.

Immediately after Shevchenko's death, Ukrainians began to search for his unknown poems and for documents pertaining to his life, to assemble bibliographical data, to research names, dates, and events mentioned in his diary. Although by the beginning of the 1870s almost all of Shevchenko's manuscripts had been found, the first scholarly edition of *Kobzar*, edited by Viktor Domanytsky, was published as late as 1907. Only towards the end of the last century and the beginning of the twentieth were Ukrainian scholars ready to write serious scholarly studies on Shevchenko's work.

In the 1870s and the 1880s Ukrainians continued to do research, and to develop definitions of – or rather, approaches to – Shevchenko. His posthumous progress from a folk poet through a people's poet to a national poet and founder of a national literature was charted again and again, with increasing impact and on occasion, with increasing impatience and exaggeration. Sumtsov, for example, brilliantly demonstrated how Shevchenko's poetry incorporates foreign themes and motifs. Following the romantics, Sumtsov considered that capability an inner energy of *narodnist*, as differentiated from incidental 'outward' borrowings of themes, images, or rhythms from folk poetry. Iakovenko compared Shevchenko with Shakespeare on the basis that both embodied the spirit of their nations in every line that they wrote. In Ukrainian literature itself, the 1870s and 1880s were marked by countless imitations of Shevchenko's poetry; such imitations, in fact, became detrimental to the literary process of that time.

Parallel to such activities, as early as the 1870s new attitudes towards Shevchenko were taking shape. The literary scene then was under the spell of the political theorist Mykhailo Drahomanov; in the words of a contemporary critic, all threads of Ukrainian public life came together in his hand. Drahomanov, influenced by nineteenth-century French socialists, envisioned Ukraine as part of a community separated from the rest of the world only by ethnic and cultural differences; there were to be no borders and eventually no governments. Ukraine, like every other country, would be divided into self-sufficient and self-governing communities. An intellectual heir of the French Enlightenment, as his teachers had been, Drahomanov believed in the power of education to transform 'irrational' acts of violence and oppression into 'rational,' productive, planned activity. In his numerous articles on the mission of Ukrainian literature, he defined literature as the most eloquent instrument of 'scientific' education in the principles of liberty and equality. In its maturity, which Drahomanov put into the distant future, Ukrainian literature would be 'national in form and universal in content.' Deeply rooted in the language and culture of the people, it would 'reach with its uppermost boughs the sky of reason,' which for Drahomanov meant the highest ideals of social justice.

Drahomanov's friend Fedir Vovk, a noted ethnographer who wrote literary criticism under the pseudonym of Sirko, in 1878 sent a long article on Shevchenko to the journal *Hromada*, which Drahomanov was then editing in Geneva. Evidently Vovk attempted to interpret the poet according to Drahomanov's own formula, although a dangerous admixture of Marx, Drahomanov's formidable adversary, cannot be missed in his article. Vovk interpreted Shevchenko as an atheistic rationalist, an enemy of institutions such as marriage and government, a believer in a depoliticized Ukraine in close federation with neighbouring nations, and in economic matters a radical socialist. Finally, he believed *Kobzar* to be a clarion call to revolution. Drahomanov published Vovk's article but followed it with his own angry rebuttal, excerpts of which are in this volume. It is obvious, incidentally, that his controversy with Vovk covertly challenges views from the diametrically opposite ideological camp, namely Kulish's opinions on Shevchenko.

Drahomanov's impatient attack not only on Shevchenko's 'cult' but on the poet's person and work has little intrinsic value for our time. Iurii Lavrynenko justly remarks: 'Sensible and interesting when condemning the cult, Drahomanov becomes a boring, pompous doctrinaire when he attempts to diminish the stature of the poet.'[4] Also, one cannot help agreeing with Pavlo Fylypovych's statement that only Drahomanov's claim that the poet is a product of his environment has some significance.[5] And Ivan Franko wrote as early as 1906 that all his life Drahomanov failed to see Shevchenko's value beyond the framework of serfdom and peasant freedom.[6] Drahomanov, who considers literature only as a vehicle for social philosophy or political indoctrination, simply does not imagine the indirect but nevertheless tremendous political impact of a genius like Shevchenko and, more important, the *modus operandi* of such an individual. This is obvious when, in the censorious tones of a schoolteacher, Drahomanov chastises the poet for not having read Saint-Simon. And when he writes about 'Son' (The Dream) – surely one of the greatest satirical poems in world literature – that 'it is even pitiful to witness the childish ineptitude with which the poet dealt with living people and scenes from real life,' we tend to pity Drahomanov's own childish ineptitude face-to-face with a work of art.

Yet the inclusion of the Drahomanov material in this volume is appropriate for several reasons. It points out some Ukrainians' readiness not only to promote an image of Shevchenko in direct opposition to that of minstrel Taras, as Vovk did, but also thoroughly negates this new image. This shows a degree of intellectual freedom far beyond the narrow-minded wholesale rejection of Shevchenko by the majority of Russian critics on the one hand, and on the other the strait-jacketed thinking about the poet in today's Soviet Ukraine. Drahomanov's excerpts, furthermore, suggest a desire on the part of Ukrainians to reconstruct their country as a modern and Western nation, in which the fetish of Shevchenko stands in the way of progress. The Drahomanov selection, in short, tells us more about the critic's own intellectual climate than about Shevchenko's work. It is interesting that in 1906 Kost Arabazhyn, a follower of Drahomanov and subsequently a Marxist, continued to argue that *Kobzar* is an ineffectual pointer 'to a true path leading onto the highway of progress towards freedom.'[7] Arabazhyn, however, hastened to emphasize that no poetry should be expected to perform such tasks. In the thirty years dividing Drahomanov's and Arabazhyn's articles, Ukrainian critics (even those dedicated to the sociological mode of literary interpretation) learned much, not only about Shevchenko's poetry but about the nature of literature.

Many lessons also had to be learned in regard to Shevchenko's frequent, and frequently self-contradictory, poetic interpretations of historical themes. His deeply concerned and yet disturbingly shifting attitudes towards the Zaporozhian cossacks, the mainland Hetmanate, and the revolts of the later haidamaks obviously bore directly upon the self-definition of the Ukrainian people. Notice in Kulish's articles, his interest in Shevchenko's historical views. As Mohyliansky shows, it is precisely that problem which kept Kulish changing his mind about Shevchenko's work. Notice also how disturbed Drahomanov was by Shevchenko's 'historiography.' In such impassioned comments is an intriguing trend, symptomatic both of Shevchenko's tremendous reputation and of the intellectual climate in which nineteenth-century critics worked: most of them took Shevchenko's views on history literally, as if the poet were engaged in scholarly research, instead of art. It was Volodymyr Antonovych, a talented historian and activist, who attempted to put Shevchenko's 'historiography' in perspective. His article in this volume is also important as an indirect refutation of Drahomanov's views on Shevchenko.

Antonovych begins with a careful summary of the romantic definition of the historical poem as a sub-genre, subsequently combining that definition with the minstrel Taras image. Following Antonovych's argument, it is not difficult to construct a model of Shevchenko's 'historiography' as a post-romantic critic would see it. The individual genius of the poet unconsciously intuits the deep strata of the collective national psyche, hidden from the scholar's lucid scrutiny. The poetic synthesis of disparate fragments from such strata in language is equally intuitive. In his metaphors, therefore, the poet embodies the essence or the idea of an epoch that is veiled from other modes of perception. Antonovych warns that in authentic poetry, factual accuracy must give way to such a synthesized or metaphorical image of the epoch: all aspects of that image will organically belong to it and therefore will seem mimetically 'right' or 'possible' as history. Hence, although a scholar has little trouble spotting many factual errors or instances of deliberate reshaping of historical material in Shevchenko's work, it would be superfluous pedantry to enumerate them, since Shevchenko's vision, in its metaphorical embodiment, is consistently faithful to the spirit of historical reality. Shevchenko's self-contradictions, furthermore, should be understood as instances of the dialectical movement within the total synthesis of the poet's specific vision of Ukraine, as intuited by his genius and as it restlessly grows with his own artistic development.

At their best, countless subsequent scholarly commentaries on Shevchenko's historical poems have either usefully elucidated historical sources, events, and people to which the poet alludes, or, following Antonovych, have interpreted such works primarily as artistic embodiments of historical themes. One of the best examples of the former procedure is the archaeologist Dmytro Iiavornytsky's seminal article on the Cossacks' and haidamaks' way of life compared to Shevchenko's treatment of them.[8] As to the interpretations of historical poems in terms of art, only in rare instances do critics avoid the various traps that history conceals for the literary interpreter. In the main, Shevchenko's historical poems, perhaps more than any other thematic group, have provided both Soviet and Western commentators with excuses for more or less clever ideological harangues.

The central star in the firmament of pre-revolutionary Shevchenko criticism is Ivan Franko. There is something symbolic in the fact that the second greatest poet in Ukrainian literature, and object of a cult of his own, became one of the most important interpreters of the greatest Ukrainian poet. On his tortuous road from early fascination with Drahomanov and Marx to a much profounder and broader humanism in his later years, Franko used Shevchenko as a guideline as well as a point of resistance. The latter term, incidentally, has some interesting implications, since there is occasional competition with 'father Taras' both in Franko's critical writings (we see this in the very fact of his almost obsessive interest in *Kobzar*) and in his own poetry: a study of 'misprision,' à la Harold Bloom, simply begs to be written on that subject.

In Franko's prodigious output are over sixty prose pieces on Shevchenko, in Ukrainian, Polish, German, English, and Russian. He also dedicated some poems to Shevchenko's memory, in which his emotional difficulties with the master are even more obvious than in the articles; moreover, numerous incidental references to Shevchenko are scattered throughout his gigantic *oeuvre*. In the critical and scholarly works are several thematic and methodological directions: meditations on Shevchenko's philosophy, discussions of his political and ideological significance, thematic interpretations, harsh comments on contemporary Shevchenko criticism and scholarship, formal analyses, close textual readings of single works, and a number of comparative studies. In the last group are articles on the relationship of *Kobzar* to mythology and folklore, classical literature, and Western European and Slavic (particularly Polish) romanticism.

Throughout his career, which was marked by ideological and philosophical shifts and adjustments and always conditioned by his highly tuned emotional nature, Franko seemed to have touched upon all four symbols of Shevchenko named by Malaniuk. In his early youth, under the influence of the cult, he committed most of *Kobzar* to memory. He began his career as a writer under the influence of Drahomanov and Marx, and consequently ignored Shevchenko altogether. In the early 1880s he addressed Shevchenko as the 'megaphone of the masses,' whose greatest value was in unmasking the Russian tyranny over the Ukrainian peasants. That attitude was soon replaced by the image of minstrel Taras, evident in several important studies on the influence on Shevchenko of Ukrainian folklore and mythology. As for political and ideological interpretations of Shevchenko's poetry in Franko's late criticism, he was the first to speak openly and courageously of Shevchenko's role as a 'spark and conflagration,' of the poet's decisive influence not only on the ethnic and cultural self-awareness of Ukrainians but on their struggle for unconditional political independence from all oppressors.

It is Shevchenko's fourth image, that of poet, that Franko developed most consistently. He certainly would not have agreed with Malaniuk that to call Shevchenko a poet is 'painfully insufficient.' To place *Kobzar* beside the great masterpieces of world literature, where it belongs, meant to see Ukraine itself 'in the circle of free nations': to prove Shevchenko's great worth as a poet in itself would support his image as spark and conflagration in Franko's thoroughly modern vision of the Ukrainian nation. In the essay included in this volume, although Franko mentions the importance of minstrels (kobzars) in Shevchenko's work, the image of minstrel Taras as such is undermined by his just opposition between the collective spirit of folk art and the romantic poet's powerful individuality. As could be expected, cultists of the minstrel Taras ikon immediately reacted in patriotic vituperation against Franko's 'internationalization' of the singer Perebendia.

In the first years of the twentieth century the two images of Shevchenko suggested in Franko's mature criticism, of spark and conflagration and of poet, were maintained by younger critics. The uncertain period in which Ukraine was defined merely as a cultural and ethnic entity was definitely over: poets, political thinkers, and civic leaders began to speak more openly of Ukraine's future as an independent state. Shevchenko's name, of course, symbolized such unreservedly nationalistic sentiments. Borys Hrinchenko's contribution to this collection is a rather mild example of that new revolutionary stance. This article, and his other critical pieces on Shevchenko, are in the tradition of Kulish, although that tradition is revised almost beyond recognition. Hrinchenko agreed with Kulish that Shevchenko was a national poet, rather than an advocate of a single social class. But he doubted Kulish's assertion that a peasant, unaided, could understand *Kobzar*: Shevchenko was a poet of the intelligentsia, since he wrote primarily for its members, attempting to convert them from being lackeys of foreigners to proud members of their own nation. Furthermore, Hrinchenko, like Franko, understood that Shevchenko's spark and conflagration image was based upon his greatness as a verbal artist. He therefore castigated patriots who limited their view of the poet to his political message. No wonder Hrinchenko's views on Shevchenko, like those of the mature Franko, had many opponents among Ukrainian activists. The article in this volume was attacked particularly vehemently by the younger and very talented short story writer Stepan Vasylchenko, who

resented Hrinchenko's reformed and modernized populist views and
defended Shevchenko's 'classical' image as minstrel Taras.

Concurrent with Ukrainians' heightened awareness of the significance of
their nation as a modern political entity, and the increasing importance of
the intelligentsia in that new ideological climate, there was at the very end
of the nineteenth and the first fifteen years of the twentieth centuries a
radical modernization of Ukrainian literature. Lesia Ukrainka, Mykhailo
Kotsiubynsky, Mykhailo Iatskiv, Vasyl Stefanyk, Marko Cheremshyna,
Olha Kobylianska, Hnat Khotkevych, and other talented representatives of
modern Ukrainian prose embodied themes from the life of the Ukrainian
intelligentsia and peasantry in a 'modernist,' sometimes experimental,
idiom, meant exclusively for the educated reader. Like Ukrainian writers of
any generation, they found it necessary to discuss the significance of
Shevchenko in Ukrainian literature as a whole and in their own work in
particular. Short pieces on Shevchenko by Kotsiubynsky, Stefanyk, and
Cheremshyna are particularly interesting in this respect.

In the second decade of the twentieth century, even more extreme
modernists appeared on the scene. Although their careers were short-lived,
they nevertheless left behind a modest but interesting body of work,
impressive in its earnest attempts to introduce into Ukrainian literature the
tradition of the anti-traditional. The groups Ukrainska Khata (The Ukrainian House), later Dzvin (The Bell), and the Futurists (who lasted until the
beginning of the 1930s and were destroyed in Stalin's purges) in Russian-
occupied Ukraine, and Moloda Muza (The Young Muse) in Western
Ukraine worshipped 'art for art's sake' and proclaimed the independence of
literature from social concerns. One can imagine how they were received
among civic-minded Ukrainian intellectuals, let alone the common reader:
it was the essentially modernist older writers Franko and Ukrainka who
became their most dangerous, because the most erudite, adversaries.

Those writers too found it unavoidable to take a stand on Shevchenko.
Mykyta Shapoval, leader of Ukrainska Khata and editor of the journal by
that name, who wrote under the pseudonym Sribliansky, simply negated
any influence by Shevchenko and other nineteenth-century Ukrainian
writers on modern times. A follower of Nietzsche, Shapoval claimed that
Shevchenko's poetry was too weak, too tear-stained, and too provincial to
announce the coming of the new Ukrainian personality, the new Ukrainian

political community, and the new Ukrainian culture. Shevchenko's 'ethnographism' had been standing in the way of a truly modern and virile literature long enough; it must be removed.

Similar ideas, but without Nietzsche or politics, were expressed by the leader of the futurists, Mykhailo Semenko. A bitter enemy of Ukrainska Khata and other pre-symbolist groups, Semenko could not understand why Shapoval should reject Shevchenko to begin with, since his poetry was as boring and inconsequential as that of Ukrainska Khata itself. Admitting that Shevchenko was innovative for his time (all of his modernist opponents conceded that), Semenko claimed that now his place was in academic reports and certainly not as a cult figure in twentieth-century Ukraine. In a sarcastic gesture, the futurist leader called his own collection of experimental poetry *Kobzar*.

Most 'modernists,' however, immediately accepted Shevchenko. For example, Sydir Tverdokhlib, member of Moloda Muza and one of the most experimental prose writers of his time, made accomplished Polish translations of his poetry. They even proclaimed him a precursor of their own revolution in art, just as the Poles interpreted Norwid, the Czechs Macha, the Germans Hölderlin, the French some of Hugo's poetry and later that of Isidore Ducasse, Allen Ginsberg, and William Blake. The futurist Geo Shkurupii even wrote a programmatic poem, welcoming Shevchenko into the ranks of his group.

Doubtless, such reconciliation with Shevchenko is the purpose of Mykola Ievshan's thoughtful article in this volume. His other purpose, surely, is to stem the irresponsible pronouncements by Shapoval and other modernists. Ievshan, whose real name was Mykola Fediushka, produced in his relatively short life an impressive body of criticism, some of it collected in his book with the ironic, politically provocative title *Pid praporom mystetstva* (Under the Flag of Art, 1910) and the rest scattered in many contemporary journals. Although Ievshan himself was a Western Ukrainian, he did not like the passive, melancholy, 'decadent' poses that members of the Western Ukrainian group Moloda Muza kept trying out: influenced by Nietzsche but also an active Christian, he preferred the doctrine of 'strong individuality' preached by Shapoval and other members of the group around the journal *Ukrainska Khata*. In his criticism, however, Ievshan did not particularly promote that ideology; his main concern was the examination of psychological motivations of writers, as reflected in literary forms.

The motives of the article reprinted here are delicately understated. It begins with praise of Kulish: his poetry is intellectual, tough, the work of a willed individual who clearly foresees the future of his nation. Needless to say, this is precisely how most Ukrainians would characterize Shevchenko's poetry. Ievshan, however, refuses to characterize him thus: as Drahomanov negated Shevchenko as a socialist and as Richytsky, some years later, negated him as a 'Red proletarian' – Ievshan here negates him as a voluntaristic superman. By this subtle manœuver, he indirectly attacks the cult of Shevchenko among Ukrainians that Kulish himself helped to found, and, almost by the way, dismisses Shevchenko's interpreters and detractors who followed the Drahomanov line.

Even more surprisingly, next step, Ievshan returns Shevchenko to his minstrel Taras image: how else are we to understand the statement that 'manipulation of aesthetic qualities ... constitutes the similarity between his poetry and the folk song.' Following the stress on intuition in the Western and Polish theories of literature around 1910, Ievshan takes this step in order to proclaim the primacy of the unconscious in Shevchenko, and to go on to describe him as an authentic genius. Having nothing to do with philosophy or even rational thought, where he is singularly helpless, Shevchenko is a true genius because, like the folk singer, he relies exclusively on the highest and lowest registers of human consciousness where language meets the ineffable. (Ievshan here seems to forget Franko's significant distinction between the collective consciousness of folk literature and the individuality of a romantic poet.) As a true poet in the modernist – specifically symbolist – tradition, Shevchenko is inspired exclusively by the present and therefore by the pure lyrical principle (in the fashion current at the beginning of the century, the epic mode was the genre of the past, the lyric of the present, and the dramatic of the future). The lyrical nature of Shevchenko's *œuvre* is supported by the fact that no matter how many themes the poet may tackle in his work, the only successful subjects are himself, his self-confessions, and his inexpressible yearning for the most distant horizons of his own existence. Ephemeral as emotion itself, his world view changes from one poem to the next; hence he cannot be trusted as an ideological leader. Having thus drawn dangerously near to Drahomanov's opinions of Shevchenko's poetry, but for diametrically opposite reasons, Ievshan does not even bother to state his conclusion, that we should save ideological interpretations for the work of uninspired but wilful

Salieris like Kulish, and read Shevchenko as a fierce artist who ultimately wrote not for the sake of content, but for the sake of pure expression or, in short, art.

Doubtless no serious reader of Shevchenko would agree wholly with Ievshan's conception of *Kobzar*. There is equally little doubt, however, that he ably characterizes a single strain of Shevchenko's genius – the lyrical strain – and that he thus adds an important trait to the composite portrait of the poet presented by this volume. The article is also important as a document of its time. It is, after all, an alternative to prevalent Shevchenko criticism and also an ingenious way of wrestling with the giant which, I believe, is a secret wish of quite a few Shevchenko critics.

In his study *Iz sekretiv poetychnoi tvorchosty* (Some Secrets of Poetic Creativity, 1898), devoted in the main to comments on Shevchenko's creative process and the formal aspects of his poetry, Franko makes some interesting observations on the role of the unconscious in the poet's work. Ievshan's contribution is obviously grounded in speculations on the activity of the unconscious in creativity. The most important, and, in fact, the only sustained study of Shevchenko's unconscious to date, written from a moderately Freudian but heavily Christianized point of view, is Stepan Balei's *Z psykhologii tvorchosti Shevchenka* (From the Psychology of Shevchenko's Work, 1916). Although on the whole somewhat superficial, it contains many valuable and exciting observations, particularly in confrontation with the monumental and hardly human effigy of Shevchenko on which most contemporary Ukrainians have been brought up. It is interesting that not the poet's person but the text is 'psychoanalysed,' and references to Shevchenko's biography are rarely made: rather, the 'blindness' of his reason is contrasted with the 'insight' of his psyche on the basis of comparisons of images and poetic statements from *Kobzar*.

Whereas Franko, Ievshan, and later Balei concentrate on Shevchenko's individual psyche, Kornei Chukovsky, an important Russian critic and talented translator of Shevchenko's poems, attempts in the selection included here something close to an investigation of 'archetypal remnants' in *Kobzar*. Chukovsky's article is a good example of serious thematic criticism: he takes a single motif – of abandonment – and discusses its development throughout the *oeuvre*. Using records of Shevchenko's early years to prove that the poet had no personal reasons to feel abandoned in glittering Petersburg, since he was 'a Petersburgian to the very marrow of his bones,' Chukovsky suggests that in his frequent metaphorical embodiments of the feeling of abandonment Shevchenko unconsciously reveals the age-old plight of his people: the feeling of abandonment on this earth in an absurd universe ruled by an indifferent God. Using parallels to folklore with a purpose directly opposite to that of Ievshan, Chukovsky claims that throughout *Kobzar* Shevchenko's own pressing interests are bracketed, and that he becomes a sensitive membrane artistically transmitting collective and unconscious images of the tragedy of his people, as ancient folk song transmits them.

Although abandonment becomes in Chukovsky's interpretation a profound, proto-Heideggerian philosophical problem, we nevertheless see here an intelligent and sensitive version of the Russians' grosser 'theories' from forty years earlier: Shevchenko, the 'Petersburgian to the marrow of his bones,' is in reality minstrel Taras, 'blindly' singing out the folk motifs of his people. The possibility that the recent serf might have been consciously tired of the 'sheepskin coat, not cut out for him,' of the supercilious patronizing attitudes of assorted 'liberals' in the salons of Petersburg, and that he might have been 'rationally' aware that the political plight of his nation parallelled his own 'abandonment' in the foreign and hostile city, is inadmissible in the world view of the hypercivilized companion of Bely and Blok.

Thus, at the end of the nineteenth century and at the beginning of the twentieth, prior to the two Ukrainian revolutions and the ensuing civil war, Shevchenko scholarship and criticism won many victories over the superficiality, vulgarity, and occasional bad faith found in earlier treatments of his work. Concurrently, however, the cult of Shevchenko became more firmly rooted both in Russian-occupied and Western Ukraine; it was now fed by the Ukrainians' growing awareness of the possibility of their independence from Russia, as that hope became increasingly viable with the rapid development of events in the second decade of the twentieth century. The spark of Shevchenko's word would finally ignite the conflagration for which the Ukrainian people had been waiting so long.

In the first few years of the Communist régime in central and eastern Ukrainian territories Shevchenko was proscribed, his portraits trampled, and copies of *Kobzar* burned. This, however, did not last long. The Soviets soon realized that they could not undo the poet's tremendous influence among the people. Consequently, Shevchenko as the megaphone of the masses, a Soviet partisan and John the Baptist of the revolution, became for a time the only ikon allowed in the land. The new religious cult of 'the Red Shevchenko' spread alarmingly. 'The Red Christ' was the title of one article on the poet, another author referred to him as 'the Evangelist of equality,' while 'the apostle of day labourers and hired hands' and 'the proletarian poet' became standard appellations. Along with such unabashed 'proletarization' (or what later Soviet critics called 'modernization') of Shevchenko, all traces of his image as a prophet of national independence, so popular in Ukraine only a few years before, had to be rapidly erased. Since hundreds of thousands of Ukrainians, both in Western Ukraine and in the massive political emigration of 1919-21, now adhered to that version of the cult more tenaciously than ever, and since military courts and firing squads could not resolve the 'ideological errors' of those people living beyond Soviet borders, the battle against Shevchenko as a 'nationalist' had to be continued relentlessly from one decade to the next. Thus the destructive 'struggle for Shevchenko,' which is now as strong as ever, was born and grew.

Andrii Richytsky (whose real name was Anatol Pisotsky) wrote his book, from which a chapter is translated in this volume, in order to counter the 'Red cult' of Shevchenko. The nature of his motives, therefore, is similar to Drahomanov's, although the circumstances in which the two authors wrote were obviously different. Richytsky's political credentials were impeccable: he was an Old Guard revolutionary, one of the founders of the original Ukrainian Communist Party, and a well-known journalist and activist. They did not, however, save him from eventual execution by a firing squad in the 1934 purges, mostly as a result of his book on Shevchenko.

Richytsky starts from the premise – compromised, as we have seen, as early as the 1870s – that Shevchenko was a peasant poet. Relying on Lenin's distrust of the peasants as a reactionary force, the author claims that Shevchenko's work contains not only non-proletarian but anti-proletarian elements: the cult of the patriarchal family, whose insularity extends to the cult of the nation; animistic and anthropomorphic religiosity in which God is identified not only with nature but with the land-owner, thus existing as a powerful patriarchal entity; fetishism of the land and the stability that it implies; fear and distrust of foreigners, represented by the industrialized Germans. To be sure, Shevchenko occasionally managed to transcend such unproductive limitations of his 'peasant philosophy,' but he could never abandon its premises. Richytsky, therefore, allows that Shevchenko might have been a 'pre-proletarian poet' but never a proletarian one.

Richytsky's book was immediately dissected by serious scholars. One of the first was Pavlo Fylypovych, who pointed out that even as 'vulgar sociologism' the work is wrong-headed, since it concentrates on the poet's social origin without accounting for his social environment. Surely a man who spent most of his life among artists, writers, and intellectuals did not think and behave like a backwoods *muzhyk*. Oleksander Doroshkevych, a serious practitioner of the sociological method, accused Richytsky of taking as his model the old minstrel Taras ikon. Somewhat later, the powers that be officially labeled the book apocryphal and heretical, and its author as a traitor to the state, a counter-revolutionary, and a spy.

Richytsky's interpretation, obviously, does not tell us much about Shevchenko. As in the case of Drahomanov, however, it does suggest a great deal about its own period and intellectual environment. In it is the naïve but enthusiastic Marxism of early Soviet Ukraine, when issues around Shevchenko's poetry, together with other problems of Ukrainian culture, were still alive and open to debate. Indeed, the years 1923-31 were extraordinarily productive and exciting in Soviet-Ukrainian culture; there was a great deal of activity in scholarship, literature, painting, theatre, and film. Many intellectuals believed that Lenin's promises regarding the status of 'nationalities' within the Soviet Union had been sincere, and that history was offering Ukrainians the opportunity to build a truly modern communist society and culture, oriented not towards the East but towards the West. Shevchenko scholarship did not lag, an astonishing amount of good work was done in that short period, most of it now either lost or locked up in 'special collections' of Soviet libraries, unavailable for impartial examination and interpretation.

An interesting and characteristic phenomenon of early Soviet literary criticism and scholarship, including that dealing with Shevchenko, was the ongoing debate between the 'sociologists' and the 'formalists.' In the end, of course, both sides lost, and most combatants ended up either dead or in Siberia. But the enthusiasm of polemical forays in that debate yielded an impressive and alive intellectual legacy. True, the journalistic or, more accurately, propagandistic branch of the sociological 'school' was quite distant from authentic criticism. Its proponents tirelessly 'struggled for Shevchenko': they battled both the pre-revolutionary cult of Shevchenko and his 'red cult,' 'exposed' 'bourgeois-nationalistic' strains in Shevchenko criticism abroad and within Soviet scholarship, castigated all academic scholars for wasting their own and their readers' time, which could be applied to more useful socialist production, and in the mid-1930s wrote denunciations against Shevchenko scholars from other 'camps' and finally against each other. Even such 'loyalty' did not save them in the Iezhov terror of 1937.

There was one refreshing aspect of their activities – their seemingly unquestionable patriotism. Volodymyr Koriak, for example, took the formalists to task for their 'all-Russian' tendencies in that they followed in the footsteps of their Russian colleagues (the ties between Ukrainian and Russian formalists were indeed close: some members of the Russian group, like Balukhaty, were Ukrainians, Shklovsky wrote a short study of Shevchenko's prose, and Eikhenbaum published his now celebrated definition of formalism in a Ukrainian journal). When Vasyl Desniak accused certain 'academics' of advancing Kulish at Shevchenko's expense – probably meaning a collection of essays that included the material by Mohyliansky in this volume and an important essay on Kulish by Mykola Zerov – he said nothing about Kulish's obvious anti-Russian stance but spoke only about his landed gentleman's lack of sympathy with socialism. What is striking in all this is that at that time it was still possible to compromise an adversary by accusing him of a pro-Russian bias. Imagine such a 'pejorative' argument in present-day Ukraine!

In 'academic' sociological Shevchenko criticism there was some serious activity, which was often directed against the 'vulgar sociologism' of the journalists. Its leader, Doroshkevych, was a capable scholar but by no means beyond occasional duplicity in political and ideological matters. Not limiting his investigations to thematic concerns, he called for 'sociological' analyses of Shevchenko's style. His colleagues heeded his call. Borys O. Navrotsky concentrated on the 'sociology' of Shevchenko's verse forms, while Borys B. Iakubsky, although 'officially' a 'sociologist' (it was safer to be known as a 'sociological critic' than as a 'formalist') was almost totally committed to the formal analysis of Shevchenko's poetry. Doroshkevych's, Navrotsky's, and particularly Iakubsky's 'sociological' analyses can be compared with the later Tynianov and younger Russian formalists like Propp, Bakhtin, and Balukhaty. It would be extremely useful to find, translate, and publish the most representative examples of such a 'formal-sociological' method as it was applied to Shevchenko.

Although the work on Shevchenko's 'sociology of style' is occasionally difficult to distinguish from formalism, not only journalists but also scholars took frequent swipes at the formalist method, possibly as a self-protective measure: in time, 'formalist' became merely a pejorative term, as it did in the 1930s in Russia. Nevertheless, there was a large group of scholars who devoted their careers to the investigation of purely formal aspects of Shevchenko's poetry by rigorous, frequently statistical methods: the poets Dmytro Zahul and Andrii Paniv, Rodzevych, Dudar, and Savchenko are a few more prominent names in that large group.

The fact that in the 1930s formalism ceased to mean anything is attested to by the 'vulgar sociologists'' use of it against Fylypovych. The author of a purely 'sociological' study on Shevchenko's audience and its potential influence on the poet's own work, but on the whole a student of Peretts's 'philological method,' Fylypovych was disliked by the 'literary establishment' from the start. His fine poetry, redolent of neo-symbolism or even neo-romanticism, was branded by another meaningless but emotionally loaded label – 'neo-classicist.' His elegant dignity and his demands for excellence in art and scholarship must have irritated the 'proletarians' beyond belief. No doubt his talent as poet and his prodigious scholarly output provoked much envy among influential colleagues. By 1936, when at the age of forty-four he was imprisoned in a Russian concentration camp, Fylypovych had published three book-length studies, over a hundred scholarly articles and reviews, and edited a number of collections in all periods of Ukrainian literature; approximately twenty titles in his bibliography are devoted to Shevchenko. (Fylypovych's full bibliography is impossible to assess in the West and his work is proscribed in the Soviet Union.)

Fylypovych makes a number of valuable discoveries in the article included here; I find his discussion of the composition of Shevchenko's longer poems particularly useful. Steeped in neo-classical poetics, early critics invariably saw the 'spatial' or 'prismatic' composition of Shevchenko's narrative poems as a drawback. Using the example of Byron, Fylypovych shows that Shevchenko's method of composition is in fact an intrinsic feature of romantic poetics. Armed with such studies of twentieth-century literature as Joseph Frank's 'Spatial Form in Modern Literature' or Albert Cook's *Prisms*, we are prepared to take Fylypovych's thesis even farther than he himself did: Shevchenko overtakes Byron, antedating the experimental composition of some twentieth-century modernist narrative poetry.[9]

In another insight, Fylypovych implies that models of the Byronic hero are recognizable in Shevchenko's Russian works, while in his Ukrainian poems the hero's metaphysical protest is channeled into action. One may go on to say that Shevchenko's alienated attitude towards his own Russian-language material and his consequent rather passive reliance on influences is opposed to the mastery in his Ukrainian poems and the ensuing active transformation of all foreign influences to conform to his unique poetic world. Grabowicz's article in this volume takes up the contrast between Shevchenko's Russian-language and Ukrainian-language works. Finally, developing Franko's thesis, Fylypovych makes the important point that Shevchenko's minstrel-Taras pose has less to do with his rural origin than with purely literary, romantic influences.

Serhii Iefremov and Mykhailo Mohyliansky belong to the older genera-tion of critics who made their reputation in pre-revolutionary literature. Mohyliansky's article in this volume is a fine piece of research, supplying a number of new details to the biographies of Shevchenko and Kulish, and discussing particularly well the latter's stormy and psychologically revealing attitudes towards Shevchenko's reputation after his death, in which Push-kin's Mozart-Salieri opposition of artistic types seemed to have been imitated by reality. Iefremov, an uncommonly prolific scholar and critic, is a direct heir of later, reformed Ukrainian populism, more particularly, of Hrinchenko's enlightened civic criticism. Iefremov seems to have had no emotional or intellectual ties with the Soviet revolution. Although he worked hard and published much (particularly on Shevchenko) under the Soviet régime, he treated his surroundings with the mild but by no means hidden disdain of an old liberal. It is small wonder that he was the first important intellectual to have fallen in the purges. Some details of Shev-chenko's biography that Iefremov reports are interesting but on the other hand, one misses in his impassioned 'retelling of events' and rather shallow psychological observations the counterbalance of formal or formal-psycho-logical analysis, which in the case of Shevchenko's letters could have yielded particularly revealing results. I am aware of no such study of the epistolary genre in Shevchenko: this seems to be another project awaiting the attention of future Shevchenko scholars.

Besides the scholars of that period mentioned above, I. Aizenshtok did valuable work in textual research, the noted historians D. Bahalii, M. Markovsky, I. Zhytetsky, V. Miiakovsky, and especially M. Novytsky researched Shevchenko's biography and his intellectual environment, P. Tykhovsky and L. Koshova wrote studies on the sources of Shevchenko's historical poems, M. Bohush and F. Samonenko attempted psychological studies of *Kobzar*, M. Iashek assembled a bibliography of Shevchenko's scholarship (1903-21), and there was much other scholarly activity. Hundreds of people were involved in Shevchenko scholarship, writing not only on Shevchenko's poetical output but also on his plays, prose, diary, letters, painting, drawing, and sculpture, on Shevchenko in the classroom, Shevchenko in the theatre, Shevchenko on film.

There was a department of Shevchenko studies at the Ukrainian Academy of Sciences: since it was considered too 'academic' and, more important, since it was headed by the 'nationalists' Mykhailo Hrushevsky and Iefremov, a special Institute for Shevchenko Studies was established in Kharkhiv. Later its even more 'sociological' and 'Marxist' branch was founded in Kiev. The Academy published variorum editions of Shevchenko's texts and biographical documents, while the Institute put out four book-length studies and collections of articles by single authors, four anthologies of articles by various hands, containing some of the most valuable shorter studies of the poet's work to date, and two volumes of the annual publication *Shevchenko*. A large number of shorter studies also appeared in various philological and literary journals, such as *Ukraina*, *Zhyttia i revoliutsiia*, and *Chervonyi shliakh*, and non-academic publishing houses put out three book-length studies on Shevchenko by D. Bahalii, O. Bahrii, and P. Fylypovych. In 1923 a plan of the first multi-volume academic edition of Shevchenko's works was prepared, and two volumes of it published. When we remember that the time span of this activity was less than a decade, and when we think about the first-rate quality of much of the work produced then, we must consider that period the zenith of the history of Shevchenko scholarship: attempts by contemporary Soviet scholars to play down that activity, to claim that not much was done and that whatever was accomplished is 'incorrect,' cannot help but provoke amusement.

It is plain that they cannot speak otherwise. The first steps in the liquidation of Ukrainian culture by the Russians, a holocaust that raged through the 1930s, were taken against scholars engaged in Shevchenko studies, for they were obviously working in the most sensitive area of Ukrainian culture. In view of Stalin's 'nationalities' program,' the Russian police simply had no choice; the least they could do was to liquidate honest Shevchenko scholarship, since attempting once again to 'liquidate' Shevchenko himself, to erase all traces of Ukrainians' memory of him, was patently impossible, as the experience of their tsarist forerunners had taught them. In the radical revamping and standardizing of Shevchenko's image, all present investigators of Shevchenko had to be destroyed. Simply put, control of Ukraine directly depended upon controlling Shevchenko's heritage and its influence upon the masses.

In the 1930s the Soviet régime progressively contained the 'chaos' of Ukrainian cultural life by the framework of party directives, in order to manage more easily its program of total 'Sovietization,' which in practice has meant total russification. Hence it substituted divergent interpretations of Shevchenko by early Soviet critics, from which a living, authentically *dialectical* portrait of the poet had been emerging, under a two-dimensional sign to be 'objectively' described, superficially 'corrected,' but never interpreted, illuminated, or thought about. After all, not only Shevchenko but Lenin himself was much safer in a mausoleum. Hence a new image of the poet was taking shape – an image that Malaniuk's stanza, written in 1925, could not predict – the image of Shevchenko as mannequin. That image has been obligatory in Shevchenko scholarship for the last forty-five years. It has been rather arbitrarily christened as that of a 'revolutionary democrat,' which is a blatant misuse of Lenin's term for the Russian radical journalists of the 1860s.

Shevchenko as mannequin was introduced not by scholars, nor even by hacks, but by the Department of Culture and Propaganda of the Communist Party of Ukraine, in a document known as *The Theses of 1934*. The catch-phrase 'revolutionary democrat' was supposed to cover the following official opinions: Shevchenko was a materialist; having shed the romantic delusions of romanticism in his youth, he soon became a 'critical realist'; his literary production depends directly on Russian literature, and he himself was forever grateful to the Russians for having taught him the art of poetry; he was a 'People's poet,' using folklore 'critically,' to discover and identify in it revolutionary moments; since he worked in unenlightened conditions, and therefore could not help making 'ideological errors,' such as his nationalism, his problematic religiosity, or his failure to work out a program against the bourgeois foundation of his society, those 'errors' were to be 'unmasked' and 'correctly illuminated.'

The countless 'misunderstandings' and 'counter-misunderstandings' in the 'finalizing' of Shevchenko's mannequin image cease to amuse the moment that we recall the number of lives that they cost: literary matters were grotesquely metamorphosed into horrible crimes, in principle no different from the Nazi holocaust, the only important difference being that the Germans have recognized the horrors of their deeds, while in 1980 Shevchenko scholars are still forced with cynical callousness to call the 1930s a 'period of ideological adjustment.'[10] It is symbolic in the history of Ukraine that the Shevchenko scholars shared a fate similar to his own. It is equally significant that a humanist poet's heritage was thus involved; one can imagine his own reaction to such murderous misuse of his poetry.

The first wave of purges took place in 1930, with the 'liquidation' of Serhii Iefremov and a number of other older intellectuals. Beginning with 1933, each year brought new repressions. Finally, in 1937, those who had hounded and denounced everyone else were themselves 'liquidated.' In the years 1917-37 (but mainly in the 1930s), 107 Ukrainian literary scholars and critics were either killed or exiled to Siberia. Eleven switched to the Russian language. Seventy-four dropped out of scholarship entirely. Twenty-five emigrated, mostly in the early 1920s. Altogether, 202 scholars and critics, most of them having worked either exclusively or partially on Shevchenko, were lost to Soviet Ukrainian scholarship. Only *fifteen* more or less notable scholars of Ukrainian literature, who had begun their careers before the purges, survived and sporadically continued their work until the beginning of World War II.[11]

It stands to reason that in the years 1935-9, Shevchenko scholarship, together with all other serious work in Ukrainian culture, came to a standstill. The few articles that did appear in those years dealt with Shevchenko's prose (written in Russian), with his painting, and with music composed to his poems. As for 'ideology,' a typical contribution of that time to Shevchenko scholarship was an address, 'Dvi zhinochykh doli' (Two Fates of Women), about the miserable life of serf women as described in *Kobzar*, in contrast to the glorious life of a female collective farm worker, and delivered at a scholarly conference by the collective farm worker Mariia Bondar.

The Party used the year 1939 (which marked the 125th anniversary of the poet's birth) for artificial resuscitaton of Shevchenko scholarship. This was necessary for several reasons: to show that the massacre of Ukrainian intellectuals was not a great loss; to support the mannequin image with permanent ideological scaffolding; and to prepare that mannequin for use as a rallying point in the impending war. The deluge of propagandistic material, in Russian and Ukrainian, 'firmly established' Shevchenko as a friend of the Russians; 'reinterpreted' Shevchenko's unkind references to the tsars as criticism of abstract autocracy, with absolutely no bearing on the tsars' nationality; criticized the party's *Theses of 1934* for dragging out Shevchenko's 'errors,' instead of concentrating on the 'positive' aspects of his work, especially his slavish submission to Chernyshevsky's ideas; and falsified facts in order to 'prove' that Belinsky was a great admirer of Shevchenko's poetry.

Nevertheless, some scholarly work was done in 1939 and 1940. Professional linguistic analyses of Shevchenko's style appeared, dealing with narrow factual topics. Some articles were published in the comparative literature branch of Shevchenko scholarship; most remarkable here is the synthetic essay by Oleksander Biletsky on Shevchenko and world literature and an article by Serhii Savchenko on the poet and romanticism; the latter author returned to Fylypovych's researches on Shevchenko and Byron, reviewed the problem of Shevchenko and English romanticism in general, and made some discoveries in Shevchenko's own reading of the romantic poets. Another interesting contribution in comparative literature was Chubach's study on Shevchenko and ancient literatures. Soviet scholars continued to investigate Shevchenko in conjunction with other Ukrainian writers: two fresh topics, namely Shevchenko and Skovoroda (by Popov) and Shevchenko and Franko (by Semenenko and Kobyletsky) opened new possibilities for research. In 1940 a collection of textual and critical studies by Aizenshtok, *Iak pratsiuvav Shevchenko* (How Shevchenko Worked) was published in Kiev.

No fewer than eight book-length biographical studies of Shevchenko appeared in 1939. It is in them that most of the distortions and falsifications of the poet's life, indispensable to the support of·his new image as mannequin, occur. On the other hand, in 1941 Marietta Shaginian, a novelist and scholar who works in the Russian language, published a series of excellent studies on Shevchenko's life and work under the title *Taras Shevchenko*. She openly used and even quoted ideas from the superlative biography of the poet by the émigré scholar Pavlo Zaitsev; she denied Pushkin's influence on Shevchenko's versification; and she showed convincingly that it was not Chernyshevsky who influenced Shevchenko but the other way around. Probably following Fylypovych, she also claimed that Shevchenko's Russian writings rather passively follow the literary current of his time, while his Ukrainian poems are far ahead of it. Besides her astonishing sense of intellectual freedom, Shaginian demonstrated a gift for solid and patient research: she discovered, in particular, new facts about the women in Shevchenko's life and about his existence in exile. It is characteristic that many of her 'errors' were corrected in the second edition of her work which came out in 1946.

During the war, and particularly during the German occupation of Ukraine, Shevchenko was allowed once again to become the megaphone of the masses in a very specific sense: he was recruited to spur the Ukrainians in the struggle against the Nazis. Authors of speeches and propagandistic articles were allowed to play up Shevchenko's devotion to the idea of Ukrainian autonomy, even at the expense of temporarily suspending the peddling of fabrications about his servile attitude towards Russian culture. Immediately after the war, however, Andrei Zhdanov was assigned to whip Soviet culture, including Shevchenko scholarship, back into the party line.

In the selection included here, Hudzii, an important Ukrainian scholar who worked both in Ukrainian and Russian literature, attempts to civilize, as it were, the post-war orgy of flunkeyism and self-abasement on the part of Ukrainian intellectuals. He does not claim, for example, that Herzen and Chernyshevsky taught Shevchenko all that he knew, as less sophisticated Soviet authors constantly do; instead, he hints at a 'mutual attraction' between Herzen and Shevchenko or at a 'similarity of views' between Chernyshevsky and the Ukrainian poet. What Hudzii neglects to point out, and what Shaginian stresses in the first edition of her book, is that although Chernyshevsky frequently mentioned Shevchenko with admiration, Shevchenko never referred to Chernyshevsky. Considering Shevchenko's views on life, it is indeed difficult to imagine the poet admiring Chernyshevsky's aesthetic theories or his novel *Chto delat* (*What is to be Done*).

Even when Hudzii suggests that revolutionary ideas may have arisen 'polygenetically' for the Russian radicals and for Shevchenko, he nevertheless hastens to add that the 'revolutionary democrats' helped Shevchenko to put his intuitive notions into proper perspective. Witness also Hudzii's completely unsubstantiated implication that in allying himself with the representatives of the Russian 'revolutionary-democratic' movement in Petersburg, Shevchenko simultaneously drew away from his liberal friends Kostomarov and Kulish . Hudzii plainly suggests that the one action depended directly upon the other, although we know that Shevchenko's occasional disagreements with Kulish and Kostomarov centred rather on the poet's impatience with his friends' excessive respect for the Russians and their views on the role of Russia in Ukrainian history.

As in the case of Drahomanov's and Richytsky's contributions, we should be grateful to the editor for including the piece by Hudzii more as an illustration of the time of its writing than of Shevchenko's time. It provides a fairly clear definition of the murky term 'revolutionary democrat'; it shows, by the author's gentle reservations and careful adjustments, the distance to which his more servile colleagues have been willing to take the term, and it is, on the whole, a telling example of more or less responsible mainstream Shevchenko criticism in post-war Soviet Ukraine.

The 1950s saw a rush of books on the 'world view' of Shevchenko. The main purpose of such 'studies' was once again to turn the poet, as one of them had it, into a 'stepchild of Russian culture.' In his careful description of Soviet scholarship on Shevchenko, the émigré critic Petro Odarchenko quotes a series of blatant falsifications of Shevchenko's diary, letters, and documents pertinent to his life, which were meant to 'prove' the poet's loyalty to Russia.[12] Even the Soviet scholar Oleksander Biletsky angrily spoke out against such distortions: 'The basic tendency of the majority of such works about Shevchenko's world view is to correct at any cost ... the poet's views in order to pull him up, by any means available, to our own times.'[13] Having quoted that passage, the authors of a Soviet report on contemporary Shevchenko scholarship interestingly remark: 'Although they were generally typical of ... the first [post-war] decade, such errors have not been totally eliminated in subsequent works on Shevchenko's world view.'[14]

It is characteristic that the first post-war decade of Shevchenko scholarship in Soviet Ukraine is currently criticized by Soviet commentators in almost the same way that 'vulgar sociologism' had been censured in the

1930s: Shevchenko's religiosity was treated too simplistically, his 'revolutionary democratism' was not thoroughly understood, the Ukrainian romantic movement as a whole was described one-sidedly, and Shevchenko was 'modernized,' made to conform too closely to the contemporary vision of Soviet communism. It is such anti-dialectical 'corrections' and 'adjustments' of the mannequin that characterize the ideological profile of Shevchenko scholarship in Soviet Ukraine from the end of the war to our days. They are anti-dialectical in that they stem from postulates outside Shevchenko's work – from an artificially posited structure, to which every mind must conform – rather than from the texts themselves.

True, there were more serious examples of Shevchenko scholarship in the first post-war decade. There was, for instance, a considerable number of articles on Shevchenko and the various nationalities within the Soviet Union: Belorussia, Lithuania, Latvia, Georgia, Kazakhstan, and the Kirghiz republic, etc. We do not know to what extent Shevchenko – that exemplary enemy of all enforcement – was forced, together with Pushkin and Lermontov, on the Kazakhs or the Kirghiz; such studies, nevertheless, are interesting. The complete ten-volume edition of Shevchenko's works, repeatedly attempted between the wars, was resumed. Beginning in 1952, Shevchenko conferences have been organized by the Literary Institute at the Ukrainian Academy of Sciences; with some recent interruptions, they have been held annually in various cities of the Soviet Union. Except for the first two years, the papers from each conference have been published in a separate volume.

As a result of some alleviation of restraints upon Soviet Ukrainian culture at the end of the 1950s, Shevchenko studies were perceptibly improving from year to year. In addition to the ten-volume edition of the poet's works and a four-volume supplement on his paintings, drawings, and prints, the Academy of Sciences published well-produced facsimiles of some of his manuscripts, the value of which cannot be overestimated. Other documentary publications, such as memoirs by the poet's contemporaries or day-by-day chronicles of his life, can be helpful only when used with discrimination, based on some previous knowledge of the subject matter. Several older publications of this type are already branded as 'incorrect.' We never know that the source published three or four months ago will not be condemned for falsifications, called by whatever euphemism, ten years from now. The two-volume bibliography of Shevchenko scholarship and criticism (1889-1959) which appeared in the 1960s is useful only for the material of which current Soviet policy more or less approves. An additional hefty volume probably could be compiled of Western Ukrainian criticism (represented in the given publication very sketchily), émigré criticism (not represented at all), work by non-Ukrainian scholars in the West (also not represented), and numerous contributions by Soviet scholars of the 1920s that have been suppressed. The editors attempt to avoid trouble by restricting their bibliography to the present borders of Soviet Ukraine. Although this manœuver, even at the risk of a charge of rampant xenophobia, eliminates émigré scholarship, the suppression of thousands of Western Ukrainian and Soviet titles remains unexplained.

By far the most valuable and dependable are various contributions to the study of Shevchenko's language and style, although here too we must be wary of claims that the Russian language was crucial in Shevchenko's development. The two-volume dictionary of Shevchenko's lexical usage, with ample cross-references, is very useful in the study of the poet's semantics and its development. Some stylistic studies by individual authors have become extremely narrow but none the less valuable for that. All are rigorously descriptive and many statistical: here one would search in vain for the excitingly inventive use of linguistics in literary criticism that we see in the early Soviet formalists, let alone the French structuralists. Most recent Soviet work on Shevchenko's form has also remained 'scientifically' descriptive, frequently statistical, and almost invariably dry. Much attention has been devoted to textual criticism, and a number of descriptions of Shevchenko's manuscripts have appeared. Here again, one would wish for bolder speculation, particularly in the area of literary psychology, which textual investigations could yield.

Biographical researchers, when they are not busy perverting facts (which now happens more rarely, although many earlier distortions have entered the critical canon), are busy almost literally counting every button on every shirt that Shevchenko owned, and, more important, listing every Russian journalist and pamphleteer with whom he could have possibly exchanged a greeting. This practice inspired Oleksander Biletsky's ironic ire. He pointed out that the reader is surely more interested in what Shevchenko wrote than in where he went and whom he met every day of his life, and that scholars should be more concerned with the study of the literary

process in which the poet participated than with the trivia of his daily life.[15]
Strangely enough, such meticulous research does not obtain in every area
of the poet's activities; even Soviet commentators themselves complain that
in the poet's biography there are still a number of lacunae, such as his
relationship with the Brotherhood of Sts Cyril and Methodius. Neither the
wide research in that specific problem by historians and literary scholars in
the 1920s, nor (needless to say!) Miiakovsky's solid contribution, included
in this volume, are taken into consideration. In a word, there are safer and
less safe areas of the poet's life to investigate.

An amazing phenomenon in the area of biography, surely opposed to
every definition of historiography, is the practice of writing Shevchenko's
biography by committee or brigade. There are two such 'collective' biographies to date: H. Viazovsky, K. Danylko, I. Duz, M. Levchenko, A.
Nedzvidsky, and V. Nestorenko, *Taras Hryhorovych Shevchenko: Biohrafiia*
(1960) and Ie. Kyryliuk, Ie. Shabliovsky, and V. Shubravsky, *T.H. Shevchenko: Biohrafiia* (1964). Even the titles of the two books are almost
identical. That 'group activity' is linked with commentators' repeated
assurances that Soviet scholars were not 'ready' to write a full biography of
Shevchenko until the 1960s. Reasons for this astonishing lack of readiness
become plain when we recall that they depend on the readiness of the
mannequin that was being constructed between 1939 and 1959 and on the
progress of the 'ideological adjustments' that kept taking place in its
fabrication. Hence it also becomes plain why Shevchenko's 'life' is to be
written not from a single point of view, but as an 'objective' scientific
report. All this becomes even more curious when we recall that as early as
1939 the émigré scholar Pavlo Zaitsev was 'ready' for a definitive biography of the poet, a beautifully written and impeccably researched work,
which in every respect stands head and shoulders above the two collective
efforts by the Soviets.

Some new work has been done in Soviet Ukraine on Shevchenko and
the Ukrainian literary process, for instance P. Prykhodko's *Shevchenko i
ukrainskyi romantyzm* (Shevchenko and Ukrainian Romanticism, 1963) and
several articles on this problem. The trouble here is that the definition of
romanticism in such works becomes considerably more narrow and distorted than in the 1920s, in order to get Shevchenko out of it and send him
on his way to 'critical realism' as quickly as possible. The other problem in
such works is obvious historical distortion of Ukrainian romanticism and of

its individual representatives. Although Soviet commentators keep saying that they have finally 'corrected' the 'ideological errors' of their predecessors in recognizing that not all Ukrainian romantics were reactionary land-owners, matters in that area are still far from 'objective.'

As for comparative studies, the nineteenth-century French model of proof of influence obtains in methodology, and speculative attempts to search for parallels or analogies are rigorously excluded. Work on Shevchenko's relationship to Western literatures has been severely curtailed, while investigations of his ties with Slavic literatures and the literatures of the peoples of the Soviet Union and the satellite countries are greatly expanded. In the collection of papers of the twelfth Shevchenko conference, for example, there is a useful contribution by D.S. Nalyvaiko on Shevchenko in French criticism of the end of the nineteenth and the beginning of the twentieth centuries, and M.M. Pavliuk's report on nineteenth-century translations of Shevchenko in German. On the whole, however, Oleksander Biletsky's article 'Shevchenko i svitova literatura' (Shevchenko and World Literature), published in 1939, remains the most interesting Soviet piece on that subject, and his more recent call to study Shevchenko against the background of world literature, by and large, remains unheeded. On the other hand, a substantial number of studies on Shevchenko and Slavic literatures, particularly Polish, but also Bulgarian, Czech, Slovak, Belorussian, Serbian, and Slovenian, have appeared in recent years. Exercises on Shevchenko and the literatures of non-Slavic nations of the Soviet Union have increased spectacularly since the first post-war decade; there are scores of articles on Shevchenko and Tadzikistan, Uzbekistan, Azerbaidzhan, the Turkmen Republic, and many similar exotic places. Although the value of such efforts (mostly appreciations by native writers and scholars, some doubtless 'made to order' to underscore the brotherhood of Soviet peoples) is in principle beyond doubt, the situation becomes rather lopsided when we recall that the volume of serious and often first-rate scholarship being done on Shevchenko by native and émigré authors in Canada, the United States, western Europe, and South America is generally ignored, and the study of the relationship of *Kobzar* to Western European literatures badly underdeveloped.

There is little of lasting value in literary interpretation of Shevchenko's poetry in Soviet Ukraine: scholars and critics shy away from discussing the text of a Shevchenko poem. It seems safer to list the poet's Russian friends

than to venture into areas where one has the uncomfortable choice of
denying one's personal convictions or risking employment as 'inspector of
the Northern Lights' (as Soviet wits call imprisonment in concentration
camps in the northern regions of the Union). It is difficult not to notice
Soviet scholars' avoidance of such a choice in their preference for the
technical, statistical, 'objective' aspects of Shevchenko studies, and it is
equally difficult, in view of their situation, to blame them for this. Furthermore, syntactic parallels, alliterative patterns, or the predominance of the
iambic foot in Shevchenko's poetry are likely to remain pretty much the
same, while official attitudes towards his symbol of the three ravens, let
alone towards his association with Kostomarov, may change overnight,
burying forever the long years of a scholar's work and, in extreme cases,
the scholar himself. And, finally, how else but by formulas is one to
describe the systems that activate a mannequin?

Iurii Ivakin's book-length study on Shevchenko's satire (1959, second
'corrected' edition 1964) has moments of literary interest, especially in the
author's careful differentiation between satire as genre and as mode, and in
his analysis of some key images, but it is marred throughout by an insistent political bias that does not avoid distortion. This is particularly unfortunate, since Ivakin seems to be one of the most responsible scholars in the
'top-level establishment' of Soviet Shevchenko studies. An impressively
produced two-volume encyclopedic dictionary on Shevchenko's work, biography, environment, and Shevchenko scholarship came out in 1978.
Although on the whole it is a comprehensive and rather impressive work,
it too is spoiled by countless distortions and perversions of the poet's
writings.

In the late 1950s and early 1960s an occasional Soviet article would
astonish us by its devotion to the text, its calm authority, and its profundity of interpretation. Mykhailyna Kotsiubynska's reading of the poem
'Ne kydai materi' (Do not Abandon Your Mother), published in the collection of papers of the Tenth Shevchenko Conference (1962), is one of
the best examples of Soviet literary criticism after the war. The articles in
this volume by Rylsky and Nenadkevych show a level of excellence
reminiscent of the kind of work done in Ukraine in the 1920s. At the time
of their publication, the authors were old men who had gone through
the purges and now probably felt that they could afford to speak
calmly about literature. Besides, 1959 was the year of liberalization in

Ukraine, when many interesting things in culture began to happen. Now that the 'thaw' of 1959 has been refrozen, Nenadkevych's and Rylsky's articles in their turn belong to history. What remains is the 'objective,' mannequin-building mockery of literary criticism, whose overall effect, in contrast to the early Soviet debates which in spite of their many instances of irresponsibility had the revolutionary spirit of authenticity, enthusiasm, and excitement, is one of unrelieved boredom.

Shevchenko's name was known and began to be venerated in Western Ukraine, then part of the Austro-Hungarian Empire, during the poet's lifetime. Later, in the 1860s and early 1870s, Western Ukrainian populists set about to develop a lively cult of Shevchenko among the people, canonizing him, building an entire educational program of the masses around his name, and at the same time making forays into serious scholarship. When, in the 1870s, intellectuals from Russian-occupied Ukraine were forced by repressions to place their writings in Western Ukrainian publications, to travel to Western Ukraine and, in some cases, to settle there, Shevchenko scholarship, together with other aspects of Ukrainian culture, became a single stream, transcending the artificial borders set up by the respective foreign powers dividing the land among themselves.

In the 1870s, pioneering efforts in Shevchenko studies were connected with the Western Ukrainian journal *Pravda* and the cultural and educational association Prosvita. In 1873 Drahomanov and other émigrés from the Russian Empire, together with Western Ukrainian intellectuals, founded in Lviv the Shevchenko Literary Society, which in 1892 was reorganized as the Shevchenko Scientific Society. The Society's voluminous publications, particularly in the first two decades of the century, remain a useful source of Ukrainian studies. It was that organization which promoted Shevchenko scholarship for many years. In 1898 Franko and others established the journal *Literaturno naukovyi vistnyk*, which published scholarly articles on Shevchenko's life and work.

After the revolutions in Russian-occupied Ukraine and the Polish occupation of Western Ukrainian territories, political borders divided Ukrainians more rigidly than ever before. Western Ukrainian scholars did not enjoy the kind of fully developed academic environment in which Soviet scholars worked in the 1920s. Most important, many of them (and after 1934, practically all of them) were forbidden entry into Soviet Ukraine and thus were cut off from all primary sources. Moreover, only a few were connected with universities or research institutes. The Polish occupation of Western Ukraine forbade higher education in Ukrainian: before World War II, an underground Ukrainian university existed in Lviv, but obviously it could not provide the facilities of a normal academic institution. Most scholars were forced either to teach in secondary schools or to hold non-academic jobs. All the funds that they managed to scrape together from private donations went into publishing their work and maintaining their scholarly organizations. Ironically, the Western Ukrainian scholars and émigrés who resided beyond Ukraine had a greater opportunity to teach in institutions of higher learning than those who lived in Western Ukraine itself. The celebrated Slavicist Dmytro Chyzhevsky taught in various German universities; Lepky at the University of Cracow; Smal-Stotsky, O. Kolessa, and Biletsky at Charles University in Prague and the Ukrainian Free University (supported by the Czech government) in the Czech town of Podebrady. In the 1920s the prominent Western Ukrainian scholars Smal-Stotsky, F. Kolessa, Vozniak, Shchurat, and Studynsky were corresponding members of the Kievan Academy of Sciences, but during the purges they, together with most of the established Soviet scholars, were deprived of their membership in that prestigious institution. Needless to say, in the 1930s Western Ukrainian and émigré scholars were not forced to follow Shevchenko's footsteps to Siberia, and the responsibility of carrying on the work of Ukrainian scholarship fell entirely upon their shoulders.

Between the wars there were three important centres of Shevchenko studies in the West. The original base was in Lviv, with Shchurat, F. Kolessa, Studynsky, Hordynsky, the émigré Doroshenko, and a great number of other scholars. With the influx of émigrés from the newly formed Soviet Ukraine, a strong centre developed in Czechoslovakia, connected with the Ukrainian Free University and led by Biletsky, Antonovych, and Bohatsky; somewhat later, they were joined by the Western Ukrainian scholar, Smal-Stotsky. In Warsaw, the émigré from Kiev, Zaitsev, and other scholars joined the Institute of Ukrainian Studies and used its facilities to prepare the definitive edition of Shevchenko's works which was published in 1937.

As early as the 1870s and particularly in the 1880s, Western Ukrainian populists – that is, most of the prominent intellectuals, with the exception of some young socialists and followers of Drahomanov – regarded Shevchenko primarily as a 'prophet' of Ukrainian autonomous statehood. Hence in Western Ukraine, somewhat sooner than in the Russian-occupied Ukrainian territories, the cultural image of minstrel Taras turned into the revolutionary spark and conflagration image of national rebirth. In the 1870s the literary historian Ohonovsky and the critic Barvinsky were already far beyond the stage of speculation about Shevchenko's work as a re-embodiment of folklore sources of of Ukrainian ethnicity, unequivocally reading the poet's 'message' as the central expression of Ukrainians' struggle for independence. That line of interpretation of Shevchenko's poetry was continued in Western Ukraine until the beginning of World War II by scholars like Lototsky, Simovych, Lepky, Hrytsai, and many others; it prevails in the émigré view of Shevchenko in our time. In the 1930s, avowed or 'integral' nationalist critics, enthusiastically doing their part in the 'struggle for Shevchenko,' took that line of criticism to its limit or perhaps even beyond it: in some of their writings there is a new image of the poet as a mystical spirit of the cossack élite, hovering over the Ukrainian people in order to cause, at the appropriate moment, their miraculous resurrection.

Smal-Stotsky's interpretive essay in this volume, taken from his collection of articles which has the distinction of drawing the most frequent Soviet fire even in 1980, is based on a rigorous philological method designed to support the author's relatively mild nationalistic bias: the image of Shevchenko as spark and conflagration is present on every page of that book. Smal-Stotsky warns the interpreter not to bring any 'forestructures' to the text. Indeed, he does not seem to veer from the text at all, even while proclaiming his message. He uses a sort of hermeneutical circle: claiming to have observed a uniform ideological direction in Shevchenko's œuvre, he then proceeds, on the basis of careful readings of single poems, to find their place in that ideology. Nevertheless, on occasion the treatment of a given text is somewhat too obviously guided by the interpreter's ideological conviction. In the essay included here, this is evident particularly in Smal-Stotsky's provocative but rather fanciful conclusion that 'Ukraine had liberty and will have it again but only Ukrainians *with Cossack eyes* will return to freedom – those with their eyes plucked out or those who are corpses will *never again* return to liberty!'

Although, as should be plain by now, politically uncommitted interpretations of Shevchenko's poetry are rare in Ukrainian criticism (even stylistic, formal, and textological studies are frequently so committed), a number of Western Ukrainian and émigré scholars between the wars treated Shevchenko primarily as an artist. A number of them, for example, researched the poet's life and intellectual environment. Simovych wrote on Shevchenko and the early Ukrainian romantics, Doroshenko speculated on his relationship with the educational system of his time (concentrating on his interest in Ukrainian textbooks in the last years of his life), and P. Bohatsky reported on new documents pertaining to his life. Shchurat, Vozniak, and Zaitsev did significant work in that area of Shevchenko studies. Shchurat wrote a number of articles on Shevchenko's Polish friends in Kiev and elsewhere: some of those pieces were subsequently collected in his volume *Z zhyttia i tvorchosti Tarasa Shevchenka* (From Shevchenko's Life and Work, Lviv 1914). Vozniak, a scholar who did valuable work in many areas of Ukrainian literature, prepared a series of short, meticulously researched studies on Shevchenko's intellectual environment, his imprisonment, and on other factual topics. Even before his emigration to Poland in 1919, Zaitsev published some valuable biographical studies on Shevchenko, particularly bearing on the peasant girl Oksana Kovalenko, who had played such an important and mysterious role in the poet's childhood and early youth. In 1939 Zaitsev's excellent biography of Shevchenko was printed in Lviv. In October of that year, when the signatures were ready for the binder, the Soviet Army occupied Lviv and confiscated the whole edition. Soviet scholars in Kiev obviously had immediate access to copies of the unbound book, because even in the early 1940s they began pillaging it; Marietta Shaginian, as mentioned above, was the only author courageous enough to acknowledge quotations from it. It was finally reprinted by the Shevchenko Scientific Society in 1955, from one of the few sets of signatures brought to Western Europe during the war.

Understandably, Western Ukrainian scholars devoted a great deal of attention to the history of the proliferation of Shevchenko's poetry in Western Ukraine. In 1930 Vozniak showed that as early as 1843 Shevchenko himself was interested in the cultural life of Western Ukrainians, and during World War II, Ie. Iu. Pelensky published a book-length study on the dissemination of Shevchenko's poetry in Western Ukraine over the years. Shevchenko and Poland was another lively topic in Western Ukraine and in the emigration. Besides his numerous articles on that problem, mentioned above, Shchurat brought out a monograph on Shevchenko and the Poles in 1917; in 1934 Zaitsev published a book on that topic in Polish. As well, Oleksander Kolessa did some valuable work on Shevchenko and Mickiewicz. Considering the circumstances, surprisingly little was written on Shevchenko and Western literatures, certainly much less than had been done in Soviet Ukraine in the 1920s. The excellent critic and comparatist Mykhailo Rudnytsky wrote articles on translations of Shevchenko (1924) and on Shevchenko and Western European critics (1931); I have not come across more substantial Western Ukrainian or émigré work in that area from the period between the wars. During the war, Ie. Iu. Pelensky published a provocative study, *Shevchenko-kliasyk* (Cracow 1942), in which he attempts to dismiss Shevchenko's importance as a romantic in favour of Western European neoclassicism.

Western Ukrainian and émigré critics did some significant work on Shevchenko's language and form. Ohiienko, Simovych, F. Kolessa, and many younger scholars discussed the poet's use of Ukrainian and his contributions to the development of the language. As early as 1925, Smal-Stotsky published a book-length analysis of Shevchenko's rhythm, in which he traces its sources to Ukrainian folklore. In the 1930s, Nykyforiak and Chekhovych reviewed that problem in important articles. But it is F. Kolessa who described the connections of Shevchenko's rhythm and folklore most broadly. His collection of long articles, published under the collective title *Studii nad poetychnoiu tvorchistiu T. Shevchenka* (Studies of the Poetry of Taras Shevchenko) in 1939, is perhaps the most meticulous work on Shevchenko and folklore. In the first article, the author compares hundreds of quotations from folk songs to excerpts from *Kobzar*, showing numerous thematic and particularly melodic parallels. In the second article, using musical (instead of the standard metrical) notation, the author carefully discusses parallels between Shevchenko's rhythm and that of Ukrainian folk songs. In his article included in this volume, Chyzhevsky combines the two approaches, claiming the derivation of Shevchenko's rhythms from folk songs, and yet analysing them in the conventional manner.

Other problems in Shevchenko scholarship were treated equally interestingly in Western Ukraine and by émigrés between the wars. I have already mentioned Balei's psychological study of *Kobzar*. Dmytro Antonovych, Volodymyr Sichynsky, and Sviatoslav Hordynsky made important contributions to the topic of Shevchenko as an artist. Volodymyr Doroshenko's work in Shevchenko bibliography is also valuable.

By far the most ambitious contribution to Shevchenko studies by
Western Ukrainian and émigré scholars is the monumental sixteen-
volume edition of his collected works, completed by the Ukrainian
Scientific Institute in Warsaw in 1937. Prior to that edition, the most
reliable was the one-volume *Kobzar*, prepared by the Western Ukrainian
scholar Simovych and published in Katerynoslav in 1921. Although the
editor's long introduction and copious annotations are intended for the
'common reader' and, in some instances, may now sound naïve and
superfluous, many of the textual glosses are still useful. In any event, that
edition has served supremely well as an educational tool: although it is
banned in the Soviet Union, its post-war reissue in Canada is still used in
many Ukrainian-language schools in the West. The Warsaw academic
edition, obviously, has quite a different purpose. Annotations are brief and
scrupulously factual, while textual variants are abundant and well explained. By far the most valuable element of the edition is the nearly fifty
interpretative essays, by Zaitsev himself and a large number of émigré
and Western Ukrainian scholars, dealing with every major work, as well as
with larger aspects of Shevchenko's œuvre. Together with the collections of
scholarly articles on Shevchenko published in the 1920s and early 1930s in
Soviet Ukraine, the short studies in that edition are the most important
source of Shevchenko criticism. In the 1960s a thoroughly revised edition
came out in the United States. The editor, Bohdan Kravtsiv, greatly
expanded the original, bringing all pertinent information up to date, and
adding a number of new articles and a whole new volume of sixteen short
studies, including some Soviet authors whom the original editors, in the
throes of 'the struggle for Shevchenko,' had conspicuously ignored.
Kravtsiv added a volume of translations of Shevchenko's poetry in many
languages, with an informative introduction that is the most reliable survey
to date of *Kobzar*'s career in the world.

Dmytro Chyzhevsky, an émigré who left Ukraine at the beginning of
the 1920s and who subsequently became one of the leading Slavic scholars
of our time, in his article on Shevchenko and religion tackles one of the
most ticklish issues of both the 'cult' and the scholarship. In the 1870s, as
pointed out earlier, some Western Ukrainians had been known to 'amend'
Kobzar in order to 'tone down' the tension of the poet's passionate quarrels
with God. In the same decade, Vovk claimed that Shevchenko was an
atheist, while Drahomanov pointed out that, regrettably, he was a believer.
In our century, Kornei Chukovsky described all of Shevchenko's poetry as

a prolonged cry *to* God and *for* God, and Ievshan, in an interesting article on Shevchenko's religion, similarly claimed that Shevchenko's basic aesthetic impulse, like that of all authentic art, was religious. Shchurat wrote voluminously on Shevchenko's religion: his 'Shevchenko and the Bible,' for example, is an interesting contribution to comparative studies of Shevchenko, since he supports his thesis with a battery of valid textual parallels between the two sources. In 1914, on the other hand, the Russian Orthodox archbishop Nikon published a formal denunciation of Shevchenko as an atheist, which gave rise to the notorious official repressions of the 'cult' of Shevchenko in Russian-occupied Ukraine, begun in that year. In Soviet criticism the Shevchenko and God motif has been constant; it began, as pointed out above, with a combination of Communism and religious messianism. More recently, journalists have proclaimed Shevchenko's atheism, while responsible critics like Oleksander Biletsky have warned that the issue is not so simple. In Western Ukrainian and émigré criticism that problem is also current. Since the war, two notable studies on it have appeared: Leonid Biletsky's *Viruiuchyi Shevchenko* (The Believing Shevchenko, 1949) and Vasyl Barka's *Pravda Kobzaria* (The Truth of 'Kobzar,' 1961).

Chyzhevsky's thesis, in its general outline, was not new in the 1930s. His apology for Shevchenko as a 'mere' poet, relying on his emotions and the truth of the heart rather than on his intellect, had been heard since the early 1870s. As for the core of Chyzhevsky's argument, as early as 1915 O. Kalyshevsky had been saying, similarly, that Shevchenko's attitude towards God was extremely personal and based directly on human suffering; that Shevchenko believed God should not be a distant emperor before whom people tremble but rather the God of the insulted and the suffering of this world. What is very interesting in Chyzhevsky's work, however, is the direction of the argument and the profound conclusion in the last few paragraphs, based on the author's careful and imaginative use of sources. Chyzhevsky's central claim is that in religion Shevchenko prefers content over form. Although we indeed find many instances of critique and even ridicule of religious institutions in *Kobzar*, I do not believe that this is the most important issue, as Chyzhevsky intimates: Shevchenko's most bitter accusation is that God is indifferent to human suffering; in my opinion, this has to do less with the empty liturgical forms of the imperial Russian Church than with the extremely bold charge of divine omission or, more bluntly, divine dishonesty. Even if we grant Chyzhevsky his point, we soon see that he takes a direction diametrically opposite that of the usual social or humanist views on Shevchenko's religion. He implies that the basis of Shevchenko's belief, inherited from thinkers like Rousseau or Diderot, is anthropocentric and therefore unfaithful to authentic religiosity; it is based on human freedom and hence on human history, which are not authentic religious concerns. Almost like Drahomanov, but more gently and with an opposite intent, Chyzhevsky chides Shevchenko for not having appreciated philosophy enough to understand correctly the transcendental, essentially ahuman, nature of God.

Whether we agree with Chyzhevsky or not, his wealth of information, skilful interpretation of texts, and deliberately 'baroque' style make the article a masterpiece of informed and elegant critical writing. Moreover, Chyzhevsky's basic bias, carefully concealed beneath the mantle of 'scientific objectivity,' tells us much about his own view of the world, which in itself is important. In most of his interpretations, the great scholar prefers the ascetic, the transcendental, the medieval to the anthropocentric, the earthly, the renaissance: his renaissance comes out as essentially medieval, and his baroque is certainly much more Miltonic than late Shakespearean. This is perhaps why Chyzhevsky wrote so little on Shevchenko: his view of the world is as different from Shevchenko's as night from day.

During World War II, in the mass exodus of Ukrainians, many Soviet scholars escaped to the West and joined Western Ukrainians and earlier émigrés in various countries and on various continents: Volodymyr Miiakovsky, who had written on Shevchenko even before the Revolution, and who had been exiled to Siberia in the Soviet purges; Viktor Petrov, ethnographer, novelist, critic, and sometime philosopher who in the 1920s and the early 1930s published articles on Shevchenko's intellectual environment; Volodymyr Derzhavyn, a noted critic and scholar of classical literature, who had contributed an article to one of the collections edited by Fylypovych in the 1920s and had done other occasional work on the poet; Hryhorii Kostiuk, a corresponding member of the Shevchenko Institute in the early 1930s and Soviet concentration camp prisoner; Petro Odarchenko, who had done some work on Shevchenko in the late 1920s, before his exile to Kazakhstan; Iurii Shevelov, a noted linguist and literary critic, whose occasional contributions to Shevchenko studies are of the highest quality; Stepan Iu. Haievsky, Iurii Boiko-Blokhyn, and many others.

Shevchenko scholarship, along with the feverish mimeograph publishing of popular editions of his selected works, resumed immediately after the war, as if the survival of the Ukrainian spirit in the West depended directly on the constant presence of the poet's images and rhythms. When the Ukrainian Free Academy of Arts and Sciences was founded in Bavaria in 1946, its first concern was the organization of Shevchenko conferences and the mimeographing of the papers presented for wide distribution. Some useful short studies appeared in that series, notably Viktor Petrov's paper on the main stages in the history of Shevchenko scholarship (1946); Dmytro Chyzhevsky's study of Shevchenko's versification (1947), translated for this volume; Ia. Rudnytsky's analysis of stress in Shevchenko's poetry (1947); Leonid Biletsky's contribution to Shevchenko's biography 'Shevchenko in Iahotyn' (1949), and other works. In 1947 the Academy also published a collection of articles, called *Shevchenko i ioho doba* (Shevchenko and His Age). The Shevchenko Scientific Society, reorganized immediately after the war, published some material on Shevchenko in its *Zapysky* (Memoirs) and its journal *Siohochasne i Mynule* (The Present and the Past). The prestigious literary journal *Arka* contained several excellent articles on Shevchenko, particularly Viktor Petrov's study on his aesthetics, as expressed in his central image of the heart (1948). In the four-year transition period (1946-50), a large number of articles on the poet appeared in other émigré periodicals.

Immediately after resettlement in the United States, Canada, South America, and Australia, Ukrainians created new conditions both for the cult of and scholarship on Shevchenko. Although the former had been very strong already among emigrants who had settled in the United States and Canada before World War II, little scholarship had been done at that time; as far as the cult itself was concerned, the newcomers gave it their own stamp. The Free Academy of Arts and Sciences and the Shevchenko Scientific Society renewed their activities. As early as 1949, Leonid Biletsky's study *Viruiuchyi Shevchenko* (The Believing Schevchenko) was published in Winnipeg by the Canadian branch of the Academy. In the years 1952-4 that branch published a well-produced four-volume edition of Shevchenko's *Kobzar*, edited and annotated by Leonid Biletsky. Subsequently, more specialized scholarly editions of *Kobzar* came out: *The First 'Kobzar' of 1840*, edited by K. Bida (Ottawa 1961), *The 'Kobzar' of 1860* (Winnipeg 1960), and *The 'Kobzar' of 'Osnova,' 1861*, the last two edited by J.B.

Rudnyckyj (Winnipeg 1961). The Canadian branch of the Academy also published a series of short studies on Shevchenko in pamphlet form. The United States branch of the Academy established a short-lived Institute of Shevchenko Studies, which published ten annual collections of articles and studies on Shevchenko, a facsimile of the manuscript of two poems owned by the Academy, and, together with the Shevchenko Scientific Society, reprinted Smal-Stotsky's *Interpretations*. Perhaps the most valuable publication on Shevchenko by the Academy is an English-language collection of nine articles, published in 1962, all but two written especially for the occasion. I have already quoted from Lawrynenko's and Odarchenko's contributions, and Miiakovsky's and Shevelov's articles are reprinted in this volume. The Academy sponsors annual Shevchenko conferences in New York.

The Shevchenko Scientific Society, with strong branches in Europe and the United States, has also promoted the poet's work. Several studies have appeared in its *Zapysky* (Memoirs) since 1950, particularly Volodymyr Ianiv's ethnopsychological inquiries into the problem of Shevchenko and the Ukrainian nation. Oleksander Kulchytsky, a senior member of the Society, has done some interesting work in the archetypal (more specifically Jungian) interpretation of Shevchenko's poems. The Society's most important contribution was the publication, in 1955, of Zaitsev's biography of Shevchenko. The Society also organizes annual Shevchenko conferences.

Outside these two organizations, but with their close co-operation, a number of other major efforts in Shevchenko studies have been undertaken. I think the expanded and corrected edition of the Warsaw collected works is the single most important post-war achievement in Shevchenko studies by émigrés. Several attempts to translate Shevchenko's poetry into English should also be noted here. The most important is a comprehensive volume of Shevchenko's translations by Watson Kirkconnell (1964). This generally excellent work suffers on occasion from the translator's penchant for the English Victorians; he makes Shevchenko sound much more like Tennyson than like Shevchenko. In order to capture the poet's images and ideas, Vera Rich, in her slim volume *Song Out of Darkness* (1961), rendered Shevchenko's poems in loose prosody, occasionally bordering on free verse. The Canadian Communist author John Weir (Vyviursky), in his *Taras Shevchenko: Selections* (1961), achieved some truly impressive translations. The volume, however, is marred by a doctrinaire introduction, whose perversion of facts to please the Soviet régime was censured even by Soviet critics.

In recent years, the centre of Shevchenko scholarship has shifted from learned societies to American and Canadian universities, as the possibilities of Ukrainian studies within the North American academic structure are becoming more and more viable. Although this shift is too new to have given many significant results, nevertheless George Luckyj's useful study *Between Gogol' and Ševčenko* (Harvard Ukrainian Studies 1971), as well as the volume in hand, show that serious work in that sector is under way.

The last part of the volume addresses itself exclusively to Shevchenko as man and poet. Both Miiakovsky's study and the rigorously scientific report by Swoboda are models of biographical research. The pieces by Shevelov, Luckyj, Schneider, and Pliushch treat *Kobzar* primarily as a literary text. Shevelov's article belongs to the philological-hermeneutic tradition, in which stylistic analysis allusively suggests the poet's calm, concentrated philosophical world view before his death. By comparing the 1860 texts with earlier poems, Shevelov unveils not only the synchronic frame of Shevchenko's last phase but the diachronic process of development which led up to it: The author interprets on the basis of careful observations on Shevchenko's style, which in turn leads him to discuss the poet's growth from restless revolutionary youth into balanced philosophical maturity. Luckyj applies methods of archetypal criticism, with a sociological approach to the theme of the bastard in Shevchenko's *œuvre*, which for Shevchenko symbolizes the destruction of the family as an institution. This is a continuation and refinement of Kulchytsky's pioneering effort mentioned above.

Pliushch's contribution to this volume is indeed a surprise. The author spent a good part of his mature life in Soviet insane asylums for radical political dissent. Although he repeated Shevchenko's bitter destiny in his own life, he does not worship a ready-made cultist image of the poet or erect a new one. There is no trace of bitterness or pathos in his writing: what we have instead is a thoughtful interpretation of a poem from a modified structuralist approach, based in the main on Bakhtin and Propp, which, if not mastered, is exciting, dynamic, and alive. It is significant and even somewhat disturbing that a man who has lived in the West for only a little over two years, and who, when he found time, studied mathematics, provides 'Westerners' of many years' standing a truly contemporary insight into Shevchenko's work. It would take too long to list all the discoveries Pliushch lightly tosses off in his article; following are a few instances worthy of development in fuller studies. Shevchenko 'raised the genre' of the sentimental ballads, as Shklovsky would put it, and forced it to embody interests quite different from sentimentalism. Shevchenko put the 'dialogue' form of his poetic discourse to various psychological and philosophical uses, all aimed at harmonizing poetically an initially discordant world view. In his most important discovery, Pliushch uses the central structuralist idea of 'transformation' to connect it with the 'indeterminate,' dialectical fluidity of the dialogue form, and to show how it uses plot, image, meaning, and motif, sometimes ending in complete inversion (or formal denial) of elements found in earlier works. Pliushch's application of transformation to the problems of good and evil, and to Shevchenko's view on religion, is thoroughly convincing and profound. Finally, Pliushch shows how Shevchenko's seemingly pure Ukrainian situations are 'transformed' into universal manifestations of the tragedy of life, an insight which goes directly against Chyzhevsky's view of Shevchenko. According to Pliushch, it is in this fatalistic evaluation of human life that Shevchenko finds the final meaning of existence. The only hope for human dignity in the midst of a tragic existence is the metaphorical transformation of evil into good and distrust into love. Perhaps here is the implied reason for Pliushch's own refusal to use his pen as an instrument of vengeance.

I have endeavoured to show, on the basis of the volume in hand, how much has been done in Shevchenko studies in the past hundred and thirty years. It should be equally obvious that whatever has been done is not enough. Soviet scholars are chronically handicapped by their régime, and dissident writings on Shevchenko from the Soviet Union that occasionally reach us – the early Dziuba, Sverstiuk, and Svitlychny – suggest what powerful work would be accomplished there given freedom. Emigré scholars, on the other hand, seem to miss many opportunities for research, for which the absence of manuscript collections or complete libraries of Shevchenko's criticism is insufficient excuse: their living in the West may be of even more aid in the work that needs to be done than being near comprehensive libraries and concentration camps. Perhaps the most obvious gap in Shevchenko scholarship is a series of studies on Shevchenko and Western romanticism, based not on the outdated method of direct influences but on an imaginative development of affinities. Iurii Boiko's brief report on Shevchenko and Western literatures, Mykola Hlobenko's equally brief essay 'Zhyvyi Shevchenko' (The Living Shevchenko), and notes on Shevchenko and Robert Burns by J.B. Rudnyckyj are practically all that we have in that area. It is embarrassing that the Soviet scholar Oleksander Biletsky's incidental essay of 1939 remains the best, and the most frequently quoted, work on that subject.

Innovative and imaginative readings of Shevchenko, obviously impossible in the Soviet Union, are also practically non-existent in the West; it is as if we were afraid to tamper with canonical interpretations of sacred texts. We should also take stock, by publishing bibliographies, of important studies on Shevchenko available in the West, and develop a program to reprint the best and most useful of that material. This would help younger scholars to wean themselves from dependence on contemporary 'predigested' Soviet reports on sources, reports that are obviously undependable. We should reveal the influence of Shevchenko in twentieth-century Ukrainian literature beyond the Soviet framework. Only we in the West can build an adequate corpus of translations of Shevchenko into foreign languages, particularly into English; the co-operation of native poets is imperative in that endeavour. We should collaborate more closely with historians of the period and of the problems bearing more or less directly on Shevchenko, in order to establish interdisciplinary study. Finally, by scholarly reviews of Soviet works on Shevchenko, we should endeavour to counteract the 'objectivizing' petrification of his image. To accomplish all this, or at least a part of it, we sorely need a clearing-house of information, which can be created only within a research institute of Shevchenko studies.

Much remains to be done. Meanwhile, this volume is an important step towards a mature and discriminating phase of Shevchenko scholarship in the West. It performs many useful tasks that in turn call for assimilation and development, charting ever more daring journeys into the mysterious and vast country of Shevchenko's imagination.

NOTES

1 Czesław Miłosz, *The History of Polish Literature* (New York: Macmillan Publishing Co. 1969) 203.

2 A. Pleshcheev, 'Zametki koe o chem,' *Moskovskii vestnik*, 13 (April 1860) 208. Cited in V. Ie. Shubravsky, 'Pryzhyttieva krytyka,' in *Shevchenkoznavstvo: Pidsumky i problemy* Ie. P. Kyryliuk, ed., 'Akademiia nauk Ukrainskoi RSR, Instytut literatury im. T.H. Shevchenka' (Kiev: Naukova dumka 1975) 24.

3 Interesting discussions of Kotliarevsky's significance in the twentieth century can be found in Dmytro Čyževs'kyj, *A History of Ukrainian Literature* (Littleton: Ukrainian Academic Press 1975) 381-403, Mykola Zerov, *Nove ukrainske pysmenstvo: Istorychnyi narys* (1924; Munich: Instytut literatury 1960) 39-94, and Ievhen Sverstiuk, *Clandestine Essays* (Cambridge, MA: Harvard Ukrainian Research Institute 1976) 69-96.

4 Jurii Lawrynenko, 'Shevchenko and His *Kobzar*,' in *Taras Ševčenko: 1814-1861*, Volodymyr Mijakovs'kyj and George Y. Shevelov, eds, 'Slavic Printings and Reprintings' ('S-Gravenhage: Mouton 1962) 197. This article is a thoughtful and extremely useful survey of nineteenth-century Ukrainian attitudes towards Shevchenko's work; it is exceptionally good on Drahomanov and Franko.

5 Cited in *ibid*. 200.

6 Ivan Franko, 'Suspilno-Politychni pohliady M. Drahomanova,' *Literaturno-naukovyi vistnyk*, 8 (1906) 227.

7 K. Ne-ia [K. Arabazhyn], 'Ukrainskyi Prometei: Z pryvodu 45-kh rokovyn smerti Tarasa Shevchenka,' *Vilna Ukraina*, 3 (1906) 5-16. Cited in V. Ie. Shubravsky, 'Shevchenko v krytytsi kintsia XIX-pochatku XX st.,' in *Shevchenkoznavstvo* 103.

8 D.I. Evarnitsky, 'Zaporozhtsy v poezii T.G. Shevchenko,' *Letopis Ekaterynoslavskoi uchenoi arkheologicheskoi kommissii*, VIII (1912) 102-59.

9 In Frank's *The Widening Gyre: Crisis and Mastery in Modern Literature* (New Brunswick: Rutgers University Press 1963) 3-62; Albert Cook, *Prisms* (Bloomington, Ind.: Indiana University Press 1967).

10 See, for example, Iu. O. Ivakin, 'Etapy rozvytku radianskoho Shevchenkoznavstva,' in *Shevchenkoznavstvo*, 175. In this case such obscene 'euphemisms' are that much more shocking since Ivakin's article is an informative, useful, and – considering the conditions in which the author worked – fairly honest account of Soviet Shevchenko scholarship.

11 See Bohdan Kravtsiv's detailed report on the destruction of Ukrainian scholarship in the 1930s, 'Rozhrom ukrainskoho literaturoznavstva 1917-1937 rr.,' in *Zbirnyk na poshanu ukrainskykh uchenykh znyshchenykh bolshevytskoiu Moskvoiu*, Mariia Ovcharenko, ed., Zapysky Naukovoho tovarystva im. Shevchenka, 173 (Paris, Chicago: NTSh 1962) 217-307. Also see Hryhorii

Kostiuk, 'Ukrainske naukove literaturoznavstvo v pershe porevoliutsiine desiatylittia,' in *Zbirnyk* 185-216.

12 Petro Odarchenko, 'Shevchenko in Soviet Literary Criticism,' in *Taras Ševčenko* 284-91.

13 O. Biletsky, 'Zavdannia i perspektyvy vyvchennia Shevchenka,' in *Zbirnyk prats IX naukovoi shevchenkivskoi konferentsii*, Akademiia nauk Ukrainskoi RSR, Instytut literatury im. T.H. Shevchenka (Kiev: AN USSR 1961) 19.

14 [Authors' Collective], 'Shevchenkoznavstvo v pisliavoienni roky (1945-1970),' in *Shevchenkoznavstvo* 214.

15 Biletsky, 'Zavdannia i perspektyvy ...' 17.

2

Graveside Oration

PANTELEIMON KULISH

No one among us is worthy of speaking in our native Ukrainian at Shevchenko's graveside: all the power and beauty of our language was revealed to him alone.[1] Yet, through him we have been granted a great and cherished right – the right to proclaim the native Ukrainian word over this vast land.

A poet such as Shevchenko is beloved not only by Ukrainians. Wherever he would have died in the immense Slavic world, whether in Serbia, in Bulgaria, or among the Czechs, he would have been at home. You were afraid, Taras, that you would die in a foreign place, among foreigners. This could not be! In the midst of your large family you went to your eternal resting place. No Ukrainian has had such a large family as you; no one ever received a farewell like yours. There have been great warriors in our native Ukraine; there have been great rulers. But you rise above them all and your family is the largest. For you, Taras, taught us that people were not made to be driven to their deaths, cities and villages were not made to be mere possessions; you taught us the sacred, life-giving truth. ... And because of your instruction, people of all tongues have gathered around you, like children around a father; because of your teaching you are kinsman to them all and they conduct you to the next world with tears and immense sorrow. We thank our Holy Father that we do not live in an age when, for the sake of truth, men were crucified upon the cross or burned at the stake. In neither catacombs nor caves have we gathered to praise a great man for his just teaching: we have gathered in the light of day in a great capital and together voice our sincere gratitude for his life-giving word.

Rejoice, Taras, that you have not been laid to rest in a foreign place, for no foreign place exists for you in the Slavic world, and foreigners do not consign you to the grave, for each good and wise soul is your kinsman. It was your wish to be buried on the bank overlooking the Dnipro-Slavuta, for you loved it and painted it and glorified it in resounding words. We have faith that with the help of the Lord we will be able to fulfil this wish. You will lie in your native Ukrainian soil, on the bank of the famous Dnipro, for you have wedded its name to your own for all eternity. ... And yet you left one other testament for us, Taras. You said to your perfect muse:

> My ne lukavyly z toboiu,
> My prosto ishly, – u nas nema
> Zerna nepravdy za soboiu ...

We were not cunning, you and I; / We walked a true path, – there is not a grain of untruth behind us ...

A great and sacred testament! Be confident, Taras, that we will observe it and will never turn from the path you indicated. Should we ever lack the strength to follow in your path, should it ever become impossible for us to proclaim the sacred truth without trepidation as you have done, then it would be far better for us to remain silent and allow your great words alone to speak the pure, unadulterated truth for all eternity.

(1861)

NOTES

1 This is the eulogy delivered in 1861 by Kulish at Shevchenko's original place of burial in St Petersburg. The translation is based on the text included in P. Kulish, *Tvory* (Lviv 1910) VI.

3

Why Shevchenko is a Poet of Our People

PANTELEIMON KULISH

News of the death of Taras Shevchenko has reached even those of us who live in the country.[1] It is a grievous misfortune that this great poet is no longer with us, and every tear that fell on his grave is blessed in the eyes of God: our accumulated tears have established the worth of this champion of our native word, which alone constitutes our strength as a people, our glory as a people, and alone gives us the right to a separate place among other nations. As long as Shevchenko was with us, we gave him the reverence due a great poet and turned a blind eye to all the mistakes and lapses along his lonely, arduous path; how great was the deed that he performed for us as Ukrainians and what we would be without Shevchenko has only now been fully revealed to us.

Literate townspeople have long neglected the illiterate villagers and their unprinted language; intellectually they embraced strangers, those who, in the vast community of the uneducated, keep together in a small group and, like an assembly of Jewish elders, understand only each other and do not care at all that they have left far behind them countless thousands of the illiterate. Our writers, too, have trailed behind these townspeople and with them written academic books and given themselves airs because they have managed to cast a net over human souls from sea unto sea with a single, bookish, academic language. These great writers and creators of the written word did not care that because of this net all our ordinary people appeared tongue-tied. They did not care that for these simple people there was no path to literature other than renunciation of the simple and easily understood native word. When our country people put their children in Russian schools, it was the same as sending them to the Russian army for because

of this illusory education the numbers of those who speak as we do, look
at God's world as we do, and live among the peasantry as we do grew
smaller.

The townspeople were muddying our common sense and unsullied taste
with their books and then, behold, there came into our simple cottage a
little man, dressed in our fashion, seemingly sharing our customs and our
language, who slowly spelled out the words of who knows what kind of
verses about some Aeneas.[2] It looked as if we should rejoice! The man is
writing verses in our language! But hardly! God save us from versification
like that! Soon some of us realized what sort of wonder that was. 'Just look
at this man closely,' they began to say. 'He is a little gentleman from town
dressed up like us. Look: he has the bearing of a gentleman and his character is entirely that of a gentleman. He simply imitates us with his words
and holds us up to ridicule. He is making fun of our customs, of our native
land, of our simplicity in not having genteel tastes – imagine that! – not
having genteel whims and spurning genteel bonbons. Look: his Aeneas says
such things about his own mother in public that it makes you want to run
out of the house; listen to the way he derides our customs, how he mangles
our Ukrainian language. The gentlefolk have presented us with the kind of
mirror that, when a simple man looks into it, he cannot even recognize
himself.'

This was the judgment handed down by our wise people on these verses
and every clear-thinking soul turned away from this Aeneas dishevelled in
God only knows what fashion. But then Kvitka's 'Marusia' dropped in on
us for a visit.[3] Dear heart, how lovely and dignified you seemed to us after
that Trojan gypsy! It was our soul nestled against God's breast speaking in
our language. It was the first book to breathe the same spirit as the word of
our blessed Teacher. Kvitka cast upon us simple folk the same gaze as that
great lover of man. We were amazed at how brightly our image as a people
shone forth, even though a plowman's sweat had settled upon it like a thick
layer of dust. We gazed deeply with Kvitka into the soul of our simple folk
and wondered where its inexpressible depth came from.

We were pondering this when suddenly Shevchenko called out loudly
all over Ukraine. It was as if all the folk songs and all human tears had
spoken in unison. He raised our silent memory from the grave, summoned
up our silent antiquity to judge, and set before it the Ukrainian as he is
now, as he has been moulded by history. Who could not make an effort to

understand, or feel in his soul that, having bathed in their own blood and endured devastation and conflagration numberless times, our forefathers must have drawn into their souls much from ancient times. Whether he described himself in his meditative poems, or old Perebendia, Kateryna's mother and father, or even Kateryna herself with her sincere feelings of love and her immense torment, Shevchenko immediately demonstrated a unique way of painting portraits in words, for both his own spiritual portrait and this entire family of kindred spirits were all children of our history. He took the sound and structure of his masterful language from those songs and *dumy* (historical songs) which only we in the country still listened to and understood in our hearts; the soul of our unwritten folk poetry became his muse's soul. His far-reaching embrace encompassed Ukraine with its bloody burial mounds and awesome glory and in his hands the language of the folk songs was transformed into images of what was and is in Ukraine. Our whole people sang of their fate with his lips: his words reverberated wherever our blood had flowed, wherever our bones lay; every heart was awakened by his song.

Kvitka was the first to understand that the poetry of our folk customs was that of a blessed and truly human family. Shevchenko presented us with the poetry of our life as a people. Kvitka surprised us all by revealing the noble, heroic soul of the quiet, meek plowman, of simple village life. Shevchenko allowed us to plumb its mysterious depths, recalled to us our forgotten Ukrainian history, and showed that this meek soul had existed in misery not for days or hours but for centuries and had not become contemptible, did not crouch timidly, had not become the servant of evil, but had retreated deep into itself and, standing among evil people with lowered gaze, silently bided its time, and awaited its fate. Thus, when Shevchenko's fiery poetry illuminated Kvitka's native works, then we realized that Naum Drot[4] is that same folk hero Samiilo Kishka[5] for, living in foreign parts, he endured a test no less demanding than Samiilo's and, suffering through century after century, did not bend, did not allow his steadfast and noble spirit to be diminished in stature.

Shevchenko is our poet and our first historian. He was the first to inquire of our silent burial mounds what they were and to him alone they gave an answer as clear as God's word. Shevchenko was the first to understand where the glory of our history lay and the reasons why future generations would curse it. Just as the folk song set the tone for his masterful language, so he gave us all the true tone upon which to tune our word. High above us, Shevchenko raised his poetic light, and everywhere in Ukraine the direction in which each of us must proceed became clear. In this light everyone came to understand how truly glorious and great in its simplicity is the village world from which Kvitka had selected his Marusia and her poetic family. In this light, everyone could see that our folk customs are one with the history of our spirit, our folk songs, and the folk *duma*, but only to the more lofty poetic gaze is their beauty and dignity revealed. Everyone with any claim to wisdom understood that in our letters we were not to follow in any footsteps other than those of our folk genius, which is silent in the chronicles of our gentry and monks but lives secretly in our customs and speaks loudly only in the folk song and *duma*.

There was Konysky who, with his *Istoriia Rusov* (A History of the Russes),[6] obscured our history with an ornate curtain until Shevchenko rent that curtain, tore it apart. Immediately after him came Kotliarevsky who, in his *Eneida*, made our simple life and wise customs seem like the refuse heap outside the gentry's doors. Both our poets turned away from this refuse heap and showed us different Ukrainians with their Ukrainian women in 'Marusia,' 'Serdeshnia Oksana' (Poor Oksana), 'Kozyr-Divka' (A Lively Wench), 'Kateryna,' 'Naimychka' (The Servant Girl), and other genuinely poetic works.

Kvitka was the first to draw tears from Ukrainians by using the Ukrainian language and in doing so showed us that we have not yet been reduced to numbers; there really are things to be told in our language, things over which to shed tears. And perhaps our simple folk in their homespun peasant cloaks are worthy of greatness if, joining this family, the wisest and most educated among us regards it as his own – if the strongest and most celebrated among us, the noblest and purest in spirit, does not refuse to call Marusia his own sister, her mother – his mother and her father his father. These are the poor, meek people whom Kvitka praised before the entire world; is their equal anywhere on this vast earth?

We crowded around Kvitka, however many of us there were then of like mind and sharing the same faith. We were few, because some had been blighted by the false learning of the towns and others necessarily tethered to the land; but all the same Shevchenko found us ready to listen to his mournful meditations and began to summon into our small circle our countrymen from all over the world.

They responded to our *kobzar* with cordial greetings in the Caucasus, in Siberia, from beyond Bendery, and the Sluch and Danube rivers. Ukrainians throughout the world were aroused, pricked up their ears, and accepted the good tidings of their *narodnist* (identity as a people). Shevchenko was like a lofty banner among a people scattered over thousands of miles and since then we have divided into the living and the dead and will long continue to do so.[7] His life-giving word became the kernel of a new force never dreamed of by the wisest among our countrymen before Kotliarevsky and that new force is *narodnist*. It made kinsmen of us, united us, and affirmed our Ukrainian being for all time. With this great feat in the realm of letters, Shevchenko completed the deed that our hetmans, with their impure hearts, had attempted. Having raised our resonant Ukrainian language out of its decline, Shevchenko marked out generous boundaries for our national spirit. No longer is our right to be a people carved by the sword on enemy fortresses; not only by old documents and seals is it secured against human subterfuge; it lies protected in thousands of faithful Ukrainian souls and is sealed by recollections a thousand years old.

Only our native word restored us to a respected position among nations and laid a new foundation for our existence as a historical entity. For Shevchenko took his language with its miraculous power not from the large towns, not from the self-acclaimed academies, not from the midst of the luminaries and the powerful; he passed them all by, disregarded, and forsook them. The language of the country and the village alone served his purposes; only in the villages, in simple cottages, did he search out people for his poems, people noble in spirit, pure of heart, dignified, of high repute. Through these people, through their poetic and righteous souls, the mystery of our past was revealed to him; these people, forgotten by the gentry, gave him the strength to open ancient graves and from our blood-stained land, as though from parchment, to read the sacred truth. Through their independent spirit he was able to rise to those great works which, without benefit of a printer, circulate throughout the world and in fiery letters are imprinted upon all sincere Ukrainian hearts. They gave him the wings to rise above the earth like an exalted, other-worldly phantom and survey from the heights all human souls and mourn them. Our living history and our renowned chronicles also placed before him Prometheus, whose bloodied heart dies each hour and each hour revives. Their eternal souls taught him to speak both to the dead and to the unborn.

Taking our history as viewed by the simple, sound mind of the people, Shevchenko gave it a new image – not the one found in Konysky – taking our people through their history, he reveals them to be other than they are in Kotliarevsky. He cleansed our history of all deception by means of the righteous and noble spirit of the folk, and gave it dignity in the eyes of the wise through his memories of the old world. After that time Ukraine entered upon a new life and whoever undertook to work on behalf of the community and was not dim-sighted knew very well where to set to work and where to go. Our popular efforts made great advances, if not in the name of all those who lived in Ukraine, then in the name of all loyal Ukrainian souls. It was as if under Shevchenko's banner we had returned to our sacred hearth from foreign lands and our native literature had become the servant of God's truth. After Shevchenko's majestic and sacred word, Kotliarevsky and his followers seemed an affront to all that we hold most sacred, and only those who were not afraid of disturbing the prayer of our *narod* with their pitiful clamour continued to babble the frivolous little verses of our sterile flowers, like children. Our literature fell silent for some time, listening attentively to the solemnly joyous proclamation of Taras's poetry, and the silence in which the poet presented us with the new canons for the Ukrainian word was life-giving. He performed no small feat with this joyous proclamation; he summoned the forgotten into the family, into the midst of those whom we justly exalt. That word was a test for the forgotten, a test of whether they were worthy of such company, of whether they would rise from that sleep which had lasted for tens and even hundreds of years. That word was their eternal right to have dominion over that which no one can either confer or destroy. Through the word a new fraternal union, a new Ukrainian family, was affirmed.

This was Shevchenko's feat! This was Taras's place in our life as a people. Making the majestic soul of the *narod* the supreme model for his creativity, he designated a simple path, a path chosen without others' advice. Only now will the efforts of those who lead our great national community, who know its spiritual needs, share its pure tastes, and look upon the world with its righteous gaze not be insignificant. For this reason only those from the country and villages know best and feel in their hearts the true value of Shevchenko. He led them, like another Israel, out of their bondage to that bookishness from which the literate townsfolk obtained all their instruction. He cast off the ignominy for which they were known the world over, that they were a good-for-nothing people. He extolled their spiritual image and offered it as an example to the civilized world: behold, enlightened lands and states, this indigent people can trace its existence to a thousand years ago and for a thousand years it submitted in its darkness and need to the representatives of authority. It did not bow down before those who sought to rise above it and distinguish themselves by putting on lordly airs; it spat them out like bad blood; only the community was extolled as 'the great one.' This great and just word, which will remain unblemished for all time, I proclaimed to the poor and simple and they understood it, showered and sanctified it with their burning tears and for them this word of mine will become an unconquerable power. No earthly force will lessen its power and, as long as the sun continues to rise, it will not be forgotten. Some day the celebrated deeds and triumphs of the great townsmen, who from time to time look down at you, my poor orphans, from their lofty heights, will pass into oblivion but through my word your spiritual image will never be forgotten. Through my word I created for you an eternal memory and from you fashioned eternal remembrance among the living.

Thus does Taras's spirit speak to our sorrowing souls. His death gave his poetry fresh force and here in the country and in villages it is being read again. All his words are now illuminated by a new light and it seems strange to us that only a short time ago such a poet lived in our midst. A small volume of his writings will appear and a volume tenfold larger can be written about it.[8] Let others abler than we take up this task; as for us, it is enough that we wrote in our simple way what we thought about Taras and what we felt in our hearts. Renown will be yours, Taras, as long as there is one young lass in Ukraine to sing our native songs, as long as there is one mother to fondle her child in our way, as long as there is one father to tell his son about our ancient burial mounds in words not foreign to our ears.

(1861)

NOTES

1 This piece, the third letter in *Letters from a Country Homestead* (1861), was first published as 'Lysty z khutora: Lyst III (Choho stoit Shevchenko iako poet narodnyi),' *Osnova*, 3 (1861) 25-32. It is upon this text that the translation is based.

2 The reference is, of course, to Ivan Kotliarevsky's *Eneida*, which began to appear in 1798 and was printed in full in 1842. A burlesque poem based on Virgil's *Aeneid*, it was the first long poetic work in the Ukrainian language and marks the beginning of modern Ukrainian literature. Although Kotliarevsky's *Eneida* was generally received with enthusiasm, Kulish was among those who came to feel that in its comic treatment of the Ukrainian folk it desecrated the sacred image of his people and did his nation a great disservice (ed.).

3 A short story in the sentimental style from 1833. Sometimes regarded as the beginning of modern Ukrainian prose, Hryhorii Kvitka-Osnovianenko's 'Marusia' was written partly to demonstrate that the Ukrainian language could be used to portray lofty emotions as well as to depict the customs and the moral character of the peasants. It is for its accomplishments in this domain that Kulish holds the work in such high esteem (ed.).

4 Naum Drot is Marusia's father, a rich peasant who does not want his daughter to marry the poor boy Vasyl, whom she loves. For Kulish, Naum Drot and Samiilo Kishka are symbolic figures of the heroic past who upheld patriarchal village life and the Cossack ethos, faced by the overwhelming odds of foreign domination (ed.).

5 Samiilo Kishka, hetman of the Ukrainian Cossacks from 1600 to 1602 (ed.).

6 This history of Ukraine, which served to stimulate the national revival, is of uncertain origin. Most likely written in the first decade of the nineteenth century, it was printed in 1846 after circulating in manuscript form in the 1820s and 1830s. At first it was attributed to Archbishop Heorhii Konysky. Subsequently, because of its libertarian and nationalistic tone, other possible authors were suggested, most frequently Hryhorii Poletyka (1725-84) (ed.).

7 A reference to Shevchenko's poem 'To My Dead and Living and Yet Unborn Countrymen in Ukraine and not in Ukraine My Friendly Epistle' (ed.).

8 Kulish is perhaps alluding to the new edition of *Kobzar* that he was finally able to have printed in 1860 (ed.).

4

Excerpts from *Shevchenko, the Ukrainophiles, and Socialism*

MYKHAILO DRAHOMANOV

A proper estimation of any man, of any writer, can only be made when he is examined from a historical and objective perspective as well as from within the context of the community from which he sprang and in which he worked.[1] Studies of this type have demonstrated that never, in any era, have there been prophets who in fact gave full expression to their nation. These studies destroy idols and sacred relics but in return provide a true picture of the prophets of the past and direct us to examine in the future, not personalities with all their temporal and individual peculiarities and flaws, but rather ideas.

Neither as poet nor public personality has Shevchenko yet been subjected to an objective historical examination of this sort. To do so is indeed not an easy task, for those close to him did not provide the foundation necessary for such a study, neither detailed information nor even a complete and well organized edition of all that he wrote....

Not only Shevchenko's youth, but also that middle period of his life when he lived in Kiev and moved in the 'better' Ukrainian circles, are still obscure. Only now is what Shevchenko learned in Poland, from the Poles and from Polish literature, beginning to be discussed. Sirko talks about what Shevchenko derived from his stay in Warsaw during the revolution of 1830.[2] For us all this is obscure. Little is known about Shevchenko's life in Petersburg, about what he learned there and what he thought of those Russian writers such as S. Burachek, Zhukovsky, and others whom he knew. Were someone to tell us which books Shevchenko read most frequently at which times during those years when his literary and social personalities were being formed, even if they could not say with whom and what he talked and wrote about in his letters, then it would be possible to make some positive judgments about his intellectual development in his early and middle years.

The strongest influences upon Shevchenko in his middle period were undoubtedly his Kievan companions of 1845-6, men far more educated than he, and his many friends of noble extraction in the provinces of Chernihiv and Poltava....

[From accounts of the relationship between Shevchenko and the Brotherhood of Saints Cyril and Methodius] it can be concluded that it was not the educated members of society who led the way but Shevchenko. Why? Certainly not because of his learning but rather because of his fiery temperament and the fact that it fell to him to experience personally the fate of Ukraine. It was 'sweet' for the educated members of the Brotherhood to hear his 'unpublished' works, and 'awesome' as well![3] Perhaps it was for this reason that they 'kept him at a distance from the Brotherhood,' because the fiery-tempered poet would very quickly have impelled these learned Slavonists 'into politics,' and *muzhik* (peasant) politics at that.[4] That Shevchenko occasionally became annoyed with his learned friends can be seen from the following lines from his 'Epistle' (I mertvym, i zhyvym, i nenarodzhenym zemliakam moim v Ukraini i ne v Ukraini moie druzhnieie poslaniie / To My Dead and Living and Yet Unborn Countrymen in Ukraine and not in Ukraine My Friendly Epistle):

I Koliara chytaiete
Z usiiei syly,
I Shafaryka, i Hanku,
I v slovianofily
Tak i pretes ... I vsi movy
Slavianskoho liudu,
Vsi znaiete. A svoiei
Dast-bih!...

And you read Kollar / With all your might / And Šafařik and Hanka / And elbow your way / Into the ranks of the Slavophiles. ... And all the languages / Of the Slavic peoples, / All of them do you know. As for your own / – Be it as God grants!...

The *muzhik* Shevchenko was the most noteworthy among his educated friends, the Kievan Slavophiles, both in his passionate social thought and his equally passionate Ukrainianism. In addition, he had seen more of the peasant world, and also more of Russia, than they. He had seen Petersburg with its tsar and the nobility in whom the members of the Brotherhood placed their hopes. In fact, the poem 'Son' (The Dream), in which Shevchenko clearly took a stand against tsarism, was written in 1844 when he was still in Petersburg and before he met Kostomarov (1845), who was undoubtedly the leading member of the Kievan Slavophile circle. There is indeed a great deal of truth in the words of the countryman of Shevchenko mentioned by Sirko, who indicated that Shevchenko came to Ukraine from Petersburg with his ideas already developed about the liberation of Ukraine from the Muscovite tsars. We know that in Petersburg Shevchenko lived among people far more educated than he, people whom he apparently respected but who were far from being republicans. Briullov alone may have occasionally expressed his annoyance with Tsar Nicholas I, his 'patron.' Yet it is a long way from this to what is to be found in Shevchenko's 'The Dream.' Clearly, while in Petersburg Shevchenko must have developed his anti-tsarist ideas more 'out of his own head' than with the help of learning and those more learned than he.

It was almost the same in Kiev where, if in fact he did learn anything new, it must have been something about Slavdom, which he had already begun to think about in Petersburg, observing in his 'Haidamaky' (The Haidamaks) how sad it was that 'the children of the ancient Slavs had become drunk with blood' (Starykh slovian dity / Vpylys kroviu). It could even be concluded from Shevchenko's 'Epistle' and the observations of Kulish and Kostomarov that, after his arrival in Kiev, Shevchenko began to lose his admiration for the Cossacks, not so much from having learned the history of Ukraine from his educated friends and acquaintances as from a sense of annoyance with their vainglorious self-image as 'the Ukrainian Brutuses and Cocleses.' And here too the semi-*muzhik* Shevchenko had to find his own way to the truth, without the help of learning or his learned friends.

Besides those belonging to the Kievan university circle, there was another group of people in Ukraine with whom Shevchenko associated, another group of Ukrainophiles – the land-owners of the Left Bank, among whom Shevchenko was well known and well received....

This society was headed by several noble families whose aristocratic French education had already given rise to the beginnings of something higher. Yet, because of serfdom, which ruined the character of the nobleman by making him lazy, and the political order, which did not allow a capable man to do anything for the community, even those who had absorbed not merely France's fashions and dances but also her libertarian ideas were severely crippled. O. Afanasiev-Chuzhbynsky describes these people as follows:

Here a few words must be said about the small circle which took Shevchenko up. This small circle of intelligent and noble people, most of whom were humane and enjoyed universal favour, belonged to that category of boon companions who, unable to devote themselves to social endeavours and renounce their youthful, dissipated life, found their only joy in drunkenness, choosing as their motto the Latin proverb *in vino veritas*. This weakness, for which allowances were made among the aristocracy and which at the same time merited special praise because of its harmless character, did not, however, prevent the members of the circle from being pleasant conversationalists throughout the day, as they could drink a great deal and only attain to the state when the tongue refuses to function and objects double before the eyes in the evening. This circle was called 'the society of whistle-wetters'....[5]

Among the nobles from whose numbers these men came there were people who, in addition to being sincere and non-bureaucratic, possessed certain libertarian ideas which they derived from the works of Hugo, Lamartine, and others. For instance, they thought highly of a book by Mickiewicz that had been banned. Among them too were women who understood Shevchenko and who, he always believed, would appreciate his work (for example, S.A. Zakrevska, author of the story 'Institutka' [The College Girl], published in *Otechestvennye zapiski*). There was Prince Repnin, a man descended from the Decembrists and even perhaps the author of *Istoriia Rusov* (History of the Russes), a book which profoundly influenced Shevchenko; there were also men whom Nicholas I had exiled to the Caucasus, such as Count Iakov Balmen, to whom Shevchenko dedicated his poem 'Kavkaz' (The Caucasus), and others like V. Zakrevsky (honoured by the society of whistle-wetters with the title 'His Drunken Eminence'), who were taken to the Third Section for praising the French

Republic. We venture to conclude that Shevchenko heard more daring libertarian European ideas (not systematic political thought but at least biting witticisms directed at church and government) from these people than from his Kievan university friends to whom, from all indications, non-specialized European writing was rather unfamiliar. These fragments of European political thought which Shevchenko heard from the nobility of Poltava province were more valuable to him than quotations from Šafařik and Hanka, whose works the poet certainly never held in his hands, or Kostomarov's *Slavianskaia mifologiia* (Slavic Mythology), which was printed in Church Slavonic script.

Shevchenko ridiculed the Ukrainian land-owners 'who thronged to foreign lands in search of the highest good, the sacred good, liberty, liberty and fraternal brotherhood' (kotre perlos na chuzhynu / Shukaty dobroho dobra, / Dobra sviatoho. Voli! Voli! / Braterstva bratnoho!), and who crawled into the heavens and said: 'There is no hell, no paradise' (Nema ni pekla, ani raiu). And he was right when he upbraided them because from foreign parts they 'brought to Ukraine many big words and nothing else' (v Ukrainu prynesly / Velykykh sliv velyku sylu, / Ta i bilsh nichoho), because they cried out that God had not created them to bend the knee to falsehood – yet all the same they bent as they did before and tore the hide off their unseeing peasant brothers. However, when these noblemen are compared with those belonging to the Petersburg *Maiak*[6] circle which Shevchenko happened upon following those of his countrymen who were followers of Kvitka or even with the evangelical Kievan Slavophiles, then it must be said that some of these noblemen, if only because of those 'big words' brought from foreign parts, were useful to Shevchenko, because later he himself began to say many of the things he had heard from his high-born countrymen, things that had once made him angry with them....

According to Afanasiev-Chuzhbynsky's account, Shevchenko's life in Ukraine from 1843-7 emerges as a period of rather aimless semi-aristocratic idleness spent in the company of the country nobility, a time spent in drinking with the men, dancing and enjoying music with the women attending balls at the governor's mansion in Chernihiv, composing caricatures of young provincial women at various clubs, whiling away the time with students in Nizhyn, and so on, and occasionally, to use Shevchenko's own words, 'carousing' all day in bed. The only relief from all this was the leisurely reading of whatever books chanced to be at hand and thoughts and dreams about 'floating down the Dnipro on an oak log to Zaporizhzhia, then to Lyman, to search for remnants of antiquity,' perhaps sketching a church, etc. If the muse happens by, then a poem gets written; if the occasion arises – a witty remark is uttered in the company of friends or to a group of *muzhiks* (for example, that a fire at a Jew's house also ought to be extinguished); if not, then the poet will resign himself to playing with children. From what his close friends tell us about this best period of his life, no plan for his work or life can be perceived because Shevchenko had none of those methodical views about life and work which only a systematic education can provide....

[In light of this we may] ask: did Shevchenko belong to the school of simple and hence peasant writers? ... [Did] Shevchenko write his poems for the *muzhik*, or rather, did he deliberately write in so simple a fashion that even the *muzhik* could understand him?

Anyone who reads the most beloved of Shevchenko's poems, especially those containing social ideas, will know that the poet intended them least of all for the *muzhik*. Why else would he bring in not only the 'Polish confederates' but all those Apollos, Cencis, and Coliseums, which he occasionally so sacrilegeously confused, knowing so little about both history and the mythology which he greedily consumed at the Academy. In a good half of the works that he wrote with the greatest fervour, Shevchenko emerges least of all as a poet writing for the *muzhik*. Just try, for example, to read his 'Epistle,' which some consider the very essence of Shevchenko, to the *muzhik*! And there is nothing surprising in this. When, as is now the case, the distance between people with respect to education is as great as it is between the land-owner and the *muzhik*, then it is not possible for the writer, and especially the writer who wishes to influence the community, to write so that he is understood equally well by the *muzhik* and the land-owner. To be sure, a literary school favouring a simple manner can dispose a poet or prose writer to write as simply as possible. Thus the literary school to which Shevchenko belonged turned him against simplicity. Of Shevchenko as a painter, Mikeshin and Prakhov (*Pchela*, 16 [1876]) write: 'Shevchenko lost little time in making the transition from Briullov's academic classicism to realism, the manner natural and native to his talent.' The same can be said about Shevchenko as a writer who learned to write by reading Zhukovsky and Mickiewicz. Shevchenko's canvases, their genre aside, reveal that he was never able to break completely with classicism; occasionally he only blended classicism with realism, 'the French with the Nizhnii Novgorodian' as, for example, in the canvas depicting water nymphs (Mikeshin and Prakhov). The same can be said about many of his later works, such as 'Neofity' (The Neophytes).

In saying this, we do not wish to imply that there are no 'unmannered' scenes in Shevchenko, which are occasionally so simple in their language that the most ignorant and unlettered person could in fact understand them. Such is the case, for example, in most of his *non-political* poems. It must be said, however, that their simplicity is owing more to chance than to design and more to the nature of poetry (which always tends towards simplicity), than to the school to which the poet belonged, a school that was anything but simple.

The same can be said about the *subject matter* of Shevchenko's poetry. Our *kobzar* began as a romantic, and romantic writers did not primarily strive to select subjects that were ordinary and hence typical. When Shevchenko was beginning to write, Russian literature had all but bid *adieu* to the romanticism of Zhukovsky, Kozlov, etc. Gogol brought romanticism to an end in Russia, while the remaining traces were dispelled by the truly 'social *belles-lettres*' of the first half of the 1840s (the literature that came between Gogol, on the one hand, and Turgenev, Ostrovsky, etc., on the other) and the criticism of Belinsky, that is, the criticism of the 'natural' and later of the 'social' schools. The natural school urged writers to portray people as they really were, and people who were ordinary rather than exceptional. The social school required that even social evil be depicted through ordinary people and preferably through ordinary people who were relatively good rather than evil. In this way it appeared not only more truthful but also had a greater impact upon the community, inciting it against existing conditions rather than extraordinary crimes. Such, for example, are the descriptions of the serfs and land-owners in Turgenev's 'Dva pomeshchika' (Two Land-owners), 'Mumu' (Moomoo), etc. Those familiar with Russian prose of the 1840s (P. Nestroev-Kudriavtsev, Sto Odin [A.D. Galakhov], Iskander [Herzen], Dostoevsky, etc.) will know that of all the European socialist ideas these writers were most taken by Robert Owen's idea that man is not to blame for what he has become or what he does, since he is what he is because of the environment in which he grew up and the conditions in which he lives. It was this notion that made the 'social' school of new Russian writers as described here.

This new idea was completely unknown to Shevchenko. He continued to judge and condemn people in the old way and even wished to 'terrify Hell and amaze old Dante with our magnates and lordlings.' Shevchenko never on his own attained the ideas of the natural and social schools and there was (and still is) no Ukrainian criticism similar to Belinsky's. Belinsky himself was disliked in Ukrainian circles partly because Ukrainians, whom the forces of history had made into provincials, that is, into involuntary followers, were not yet ready for him and partly because Belinsky, having been misled by conventional Muscovite belief and the Hegelian concept of statehood, would have nothing to do with 'literature of the provincial type.'[7] In his earlier poems, Shevchenko was unreservedly a romantic ('Pry- chynna' / The Bewitched Woman; 'Topolia' / The Poplar; 'Utoplena' / The Drowned Maiden). Subsequently his work became more realistic, but he still succumbed to melodrama as, for example, in 'Kateryna' (the passage beginning 'Her father sits at the end of the table' / 'Sydyt batko v kinets stola' and even the scene in which Kateryna meets the wagoners and soldiers), in 'The Haidamaks' (when Honta buries his children), 'Vidma' (The Witch; the death of her father) and even in 'Naimychka' (The Servant Girl), the simplest and most life-like of all his narrative poems (the death of the servant girl). Until the very end Shevchenko occasionally selected completely unrealistic subjects. He stooped to using allegories quite inimical to poetry (for example, 'Velykyi lokh' / The Great Vault), or to obscure language [for example, 'Isaia. Hlava 35 (Podrazhaniie)' / Isaiah 35 (An Imitation), etc.]. Sometimes it is even pitiful to witness the childish ineptitude with which the poet dealt with living people and scenes from real life [for example, 'Sotnyk' / The Captain; 'The Dream' (1844) from which we need only cite the scene depicting the tsar's court, especially the passage noted by Sirko where 'the Tsar approaches the greatest of the lords ... and smashes him in the face' (tsar pidkhodyt / Do naistarshoho ... ta v pyku / Ioho iak zatopyt'), etc; 'Vo Iudei vo dni oni' / 'In Judea in those far-off days' when Herod licks the lictor's boots and begs for a half dinar for a drink]. Seeking to portray the loathsomeness of the land- owners, Shevchenko always selected their most exceptional evil deeds (for example, 'Kniazhna' / The Princess; 'Varnak' / The Convict) and usually resorted to the 'sin of fornication,' neglecting other no less significant sins not so much of individual land-owners as of the land-owners as a group, ordinary sins, all the more serious for being committed by groups, not individuals.

I must repeat that in spite of this, Shevchenko gave us the most vivid scenes of everyday life (it will suffice to point to the old man, woman, and boy in 'The Servant Girl,' to 'Sadok vyshnevyi kolo khaty' / 'A cherry orchard by the house,' to 'Teche voda z-pid iavora' / 'Water flows past a maple tree'), and sketches portraits of officials, land-owners, soldiers, 'Muscovites,' Ukrainians, young girls (two types: Kateryna, the Servant Girl, etc. and Nastia in 'The Captain,' the girls in 'Iak by meni chere-vyky' / 'If I had a pair of shoes' and 'Iakby meni, mamo, namysto' / 'If I had a string of corals, mother'). He revealed a great deal of everyday hardship resulting from existing conditions – social hardship, the hardship of the soldier's life ('Pustka' / 'A Deserted Cottage,' etc.) and that of servants ('If I had a pair of shoes') – in the simplest and most life-like manner. This, too, was a gift of the poet's nature and to some extent, as we know, of the times whose influence not even our poet could escape, but it was not a result of the school from which he came and whose influence his countrymen, his community, and its critics were unable to counteract. We have seen that it was quite beyond the capabilities of the Ukrainian community to provide Shevchenko with the education necessary for him in his era. Neither did it regularly assist him with its literary criticism. When our poet was in his formative years, foreign critics ridiculed him and his countrymen were only capable of bowing down before him just as they do to this day. The treasure which Shevchenko gave us he found within himself and it is a part of our heritage rather in spite of his school and his lettered countrymen than because of them....

[In] his early writing Shevchenko revealed himself to be just as pious as Kvitka and did not demonstrate that he was not taken with the attitude of the writers associated with the journal *Maiak*. The Slavophile circle in Kiev drew him even further into 'holy writ,' which left its mark on him for all time.[8] To be sure, Shevchenko subsequently became an 'evangelical' Christian rather than a devotee of Orthodox 'Byzantism' and sought in the Bible the spirit of populist prophecy, those biblical sermons which speak of God's punishment of the unjust. We would not be far wrong were we to compare Shevchenko's faith during his middle years with that of an eighteenth-century Puritan Independent, adding only that as a poet, painter, and Orthodox Christian Shevchenko could thrust from his mind neither the Mother of God nor even the divine service.[9] Shevchenko generally remained a 'man of the Bible' until his death, as can be seen, for example, from his 'Isaiah 35 (An Imitation),' written in 1859 or 'In Judea in those far-off days,' which ends with an apostrophe to Christ beginning with the lines 'Save us, blessed, mighty Child' (Spasy ty nas, mladenche pravednyi, velykyi!). Even in 'Mariia,' where Shevchenko moved furthest from the gospels, there occurs the following passage, which causes some critics to say that Shevchenko never ceased to be a Christian:

> Vse upovaniie moie
> Na tebe, mii presvitlyi raiu,
> Na myloserdiie tvoie,
> Vse upovaniie moie,
> Na tebe, maty, vozlahaiu,
> Sviataia sylo vsikh sviatykh!
> Preneporochnaia, blahaia!

All my hope / In you, my glorious Paradise, / In your mercy / All my hope / I place in you, Mother. / The holy power of all saints, / Immaculate and blessed!

These words could not have been written by an unwavering rationalist. The kind of rationalist that our friend [Sirko] reveals Shevchenko to have been, our poet never was nor could have been, for in order for this to be the case Shevchenko would have had to undergo a different schooling and to have kept different company. All those anti-Christian and even impious words and scenes to which our friend points are simply outbursts of despair uttered by a man of fiery temperament who does not see God's promises realized on earth. They are the blasphemies of a free-thinker or a poet's daring assaults. This is the same *beginning* of rationalism that we see in our folk tales and songs, which does not prevent the *muzhik* from going to church or seeking a priest's advice, but it is not something that can properly be called rationalism, for this term refers to consistent (consequential) and ordered (systematic) thought. We see Shevchenko jumping from impious outbursts to faith in the judgment of God. Even 'Mariia' demonstrates that he did not break with Christianity, but reveals his desire to reinterpret Christian faith to suit his own image of it and transform it into the handmaiden of his *muzhik* perception of the world. A consistent rationalist cannot have such dreams.

These conclusions can be supported by a year-by-year review of what both his friends and he himself have written and not only by excerpts from the 'uncensored' works contained in the second volume of the Prague edition of *Kobzar*, on the basis of which Sirko makes of Shevchenko both a deist and a rationalist.[10]

We have already noted how in 1845 in his 'Epistle' Shevchenko vented his anger against the Europeanized 'unbelieving' nobles. On this and perhaps also the subsequent periods of Shevchenko's life the following account by Kozachkovsky should be brought to bear: 'I was witness to an occasion when, having listened to the blasphemy of the master of the house in which he resided, he said: "Scoffing at ethico-religious beliefs consecrated by the centuries and millions of people is foolish and criminal".' And, obviously, not only deism but everything related to the Church, even all the facets of Byzantism, are consecrated by the centuries and the millions.

Only later, reflecting on the fact that 'God's punishment' and 'God's truth' were slow to come, does Shevchenko exclaim:

A boh kunaie. Bo tse bulo b dyvo,
Shchob chuty i bachyt i ne pokarat!
Abo vzhe azh nadto dovhoterpelyvyi ...
('The Princess')

And God slumbers. For it would be strange / Were He to hear and see but not punish! / Or else He is overly patient ...[11]

'The Princess' was written in 1847 and the introduction to it in 1858. Whether written in 1847 or inserted later, perhaps in 1858, these words are important as a revelation of the fact that it was Shevchenko's complaining about the absence of punishment for sin that produced the first bright sparks of his free-thinking assaults against the Christian God. During his exile this idea increasingly gave Shevchenko pause and in 1850 he concluded his poem 'Iakby vy znaly, panychi' (If you but knew, lordlings) with the following outburst:

Ni! Ni! nichoho
Nema sviatoho na zemli!
Meni zdaietsia, shcho i samoho
Tebe vzhe liude proklialy!

No! no! there is nothing / Sacred on this earth! / It seems to me that men / Have cursed even You!

At the same time, however, attempting to console Kozachkovsky following a death in his family, Shevchenko wrote: 'believe deeply, wisely!' Even in 1857 in his poem 'The Neophytes,' Shevchenko still stood upon a foundation of Christian faith and even worshipped the Holy Cross, in no way revealing himself to have been a rationalist, as Sirko claims. Although in this poem he does say: 'All is a lie: the kings and the priests alike!' (Vse brekhnia: i tsari i popy!) he says this about the ancient Roman priests with their idols 'of stone'; he disallows prayer to anybody or anything on earth except truth (and not to kings) and when it comes to the heavens he issues the call: 'pray to our blessed Lord' (molites Bohovi sviatomu). How Sirko could have excluded these words, which stand immediately next to the passage from 'The Neophytes' which he introduces in his article (p 63) as proof of 'Shevchenko's full-fledged rationalism,' is beyond our comprehension. Only in 1859 while in Petersburg did Shevchenko begin to break out of the confines of Christianity and not simply Byzantism. This occurred, in our opinion, because Shevchenko was growing progressively more troubled by the absence of truth on earth and because in Petersburg he encountered that series of social ideas which prompted him to read Herzen, Karl Vogt, Ludwig Büchner, Feuerbach, etc. At this time too the devout Slavophiles began to irritate him. (See, for example, his prayer, 'Umre muzh velii v vlasianytsi' / The great man in the haircloth shirt will die), on the death of Metropolitan Grigorii, whom Shevchenko, following Herzen's *Kolokol*, calls a 'skirt chaser.'[12] In Petersburg, Shevchenko also began to mix to some extent with the group associated with the journal *Sovremennik*, which promulgated, as best it could, the new European philosophical ideas. Yet, whether it was his own lack of audacity and knowledge that prevented him from breaking with Christianity or the spirited opposition of his friends [one of whom, Kostomarov, took a stand against 'the fashionable progressives for whom it is convenient to ascribe materialism to the people'],

Shevchenko, as S. Krapyvyna (*Pravda*, 3 [1876] 104) testifies, was still praying to God each day, even in 1859 when he was already writing 'Mariia,' while in 1860 he published his *Bukvar Iuzhnorusskyi* (South Russian Primer) with its prayers and a new kind of 'Byzantism....'

Shevchenko went furthest in his thinking about freedom for the nation and the community in his ideas about the rich and the poor. Here he was impelled both by his own fate and the fate of Ukraine. Here, too, the little schooling he had greedily absorbed from the people stood him in good stead. The Pole, Gordon, is correct when he says that in his social views Shevchenko belongs in the ranks of the purest reds.[13] Shevchenko became one very early, in 1843-4, but we do not know how (undoubtedly largely on his own, without guidance). Shevchenko progressively became a more thoroughgoing red republican and democrat, tackling not only the problem of enslavement but also that of poverty.

We need not discuss the how and why: Sirko has done so in detail. We need only accurately fix the dividing lines between the stages through which Shevchenko's thinking about the Ukrainian nation and community passed in the middle and final years of his life. This can be done easily by means of a cursory examination of his writings, year by year.

Shevchenko's first poems expressed his longing for his native land ('Na vichnu pamiat Kotliarevskomu' / 'In Eternal Memory of Kotliarevsky'). Then came recollections of her fate and, of course, of the Cossacks and their wars with the Turks and the Poles (Ivan Pidkova; Tarasova nich / The Night of Taras; Hamaliia; The Haidamaks). And these recollections gave rise to the thought: how did it all end? Who took away Cossack liberty? Has it fallen into an eternal slumber? The answers to these questions appeared in his epistle 'Do Osnovianenka' (To Osnovianenko, 1840). At first the poet believed only that the glory of Ukraine 'will not die, will not pass into oblivion' (ne vmre, ne zahyne), that it would be recalled by bards such as Kvitka-Osnovianenko, who with their poetic voices and songs would take on the Muscovites more skilfully than he. Several years later in 'Chyhyryn' (1844), he recorded the expectation that his words would fashion knives which 'will cut out the bad, rotting heart' (rozpanakhaiut pohane, / Hnyle sertse) from the breasts of those of his countrymen who had forgotten their Ukraine, would drain the blood from it and fill it with living Cossack blood (cf. Isaiah 6). In the earlier poem, 'To Osnovianenko,' no political idea is evident and the poet emerges simply as a defender of his country, race, and language. In 'Chyhyryn' (Moscow, 19 February 1844), he speaks about 'the poison to our liberty' (voli nashoi otruta). In 'The Dream' (St Petersburg, 8 June 1844) Shevchenko already takes a stand against the Moscow-Petersburg tsars, executioners, and blood-suckers who have crucified Ukraine, attacking Peter I and Catherine II with the utmost vehemence and selecting images from *Istoriia Rusov* (A History of the Russes) for his onslaughts against the former.

All this makes it apparent that before the publication of the first edition of *Kobzar* (1840) Shevchenko had already come upon those countrymen in whose possession he was to find not only the works of Kotliarevsky and Kvitka, works which struck a responsive chord in the heart of this Ukrainian periodically overcome by melancholy in a land not his own and impelled him to write in Ukrainian, but also historical works such as Dmytro Bantysh-Kamensky's *Istoriia Maloi Rossii* (A History of Little Russia), which reawakened the poet's recollections about the Cossack burial mounds, the Haidamak era, and the like, recollections that he brought with him from the village, the legacy of his grandfather and others. Furthermore, between 1840 and 1844 Shevchenko became acquainted with *A History of the Russes*, attributed at that time to Archbishop Heorhii Konysky. This work captured his imagination with its Ukrainian autonomist ideas and Cossack republicanism, with its spirit in which the patriotism of the Cossack chroniclers of the seventeenth and eighteenth centuries and the *dumy* (epic songs) of the *kobzars* was blended with European republicanism of the Decembrist era. Shevchenko took entire scenes from *A History of the Russes*. In the years 1844-5 nothing, with the exception of the Bible, had such an influence on his thinking.

In 'The Great Vault' (Myrhorod 1845) Shevchenko emerged as a critic of Bohdan Khmelnytsky, who swore allegiance to Moscow, and as a supporter of both Mazepa, whose warriors were slaughtered by Moscow in Baturyn and near Poltava, and especially of the famous Polubotok, whom *A History of the Russes* portrays as the last Cato of the Cossack republic.

It cannot be held, as Kostomarov does, that Shevchenko never had 'dreams of local independence.' In all he wrote in 1845 ('The Great Vault'; 'Rozryta mohyla' / The Ransacked Grave; 'The Caucasus') Shevchenko expressed what was later called Ukrainian 'separatism.' It can even be said that his separatism was largely Cossack in character, although without that somewhat seignorial spirit which the Cossack elders began to manifest in the eighteenth century. It was a more democratic separatism, very much like that in *A History of the Russes*, yet above all a separatism which traced all evil in Ukraine and even the existence of the nobility to *foreigners*, to the Muscovite, to Moscow's tsars. When it came to the Ukrainian nobility and officials, Shevchenko was especially stung by the fact that they were 'turncoats who helped the Muscovite to administer and torment their motherland,' Ukraine, that they chattered ineptly in Russian and scoffed at their own language ('The Ransacked Grave,' 'The Dream'). In 'The Great Vault' Shevchenko prophesied the birth of a new Honta who would let freedom loose throughout Ukraine; in 'The Ransacked Grave' he clearly led us to understand that, if 'what had been buried in the grave by our old fathers' were to be found, that is, the Cossack state interred there by Khmelnytsky, then 'the children would not cry, the mother would not worry' (Ne plakaly b dity, maty b ne zhurylas); and in 'Zapovit' (My Testament) ... he openly urged his countrymen: 'arise, rend asunder your chains / And baptize freedom with the blood of the foe' (vstavaite, / Kaidany porvite / I vrazhoiu zloiu kroviu / Voliu okropite). On everything that Shevchenko wrote in 1845 there is the imprint of his concern with liberty and, most particularly, liberty for his race and country, for the Ukrainian national entity, and for the Ukrainian state.

In the works written in Ukraine towards the end of 1845 ('The Caucasus,' Viunyshche, 14 December; 'Kholodnyi Iar' / 'The Cold Ravine,' Viunyshche, 17 December), Shevchenko concentrated on serfdom (the reason needs no explanation), a theme that he had already touched on earlier ('A Dream,' 1844; 'The Great Vault'), but not to the same extent as here. This focus on serfdom and Kostomarov's Pan-Slavism, which engulfed him in 1845 [following 'Shafarykovi (Ieretyk)' / 'To Šafařík (The Heretic)' there stands the notation Pereiaslavl, 22 November 1845] divested Shevchenko to some extent of his 'separatism' and diverted his verbal arrows from 'foreign people,' from the 'Muscovites,' and in the direction of his own nobility, those high-born Ukrainophiles and admirers of the Cossacks whose numbers he, above all, had caused to swell through his fiery word. In his 'Epistle,' Shevchenko 'scoffed at the glory of the Ukrainian Cossacks like no one else,' as Panteleimon Kulish says, while it was his own historical Ukrainian separatism derived from *A History of the Russes* that most significantly undercut his favourable opinion of the Hetmanate.[14]

After Shevchenko had distanced himself from the Hetmanate, the further development of his admiration for the Cossacks involved the transfer of his sympathies to the Zaporozhians of the end of the seventeenth century, who opposed both Muscovite bondage and the increasingly undemocratic urban-oriented Hetmanate, which was prepared to give up a portion of Ukraine's liberty, especially the liberty of the 'good-for-nothings' (the rank and file Cossacks and the Zaporozhians) to preserve its dominion. (See 'Son' / 'The Dream,' 1847; 'Za bairakom bairak' / 'Beyond the ravine another ravine,' 1847 and compare them with the Zaporozhian edicts contained in *Hromada* I, 12).[15] The spirit emanating from Shevchenko's 1846-7 works, more akin to that of the rank and file Cossacks and Zaporozhians than the urban-oriented Hetmanate, reveals that Shevchenko had a truly unusual understanding, even an historian's understanding, for events....

Shevchenko's views concerning Ukraine's neighbours, those who had ruled and continued to rule her – Poland and the Poles, Russia and the Russians – underwent a similar development and modification because they were tightly bound up with his thinking about the Ukrainian state and nation. His early acquaintance with Polish noblemen and stewards, on the one hand, and Russian land-owners and officials, on the other, could not have left him with pleasant memories. A suspicion of and hostility towards foreigners, towards Ukraine's neighbours – what is called 'discrimination' – remained with Shevchenko until the end; in any case, not only these foreigners but even Shevchenko himself discusses this. Thus, the Pole, Gordon, who saw Shevchenko in 1850 in Uralsk, says that Shevchenko 'hates Muscovites, dislikes Poles.' [Gordon's *Soldat* is mentioned in Gwido Battaglia, *Taras Szewczenko* (Lviv 1865).] In Afanasiev-Chuzhbynsky we read the following:

He did not like Poles but was somehow drawn towards Mickiewicz. On several occasions he began to translate Mickiewicz's lyrical dramas but never completed his work and tore the pages into tiny pieces so that not even a trace would remain. Some lines would turn out unusually well but if just one seemed laboured or false, Shevchenko would cast aside and destroy all those that went before.

'Perhaps fate itself does not wish me to translate Polack songs,' he would say.

Shevchenko's attacks on Muscovites are sufficiently detailed in the article by our friend....

We regard Shevchenko's 'hatred of Muscovites and dislike of Poles' as a natural circumstance and those unsympathetic aspects of these feelings (for example, about Muscovites) pointed out by Sirko as indeed being present. The problem is that Shevchenko has come to be regarded as a figure in public life offering 'guiding ideas' to his countrymen and even as a socialist.

The man with political ideas subordinates his emotions to his ideas. The man who holds the wide-ranging ideas of these new times, and is a socialist at that, cannot elevate one race so much above the others as Shevchenko did when he said: 'There is no other Ukraine in the world, no other Dnipro' (Nema na sviti Ukrainy, nemaie druhoho Dnipra), cannot perceive and reveal in other races only the bad side of their national spirit. And for these reasons a man of this type will come to accept the guiding idea that all races share in the aspiration to replace the current unfavourable order with something better or, more accurately, will come to accept a whole series of guiding ideas which specify how this aspiration can be realized. None of this is to be found in Shevchenko – and because of this his national ideas as well as his ideas about the state went through the same process: that is, having initially proclaimed a discriminatory Ukrainianism, he then began to abandon it, formulated several wide-ranging ideas but did not develop them, did not provide all the particulars, and left his would-be followers without guiding principles concerning the national question in circumstances like those in which Ukraine found herself in the 1860s and 1870s.

Thus Shevchenko, like the early historians of 'Little Russia,' initially approached the Poles more from the perspective of an Orthodox Cossack patriot than from that of a son of serfs belonging to a Polish estate. In his early poems about the Cossacks, even the words 'Polack lordlings' (liashky-panky) simply represent an adherence to the traditions of the old folk songs, while the main concern is with the violation of Cossack rights and, to an even greater extent, the Union, rather than the peasants, who, even in the sixteenth and seventeenth centuries, suffered at the hands of both Orthodox and Uniate squires. Even in 'The Haidamaks' (1841), we see the same thing except that here the poet's good-heartedness prevailed and, enjoining him to weep over the fact that 'the children of the old Slavs had become drunk with blood' (starykh slovian dity vpylys kroviu), set him on the path to wider-ranging ideas, a path which, with the aid of Kostomarov's Slavism, led him to hope 'that all Slavs will become good brothers' (shchob vsi sloviany staly dobrymy bratamy, 1845). His scoffing at the Hetmanate (1846), which brought Poland down and was then itself destroyed, and later the punishment which Shevchenko shared with a number of Poles (Bronisław Zaleski, Gordon, etc.) further softened his hatred of the Poles and he wrote his epistle to Zaleski, 'Shche iak buly my kozakamy' (When we were still Cossacks). Here the Cossack extends his hand to the Pole, requesting in return his hand and a pure heart so that in the name of Christ that quiet paradise may be renewed, the paradise which ostensibly existed in Ukraine in relations with the Poles and Cossacks until 'unsatiated priests and magnates set us at odds, divided us' (nesytii ksondzy, mahnaty nas rozluchyly, rozvely)....

This is also the case with Shevchenko's thoughts about 'Muscovites.' Here, too, the wave of Pan-Slavism which engulfed him and his critical reassessment of 'Cossack glory' and the Hetmanate softened his Cossack heart. Perhaps even more important in this regard were the friendship and respect shown him by 'Muscovites' in his final years in Nizhny Novgorod, Moscow, and Petersburg. But this new, more favourable view of Russians was not expressed in his poetry. Living with Russian soldiers who were *muzhiks* like him and in bondage like him, Shevchenko, unlike other exiles such as Dostoevsky, did not leave us even one portrait of such a 'Muscovite'; the Russian *muzhik* given into military service by his master is portrayed by Shevchenko simply as one who recalls of his beloved that 'she was a rough one and did not forgive any more than another' [taka ukhabista soboi, i menshe beloi ne darila; see 'Ne spalosia, – a nich iak more' – (I could not sleep, – the night was like a sea), 1847]. The 'Muscovite' welcomed by the haughty Tytarivna-Nemyrivna was still only a vagabond for Shevchenko as late as 1860, just as in 1840 he had been a stranger. Clearly, if national poets talk of their neighbours in such terms, it will be difficult for the hope 'that all Slavs should become good brothers' to come true. This is why we doubt that Shevchenko could really have brought us together into a 'new, free,' and international family.

Shevchenko could have gone further in those social matters which relate to the liberation of the *muzhik*. His love for the peasants, for those in bondage, and later for the poor, was Shevchenko's guide both in his poetry and in his life. From the very beginning of his career as a poet, even immediately after gaining his freedom when, as Soshenko recounts, he behaved very much like a dandy, Shevchenko, like every living Ukrainian

poet without exception, wrote about the *muzhik*. And throughout his life
Shevchenko wrote most often about the *muzhik*, imitating *muzhik* tales and
songs at first ('The Bewitched Woman,' 'The Poplar') and subsequently
portraying the life of the *muzhik* ('The Servant Girl,' etc.) primarily
in order to defend him against those foreign ('Kateryna') and native
('Epistle') land-owners who had wronged him and, secondarily, in order to
provide the land-owners with an example to follow, concluding his narrative with the following words: 'Learn to forgive your enemies, people,
like this uneducated one' (Ottak liudy nauchaites voroham proshchaty, iak
tsei neuk). Shevchenko came very early to equate 'our Ukraine' with the
Ukrainian *muzhik* and 'our truth' with a free and happy life for this
muzhik. But we need not discuss this at length; it is a well-known fact
and is discussed in detail by Sirko.

We need only pause to consider whether, as our friends, Sirko among
them, often state, Shevchenko in fact thought about 'truth and liberty' and
their materialization in the manner of a socialist. We will never agree that
Shevchenko was a socialist. Indeed, we even venture to think that to agree
would be harmful to the cause of socialism in Ukraine, as this would create
a misconception about what socialism is.

In the first instance, there can be no genuine, indigenously based
socialism in a community where serfdom has not yet been abolished and
the economy is still not totally founded upon free, hired labour. We would
add that there can be no indigenously based socialism where there is no
statutory parliamentary state which alone can expose the dominion of the
rich. Where serfdom and tsarist autocracy reign, socialism can only come
from outside and will be more bookish than indigenous, more familiar, on
occasion, with the thinking directed against serfdom and the governmental
bureaucracy than with that of a truly socialist, anti-plutocratic character.
This was the socialism of the Moscow and Petersburg circles in the years
1830-60, a socialism gleaned from French books; this, in certain respects,
is the new socialism in Russia, although a foundation for it has begun to
develop since the abolition of serfdom. Shevchenko wrote during the era of
serfdom and was too closely in touch with the realities of his time not to
direct more of his attention to the millions of enslaved serfs than to the
hundreds of free hired men. Furthermore, there is no evidence that Shevchenko knew anything about Saint-Simon, Fourier, Louis Blanc, Proudhon,
etc., nor even the social novels of George Sand, which in the 1840s were

already being read in Moscow and Petersburg and towards the end of the 1850s to some extent in Kiev as well. There is no evidence that Shevchenko's more learned friends intended to acquaint him with the ideas of these European socialists because in their own writings there is no indication that they had any interest in these socialists and the issues of the working class in Europe which they raised. Consequently, Shevchenko would have had to become a socialist through his own efforts, and the wisest intellect could not have developed the precepts of socialism simply from what Shevchenko saw in the Russia of his own time, when there was not only autocratic rule administered by tsarist bureaucracy but serfdom as well.

Shevchenko bore down upon both – and while he took a stand not only against bondage but also against the legalized extortion that it involved (that is, revealed the economic aspect of serfdom, as Sirko says), this does not in the least make him a socialist. And, further, can an opponent of tsarism avoid discussing the poll tax? Although, as Sirko says, Shevchenko did not regard tsars 'from the *muzhik* point of view' but rather 'as the source of all the extortion' (for the *muzhik* believes conversely that the tsar only wishes the peasant good and that the land-owners and officials do all the fleecing), a socialist also regards the state as in large (if not full) measure merely a fortress for the defence of the rich's dominion. It is not the legalized extortion that Shevchenko most denounced but rather the bondage and lack of respect for the individual manifested by the land-owners, who in his works most frequently appear as violators of women and girls. The tsars are no better and are indeed violators of entire peoples, and murderers to boot. But the distance from this point to socialism is still great. What Shevchenko says about the rich and the poor, 'the goods stolen by your grandfathers' (didamy kradene dobro), and even the industrious and the 'earth, bequeathed to all' (zemliu vsim dannuiu) does not change one iota of what has been said above. Even in the Cossack *duma* of the seventeenth century we find Handzha Andyber complaining that the magnates 'took the shrubland and the meadows for themselves' (pozabyraly luhy i luky) and it would be strange indeed to speak of the socialism of the seventeenth-century Cossacks. Much has been written against the rich and the injustice of the rich, not only by medieval priests, but also by the Hebrew prophets. Yet, were we to include them among the socialists, the image of socialism would lose all its clarity and we would find ourselves in precisely that trap set by the enemies of socialism when they say that, in their opinion, socialism is merely the complaining of the poor against the rich and *not a matter of the organization of all labour required by the community.*

Even the Old Testament prophet Amos, for example, reproves those who trample the needy, grind the bones of the poor into flour, oppress them with taxes, possess magnificent vineyards and have large buildings constructed for them, pile injustice upon injustice, and heap spoils upon spoils in their palaces, etc.[16] The same is true of Hosea, Isaiah, and a number of other prophets. Hosea 10:12, for example, almost could have been written by Shevchenko. Shevchenko's lines about God's judgment of the wicked are very much like the well-known psalm, 'Arise, O Lord!'[17] In Shevchenko's descriptions of the 'kingdom of truth,' all that is lacking is the image found in Isaiah of the wolf lying down beside the sheep.[18]

Shevchenko loved the Hebrew prophets (see Kozachkovsky) and the psalter so much because he thought about social questions in their terms. Like a biblical prophet speaking of the tiny Jewish kingdom and the immense Assyrian or Babylonian powers, Shevchenko says to the Circassians: '... mighty knights, by God not forgotten! Fight on – you will be victorious! God is with you' (... lytsari velyki, Bohom ne zabuti! Boritesia – poborete! Vam Boh pomahaie; 'The Caucasus,' 1845). He considers what is now called 'social revolution,' 'social upheaval,' etc. in biblical terms:

> Koly zh odpochyty
> Dasy, bozhe, utomlenym
> I nam dasy zhyty!
> My viruiem Tvoii syli
> I dukhu zhyvomu.
> Vstane pravda! vstane volia!
> I Tobi odnomu
> Pokloniatsia vsi iazyky
> Voviky i viky!

When will you grant the weary leave to rest, / O Lord, / And grant us leave to live! / We have faith in your power and living spirit. / Truth will arise! Freedom will arise! / And to you alone / Will all the tongues bow down / For ever and ever!

Even in 1859, Shevchenko portrayed the 'wonders of the Lord' (dyva Hospodnii) – how God would judge, free the long-suffering, and repay the wicked for their wickedness – while just before his death he wondered when 'the apostle of truth and light' (Apostol pravdy i nauky) would come. During the periods when Shevchenko doubted that the judgment day and the messiah he awaited would ever come, he was still impelled to portray thoroughly biblical scenes of impending catastrophe, even though Jehovah was absent from them: 'Will there be a day of judgment!? Will there be punishment for the kings and princes on earth? Will there be truth among people? ... There should be! ... for the sun will rise and consume the defiled earth!' (Chy bude sud!? Chy bude *kara* tsariam, tsariatam na zemli? Chy bude pravda mezh liudmy? ... Povynna but! ... bo sontse stane i oskvernenu zemliu spalyt!) [19]

Together with Shevchenko's biblical vision or, more accurately, within it, there were the recollections of the Dnipro peasant about the Haidamaks' vengeance upon the gentry – and Shevchenko moved from biblical images of God's judgment and the Messiah to descriptions when 'the unlettered eye would gaze deep, deep into its master's soul, when the blood of the nobles' children would flow into the blue sea in hundreds of streams.' Yet even this Haidamak image is forced into the biblical mould: 'The day of judgment will come – the Dnipro and the hills will raise their voices!' (Nastane sud – zahovoriat i Dnipro i hory!) Because his thinking was almost totally governed by the biblical prophets and by recollections of the era of the Haidamaks, Shevchenko cannot be included among nineteenth-century socialists.

True socialist thought and endeavour came into being in the nineteenth century because only now – after the great political changes and revolutions of the sixteenth to the eighteenth centuries – has free capital and free hired labour in the employ of the rich assumed control of the state and because only now have the ideas of the leading thinkers of the eighteenth century concerning *progress* – the natural, unceasing *advance* of society in the spheres of economics, social organization, science, and learning – taken on definitive form and been confirmed.... [Shevchenko] had no clear and definite notion of historical progress because he was a man whose thinking was grounded in the Church; he lacked a European education and knew only Russian life of the period of Nicholas I. A man like that could not have become a true revolutionary or even a permanent public figure of the sort that existed in nineteenth-century Europe. To be sure, Shevchenko could have become a revolutionary for the independence of his people and country, a revolutionary of the type to be seen, for example, among the Poles, who can sometimes even do without faith in progress and is expressly drawn towards his nation's past. But we must not forget that the feelings of the Ukrainians concerning racial distinctness and political independence were never as strong as those of the Poles, while after the destruction of the Cossack state in the eighteenth century those feelings weakened further, so that in the period when he was most attracted by the ancient Cossack order Shevchenko himself could say: 'It existed once! But what of it?! It will not return!' (Bulo kolys! Ta shcho z toho?! Ne vernetsia!) In the final analysis it must be said that, no matter how passionately he felt about this cause, Shevchenko was nonetheless almost alone in his feelings, for there cannot be many people passionately committed to working in a community where there are as yet few members with well-formed ideas about the work to be done and where the total destruction of the community of interests shared by the people and national enslavement have weakened the spirit of comradeship and voluntary action. One man – or even two or three – cannot be warriors on the field of battle nor even organizers of the coming battle against all that is around them.

Thus, while Shevchenko was a man with admirable social aspirations and occasional dreams of rebellion, he did not become a sociopolitical or still less a revolutionary activist of the sort that a poet could become. Prior to 1847 only his friends were beginning to see the mighty destiny of Shevchenko's work and from then until 1876 it remained obscure, lying untouched for almost too long. We have already noted (*Hromada*, no. 2) that this did not happen with poet-revolutionaries such as Victor Hugo or – in the Slavic context – Mickiewicz.

This in no way diminishes Shevchenko as a man, but merely indicates the point beyond which his community had not developed (for whatever reason). To reproach it for not being one way or another is nonsense. The only sensible thing that might be done here is to examine what this community was like in order to understand what sort of person a man like Shevchenko could and had to become.

(1879)

NOTES

1 Translation of excerpts from 'Shevchenko, ukrainofily i sotsializm' in Drahomanov, *Literaturno-publitsystychni pratsi* (Kiev 1970) II. The article first appeared in *Hromada* 4 (1879).

2 Sirko was the pseudonym of Fedir Vovk, author of an article on Shevchenko to which Drahomanov's study is a reply (ed.).

3 The words in quotation marks were employed by Kostomarov in his 'Vospominaniia o dvukh maliarakh' (Reminiscences about Two Painters) (ed.).

4 An observation made in 'Zhyzn Kulisha' (The Life of Kulish; *Pravda* 1868) and quoted more extensively by Drahomanov in a section of his study not included in this edited version (ed.).

5 A. Afanasiev-Chuzhbinsky, *Vospominaniia o T. Gr. Shevchenke* (St Petersburg 1861) (ed.).

6 Edited by S. Burachek, the journal *Maiak* fostered the fashionable idea of 'official nationality' (ed.).

7 Kozachkovsky recounts that Shevchenko also did not like Gogol or, as he puts it, 'was not sympathetic towards Gogol: in his words, Gogol's failure to realize his ambitions were the cause of his mental derangement.' Gogol is also disliked by other Ukrainophiles because he did not write in Ukrainian. The only problem is that the Russian poets and prose writers of today would not exist were it not for the Gogolian school. Among other things, it is because they have not gone through the Gogolian school that Ukrainian writers in Russia and Galicia lag behind their Russian counterparts.

8 Recalling the time in 1845 when Shevchenko stayed with him, Kozachkovsky writes: 'On occasion he would read the Bible, taking note of passages that impressed him with the exceptional greatness of the thoughts they contained. Of the projects that he was then planning I can recall two that were never realized: the first – a large canvas which was to depict "Ezekiel's vision in the desert filled with dry bones".'

9 In a passage from his 'Vospominaniia o T. Gr. Shevchenke' (*Kievskii telegraf*, no. 25, 1875), removed by the censor, Kozachkovsky said that Shevchenko both praised the Protestant faith and criticized Orthodox believers for their submissiveness to the authorities and the land-owners. It is regrettable that Kozachkovsky does not say when Shevchenko expressed this thought, whether in 1845-6 or in 1859.

10 Taras Shevchenko, *Kobzar*, 2 vols (Prague 1876).
11 Here and elsewhere Drahomanov quotes lines from Shevchenko's poetry which have not been included in Shevchenko's definitive texts, established by scholars much later (ed.).
12 A rather inadequate translation of Herzen's special word 'iubkoborets,' which implies 'wrestling' with a skirt in more than one sense (ed.).
13 Jakob Gordon was the pseudonym of Maximilian Jatowt, a Polish political prisoner whom Shevchenko met in exile (ed.).
14 The change in Shevchenko's ideas about the Ukrainian past is best revealed by comparing his words in 'To Osnovianenko' (1841):

> Slava ne poliazhe,
> Ne poliazhe, a rozkazhe,
> Shcho diialos v sviti,
> ...
> I chyi my dity.

Glory will not fall, / Will not fall but will recount / What happened in the world ... and whose children we are.

with the following passage from his 'Epistle':

> Vse rozberit, ta spytaite
> Todi sebe: shcho my?
> Chyi syny, iakykh batkiv,
> Kym, za shcho zakuti?
> To i pobachyte, shcho os shcho
> Vashi slavni Bruty:
> Raby, pidnizhky, hriaz Moskvy
> Varshavske smittia vashi pany
> Iasnovelmozhnii hetmany!
> ...
> Ia rydaiu, iak zhadaiu
> Dila nezabutni
> Didiv nashykh: tiazhki dila!
> Iakby ikh zabuty,
> Ia oddav by veseloho
> Viku polovynu!

Consider everything and ask yourselves then: / Who are we / Whose sons? of what fathers? / By whom, for what enslaved? / Then you will see that such are your renowned

Brutuses – / Slaves, toadies, the scum of Moscow, / Warsaw's refuse / Are your masters, / The illustrious Hetmans! ... I weep when I recall / The unforgotten deeds / Of our grandfathers: burdensome deeds! / To forget them / I would give half / Of my happy life!

15 *Hromada* was a journal published by Drahomanov in Geneva (1878-82) (ed.).

16 Amos 8:4, 5, 2; 6:12, 1-7, 14, etc.

17 Also Isaiah 5:8, 'Woe to those who join house to house, who add field to field,' etc.; Isaiah 10:1, 2, about the judgment of wickedness.

18 Shevchenko's entire poem, 'Raduisia, nyvo' (Rejoice, verdant field, 1859), dealing with God's judgment of the wicked and the freeing of slaves is nothing more than Isaiah 35 with a few alterations (for example, the conclusion). Anyone wishing to be convinced of the hold that the Bible had upon Shevchenko to the very end need only make a word-by-word comparison of Shevchenko's psalm with Isaiah 35.

19 Cf. in Isaiah 33 the depiction of the vengeance for injustice, especially the description of how the stars in the heavens will be extinguished, the rivers turned into pitch, the soil into brimstone, and the land into burning pitch. In connection with the burning of the earth, see also Isaiah 24:6.

5

Shevchenko and Ukrainian History

VOLODYMYR ANTONOVYCH

Those segments of Shevchenko's works which recreate historical events are undoubtedly of greatest interest to the Historical Society of Nestor the Chronicler.[1] These works met with the same response as the works of all those talented writers and poets who selected historical subjects as their themes. Captivated by the artistic recreation of bygone years and sensing a truthfulness in the depiction of the historical era recreated by the artist, the educated public with no serious interest in the study of history has always regarded the artist's work as an historical document and, charmed by the overall view of life presented, believed the details and images to be historically accurate, evincing no concern for the verification of individual facts, whether major or minor. With Shevchenko's works, a public response of this nature appears all the more natural when it is remembered that the poet frequently recreated historical incidents which were at that time, and still remain, almost totally untouched by scholarship. There is no doubt in my mind that the majority of the educated public who have read Shevchenko are convinced, for example, that Honta executed his own children, that Palii ended his life in the monastery in Mezhyhiria, that Pidkova and Hamaliia led campaigns against Constantinople and Skutari, and so on. Neither was the general reading public alone in its readiness to see in Shevchenko's poetic works exact, factual recreations of historical events; occasionally even those who wrote on historical subjects expressed the same view (for example, D. Mordovtsev in his history of the Haidamak era).

From the perspective of a rigorously critical analysis of the facts, such an appraisal of Shevchenko's works would naturally be revealed to be erroneous. It was, of course, not the poet in his artistic recreations of the life of the people who was at fault in this case. Rather, the error, a very natural one, originated with the readers themselves. The poet must not be equated with the historian; a poet is an artist – it is not for him to establish the individual facts of life in the past by means of critical analysis and continuous, painstaking work and then generalize these facts in the form of a historico-philosophical synthesis. Were he to devote himself to this type of work, the poet or artist would squander a significant portion of his talent and probably produce only a mediocre historical work. It is well known that Gogol, for example, sought to become a historian, but with little success. The endowments bestowed upon the poet by nature direct his activity along a different, but no less fruitful, path – the restoration of the historical life of a nation by the fusion of traits that are significant to a high degree but inaccessible to the historian and critic, traits which accrue from the keen powers of observation and creative capacity of the poet himself. The poet recreates a living, integral image of an epoch, brings to life and presents to the reader's view individual characters and entire generations; in his works, epochs and peoples, their flesh and spirit, their emotions and thoughts are brought to life. In a word, for the artist the factual accuracy of the details he employs is unimportant; what matters is that they be possible in the context of the epoch he has chosen to portray.

Applying all this to Shevchenko's literary canon – to his historical works – it is necessary to single out the wide-ranging artistic recreations of given epochs, the characters of which are always accurately understood by the poet. Historical studies merely verify the truthfulness of his tableaux and they will undoubtedly verify much more in the future. From this perspective, the many factual errors and inaccuracies of detail are of no consequence. To convince ourselves of this let us examine those of Shevchenko's works with a historical subject matter. There are only a few: two narrative poems – 'Haidamaky' (The Haidamaks) and 'Hamaliia' – and several short rhapsodies and episodes – 'Ivan Pidkova,' 'Taras Triasylo,' 'Nevolnyk' (The Captive), the election of a hetman, 'Chernets' (The Monk), the dead man's tale, 'Shvachka,' 'The Surrender of Doroshenko.'

In almost every poem small factual errors are to be found. This is explained by the fact that the poet had few historical materials. He was forced to rely in large measure on the apocryphal *History of the Russes* attributed to Konysky, the works of Markevych, Bantysh-Kamensky, and a few fragments of incomplete works like Ruban's Chronicle. This represented the complete library of historical materials Shevchenko had at hand and thus it is not surprising that there are notable factual errors in his works. I will point out a few of them. If they did indeed actually exist, Pidkova and Hamaliia did not undertake campaigns against Constantinople and Skutari. There are inaccuracies, too, in the description of the election of hetmans Loboda and Nalyvaiko: the poet depicts the transfer of the title of hetman from the old hetman to the new one, and attributes this to Loboda and Nalyvaiko. In actual fact, something of the sort is encountered thirty or forty years later in the story of Pavliuk and Tomalenko. The entire structure of 'The Monk' revolves around the story of Palii's death in Mezhhiria – something that never happened; yet, in this poem we find the historically truthful account of the Zaporozhian's leave-taking. Similarly, there are more than a few errors in various parts of 'The Haidamaks.' The death of the sexton, for example, is an event that did occur, but in a different form. The events described in 'The Haidamaks' occupy almost a year; in reality, they were played out in no more than two months.

The artist frequently divines those things which are established by historical analysis many years later. In his novel *Ivanhoe*, Walter Scott introduced motifs from the life of the Anglo-Saxon tribes which historical research in his time had not touched upon but which were later explained by Augustin Thierry.[2] I will indicate a few instances where Shevchenko's powerful poetic talent results in similar intuitions. When checked against the historical data available to us now, some components of Shevchenko's historical poems are revealed to be absolutely true to fact – for example, the entire series of scenes devoted to the portrayal of Zaporizhzhia: we see what the people of Zaporizhzhia strove for, what life was like there, and how the Zaporozhian ended his days. For the people, Zaporizhzhia represented the materialization of the ideal social order. Hence its numbers were always replenished. Shevchenko's portrayal of the otaman's relationship with the rest of the Zaporozhians is of interest: it consisted at one and the same time of both an absolute dictatorship and the absolute dependence of this dictator upon his electorate. Shevchenko understood and portrayed the spirit of Zaporizhzhia in the best possible way. The elected otaman was conscious of the fact that he represented public opinion, was prepared to be governed by it, and treated the members of the community as friends and equals. That Shevchenko conceived of the Zaporozhian system in this way can be seen from his 'Ivan Pidkova,' where the otaman brings his flotilla to a halt at the mouth of the Dnipro, delivers a speech to his companions explaining the objective of the campaign, and puts to them the question of whether to continue the campaign, although he knows in advance that their answer will be affirmative. A climate of total confidence in the elected otaman held sway. This motif comes to the fore in the poem describing the election of a hetman. The old hetman notes his advanced age and asks that someone else be chosen to take his place. Other scenes can also be noted. In the poem which I call 'The Surrender of Doroshenko,' the period of the Ruin is depicted so vividly that an equally graphic representation could be pieced together only after reading the substantial monograph by Kostomarov.[3] The struggle against the all-powerful Polish first estate which occurred in the first half of the seventeenth century is masterfully sketched out in what I will call 'the dead man's tale.'

I should also like to say a few words about 'The Haidamaks,' the most significant poem from the point of view of length. It is concerned with a not very distant epoch. The poet himself remarks that he heard a great deal about that time from his ninety-year-old grandfather. Here all the truly tragic circumstances that existed in our land in the second half of the eighteenth century are accurately understood and portrayed. The people who had developed those well-known ideals and views were ruled by a small group of noblemen. The Jews constituted the intermediate group. There were thus three groups in the land, each distant from the other two. The heterogeneity of their interests notwithstanding, the universal laws of history allow that separate groups such as these may develop mutual respect, that renowned *modus vivendi*, but this is possible only when the ruling group is endowed with sufficient wisdom, recognizes that it cannot go far by exploitation alone and is prepared to make certain concessions. The Polish gentry possessed no such tact; the Jews even less. The result was an unfortunate organization of relations which erupted into the tragedy of the second half of the eighteenth century. Shevchenko understood fully the situation of these three segments of the population at that time and depicted the attitude of the peasants to the nobility and Jews, sketched out the gentry's reaction to the schismatics and Jews, and conceived the character of the Jew in relation to the Cossack and the gentry. The nobility is represented in the poem as an all-powerful estate unable to use its authority judiciously, as a wilful group with no respect for the individual. We see a group of Confederates catching a Jew and mocking him, breaking into the home of a venerable church warden and torturing him out of mercenary motives.[4] The second group is composed of Jews. They bow down before the gentry but despise them, fully convinced of their own superior wisdom. There are also peasant types – people without education but with a sense of their own rightness, whose lengthy oppression had given rise to bitterness that occasionally erupted into inhuman hatred. The peasant is most prominently depicted by the author as a brother who is the victim of injustice. There are thus the Zalizniak and Honta[5] types, the latter revealing his capacity for extreme self-sacrifice in the scene in which he kills his sons for the general good, a scene which, incidentally, is incorrectly understood. But along with these, we encounter images of greater depth, such as that of the archpriest who sanctifies the people's truth with his studied word. This archpriest was modelled on Melkhisedek Iavorsky.[6] Shevchenko has been reproached for the apparent sympathy with which he depicted the brutality involved here. This is unjust. Two breaks are to be found in the poem where, in the midst of the account of events, we read moving lyrical lines that speak of how people could get along together in this rich land were the relations between them not so deeply tinged with discrimination. On two occasions the poet expresses this sentiment and one cannot but agree with him.

(1888)

NOTES

1 Translation of a summary of V. Antonovych's lecture, printed in *Chtenie v istoricheskom obshchestve Nestora letopistsa* (1888) II, 145-9.
2 Augustin Thierry (1795-1856), French historian, author of a major work on the Norman conquest of England (ed.).
3 'The Ruin' was the period of decline of the Cossack state after the death of Bohdan Khmelnytsky in 1657 (ed.).
4 Confederates were members of a Polish military union (ed.).
5 Zalizniak and Honta were the leaders of the *haidamak* rebellion of 1768, also known as *Koliivshchyna* (ed.).
6 Melkhisedek Znacho-Iavorsky (c. 1716-1809), abbot of the Motronynsky monastery near Chyhyryn who was very sympathetic to the *haidamak* rebellion (ed.).

6

Foreword to Shevchenko's 'Perebendia'

IVAN FRANKO

In recent years a heated debate about the newer Ukrainian literature, its genesis and evolution, has been waged in Russian academic circles.[1] How did this literature come into being, what influenced it, what facilitated or hindered its development? These questions are hardly new; indeed, they have been asked almost from the beginning, but they have been discussed on the basis of guesswork rather than solid factual research.

With the appearance of the first more or less complete biography of Shevchenko (by M. Chaly), however, which has prompted many detailed memoirs of the poet (for a list see Komarov, 'Bibliohrafiia T. Shevchenka,' in *Kievskaia starina* [March 1886] 570; [April] 778) and with the appearance of Petrov's *Ocherki istorii ukrainskoi literatury XIX stol.* (1884), and the memoirs of Kostomarov and Kulish, among others, a scholarly answer to these questions is at last possible.

It is patently obvious that in Russia these questions are corollaries to the basic question whether Ukrainian literature is separatist or not. This is, indeed, the biggest difficulty in Russia's state organization today. In its *ukaz* of 18 May 1876, the government of Russia declared that Ukrainian literature is separatist and therefore, for reasons of state, ought not to exist. The Russians, especially the well-educated of progressive European bent, are aware of and deeply affected by this unjust proscription of Ukrainian writing by their government and consequently attempt in scholarly articles to put forward as many arguments as they can to show that Ukrainian literature is not separatist and that its development does not threaten Russian unity, but on the contrary, constitutes a proof of Russia's power and diversity (see A.N. Pypin in *Vestnik Evropy* [February 1887] 684 ff.). Or, they argue that it is only a weak echo of Russian literature or merely its offshoot which cannot separate (Petrov). M. Dashkevych, a talented new historian of Ukrainian literature, also supports this argument. His voluminous review of Petrov's book offers valuable, original, and far-reaching insights into many as yet unexamined or unexplained problems in Ukrainian literary history. Contradicting Petrov, Dashkevych states that Ukrainian literature is not the product of foreign influence, but arose as a result of local conditions, from a positive national awareness (*narodnist*) and from the need for self-knowledge and self-expression. Dashkevych does not deny the influence of Russian literature, but he notes in all fairness that if Russian influence is mentioned, the unmediated Polish and Western European influences must be regarded as equally important. But Dashkevych's book concludes that for Ukraine, cultural and literary development is possible only as long as the ties with Russia are maintained and that all, or almost all Ukrainian literature until now has tended towards unification with Russia and has drawn its strength from this bond. At the end of his book the author even expresses the view that Ukrainian literature will atrophy with time, as the ties between Russians and Ukrainians become stronger, the population becomes better educated, and so forth (*Otzyv* 232). I do not intend to express an opinion here on Dashkevych's remarks about the eventual results of better education and reciprocal international relations, which supposedly minimize or even level the differences between peoples. But in this regard I could mention the dominance of French culture in the seventeenth and eighteenth centuries and its current decline in the face of widespread education. Another counter-example is the enmity between the most nationally aware European peoples (the Germans and French, Germans and Czechs, French and Italians, etc.). This testifies to a positive insistence upon retaining their national peculiarities on the part of peoples who live side by side and under the most liberal constitution in Europe (Switzerland *et al.*). Still, it cannot be denied that this scholar's conclusions are to a great extent valid and constitute the most fundamental and all-encompassing ideas yet put forward on the subject. Indeed, they must be accepted as the basis for further research in Ukrainian literary history. As Naumenko, following Maksymovych's lead, has pointed out, the existence before Kotliarevsky of oral and written works in Ukrainian, far from contradicting, confirms M. Dashkevych's views. For the love for his own people and language that made Kotliarevsky write in Ukrainian, and the public read and appreciate his work, did not appear overnight, but had to be the result of Ukraine's long and illustrious history.

Shevchenko's role in the development of Ukrainian literature cannot be discussed here. This subject, among other, is masterfully elucidated in Drahomanov's article as well as in Petrov and Dashkevych.[2] The latter has quite rightly indicated that in order to understand Shevchenko's poetic genius fully, as well as (what is most important) tradition in local Ukrainian influence and (the much less important) Russian influence, the influence of Polish literature must also be studied. This influence was especially strong during Shevchenko's early creative period, which spanned the era of romantic nationalism (up to 1843), political radicalism, and Pan-Slavism (up to and including 1847). I have discussed these influences in my article 'Mickiewicz w literaturze rusinskiej' (*Kraj* [1886] no. 46). Here it is essential to consider Mickiewicz's influence. Dashkevych points out that the effects of his influence are mainly evident in the ballads (eg, 'Prychynna' (The Bewitched Woman), 'Utoplena' (The Drowned Maiden), 'Rusalka' (The Mermaid), and 'Lileia' (The Lily). The theme of 'Kateryna' (Catherine) (in undeveloped form) appears in Mickiewicz's ballad 'Rybka' (The Little Fish). Shevchenko found models for his poems against serfdom and his political poems in Mickiewicz's work. For this reason Dashkevych compares Mickiewicz's poems 'Ustęp' and 'Petersburg' with Shevchenko's 'Son' (The Dream) (*Otzyv* 173-4).

Shevchenko's short but beautiful poem 'Perebendia' is a typical example of his early work, where the most varied influences come together and, thanks to his genius, are shaped into an organic and profoundly poetic whole. A detailed analysis of 'Perebendia' is very important to a characterization both of Shevchenko's poetic talent and of an entire epoch in our literature.

Shevchenko wrote 'Perebendia' in the first two years after his emancipation, between 1838 and 1840, and the poem was published in the 1840 edition of *Kobzar*. Its theme is the ancient one of the poet's opposition to society. It is interesting that this theme is completely foreign to all folk poetry, in which tradition and collective creativity entirely obliterate all traces of individuality. The theme can be found neither in folk songs nor in the partially-folk Indian and Greek epics; it occurs only in the literature of societies well enough developed to give rise to sharply divided social strata. How slowly and with what difficulty individualism in poetry struggled out from under the pressure of formulae and tradition during the Middle Ages is documented in Kareev's book *Literaturnaia evoliutsiia na zapade* (St Petersburg 1886); a similar process in Greece is described in Korsh's 'Istoriia grecheskoi literatury' in *Vseobshchaia istoriia literatury pod redaktsiei V. Korsha i Kiprichnikova*. Horace's ode 'Odi profanum vulgus et arceo' is a definitive representation of the poet's opposition to society as a whole. Centuries later, this ode served many poets as the starting point and theme for more or less contemptuous utterances about the 'mob' and the 'rabble.' The Russian poet Pushkin's 'Chern' (The Mob) is perhaps the most sharply worded modern version of Horace's ode. I shall refer to it again later.

As early as the eighteenth century there occurred a decisive change in views on the poet's relationship to society. The century which brought into being the magnificent writings of Rousseau on the upbringing of the normal human individual (*Emile*) and on the return of society to the bosom of nature, the century which proclaimed the rights of man as the basis of all social organization, had to give supreme importance to the individual. It took upon itself the battle with ancient, decaying orders, not only in the political sphere (the French Revolution) but also in literature (Schiller's 'Räuber' and 'Kabale und Liebe'). Poetic creativity turned away from the often noisy and empty-headed treatment of 'weighty matters' ('Haupt und Staats-Aktionen') to analysing the thoughts, feelings, and wishes of the individual (Goethe's 'Werthers Leiden' and 'Stella'; 'Egmont' is an especially interesting example of the individualization of formerly 'weighty' matters). Obviously, when the 'mob' that had formerly been contemptible broke into a multitude of individuals, each of whom had the same rights to life and all its joys, then even the poets had to change their attitude. In his poem 'Zueignung' (1784), Goethe clearly indicated his new outlook on poetry when he wrote: 'Für andere wächts in mir das edle Gut, Ich kann und will den Pfund nicht mehr vergraben! Warum sucht' ich den Weg so sensuchtvoll, Wenn ich ihn nicht den Brüdern zeigen soll?' Poetry here has a social, utilitarian (in the more exalted sense of the word) function; it uplifts the hearts and minds of that same mob whose members have now become the poet's *brothers*. It is in this twofold direction – towards the greater autonomy and advantage of the individual – that our views have been progressively developing since the end of the eighteenth century. The development of so-called political Jacobinism in France constituted a great step forward. This movement held that certain powerful individuals could and ought, by a single decree, to revolutionize the way of life and even the thinking of the masses and ensure their happiness. In politics these ideas went out of fashion quite quickly, but in poetry they remained and became part of the basis of romanticism. Romanticism in literature, like Jacobinism in politics, implied the triumph of genius over the masses, over talent and hard work, and consequently the triumph of flashes of genius, emotion, and enthusiasm over the steady but feeble light of ordinary intellect. The poet's individuality became the ultimate strength and broke the bonds of society's rules; poetry became a kind of inspiration or clairvoyance, something holy and immortal. Mickiewicz's 'Improwizacja' in Part Three of *Dziady* (The Ancestors, early 1832) is a typical romantic poem: 'Such songs are worthy of God and nature! Such songs are a great creation. Such songs are strong and brave! Such songs are immortal! I feel this immortality, I create it. Could you create anything greater, God?' (Boga, natury godne takie pienie! Pieśń to wielka, pieśń-tworzenie. Taka pieśń jest siła, dzielność. Taka pieśń jest nieśmiertelność! Ja czuje nieśmiertelność, nieśmiertelność tworzę. Cóż ty większego mogłeś zrobić Boże?)

The romantic poet shares certain characteristics with Horace's poet; he regards himself as far superior to the rabble, which is concerned with everyday things and is quite unable to understand him (Solitude! ... What of people? What kind of singer am I for them? / Samotność! ... Cóż po ludziach? Czym śpiewak dla ludzi?). But he is not proud of this – on the contrary, it pains him – he sees in it his misfortune (Unhappy is he who uses his voice and his language for the people / Nieszczęsny, kto dla ludzi głos i język trudzi). He is not contemptuous of the mob; rather, he wishes to do something for it, to serve it (I want to lift it up, to make it happy, to astonish the world with it / Chcę go podnieść, uszczęsliwić; Chcę nim cały świat zadziwić). His misery is the misery of his people; as one of the elect his sorrows and joys are infinitely more profound than those of the common man. He, the representative of the people, suffers for the entire nation (My name is 'million' for I love and suffer for millions / Nazywam się milion, bo za miliony kocham i cierpię katusze). The poet's lofty individualism quite naturally draws to itself the companion ideas of Jacobinism and messianism. The poet wishes to uplift his people and ensure their happiness by means of his personal will and strength (Let them guess, fulfil, and be happy with what I wish and if they reject me let them perish. / Co ja zechcę, niech wnet zgadną, spełną, tem się uszczęśliwia, a jeżeli się sprzeciwią, niechaj zginą i prezepadną.) and thus shows himself to be a true Jacobin. The poet wants to uplift his people not by means of physical strength, learning, or science. Rather, he wishes to 'redeem' them through the miracle of his own omnipotent emotion. Thus he becomes the messiah, prophet, and redeemer of the nation.

I have examined Mickiewicz's 'Improvisation' at length because I will attempt to prove that this poem influenced to some degree the main idea of Shevchenko's 'Perebendia.' There exist several important clues that Shevchenko knew and thought highly of Mickiewicz's poetry. Petrov ('Ocherki' 303) states that in later life Shevchenko read Mickiewicz and Libelt in the original. Of more importance to us, however, is the testimony of Afanasiev-Chuzhbynsky, who, in 'Vospominaniia o T.G. Shevchenko' (p 10) recalls how he, together with Shevchenko, read *Dziady* (The Ancestors) in 1848. Shevchenko's own testimony leads us even further back; in his novel *Khudozhnik* (The Artist), Shevchenko described the first stirrings of his creativity, that is, the years 1838-40, his emancipation from serfdom, and his life in Petersburg in the company of Briullov, Sternberg, *et al.* An especially significant passage in this autobiographical novel describes Shevchenko's acquaintance with members of a Polish circle in Petersburg, especially his friendship with the learned and amicable Leonard Demski, whose library contained works by Lelewel and a volume by Mickiewicz. What is more, in 1829 Shevchenko spent some time in Vilnius and in one of his poems ('U Vilni, horodi preslavnim' / 'In the glorious town of Vilno') describes an incident that took place during his stay or just before it ('there was still a university' / 'shche buv todi universytet,' which later was turned into 'quite a hospital' / 'zdorovii-prezdorovii lazaret,' as a result of student activities in which Mickiewicz took part). It is hard to suppose that during his stay Shevchenko would have heard nothing of Mickiewicz or would not have known at least some of his poems. The same must be said of his later visit to Warsaw (1830), where an attempt definitely was made to acquaint the poet with Polish language and literature (see *Osnova* [May 1862] 53).

A comparison of Shevchenko's 'Perebendia' with Mickiewicz's 'Improvisation' reveals distinct similarities in the ideas contained in both poems. Just as Mickiewicz's poet is far superior to the mass of common people,

who do not understand him, so too is Shevchenko's Perebendia, who
appears as a poor, blind Ukrainian *kobzar* rather than as an unidentified,
cosmopolitan figure. 'No one in the world welcomes him' (Ioho na sim sviti
nikhto ne pryima) says Shevchenko – 'Like the sun, he is alone among
men. People know him because he walks upon the earth' (Odyn vin mizh
liudmy, iak sontse vysoke. Ioho znaiut liudy, bo nosyt zemlia) – that is,
they know him only superficially, not knowing his soul or his secret
thoughts. This is how we must construe the opening line 'Perebendia is old
and blind, – who does not know him?' (Perebendia staryi, slipyi, khto ioho
ne znaie?) Just as Mickiewicz's poet has an all-encompassing knowledge of
the world, so Perebendia 'knows all, hears all: what the sea says, where the
sun sleeps' (vse znaie, vse chuie, shcho more hovoryt, de sontse nochuie).
Just as Mickiewicz's poet regards himself as the chosen mediator between
his people and God and even argues with God in their favour and threatens
Him with war, so Perebendia, alone on the Ukrainian steppe, voices 'the
word of God – thus the heart speaks to God at will' (Bozhe slovo – to
sertse po voli z Bohom rozmovlia).

As Mickiewicz's poet journeys in thought beyond the world to the
'boundary between God and nature' (gdzie graniczą Stwórca i natura;
compare Schiller's 'Bis am Strande ihre Schöpfung ich lande ... Anker
werf', wo kein Hauch mehr weht und der Markstein der Schöpfung
steht'), so Perebendia's 'thought frolics on a cloud at the edge of the
world; it flies like the blue-winged eagle, soaring, touching the sky with its
wings' (Dumka krai svitu na khmari hulia, orlom syzokrylym litaie,
shyriaie, azh nebo blakytne shyrokymy bie). As Mickiewicz's poet feels
'unhappy, wearing out his voice and his tongue for the people' (nesh-
chasnym, trudiachy holos i iazyk dlia liudei), so Perebendia feels an inner
conflict, and although he often tries to dissemble his profound sorrow by
joking and singing happy songs, nevertheless 'he will sing and laugh, but
returns to tears' (zaspivaie, zasmiietsia, a na sliozy verne). Perebendia's
sorrow springs from the same source as that of Mickiewicz's poet's, that is,
from his isolation. 'He is alone among [people]' says Shevchenko, 'he has
no home on this earth,' 'no one in the world welcomes him' (Odyn vin
mizh nymy ... nema iomu v sviti khaty ... ioho na sim sviti nikhto ne
pryima).

In spite of all these similarities, there are important differences between
Perebendia and Mickiewicz's poet. In the first place, in Perebendia not a

trace of the Jacobin view of the people as a mob that should and must be rendered happy by decree from above can be found, nor is there even a shadow of messianic pretension, or the need to be the saviour or prophet of his people. Perebendia unassumingly carries out his modest but valuable service to society; he dispels the sorrows of the people. Thus, Shevchenko describes the sphere of activity of his *kobzar*, and it is only from the facts he enumerates later that we get an idea of the *kobzar*'s other activities. In these short verses, which are nevertheless masterpieces of characterization, the *kobzar* is shown in various situations and before different audiences. In every case Perebendia comports himself appropriately and chooses the songs which his audience will most likely prefer and which best serve his purpose. Thus, we first see him 'with the girls in the pasture' where he sings 'Hryts' and a spring song. 'Hryts' is of course the well-known song 'Do not go, Hryts, to the evening gatherings' (Ne khody, Hrytsiu, na vechernytsi).

Next, we see Perebendia at the inn where the young men are making merry. There he sings two songs, 'Serbyn' (The Serb) and 'Shynkarka' (The Tavern Girl). The first is one of the countless versions of the well-known song about a Ukrainian who has become a Turk, buying a woman prisoner of war at the market-place. The woman turns out to be his sister. In most versions the brother is called a Turk, but in some he is a Serb. Five versions, with valuable annotations, are included in the collection of historical songs edited by Antonovych and Drahomanov (I, pp 275-80; annotations pp 280-6); version E replaces 'Turk' with 'Serb.' 'This song' (I quote from Antonovych and Drahomanov's note), 'belongs to the pan-European cycle of stories about incest. In elaborating this theme, Ukrainian folk poetry is both original and testifies to Southern Rus's poetic and cultural ties with many peoples, the result of its geographical location and ethnographic composition.' The very description of the buyer ('a Serb') and the Serbian-Bulgarian cry 'bre!' repeated at the end of every line indicates its southern Slavic origin. Indeed, many Bulgarian and Serbian songs contain similar descriptions of the slave trade in women. This subject came into Ukrainian folklore as a result of the historical factors that forced thousands of our people onto the Crimean and Asian slave markets. The incest legend found here is literary in origin and derives mainly from the apocryphal life of St Gregory, which, in turn, is a reworking of the ancient Greek legend of Oedipus. Sung by the folk rhapsodist Perebendia, 'a man of God,' this song has a dual import. Firstly, it is an historical memoir of the dreadful period of Turkish and Tatar invasions and secondly, it is a purely poetic description of abnormal social relations (Such is the world now that a brother cannot recognize his own sister / Takyi teper svit nastaie, shcho brat sestry ne piznaie), abnormal because a woman, a human being, becomes an object and is bought and sold in the market-place. The woman's sad fate in such circumstances moves the listeners; I myself used to weep every time the girls sang this song at evening gatherings. The song's highly poetic and moral meaning lies in its power to move, and this is why Shevchenko has Perebendia sing it.

This tendency towards purely poetic moralizing, that is, towards an appreciation of human dignity and of sympathy for the wronged and unfortunate, is also found in the second song that Perebendia sings to the young men. It is about the tavern girl (Khaiunia, Rezia) whom the Cossacks (Don Cossacks, Chornomortsi, or foreigners) persuade to travel with them and whom they eventually betray and murder either by drowning her in the Danube, or, in other versions, 'they tied her to a pine tree with her long hair' (pryviazaly do sosny kosamy) and 'set the pine afire from top to bottom' (zapalyly sosnu z verkhu azh do nyzu). This also ranks among the most popular folk songs (see Holovatsky, II, 87; Kolberg: *Pokucie*, II, 22-3; *Kievskaia starina*, 1883, I, Chubynsky, V, 1082, *et al.*). The subject is, like that of the preceding song, not Ukrainian but foreign in origin; Potebnia has enumerated and commented upon the Slavic versions ('Obiasneniia,' II, 512-24), although, typically, he pays no attention to the non-Slavic origins of this subject and favours a mythological interpretation of the song. I do not intend to discuss this interpretation, but shall simply note that the song owes its popularity to its eloquent description of the fate of this unfortunate, betrayed girl and also, of course, to the moralizing tendency evident in its ending: 'Whoever has children, let him teach them and not let them go to the tavern in the evenings' (Oi khto dity maie, nai ikh nauchaie, zvechora do korchmy nai ikh ne pushchaie). Savage violence here is described in simple, powerful, and deeply affecting language.

By singing these songs to the young men carousing at the tavern, Perebendia (in Shevchenko's interpretation) wishes to use these terrifying scenes to make drunken brains think, to sober rational faculties, and to rein in sexual desires and passions, which under the influence of drink and noisy company are most likely to explode and exceed their bounds.

The same notion of the *kobzar* as guardian of the purity of village life, of humane and sincere relations between people, is the basis for the later scene where the poet shows us Perebendia 'with the married couple and the evil mother-in-law at the feast' (z zhonatymy na benketi, de svykrukha zlaia). Here Perebendia sings 'of the poplar tree, of evil fate' (pro topol-iu – lykhu doliu) that is, about the mother-in-law who, taking a dislike to her son's wife, sends her into the fields to gather flax and puts a curse on her, that if by evening she has not gathered all the flax she will turn into a poplar in the field. There are a great many versions of this song particularly in Galicia. Dashkevych recorded one from the province of Volyn (see 'Otzyv' 133-4). Naturally Shevchenko was familiar with this song and he must have been very fond of it because, changing its motif somewhat, he reworked the subject in his famous ballad 'Topolia' (The Poplar). We cannot precisely identify the song that begins 'In the grove' (U haiu); there are many such songs. It appears that Shevchenko was thinking of the many versions of this song reprinted in Chubynsky's book (*Trudy*, v, 727-34). This song was also known in Galicia (one version in Chubynsky's book begins 'In the meadow [grove] a guelder-rose rustled' (Oi u luzi [haiu] kalyna shumila). It tells how a mother persuades her son to beat his wife. ('My son, take the wire reins and tie your beloved's hands and feet; My son, take the wire whip and thrash your beloved black and blue.' / Ozmy, synu, drotiani vizhky, zviazhy mylii ruchenky i nizhky; Ozmy, synu, nahaiku-drotianku, spyshy mylu, iak chornu kytaiku). The son, obeying his mother, beats his wife to death and later dies for it. This song derives exclusively from folk custom and seems to be an original creation of the Ukrainian people. That so many versions of it exist indicates that it is greatly loved and widely known; it is without doubt among the most beautiful of our folk songs and is perfectly suited to the end for which the poet makes Perebendia use it – to move people by means of these dreadful scenes, to awaken their fear and sympathy and thus to uplift and ennoble them.

Finally, Shevchenko depicts his *kobzar* before a large crowd in the market-place. Here, he sings 'of Lazarus ... or, so that they should know about it, heavily, ponderously, of the destruction of the Sich' / pro Laz-aria ... abo, shchob te znaly, tiazhko – vazhko zaspivaie, iak Sich ruinuvaly). The song about Lazarus is also well known in Galicia. It is a lyrical reworking of the evangelical parable about the rich man and the poor man, from Luke 16: 19-31. I shall not enter into the history of the literary reworkings and wanderings of this parable. I only wish to point out that in its Ukrainian version the emphasis is upon the contrast in social position of the two brothers and on the need for humane, brotherly attitudes towards the poor and the sick. One of the experts in the field of Ukrainian folk culture, T. Rylsky, writes that this song – or better, this *duma* – is very popular ('K izucheniiu ukrainskogo narodnogo mirovozzreniia,' *Kievskaia starina*, 1888, XXIII, 284-5). Every lyre player knows it perfectly. The audience of simple village folk listens with great attention and feeling when the lyre player, accompanied by the mournful sounds of his instrument, tells the story of the humiliation of the poor brother by the rich man who 'did not consider his brother Lazarus a brother' (brata svoho Lazaria za brata ne mav) and of the poor man's reward after death ('in honour and glory' / v chesti ta v khvali). Finally, the song 'about the devastation of the Sich' which is sung 'heavily, ponderously,' that is, with a consciousness of the full meaning of that fact for the independent development of Ukraine, shows us Perebendia as a patriot who preserves the spirit and tradition of the people's historical memory and attempts to pass on these sacred things to succeeding generations.

Such is Shevchenko's description of the *kobzar* and his service to the people. The awakening of sincere, humanitarian feelings in his countrymen, the ennobling of their hearts and minds, the preservation of historical memory, and the passing on of the finest achievements of the past to new generations – this is what constitutes his service – these are the activities of the *kobzar*, the popular minstrel whom Shevchenko described in 'Pere-bendia' and whom he himself evidently wished to emulate at the time. Shevchenko's minstrel differs from Mickiewicz's poet in 'Improvisation' not only in sphere and method of activity, but also because he is a thoroughly realistic figure taken from actual Ukrainian life. Konrad (the hero of 'Improvisation') is a mystical and allegorical figure, the creation of a fertile romantic imagination. He belongs to no specific locality. He does not, so to speak, wear a national costume. Shevchenko, who falls far short of Mickiewicz in breadth of conception, scale of setting, and imaginative power, nevertheless equals him in the dexterity of his characterization of the hero and outstrips him in the quality and realism of his poetic vision.

The reasons for this must be sought in the poet's origins and in his literary education before writing 'Perebendia.' Shevchenko's origin in a simple peasant family and his youth spent in serfdom had a great influence upon all his thoughts and attitudes and the direction and character of his poetic creativity. This influence has not yet been fully studied. It has not yet been shown what Shevchenko derived from his family origins and his life as a serf, although in all his work there are many indications of it. Although critics and biographers (Drahomanov, Chaly, Petrov, and Dash-kevych) have attempted broadly to characterize this influence, they have done so only superficially and not systematically. It is impossible to close the gap here, for this would demand special and exacting research. But we cannot pass over certain details which will help to elucidate Shevchenko's concept of the *kobzar* Perebendia. The authority and respect accorded *kobzars* and lyre players by the Ukrainian community is well known. Kulish, in 'Zapiski o iuzhnoi Rusi' (1,43), wrote of their significance, of their 'poetic and philosophic frame of mind' and their 'reminding people of God and good deeds.'

It is certain that the people also regarded the *kobzars* in this way, as did Shevchenko in his youth. In his writings and memoirs there is no hint of close personal ties with any one *kobzar*, but Shevchenko must have met many in his travels about Zvenyhorod province. It is a well-known fact that *kobzars* and lyre players most often gather at monasteries where people come on pilgrimages; and there is such a monastery, the Motronynsky, not far from Shevchenko's native village. 'Slipyi Volokh' (The Blind Walla-chian) in 'Haidamaky' may have been based upon Shevchenko's recollec-tion of one such *kobzar*. Vivid accounts of similar meetings abound in the foreword to 'Haidamaky,' where Shevchenko writes: 'It gladdens one to see the blind *kobzar* sitting with a boy by a fence, and it gladdens one to hear him sing a *duma* about things that happened long ago.'

Shevchenko's impressions of the *kobzars* and their songs must have been numerous and vivid for, even after being away from Ukraine for ten years (1829-39), when he began his literary work he almost always portrayed the *kobzars*. We meet them in 'Kateryna,' 'Perebendia,' 'Tarasova nich' (The Night of Taras), 'Haidamaky,' and 'Chernytsia Mariiana' (The Nun Mariana). Shevchenko even entitled his anthology of verse *Kobzar* and in the person of Perebendia we perceive to a great extent his own thoughts about the minstrel's fate among the people.

Still, no matter how powerful and numerous Shevchenko's youthful impressions, to my mind they cannot fully account for his fondness for

kobzars and his delight in them at the time he was writing 'Perebendia.'
Anyone who appreciates how slowly and with what difficulty certain images
and forms are created in literature and how rare it is for the most ordinary
everyday phenomena to become poetic conventions (during the romantic
era when Shevchenko began writing this was even more difficult than it is
today) will agree. That the *kobzar* did not occupy Shevchenko's imagination exclusively (as one might suppose on examining his poems) is
attested to by his many drawings from that period. There are no drawings
of the Ukrainian *kobzar*; instead Shevchenko invariably chooses subjects
favoured by the school where he learned to draw (see *Khudozhnik* / The
Artist). This leads us to suppose that Shevchenko's poetic representation of
these *kobzars* was also influenced by an unspecified literary movement to
which he adhered, and that he was not concerned about uniting the literary
doctrine with the artistic. The literary movement that provided Shevchenko
with ready-made concepts and types was the so-called 'Ukrainian school,' a
Polish movement whose chief representatives had begun to expound their
views on literature in the mid-1820s.

The poets of this school first introduced the figure of the idealized
mendicant *banduryst* (Dashkevych, *Otzyv* 177). In 1824 Padura wrote his
dumka (a short poem) 'Lirnyk' (The Lyrist) which he dedicated 'to the
spirit of Ivan Mazepa, hetman of the region beyond the Dnieper.' This
dumka, which begins, 'Fear not, my host, I am not asking for charity' (Ne
zhurysia, mii khoziaiu, ne za datkom ia idu), quickly became a folk song
and was performed mainly at the houses of noblemen and the clergy. By
the 1820s and 1830s the song had popularized the figure of the lyre player
Vidort, in whose songs 'dead people and times gone by are resurrected' (v
pisniakh voskresaiut zmerli i chas). Vidort asks to be admitted to the castle
in the following words: 'Open the castle gates, let the song resound within.
The singer will lament with you, he will lament and take his leave' (Vid-
chynaite zamku bramy, nekhai pisn v nim zahude: Pozhurytsia spivak z
vamy, pozhurytsia ta i pide). Worry and longing are the main themes in
the songs of the first lyre player in our literature. It is interesting, moreover, that already he is referred to here as an 'apostle.' ('Where they invite
the apostle in, the house will be blessed' / De apostola zaprosiat, blahos-
loven bude dim.) Thus, the author uses a poor, elderly mendicant to
express his views on poetry, on the past and the future. We know that
Shevchenko, even as a serf, perhaps even in Engelhardt's service, got to

know Padura's songs. Evidence of this can be found in the story 'Progulka s udovolstviem i ne bez morali' (An Excursion, pleasant, and not without a moral lesson). Although it is late evidence (1858), it is nevertheless important because Shevchenko, writing the story in exile, quotes (from memory) Padura's poem 'Cossack, in the name of God' (Hei, kozache, v imia Boha) and states 'I knew Padura's poetry very well.'

In his poem 'Zamek Kaniowski' (The Castle of Kaniow) published in Warsaw in 1828, Severyn Goszczynski gave a powerful and effective description of the mendicant bandurist. It is not clear whether Shevchenko knew this poem, but it seems he did; this is shown, even though at second hand, by the many parallels between 'Zamek Kaniowski' and 'Haidamaky' which have been documented in O. Ohonovsky's analysis of Shevchenko's poem. Goszczynski's poem made a great impact immediately upon publication in Warsaw, so it would have been strange if Shevchenko, being in Warsaw in 1830, had not read a poem which dealt with his native Ukraine. As Konysky relates, Goszczynski's poem was very popular among Ukrainian youth in Kiev during the 1840s and even some left-bank Ukrainians such as Pylchykov had memorized the original version.

What is perhaps most important here is Shevchenko's acquaintance with the work of another Polish writer of the Ukrainian school, Michał Czajkowski, whose influential and, in its day, widely-read novel *Wernyhora* gave primary importance to the *kobzar*, endowed him with highly idealistic qualities, and in the end made him a prophet and a Polish patriot. Shevchenko never explicitly refers to this novel, but his poem 'Haidamaky,' and the remarks appended to it, testify only too clearly that the poet not only knew the novel but in certain passages copied entire sections almost verbatim and imitated it in his poem in many important details (this is shown at length by Dashkevych in 'Otzyv' 188-9). In 'Perebendia,' of course, Shevchenko had no need to borrow directly from Padura, Goszczynski, or Czajkowski, but this is not a point that I intend to prove.

Here it is important merely to affirm that long before Shevchenko, the personage of the *kobzar* was made use of and described in literature in a way similar to that which we find in his work. In creating Perebendia, he followed in the footsteps of others, taking in a poetic tradition, accepting some aspects, rejecting others, in places enriching it in accordance with his talent but at the same time including his feelings, his life experience, and his impressions.

It would be wrong to maintain that everything deriving from tradition in Shevchenko's poetry is taken from Polish literature. If not the basic concept and description of the *kobzar*, then certainly his method of dealing with the notion was to some extent influenced by the Russian school to which Shevchenko, living in Petersburg after 1831, was exposed. There is valuable evidence as to Shevchenko's acquaintance with Russian and foreign writers (in Russian translation) during the years 1838-43 in his autobiographical novel *Khudozhnik*. The novel, although written in 1856, appears to have been based on Shevchenko's letters to Soshenko, and on his day-to-day notes. I will cite all that the novel contains about Shevchenko's knowledge of Russian literature. He refers to reading the works of Ozerov, a Russian dramatist of the pre-Pushkin era, and that he especially liked his *Edip v Afinakh* (Oedipus in Athens). He also quotes from Zhukovsky's 'Shilonsky uznik' (The Prisoner of Chillon). Briullov gave a reading of Pushkin's poem 'Angelo.' Later, he mentions Zhukovsky's ballad 'Dvenadtsat spiashchikh dev' (The Twelve Sleeping Maidens); he also refers to Gogol. In another story, Shevchenko quotes a poem of Pushkin's from memory 'Not for Trepidations, not for Struggles' (Ne dlia volnenii, ne dlia bitv). Shortly after Shevchenko's death, Kulish wrote: 'He knew Pushkin by heart.' The poet's opposition to society is powerfully represented in Pushkin's poetry. Pushkin, at first a liberal and a Decembrist sympathizer, author of various anti-tsarist and anti-despotic epigrams which were transmitted orally and circulated in manuscript form throughout Russia, changed his political outlook after 1825. Under the influence of the Moscow circle led by the poet Venevitinov, Pushkin began to concern himself with the philosophical and aesthetic ideas of Schelling, who advocated 'art for art's sake.' and 'objectivity of representation regardless of what is represented,' and held that 'poetry is not the servant of reality and its interests, but a kingdom unto itself.'

This change is most clearly evident in 'Prorok' (The Prophet, 1826), 'Poet' (1827), and 'Chern' (The Mob, 1828). In the first poem, Pushkin, still a liberal, eloquently describes the ideal of the poet-prophet, fearless accuser of all injustice and bearer of the divine word. God himself speaks to him: 'Arise, o prophet, watch and hear, Filled with my Will, roam sea and land and with the Word inflame the hearts of men' (Vosstan, prorok, i vizhd, i vnemli, Ispolnis voleiu moiei, I, obkhodia moria i zemli, *Glagolom zhgi serdtsa liudei*). True, Pushkin does not clearly indicate to what end and in what words the poet-prophet must inflame the hearts of men but it is certain that those words are meant to further social reform. Especially interesting is the poet's description of himself: 'I heard the heaven's chiming, / The angels in their soaring sweep, / The monsters moving in the deep, / The vegetation of the vine' (I vnial ia neba sodroganie, / I gornii angelov polet, / I gad morskikh podvodnyi khod, / I dolnei lozy proziabanie). Shevchenko was thinking of these words when he wrote in 'Perebendia': 'His thought frolics on a cloud at the edge of the world; it flies like the blue-winged eagle, soaring, touching the sky with its wings. It alights upon the sun and asks where it sleeps and how it rises. It listens to what the sea says; it asks the black mountain: why are you silent?' (A dumka krai svitu na khmari hulia, Orlom syzokrylym litaie, shyriaie, Azh nebo blakytne shyrokymy bie; Spochyne na sontsi, ioho zapytaie: De vono nochuie, iak vono vstaie; Poslukhaie moria, shcho vono hovoryt; Spyta chornu horu: choho ty nima?). Later, he says that Perebendia 'knows all, hears all – what the sea says, where the sun sleeps' (use znaie, use chuie, shcho more hovoryt, de sontse nochuie). Perebendia's role is more modest than that of Pushkin's poet, but it is more clearly defined and more realistic. His word does not 'inflame the hearts of men,' but dispels their sadness and teaches them to live peacefully, humanely, and honestly.

In 'Poet' and 'Chern,' Pushkin characteristically turns the reformer, the didactic poet-prophet, into the pagan priest. He serves, not the mob (chern) but art alone. Pushkin repeats Horace's 'odi profanum vulgus' with brutal vehemence. 'Go away,' he shouts to the crowd, 'what has a peaceful poet to do with you?' (Podite proch ... kakoe delo Poetu mirnomu do vas? ...). Pushkin's poet is horrified at the thought of playing a role in society: 'Does a priest take your broom?' (zhretsi l u vas metlu berut?). The poet is beyond judgment and does not need the people's love: 'Thou shalt not prize the people's love' (Poet, ne dorozhi liuboviiu narodnoi). Pushkin also criticized Mickiewicz, with whom he earlier had been friendly, censuring him specifically because 'he sings for the rabble' (v ugodu buinoi cherni on napoiaet). Of course, Shevchenko's entire being, full of love for the poor and unfortunate and hatred for their oppressors, reacted against Pushkin's extremely objectivist views. Shevchenko could not follow him. But in spite of this, the shadow of objectivism was cast upon our poet. We should not forget that as a painter, Shevchenko was then studying at the Academy of Art, where spurious pseudo-classicism was dominant. This style was the antithesis of the realism that Shevchenko almost unconsciously espoused in his poetry. At the Academy, he must have acquired certain aesthetic formulae concerning 'pure, divine art' from Briullov and others. The unfortunate effect of these formulae is that they always give rise to contempt or at least disregard for real people and their needs. A hint of disregard, which is not quite in the spirit of the rest of the poem, is met with at the end of 'Perebendia,' where the poet praises his *kobzar* for singing his most beautiful songs upon a grave in the steppe 'so that no one will hear' (shchob liudy ne chuly). He counsels him thus: 'And so they will not shun you / Indulge them, brother! / Jump, you devil, at the master's command / For that is he wealthy!' (A shchob tebe ne tsuralys, / Poturai im, brate! / Skachy, vrazhe, iak pan kazhe: / Na te vin bahatyi!). This is an unmistakable echo of Pushkin's 'the lyre's sound will not enliven you' (ne ozhivit vas liri glas) and arises from the same romantic notion as the line in Mickiewicz's 'Improvisation': 'Unfortunate is he who wearies his voice and his tongue for men' (Nieszczęsny, kto dla ludzi głos i język trudzi), that is, that the 'rabble' is incapable of understanding the poet's lofty thoughts and can receive them only with derision. Shevchenko soon abandoned this view and learned from his own experience that the 'rabble,' and especially the intelligent 'rabble' is not at all such a barren field for the seed of 'God's word' and that the poet, like any other public activist (*narodnyi diiach*), must 'plow his field' and 'sow the word'; he must speak 'in fiery words, so that the word may be set aflame / So that men's hearts may soften ... Such a word is the censer of God, / The censer of truth' (ohnennymy slovamy, shchob slovo plamenem vzialos, / Shchob liudiam sertse rostopylo ... Te slovo, Bozheie kadylo, / Kadylo istyny). These quotations from the end of 'Perebendia' show that the poet did not yet completely understand his task as a poet or that he adhered too closely to the romantic or 'objectivist,' antisocial school.

Nevertheless, I do not hesitate to include 'Perebendia' among Shevchenko's finest early works, considering it from a purely artistic viewpoint. Later he wrote poems far more profound in feeling and broader and clearer in outlook, but few were more harmonious in their artistic unity, or more limpid in composition and detail. All the unique qualities of his poetry – his heartfelt sincerity, his simplicity and plasticity of expression, the purity of his language, and the delicate, melancholy humour he derived from

Ukrainian folk songs – are already present in their full brilliance in 'Perebendia.' The description of the Ukrainian steppe, short as it is, paints a delightful picture which can easily be compared with similar descriptions in Zaleski. (Compare his 'Step' / The Steppe, which begins: 'The grass rustles ... mounds rise like waves ... the steppe is like a sea ...' / Szumią trawy ... Jako fale wciąż kurhany, Step ... Morze ...' – and Shevchenko's 'about him the steppe, like a great sea, darkens; / One burial mound after another stands, / And there, it dreams on' / kruhom ioho *step, iak more* shyroke, syniie; *Za mohyloiu mohyla*, A tam,-tilky mriie. There can be no question here of imitation despite the similarity of the descriptions.)

Our investigation of the literary history of the theme and individual characteristics of this poem has shown that Shevchenko entered the literary field with many ideas and impressions taken from life and from his reading, and certainly with far larger spiritual baggage than most other Ukrainian poets, whose lives had been happier than Shevchenko's under his father's roof. At school, in his wanderings among people 'who would teach him about good' and in his master's house, besides witnessing sorrowful scenes of serfdom, Shevchenko must have seen and heard much that enriched his knowledge of the world and people. In his travels to cities like Vilno and Warsaw, even as a serf, he must have learned a great deal because of his talents and curiosity. His life with painters in the capitals (Warsaw and St Petersburg) and the circles he frequented after being emancipated (the Ukrainophile circle of Hrebinka and the artistic circle surrounding Briullov) all constituted the school of life that Shevchenko attended before entering the world of literature. Drahomanov rightly noted that on the whole, Shevchenko 'saw more of the world, both as a serf, and while in Russia, than his learned friends in Kiev.' We have already seen from what a wide circle of thought Shevchenko derived the impetus and direction for his early work, perhaps even unconsciously reworking the turbulent romanticism of Mickiewicz and Goszczynski, the aristocratic Ukrainophile views of Padura and the liberal impulses and reactionary objectivism of Pushkin. And even though it does not hold to a single ideological viewpoint, from the artistic perspective Shevchenko's poem, with its simplicity and unpretentiousness, completely satisfies all critical demands.

(1889)

NOTES

1 Translation of 'Perednie slovo (Do "Perebendi" T.H. Shevchenka)' in *Svitova velych Shevchenka* (Kiev 1964) I. Most of Franko's own documentation has been retained in the text. Supplementary notes have been omitted.
2 Excerpts from Drahomanov's article appear in this book (ed.).

7

What Were Shevchenko's National Ideals?

BORYS HRINCHENKO

First I must warn the reader that I reject the notion that Shevchenko's views on nationalism can be divided into two periods: the period in which his Ukrainian patriotism was marked by an 'ancient Cossack' influence and the period in which this influence was lost, that is, when 'he was very much influenced by the humanistic ideas of the Brotherhood of Sts Cyril and Methodius' (Ohonovsky).[1] At this point the thought, 'Who has taken Ukraine's freedom?' is first supposed to have occurred to him, and only then did his 'antagonism to the Tsar' and his 'genuine Ukrainian patriotism' come into being. As I have already stated, it is utterly mistaken to think that Shevchenko's views were altered by Kostomarov and the Brotherhood, and, moreover, although Shevchenko did in fact change his opinion of the Cossack commanders and the hetmans (although only of some), he was always favourably disposed towards the *hetmanshchyna* (the hetman state) as an autonomous form of Ukrainian political life. He regarded the popular Cossack movements even more favourably, although he was always aware of the evils resulting from them (see 'Hupalivsh-chyna' in 'Haidamaky'). Shevchenko was always an admirer of the Cossacks. This is attested to by the fact that when he wrote the 'Friendly Epistle' in which he called their highnesses the hetmans 'the refuse of Warsaw, slaves, toadies, the scum of Moscow' (Varshavske smittia, raby, pidnizhky, hriaz Moskvy) he also wrote 'To Osnovianenko,' where the following lines occur:

Ne vernutsia spodivani,
Ne vernetsia volia,

Ne vernetsia kozachchyna,
Ne vstanut hetmany,
Ne pokryiut Ukrainu
Chervoni zhupany.

Those awaited [the Cossacks] will not return,
Freedom will not return,
Cossack rule will not return,
The hetmans will not arise,
Ukraine will not be covered in red mantles.

(And because of this, Ukraine)

Obidrana, syrotoiu
Ponad Dniprom plache ...

A ragged orphan,
Weeps beside the Dnipro.

Afterwards, Shevchenko wrote poems such as 'The Dream' (Son, the second poem of that title, written in 1847), in which he described Cossack fame as a 'glorious fame'; 'The Monk' (Chernets, 1848); 'I do not know how the Poles live now' (Ne znaiu, iak teper liakhy zhyvut, 1848); 'Oh why have you darkened' (Oi choho ty pochornilo, 1849); 'On holy Sunday' (U nedilenku sviatuiu, 1849); 'Shvachka' (1849); 'A black cloud has arisen' (Zastupyla chorna khmara, 1850); 'Sometimes in captivity I remember' (Buvaie v nevoli inodi zhadaiu, 1850, in which he stated that Ukraine's freedom perished with the Cossacks). In these poems he sang the praises of Cossack rule. Shevchenko never renounced his past; he correctly perceived the standpoint from which our past should be regarded. He branded as infamous those who were 'the scum of Moscow' and 'the refuse of Warsaw.' He censured individuals, but strongly supported the popular national movement, whose aims were freedom for all peoples and national freedom for Ukraine. He did not barter these sacred things for the 'scrap of rotten meat' that some regarded as 'a higher culture.' He voiced the will of the people and their national self-awareness (manifested even in such imperfect forms as the Hetmanate and the Sich). He did not give up in the face of the ruinous despotism of Peter I and Catherine II, of whom he wrote in 'The Dream.' It is shameful to relate that some ten years ago, crudely adulatory odes were addressed to them in Ukrainian, reminding one of the old panegyrics to Ukrainian land-owners or the 'Ode to Prince Kurakin.'[2] Shevchenko did not cut himself off from our historical background for he knew that this must not be done; he clearly saw the flag of his nation when no one else did. Shevchenko was the focus on which popular wisdom, feeling, and hope converged. In his soul he encompassed all that could be found in the souls of millions of Ukrainians wearied by slavery, and this is why we call him a genius.

I repeat that, regardless of minor faults in his work (and whose work is faultless?), Shevchenko's national awareness made him a genius, and his immeasurable importance and significance in the national rebirth of his country made him a phenomenon unique, perhaps, in the entire world. At a time when his predecessors hardly dared mention Ukrainian independence in their work, and if they did, understood the notion not as national independence but as the very limited independence of a part of the 'united and indivisible Russian people,' an independence contingent upon the good grace of that 'united' nation, that 'elder brother,' Shevchenko in his work clearly presented our independence as a nation.

He regarded all Slavic peoples as a single family. He considered them brothers and wept bitterly to see how disunited they had become, how 'the children of the ancient Slavs are drunk with blood' (Haidamaky). He hoped

Shchob usi slaviane staly
Dobrymy bratamy
I synamy sontsia pravdy
I ieretykamy
Ottakymy, iak Konstansky
Ieretyk velykyi!...
Myr myrovi podaruiut
I slavu vo viky!...

That all Slavs will become
Good brothers
And sons of the sun of truth
And heretics

Like the one from Constance –
A great heretic!
They will bring peace to the world
And eternal fame!
        ('Poslanie do Shafaryka' / 'Letter to Šafařík')

He thanked Šafařík for guiding 'the Slavic rivers into one sea.' Šafařík showed the Slavs the way to unity and united action; he showed them a common goal. No proof is needed that Shevchenko recognized each Slavic people's right to complete national independence, and above all the right of the Ukrainian people to it. He fiercely defended this independence against interference from either the Russian or the Polish side and the spectre of the 'one and indivisible' people did not hold him back in any way. He began as a supporter of Pan-Slavic unity and brotherhood but soon perceived that unity with one brother, the Muscovite, would be not brotherhood but slavery. Then he immediately opposed this 'unity and indivisibility' and did not hesitate to accuse Bohdan Khmelnytsky of capitulating to Moscow.

Oi Bohdane, Bohdanochku,
Iak by bula znala, –
U kolystsi b prydushyla,
Pid sertsem pryspala!

Oh Bohdan, little Bohdan, (says Ukraine)
If I had known
I would have smothered you in the cradle,
At my bosom lulled you to sleep!

The poet fiercely opposed all despotism (see, for example, 'Tsari' [The Kings]) and specifically the despotism of the contemporary Russian regime. In 'The Dream' (Son), he described the dreadful wrongs done to Ukraine and expressed the hope that her natural rights to nationhood would be restored. He perceived that Ukraine had been brought to this state by her own indolent leaders and he did not hesitate to seem unpatriotic in saying to his countrymen:

Vse rozberit ta i spytaite
Todi sebe: shcho my?
Chyi syny? iakykh batkiv?
Kym? za shcho zakuti?

Consider everything and ask
Yourselves then: who are we?
Whose sons? of what fathers?
By whom, for what enslaved?

Thus they would see that

Vashi slavni Bruty –
Raby, pidnizhky, hriaz Moskvy,
Varshavske smittia vashi pany,
Iasnovelmozhnii hetmany!

Your renowned Brutuses –
Slaves, toadies, the scum of Moscow,
Warsaw's refuse are your masters
The illustrious hetmans!
('Poslanie' / 'Epistle')

But this did not prevent him from defending those hetmans he thought had fought for Ukraine's independence. He praised Petro Doroshenko for this (in 'A black cloud has arisen' / 'Zastupyla chorna khmara'). Still, he perceived few like Doroshenko and the fact that some hetmans could 'trounce Poland' did not gladden him as it did other writers. Unlike Kvitka or Hulak-Artemovsky, he advised his countrymen not to rejoice in their supposed victory over Poland:

Chvanytesia, shcho my Polshchu
Kolys zavalyly!...
Pravda vasha: Polshcha vpala
Ta i vas rozdavyla!

You boast: We once
Ruined Poland!...

You are right: Poland fell
And crushed you! (*ibid*.)

Such a victory should not be celebrated but regretted, for neither the Poles
nor the Ukrainians derived any benefit from it; it resulted in bondage for
both nations:

Choho zh vy chvanytesia, vy,
Syny serdeshnoi Ukrainy?
Shcho dobre khodyte v iarmi,
Shche luchche, nizh batky khodyly?

Of what do you boast, you,
Sons of poor Ukraine?
That you wear your yoke
Even better than your fathers?

The poet fearlessly called his countrymen slaves and blamed them
directly for the misfortune of their native land:

Hirshe liakha svoi dity
Ii rospyniaiut!

More cruelly than the Pole her own children
Crucify her!

Shevchenko could not be taken in by superficial patriotism. He often
argued vehemently against provincial patriots whom he hated and eventually he painted the following picture of a so-called 'patriot':

Potomok hetmana durnoho
I prezavziatyi patriot
Ta i khrystiianyn shche do toho –
U Kyiv izdyt vsiakyi hod!
U svyti khodyt mizh panamy
I pie horilku z muzhykamy.
I volnodumstvuie v shynku –

Ottut vin vves – khoch nadrukui!
Ta shche v seli svoikh divchatok
Perebiraie; ta zprosta
Taky svoikh baistriat z desiatok
U hod poderzhyt do khresta
Ta i tilky zh to ... Kruhom paskuda!

Descendant of a stupid hetman
An overeager patriot
And a Christian to boot –
He travels to Kiev each year!
He wears a homespun cloak among the land-owners
And drinks whisky with the peasants
And is a tavern philosopher.
There he is, complete – ready to be printed.
And in his village he has his pick
Of young girls, and openly christens
Ten of his bastards a year.
If that were all! ... He is a thorough villain! ('P.S.')

Shevchenko had no use for the simple-minded patriotism found so frequently among our early writers. He demanded something different from Ukrainians. 'Rozkuitesia! Brataitesia!' (Cast off your chains! Be brothers!) he exclaims. To 'cast off chains' is to cease being the 'scum of Moscow' and the 'refuse of Warsaw' and to realize that we are the sons of a great, independent nation, to cease bowing down before Moscow and Warsaw and to turn our attention to achieving national independence. But what is national independence? Shevchenko had a completely original conception of it and, significantly, his conception was correct. As he understood it, a nation was a family of brothers endowed with equal rights and only when all (and not only a few) are truly free can their nation also be free:

Ne verstovii
A volnii, shyrokii
Skriz shliakhy sviatii
Prosteliutsia, i ne naidut
Shliakhiv tykh vladyky,

A raby tymy shliakhamy,
Bez hvaltu i kryku,
Pozikhodiutsia dokupy
Radi ta veseli
I pustyniu opanuiut
Veselii sela, –

                  Unmarked,
But broad and free
The sacred roads throughout
Will lie, and the rulers
Will not find them,
But down the roads the serfs
Without cries or alarms
Will come together
Full of gladness and cheer,
And joyful villages
Will conquer the desert. ('Rejoice, o Field')

This is why the poet, urging us 'not to forget our Mother' and, calling down heavenly vengeance on the turncoats who sell their children to the Muscovite butchers ('Za dumoiu duma' / 'Thought after thought') also protested against all the barriers invented between people and exhorted the land-owners thus:

Obnimite, braty moi,
Naimenshoho brata, –
Nekhai Maty usmikhnetsia,
Zaplakana Maty!

My brothers, embrace
Your youngest brother, –
So that our mother will smile,
Our tearful mother! ('Epistle')

Only when there are no more masters or peasants but a unified, educated Ukrainian family will Ukrainian national independence be possible and only then

Ozhyve dobra slava
Slava Ukrainy.

Her good name will be reborn,
The honour of Ukraine. (*ibid*.)

This was the road to freedom that the poet pointed out to his countrymen, and a wide-ranging reform of social relations was the only means of achieving this freedom. It would be wrong to think that Shevchenko would have been satisfied with, for instance, merely the abolition of serfdom or that his words, quoted above, have no wider significance. He boldly rejected even the seemingly most sacred forms of social organization as soon as he was convinced that they were not in harmony with truth and that they were harmful to people. He saw no truth in the existing forms of social organization.

Molites Bohovi odnomu,
Molites pravdi na zemli,
A bilshe na zemli nikomu
Ne poklonites: vse brekhnia!

Pray to God alone,
Pray to truth on this earth,
And on earth never again
Bow before anyone: it is all lies! ('The Neophytes')

The poet perceived another social order and a truth other than that upheld by priests and police. As he said in his 'Testament':

Pokhovaite ta vstavaite,
Kaidany porvite
I vrazhoiu zloiu kroviu
Voliu okropite.
I mene v semi velykii,
V semi vilnii novii
Ne zabudte pomianuty
Ne zlym – tykhym slovom.

Bury me and arise,
Rend asunder your chains
And baptize freedom
With the blood of the foe.
And in the great household,
In the new, free household
Do not neglect to speak of me
With a kind and quiet word.

This new household will come into being only when

Liude vyrostut. Umrut
Shche nezachatii tsariata.
A na onovlenii zemli
Vraha ne bude supostata,
A bude syn i bude maty,
I budut liude na zemli!

The people will grow up.
The not yet conceived princes will die
And on the renewed earth
There will be no foe and adversary
But there will be a son, and there will be a mother
And there will be people on the earth.

Nothing must be allowed to stand in the way of a reform of interpersonal relations in Ukraine; even the Church, which strikes its roots deepest into the soul of the people, must be reorganized. Shevchenko refused to believe in the God venerated by the priests and he wanted no part of the church they had established.

Rai u vichi lize,
A my v tserkvu lizem,
Zapliushchyvshy ochi!

Paradise is before our eyes
But we creep to church
Our eyes tightly closed.

The existing 'tomb of a church' must be destroyed so that a new, free church can be established in its place.

> Tserkva-domovyna
> Rozvalytsia ... A z pid nei
> Vstane Ukraina
> I rózviie tmu nevoli,
> Svit pravdy zasvityt,
> I pomoliutsia na voli
> Nevolnychi dity.

> This tomb of a church
> Will fall into ruin ... And from beneath it
> Ukraine will arise
> And disperse the gloom of slavery,
> A world of truth will shine forth,
> And the children of slaves
> Will worship in freedom.

Only when men become free brothers and when lies no longer prevail in our land, when master and peasant are no more, will national freedom be possible for Ukraine. It follows from this that if we want freedom from national enslavement we must work for the good of the common, uneducated people, who are oppressed by their evil fate, and if we neglect to do this nothing will result from our work except an empty provincial patriotism.

These, in short, are Shevchenko's thoughts on nationalism. They reveal no chauvinism or provincial patriotism, nor are they tinged with the slavish mentality of his predecessors. Throughout, Shevchenko saw the Ukrainian people as an independent nation and he demanded for them the rights that belong to every nation as a matter of course. His independence and hatred of slavery made him despise it everywhere he saw it, even when his enemies were enslaved. Shevchenko harboured no hostility towards the Muscovites as a nation, nor to the Poles as such. He rebelled against Muscovite oppression but not against the Muscovite nation. He rebelled against Polish oppression in the past but not against the Polish nation. And in his poem 'To the Poles,' he said:

Podai zhe ruku kozakovi
I sertse chysteie podai
I znovu imenem Khrystovym
Vozobnovym nash tykhyi rai!

Give your hand to the Cossack
And your pure heart
And again, in the name of Christ
We shall renew our peaceful paradise!

How far removed this is from Kvitka's or Hulak-Artemovsky's wild notions about the Polish situation!

Shevchenko was the first to express clearly the idea of Ukraine's complete independence as a nation, and along with this he maintained a consistent tolerance of other nations; he expressed something completely new and previously unheard-of in the Ukrainian writers who preceded him. The poet dispersed the tissue of lies which until then had obscured the issue of national independence. He was the first Ukrainian with a real national awareness and no one assisted as he did in the creation of a healthy Ukrainian national outlook.

The greatness of his deed can be appreciated only when we understand what darkness prevailed in our land before Shevchenko. His description of Šafařik can be far more justly applied to himself, for it was he who lit 'Svitlo pravdy, voli,' / 'The light of truth and freedom,' and he became

     Iiezekiilem.
I, o dyvo! trupy vstaly
I ochi rozkryly.

     Ezekiel.
And wonder to behold, the corpses arose
And opened their eyes.

Shevchenko transformed the dead into live human beings, for what were the members of the Ukrainian intelligentsia as Ukrainians if not corpses? This is why we call him our national prophet and see him as a phenomenon perhaps unique in history. Ukrainian literature will surely produce many more writers as talented as Shevchenko but never again will there be one as significant for the national renaissance; there will be other great writers but never again a prophet.

(1892)

NOTES

1 This article is a translation of chapter six of B. Hrinchenko, 'Lysty z Ukrainy naddniprianskoi,' in *Bukovyna* (Chernivtsi 1892-3). Hrinchenko's tract prompted Drahomanov to write 'Lysty na naddnipriansku Ukrainu,' *Narod* (Kolomyia 1893). Omelian Ohonovsky (1833-94) was a prominent Galician scholar and a professor at the University of Lviv.
2 I. Kotliarevsky, 'Pisnia na novy 1805 hod panu nashomu i batku kniaziu Alekseiu Borysovychu Kurakinu,' 1849 (ed.).

8

Shevchenko as a Poet

MYKOLA IEVSHAN

Shevchenko's creative output can be understood only when the poet's life is taken into consideration.[1] His work is not self-contained; rather, it depends on, grows out of, and is tightly bound up with the poet's life and character. For this reason it loses *a priori* any intrinsic logical continuity and becomes occasional, in Goethe's sense of the word. 'All my poems,' Goethe said to Eckermann, 'are occasional; they originate in reality and in reality they find their *raison d'être*. I do not think highly of poems snatched out of the air.' Shevchenko might have said those words. Only his deepest feelings ever found a place in his work. This is why his poetry is so forceful, so fiery, so full of temperament and feeling not blunted by dispassionate reflection. His work is pure emotion; we can perceive its birth and its thrust. His poetry is of the present moment, and the present moment is the essence of the lyric. Unlike epic poetry, it does not depict scenes from the past, nor does it describe passionate conflicts, which are the basis of drama. For these require that the poet transcend himself and objectively describe other lives, not his own. But in fact the opposite occurs; the poet seeks himself and in lyric poetry finds only himself. A centripetal movement takes place and this movement becomes the main theme of creative expression. Therefore, if we wish to discover the foundations of the creativity of individual writers we must first consider those passages that could be called lyrical: we must seek the creator where he fully discloses himself, where he confesses to himself. This is especially necessary with Shevchenko, who reaches the greatest heights only in his immortal lyrics. By treating Shevchenko's lyrics as the keystone of his creativity we shall come as close as possible to the whole truth about him, and will be able to characterize him, at least in general terms.

Like all creative people, Shevchenko was never without more or less wide-ranging plans. He intended his work to be useful to society and to point the way towards the beautiful and the ideal. With Shevchenko there occurs the same process to be observed in the creative endeavours of other great poets. They wish to serve their people and to put their God-given talent to use. And this is precisely why, on the whole, they end by burying their gift, for they block that unconscious, natural flow that is their inspiration. Usually their plans fail or are only partly realized. Their works are then judged unworthy of their genius even though they reveal an uncommon ability. On the other hand, they create immortal works almost unconsciously when they are not thinking of any ultimate goal, but heed only their inner voice. Thus, the real worth of the artist is disclosed when he stops speaking, or rather, that which is most vauable in art remains unexpressed. The artist cannot reveal his thoughts concretely; he must always leave them incomplete, in their beginning stages. We measure the greatness of a work according to the degree of its longing to express these thoughts. This longing is nevertheless to be found in every work; it constitutes the work's dynamism, its potential force, its inner rhythm. This longing unites us with the work of art and with the very soul of the poet; it reveals his world to us. How gladly we put aside the part of Shevchenko's work in which he labours to discover paths of righteousness and ideals, where he attempts to show men the way out of the morasses and labyrinths of contemporary life. Thus, we take account of the poems which are epistles to himself, where he is beyond playing roles, disclaims leadership, and confesses to his soul in solitude. Shevchenko told the whole truth about himself when he wrote in a letter:

> Ne dlia liudei, i ne dlia slavy,
> Merezhani ta kucheriavi
> Otsi virshi virshuiu ia, –
> Dlia sebe, bratiia moia!

> Not for men, and not for fame
> Do I write these embroidered and embellished verses,
> But for myself, my brothers!

It was indeed for himself that he wrote. Anything not intended solely for himself was not for anyone else either. No one derives benefit from the stories he wrote in Russian and no one could derive benefit from the great poem that he intended to write in the common Slavic language. Poets ten times lesser than Shevchenko could realize all sorts of ideals in their work and consequently succeed in expounding entire philosophical systems or world views. Shevchenko, fortunately, had no 'ideals,' and when he appeared in the role of propagandist for certain catch-phrases he was not even able to formulate these as well as the average party agitator. No *Weltanschauung* is to be found in Shevchenko's poetry. His creative efforts were directed towards achieving an ever-higher degree of spiritual perfection, to create an equilibrium which he did not find in life.

Everything he expresses is a revelation of his emotional state, only a momentary cry, a transient 'philosophy,' and an ephemeral truth, for the next moment and the following mood will dictate otherwise and compel him to champion another cause. Why does the poet struggle and protest against the circumstances of life? Not in order to prophesy, nor to instruct others, nor to explain a program, but to ease his heart and soul. We can truly know the poet only by examining his emotions and not his words. It is the negative side of his efforts that will guide us in our search for his wandering spirit. And in the end all this will serve no purpose and will yield no guiding thread through the labyrinth of his work. Whatever conclusions or practical deductions we should try to reach from the poems would all be false. For here we are dealing with the expression of the state of the poet's soul, with his ever-changing moods and his efforts to break out of life's enchanted circle in order to find a personal harmony.

Here creativity is always a constant reaction to life, a constant competition with oneself, a constant unrest. The basis for this poetry obviously consists only of the deepest personal experiences and never of any rational elements. Poetry such as this is always the outflow of pent-up energy, an emotive creativeness, in which the aim of the creative process cannot be, as Ovsianiko-Kulikovsky[2] states, 'the creation of ideas, but a higher spiritual harmony.' And here Shevchenko's constant vacillating from the aesthetic to the ethical, that eternal passing from contemplation of the beautiful to more or less religious moods, is explained. No sight could give him peace or calm his sensitive soul; he always searched for an underlying mood, became obsessed by it, and plunged headlong into ecstasy instead of remaining in contemplation of the scene. And thus he found himself suddenly 'on the other side' and became aware of it only when all his spiritual energy was spent. But then he had no strength left to turn back and begin again; the road had been travelled, the poet's intensity of feeling had gone. Emptiness and a desire for peace and spiritual calm remained.

Here Shevchenko unconsciously touches upon a religious ideal, that is, the notion of a mysterious, superior, and unique power that is able to uplift the poet and make him conscious of his own strength in submitting to it, reviving the exhausted spirit and reconciling it with life. This phenomenon, in the idiom of those 'severe' and disciplined people who have taken it upon themselves to comment ironically upon all ecstatic experience and to disparage any truth they cannot understand, is termed *Fahnenflucht*, that is, deserting the field. But this is neither a desertion nor an unworthy act for the artist. On the contrary, it is a necessary stage for every artist of Shevchenko's type; it is his only possible means of self-knowledge and self-elevation. In this moment all the *disjecta membra* of his experiences and emotions find their justification and synthesis. This is giving oneself a goal, redeeming the spiritual values that the poet incorporates into everything he feels. It is the supreme summing up of strength, and experiencing in a single moment that which can constitute the content and worth of an entire life.

These qualities are decisive in Shevchenko's creative character and in the creative type as defined by Ribot.[3] Shevchenko's aesthetic feelings are in disproportion to his own feelings. Hence his powerful lyricism grows in opposition to his aesthetic sensibility. Sometimes it seems that the quality in poets that we like to call 'thinking in images' was positively foreign to our poet. His thinking by its very nature was not, and could not, have been visual. And the essence of Shevchenko's creativity is not to be found in artistic scenes and images. He was above all a *raconteur*. Pictorial images would dissolve before his eyes, but he would capture their music and their echo and express them in his inimitable way, in a form less clearly determined for the eye, but unmistakable to the ear of the hearer. His lyricism might be termed auditory and musical. Only by his own efforts could the reader transform these impressions into pictorial images more congenial for the eye. Lyrical emotion for its own sake predominates in Shevchenko's poetry; his visual imagination does not match it. What is more, the stronger his voice becomes and the more affectingly his passion speaks, the more do the poetic images lose their form and dissolve: the intensity of the creative process destroys plasticity. In a word, if we accept Ribot's terminology, Shevchenko's sort of creativeness may be termed 'overflowing.' The methods Shevchenko uses to create his effects are, of course, adapted accordingly. Not being able to make use of the plasticity, the visual effect of his images, he had to use their passion and power. Even when the value of the work is threatened by its excess and chaos (for example, in the 'Epistle'), Shevchenko is able by his strength of expression so to synthesize all the various moments and feelings that he achieves unexpectedly powerful results. This is what makes his poetry so energetic, so thoroughly vital, its eloquence and force equalled only, perhaps, in the works of the Jewish prophets.

As a result, Shevchenko's lyrics were fated to appear in the wider arena of national interests and to make powerful statements about untruth and evil. Thus, without writing a national epic or using any grandiose poetic form, as did other national poets, Shevchenko became our greatest national poet.

These considerations give rise to a rather interesting observation about our poetry as a whole, although Shevchenko's poetry is still its highest achievement. Even now our poetry does not transcend the largely suggestive and somewhat passive stage. It has never been strong in content, but rather in the way it evokes feeling. Even now it cannot transcend the content supplied to it by everyday life and the ethnographer. Throughout, man remains under the sway of primitive emotions; he has not freed himself from his nature. Even in those cases where a new element, purely cultural, has been introduced, man still has not lost his primitive, unrefined traits. After Shevchenko's death, Kulish was the first to enter the larger arena and to widen the perspective of Ukrainian poetry. He tried to change it from a confession, a reflection of ever-changing moods, into an expression of the spirit which wings its way into the distant future, discovering new cultural horizons. He even abandoned that trite, attractive lyricism which Shevchenko raised to such heights in order to give a much more lyrical quality to his grandiose poems.

What a lack of response there has been to his truly great and highly poetic plans! How isolated they are in Ukrainian poetry, which has no desire to transcend lyricism. Kulish attempted to 'cleanse' our poetry of the instinctive element; he wished to raise it to a stage where poetry ceases to be pure instinct, merely an expression of man's elemental nature, and becomes the harmonious sound of the ideal. He wanted to give it greater inner strength and endurance so that it would not bend before the winds of life. But Shevchenko's poetry had greater force and became the model for national poetry.

What does this mean? It merely means that the stage Shevchenko lived through in his creative life was closer to reality, and more in harmony with the stage at which Ukrainian poetry found itself at the time. Kulish's efforts might have been premature, in advance of that type of poetry or even perhaps ushering in a new style which at that time must have seemed somewhat abstract. Even now considerable sophistication is needed to appreciate Kulish's poetry. But every heart and soul responds to Shevchenko's poetry. In this respect, especially in its popularity and accessibility, it is unparalleled. It is almost on the same level as folk poetry, for there everyone finds a pre-existing framework into which he can fit both content and experience. But this is not all. At its best, folk poetry has a quality which might be called sensuality, which tremendously facilitates the approach for everyone. In some cases it may act directly upon the senses, like the scent of a flower. Its effect is not achieved by superficial picturesqueness or a richness of form and expression, for these are poor and simple. But Shevchenko's work is that much more powerful precisely because of its simplicity and economy. And Shevchenko, without the artistic education of the average artist of our time, influenced millions of Ukrainians. What others achieved by the plasticity and harmony of their poetic vision he achieved by the force of his poetry and the rhythm of his *dumy*. Whatever aesthetic sensitivity, the product of long ages of history and artistic culture, gave to others, was given to Shevchenko by the aesthetic of the word, and the manipulation of its aesthetic qualities, which is the similarity between his poetry and the folk song. Truly, a prophetic soul is required to understand the power of poetry as Shevchenko understood it, when he wrote after reading the eleventh Psalm:

> ... Voskresnu nyni, rady ikh,
> Liudei zakovanykh moikh –
> Ubohykh-nyshchykh ... Vozvelychu
> Malykh ottykh rabiv nimykh
> Ia na storozhi kolo ikh
> Postavliu slovo ...

Today I shall arise from the dead for their sake,
For my enchained people,
Poor and humble. I shall extol
Those lowly, silent slaves.
I shall place my word
On guard beside them.

(1911)

NOTES

1 Translation of an excerpt from M. Ievshan, 'Taras Shevchenko,' *Ukrainska khata* (1911).
2 D.N. Ovsianiko-Kulikovsky (1853-1920), a prominent Russian literary historian, professor at Kharkiv University (ed.).
3 Theodule Ribot (1839-1916), French psychologist, author of *Essai sur l'imagination créatrice* (1900) (ed.).

9

Shevchenko's 'Abandonment'

KORNEI CHUKOVSKY

We have been forsaken by God, God has forgotten us.[1] This is the most terrifying knowledge that Shevchenko possesses about God. For, of all the types of human suffering, the most painful to him is precisely this: being forsaken. All those in the land of the suffering were close and dear to him but closer and dearer than most were those whom he called 'poor wretches' (siromakhy, siromy), the 'miserable orphans' (syri syroty), all the forgotten and forsaken. And when you read his *Kobzar*, the most poignant circumstance seems to be neither hunger nor madness, neither sickness nor death but being orphaned, the state of orphanhood, when one is cast aside, rejected. How terrifying, then, must be the thought that God has rejected His people! Those who have been rejected by someone for some reason – those poor wretches alone did Shevchenko admit to his page. Come to me, all you who have been forsaken, I alone will not forsake you!

Everyone remembers Kateryna from his *Kobzar*: 'having taken his pleasure, the Russian soldier abandoned Katrusia' (zhartuiuchy kynuv Katrusiu moskal). But even Oksana – 'so small, curly-haired' (taku malenku, kucheriavu), Shevchenko's childhood friend – is abandoned by just such a Russian soldier, and Tytarivna-Nemyrivna as well. Tytarivna-Nemyrivna continues to await the return of her Russian soldier, while Kateryna throws herself into an icy pond, Oksana goes mad, Lukiia from the poem 'Vidma' (The Witch) becomes simple-minded and the bewitched maiden ('Prychynna' / 'The Bewitched Woman'), abandoned by her Cossack, or rather, not actually abandoned but concluding she has been abandoned, joins the water nymphs in the river.

The most fortunate of Shevchenko's abandoned maidens enters a convent; for the others, madness or suicide is the inevitable end. 'Martyr!' is what Shevchenko calls the girl forsaken by the land-owner's son. She dies by a fence in winter, in the freezing cold. The spectacle of an abandoned woman is so unbearable for Shevchenko that he was even led to exclaim on one occasion:

> Ochi, ochi!
> Na shcho vy zdalysia?
> Chom vy zmalku ne vysokhly,
> Slizmy ne zlylysia?

Eyes, eyes! / What good are you? / Why did you not dry up in childhood, / Not exhaust your tears?

There is much in this that perplexes me and much that I fail to understand. To be sure, an orphan himself, motherless at the age of nine and fatherless at twelve, having experienced in full measure the horror of yearning and abandonment in 'the God-forsaken wilderness' in Kos-Aral and Novo-Petrovsk, having no one show him any kindness in his final years, Shevchenko was naturally attracted to characters who were orphans like himself. Yet, all the same, why do words such as the following, which normally do not convey dread, always sound so inexpressibly sinister in his poetry? 'And he *forsook* me' (A vin mene i *pokynuv*); 'He went somewhere far away and *forsook* me' (Vin poikhav des daleko, a mene *pokynuv*); 'Petro has not come, there is no news about Petro, has he perhaps *forsaken* me?' (Nema Petra, ne chut Petra, ne vzhe zh to *pokynuv*?); 'They *forsook* their old mother, he his wife *forsook*' (*Pokynuly* staru matir, toi zhinku *pokynuv*); 'Do not *forsake* your mother, they told you. – But you *forsook* her, ran away' (Ne kydai materi, kazaly. – A ty pokynula, vtekla).[2]

Why, in fact, do Shevchenko's characters have such an irrational fear of being abandoned? Why in the poem 'Nevolnyk' (The Captive) does the old man, a 'grey-haired, wealthy orphan,' weep so much when he learns that his daughter, 'his only child, plans to *forsake* him' (Ioho iedynaia dytyna / Pokynut khoche)?

'With whom am I to live out my days, with whom complete my life's term?' (Z kym dozhyt, dobuty viku vikovoho?) Even for Honta, a man who puts his own sons to the sword, the most awesome fact is that without them he is an orphan! 'And who will bury me in this foreign tract, who will weep over me?' (A khto mene pokhovaie na chuzhomu poli, khto zaplache nado mnoiu?), the murderer of his own children laments over their bodies. Why, even in his youth, did those discarded in old age appear to Shevchenko as a constant and terrifying spectre? He was twenty-four when he wrote in 'Kateryna' that after their daughter's departure, 'they became orphans, her old father and mother' (Ostalysia syrotamy / Staryi batko i maty). And from then until the end of his life he ushered a whole string of orphaned old men and women into his *Kobzar*, all of whom die on top of a stove in a cold, dark peasant hut:

> Pokynuta starukha-mat:
> Nikto ei ne istopit khaty
> I ne prikroet driakhlykh plech.
> A ei uzh trudno vstat – zazhech
> Ogon bezsilnymi rukami.[3]

She has been forsaken, the old mother: / There is no one to heat the house / Or cover her decrepit shoulders. / And it is hard for her to rise / And light the fire with her feeble arms.

In 'The Witch,' the girl's old father dies and 'there is no one to make the sign of the cross over him, no one to fold his arms.' In another poem an old woman is alone on top of the stove; the poor soul dies, the peasant hut slumps and rots. Another old woman, Kostomarov's mother, who has been deprived of her son,

> Chornisha chornoi zemli
> Ide, z Khresta nenache zniata

Walks, blacker than the black soil, / As if taken down from the Cross.

In 'Kniazhna' (The Princess) there is the dying prince, forsaken by his daughter. In 'Sova' (The Owl), the mother whose son was conscripted sits by the door for days on end, staring at the path through the field: 'But her son, the soldier, does not come, does not come' (a moskalia, ii syna, nemaie, nemaie) and in the end she goes mad, makes a doll for herself, and cares for it as if it were a child. Having lost her son, yet another mother, the mother from 'Neofity' (The Neophytes), pounds her head against a wall and falls to the ground in a dead faint. Our loved ones leave us, our loved ones die, our loved ones are taken from us – why did these images form a constant theme in Shevchenko's works, a theme to which he persistently reverted with continuing surges of emotion?

Strange as it may seem, Shevchenko was also in some inexplicable way drawn towards abandoned things, abandoned inanimate objects. The nest, left behind by a nightingale, swaying alone on the branches of a guelder rose; the abandoned boat, carried by the wind; the poetic 'poplar,' which 'alone, all alone, like an orphan, dies in foreign parts' (odna, odna, iak syrota na chuzhyni hyne); the orphaned hills and the orphaned sea; the orphaned groves – 'do not leave me an orphan as you left the groves' (Ne kyn syrotoiu, iak kynuv dibrovy); the orphaned burial mounds in the steppe, the Dnipro rapids, and that most holy of holies, Ukraine, which

> Obidrana *syrotoiu*
> Ponad Dniprom plache.
> Tiazhko, vazhko *syrotyni*,
> A nikhto i ne bachyt.

A ragged orphan, / Weeps beside the Dnipro. / It is hard, it is burdensome for the orphan / But no one even sees.

The main thing is that 'no one even sees.' This is what the poet is drawn towards; this is what attracts him more than anything else. And then there are those orphaned peasant huts which in Ukrainian are so ominously called *pustky* (deserted houses): 'The deserted house near the village had swung a little to one side' (Tilky pustka krai sela na bik pokhylylas); 'And the cottage smells of the deserted house' (I khata pustkoiu smerdyt); 'And the deserted house rots in emptiness' (I khata pustkoiu hnyie).

The peasant houses inhabited not by people, but by owls, the ponds that are drying up, the tumbledown well, the path overgrown with grass, the bell tower abandoned by the bell-ringer,[4] the open gates through which no one enters; the mothers forsaken by their children, the girls abandoned by their lovers, the universe forsaken by God, rejected and orphaned by the

Almighty – all these images are, of course, symbols, likenesses, the external images through which Shevchenko unconsciously strove to convey at least to some degree his inescapable and persistent feeling of an inhuman aloneness. Yet, all the same, one detail, one little circumstance, which hardly merits comment, constantly disturbs me and, venturing to interrupt myself here, I hasten to take note of it.

Imagine for a moment Taras as a youth here in Petersburg; he scurries about on Gorokhovaia, Liteinaia, and Meshchanskaia in a cotton smock with a bucket and paintbrush in his hand, bespattered with whitewash and ochre, a pupil of the house-painter and master of pictorial arts, Shiriaev. 'Taras, some beer!' 'Taras, some tobacco!' He sleeps and eats with glass-cutters and roofers – from Kaluga, from Kostroma – in a filthy garret and then, too, there are the usual kicks and cuffs. The typical Petersburg boy – he scurries about here on Gorokhovaia for a year, a second, a third, and a fourth – a serf-slave, an uneducated youth:

> Ne znav siromakha, shcho vyrosly kryla,
> Shcho neba dostane, koly poletyt,
> Ne znav, nahynavsia ...

The poor wretch did not know that he had grown wings, / That he will reach the heavens when he flies, / He did not know, he stooped ...

Naturally, they give him something for tea – here's a ten-kopek piece! Naturally, he kisses their hands (he came to see Ivan Soshenko and kissed his hand) and, while kissing them, worries that he may be struck (when Soshenko pulled his hand away, Taras took fright and ran off) – a cowed and maltreated slave who was whipped in the stable and, as a child, was driven by hunger to eat clay. And suddenly a miracle happens, his wildest dreams – 'that which was not,' 'that which could not be' – came to pass: some people gather around him like angels – he had not even suspected that such people existed, such wizards and sorcerers – and say to him: you are free! And they give him a charter of freedom, some sort of magical document; you are freed from the house-painter Shiriaev, from the land-owner Pavel Engelhardt, from the ochre, and from the inveterate swearers. The benevolent Zhukovsky, the magnificent Briullov, Count Velgorsky, Countess Baranova, Vice-President Grigorovich, the artist Venetsianov, all come to him, all are concerned about him, buy freedom for him from his master. They are affectionate, they are kind-hearted as no one else has ever been. And when, for one moment, even if only of the shortest duration, these kindly hands reached out to him from all sides, his ever-present feeling of having been deserted should have been silenced because he was not deserted then, because even twenty years later it would be beyond his powers to forget his bliss at that time, because even after twenty years he would still be amazed by what had happened: 'It is hard for me to believe now,' he would write in his diary, 'but it actually happened. From a dirty garret I, an insignificant sloven, flew into the magical halls of the academy of arts. A swift passage for a coarse *muzhik* house-painter from a garret to the magnificent studio of the greatest painter of our century!'

There was April and then May. There were the white nights. And, with his coat undoubtedly flung open, Shevchenko scudded about all Petersburg, along Liteinaia, along Gorokhovaia. In his pocket, his remittal, his charter of independence. He pulls it out and kisses it, makes the sign of the cross and kisses it again, is already scribbling on some scraps of paper. Read carefully the lines written in the months immediately following his redemption:

> Bo ia odynokyi
> Syrota na sviti v chuzhomu kraiu.

For in this world / I am a lone orphan in a strange land.

This is what he writes on these pages. And again: 'It is hard for me to live in this world as an orphan' (Tiazhko meni syrotoiu na sim sviti zhyty); 'For the orphan the sun shines, shines but gives no warmth' (Syrotyni sontse svityt, svityt ta ne hriie); 'People would block the sun so that it could not shine for the orphan' (Liudy b sontse zastupyly, shchob syroti ne svitylo).

Oh, naturally, he is overflowing with gratitude for the kindness of those who took him to their bosoms. He dedicates almost all his poetic lines to them: 'Kateryna' to Zhukovsky, 'Haidamaky' to Grigorovich.[5] But in these poems he discusses only one thing: his orphanhood, how terrifying it is for him to live among strangers in a strange land. 'Chuzhiie liudy' (strange people) is a common phrase in his poetry at that time. Who was a stranger to him then? Count Iakiv de Balmen? Petrovsky? Hrebinka? Shternberg? Or was it Soshenko? They share everything with him, work with him, go hungry with him. Altogether, he has so many friends that, as he later wrote, 'you aim at a dog and strike a friend.' These were not merely 'acquaintances' but friends of the staunchest and most devoted sort. And, then, how many more were there later in Ukraine? Kulish, Kostomarov, Bilozersky, Princess Repnina, Kozachkovsky, Tarnovsky – yet, on every page all he can do is complain and lament about his cruel orphanhood: 'Around me, wherever I look, are not people but serpents' (Kruhom mene, de ne hlianu, ne liudy, a zmii).

Read carefully those first poems written in Petersburg, the lines from his first years as a poet: always that same set of images, that same theme of abandonment. A girl roams along the shore overlooking the sea, sobbing: 'because my dark-browed one has perished, I am perishing too' (koly zh zhynuv chornobryvyi, to i ia pohybaiu). And another, no different from the first, and also at a spot overlooking the sea: 'let the orphan cry, let her waste her years' (nekhai plache syrotyna, nekhai lita tratyt). And a third, no different from the first: 'a year passed and then a second, still the Cossack did not return' (mynuv i rik, mynuv druhyi, kozaka nemaie).

Then, those constant refrains: 'I am an orphan, my dear one' (ia syrota, mii holube); 'I am an orphan from Vilshana, I am an orphan without a mother, an orphan, granny' (Ia syrota z Vilshanoi, ia syrota bez materi, babusiu).

It's simply amazing. Open arms greet him wherever he turns, but he seems not to notice. Shchepkin, Kukharenko, Bodiansky, Maksymovych – did he really not remember them, had he forgotten them when he wrote subsequently from his barracks: 'no one loved me, no one hailed me and I leaned upon no one' (nikhto liubyv mene, vitav, i ia khylyvsia ni do koho)? So affectionate a man, but not responsive to the affection of others! Or, rather, responsive but not here, in his *Kobzar*. Where did this negative feeling of Shevchenko's come from? For a long time I could not understand this but now I think I do. Delve deeply into Ukrainian folk song, listen attentively to it. Take even Maksymovych himself, that collector of antiquities in whom Gogol had once delighted, and you will be amazed to discover that in the folklore of the Ukrainian people *desertion and orphanhood also dominate all the other emotions*:

Oi, poikhav v Moskovshchynu
  Ta tam i zahynuv.
Svoiu mylu Ukrainu
  Na viky pokynuv.

Oh, to Muscovy did he go / And there perished. / His beloved Ukraine / For eternity abandoned.

This is from the very first song, but could it not just as easily have come from *Kobzar*? Then, there is the second song: a son vows to return to his mother only after the sand sown on the earth and watered by her tears sprouts; and the third: he will return when the peacock's quill sinks to the bottom and the miller's millstone floats. Indeed, how can Ukrainian folk songs not be songs of parting and abandonment?

Call to mind the wife of Taras Bulba: 'she had lived in a paradise of love for only an instant, only in the first heat of passion, and already her grim tempter was deserting her for the sword, for his friends, for the life of revelry. ... The sexes shared only the most fleeting of encounters and then separated for years. For the women these were years of longing and waiting for the return of their husbands and lovers who had flashed before them like visions, like a dream.' Is this not the source of that longing, that affliction, that constant 'lament of Iaroslavna' for her beloved, Sviatoslav, which is heard in Ukrainian melodies?

In Chubynsky's classic tomes on the southwestern area I discovered only fourteen songs about jealousy and thirty about unhappy affairs of the heart, but 240 concerned with parting![6]

It is indeed remarkable that, independently of the facts of his own biography and even *in opposition* to them, Shevchenko took to himself and expressed only these national feelings; all the others, all those uncharacteristic of his people, even those that he himself experienced, he did not feel keenly and they were excluded from his *Kobzar*, remained outside its covers. It was as if Shevchenko had no words to express them, no images, no rhythms, no poetry! All feelings and thoughts not shared by his nation somehow dimmed and died away as soon as he took pen in hand.

But this is a miracle of sorts! Shevchenko lives on Vasilevsky Island in Petersburg for sixteen years, he is a Petersburgian to the very marrow of his bones. But where is Vasilevsky Island in his *Kobzar*? In which of even

the least significant psychological details is it to be found? Where in
Kobzar is Briullov, the academy of arts? Shevchenko can live with Briullov
for ten years, regard him with reverence, copy him in a varietyof ways, in
his paintings, in his dress, in the cut of his hair, discuss Dürer, Guido
Reni, Teniers with him, but here he takes pen in hand and where are you
then, Briullov? Where is Jurgens's restaurant then? Where is Izler, the
Aleksandrinsky Theatre and Karatygin? Where is *Severnaia pchela* (The
Northern Bee), 'Zolotoi iakor' (The Golden Anchor)? Where is Nikolai
Polevoi, Count Iakiv de Balmen, Dal, Petrovsky, Pletnev, the small fish
patties, Adolfinka?[7] All this is shed like some external covering and in that
magical moment there is not a single gesture in Shevchenko, not even a
slight hint, not even the smallest touch of anything which could not exist in
that Dnieprovian Ostap, Maksym, or Iarema. He stripped all this away as,
you will recall, did Tolstoi's Natasha Rostova. When she launched into a
Russian dance, this French-educated countess flung off her noble title and
her usual psychological identity and the laughing peasant, Anisia, was
reduced to tears as she watched this girl, now a stranger to her, this
countess accustomed to silk and velvet, who could comprehend and express
with every gesture, whatever lay within Anisia, her father, her aunt, and
her mother. And this very gift, this capacity to suspend the characteristics
peculiar to one's own personal 'I,' Shevchenko possessed above everyone
else and from this derives the unique character of his *Kobzar*, in which, no
matter how close your examination, you find almost no trace of the poet's
personality, nothing characteristic of him alone, belonging to him alone.
Whatever you attribute to him *as a poet, as an author*, you will find that,
no, it belongs not to him but to the entire Ukrainian people.

(1914)

NOTES

1 Translation of chapter 6 of K. Chukovsky, 'Shevchenko,' *Litsa i maski*
  (St Petersburg 1914). The title has been added.
2 In only three instances in *Kobzar* does the person who leaves return. But he
  returns either a blind man ('Nevolnyk' / 'The Captive'), a dead man
  ('Khustyna' / 'The Kerchief') or, even worse, a man who has been deceived

('Mizh skalamy, nenachy zlodii' / 'Between the cliffs, like a thief'). From the standpoint of *Kobzar* there appears to exist an abiding law to the effect that one who leaves may not return.

3 Chukovsky here is quoting some lines from A. Koltonovsky's translation of Shevchenko's poem 'U nashim rai na zemli' (In Our Heaven on Earth) (ed.).

4 The empty bell tower appears in 'Chuma' (Tḥe Plague): 'Long has the bell not been heard. / Chimneys sorrow without smoke' (Bo dzvona vzhe davno ne chut. / Sumuiut komyny bez dymu). Generally characteristic of this feeling for abandoned objects are 'The Plague,' 'Ne kydai materi! – kazaly' (Do not forsake your mother! – they told you), 'Chyhyryn,' and many others. In every little piece there are up to ten or fifteen objects that have been discarded.

5 Later in his *Kobzar* he recalled Grigorovich's good deed: 'Had I not met him at that unfortunate hour, they would have buried me long ago in the snow in a foreign land' (Iak by ne vin spitkav mene pry lykhii hodyni, davno b dosi zakhovaly v snihu na chuzhyni). And again: he 'did not allow me to die in a foreign land' (meni na chuzhyni ne dav pohybaty).

6 P.P. Chubinsky, ed., *Trudy etnografichesko-statisticheskoi ekspeditsii v zapadno-russkii krai* (St Petersburg 1878) V.

7 Adolphina or Adolfinka is mentioned in Shevchenko's letters. He knew her as a woman of easy virtue during his student days in St Petersburg. See also p 251 (ed.).

10

Muzhik Philosophy

ANDRII RICHYTSKY

As is to be expected, the fundamental elements of Shevchenko's world view derive from the peasantry, that segment of society from which he himself came.[1] To be sure, his general level of consciousness transcended that of his own social stratum and his world view thus was also broader, yet, all the same, his feet were firmly planted upon *muzhik* (peasant) soil. A Ukraine choking under the tsarist yoke, the recollections of a 'centenarian' (stolitnoho dida), the sight of the enslaved peasantry, memories of the 'Cossack liberty' (kozatska volia) of yore, gave rise to his nationalism and Ukrainian patriotism. But even in his nationalism, the *muzhik* Shevchenko stood opposed to the patriotism of the land-owning class, a patriotism which combined fidelity to 'the throne' and 'the fatherland' with an interest in ethnography.

Because of his fiery cult of oppressed Ukraine, which, 'a ragged orphan, weeps beside the Dnipro' (obidrana syrotoiu ponad Dniprom plache), because of his passionate love for her ('so do I love her, so do I love my poor Ukraine' / 'ia tak ii, ia tak liubliu moiu Ukrainu ubohu'), Shevchenko came to hold a view sharply opposed to the land-owners' 'appreciative love of the common fatherland' (vdiachnoi liubovy do spilnoi batkivshchyny), tsarist Russia. If Shevchenko's nationalism is viewed in isolation from his era and its social base – the oppressed and enslaved peasantry – apostrophes to Ukraine such as 'quiet world, beloved country, my Ukraine' (Svite tykhyi, kraiu mylyi, / Moia Ukraino!) or 'Ukraine, Ukraine, dear mother mine' (Ukraino, Ukraino, / Nenko moia, nenko!) and his poetry as a whole provide the foundation for latter-day bourgeois nationalism. Needless to say, the fact that his nationalism is founded upon a base that was revolutionary for its time in no way refutes its narrow, limited, and obtusely insular character. Elements such as national exclusivity, insularity, and hostility to everything unfamiliar are characteristic in general of the peasant outlook produced by the limited and insular nature of an economic organization founded upon the small peasant farm. As a consequence of such an outlook, the peasant regarded all foreigners as pagans and infidels, indeed, as enemies, and all the more so when for the peasantry the coming of foreigners meant exploitation and enslavement.

National insularity is manifested in unadulterated classical form in Shevchenko's works. His epistle to his countrymen (I mertvym, i zhyvym, i nenarodzhennym zemliakam moim v Ukraini i ne v Ukraini moie druzhnieie poslaniie / To My Dead and Living and Yet Unborn Countrymen in Ukraine and not in Ukraine My Friendly Epistle) offers examples of *muzhik* wisdom such as the following:

U chuzhomu kraiu
Ne shukaite, ne pytaite
Toho, shcho nemaie
I na nebi, a ne tilky
Na chuzhomu poli ...
V svoii khati – svoia pravda,
I syla, i volia.

Nema na sviti Ukrainy,
Nemaie druhoho Dnipra;
A vy pretesia na chuzhynu
Shukaty dobroho dobra,
Dobra sviatoho, voli, voli,
Braterstva bratnoho!

In a foreign land / Do not seek, do not inquire / After that which does not exist / Even in the heavens, not only / Not in a foreign plot of land .... / In your own house is your own truth, / Strength, and liberty. / There is no other Ukraine in this world, / No other Dnipro, / But you throng to foreign parts / In search of the highest good, / The sacred good, liberty, liberty, / And fraternal brotherhood!

The pronouncement 'in your own house is your own truth, strength and liberty' (V svoii khati – svoia pravda, / I syla, i volia) contains the very essence of *muzhik* philosophy, a philosophy confined behind an enclosure fencing off the peasant's 'cottage in the garden' (khatynochka v haiu) and his 'cherry orchard by the cottage' (Sadok vyshnevyi kolo khaty) from the rest of the world. The *muzhik* farmer does not like to seek 'the highest good' (dobroho dobra) beyond the confines of that enclosure. Hence, he is scornful of the gentry who swarm to foreign lands.

It goes without saying that hand in hand with such national isolationism goes hostility towards those foreigners who penetrate the enclosure. The peasant encounters these foreigners sometimes in the form of Muscovites (Russian soldiers) – occupying armies with their demands for lodgings, their requisitions, their recruiting levies – sometimes as Polish noblemen, sometimes as Jewish leaseholders, tavern-keepers or money-lenders, sometimes as German colonizers or manufacturers. These various social elements press upon the peasant farm from various sides, exploiting the *muzhik*, and this class antagonism indiscriminately carries over to entire peoples. Thus Shevchenko begins his poem 'Kateryna':

> Kokhaitesia, chornobryvi,
> Ta ne z moskaliamy,
> Bo moskali – chuzhi liudy,
> Robliat lykho z vamy ...

Fall in love, my dark-haired beauties, / But not with Russian soldiers, / For Russian soldiers are alien people / And will do you wrong ...

Typically, the Russian soldier with whom Kateryna falls in love is at the end of the poem unexpectedly transformed into a man of the land-owning class en route to Kiev in a carriage drawn by six horses. Here Shevchenko did not remain true to his *muzhik* mentality; he could not refrain from introducing the underlying class antagonisms of the social base in portraying the Russian soldier. In Shevchenko's works this Muscovitophobia becomes mockery when he sees his countrymen in clothing adorned 'with zinc buttons' (z tsynkovymy gudzykamy), 'jabbering in the Muscovite fashion' (po moskovsky tak i cheshut), going so far as to abuse 'their parents for not teaching them to chatter in German from childhood' (Batkiv svoikh, shcho z-malechku / Tsvenkaty ne vchyly / Po nimetsky), and Shevchenko so masterfully places Russian in the mouths of these pitiful countrymen of his that it is simply pure mockery.

The *muzhik* in Shevchenko assumes a somewhat ironic and sceptical attitude towards everything beyond the limits of his ideological neighbourhood, towards the wisdom of foreign lands, towards everything that goes counter to long-standing peasant beliefs about God, hell, and heaven. And he reproaches his countrymen thus:

Iakby vy vchylys tak, iak treba,
To i mudrost by bula svoia;
A to zalizete na nebo:
I my – ne my, i ia – ne ia.
I vse te bachyv, vse te znaiu:
Nemaie pekla, ani raiu,
Nemaie i Boha, tilky ia
Ta kutsyi nimets uzlovatyi,
A bilsh nichoho ...

Were you to learn as you should, / Then you would possess wisdom of your own; / But you climb into the heavens: / We are not we, I am not I. / I have seen everything, I know everything: / There is no hell, no paradise, / There is no God, only me / And the awkward little German / And nothing else ...

Thus, it is the German who is always behind all the Devil's work. It is not by chance that the Devil in one of Gogol's stories from the collection *Vechera na khutore bliz Dikanki* (Evenings on a Farm near Dikanka) resembles a German. In the peasant consciousness the pagan German is believed to be in league with the Devil because he operates various kinds of clever machinery and economically and culturally stands higher than the Slavic *muzhik*. For the peasant all that is incomprehensible to him is either from God or the Devil.

A product of historical development, the universal Germanophobia of the Slavic peoples is deeply embedded in Shevchenko's consciousness. Linked to a degree with his Slavism, however, it emerges in bolder relief and in sharper form than his Slavist ideas. But this is to be expected. This Germanophobia was reflected in the negative, destructive element of the social psyche of the peasant. Slavism endeavoured to offer some kind of constructive system, some kind of positive program. As we know, the peasantry functions as an excellent destructive force in any social movement but has no positive program for social reconstruction [acquiring this only when united with an organized urban class and under the latter's leadership. During bourgeois revolutions that leadership is exercised by the bourgeoisie, during proletarian revolutions, by the proletariat]. This is also manifested in *Kobzar*. Criticism, rebellion, protest, and harsh condemnation of social injustice are expressed with unusual vividness. The elements of a positive program for social reconstruction, on the other hand, are laid out vaguely. Likewise, Germanophobia, as the negative side of Slavism, is thickly sown in Taras's poetic field and illustrated by concrete examples and facts, while Pan-Slavism in all its manifestations and facts makes only a fleeting appearance.

[In addition, it should be noted that, while standing firmly upon the base of peasant consciousness, Shevchenko rises above it. For this reason his rejection of all foreign things and his Germanophobia are not as indiscriminate as those of the peasant masses. He recommends that foreign things be learned, that we ought to be familiar with foreign peoples, and he recognizes that there are some fine people among the Germans. In his story 'Khudozhnik' (The Artist) he writes: 'Very likely you have noticed that all my acquaintances are Germans, but what fine Germans they are! I am quite simply in love with these Germans.' The tone of this passage is most interesting, as the overall effect is not to refute but rather to affirm the poet's universal Germanophobia. He speaks, as it were, with the lips of the *muzhik*, saying, so to speak, although he's a German, he's still a fine fellow.]

In his 'Epistle,' the countrymen to whom the poem is addressed are especially attacked for thronging 'to German lands to contemplate the light of truth' (... sontsia-pravdy dozrivat / V nimetski zemli ...). The 'German' is always the enemy of Ukraine (my steppes have been sold to Jews, to Germans / stepy moi zaprodani zhydovi, nimoti); of Slavdom [So did the Germans set the vast house aflame and separated the family, the family of Slavs; Otak nimota zapalyla / Velyku khatu. I simiu, / Simiu slavian roziednala; And German gentry divided up the burned-out shell and the orphans; A nimchyky pozharyshche / I syrot rozdilyly; see Ieretyk (Shafarykovi) / The Heretic (To Šafařik)].[2] He grieves that 'the wise German plants potatoes on the Sich' (I na Sichi mudryi nimets / Kartopelku sadyt); he juxtaposes Germans to people, regards the word 'German' as a term of abuse. 'I have no hope for Ukraine; there are no people there, only accursed Germans and nothing else,' he wrote to his friend Iakiv Kukharenko on 24 March 1844. Pavel Šafařik, on the other hand, is praised in the poem dedicated to him 'because you did not allow our truth to drown in the German sea' (Shcho ne dav ty potonuty / V nimetskii puchyni / Nashii pravdi).

From his purely *muzhik* point of view Shevchenko reacts negatively to any imitation of foreign and, here again, German culture, seeing in this merely the aspiration on the part of the ruling classes – the noble land-owners – to obscure its oppression of his 'poor Ukraine' (Ukrainy ubohoi):

Hirshe liakha svoi dity
Ii rozpynaiut;
Zamist pyva – pravednuiu
Krov iz reber tochat, –
Prosvityty, bachysh, khochut
Materynski ochi
Sovremennymy ohniamy,
Povesty za vikom,
Za nimtsiamy nedoriku,
Slipuiu kaliku. ('Epistle')

More cruelly than the Pole do her own children / Crucify her; / Like beer they / Tap her righteous blood from her breast – / They wish, you see, to enlighten / Her maternal eyes / With contemporary fires, / To lead the stutterer, the blind cripple, / Into step with the age, / Into step with the Germans.

Muscovitophobia and Germanophobia often stand together in Shevchenko's works [appearing not only in the form of the historically formed Slavic idealogy of the *muzhik* but also as the protest of that self-same *muzhik* against the serfdom and bureaucratic absolutism of his time. And to a large extent at the core of Shevchenko's Germanophobia lies his hatred of the upper echelons of the tsarist bureaucracy, recruited in abundance from among the Baltic German barons]. Of his countrymen who formed part of the St Petersburg bureaucracy, Shevchenko scornfully writes that they 'are drowned in ink, tormented by Muscovite henbane in German buttonholes' (chornylom polyti, / Moskovskoiu blekotoiu, / V nimetskykh petlytsiakh / Zamucheni). And more than this, in the spirit of the Slavophile belief that

Russia had forsaken her independent Slavic path and given herself over to the Germans, Shevchenko follows *Knyhy bytiia ukrainskoho narodu* (Books of Genesis of the Ukrainian People), which strongly derogate 'the German tsaritsa, Catherine.' His 'third raven' (the evil spirit of Russia) in the poem 'Velykyi Lokh' (The Great Vault) speaks thus of her deeds:

> 'I ia taki pozhila:
> S tatarami pomutila,
> S Muchitelem pokutila
> S Petrukhoiu popila,
> Da vse nemtsam prodala.'

'And I too have lived it up: / With the Tatars I muddied the waters, / With the Terrible caroused, / With dear Peter imbibed / And sold everything to the Germans.'

To this the 'first raven' (the evil spirit of Ukraine) replies:

> 'Tai ty dobre natvoryla:
> Tak katsapiv zakripyla
> U nimetski kaidany, –
> Khoch liahai ta i zasny.'

'And you did well: / You shackled those Russians (Katsapy) / In German chains so well that all they could do / Was to lie down and sleep.'

Thus was Russian oppression of the Slavic peoples under her control explained in terms of German domination of the antipathetic 'Slavic spirit,' such an explanation being necessary for the Ukrainian Slavophiles so that the precarious position of Slavic union could somehow be retained. In this area Shevchenko followed in the footsteps of the Ukrainian Slavophiles; unmasking the betrayal of Ukraine by his countrymen and their indifference, he speaks of the fact that a father, having lovingly nurtured his son,

> Ta i prodast v riznytsiu
> Moskalevi ... Seb-to, bachysh,
> Lepta udovytsi[3]

Prestolovi, 'otechestvu'
Ta nimoti plata ...

Goes and sells him into Muscovite slaughterhouses ... / That is, you see, / The widow's mite, / Payment to the throne, / 'The fatherland' and the Germans ...[4]

To be sure, his active nationalism and concomitant view of the Muscovite as the most immediate enemy did not allow Shevchenko to regard the Germans as the sole cause of the oppression of Slavs (Ukraine) by other Slavs (Russia). His 'first raven' in the above poem boasts that 'even their devilish Sich is overgrown with Germans' (Uzhe zh i Sich ikh bisnuvata / Nimotoiu porosla) and, unable to contain herself, adds:

'Ta i moskal – nezhirsha shtuka:
Dobre vmiie hrity ruky.
I ia liuta, a vse taky
Toho ne zumiiu,
Shcho moskali v Ukraini
Z kozakamy diiut.'

'And the Muscovite is not to be sneezed at either: / He well knows how to warm his hands. / I am fierce too, / but could not do / What the Muscovites are doing / With the Cossacks in Ukraine.'

This central concept in Shevchenko's world view – Ukrainian nationalism as a liberating if insular force – remained constant throughout his life, although its social foundations, or better, the sharpness of their contours, evolved over time. His is the nationalism of a poor people and not that of its class oppressors, a *muzhik* nationalism, which grew sharper particularly during the period of his exile when the poet-soldier was sustained by dreams of being able

Khoch hlianut
Na narod otoi ubohyi,
Na tuiu Ukrainu.

At least to gaze upon / That poor people, / That Ukraine.[5]

The prime constituent of the peasant world view, then, is its national insularity and exclusivity. After this comes religion. All modes of peasant life are so thoroughly permeated by it that there is even a proverb which reads 'bez Boha ni do poroha' (without God's help you can't even get to the doorstep). But in its fundamentals the peasant religious world view is far removed from dogmatic Christianity. To all intents and purposes, abstractions do not exist for the peasant. For him even God is concrete, something upon which his day-to-day life as a peasant farmer depends. Thus, his God is incarnated in the forces of nature which hold sway over his life or is their ruler. In this regard, from its pre-feudal beginnings throughout the Christian era, the ideology of the peasant tiller of the soil remained unchanged. The ancient pagan view of the forces of nature as spiritual entities demanding worship (animism) simply lay hidden beneath the Christian cult, which appeared in Rus owing to the requirements of a nascent feudalism. God sends rain and foul weather; one must pray to Him for a good harvest. The stock phrase 'iak Boh dast' (as God grants) is fairly widespread among the peasantry. The peasant fulfils his obligations before God as he would those owing to his land-owner. He prays to him and brings offerings to fill the priest's pockets; he has grown accustomed to God as another indispensable element of his daily life (*pobut*). Yet, in the religious cult of the peasantry as a whole, the formal and normative element predominates. In so far as God is believed to be the ruler of the world, the land-owner is the ruler of his serf 'souls,' and the peasant of his farm and family, then rebellion against the powers that be is permissible if these powers do not serve the interests of the peasant farm economy, that is, if God permits the existence of a social order that chokes the peasant; such rebellion against God is embodied in stock phrases such as 'nemaie Hospoda na nebi' ('there is no God in the heavens,' that is, the social order desired by the peasant does not exist, truth does not exist, etc.) or in protests against God ('hnivyty Boha' / 'to anger God').

Like the peasant *pobut*, Shevchenko's poetry is filled with God. God figures in his works all too frequently. The image of God emerging from Shevchenko's poetry is fundamentally the same as that of the peasant. To be sure, Shevchenko went far beyond primitive peasant conceptions. Especially towards the end of his life, he was resolutely opposed to organized religion and Byzantism. Furthermore, he came close to an outright rejection of religion and treated religious themes from the point of view of social relations and in their capacity as earthly social phenomena, rather than heavenly manifestations.

While it will be necessary to consider this point again when analysing the social evolution of Shevchenko's views, it can be said in general that his religious conceptions are part of his *muzhik* understanding of the world. To be sure, traces of pantheism are to be found in his poetry, but its roots also lie in the peasant social milieu. His God hovers above nature or is simply incarnated in it; moreover, it is in nature and the peasant life and *pobut* with which it is tightly interwoven that this divinity is most often revealed. This finds its most vivid expression in the following lines from the poem 'Kniazhna' (The Princess):

> Selo! I sertse odpochyne ...
> Selo na nashii Ukraini –
> Nenache pysanka: selo
> Zelenym haiem poroslo;
> Tsvitut sady, biliiut khaty,
> A na hori stoiat palaty,
> Nenache dyvo, a kruhom
> Shyrokolystii topoli;
> A tam i lis, – i lis, i pole
> I syni hory za Dniprom;
> Sam Boh vytaie nad selom!

The village! And the heart will rest ... / A village in our Ukraine – / Is like a coloured Easter egg: the village / Is overgrown by a green grove; / Orchards blossom, white houses gleam here and there / and on the hill is a mansion / as beautiful as a vision and around it / Broad-leaved poplars; / And over there – forest, more forest and a field. / And blue hills beyond the Dnipro; / Over the village God himself hovers!

So magnificent that in them and hovering over them the poet sees God, these idyllic scenes from nature and the peasant environment are still not everything. Cruel and unhappy social relations unfold beyond them, social relations which rest upon the same 'mansions, charming at a distance' (Veseli zdaleka palaty) denounced by the *muzhik*-poet (May you become

overgrown with blackthorns / Bodai vy ternom porosly) as the source from
which the yoke and the fleecing of the 'poor brother,' the serf, proceed and
as that place where the nobleman-land-owner sits and 'takes from the
muzhik his daughter and his heifer' (Dochku i telychku odnimaie / U
muzhyka ...). Against the background of social relations like these, at one
pole of which 'lively music plays, rivers of wine drench the insatiable
guests' (Muzyka tne, vyno rikoiu / Hostei nesytykh nalyva ...) and at the
other '*muzhik* souls can only squeak' ('Muzhytski dushi azh pyshchat'),
against a background of such an unhappy peasant social life even God
himself takes on a different character, revealing his indifference to this
social misery, for perhaps

> I Boh ne znaie ...
> A mozhe znaie, ta movchyt!

God does not know ... / Or perhaps he knows but keeps silent!

In another place and at another time we find a similar example of such
an association of God with nature. Shevchenko flees in disgust from the
Christian Church, from its 'pagan temple,' but when 'against the dark
background of a broad meadow the glistening Volga, that gracefully
winding beauty' appears before him, his religious sentiments are fulfilled. 'I
took a deep breath,' the poet says, 'involuntarily crossed myself, and went
home.'[6]

This 'divine' nature, which sends light, warmth, and dew down upon the
muzhik's miserable little field, alone offers the poet repose from human
injustice, from a world in which the rich are given the power and authority
to oppress the poor and tear their hides off. But when the poet gazes upon
these human relationships, then we have standing before us in all his glory
the peasant-serf, who in his quest for salvation in God reveals a religious
range extending from submissive prayer to God to denunciations of him.
The hopelessness of the wretched situation of the peasantry becomes either
resignation or outbursts of despair. We offer some examples of such fluc-
tuations of Shevchenko's religious sentiments from *Kobzar*.

When catastrophe befell the poet himself, when he was thrown into the
prison dungeon, Shevchenko in the poem 'Chy my shche ziidemosia
znovu?' (Will we meet once again?) bowed to his fate. 'It is the will of

God. Please God! submit to him, pray to him.' (To volia Hospoda. Hodit! / Smyritesia, molites Bohu ...), he advises those of his friends forced to endure the same misfortune and, above all, on behalf of Ukraine he beseeches them to 'pray to God for her!...' (Za nei Hospoda molit!...). Or he turns to God:

> 'Molius Tobi, Bozhe mylyi,
> Hospody velykyi!
> Shcho ne dav meni zahynut,
> Nebesnyi vladyko.
> Shcho dav meni dobru sylu
> Peresylyt hore ...' ('Son' / A Dream, 1847)

'To you, dear Lord, o, God almighty, / I offer my prayers of gratitude / That you did not let me perish, / O, heavenly ruler, / That you granted unto me enough strength / To overcome my sorrow ...'

Yet, striving to overcome his sorrow (largely social) and praying to his God, the *muzhik*-poet is not unexpectedly led to ask the following question: 'Does God see our tears, our misfortune from behind his clouds?' (Chy Boh bachyt iz-za khmary / Nashi slozy, hore?) and replies:

> Mozhe i bachyt, ta pomaha –
> Iak i oti hory
> Predkovichni, shcho polyti
> Kroviiu liudskoiu! (*ibid.*)

Perhaps he does, but comes to our aid / Like those timeless hills / Watered by human blood!

Here already are the beginnings of a criticism of God. The comparison of his role with that of inanimate nature when human blood is spilt is characteristic; that is, the reduction of the 'living' God to inanimate nature. After this come complaints against God, who 'perhaps knows of the misfortunes of man but keeps silent':

> Mozhe Boh tak khoche?
> Bozhe! Bozhe! Daiesh voliu

I rozum na sviti,
Krasu daiesh, sertse chyste,
Ta ne daiesh zhyty! (The Princess)

Can it be that this is how God would have it? / O, Lord, Lord! You allow us freedom / And intelligence in this world, / You allow us beauty and a pure heart, / But you do not allow us to live.

What kind of a God is this who does not allow people to live? Or, in Shevchenko's own words on the subject of the Christian thesis 'all is from God':

I vse-to te lykho, vse, kazhut, od Boha!
Chy vzhe zh iomu liubo liudei morduvat? ('Irzhavets')

And all misfortune, all of it, they say, is from God! / Is it possible that he enjoys tormenting people?

Does this 'just, implacable, indifferent' God torment all men equally? In this context Shevchenko's class affiliation becomes clearly apparent:

Huliaie kniaz, huliaiut hosti;
Revut palaty na pomosti,
A holod stohne na seli ...
I stohne vin, stohne po vsii Ukraini,
Kara Hospodeva; tysiachamy hynut
Holodnii liude. A skyrty hnyiut,
A pany i polovu zhydam prodaiut,
Ta holodu radi, ta Boha blahaiut,
Shchob shche khoch hodochok khlibets ne rozhav, –
Todi b i v Paryzhi, i v inshomu krai
Nash brat khutorianyn sebe pokazav!
Chy Boh teie znaie? – bo se bulo b dyvo,
Shchob chuty i bachyt, i ne pokarat!
Abo vzhe azh nadto dovhoterpelyvyi! (The Princess)

The prince makes merry, the guests make merry; / In the mansion the wooden floor groans, / While in the village hunger moans. ... / And it moans, it moans throughout Ukraine, / This punishment of the Lord; by the thousands / Do starving people die. And stacks of grain decay, / Yet the lords sell even the chaff to Jews / And rejoice at the famine and beseech God / That the harvest be poor for one more little year – / Then in Paris and in another land / Our brother the homesteader would parade! / Does God know of this? – / It would be strange to hear and to see but not to bring punishment to bear! / Or is he overly patient here!

It appears that the 'punishment of the Lord' is meted out only to the hungry, the *muzhik*. The nobility are pleased by it because it brings in profits (even from the chaff). People die while the land-owners' stacks of grain rot and God does not punish them. Of this God he inquires:

> A mozhe i sam na nebesy
> Smiieshsia, bratechku, nad namy,
> Ta mozhe radyshsia z panamy,
> Iak pravyt myrom? – ('Iakby vy znaly, panychi' / 'If you but knew, lordlings')

And are you not perhaps / Laughing at us, brother, up in your heavens / And are you not perhaps taking counsel from the gentry / On how to run the world?

Not without reason do the Ukrainian peasants call him 'our Lord God' (Pan-Boh).

This God of the nobility bestows his bounty upon the land-owners alone and they accept it as their due without even appreciating his munificence, procured for them by the serf's sweat and blood:

> Daiesh ty, Hospody iedynyi,
> Sady panam v tvoim raiu,
> Daiesh vysokii palaty, –
> Pany zh, nesytii, puzati,
> Na rai tvii, Hospody, pliuiut.
> I nam dyvytys ne daiut
> Z ubohoi maloi khaty. (Ne molylasia za mene / My mother did not pray for me)

To the nobility you give, o Lord, our only God, / The orchards in your paradise, / You give the lofty mansions – / The nobility, pot-bellied and insatiable, o Lord, / Spit upon your peaceful paradise. / But to us they allow not even a glimpse / From our miserable little hut.

After all this, only tell-tale traces of religion remain. In a moment of despair Shevchenko proclaims: 'There is no God in the heavens' (nemaie Hospoda na nebi). Later, towards the end of his life, he even takes God down from the heavens and scornfully places him in an 'icon case.' Thus he mocks this 'all-seeing eye' (vsevydiashcheie oko) in 'Iurodyvyi' (God's Fool):

A ty, vsevydiashcheie oko!
Chy ty dyvylosia zvysoka,
Iak sotniamy v kaidanakh hnaly
V Sybir nevilnykiv sviatykh,
Iak morduvaly, rozpynaly
I vishaly? ... A ty ne znalo?
I ty dyvylosia na nykh
I ne osliplo?! Oko, oko!
Ne duzhe bachysh ty hlyboko!
Ty spysh v kioti ...

And you, you all-seeing eye! / Were you not looking down from on high / When the holy captives by the hundreds / Were being driven to Siberia in shackles, / When they were being tortured to death, crucified and hanged? ... / And you did not know this? / And you gazed upon them and were not blinded? / Eye, o eye, how unpenetrating is your vision! / You are asleep in your icon case ...

Yet, all the same, Shevchenko did not banish God from his world view. Just as *muzhik* ideology was unthinkable without an external controlling force, in this instance, in the form of God; just as the peasant *pobut* is permeated with God; just as the corner of the peasant house is crammed with images of him – so too is Shevchenko's poetry filled with images of God, even though the poet denies him and scoffs at him. His blasphemy did not develop into a definite rejection of the religious view of the world, although it was fertile soil for such a transformation. The poet himself, recalling his childhood and his mother, says:

Luchche bulo b ne rodyty
Abo utopyty,
Iak mavby ia u nevoli
Hospoda hnivyty. (Ne molylasia za mene)

Better not to have borne me / Or to have drowned me / Than that I should in my exile / Anger God.

In this notion of 'angering God,' in this short phrase, the *muzhik* character of Shevchenko's philosophy as regards religion emerges in bold relief, despite the fact that his philosophy contained elements of a rejection of religion.

An even stronger reflection in Shevchenko's poetry than his religious views are those on the family and women. These views are also marked with a *muzhik* attitude, although here too Shevchenko advanced beyond his social environment. In the life and consciousness of the peasant the family is the basic unit of economic and social organization, its most sacred foundation. House, field, wife, and children define the range of the peasant's ideals. Only by realizing them does he become a good master of the household and to become this is his life-long task. The peasant ideology is centred upon house, field, and patriarchal family; as to a centre of gravity it is impelled towards the individualistic, petty, proprietary system of economic organization. Consecrated by time and religious tradition, this ideology imprisons the *muzhik* within the narrow confines of these narrow horizons, moulding him into a buttress for economic and social conservatism and a great variety of prejudices. Our poet-*kobzar* remained true to this *muzhik* ideology until the very end. He asks of God:

... Tilko khatu,
Odnu khatynochku v haiu,
Ta dvi topoli kolo nei,
Ta beztalannuiu moiu,
Moiu Oksanochku ... (Ne molylasia za mene)

Only a cottage, / One little cottage in a grove / With two poplars nearby / And my dear ill-starred one, / My dear Oksana ...

In his poem 'Na panshchyni pshenytsiu zhala' (In serfdom grain she reaped), the serf girl's fondest hopes for her young son's future are expressed in a dream:

I snytsia ii: toi syn Ivan
I urodlyvyi, i bahatyi,

Uzhe zasvatanyi, zhonatyi,
Na volnii, bachytsia – bo i sam
Uzhe ne panskyi, a na voli;
I na svoim veselim poli
U-dvokh sobi pshenytsiu zhnut.
A ditochky obid nesut ...

And she dreams: that son of hers, Ivan, / Is both handsome and rich, / Already betrothed, even married, / To a free woman, it appears – for he / No longer serves a master, he is free; / And on their happy field / Both are reaping wheat. / Their little children bring them their meal ...

To this ideal of peasant well-being upon a scrap of one's own land, in 'a house in this paradise' (khatochtsi v tim rai) and with a family of one's own, Shevchenko aspired both in his poetry and personal life, especially in his final years, when he devoted much energy to purchasing a small country homestead on the Dnipro, constructing a house, and arranging a marriage to a simple peasant girl. He sees his 'blessed state' (blahodat) thus:

Postavliu khatu i kimnatu,
Sadok-raiochok nasadzhu;
Posyzhu ia i pokhozhu
V svoii malenkii blahodati ...

I shall build myself a one-roomed cottage, / Plant a heavenly garden. / I shall sit and I shall stroll / In my little paradise ...

These lines were written towards the end of 1860, when the realization of this dream was close at hand. Earlier, during his exile, when there was no hope of his ever having a house, he could only envy those who had:

Blaho tobi, druzhe-brate,
Iak ie v tebe khata!
Blaho tobi, iak u khati
Ie z kym rozmovliaty,
Khoch dytyna nemovliashcha ...

Blessed are you, my friend and brother, / If you have a house. / Blessed are you, if in that house / There is someone with whom to commune, / Even if it be a speechless baby ...

Among people with such notions about the bases of economic and social life, about home and children, every infringement of patriarchal family customs consecrated by the *muzhik* consciousness must be considered an offence. Indeed, the *muzhik* community severely punishes the offender: the unwed mother (pokrytka) is banished from its midst; the illegitimate child (baistria) is condemned to a miserable life as a guide to destitute blind men, and to everlasting disdain.

Here Shevchenko could not fully follow the principles governing his community. In his poetry the *pokrytka* and the illegitimate child emerge as the most aggrieved, the most ill-starred elements of society, the products of bad social relations, and for this reason the poet sheds tears over their unfortunate fates. These two social types appear very frequently in his poetry and are always presented either as the products of the yoke of serfdom or of the love of peasant girls for land-owners and gentry. With what anguish Shevchenko writes of these social products of serfdom:

A on bachysh? Ochi, ochi!
Na-shcho vy zdalysia?
Chom vy z-malku ne vysokhly,
Slizmy ne zlylysia?
To pokrytka po-pid-tynniu
Z baistriam shkandybaie, –
Batko i maty odtsuralys,
I chuzhi ne pryimaiut,
Startsi navit tsuraiutsia ...
A panych ne znaie:
Z dvadtsiatoiu nedoliudok
Dushi propyvaie.

And do you see? Eyes, eyes! / What good are you? / Why did you not dry up in childhood, / Exhaust your tears? / That is a *pokrytka* with her bastard child / Limping along by the fence, – / Her father and mother have renounced her / And strangers will not take her in, / Even the old people shun her ... / And the gentleman does not know: / With his twentieth girl the beast / Is drinking away serfs.

After returning to Ukraine with her illegitimate children by a land-owner, her locks shorn, the witch in the poem of the same name recalls with horror a life of precisely this sort:

> ... I shcho z mene
> Liudy nasmiialys!...
> Trokhy bula ne vtopylas,
> Ta zhal bulo kynut
> Blyzniatochok.

... And how the people mocked me! / I almost drowned myself / But could not bear to desert my twins.

After this, *pokrytka* dies – after 'demons drowned the old witch in a pool' (u kaliuzhi staru vidmu chorty utopyly) from the point of view of peasant society – then 'an aspen stake was driven' (osykovyi kilok zabyvaly) into her grave. For this reason the poet urges young girls:

> ... ne kvaptesia
> Na paniv lukavykh,
> Bo zhynete osmiiani ...

Do not let cunning lords entice you / Else you will be ridiculed to your dying day.

and fervently advises:

> ... Kokhaitesia
> Khoch iz naimytamy, –
> Z kym khochete, moi liubi,
> Tilky ne z panamy!

Fall in love / With hired men, / Whomever you wish, my dear ones, / Only not with lords!

In such a social environment the fate of the *pokrytka* is hopeless. She leads a miserable existence until she dies

> Mezhy psamy, na morozi,
> De-nebud pid tynom. ('U nashim raiu na zemli' / 'In Our Heaven on Earth')

Among the dogs out in the cold, / Somewhere by a fence.

Neither will anything come of her child; he too is regarded as a lost cause by the community:

> I nikoly iz baistriaty
> Ne matyme maty
> Sobi dobroi dytyny ...

And never will the mother of a bastard / Have a good child ...

Shevchenko even presents 'the Mother of God,' Mary, as a hired girl working in the house of 'Joseph the carpenter,' 'who bears joyous tidings' as a result of her love for the 'happy young guest.' And if she too did not become a *pokrytka* it was only because the old carpenter covered her 'gladsome sin' by marrying her. Otherwise, the people would have killed her and there would have been no Messiah. Thus,

> Ne od Siona blahodat,
> A z tykhoi tvoiei khaty
> Nam vozvistylasia. Iak by
> Prechystii ii ne dav ty ruku,
> Rabamy b bidnii raby
> I dosi merly b. ('Mariia')

Not from Zion came this grace / But from a quiet house / Was it announced. / Had he not given his hand to the Immaculate One, / To this day we, poor slaves, / Would die as slaves.

But all the same, Mariia-Mary 'by a fence, grieving, amidst weeds, died of hunger' (... pid tynom, / Sumuiuchy, u buriani / Umerla z holodu).

Such a human and, more particularly, such a *muzhik* treatment of this religious legend could only have been born in a mind well endowed with *muzhik* wisdom. Yet it does not even occur to this mind to condemn his own community for driving from its midst the girl-mother and spurning those who violate the norms of peasant behaviour. Not a word of condemnation does he utter against this barbaric morality! The poet accepts it

as necessary, inviolable, and beyond criticism. All his anger is directed
solely at the land-owners, who turn young girls into *pokrytkas* and father
their illegitimate children.

In the epic tones of a tragic character the poet presents the scene in which
Kateryna's father and mother drive her and her child out of their home:

> 'Doniu moia!
> Shcho ty narobyla? ...
> Oddiachyla! Idy zh shukai
> U Moskvi svekrukhy!
> Ne slukhala moikh richei,
> To ii poslukhai!
>
> ...
>
>   Idy od nas!...'
> Ledvy-ledvy
> Poblahoslovyla:
> 'Boh z toboiu!' – ta, iak mertva,
> Na dil povalylas.
> Obizvavsia staryi batko:
> 'Choho zhdesh, neboho?'

'O, daughter mine! / What have you done? ... / Fine is your recompense! / Go to
Moscow to your mother-in-law! / My words you did not heed, / Now go and obey
hers!... / Depart from us!...' / Barely, barely did she find the strength to bless
her: / 'God be with you!' and then, as though dead, / She fell to the ground. / Said
her old father: / 'What are you waiting for, my poor dear?'

Kateryna begins to sob and begs forgiveness of her father, but he replies:

> 'Nekhai tebe Boh proshchaie
> Ta dobryi liude!
> Molys Bohu ta idy sobi –
> Meni lehshe bude.'

'May God and the good people forgive you! / Pray to God and be on your way – /
So it will be easier for me.'

To this the poet appends his epic commentary:

Otake-to na sim sviti
Robliat liudiam liude.

So do people / Unto others in this world.

There is no rebellion in his words, no protest. All that remains to him is 'to pour forth his sorrow in fine, bitter tears' (dribnymy slozamy lykho vylyvaty).

[While Shevchenko lacks the strength to rise up against the inhuman laws of the peasant community, all his sympathies are nonetheless on the side of those same unfortunate members of serf society, on the side of the *pokrytka* and the illegitimate child, whom he elevates to the heights of his poetic creation from their positions of utter contempt and ostracism.] In the poem 'Oi, kryknuly siri husy' (O, the grey geese called out), the poet speaks of the fact that 'bad rumours about that widow spread over the whole village' (Stala slava na vse selo / Pro tuiu vdovu), a widow who chooses to love a Cossack and subsequently gives birth to his son. This widow, however, did not wish to be held in disdain in her social environment and issued a challenge to her enemies: she treasured her son,

Odiahla ioho v chervonyi
zhupan dorohyi,
Posadyla na konyka:
'Hliante, vorohy!
Podyvites!' Ta i povela
Konia vzdovzh sela ...

In a costly red mantle / She clad him, / Upon a fine horse seated him: / 'Behold, enemies of mine! / Look here!' And she led / The horse the length of the village ...

In these lines Shevchenko demonstrates that he was far removed from lower middle class and serf morality. In his poetic epistle to a close friend (Nadiia Tarnovska) he even writes the following:

Nachkhai na tu divochu slavu,
Ta shchyrym sertsem, ne lukavo,
Khoch raz, serdeho, sobludy.
['N.T. (Velykomuchenytse kumo!)' / To N.T. ('Dear, Long-Suffering Friend')]

Don't give a damn for your maiden reputation and sincerely, / Without evil, err, my dear, woman, if only once.

[All this notwithstanding, Shevchenko speaks of the 'ill repute' of women, of the widow (typically not a maiden) who bears a Cossack's child out of wedlock, and in the final analysis this widow too 'made a pilgrimage to Kiev and became a nun' (... sama na proshchu v Kyiv, / V chernytsi pishla), undoubtedly to wash away the 'sin of her fornication.']

In his views on women and the family, Shevchenko always stood upon the foundations of *muzhik* philosophy. A serf himself and an enemy of serfdom, this poet-*muzhik* found it impossible to rebel against the prejudices and unenlightened philosophy of his own 'community in homespun cloaks.'

(1923)

NOTES

1 Translation of the chapter 'Muzhytska filosofiia,' from A. Richytsky, *Taras Shevchenko v svitli epokhy* (Kharkiv 1923). Throughout this article, the word *muzhik* (peasant) has been retained in its Russian variant. Occasionally passages have been added here (marked [ ]) from a later Russian translation of Richytsky's article.

2 Richytsky uses the derogatory term, *nemota* (the 'German'), frequently employed by Shevchenko. Often, the term 'Germans' was used by Shevchenko to refer to foreigners and Russian bureaucrats (ed.).

3 The word *udovytsia* (widow) is apparently meant to be understood as 'Ukraine.'

4 In the later Russian edition the initial lines of this quotation, referring to the 'Muscovite slaughterhouses,' are deleted (ed.).

5 In the later Russian edition this paragraph is couched in more strongly Marxian jargon, with the emphasis falling much more markedly on the revolutionary character of Shevchenko's nationalism. The fact that the quotation which expressed Shevchenko's longing for his native land was omitted is revealing (ed.).

6 See Shevchenko's diary for 27 September 1857.

11

Shevchenko and Romanticism

PAVLO FYLYPOVYCH

There is no question that romanticism with its more than purely literary significance played an immense role in the development of European culture in the nineteenth and early twentieth centuries.[1] 'All of us whose lives are not spent in worries over our daily bread, all of us, to a greater or lesser extent, are the students and heirs of romanticism,' the author of one of the best articles on German romanticism has written.[2] The romantics have bequeathed their rich heritage not only to literature, art, and aesthetics, he observes. Literary history, a discipline based upon a broad, comparative methodology (its scope – world literature), the contemporary philosophy of nature, psychology and neuropathology, folklore, comparative linguistics, the new understanding of the idea of nationality – early German romanticism prepared the way for all this.

It came into flower at the turn of the eighteenth century, with the romantic current moving triumphantly across Europe and attaining luminous pinnacles in the works of Byron, Hugo, Leopardi, Lermontov, Mickiewicz, and many other first-rate writers. Even Heine, who scoffed at his romantic predecessors, felt their influence and attempted, as he acknowledged in a letter in 1842, to reintroduce the old romanticism into literature. At the end of the nineteenth century and in the twentieth, romanticism has experienced a renaissance in a new symbolist form in Maeterlinck, Ibsen, Verlaine, Blok, and others. Our revolutionary era has not escaped its influence; on the contrary, discussions about revolutionary romanticism are often heard, especially in connection with the theatre. 'Our theatre elevates human culture to the heights it truly merits. The course taken by romantic drama can yield the most prodigious results,' A.V.

Lunacharsky writes.[3] The repertory section of the TEO (Teatralnyi otdel Narodnogo Komissariata Prosveshcheniia / Theatre Department of the People's Commissariat of Education) advocates the staging of many plays of 'a heroic character.'[4] New romantic tragedies such as *Bertrand de Born*, by the Serapion Brother, L. Lunts, make their appearance.[5]

Quite a few monographs and articles about romanticism and individual romantics have appeared in the last decade. Establishing its existence in this century, one scholar, la Bart,[6] notes that it is not a random occurrence and is explained by the general character of western European thought.

The understanding of romanticism has gained significantly in depth. Earlier historians of Russian literature, for example, simply described Zhukovsky as a romantic, while A.N. Veselovsky[7] has recently demonstrated that 'the poetic uncle of the German demons and witches' was rather a sentimentalist than a romantic because he lacked the symbolic component of the German romantics, their experience of the transcendent, their perception of an internal relationship between phenomena seemingly torn asunder in nature. Zhukovsky is significantly simpler than the German romantics, to whom the Russian symbolists can now be compared.[8]

But even now, when the study of romanticism has become more widespread and has gained in depth, many unresolved issues remain. There is not, and probably never will be, a definition of romanticism which will satisfy everyone. In different countries and in the works of individual writers the characteristic features of romanticism were not displayed in the same way. While mysticism dominates in early German romanticism, it is not to be found, for example, in the French context.[9] The characterization of Romanticism as a manifestation of individualism is far too general, although the characteristic features of the style and content of romanticism doubtless can be explained in this way.[10] This feature evolved and was manifested in a historical context, a fact to which the scholar should turn his attention at the outset. The literary historian's primary concern is not with the analysis of abstract ideas, but of concrete motifs and forms. Romanticism came to the Slavic countries from the West, and on this new ground took various directions and exhibited various shades. In some respects it was not clearly defined, but was non-indigenous, alien; its expression was often obstructed in various ways. In his study, I. Zamotin observes that 'the main motifs of romantic individualism which are to be found along with idealism and nationalism and which led the romantics to the cult of a future universal happiness were also reflected in Russian social and literary life at the beginning of the century. This reflection was, however, comparatively weak.'[11] Zamotin goes on to point out that there were 'various circumstances' which did not favour the development of 'universalism' and 'revolutionary romanticism' in Russian literature. Indeed, there is now evidence[12] of the measures taken by the tsarist censorship to prevent the appearance in Russia of Byron's works, that 'ruler of men's minds.' Naturally, Byron's followers did not meet official favour either and could not touch upon motifs of rebellion and revolution nor those of a satirical character.

The lack of an organic link with the base upon which it grew, of clarity and definition in Russian romanticism may, significantly, be explained by the strong classical traditions which held sway over the most prominent writers. Today it is argued that Pushkin's poetics is totally founded upon the principles and examples of the eighteenth-century Russian neoclassicists. As B. Eikhenbaum[13] has said, 'Pushkin represents a culmination, not a new beginning.'

While Sipovsky[14] demonstrates in great detail that Pushkin had a romantic period but subsequently found a path to realism, Zhirmunsky[15] analyses Pushkin's 'Byronic poems' and finds in them the characteristically romantic technique of composition and style.

The greater the writer, the more difficult it is to assign him to a particular school. Depending upon the extent to which he evolves, a writer can sustain the influence of various literary currents; at the same time he can be both a romantic and a classicist (Pushkin) or a romantic and a realist (Gogol); he can initiate something new, while clinging to old traditions.

When Shevchenko began to write poetry, romanticism had long since reached its zenith in Europe, was not yet a thing of the past in Russian poetry (in prose, realism was beginning to take hold) and Polish poetry, and had already burgeoned in Ukraine. How was it reflected in the works of Shevchenko, 'the central figure in Ukrainian literature in the nineteenth century'?

Needless to say, Shevchenko's romanticism has been studied but largely without, among other things, much significance being accorded to the influence of romantic currents. The observation has been made that this was in his early years. The scope of Shevchenko's romanticism has been sketched out. Romantic authors were captivated by antiquity and presented it in idealized, poetic form; they also availed themselves of fantastic elements derived from folk sources. Shevchenko also wrote ballads and idealized the past – the Cossacks, the Hetmanate – but subsequently left all this behind and, furthermore, revealed, even in his early works, a predilection for themes from everyday life and for a realistic manner. Shevchenko's historical romanticism has frequently been singled out by scholars, the Ukrainian, Polish, and Russian sources note (usually only in passing), and the ballads based on fantasy have been examined in considerable detail with an eye to the influence of Polish and Russian poets. In general, however, it can be said that the issue of Shevchenko's romanticism has scarcely been explored. As an organic, enduring, and wide-ranging factor in the works of the author of *Kobzar* and in the development of Ukrainian literature, it has gone all but unrecognized. As far as possible in a short article, an attempt will be made here to define the nature of Shevchenko's romanticism.

Ukrainian authors tended to appropriate new European literary currents cautiously and by degrees, using only material for which there was an organic base in their epoch, that of the renaissance of the Ukrainian word initiated by Ivan Kotliarevsky. The beginning of romanticism in Ukrainian literature is usually said to coincide with the appearance of Petro Hulak-Artemovsky's 'Rybalka' (The Fisherman, 1827), a translation of Goethe's ballad, 'Der Fischer.' Upon sending it to Mikhail Kachenovsky, the editor of *Vestnik Evropy*, Hulak-Artemovsky included a most interesting letter. He wrote, Kachenovsky says, that

curiosity moved him to attempt to discover whether tender, noble, and elevated feelings could be communicated in the Little Russian language without causing the reader or listener to laugh, as is the case with Kotliarevsky's *Eneida* and other poems written with a similar aim. Subsequently, drawing attention to some of the tenderest Little Russian songs, he offers his ballad, of whose success he remains politely uncertain, explaining it as merely the usual type of experiment. He applied the Little Russian women's way of singing.[16]

At first sight it seems a strange scene: a poet offers his translation of a romantic work of European literature and, to demonstrate that such a translation is possible, cites Ukrainian women's folk songs. Indeed, diminutives particularly characteristic of the Ukrainian folk song and of the language as spoken by ordinary people are encountered at every step, diminutives such as, 'rybalka molodenkyi' (the young fisherman), 'serdenko' (dear heart), 'rybonky' (little fish), and so on, which cannot be found either in the German original or in Vasilii Zhukovsky's Russian translation (1817). In addition, Hulak-Artemovsky's translation contains many interjections: 'Shcho rybka *smyk*, to sertse *tokh*' (When the little fish goes jerk, his heart goes thump); 'Azh, *hulk*' (When suddenly, pop) and so on. Characteristic of folk tales, of Kotliarevsky's *Eneida*, and of Kvitka's stories of everyday life, these interjections give Hulak-Artemovsky's ballad greater liveliness, realism, and ethnographic realism; Zhukovsky, on the other hand, turns to abstraction ('the soul is full of chilly stillness'), for which the paths in Russian literature had already been made. Interjections are encountered in Hulak-Artemovsky's burlesque works, which he attempted to transcend in his 'Rybalka.' Yet, employing one of their linguistic components in his translation, he made his ballad livelier and more original.

As is evident from his letter, to this end he also consciously used linguistic forms employed in folk song to express tender feelings. The first attempt to transplant romanticism into Ukrainian poetry was thus successful because a foundation was found for it and on this foundation of folk poetry, of the oral tradition, a flower unlike the German one grew up – simpler, livelier, more tender and, it should be added, more sentimental, because sentimentalism is not a wearisome and naïve mannerism as some critics have said.[17] This sentimentality is what the ethnographer, T. Korsh, believed to be the feature which distinguished Ukrainian oral literature from Russian.

Hulak-Artemovsky's ballad was not an isolated phenomenon. A little later, Levko Borovykovsky's 'Marusia' (1829), a Ukrainianized version of Zhukovsky's 'Svetlana,' appeared. In 1828 *Vestnik Evropy* printed 'Molodytsia' (A Young Wife) by an author identified only as N.; in 1830 a fragment of a tale entitled 'Vidma' (The Witch); in 1835 in *Molva* there was the 'ditty' 'Kornii Ovara' (Iak pokantraktuvavsia kozak Kornii iz bisom i shcho z toho bulo / How the Cossack Kornii Made a Contract with the Devil and What Came of It), a reworking of Zhukovsky's 'Gromoboi' in which, as V. Kallash has observed, 'only the skeleton of the plot is retained, the circumstances and the heroes having been adapted to local surroundings.'[18]

Thus, when Shevchenko appeared on the literary stage, he had a number of predecessors in one branch of romanticism. It was thus possible for him to develop the ballad, not only by using the images from folk poetry more extensively, but also by taking his plots from fairy-tales, something that had already been done to some extent by Ukrainian poets. It is interesting to note that Shevchenko expressed thoughts similar to those of Hulak-Artemovsky. Speaking of those 'patriots from country homesteads,' who 'praise what is most worthless' in Ukrainian literature, Shevchenko says the following: 'They read a bit of *Eneida* and stroll about the tavern for a time and think that, lo and behold, we have recognized our peasants for what they are. O, no, dear brothers! Read our *dumy* and songs.'[19] To be sure, these thoughts were expressed in 1847, while Shevchenko wrote the well-known poem 'Na Vichnu Pamiat Kotliarevskomu' (In Eternal Memory of Kotliarevsky) in 1838. Yet even then he differed from the author of *Eneida*, only occasionally using ethnographic motifs and spurning the burlesque genre altogether.

It cannot be argued that Shevchenko brought folk motifs and forms into literature because he himself was a son of the people who, so to speak, continued the traditions of folk poetry. In his paintings Shevchenko did not reveal himself as the heir to the rich heritage of Ukrainian folk art, which did not receive the attention it deserved from this student of the classicist, Briullov, who submitted instead to the spirit dominating painting at the time.[20] But, as a poet, Shevchenko found himself in a romantic environment (initially there was the personal influence of Zhukovsky) and romanticism unquestionably revealed to him that the folk song, *duma*, and legend could and should be the poet's material. Ukrainian, Russian, and Polish ballads showed Shevchenko that the fantastic elements in the legends, as Kolessa has observed, 'could be brought into poetry.'[21] Indeed, Shevchenko demonstrated that the ballad was the genre to sustain romanticism in the Ukrainian setting.

At this point the characteristic features of Shevchenko's ballads ('Prychynna' / 'The Bewitched Woman'; 'Topolia' / 'The Poplar'; 'Utoplena' / 'The Drowned Maiden'; 'Lileia' / 'The Lily'; and others) should be noted. In form, they are simpler than the popular ballads of that time – Bürger's 'Lenora,' Zhukovsky's 'Svetlana,' Mickiewicz's 'Ucieczka' or 'Lilie.' They lack the characteristic ballad structure – the reliance on repetition, which strengthens the impact of the poem and focuses the reader's attention, but has a certain artificial, 'stylized' character. They are simpler, too, in their internal make-up: the fantastic elements are not overdrawn and are far removed from mysticism, occasionally combining with social details to depict the conditions of life in the age of serfdom (The Lily, Rusalka / The Mermaid), Shevchenko's theme on more than one occasion. Ivan Franko has written that Borovykovsky's original ballads (unpublished and thus known only through several Russian reworkings) were not truly ballads in the romantic sense, but were simply Ukrainian folk tales and legends presented in verse. Similarly, the works by Shevchenko mentioned above are not 'truly ballads.' Ethnographic elements, motifs, and forms from Ukrainian folk songs about love and parting and plots from folk legends unite organically in Shevchenko's ballads, giving them both a lyrical and an epic character. The lyrical digressions which they contain resemble sentimental folk songs. For example, there is the lyrical digression in 'The Bewitched Woman' which begins as follows:

Taka ii dolia, o Bozhe mii mylyi,
Za shcho ty karaiesh ii molodu ...

Such is her fate; o, dear God, / Why do you punish this young one ...

These elements from the oral tradition encountered in Shevchenko's ballads mingle with various literary influences. In his study, Kolessa refers to Polish and Russian influences (Mickiewicz, Pushkin, Kozlov, Zhukovsky, and others) without granting them an absolute significance: 'At every step he gives his ballad a local Ukrainian character. His sorceress, his Cossack, and his young girl – these are purely Ukrainian types.' [22] It should also be pointed out that with specific elements in Shevchenko's ballads it is frequently impossible to say whether they were borrowed from one poet or another. During Shevchenko's time they were already commonplace, not only among European and Russian poets, but even among their Ukrainian counterparts. In Shevchenko's depiction of the Dnipro ('Reve ta stohne Dnipr shyrokyi ...' / 'The wide Dnipro roars and moans ...'), for example, Kolessa points to an analogous passage from Zhukovsky's 'Liudmila' (Vot i mesiats velichavyi ... / And, lo, the majestic moon ...) and to the following lines from Kozlov:

Za Kievom, gde Dnepr shirokii
V krutykh bregakh kipit shumit ... ('Chernets' / 'The Monk')

Beyond Kiev where between winding banks / The broad Dnieper foams and froths ...

Vetr vyl, groza revela,
Mesiats krylsia v oblakakh,
I reka, klubias, shumela
V omrachennykh beregakh. (Son nevesty / The Bride's Dream)

The wind howled, the storm roared, / The moon hid in the clouds / And the river swirled and foamed / Between the darkened banks.

However, a similar description is to be found in Metlynsky:

Buria vyie, zavyvaie
I sosnovyi bor troshchyt,
V khmarakh blyskavka palaie,
Hrim za hromom hriakotyt.
Nich to uhlem vsia zchorniie,
To iak krov zachervoniie,
Dnipr klekoche, stohne, plache,
I hryvu syvuiu triase. ('Smert bandurysta' / 'Death of a *Bandura* Player')

The storm howls, roars, / The pine forest shatters, / In the clouds a lightning flash blazes, / Thunder rumbles bolt upon bolt. / The night grows black as coal, / Then glows red as blood, / The Dnipro gurgles, moans, wails / And shakes its grey mane.

The above ballad, 'The Young Wife,' begins as follows:

Vatahamy khodyly khmary;
Mizh nymy molodyk blukav,
Vitry v ocheretakh burkhaly
I Psol stohnav i klekotav.
Shumily verby ... rvalos lystia;
Huly vitry po-pid mostom.

Clouds passed in droves;
a new moon wandered among them,
the winds muttered in the reeds
and the Psol moaned and gurgled.
Willows rustled ... leaves were torn to shreds;
beneath the bridge the winds howled.

This is a typical Ossianic landscape, and Shevchenko knew Ossian well, even before his exile. In a letter to Bronisław Zaleski (1854) he writes:

In the bosom of virginal, solemnly beautiful nature I salute you! Many, many heartfelt prayers would I dispatch to the throne of the living God would he but allow me to pass one hour with you in a primeval pine forest beneath a dark, broad-branched shadow, as surly as an Ossianic meditation. ... Do not forget to obtain Ossian; his works, I believe, are available in a French translation. Now you will read them with delight. Your décor is perfect for Ossian.[23]

Devices from Ukrainian folk poetry are also encountered in his land-scapes.[24] Generally, in his ballads the borrowings from various European romantic poets are blended with elements from folk poetry. Thus, his four-foot iambs blend with folk rhythms, those rhythms upon which nineteenth-century Ukrainian poets before him had scarcely begun to draw.

It is apparent that the ballad was a form with an organic base in both Shevchenko's poetry and in the Ukrainian poetry of his era, that it is the Ukrainian version of this typically romantic genre. When Shevchenko ceased writing ballads, he simply freed himself from that fantastic element which hardly spoke to his soul; the lyricism, certain approaches to poetic material, the element of folk poetry, the ethnographic features encountered in his ballads – all this could evolve independently. Even while he was still writing his ballads, Shevchenko was already composing 'Kateryna' (in which the ethnographic stratum is fused with an idealized, romantic one) and lyrical poems in the spirit of folk poetry.[25]

There was an organic base, too, for the historical motifs and forms that Shevchenko took over from romanticism. The national sentiment, love of one's own antiquity, was a characteristic feature of European romanticism; it was reflected too in Russia and especially in Ukraine, where it was particularly revealed to Shevchenko in the collections of ancient folk literature (for example, Tsertelev,[26] Metlynsky).[27] It is well known that in the first three decades of the nineteenth century there was a growing interest in the Ukrainian past and its depiction in literary works, an interest shared not only by Ukrainian writers but by Russian writers, too (Ryleev,[28] Pushkin), who in some instances were of Ukrainian origin (Mykola Markevych, Gogol), and by Polish writers (the 'Ukrainian school' – Zaleski, Tymko Padura, Seweryn Goszczyński, etc.). When Shevchenko was beginning his literary activity, the view of the Ukrainian past as a source for poetry was widespread in Russia. Even Belinsky expressed it in 1840:

Little Russia is a poetic country and very original. Here all possess those feelings in which man, by his nature, abounds. Love is the basic element of life. To this add Asiatic chivalry, known under the name of courageous Cossackdom, call to mind the troubled existence of Little Russia, its struggle with Catholic Poland and the Moslems of Crimea and you will agree that it would be difficult to find a richer source for poetry than Little Russian life.[29]

But Shevchenko not only encountered this general view of his country's past; in the works of Russian, Polish, and Ukrainian (Metlynsky, Kostomarov) writers he found romantic treatments of historical motifs; here were *bandura* players and burial mounds which talked with the wind, Zaporozhian campaigns, hetmans, and so forth. *Dumy* and folk songs provided especially valuable material. Shevchenko wrote 'Ivan Pidkova,' 'Tarasova Nich' (Night of Taras), 'Do Osnovianenka' (To Osnovianenko), 'Hamaliia,' 'Haidamaky' (The Haidamaks), and other poems which offered an idealization of a brilliant past, a sad parallel to the circumstances in Shevchenko's own era. A romantic enchantment with the dazzling colours of antiquity, a quest for a bygone liberty embellished by fantasy in the recollections of the past, deliverance from a meagre and malevolent reality – all this reigned for some time in Shevchenko's poetry. In 1845 he concludes:

Raby, pidnizhky, hriaz Moskvy,
Varshavske smittia vashi pany,
Iasnovelmozhnii hetmany.

Slaves, toadies, the scum of Moscow, / Warsaw's refuse are your masters, / The illustrious hetmans.

At the same time, in 'Zastupyla chorna khmara' (A black cloud obscured, 1848) he eulogizes Hetman Doroshenko and in 'Khiba samomu napysat' (Should I attempt to write, 1849) he confesses:

> ... shche ne znaiu, shcho robliu;
> Pyshu sobi, shchob ne miniaty
> Chasa sviatoho tak-na-tak,
> To inodi staryi kozak
> Verzetsia hrishnomu – usatyi,
> Z svoieiu voleiu, meni,
> Na chornim voronim koni.

... still I know not what I do; / I write in order not to barter away / These precious hours / And sometimes an old, bewhiskered Cossack who with his freedom / Appears before me, / Sinner that I am, / Upon a raven-black horse.

Mykhailo Drahomanov noted that Shevchenko moved from a celebration of the hetmanate to Cossackophilism – to an idealization of the Zaporozhians and the Zaporozhian spirit. In addition, he indicates that Shevchenko could not be critical of the 'fictitious images of Cossackdom'[30] because historical scholarship was little developed at the time, and the author of *Kobzar* was forced to rely on *Istoriia Rusov* (A History of the Russes).[31] It could also be said that it was less the ideology underlying these 'fictitious images' than their poetic and pictoral qualities that attracted Shevchenko. In a letter to Iakiv Kukharenko in 1857, Shevchenko speaks of his keen interest in the romantic Ukrainian past:

Cossack supreme commander Panko Kulish sent me from Peter[sburg] a copy of his book entitled *Zapiski o Iuzhnoi Rusi* (Notes on Southern Rus) written in our language. I do not know whether this very wise and sincere book has yet reached the Black Sea coast. If it has not, then order it; you will have no regrets. In it our *kobzars* and hetmans and Zaporozhians and Haidamaks are cast in living images and our ancient Ukraine is exhibited as if on the palm of the hand. Kulish has added nothing of his own but only recorded what he heard from our blind *kobzars* and for this reason his book happened to be good, sincere and wise.[32]

In the romantic works by Shevchenko on historical subjects, typically romantic treatments of the théme are encountered in more emphatic form than in his ballads: here we have poses, melodramatic scenes, bloody deeds (for example, Honta's killing of his own children), explicit contrasts – all of which are also to be found in those of Shevchenko's later works which draw their themes from everyday life ('Vidma' / 'The Witch'; 'Maryna,' etc.).

A second feature of Shevchenko's historical poems is their celebration of the heroic individual who is both strong and daring. This cult of the heroic individual not only does not vanish in his later works but, rather, becomes more profound. Now internal, not external, strength begins to attract the poet, not daring for its own sake as in the early poem 'Ivan Pidkova' (1838), but heroic deeds performed in the name of human happiness, an individual's struggle against coercion and injustice. This is clearly distinguishable in those poems in which national Ukrainian motifs evolve into universally human, revolutionary ones – in 'Ivan Hus,' in 'Kavkaz' (The Caucasus). Ultimately, Prometheus, that figure beloved by the romantics, makes his appearance:

Za horamy hory, khmaramy povyti,
Zasiiani horem, kroviiu polyti.
Spokon viku Prometeia,
Tam orel karaie.

Beyond the hills more hills, swaddled in clouds, / Sown with misfortune, / Drenched with blood. / There, from time immemorial, / An eagle scourges Prometheus.

Shevchenko's unique, independent individual is above the masses, yet, at the same time, has an affinity to them, is gripped by a desire to liberate the masses, the Ukrainian people, from their yoke of serfdom and appears in the guise of the poet whose image Shevchenko paints with typically romantic strokes.

The romantic treatment of the *bandura* player, Perebendia, immediately catches the imagination; little wonder that Kolessa found his prototype in Mickiewicz. Yet, images of the lone bard whose inspired heart can be tranquil only in the midst of nature can be found quite often in the works of romantic poets and in the pre-romantic sentimental writers. Later, Shevchenko was to alter this image, transforming it into the image of a prophet, 'a critic of the ill-intentioned,' analogous to Lermontov's prophet and other romantic character types. Undoubtedly, Shevchenko had an inner sense of the power of poetry, was possessed of an inner dynamism.[33] Yet, since Metlynsky's sombre reflection that the Ukrainian language was dying ('Vzhe nasha mova konaie' / 'Already our language is dying') had re-sounded in Ukrainian poetry not long before, it is doubtful whether Shevchenko's conception of the poet in the role of reformer could have appeared without the influence of the romantic movement. Beginning with the era of the *Sturm und Drang*, romanticism formed individualities, the creative 'I' of prophets and rebels, band chieftains and revolutionaries, created the cult of the poet-leader, and Shevchenko was a son of his own time when he expressed the following fond desire after the appearance of his 'The Haidamaks': 'let me be simply a peasant poet; but let me be a poet ...'

Once he had experienced the poet, the creator, within himself and become convinced of his lofty destiny, Shevchenko understandably could not continue to celebrate the past and write variations on ballad themes. His motifs became broader in scope; he moved from a national to a revolutionary romanticism, issuing summonses to battle and revenge, to political and social protest. These motifs frequently reverberated in the works of the romantics – in Byron, whom Shevchenko knew and valued highly,[34] in the French poets, in Mickiewicz, in some Russian writers. Even in Bestuzhev-Marlinsky, whose influence O. Doroshkevych[35] perceives in the style of Shevchenko's stories, protests against feudalistic serfdom are encountered: 'You taught me to spill innocent blood at will, so do not gape at me now that I wish to drink my fill of yours in revenge,' a young knight from the story 'Zamok Eizen' (Castle Eizen) says to the baron who took from him his bride-to-be and all his possessions.

Impressions from life could have provided Shevchenko with the material for those works in which he portrays serfdom, generally lingering over scenes in which noblemen maltreat the girls they have ravished. But in these works, which seemingly portray scenes from everyday life, there are many scenes distinctly romantic in origin, powerful in their murderous cruelty, scenes in which the poet deliberately accumulates horrifying images.[36] In 'Maryna' (1848), for example, a drunken nobleman enters the chamber occupied by Maryna, his daughter by a serf-girl whom he had raped:

> Moroz liutuie azh skrypyt,
> Luna chervona pobilila,
> I storozh boiazko krychyt,
> Shchob zloho pana ne zbudyt.
> Azh hliad! – Palaty zanialysia.
> Pozhar! Pozhar! ... I de vzialysia
> Ti liudy v Boha! Mov z zemli
> Rodylysia i tut rosly,
> Nenache khvyli naplyvaly,
> Ta na pozhar toi dyvuvalys,
> Ta i dyvo tam taky bulo!
> Maryna hola na holo
> Pered budynkom tantsiuvala
> U pari z matiriu, i – strakh! –
> Z nozhem okrovlenym v rukakh,
> I pryspivuvala ...

The frost is severe, it even crackles, / The red glow fades / And the watchman shouts timidly / So as not to rouse the wicked master. / But lo! – the palace rises in flame. / Fire! Fire! And from whence / In God's world came all these people! / As if they had just sprouted and grown up out of nowhere, / They rolled in like waves / And marvelled at the conflagration / and what a wonder there was to behold! / Stark naked, Maryna / Danced before the building / With her mother and – awesome to behold – / With a blood-stained knife in her hand / She began to sing ...

'Maryna,' like 'The Witch,' is based on Shevchenko's Russian poem 'Slepaia' (The Sightless One) and the comparison of these three works allows interesting conclusions to be drawn about Shevchenko as a romantic. It should be noted that earlier comparisons of these poems were made with a different aim: to show that Shevchenko had a poor mastery of the Russian language and a good mastery of Ukrainian or to determine that 'all Maryna's dialogues were completely natural and we need only marvel at how the poet managed to paint Maryna's onerous malady with purely Shakespearean strokes. All that we find in the Russian poem is transformed into pure gold in the Ukrainian ...'[37]

But not everything in the Russian poem found its way into the Ukrainian version and those elements which did not should be of particular interest to the literary historian. Portraying in 'Maryna' and 'The Witch' the ravishing of peasant girls by their masters, even if these girls are their own daughters, Shevchenko expresses his intense wrath towards violators, something that is encountered in a number of his other Ukrainian poems. This theme is also the main component of 'The Sightless One.' At the same time, however, there are passages, generally lyrical asides, in which the poet's pessimistic view of man emerges, expressions of sentiment which unquestionably contain echoes of the *Weltschmerz* of Byron, Chateaubriand (whose works, as his letter to Countess Tolstoi reveals, Shevchenko knew well even before his exile)[38] and his beloved Lermontov:

Pridet pora, pora liubit,
A zloe sertse cheloveka
Ee liubvi ne poshchadit.

...

Ona izvedala liudei!

...

I vot ona v griazi razvrata,
Vo slavu driakhlykh vashykh dnei,
Pered tolpoiu cherni pianoi
Pet kubok ...

The time will come, the time for love, / But the evil heart of man / Will not spare her love / ... / She has come to know people! ... / And there in the filth of corruption, / Before a drunken crowd of low-born men, / To the glory of your days of yore / Her goblet drains ...

Ne toi ia stal, chto prezhde bylo:
I put unylyi bytiia,
I nosha tiazhkaia moia

Menia uzhasno izmenili.
Ia tainu zhizni razgadal,
Raskryl ia sertse cheloveka,
I ne stradaiu, kak stradal,
I ne liubliu ia: ia kaleka!

No longer am I as in time past: / My life's cheerless path / and my heavy burden / Have changed me terribly. / The mystery of life I have deciphered, / Laid open the heart of man / And do not suffer as once I did, / And do not love: a cripple am I!

In 'Trizna' (Funeral Feast), the second of Shevchenko's Russian poems, there is not only even stronger pessimism but also a melancholy titanism in the spirit of Byron and Lermontov:

Ruka, szhimaiasia, drozhala ...
O, esli b mog on shar zemnoi
Skhvatit ozloblennoi rukoi
So vsemi gadami zemnymi;
Skhvatit, izmiat i brosit v ad!...
On byl by schastliv, byl by rad.
On khokhotal, kak demon liutyi ...

His clenched hand shook ... / O, if only he could seize in his embittered hand the earthly orb / With all its vile creatures; / Seize them, crush them, and toss them into Hell! ... / He would be fortunate, would rejoice. / He roared with laughter like a malevolent demon ...

The hero of this poem

Nepostizhimoiu toskoiu
Byl postoianno udruchen ...

... was always despondent, in an unfathomable melancholy ...

These are all typically Byronic motifs, derived from Byron and especially from Pushkin's 'southern poems,' from Lermontov, Kozlov, and others. Shevchenko's Russian poems are in the then dominant Byronic tradition;

this external force possessed him and carried him in a direction remote for a son of peasant Ukraine who dreamed of the village: 'Selo – i sertse odpochyne ...' (The village – and the heart will rest ...).

Nothing of the sort, no universal pessimism, no universal reproach, no *Weltschmerz*, is carried over into the Ukrainian reworkings of 'The Sightless One,' into 'Maryna' and 'The Witch,' nor into his Ukrainian works as a whole. There was no foundation for it. Furthermore, this titanism and pessimism would have checked that tendency towards the idyllic, that sentimentalism which was deeply rooted in Shevchenko's heart even when he raised his voice in outbursts of anger and blasphemy. Shevchenko wrote two poems, dramas and, later, short stories in Russian, but confesses that the Russian language is hard, coarse ... 'I have just transcribed "The Sightless One",' Shevchenko wrote to Kukharenko in 1842, 'and cry over it: what a crime that I confess my sins to the Muscovites in coarse Muscovite words.'[39]

Casting aside all that he himself labelled a 'Byronic fog' in 'The Sightless One,' Shevchenko hastened to rework the Russian poem in Ukrainian (Maryna) and to rediscover the sentimental lyricism of his native Ukrainian folk song:

Nenache voron toi, letiachy,
Pro nepohodu liudiam kriache:
Tak ia pro slozy ta pechal
Ta pro baistrat otykh ledachykh,
Khoch i nikomu ikh ne zhal,
Rozkazuiu ta plachu ...
Meni ikh zhal ... Mii Bozhe mylyi!
Darui slovam sviatuiu sylu
Liudskeie sertse probyvat,
Liudskii slozy prolyvat:
Shchob mylost dushu osinyla,
Shchob spala tykhaia pechal
Na ochi ikh, shchob stalo zhal
Moikh divchatok, shchob navchylys
Putiamy dobrymy khodyt,
Sviatoho Hospoda liubyt,
I brata myluvat!...

Like a flying raven cawing out / A warning about bad weather, / So do I tell of
tears and sorrow / And of those poor, unlawful children / Even though they are
pitied by none, / And I cry ... / I pity them ... Dear God! / Grant to my words the
sacred power / To arouse the human heart, / To bring forth human tears: / So may
compassion guard the soul, / so may sorrow still sleep / Upon their eyes, so my
girls will be pitied, / So man will learn to tread the good path, / Love our holy
Lord, / And spare our brother.

Not all the typical motifs and forms of expression encountered in the works
of Western and Russian romantics were reflected in Shevchenko's works,
especially when only his *Kobzar*, which represents a definite point of
demarcation in the development of Ukrainian poetry, is considered. The
mystical feeling, the themes and their treatment characteristic of early
German romanticism were foreign to Shevchenko.[40] '"Mysticism" and
metaphysics were not for him,' K. Chukovsky has observed. 'The mysterious, the infinite, the world of excessive sensibility does not interest
him.'[41]

The Byronic cult of the titanic individual, disenchanted, hostile to the
masses, often villainous, was also alien to Shevchenko. Questions of individualism were of no interest to him; about the language of Russian
journalists he wrote: 'they pack in some sort of *individualisms* and the like
so that your tongue grows numb before you can pronounce them.'[42] On the
other hand, the strong individual who acts upon what he feels and whose
actions have the support of the masses (Ivan Pidkova, Honta, Zalizniak,
etc.), who fights against injustice (Ivan Hus), who leads the people in the
struggle for national and social liberation – this type of individual indeed
does captivate the poet's imagination. At the same time, many romantic,
particularly Byronic, motifs, forms, and literary devices permeate nearly all
Shevchenko's works. The folk song – folk poetry – was never forsaken by
Shevchenko even though at times he wrote purely 'literary' works. An
analysis of his *Kobzar* (a subject for a special study of major proportions)
would reveal that Shevchenko was and remained a romantic. It is true that
romantic poetics have not yet been minutely studied; the characteristic
features have, however, been outlined. It is possible to compare Shevchenko's poetic methods with those found in the Byronic poem (Byron and
others), in the case of the latter using V. Zhirmunsky's studies. On the
compositional structure of the lyrical Byronic poem Zhirmunsky writes:

The lyrical Byronic poem has the character of a novella and contemporary psychological content. It centres on one character and one event in his inner life: usually this event is love. Fragmentation of the narration, which begins in the middle of the story and jumps from one climactic point in the action to another, glossing over all intermediary developments; focusing on powerful individual situations and scenes; a lyrical overture; many lyrical monologues and dramatic dialogues – all this attests to the fact that the composition complies with the principles of lyrical and dramatic form.[43]

A similar compositional structure, which Zhirmunsky finds in the Byronic poems of Russian poets,[44] is also present in Shevchenko's *Kobzar*, especially in 'The Witch' and 'Maryna,' whose genesis in his typically Byronic Russian poems is unquestionable. What Drahomanov called 'the inept structure of other poems and their movement from one thing to another'[45] is easily explained as romantic compositional structuring.

Characteristic of Byron's emotional style and that of his imitators is a 'wealth of questions, interjections and repetitions.' This emotional style holds sway in Shevchenko's poetry. In his revolutionary poems it is encountered everywhere. Many examples where Shevchenko is 'driven beyond the point of endurance' can be found. I offer a fragment of a passage from 'Neofity' (Neophytes, 1857), which in its totality could stand as an example:

> Hore z vamy!
> Koho blahaty vy pryishly?
> Komu vy slozy prynesly?
> Komu vy prynesly z slozamy
> Svoiu nadiiu? Hore z vamy,
> Raby nezriachii! Koho,
> Koho blahaiete, blahii?

Woe to you! / Whom did you come to beseech? / To whom did you bring your tears? / To whom with your tears your hopes offer? / Woe to you, unseeing slaves! Whom, / Whom do you beseech, poor creatures?

Plasticity was lacking in the works of the romantics; the musical principle defined their style. This thesis, which has so far only been sketched in a fairly general outline, could be established in studies of individual authors. Shevchenko's works with their unusual wealth of assonance, alliteration, internal rhyme, and folk rhythm furnish the scholar with interesting materials for an exploration of this subject, materials which have already been studied to some degree.[46]

A series of other questions which have some bearing on Shevchenko's romanticism (for example, the antithesis between nature and culture) cannot be discussed here. Neither can the observations offered, which are only notes towards a synthetic study of Shevchenko's total literary production, be detailed. However, even on the basis of what has been said it can be concluded that romanticism had a great significance for Shevchenko's works, much greater than has thus far been allowed.

(1924)

NOTES

1 This article was first published as 'Shevchenko i romantyzm,' *Zapysky istorychno-filolohichnoho viddilu VUAN*, kn. 4 (Kiev 1924) 3-18 (ed.).

2 F.D. Batiushkov, F.A. Braun *et al.*, eds, *Istoriia zapadnoi literatury, 1800-1910*, I (Moscow 1912) 330.

3 See V.A. Lunacharsky in *Vestnik teatra*, 76-7 (1920) 13.

4 See *Vesnik teatra*, 75 (1920) 7.

5 See *Gorod: Sbornik*, I (Petrograd 1923) 9-48. This volume contains the text of Lunts's tragedy and a noteworthy afterword by the author on the romanticism of the *Sturm und Drang*. The Serapion Brethren was a literary group in the 1920s.

6 Ferdinand Georgievich la Bart, the author of several books on romanticism. Fylypovych does not indicate to which work by la Bart he is referring (ed.).

7 A.N. Veselovsky, *V.A. Zhukovskii: Poeziia chuvstva i 'serdechnago voobrazheniia,'* 2nd ed. (Petrograd 1918).

8 See V. Zhirmunsky, *Nemetskii romantizm i sovremennaia mistika* (St Petersburg 1914).

9 V.M. Zhirmunsky, 'Sovremennaia literatura o nemetskom romantizme,' *Russkaia mysl*, XI (1913).

10 See, for example, V. Sipovsky, 'Pushkin i romantizm,' in *Pushkin i ego sovremenniki*, XXIII-XXIV (1916).

11 I. Zamotin, *Romantizm dvadtsatykh godov XIX stol. v russkoi literature*, II (St Petersburg 1913) 79.

12 Iu. Oksman, 'Borba protiv Bairona ...,' *Nachala*, 2 (1922).

13 B. Eikhenbaum, *Poetika Pushkina* (Petrograd 1921) 78.

14 Sipovsky, 'Pushkin i romantizm.'

15 V. Zhirmunsky, *Pushkinskii sbornik* (1923).

16 See Mikhail Kachenovsky's editorial note in *Vestnik Evropy*, 20 (1827) 286-7.

17 The relationship of the sentimental style to the folk song is sketched in general terms in Robert de Souza, *La poésie populaire et le lyrisme sentimental*, 2nd ed. (Paris 1899).

18 V. Kallash, *Iz istorii malorusskoi literatury 20-kh i 30-kh godov XIX veka* (Kiev 1900-1) 6. 'Molodytsia' has since been proved to be by Borovykovsky (ed.).

19 Taras Shevchenko, *Tvory*, ed. V. Iakovenko (St Petersburg 1911) II 84.

20 See D. Antonovych, 'Estetychni pohliady Shevchenka,' *Literaturno naukovyi Visnyk*, II (1914).

21 O. Kolessa, 'Shevchenko i Mitskevych,' *Zapysky naukovoho tovarystva im. Shevchenka*, IV (1894).

22 Kolessa 80.

23 Shevchenko, *Tvory*, II ed. Iakovenko, 380-1.

24 O. Doroshkevych, 'Pryroda v poezii Shevchenka,' in *Taras Shevchenko: Zbirnyk* (Kiev 1921) 80.

25 Ivan Franko, '"Naimychka" T. Shevchenka,' *ZNTSh*, VI, kn. 2 (1895) 1-20; reprinted in Ivan Franko, *Tvory*, XVII, *Literaturno-krytychni statti*, 20 vols (Kiev 1955) 100-20.

26 Nikolai Tsertelev, *Opyt sobraniia starinnykh malorossiiskikh pesnei* (St Petersburg 1819).

27 Amvrosii Metlinsky, *Narodnye iuzhnorusskie pesni* (Kiev 1854).

28 Interesting materials on Ukrainian subjects in Russian literature are to be found in V. Maslov, *Literaturnaia deiatelnost K.O. Ryleeva* (Kiev 1912), ch. 5.

29 V.G. Belinsky, *Sochineniia* (St Petersburg 1896) I, 904.

30 See Mykhailo Drahomanov's well-known study, *Shevchenko, ukrainofily i sotsializm*, 2nd ed. (Kiev 1914) 62. [See translation in this volume (ed.).]

31 *A History of the Russes* is a history of Ukraine probably written in the first decade of the nineteenth century. After circulating in manuscript form in the 1820s and 1830s, it was printed in 1846. Of uncertain origin, this work, which covers Ukrainian history to 1769 and presents it from a national point of view, did much to stimulate a national revival in the nineteenth century (ed.).

32 T. Shevchenko, *Tvory*, ed. Iakovenko, II, 405.

33 See Pavlo Fylypovych, 'Poet ohnennoho slova,' in *Taras Shevchenko: Zbirnyk*, ed. Ie. Hryhoruk and P. Fylypovych (Kiev 1921).
34 Afanasev-Chuzhbynsky testifies that in 1843 Shevchenko was especially taken with Mickiewicz's translation of Byron's 'Childe Harold' and frequently recited the following verse which was particularly relevant to his own life:

> Teraz po świecie błądzę szerokim
> i pędzę życie tułacze;
> Czegoż mam płakać? za kim? i po kim?
> kiedy po mnie nikt nie płacze!

Now I wander over the wide world / And lead the life of an exile. / Why should I weep? For whom? / No one is weeping for me.
35 Doroshkevych 87.
36 This characteristic struck Drahomanov. About the 'melodramatic' aspect of 'Kateryna' and other poems, see Drahomanov 45. Later, Drahomanov (p 46) observes:

> Intending to portray the gentry, Shevchenko always selected their most exceptional evil deeds (for example, 'Kniazhna' / 'The Princess'; 'Varnak' / 'The Convict') and usually resorted to the 'sin of fornication,' neglecting other no less significant sins not so much of individual land-owners as of the land-owners as a group, ordinary sins, all the more serious for being committed by groups, not individuals.

37 See M. Markovsky, 'Rosiiski i ukrainski tvory Shevchenka v ikh porivnianni (Deshcho do psykholohii tvorchosti Shevchenka),' *Ukraina*, 1-2 (1918) 32-48.
38 Shevchenko, *Tvory*, ed. Iakovenko, II, 401.
39 *Ibid.* 453.
40 Shevchenko writes about Zhukovsky (in his diary for 1857) that the latter 'believes in the lifeless beauty of the paltry and everlasting German ideal.'
41 K. Chukovsky, 'Taras Shevchenko,' in his *Litsa i maski: Stati* (St Petersburg 1914) 261.
42 Shevchenko, *Tvory*, ed. Iakovenko, II, 83.
43 V. Zhirmunsky, introduction to George Gordon Byron, *Dramy* (Moscow, Petrograd 1922) 44.
44 V. Zhirmunsky, 'Baironizm Pushkina, kak istorikoliteraturnaia problema,' in *Pushkinskii sbornik pamiati prof. S.A. Vengerova*, ed. N.V. Iakovlev (Moscow, Petrograd 1923).
45 Drahomanov 107-8.
46 See B. Iakubsky, 'Forma poezii Shevchenka,' in *Taras Shevchenko: Zbirnyk* (Kiev 1921).

12

Kulish and Shevchenko

MYKHAILO MOHYLIANSKY

> Not to rage, nor to weep, but to understand. (Spinoza)

The first decades of the nineteenth-century Ukrainian cultural renaissance brought three great figures onto the public forum of literary, academic, and community life.[1] They were Kostomarov, Kulish, and Shevchenko. Today, at a distance of over a century from the birth of each and more than thirty years since the death of Kulish, who was the last to die, it behooves us to approach, *sine ira et studio*, the study of their characters, ideas, and relationships. In this undertaking, so important to our national consciousness, it is essential to keep an historical perspective. It is unnecessary to glorify or sanctify these men by depicting them as heroes, nor is it necessary to polemicize or expose their mistakes and personal faults. We need realistic descriptions in order to understand the significance of their ideas and deeds in relation to our own problems. No prayer of praise or anathemization is justified; rather, historical analysis is needed. The historian must never forget that it is harder to understand things when they occur than it is to think about them intelligently at a distance.

But an approach to the historical evaluation of the famous 'Trinity' using such seemingly primitive principles is almost an attempt to 'encompass the unencompassable.' The passions aroused by the work of the 'Trinity' have not yet died down, and this is the most eloquent testimony to the importance of their work. For this reason any attempt at objectivity remains one of those good intentions with which, as the saying has it, hell is paved. All the material needed for such an evaluation has still not been researched and published, and among those researchers who have worked on this material there have not been enough who cleared the path to historical truth, but there have certainly been too many 'gravediggers' who have made the path impassable by heaping it with earth and stones. Therefore, the time for synthesis is not yet ripe. There is not enough detailed research of the huge amount of material which constitutes an entire Mt Blanc of facts, partial topics, and problems which in their entirety will enable some future historian to produce a synthetic evaluation, this time not based on mere imaginings and obvious prejudices. The subject of this article is one of those partial topics – Kulish and Shevchenko.

The subject, or rather the problem of Kulish, is possibly the central problem in the history of the nineteenth-century Ukrainian cultural renaissance. It is significant that Drahomanov wrote, in a letter to Pavlyk, that Kulish, 'one of the Ukrainophiles, insists upon a universal humanist culture that will uplift our people.'[2] This subject demands a thorough examination because, even if we ignore all that has been written about Kulish (which is probably greater in volume than his collected works) at this point we have only the beginnings of a fair evaluation of certain features of this great man's complicated character. It is surprising that the strongest character in the famous 'Trinity,' the man whose will was most intense and constantly directed towards the fulfilment of his chosen goal, is looked upon as a chameleon capable of changing his attitude towards an issue from enthusiastic support one day to anathema the next. Even his former 'friend,' Kostomarov, writing about Kulish's 'latest literary output,' predicted that he would lose his readers' trust and affection as a result of switching to views diametrically opposed to those which 'they had already got used to hearing from him.'[3] Kulish, however, was completely single-minded throughout his long career. He was driven by a single idea, the dream of an independent Ukrainian nation which, as Iefymenko has pointed out, was passed on to him 'by his ancestors, by that Ukrainian Cossack race from which he was descended.'[4] As a champion of this idea Kulish was immeasurably more consistent, steadfast, and logical than his accuser. This is glaringly evident in the accusation brought against Kulish in the article mentioned above by the former head of the Brotherhood of Saints Cyril and Methodius.

The accusation brought against Kulish forty years later, by an author who had already completely accepted the idea of an independent Ukrainian nation (and in this, he was very possibly much influenced by Kulish) is no more convincing. I refer to S. Iefremov's ingenious attempt to characterize Kulish fully by analysing 'the drama of Kulish's life.'[5] If we ignore 'Kulish's intellectual inability to synthesize,' treating it as an inherent characteristic of his nature (and this view too must be contradicted almost entirely), we find that S. Iefremov's article restricts itself almost entirely to describing the psychological characteristics of Kulish: his misanthropy, a result of his upbringing; his fundamental antisocial attitude which progressed through all the stages 'because of his excessive egoism, arrogance, vindictiveness, and inherent insincerity and pretentiousness.' 'Kulish could not get along without playing a role, not even in his painful solitude, not even in his diary. His unbounded self-importance, the result of a cold, egocentric temperament brought up in a homegrown aristocratic environment, and of an a-synthetic way of thinking, is evident everywhere.'[6] Even the 'homegrown aristocratic environment' does not seem to contribute a social analysis. Indeed, this notion has all the earmarks of a psychological category.

Not being 'in possession of the required ability to synthesize,' Iefremov was unable to resolve the drama of Kulish's life adequately, which resulted from his [Kulish's] psychological shortcomings.[7] Without considering whether being 'in possession of the required ability to synthesize' would enable one to overcome those psychological faults of Kulish's 'egocentric self,' so heavily emphasized by our researcher, I believe that the 'drama of Kulish's life' can only be understood on the basis of a profound analysis of social factors. Iefremov's clever and original article, which ought to have cleared away the foggy notions left by years of incompetent research on the problem of Kulish, in spite of its masterful analysis and richness of thought, cannot be regarded as a completely satisfactory resolution of the problem, specifically because of the researcher's penchant for moralizing rather than for social analysis. As a result, Iefremov's article sounds accusatory on the whole, and although certain characteristics of Kulish are very clearly and faithfully described, the characterization is almost entirely that of an egocentric and antisocial Kulish whose life's drama is that of one who never came to understand his destiny. The portrait, then, has turned out to be one-sided and not entirely 'true to the original.' The stage I have reached in my study of Kulish permits me to counter Iefremov's description, which is defended by a well-argued factual analysis.

At this point I will not even attempt the necessary argumentation because I am not attracted by the easy generalizations that can be made using the popular but oversimplified and vulgarized sociological method. It is time to realize that merely postulating a direct link between ideological principles and the economic basis of society is an inadequate use of the Marxist method. The use of this method only results in the creation of that 'twilight in which all cats are grey.' Since the prospect of turning the colourful Kulish into an undistinguished member of the petty bourgeois land-owning class (a product of their society he certainly was, and it is there that one must seek the source of his 'life's drama') does not attract me, and because I am interested in his 'special characteristics,' whose interpretation demands detail, profundity, and a refined methodology, in this study I shall limit my topic and examine a page, or better, perhaps, one act ('Kulish and Shevchenko') of the larger drama 'Kulish.' It may be by chance that this particular material is most familiar to me, although I admit that even in the attempt to determine Kulish's personal characteristics the choice of this topic may be rather unfortunate mainly because it will be necessary to proceed without the appropriate amount of argumentation and to raise certain issues without fully explaining why. I will be forced to limit my discussion of existing social conditions and thus to sacrifice a certain degree of clarity, even though at no time during my analysis have I neglected to take these conditions into account. Finally, my article is far from an in-depth study and certainly does not exhaust the topic. Nevertheless, I think it has its value because the relations between such giants as Kulish and Shevchenko give rise to material which is both interesting and exciting. There is little in the history of human relationships that is equally fascinating and, in the history of our cultural renaissance there is perhaps nothing to equal it. In addition, in the relationship between Kulish and Shevchenko, the poet's attractive, expansive, brilliantly intelligent, generous, stormy and sincere, simple and genial nature was reflected as sunlight in a drop of water and in this year's anniversary celebrations I hope that my modest article will be regarded as a 'kind and quiet word' in his memory.

'Where and how Kulish and Shevchenko first became acquainted is unclear,' wrote O. Hrushevsky in his article 'Shevchenko i Kulish' in the

Shevchenkivskii zbirnyk published in St Petersburg in 1914. In two articles by Kulish, however ('Vospominaniia o N.I. Kostomarove,' November 1885, no. 13, and 'Zhyzn Kulisha,' *Pravda*, 1868) we find clear indications as to where and how they met. Until very recently the date of the event described by Kulish in the above articles was unknown, but now, on the basis of new material, V. Petrov has been able to ascertain it exactly.[8] Kulish and Shevchenko became acquainted sometime between the spring of 1843 and 29 June of that year. As to where and how they met, there is no reason why Kulish's description cannot be regarded as an account of what really happened. O. Hrushevsky and his predecessor O. Konysky, although not discounting this description, thought it necessary to interpret it completely unconvincingly in a way that does not agree with Kulish's story. The article 'Zhyzn Kulisha' in *Pravda* of 1868 is thought to have been written by Kulish. It is now time to confirm its authorship. The reason for this assertion, besides the fact that the article is written in Kulish's inimitable style, is the conviction that at the time 'Zhyzn Kulisha' appeared in *Pravda* there was no critic except Kulish himself who could have delivered such a just and faithful evaluation and would have treated his subject with due respect. Therefore, even if it were shown that the original manuscript was not in Kulish's hand, there would still be no doubt that Kulish had dictated it.

Kulish describes the meeting thus (we quote from 'Vospominaniia o Kostomarove'):

As I was sitting at my easel, immersed in the play of lines, tones, and colours, there appeared before me the as yet unfamiliar figure of Shevchenko, in a canvas coat and a cap of the same material which he wore like a Cossack hat on the back of his head. 'Guess who?' were Taras's first words, delivered in that enchantingly gay and carefree voice which so attracted women and children to him. I replied, 'Shevchenko.'

'Himself,' said Taras, laughing the way our young women do. At that time he had no mustache and his face had a markedly feminine quality. 'Do you have any *horilka?*' were his next words.

Another version of this story, which appeared in *Pravda*, goes as follows:

A man in a canvas coat came to see Kulish.
'Good day. Guess who?'
'Who if not Shevchenko?' (I had never even seen a portrait of him.)
'Yes – he! Do you have any *horilka*?'

Does either version invite any doubts? It seems not. Even before their first meeting, Kulish and Shevchenko knew of one another. Shevchenko's behaviour during the meeting is quite in character. Indeed, the meeting is so clearly and masterfully described that in reading about it we have the impression of being present during the conversation.... Kulish's story, therefore, remains the definitive account of the meeting. It is true that the two versions of the story are somewhat different. In the later version (1885) Kulish pays more attention to other people's impressions (for example, Kostomarov's, his mother's, and those of 'the faithful Thomas'), at the same time weaving in his own warm and heartfelt comments.

And it was such a 'Hanzha Andyber' that I introduced to my learned and intrigue-loving friend.[9]
    At first, Shevchenko's mannerisms, suggestive of a Zaporozhian cynicism, irritated Kostomarov. However, they soon worked out a *modus vivendi* and Kostomarov even liked to parody the well-known song about Nechai, adapting it to Shevchenko:

Kozak Taras, kozak Taras
Na to ne vvazhaie,
Sydyt movchky konets stola
Z chaiem rom kruzhaie.

Cossack Taras, Cossack Taras,
Takes no heed of that
Silently sitting at the table's end
He stirs his rum and tea.

As for Tatiana Petrovna and the faithful Thomas, they were fast friends of Cossack Taras from the time he made his first joke, sang his first song (he was constantly happy then, and used to hum while he talked), from the time they first heard his laugh, in which his naïve soul, sympathetic to all that was honest, beautiful, and

exalted, was reflected. Such was the last Ukrainian minstrel, whom I left in Kiev
with Kostomarov before continuing on to Petersburg, so mysterious and attractive
to the provincial.

Later, Kulish thinks it necessary 'to add immediately that underneath the
"outer clothing" in which Taras loved to parade before people, he wore
another habit, black in colour.' He acknowledges Shevchenko's influence
on himself and Kostomarov: 'his words infected us ... Our youthful hearts,
in a state of peaceful bliss as a result of the influence of Russian learning
and poetry, were wounded by these unknown creators of paradoxes who
are to be found in Konysky's chronicle – the renowned *Istoriia Rusov* (A
History of the Russes). Shevchenko, who had been brought up on Konysky, exacerbated this wound ...' And further on: 'Shevchenko's store of
sarcasms, anecdotes, and refrains at the expense of the unfortunate Great
Russians, whom we had so severely deprived of a share in the "patri-
mony" of the Rurykides and Romanovs, was inexhaustible.' There are
many factual mistakes, or at least misunderstandings, to be found in the
above quotations from Kulish's memoirs. Shevchenko's meeting with
Kostomarov, strictly on the basis of the latter's and Shevchenko's testimony, took place without the mediation of Kulish, who was in Petersburg
at the time. 'I met Kostomarov last spring in Kiev,' was Shevchenko's
reply during the Third Division interrogation. Kostomarov in his article
'P.A. Kulish i ego poslednaia literaturnaia deiatelnost' (P.A. Kulish and
his latest literary output) wrote: 'Kulish and Shevchenko did not participate in the conversations which took place in January 1846; Kulish was
in Petersburg at the time, and I was not yet acquainted with Shevchenko.'[10]
Kostomarov says exactly the same thing about his acquaintance with
Shevchenko in his well-known *Avtobiografiia* (Autobiography) ...

Kostomarov himself, in his earliest reminiscences about Shevchenko,
also related that he first met Shevchenko in the spring of 1845.[11] This may
have occurred during Kostomarov's stay in Kiev, that is, after the exami-
nations in Rivne and before his departure for the province of Voronezh,
and if this is the case it is conceivable that Kulish, Kostomarov, and
Shevchenko came together then. But Kulish's account of Kostomarov's
inviting him to an 'Homeric repast' at which Kostomarov's mother was
'priestess of the revelry' when 'the beautiful Little Russian autumn covered

the hills of Kiev' is contradicted by the facts as put forward in Kosto-marov's *Autobiography*. It is reasonable to suppose that the meetings between Kulish, Kostomarov, and Shevchenko took place in the spring of 1845 before Kostomarov's departure for Voronezh province, or following his return (in August), but the 'Homeric repast' could not have taken place at that time.

It is impossible to resolve all these contradictions at present. We must, however, assume that the atmosphere of friendly concord (which resounded with the 'sarcasms, anecdotes, and refrains' of Shevchenko) described by Kulish in his reminiscences about Kostomarov can be taken only as referring either to the end of 1846 or the beginning of 1847 between mid-December, when Shevchenko returned from an official journey, and the 9th of January, when he left for Borzenshchyna. Konysky, describing the meeting in Hulak's home on the first day of Christmas, 1846, includes Shevchenko and Kulish among those present. But there is no mention of Kulish's presence at this unfortunate meeting (the student Petrov eavesdropped on the conversation) in Kostomarov's *Autobiography*.[12]

To admit that Kulish's description of the meetings between Shevchenko and Kostomarov may refer to the spring of 1845 is not to admit also that Kostomarov's mother was in Kiev at the time. This forces us to regard Kulish's account as referring to the end of 1846 or the beginning of 1847. Before Kulish set out abroad with his wife and V. Bilozersky, one of their mutual friends gave him a manuscript of the *Knyhy bytiia ukrainskoho narodu* (Books of Genesis of the Ukrainian People) and Shevchenko's uncensored poems. 'Before we reached Warsaw in the mail coach,' writes Kulish, 'we all knew Shevchenko's poems by heart and, like Kostomarov, we could have got along without the compromising manuscripts. ... We were almost literally enchanted by Shevchenko. No one valued his glorious verse more highly than I.' These were not empty words, as Kulish proved not only by describing the effect of Shevchenko's poetry on himself and those close to him but by describing the social role of this poetry in 'Istorychne opovidannia' (The Historical Tale):

Shevchenko appeared among these gifted youths with a loud lament for the sad fate of his countrymen and sang: 'Quiet world, beloved country, / My Ukraine / Why have you been plundered / Why, mother, are you dying?' ('Svite tykhyi, kraiu mylyi, / Moia Ukraino / Za shcho tebe splindrovano, / Za shcho, mamo, hynesh?')

For Ukraine this song was the sound of the archangel's resurrecting trumpet. If it has ever been truly said that the heart came to life, that the eyes lit up, and that a tongue of flame appeared above a man's forehead, it was then in Kiev.[13]

No one before Kulish nor after ever spoke so passionately of Shevchenko.

In the second version of the initial meeting with Shevchenko ('Zhyzn Kulisha') after the scene quoted above, we read, 'there began a true "Sich-like gossiping," and then singing (Shevchenko had a beautiful voice, and Kulish knew an enormous number of songs). Later they started going about Kiev, sketching and fishing in the Dnieper ...' There is no further mention of Kostomarov's dislike of Shevchenko's 'cynicism.'

However, Kulish's liking for Shevchenko was tempered by a distaste for his cynicism; he tolerated the poet's capriciousness because of his brilliance. Shevchenko, for his part, did not care for Kulish's aristocratic airs. Kulish was fastidiously clean and wanted his surroundings to be so; he was also meticulously neat and punctual. He had a girlish sensibility – no one ever heard him use coarse language. One might say that a lowly Cossack from the Sich and a well-to-do Cossack from the city had come together. And they were indeed representative of the two sides of Cossack society. Shevchenko represented the Right Bank Cossacks who, after the Treaty of Andrusovo, had found themselves without a commander and under the yoke of Polish oppression. They escaped to the Sich and from there the Haidamaky would attack the nobles. In one of their last forays, on the city of Uman, they killed 18,000 Jews and nobles and consequently desired only one thing – to destroy the nobles with their own arms. But Kulish was a descendant of those Cossacks who had associated with the tsarist boyars, who had built the 'Little Russian Collegium' for Tsar Peter, who had helped Empress Catherine write the *Nakaz* and established *uchylyshcha* in Ukraine in place of the old *bursy*. The former had learned history directly from the Haidamak commanders, and his offended spirit struggled against subjection to the Polish enemy. The latter learned of Ukraine's past from those whose ancestors had never known serfdom, but had stood on the border along with the knightly Lianskoronskys, Pretvyches, and Vyshnevetskys defending Southern Rus', Lithuania, and Poland, and later had freely come to the defence of Muscovy. Their national feelings were equally profound, but Shevchenko was in a state of constant turbulence, whereas Kulish was even then seeking a balance of heart and mind, an equilibrium of desire and obligation (p 236).

I have quoted extensively from 'Zhyzn Kulisha' because I believe that the above passage contains an accurate description of the social factors indispensible to a study of Kulish.

After their first meeting Kulish and Shevchenko began real 'Sich-like gossiping,' going on excursions and sketching and fishing expeditions around Kiev. It was an idyll. But even in this idyllic atmosphere Kulish (who, as Pushkin wrote of Salieri, 'checked harmony by algebraic rules'), looking on as 'immortal genius illuminated a madman, an idle reveller' (for so Shevchenko must have seemed with his 'Zaporozhian cynicism'), must have already felt that 'there is no justice on earth nor in heaven.' Kulish was proud, ambitious, and well aware of his great talents, but he was perhaps, like Salieri, haunted all his life by the bitter realization that he was not gifted with 'immortal genius' as 'a reward for his pains and diligence.' Much later, during Shevchenko's last years, Kulish wrote a letter dated 14 February 1858, in which he suggested that Shevchenko 'write about our history': 'I would do it myself, and it wouldn't be worse than a Muscovite could do, but still my sketches would never be as good as yours. No matter how you write, it always turns out a work of art.'[14] Whoever knows, or rather, whoever understands Kulish will appreciate how difficult it was for him to acknowledge this. With regard to poetry, he felt the same way: 'Whatever I'd write wouldn't be bad, but it would not equal what Shevchenko could do. No matter what he does, it always turns out a work of art.' His pride prevented Kulish from writing poetry until after Shevchenko's death.

'No one valued his glorious verse more highly than I.' Kulish's refined appreciation of Shevchenko's poetry and the wisdom of his advice are evident in his famous letter to Shevchenko. One need only mention the changing of the line 'our bold Holovaty' ('the personage is not important enough nor well-enough known to the people and to historians') for 'our song, our *duma*' which Kulish proposed.[15] But that ability to create works of art effortlessly that had been given to Shevchenko (that 'idle reveller illuminated by immortal genius') was never given to Kulish, notwithstanding his truly great talents, his profound, well-trained intellect, and even his unceasing labour. An impassable boundary, a small step which he could not take constituted the barrier separating the brilliant, tirelessly working Kulish from genius. Was it not understandable that he should feel that 'there is no justice on earth nor in heaven'?

Of course, we must in all fairness admit that Kulish found the strength to overcome the black jealousy of Salieri, to confine his bitterness to the depths of his soul and to conserve his warm, friendly feelings towards Shevchenko. Kulish's feelings were not the usual tepid banalities of friendship. From the moment he understood Shevchenko's real worth ('in my soul I saw the poet, who was indeed the rising sun of poetry only just appearing in the crimson sky, sending out rays of light over the dewy grasses') Kulish felt obligated to watch over Shevchenko 'so that his talent would spread its wings even wider.'[16] This solicitude was expressed in both word and deed. In their plans to travel abroad, he and his young wife, 'intoxicated by Shevchenko's works, [decided] to enable him to undertake the voyage as an artist. ... Kulish's wife was as much of an enthusiast as he and as a sacrifice for Shevchenko and Ukraine gave him her entire dowry (3,000 silver rubles). They wrote to Taras, telling him to get an academic passport and saying that they would supply him with money.'[17] But then occurred the sudden catastrophe of 1847, which 'began the period of persecution of our native language in our own land.'[18] And afterwards Shevchenko's whole life was marked by Kulish's ceaseless solicitude and intelligent advice.

Although he had inherited his grandfather's 'fiery temperament,' Kulish's intellect took precedence over his emotions. Sentimentality and extreme emotionality were foreign to him. He was exacting with regard to his obligations. This exactingness which sometimes seemed to go too far, was also evident in his attitude towards Shevchenko. Kulish's above-mentioned letter to Shevchenko from Petersburg (in 1845 or 1846) illustrates this:

here in Petersburg, I read *Kobzar* and 'Haidamaky' over and over again. I delighted in them and committed many passages to memory, but at the same time I was considerably more impressed with their shortcomings than formerly. Some of these shortcomings result from your carelessness, negligence, and laziness, or similar faults; others from the fact that you have depended too much on your innate abilities and haven't tried hard enough to reconcile your talent with Art. In itself, this is insignificant, but with your God-given talent you could create marvels even more striking than Pushkin's. Your creations belong not only to you and your time; they belong to Ukraine and they will speak for her eternally. This is what gives me the right to interfere in the private dealings of your imagination and creativity.'[19]

The critical remarks and advice which follow this introduction are invaluable to the student who wishes to analyse Kulish's views on Shevchenko's poetry. But this is a topic which lies beyond the scope of the present work. The end of the letter is significant: 'I hope that you will not take amiss my severe criticism of your matchless creations and the emphatic tone of my advice. I beg you not to destroy this letter but to keep it so that in about five years' time you come upon it again, when you have had enough of universal acclaim and your inner being will desire other poetic delights, the delights of a profound awareness of the beauty of creativeness which the public is unable to approach.'[20] Kulish knew that his remarks were valuable and he was aware that the possibilities open to Shevchenko were beyond his reach: 'perhaps they [his remarks] will lead you to thoughts which I could never even dream of.' Kulish also devised a plan to publish Shevchenko's work abroad 'for the Slavic world, with a German translation and a foreword and commentary in German. Then all would praise the name of Ukraine!' When Kostomarov and others refused financial support for this project, Kulish gave his 'Cossack's oath' to publish it 'at his own expense.'

As we can see, Kulish's critical and exacting attitude did not prevent him from understanding Shevchenko's significance and dreaming about his obtaining 'universal acclaim' for Ukrainian literature. In a letter written about that time (23 May 1846) to O. Bodiansky, we can see that he was almost enraptured by Shevchenko's creativeness, how he delighted in its development, and what great hopes he invested in the poet: 'I would like to publish a Ukrainian almanac (try to think of a title). Shevchenko has sent four marvelous poems. He works wonders with the Ukrainian language.' And further on: 'Shevchenko's translations of Psalms 136 and 149 are a brilliant success.' And finally, at the end of the letter:

They are saying wonderful things about Shevchenko. They say he's written a poem, 'Ioann Hus' and many others which the Little Russians already know by heart. I believe you know that he is now in Kiev. He is working for the Archeographic Commission and earning a salary of 1,000 rubles. We should be glad of this because the Commission sends him to various places in southern Russia in order to research antiquities and this should eventually give him a Shakespearean knowledge of people, customs, etc.[21]

Even in Kulish's later letters to Shevchenko we come across many pieces of advice, as for instance in a letter dated 22 December 1857:

I have had a letter from Moscow asking that something of yours be printed in a Moscow journal. Don't worry about this for a while yet, my dear fellow. In the first place, your path to the capital must be facilitated and in the second place, you must be very careful in deciding what to publish and what to hold back. You are now at the zenith of your fame as a writer and you must produce something great. Since 1847 your countrymen have expected great things of you.[22]

This letter begins in a way which shows how highly Kulish valued Shevchenko and how interested he was in the poet's thoughts and opinions on literary matters: 'brother Taras, I include in this post the stories of Vovchok. What do you think of them? Write what you really think, because you are our leading intellect in the entire Ukraine.' The letter of 7 June 1858 from Motronivka is especially interesting in this regard. Here we find not only Kulish's usual exactingness but a great respect for Shevchenko:

What do you intend to do with your poems and *dumy*? Can they not be revealed to the world? Sit down, brother, and put your great mind to work on this, so that all will be as well thought-out as it was with Pushkin, in order that the spiritual pastures of our countrymen may be sown with good seed and not with chaff. ... It is better that you emulate Pushkin in this rather than rely on your native strength. Jealous as I am about your glory and the beauty of our poetic words, I give you this advice in the hope that your wide forehead will receive it.

After this it is hardly surprising that Kulish not only gave Shevchenko advice but sometimes even felt the need for advice from him: 'I have started writing something that no one but I could write either well or badly. If only you were here I would read it to you and you would help me with your good advice. But now I've no one to ask. Everyone is either critical or hostile, or has a lot of book-learning, but, as for someone whose knowledge comes directly from God, like you, my brother, there is no one.'[23] It is not surprising that the very controlled and unemotional Kulish even allows himself to daydream about 'what a good thing it would be if God brought us together – if we could be neighbours for just one year and if we could have Kostomarov with us. All three of us would be the wiser for it.'[24]

Shevchenko with his 'wide forehead' could not avoid realizing the value of Kulish's advice and feeling the influence and moral accuracy of his severe demands. They could do him nothing but good. All his life he sought, eagerly and painstakingly, to hear the truth about his poetry and in the end he came to understand that he would only hear it from Kulish. 'I have completed rewriting and editing the poems I wrote in 1847,' we read in Shevchenko's diary from 18 March 1858. 'What a pity there is no one here to read them to. M. S[hchepkin] is hardly a judge. He is too easily carried away. Maksymovych positively venerates my talent. Bodiansky too. I will have to wait for Kulish. He may be brutal, but he will occasionally tell the truth.'[25] Kulish's judgments and reflections always interested Shevchenko. His attitude towards Kulish's judgments was like that of a student towards a severe and exacting teacher who is feared but respected and whose opinion is sought because its worth is well-known. We find the following entry for 4 December 1857: 'I sent Kulish "The Neophytes" along with a letter. His opinion of my new poem [will] interest me.'[26] For 26 October 1857: 'In his epilogue to "Chorna Rada" (The Black Council), P.A. Kulish writes about Gogol, Kvitka, and me and calls me a great and original poet. Is this not simply out of friendship?'[27] Shevchenko clearly understood Kulish's neurotic egoism. In mentioning that 'he [Kulish] may be brutal, but he will occasionally tell the truth,' Shevchenko adds 'but for all that never tell him the truth if you want to remain on good terms with him.'[28] But the great-hearted Shevchenko was indulgent of human foibles, especially those of his friends, and he responded to warm, friendly feelings in a like manner.

It is hardly necessary, after all the above quotations from Kulish's letters to Shevchenko, to examine in detail Kulish's worries about Shevchenko's interests and all the instances where he was ready to help the poet and in fact did so. For example, there was the sale of his 'landscapes of slavery'[29] which aided the poet financially, but Kulish managed the sale so that 'the

mementoes of your exile, which is sacred to us, will remain not in for-
eigners', but in our own hands.' (It is Kulish's doing that these are now in
Chernihiv in the V.V. Tarnovsky Ukrainian museum.) What is more,
Kulish thought of sending Shevchenko abroad so that he could 'see more of
the world'; it was Kulish who edited (to be more exact, who wrote)
Shevchenko's famous autobiographical letter to the editor of *Narodnoe
Chtenie*. Indeed, it requires an excess of persecutory fervour to interpret as
proof of Kulish's 'brutality' the episode when Shevchenko, on returning
from exile, invited Kulish to visit him at Nizhny-Novgorod in order to
discuss the 'good deed' thoroughly (that is, 'making "Zapiski o iuzhnoi
Rusi" a regular publication, like a journal'), but Kulish found that his
arrival could 'injure' Shevchenko's plans (that is, his return to Petersburg).[30] Kulish in this case demonstrated a good knowledge of current
sociopolitical conditions and a cautiousness which attested to his having
reached a balance between desire and obligation. The need for caution
under these circumstances is hardly debatable.

The close of 1858 saw a certain coolness spring up between Kulish and
Shevchenko. This is reflected in the letters Kulish wrote at the end of 1858
in which he addressed Shevchenko as 'Vy' (whereas previously he had
used the informal 'Ty' – no explanation for this has as yet been discovered), but the tone of the letters remains as friendly as ever. Even these
letters are positive proof that the relationship between the two men was not
one in which Kulish played the role of the cold, superior mentor (as
certain 'interpreters' try to make out). Indeed, the excerpts from their
correspondence cited above convince us of this. Kulish never denied himself the pleasure of making the poet happy and encouraging his confidence
and belief in himself. Thus, in his letter of 10 May 1860, Kulish writes
(using the formal form of address):

I assure you that nowhere in the world will you find admirers more sincere and
sympathetic to you than in Poltava. Here it is not the gentry and the nobles, but
all literate people who regard your *Kobzar* as a priceless treasure. Soon they will
not even need books for they will have committed your verses to memory, and
your poems may even be their prayers to God.[31]

An examination of the development of Kulish's views on Shevchenko's
poetry and an historico-literary analysis of them falls beyond the scope of

this article. Therefore I will simply state that there was no one, either during Shevchenko's life or just after his death, who wrote about him as passionately as Kulish. Even later, there is little to match his writings. There was no one who worked as hard as Kulish in publicizing the poet's national, artistic, and cultural importance. The thoughtful and cautious Kostomarov wrote concerning Kulish's enthusiasm: 'even then [the time of *Osnova*] many of those who respected Shevchenko's talent found Kulish's rapture excessive.'[32]

At Shevchenko's funeral, Kulish delivered a eulogy full of emotion. He said:

you left us one testament, Taras. You said to your faultless muse: 'We were not cunning, you and I; we walked a true path, – there is not a grain of untruth behind us ...' (My ne lukavyly z toboiu, / My prosto ishly, – u nas nema / Zerna nepravdy za soboiu ...).

A great and sacred testament! Be confident, Taras, that we will observe it and will never turn from the path you indicated. Should it ever come about that we lack the strength to follow in your path, should it ever become impossible for us to proclaim the sacred truth without trepidation as you have done, then it would be far better for us to remain silent ...

In the end we do not know the secrets of Kulish's soul, but we can truly say that never during Shevchenko's life did Kulish evince the black emotions of a Salieri. Nevertheless, Kulish did attempt to 'poison' Shevchenko, even though this occurred thirteen years after the poet's death. Therefore, even though the description of the relationship between Kulish and Shevchenko is complete, we must pause to examine this instance of Kulish's enmity towards the dead poet.

The *corpus delicti* is this: in the second volume of *Istoriia vossoedineniia Rusi* (The History of the Unification of Rus), describing popular feeling towards Empress Catherine II, Kulish wrote: 'even in the sorrowful songs of the ruined Sich they retained a filial respect for her; there she is the Great World our Mother and not at all the figure Shevchenko's half-drunk Muse made her.'[33] To this brutal remark Kulish added an extensive comment in which he said, 'I know that these words will put their author in a bad light. I hasten to say that for the historian, the truth must be more important than the favour of his readers. No one has written more favourably about Shevchenko than the author of this unpolished book, but this has not prevented him from perceiving all the shortcomings of Shevchenko's undisciplined muse ...' Further on, again turning 'to the people's memory of those great warriors against the age-old enemies of Ukraine' (that is, Peter I and Catherine II) he writes:

In that instance Shevchenko, swayed by not at all poetic influences, parted ways with the Ukrainian people. Even 'among the nobodies of this world' he was often more obscure than they. In spite of all his talent he suffered a great deal in primary schooling, where he obtained what may be called, for better or worse, his education. For a long time he took the seat of the destroyers, who, according to the Hebrew original of the first psalm, are those with a bitter tongue, and before their seat there always stood an altar to the worst Olympian. This is a well-known story.[34]

Writers who have referred to Kulish's attack have not explained its real meaning. The majority have confined themselves to expressing their anger and indignation. O. Konysky did not even bother to be accurate when he wrote: 'Kulish threw mud at his illustrious friend's name, calling his muse "drunken." History cannot forgive Kulish this sin "against the soul" [of Shevchenko], although it must be admitted that he was one of those people who are not completely well and who today reject those idols which yesterday they worshipped.'[35] O. Hrushevsky is more willing to express an opinion in this case:

Kulish's famous spiritual crisis is reflected even in his opinion of Shevchenko's work. Kulish began slinging mud at the dead Shevchenko and at his muse. Then came hesitation and explanations of his behaviour. Kulish began justifying himself and taking back his remarks but there again occurred an explosion of hate and mud-slinging ...

Kulish's antagonism to the memory of the dead poet who was once his good friend creates a very unpleasant impression. This enmity obscured the former genuine friendship between the two writers and often when their relationship is mentioned it is only this last shameful episode and the blind, hateful muddying of the dead Kobzar's name that is remembered.[36]

All that is worthy of note in the above tirade is the indication of the link between Kulish's attack and what O. Hrushevsky calls 'Kulish's famous spiritual crisis,' but which I would simply designate as that principled or idealistic quality that made Kulish's attack on Shevchenko unavoidable. Indeed, in Kulish's view it was 'the inevitable subject of our historiography.' B. Hrinchenko, author of the first impartial, unemotional study of Kulish, has also noted this.[37] But Hrushevsky's description of Kulish's later attitude towards the attack he made, and even Kulish's own description of it, cannot be admitted as accurate. True, in time Kulish realized the brutality of his attack and justified himself 'with shame and contrition,' referring to his 'painful condition.' But the excuses were only for the harsh way he had expressed himself; in reality he never 'took back' his 'accusations.' In addition, as we can see from the manuscript of Volume II of *Istoriia vossoedineniia Rusi*, which he had prepared for a second printing, Kulish deleted the comment cited above with its attack on Shevchenko.[38] This, as Kulish himself explained, was done 'for a more logical sequence of ideas and not at all [as some may suppose] so that [and he crossed out 'due to the pressure of so-called liberal journalism'] due to the pressure of journalism, which has made of Shevchenko the spokesman of his race and the poet of his people, I should repudiate my views on this subject.'

In addition, the reverential dedication of *Krashanka* (The Easter Egg, 1882) to 'Taras Shevchenko and Adam Mickiewicz, those martyrs of love for mankind now departed from this vale of sorrows'[39] cannot be considered either as 'a moment of hesitation and explanation' (O. Hrushevsky) or as an attempt 'to atone for his sin' (B. Hrinchenko). Even at the time of the attack, Kulish would not have denied Shevchenko the title of 'martyr for the love of mankind.' In 1874 he would not have refused to 'make room' for Shevchenko 'in the pantheon of our talented countrymen, side by side with Gogol and Kostomarov' as he did in 1885 in 'Vospominaniia o Kostomarove' (Reminiscences of Kostomarov).[40] This is because he never hated Shevchenko. No matter how harsh and brutal his attacks in 1874 and later, to call them 'slinging mud' at Shevchenko and his muse is certainly a polemical exaggeration. This will become clearer when we examine Kulish's accusations alongside similar accusations made by other old friends and acquaintances of Shevchenko's. In the first place, Kulish's accusations cannot even be compared with those made by Maksymovych.

The latter even tried to discourage Maslov from writing a biography of Shevchenko, saying that 'there is so much filth and dissoluteness in the poet's life that a description of it would overshadow all that was decent.'[41] This same Maksymovych who, according to Shevchenko, 'positively venerated' his work and called his creations 'divine,' twelve years after Shevchenko's death regarded them as written 'by a drunken hand' and said of the poet that he was 'untutored in aesthetics and without artistic ideals.'[42] Kulish, even when he called Shevchenko uneducated, added 'an uneducated genius ...'

Finally, let us call to mind Polonsky's description. Shevchenko reminded him of 'a hog in whose heart a robin sang.' Has there not been enough of this sort of thing, and is it not high time to say to all the modern followers of Herostratus who regard Shevchenko as 'merely a drunk and a dissolute' that none of these accusations leaves the smallest stain upon the portrait of this poet of genius? As Shevchenko was in reality, so we accept and cherish him. He was, as M. Novytsky has said in another context, a man to whom nothing human, or too human, was foreign.[43] We have no need of Pavlenkov's icon, that imaginary likeness from the Lives of Famous People series. We are not afraid to admit that he drank and visited the sort of houses that are not spoken of in polite society. He was no Byzantine saint but a worldly warrior, a grown-up child who, throughout his whole life and regardless of his faults, preserved the saintliness of the pure in spirit. Although it is true, as Kulish said, that 'among the nobodies of this world' Shevchenko 'was often more obscure than they,' and, in M. Novytsky's words, that what was human, and even too human, was not foreign to him, in his closeness to this Shevchenko remains completely pure and infinitely, movingly great. That is why the philistines' efforts to categorize him by means of special investigations of, for example, how many times he was drunk in Nizhny or in Petersburg are more offensive to his memory than Kulish's sharp words. For the bourgeois it is shocking to find out that Shevchenko drank too much and visited disreputable places. But the saintly sinner Shevchenko could calmly say to every accuser and every so-called 'defender': 'I will recount every incident and every thought in my life and hide nothing, and then you do the same ...' His very sins and failings are more saintly than the virtues of many 'good' people. May he who is sinless cast the first stone!

In his *Diary*, Shevchenko created perhaps the only completely honest book in existence. Here he recounted every incident in his life, omitting nothing. Let the righteous philistines be still and stop their rejoicing and mockery, and their saying, 'He resembles us,' or 'Thank you, Lord, that you have not made me like him.' For, *horribile dictu*, the peasant son of an enslaved people fell so low as to admit openly that 'we drank a glass of gin each and ate a dozen oysters' (*Diary*, 12 April 1858, p 328);[44] 'alas, it was necessary to abandon the immaterial word and start in upon real work, i.e. a heavy dinner' (18 April, p 330); he drank champagne (11 May, p 337), 'breakfasted heartily' (6 May, p 336), lunched at Dussault's (12 May, p 338), dined at Borel's, and 'sated his passions at Adolphina's. What cynicism!' (16 May, p 340). Let the righteous philistines stop rejoicing and mocking at this, for in spite of it all the pure and unmuddied memory of Shevchenko lives on in the hearts of those who understand the torture of the 'crucifixion' that was the whole life of this great and genial martyr.

Instead of continuing with these useless accusations and justifications of Shevchenko, it is high time to approach the 'oysters,' the 'champagne,' 'the enchanting domestics of Mme Gilde,' the 'drunken gibes' and 'cynicism,' etc. by an analysis of the poet's bohemian life-style. But this by itself constitutes a subject of research which no one has yet studied. Its earliest interpretation, as put forward by Kulish (in his description of the poet as 'a Zaporozhets,' 'representative of the Right Bank Cossacks,' and so forth) cannot be regarded as exhaustive. Kulish must be respected for this, that his accusations and his biting irony were owing not to hypocritical, petty bourgeois moralizing, but to his idealistic and principled character.

(1927)

NOTES

1 Translation of 'Kulish i Shevchenko' in *Panteleimon Kulish* (Kiev 1927).
2 *Perepyska Mykhaila Drahomanova z Mykhailom Pavlykom*, VII (Chernivtsi 1911) 106.
3 *Kievskaia starina*, February 1883, 234.
4 A. Ia. Iefimenko, *P.A. Kulish, kak istorik*, n.p. 'Biblioteka Samoobrazovaniia,' 44 (1904).

5 S.O. Iefremov, 'Bez syntezu,' *Zapysky Istorychno-Filolohichnoho Viddilu Ukrainskoi Akademii Nauk*, IV (Kiev 1924).

6 S.O. Iefremov, 'Bez syntezu' 22.

7 *Ibid.*

8 V. Petrov, 'Shevchenko, Kulish, V. Bilozersky – ikh pershi strichi,' *Ukraina*, I-II (1925) 42-50.

9 Hanzha Andyber was a hero of a Cossack *duma* (ed.).

10 *Kievskaia starina*, II (1883) 230.

11 N.I. Kostomarov, 'Vospominanie o dvukh maliarakh,' *Osnova*, 4 (1861) 48.

12 N.I. Kostomarov, *Avtobiografiia* (Moscow 1922) 195.

13 'Khutorna poeziia' (Lviv 1882) 7-8.

14 *Kievskaia starina* (February 1898) 236-7.

15 *Ibid.* (September 1900) 306.

16 'Istorychne opovidannia,' in *Khutorna poeziia* 22-3.

17 'Zhyzn Kulisha,' *Pravda* (1868) 298.

18 'Istorychne opovidannia' 7.

19 *Kievskaia starina* (September 1900) 305.

20 *Ibid.* 310.

21 *Kievskaia starina* (September 1898) 399.

22 *Ibid.* (February 1898) 231.

23 *Ibid.*, 2 (1898) 230.

24 *Ibid.* 235.

25 'Dnevnik T.H. Shevchenka,' *Tvory T. Shevchenka*, II (St Petersburg 1911) 317.

26 *Ibid.* 296.

27 *Ibid.* 276.

28 *Ibid.* 317.

29 *Kievskaia starina* 2 (1898).

30 *Tvory T. Shevchenka*, II, p 419.

31 *Kievskaia starina*, 2 (1898) 238-9.

32 N.I. Kostomarov, *Istoricheskie monografii i issledovaniia*, XIV (St Petersburg 1863-89) 111. *Osnova* was a Ukrainian magazine which appeared from 1861 to 1862.

33 P.A. Kulish, *Istoriia vossoedineniia Rusi*, II (St Petersburg 1874) 24.

34 *Ibid.* 24-6.

35 A. Ia. Konissky, *Zhizn ukrainskogo poeta T.H. Shevchenko* (Odessa 1898) 237-8.

36 O.S. Hrushevsky, 'Shevchenko i Kulish,' *Shevchenkivskyi zbirnyk*, I
    (St Petersburg 1914) 17.
37 B. Grinchenko, *P.A. Kulish: Biograficheskii ocherk* (Chernihiv 1899).
38 The manuscript is in the Kulish archives of the Commission for Research
    upon Social Trends in Ukraine of the Ukrainian Academy of Sciences.
39 P. Kulish, *Krashanka Rusynam i Poliakam na Velykden 1882 r.* (Lviv 1882).
40 'Nov' 13 (1885).
41 A. Konissky 574-5.
42 *Ibid.* 575.
43 M.M. Novytsky, 'Shevchenko v protsesi 1847 r.' This article was read to the
    Literary-Historical Society of the Ukrainian Academy of Sciences. It was
    published with this section omitted in *Ukraina* 1-2 (1925).
44 All pages [from the diary] are indicated according to Iakovenko's edition of T.
    Shevchenko, *Tvory* (1911) II.

13

Shevchenko in His Correspondence

SERHII IEFREMOV

Shevchenko's journal has shown us the poet in communion with himself, alone with his thoughts.[1] His letters show him as he was in society, among his friends and acquaintances. Even more than this, the letters give added depth to the self-portrait which, with all its charming lineaments, peers out at us from the pages of his journal. In this respect the letters provide us with an even broader image of their author, for whereas the journal encompasses only a short, although most interesting, period which lasted about a year, the letters illuminate twenty years of his life, beginning from the time when he first appeared before the public as, in Kulish's words, 'a kind of heavenly lamp' to the final days he passed in the company of mortals. This forms the poet's true autobiography; granted, it is incomplete, it is made up of fragments, each individual component is fortuitously occasioned, yet it encompasses his entire conscious life, illuminating its authentic features. In his correspondence, hundreds of people as they were seen by the poet pass before us. Events that occurred throughout the entire span of his life are reflected here, sometimes in greater detail, sometimes in more concise form, sometimes merely hinted at. His reaction to those events, his relationships with people, the perturbing thoughts occasioned by one event or another – all this, illuminated by Shevchenko's own innate vision, is to be found in his correspondence.

In his own words he tells various people, in fragments, the story of his life. Simplicity and sincerity of tone, a keen mind and an unusually deep and noble nature – such is the candid image of Shevchenko revealed in these documents. Easily, naturally, without noticing it himself, he wears his genius and with it illuminates those hundreds of people who had the good fortune to correspond with him. And his correspondents were aware of their good fortune. Read the letters of Kvitka-Osnovianenko, Princess Repnina, A. Lyzohub, Bronisław Zaleski, M. Lazarevsky, Ia. Kukharenko, and M. Shchepkin and it will be clear with what devotion these uncommon people regarded the poet even during his lifetime when, as so often happens, the petty considerations of life tend to obscure genius, covering it with the dust of everyday existence. It was not thus with Shevchenko. His brilliant simplicity inspires respect, humbles, illuminates his correspondence with its rays; and they sense this and seem to grow in stature themselves when they write to him. Because of the deep humanity demonstrated on its pages, Shevchenko's correspondence continues to captivate and move the reader.

If Shevchenko's correspondence is viewed in this way, it naturally divides into three cycles which correspond in general to the three cycles in his literary canon, the stages in the development of his poetry. These are: letters from the period before his arrest in 1847, those written during his exile, and, finally, the remaining ones from his final years. ... Within the framework of these sharply defined cycles the image of the poet himself will take shape before us.

Young, happy, trusting, sensitive, energetic, ardent, possessing a great abundance of both creative and the more common sort of pure life force – that is Shevchenko in the first cycle of lettes, '*Received my freedom* from my land-owner ...' are the telling words with which his correspondence begins. And this consciousness of being free completely captivates the young poet and artist. 'I live, learn, bow before no one and fear no one except God – it is a great good fortune to be a free man: you do what you wish, no one will stop you,' he boasts to his brother, Mykyta. His entire life is before him: his brilliant debut in the literary arena; his dreams about Italy, Rome, that magnet for all artists; those companions of superior intellect; a life broad in scope, free of that deadening philistinism. ... In the literature it is often erroneously suggested that Shevchenko was a person of reserved character, that he did not easily or quickly become intimate with people, that he avoided strangers and generally only bared his soul reluctantly. This notion is founded upon the poet's behaviour in exile and clearly applies only to a certain group of people whom Shevchenko had good reason to regard with suspicion.

It is characteristic that in the poet's correspondence, a correspondence spanning a great many years and carried on with a vast number of people, only very rarely do we encounter a negative appraisal of anyone. Moroseness, withdrawal, and aloofness are completely alien to his true nature. On the contrary, few have possessed such an ability to gauge people correctly and to take hold of them so firmly with a mere letter, to give themselves over so totally to feelings of friendship. In Shevchenko's correspondence one encounters whole groups of people, like Aldridge, upon whom he immediately and impetuously bestowed his affections, often, as was the case with Kvitka, without their even knowing, people who were unquestionably worthy of his sincere feelings. Shternberg, Kukharenko, Shchepkin, Hulak-Artemovsky, Iakiv de Balmen, A. Kozachkovsky, Repnina, A. Lyzohub, M. Lazarevsky, Bronisław Zaleski, K. Hern – it is characteristic that almost all these friends in one way or another were involved with art. The majority (Shternberg, Hulak, de Balmen, Lyzohub, Zaleski, Hern) had a special interest in painting. An interest in art, or even a narrower interest in painting, provided the basis for Shevchenko's good relations even with those whose official positions opened a deep abyss between them and the poet. 'You won't believe,' he wrote on one occasion to Bronisław Zaleski, 'what bugaboos ... they seem to me now, it's simply terrible.' Yet art immediately brought him close even to these 'bugaboos.'

Perhaps the beginnings of his attachment to Uskov were born of a shared interest in art. The painter, the artist, in Shevchenko always sought out in another artistic nature those features they shared, the harmonious strings, and trustingly disclosed himself to them. This habit, acquired in his youth at the Academy, made itself felt throughout his life and he was impelled towards people who shared his interest in art, people whom he met perhaps only once in his life. For him, art was often the measure of a man and lack of interest in it such a defect that he was amazed by its absence in people he liked and made specific note of it. 'Strange,' he observes in describing Mostovsky, for example, 'he is a quiet, good, nobleman without any comprehension of beauty.' Danilevsky 'is in all respects a fine man, only one regrets that he is a scholar for otherwise he would have made a true poet.' This is not professional blindness, the narrowness of the specialist. Not in the least. While the divined artistic temperament constituted the basis, the ground, for the initial acquaintance, upon this foundation he developed a strong attachment if he found beneath the interest in art a compassionate and 'noble' disposition. The carefree, artistic, bohemian life, to which our poet was predisposed, which he himself called 'Zaporozhian,' was also predicated upon artistic beauty, upon this tendency to approach people with an artistic yardstick in hand. Yet, how few people from among, for example, the Poltava 'whistle wetters' or the Petersburg '*horilka* brotherhood' earned the poet's deeper affection! And how deeply did he later regret the time and energy he wasted in their company! He knew the value of a person and, although he did not simply shun convivial company, he gave his respect, love, and friendship only to those who, besides possessing a jovial temperament, were truly among the better people of their time, the exceptional persons in a given environment.

Shevchenko began life as an ardent and trusting person and life's broad course opened out before him. Then, suddenly – a catastrophe. He is an exile deprived of his rights. A person who from childhood has hated military men, is in the thickest of military atmospheres, in a stinking barracks and all this in the primitive times of Nicholas I. An artist without a brush, a poet beneath the ever-present heel of a coarse boot. Before, lines, pigments, musical images, that indomitable inspiration – and now parading, lining up, drills in 'loading ammunition,' peremptory 'inspections.' We are told that, thanks to the efforts of various good people, the burden of Shevchenko's military service was occasionally eased, that the poet's complaints are exaggerated, that his situation was not so very wretched or, at least, could have been far worse. There is only the factual sort of truth in this and it does not in the least ameliorate, dull, that terrible contradiction in Shevchenko's life, that unnatural circumstance of mere existence in which the poet of genius found himself.

I offer a few unembellished quotations from the correspondence of that period of exile.

'To look but not draw – this is agony of a sort that only a true artist will understand.' ... 'My fellow soldiers completed their drills, the stories began – whom they had beaten up, whom they had promised to beat up, noise, shouting, a balalaika.' ... 'No one to share a word with and nothing to read – tedium. Such tedium that it will soon drive me to the grave.' ... 'I live, one might say, a public life, mostly in the barracks, go out for drills every day, do guard duty, etc. – in a word, I'm a soldier and what a soldier – enough of one to scare a crow!' ... 'They work me, now an old man of fifty, without mercy for eight hours a day.' ... 'Everything here, beginning with the people, has so sickened me that I wish I could see nothing.' ... 'O save me, or one more year – and I am lost.' ... 'I am poor in the full sense of the word and not only materially – I am impoverished in soul and heart.'

All but an idiot – this is what that accursed exile has made of me. It is now the tenth year in which I have written nothing, drawn nothing, and read nothing; and, if you could only see with what kind of people I have passed these ten years. God grant that you never see such inhuman monsters even in your dreams! And I'm sitting here in their midst, they have me in their power; they choke me without any mercy and I am still supposed to prostrate myself before them or else they will grab me then and there and choke me to death as they would a flea between their fingernails.' ... 'Ten years! my only true friend – it's terrifying even to say, let alone to endure! And for what?'

These excerpts will suffice. An exhaustive treatment of this theme would require a total transcription of his letters. But the letters written during his exile themselves bear witness to the indignation, to those cries of despair and impotence, to the aquiline flights and trammeled wings all of which are there in abundance. In his letters Shevchenko often recalls the fate of other great men who were exiles – Ovid, Dante – and even deduces from this a general law of existence: 'An unhappy lot such as has befallen me, dullard that I am, has perhaps also been that of all minstrels.' If we follow the poet's lead and continue this analogy with world literature, we can assert boldly and without fear of exaggeration that the significance not only of Shevchenko's surreptitiously-written poems (*zakhaliavna poeziia* – the poetry written in exile and hidden from his keepers in his boot) but also the letters from the period of exile have greater depth than Ovid's *Tristia* or *Ex Ponto*. In the depth of their chilling images of life in exile, in the dazzling clarity of their depiction of the barracks milieu, especially in such desolate corners of the land as Orsk and Novopetrovsk, in the force of their indignation and in the fate of the poet himself – a passionate man forced to sink little by little to a 'fish-like cold-bloodedness,' to render himself a 'lifeless phlegmatic' and assert 'the altogether seamy side of the former Shevchenko' – in all these respects Shevchenko's letters perhaps may even be without parallel in world literature. This completely gratuitous maltreatment of a poet of genius, the strangulation of his creative energy, and the squandering of who knows how much potential, these deeds perpetrated by the truly 'evil times' in which he lived upon a man of genius born in the wrong place and the wrong time, this is the greatest of tragedy which confronts us in the letters from the period of exile. There is indeed perhaps no tragedy of comparable scope to be found anywhere in world literature.

But the tragedy comes to an end. Even before this, when only the gentle breath of the 'enchantress, freedom' had reached the agonized and enervated poet, a new tone can already be heard. 'As gold from a fire, as a baby from a baptismal font, do I set forth from my gloomy purgatory to walk a new, more noble path in life.' This is not merely the completion of the earlier cycle from which Shevchenko emerges unvanquished, his character unbroken, but also the prelude to a new and final cycle. 'I am at liberty,' 'I am free' – such wildly exultant and laconically moving exclamations begin several of the first letters in this cycle. Without the slightest affectation, without assuming a martyr's pose or stature, with all possible simplicity and directness, the poet establishes himself in his new life, a life to which he was unaccustomed but greeted with radiant joy upon his return to society from the graveyard in which he had spent ten years of his life. A tremendous effort to regain and make up for all that was lost during those ten years of exile, a new surge of creative energy in poetry and painting, renewed and even new ties, such is the substance of this final cycle.

Yet its tone is uncheerful. Here Shevchenko is no longer that carefree, wide-eyed, ardent poet who twenty years earlier had managed to shake off his master and escape to freedom. His efforts to grapple with the daily concerns of life – to see to his works, to find a final refuge for himself and his solitary heart, to secure the freedom of his kinsmen – these are the things that fill his letters. Here we see him working assiduously on his etchings, taking great pains over the publication of his poetry and the liberation from serfdom of his brothers and sister. But what comes through most forcefully is that melancholic dissatisfaction, that seeking of some sort of haven from his solitude, from an inevitable, bereaved, homeless old age, that concern to provide himself with some safeguard against future illness. The poet could not but have felt that, come what may, the high point of his life had come and gone, that the future would not be rich in happiness or attainments, that for the last time he must take from life whatever it still had to offer. Hence that fervent, purely reflexive care over the selection of a mate to protect himself against the prospect of a solitary old age; hence also those dreams of returning to live in his native land. Having undergone the burdensome trial of seeking 'a union with vile noble blood' in Nizhny

Novgorod, Shevchenko's search for a wife turns in a different direction, he dreams now of

an orphan, a serf, a servant girl. Fame is of no avail to me and I feel that were I to fail to settle down in my nest, it would immediately take me out to Makar to tend the calves [lead me into exile] ... I cannot stay in Petersburg – it will suffocate me. ... The loneliness here torments me. ... I will not be able to bear it and will marry such an ugly woman that it will make even you ashamed.

A whole series of desperate attempts to disperse that solitude unroll before us. Kharytia, Lykera, one Shuliachivna, Vytavska, and finally any sort of 'girl, even a widow, as long as she is from a decent family, not old and prudent,' or simply 'a dark-browed Poltava girl with a turned-up nose.' Thus Shevchenko gradually lowered his requirements, and all in vain: there was his age, and then his surroundings with all their demands and obstacles. So intensely painful had that terrible 'romance' with Lykera been that who can say whether it may not have hastened the poet's final reckoning with life. ... Hence the ardent, uncontrollable desire to find some sort of haven for his homeless, solitary heart, which pours forth in the unusually expressive images of poems such as 'Mynuly lita molodii' (My youthful years have passed), 'Iak by z kym sisty' (Could I but sit by someone's side), etc., in his letters is fitted to actual circumstances and living people.

The letters from Shevchenko's final period are thus the best commentary upon the poetry of that time.

> Svit shyrokyi,
> Liudei chymalo na zemli ...
> A dovedetsia odynokym
> V kholodnii khati kryvobokii
> Abo pid tynom prostiahtys!...
> Abo ... ni! Treba odruzhytys
> Khocha b na chortovii sestri!
> Bo dovedetsia odurit
> V samotyni ...

The world is wide, / There are a great many people on the earth ... / But it looks as if I must stretch out / Alone in a cold, lop-sided house or by a fence! / But, perhaps not! I could marry / Even if it were the Devil's sister! / Else in my solitude I will be brought to madness ...

Is this cry any less desperate than the following from his letter to V. Shevchenko on the subject of his courtship of Kharytia: 'be so kind as to assist me in this matter else I will not be able to bear it and will marry such an ugly woman that it will make even you ashamed.'

Its fragmentary and incomplete nature notwithstanding, Shevchenko's correspondence as a whole provides valuable, and often the only, information about his work as both poet and artist. The scanty information we have about his sculptures, for example, comes from his letters; the sculptures Shevchenko tried his hand at in Novopetrovsk – 'Trio,' 'Christ,' 'John the Baptist' – all perished. Were it not for chance references to them in letters to Hulak and Bronisław Zaleski we would perhaps know nothing at all about the poet's moving efforts to seize any opportunity to work in the field of art. ... Similarly, it is only from his letters that we know of those dozens of Shevchenko's paintings which have either not come down to us at all or are now in the possession of unknown people ('The Monk,' 'The Gypsy,' the water-colour 'Night,' 'The Daughter of a Chiosian Potter,' 'Prayer for the Dead,' a few self-portraits and much, much more). Again much that is known can only be ascertained from information derived from his correspondence, for example the 'Circassian Boy,' which Shevchenko sent as a gift to Countess Tolstoi from Novopetrovsk or his 'Karatausian Landscapes.'

Shevchenko himself lost track of these works and only learned of their fate by accident. In the history of Shevchenko's development as a painter, his productiveness, his strivings for and his superhuman efforts to avoid death in that 'stinking barracks,' the letters provide materials of such incalculable value that their equal is not to be found in any other document. The same can be said in regard to Shevchenko's literary works; in this context as well, dozens of issues can be raised and resolved only with the aid of those threads in the letters leading from him and to him. Let us simply take up the matter of Shevchenko's stories: when, how, and why were they written, what were the poet's intentions, and what did he hope to achieve? To these questions the letters and letters alone can provide answers, for all other documents are silent on this issue. The history of 'Varnak' (The Convict), 'Kniazhna' (The Princess), 'Matros' (The Sailor),

Shevchenko's efforts to have them printed, his plans for his Russian stories, are clarified only by what the poet himself told Osipov, Bronisław Zaleski, M. Lazarevsky, Kulish, and Aksakov. This material alone allows us to trace the course of these pieces and weigh their significance in the light of his works as a whole. But along with many literary episodes and literary views, we also find in the correspondence several cardinal points about Shevchenko's poetry. For example, the question Shevchenko put to Kukharenko in a letter from the first cycle: 'What are we to do, my brother and *otaman*: press on in the face of all obstacles or bury ourselves alive?' For Shevchenko, whose appearance in the literary arena elicited mixed reactions from both readers and critics, the cardinal issue was indeed 'to be or not to be.' His response would determine the direction he would take as a poet in the future. The doubts which he poured out here to Kukharenko were shortly to be resolved in a letter to Hryhorii Tarnovsky: 'They call me an enthusiast, that is, a fool. God forgive them. Let me be even a peasant poet, so long as I am a poet. I need nothing more.' Along with his reply to the unfavourable criticism of his poetry in the poetic preface to 'Haidamaky' (The Haidamaks) the passages from his correspondence quoted above most accurately demarcate and elucidate Shevchenko's creative development at a time when he was still stubbornly seeking his own individual direction and later when he finally discovered this path and planted his feet firmly upon it. Another equally important milepost, Shevchenko's return to poetry after a silence of seven years in Novopetrovsk, would be totally incomprehensible to us without those famous, often quoted words from the letter to Kukharenko written in 1857:

I myself thought that I had grown lazy and indifferent in exile. But suddenly I see that this is not so. There was simply no one to light a fire beneath my old heart, which grief had not quite finished off. And you, my friend, guessed that this was so and took a notion to toss some of these holy flames my way. ... I read your letter over and over, at least ten times, if not more, until not only my eyes but my heart, too, began to cry like a hungry child.

I doubt that this psychological process, this internal stirring, which brought this poet of genius back to literature, could be more simply or more eloquently expressed. In the absence of this laconic but psychologically definitive response to Kukharenko ('you ... took a notion to toss some of those holy flames my way,' 'my heart too began to cry') we might never have discovered the true depth of the creative torment Shevchenko experienced in exile, nor the inner process which led him back to the poetry he had so long shunned. Although Shevchenko never intentionally dwells on his works, referring to them only in passing when the occasion arises, there is scattered throughout his correspondence a wealth of both discerning and profound observations, many flashes of great insight and humanity which instantly illuminate obscure areas and will always serve as the thread allowing the scholar to find his way through the labyrinth of questions relating to Shevchenko's life, literary interests, and works.

Yet, it is not in this connection alone that Shevchenko's letters are of interest. They are worthy of attention from a purely literary standpoint, as a manifestation of a particular epistolary character, as a work with an individual literary style. ... Shevchenko was a regular and diligent letter writer. He wrote eagerly and at length, especially to favourite correspondents such as Lyzohub, Repnina, Kukharenko, M. Lazarevsky, Shchepkin, and V. Shevchenko. Although he did not polish his letters, took no pains with them, was not, as far as we can gather, even in the habit of writing drafts, doing so very rarely and then only on exceptional occasions, nevertheless he unquestionably developed an individual style which was tailored to the individual correspondent. Reminiscence and lyricism dominate in the letters to Kvitka, A. Lyzohub, and Kozachkovsky; reflection, deliberation, philosophical speculation in those to Zaleski; factual material in those to Lazarevsky, Shchepkin, and V. Shevchenko; a playful tone in those to Kukharenko, M. Maksymovych's wife, and Tkachenko. Shevchenko takes the individuality of each of his correspondents into account, selects the style he probably used in his personal encounters with each one, attunes himself to their personalities.

And this style is not confined to business dealings, making various arrangements or factual explanations. Shevchenko can always enliven the business content of his correspondence with a warm lyrical aside or an expression of indignation, offer some recollection as an illustration, embellish this material with philosophical reflection, an apt witticism, and refresh it with a deep, unaffected sincerity. And he generally does this clearly and laconically, without going on at length. Some of Shevchenko's letters can indeed be considered true masterpieces, models of epistolary style, brilliant, many-hued, boisterous. The following is an example of a humorous note to a friend: 'Am sending you two strumpets, both unfinished; won't be dropping in, can't, have no time to idle away, must take a nap. You say that you have some green plants, similar to hops or grapes, in abundance. Entrust some of them to the care of the strumpets' keeper and I, who am no strumpet, will offer you my thanks.' Examples of other types of letters – dignified or thoughtful – can be found, for example, among those to Bronisław Zaleski, one of which (containing a description of the poet's 'castles in the air') Zaleski described thus: 'Just when you were writing to me and creating that beautiful, tender poem about taking up residence in Petersburg, inspiration descended upon you.' Signs of such 'inspiration' are frequently encountered in Shevchenko's correspondence, especially in those letters where the subject is poetry or painting, and an unconstrained, expressive power radiates from them.

There are people whose public activities and personal lives are sharply segregated; they are different in public from when they are alone or with a group close to them. But Shevchenko was not one of them. Emotional candour and an amazing sincerity were fundamental features of his character and informed all his activity, whether of a public or a private nature. He erred and faltered but never dissembled, never postured either before others or himself, never thrust himself forward, never acted a part. So he is in his literary works. So he is in his journal, that most intimate documentation of a great soul. So he is in his correspondence. Shevchenko's letters are an organic part of his creative heritage inseparable from the works intended for public consumption.

(1929)

NOTES

1 Translation of 'Shevchenko v svoiemu lystuvanni' in *Povne zibrannia tvoriv Tarasa Shevchenka*, III (Kharkiv 1929).

14

The Genesis of Shevchenko's Poem 'At Catherine's'

MYKHAILO DRAI-KHMARA

Students of Shevchenko's work are almost unanimous in affirming that he had a very good knowledge of Ukrainian folklore, especially of historical, wedding, and religious songs.[1] In his diary, Shevchenko frequently mentions his fondness for them and quotes titles or snatches of the songs which appealed to him most and which he used to sing. Folk songs also appear in Shevchenko's letters to Kozachkovsky, F.M. Lazarevsky, Kukharenko, and others. Shevchenko's biographer, O. Konysky, relates that 'according to old Petro T. Shevchenko and Bondarenko, Taras loved folk songs, knew "a great many" and was capable of memorizing them instantly: "whenever he hears a new song, he learns to sing it aloud and thus retains it".'[2] Konysky also describes how the Kiev Archeographical Commission assigned Shevchenko to collect folk tales, songs, legends, and stories in Right Bank Ukraine. *Kievskaia starina* published the peasant M. Kyryliach's recollections of Shevchenko collecting songs. Traces of his annotations occur in two of Shevchenko's notebooks, now in V. Tarnovsky's collection, which were seized by the police during their search of the poet's quarters in Orenburg. The first notebook, according to Storozhenko, contains 'about twenty songs and *dumy*.'[3]

Did Shevchenko use Ukrainian folk songs in his own poetry? Undoubtedly he did. As Sumtsov writes, 'many folk songs can be found in the *Kobzar*. Some are quoted almost verbatim by the poet, either from memory or from his notes; others are reworked to a greater or lesser degree and some are only mentioned.'[4] Further on, Sumtsov lists the folk songs included in the *Kobzar*. 'The rewriting of the folk songs "I don't feel like drinking either" (oi ne piutsia pyva-medy), "There is sorrow in the street"

(Na ulytsi neveselo), and "At Catherine's" (U tiiei Kateryny) dates from
1848.'[5]

According to Sumtsov, therefore, Shevchenko's poem 'At Catherine's' is
a reworked folk song. 'Shvachka' is of course another such reworking. It
was written in 1848 in remote and sparsely inhabited Kos-Aral, where
there was nothing to read but the Bible. Shevchenko notes in his diary that
one day, while taking a walk in the garden, he quietly sang the Haidamak
song 'Shvachka the Cossack is journeying through Ukraine' (Oi poizzhaie
po Ukraini ta kozachenko Shvachka).[6] Evidently the origins of Shevchenko's poem must be sought in the song mentioned in his diary. But
there is no parallel for 'At Catherine's' in Shevchenko's notebooks or in his
diary. We must, therefore, suppose that he had memorized the folk song
that is the basis of 'At Catherine's.'

What kind of song is this and how did Shevchenko rework it? I. Franko
believes that the original is 'The Three-Leaved Herb' (Troizillia), which
dates probably from the fourteenth, and certainly not later than the seventeenth centuries. 'Everyone acquainted with Ukrainian literature knows
Shevchenko's clever little poem that begins with the words "Catherine's
house has a wooden floor",' writes Franko. 'The poem has been further
popularized by Lysenko's beautiful musical setting. But perhaps not
everyone knows that in composing this poem, in which he wished to
characterize the Cossack's depth of feeling and persistence in attaining his
goal and, lastly, his pride, which does not tolerate falsehood, Shevchenko
made use of one of the most popular Ukrainian folk songs, which is
familiar to researchers as the song about the three-leaved herb.'[7] One of the
most complete versions of this song is found in Ia. Holovatsky and three
(A, B, and C) in B. Hrinchenko.[8] By combining the first two versions and
at times adding to them from others, Franko recreates a text similar to the
original. Further on, Franko examines the versions which make up his
composite text and it becomes evident that the Ukrainian versions generally
have no introduction; this has been preserved only in the written Galician
versions. Returning to Shevchenko's reworking of the song, Franko notes
that Shevchenko changed the main theme – the quest for the three-leaved
herb – to a task in a purely Cossack spirit: Catherine proposes that the
Cossacks free her brother from a Tartar prison. Two of the Cossacks die in
this perilous undertaking but the third frees the prisoner and, on their
journey together from Crimea to Ukraine, incredibly, he does not ask
whether this man really is Catherine's brother. Not until they arrive at her

house and Catherine admits that he is not her brother but her lover does the enraged Iaroshenko behead her. The motivation for this killing is no better than for the one that occurs in the folk song, although the change of the motif from finding the three-leaved herb to the freeing of the Cossack testifies to Shevchenko's lively poetic sensibility.

Our task is to discover just how Shevchenko reworked the old Ukrainian folk song 'The Three-Leaved Herb.' This is very difficult because Shevchenko's use of folk songs was masterful. In Sumtsov's words, 'he brings them [folk songs] into close contact with his own creativeness to such degree that sometimes it is hard to tell where what has been borrowed leaves off and where his own writing begins. In this respect Shevchenko and the people are linked by an indissoluble unity of thought and sentiment.'[9]

The matter would be much simpler if we knew which version of 'The Three-Leaved Herb' Shevchenko used. But, as I have already mentioned, this version is not to be found anywhere in Shevchenko's papers. True, its first few lines occur in 'Maryna,' which was also written in Kos-Aral in 1848 (contained in the song which the half-mad Maryna sings, and also in 'Hamaliia'). Franko's composite version is unsatisfactory, if only because it is based upon just two versions. Thus, the need arises to consider all the known versions of the song about the three-leaved herb, even the incomplete ones, because any one of them may contain a parallel, even if an insignificant one, to Shevchenko's poem. I have examined sixty versions of this song.[10]

When we compare Shevchenko's poem with Franko's composite version and with all the versions of 'The Three-Leaved Herb' it is evident where the difference between them lies. The theme of obtaining the three-leaved herb does not occur in Shevchenko; it is replaced by another – freeing the Cossack from a Tatar prison. Shevchenko might have taken this theme from the *dumy*, with which he was well acquainted.

This theme is also present in Shevchenko's earlier poems, for example, in 'Hamaliia' (1842), where the Otaman Hamaliia frees his fellow Zaporozhtsi from Turkish captivity. Almost identical phrases occur in both poems: (1) two lines from 'The Three-Leaved Herb,' (2) the line 'to free his brothers from Turkish imprisonment' ('Iz Turetskoi nevoli brativ vyzvoliaty' / 'Hamaliia') can be equated with 'He frees the brother ... from cruel bondage' (Z liutoi nevoli ... brata vyzvoliaie / 'At Catherine's'). But Shevchenko retained the main theme of the punishment of the deceitful girl or the 'bloody punishment for the violation of a freely-given word' (from the title of one version). The introduction, which has been preserved only in Galician manuscripts (in Wacław z Oleska and Holovatsky it takes up the first fifteen lines) is missing in Shevchenko. This is quite under-standable because Shevchenko, naturally, was familiar with a Ukrainian version of the song. Because the theme of the quest for the three-leaved herb does not occur in Shevchenko, no mention is made, either, of the girl's illness. This also explains why his poem does not contain the con-versation with the mother, the cuckoo's song, the wedding, the musicians, the dancing, the wine, etc. The episode of the three horses, which is found in almost every version, was not used by Shevchenko, perhaps because it would have given the poem an excessively slow, epic character and would have retarded the extremely tense and dramatic action.

In no version of 'The Three-Leaved Herb' is the girl's name Catherine. She is usually called Marusia, or Marysia in the Galician versions. In one version she is called Marichka, and in two others Hannusia. Of course, Shevchenko deliberately changed Marusia to Catherine. This name occurs frequently in his poems, and especially in 'Catherine' (Kateryna) and 'The Soldier's Well' (Moskaleva krynytsia). The epithet 'black-browed Catherine' which occurs in 'At Catherine's' is also found in these two poems.

In every version of 'The Three-Leaved Herb' the three Cossacks who visit the girl are nameless. In Shevchenko they have names:

Odyn Semen Bosy
Druhyi Ivan Holy,
Tretii, slavnyi vdovychenko,
Ivan Iaroshenko.

The first is Semen Bosy, / The second Ivan Holy, / The third, a widow's famous son, / Ivan Iaroshenko.

The name Semen is perhaps linked to

Polkovnyka khvastovskoho,
Slavnoho Semena,

The Khvastiv colonel's, / The famous Semen's,

of whom the poet wrote in Kos-Aral, perhaps a few weeks or even a few days before writing 'At Catherine's.' Ivan Holy could possibly be linked to Ivan Holyk, hero of a Ukrainian folk tale.... To this name Shevchenko twice adds 'a widow's famous son.' The phrase 'the widow's son' occurs frequently in Shevchenko's poetry and, moreover, in the Kos-Aral poems of 1848. From A. Lazarevsky's accounts we know that Shevchenko was fond of singing a song which is a shorter version of the well-known *duma* about the widow's son Ivan Konovchenko. It could be that the naming of Ivan Iaroshenko, like other widows' sons in the Orsk and Kos-Aral poems, was inspired by the hero's name in the old Ukrainian *duma*.

What, apart from the main theme, did Shevchenko derive from 'The Three-Leaved Herb'? First of all, the beginning of the poem, which we find in Maryna's song in the poem 'Maryna' and the song of the Cossacks in 'Hamaliia.' In the poem 'At Catherine's' these are the opening lines:

U tiiei Kateryny
Khata na pomosti
Iz slavnoho Zaporozhzhia Naikhaly hosti.

Catherine's house has a wooden floor, / Her guests / Are renowned Zaporozhtsi.

In Maryna's song:

Khata na pomosti
Naikhaly hosti.

A house with a wooden floor, / Guests have arrived.

In the song of the Cossacks:

U Turkeni po tim botsi,
Khata na pomosti.
     Hai, hei! More, hrai,
     Revy, skeli lamai!
Poidemo v hosti.

The Turkish woman across the sea / Has a house with a wooden floor, / Hai, hei! Roar, sea, / Rage, break down the cliffs! / We shall go and visit.

In 'The Three-Leaved Herb':

U Marusi khata na pomosti,
Pryikhaly try kozaky v hosti.

Marusia has a house with a wooden floor, / Three Cossacks have come to visit.

A v Marusy khata na p'omosti
Do Marusi naiekhali hostsi.

Marusia has a house with a wooden floor, / Guests have arrived at Marusia's.

Other versions repeat exactly the same thing with minor changes. Shevchenko, therefore, borrowed from the folk song not only its parallelism but also its syntactic constructions, individual expressions, words, and even the rhyme 'pomosti-hosti.'

Three Cossacks figure in Shevchenko's poem. Similarly, there are three Cossacks in most versions of 'The Three-Leaved Herb.' In approximately twenty versions, there is only one Cossack, and in two versions only two Cossacks are mentioned (two Cossacks stand beside Marysia, and upon the embankment – three hundred; / dva kozaky kolo Marysi stoiat, a na pryspakh – trysta).

Franko's composite version also contains three Cossacks. There is no question that the versions containing only one or two Cossacks are of later, mostly western Ukrainian origin. The conversation of the Cossacks in Shevchenko's poem is longer than in the folk song, but in both, the actual words are preceded by: 'The first says,' 'The second says,' and 'The third says.' In Shevchenko we read:

Odyn kazhe: 'Brate!
Iakby ia bahatyi,
To oddav by vse zoloto
Otsii Kateryni
Za odnu hodynu.'
Druhyi kazhe: 'Druzhe!
Iakby ia buv duzhyi,
To oddav by ia vsiu sylu
Za odnu hodynu

Otsii Kateryni.'
Tretii kazhe: 'Dity!
Nema toho v sviti,
Choho b meni ne zrobyty
Dlia tsiiei Kateryny
Za odnu hodynu.'

The first says: 'Brother, if I were rich / I would give all my gold / For but one hour with Catherine.' / The second says: 'Friend, if I were strong / I would give all my strength / For but one hour with Catherine.' / The third says: 'Children, there is nothing / I would not do / For but one hour with Catherine.'

And in Franko's composite version:

Ieden kazhe: 'Oi, temnaia nichka!'
Druhyi kazhe: 'Oi, bystraia richka!'
Tretii kazhe: 'Khot-sia konia zbudu,
A v divchyny na vecheriu budu.'

The first says: 'Oh, the night is dark!' / The second says: 'Oh, the river is swift!' / The third says: 'Though I lose my horse, / I'll be at the girl's for supper.'

This formula is repeated in most versions of 'The Three-Leaved Herb.'
After the Cossacks' conversation, Catherine addresses the third, who has vowed to do anything for her, and proposes that he free her brother from a Tatar prison, adding:

Khto ioho dostane,
To toi meni, zaporozhtsi,
Druzhynoiu stane!

Whoever rescues him, Zaporozhtsi, / Shall be my mate.

In Franko's composite version the mother turns to the Cossacks with these words:

Kotryi kozak troizillia distane,
Toi z Maruse do shliubonku stane.

The Cossack who brings back the three-leaved herb / Shall marry Marusia.

In most versions these words are spoken by the girl:

Oi khto meni trii-zillia dostane,
To toi meni druzhynoiu stane.

Oh, he who brings me the three-leaved herb / Shall be my mate.

There are nine versions which repeat the lines quoted above almost word for word, and twenty-nine versions which repeat them with minor changes. Franko's version only shares rhymes with Shevchenko's poem (dostane-stane), and Kvitka's version, which has been cited above, like the other thirty-eight versions, not only shares that but also its syntactic construction, along with certain words and phrases. Shevchenko's last two lines (if we ignore the word 'zaporozhtsi') completely coincide with Kvitka's second line and with those in the other thirty-eight versions.

We must also note that the rhymes (dostane-stane) are often repeated even in the Cossack's reply (dostanu-stanu). The quoted lines in which these rhymes occur are so much a part of folk poetry that they are preserved even in the Hutsul 'kolomyika-metre' versions, which are very different from the original version of 'The Three-Leaved Herb.' It is not surprising, therefore, that the lines ending in 'dostane-stane' are retained in Shevchenko's poem.

In the passage describing the girl's death, the folk song for the most part uses parallelism. In Franko's version we have:

Na horodi makivka brenila,
To Marusi holovka zletila.

The poppies rustled in the garden, / And Marusia's head fell to the ground.

Other versions of 'The Three-Leaved Herb' use a similar image to convey the action and the poppies are replaced variously by the lily, the grass, the grove, the grave, the water, the wind, lightning, the sword, etc. But hardly a version omits a description of the girl's head being severed from her body. In Shevchenko this moment is described as follows:

... i Katryna
Dodolu skotylas
Holovonka.

... and down fell / Catherine's head.

In this case Shevchenko has not used the parallelism of the folk versions, but retained only the basic event that occurs in every version of 'The Three-Leaved Herb.'

The conversation of the Cossacks begins with the words:

Zizdyly my Polshchu
I vsiu Ukrainu.

Through Poland / And all of Ukraine we travelled.

In 'The Three-Leaved Herb' the Cossack usually rides to the sea, crosses it, and digs up the herb. Sometimes the sea is replaced by or figures along with the Danube, the Black Mountain (Chornohora), or simply 'the field.' Poland is mentioned in Zhytetsky's version, but it is perhaps impossible to link this to Shevchenko's poem because in the first place, this is a unique occurrence; in the second place, its origin is remote; and in the third place, because the name Poland could easily have been incorporated into the song at a later date.

I have already noted that Shevchenko developed and expanded the Cossacks' conversation. Yet in certain versions of 'The Three-Leaved Herb' one can already see the original form which was developed in Shevchenko's poem. Consider, for example, the third Cossack's statement. In Shevchenko's poem he says:

'... Children, there is nothing
I would not do
For but one hour with Catherine.'

In one version he says:

Tretii kazhe: shcho khochesh, dostanu
A z toboiu do shliubonku stanu.

The third says: I will bring back what you want, / But I will marry you.

The third Cossack's reply in this version corresponds to the reply in Shevchenko. Therefore we may suppose that this did not originate with Shevchenko but that he borrowed the idea from the folk song.

    The conversation of the three Cossacks who are ready to give all for 'but one hour' with Catherine is in fact a romantic stereotype. This method of representing the feelings of people in love can be found not only in the best romantic writers but also in second- and third-rate ones. ... The act of saddling the horses, which Shevchenko describes thus:

> Razom povstavaly,
> Konei posidlaly, –

Together they arose / And saddled their horses, –

is, in the folk song:

> Oi pishov vin do staienky
> Konyka sidlaty.

Oh he went to the stable / To saddle his horse.

> Ta stav zhe vin konyka sidlaty.

He began to saddle his horse.

> Oi osidlav ia konyka ta pishov horamy.

Oh I saddled my horse and rode off through the mountains.

Several other examples exist which show that Shevchenko could also have transferred this description to his poem.

    In spite of its being an imitation or rewriting of a folk song, Shevchenko's poem has its own unique rhythm. 'The Three-Leaved Herb' is written mainly in ten-syllable metre (a five-foot trochee with a caesura following the second foot, as in the Serbian *deseterci*. It belongs to the type of rhythmical song in which the theme of family life predominates, and the historical flavour is somewhat weaker than in twelve-syllable songs.

Of the sixty versions I have examined, forty-five use the ten-syllable metre, ten use the fourteen-syllable or *kolomyika* metre, and five have no specific metre. As for the fourteen-syllable metre, it is generally found in western Ukrainian, and especially in Hutsul versions which, as we have already noted, developed very differently from the original Ukrainian folk song.

Shevchenko's poem also contains the fourteen-syllable metre [(8+6)+(8+6)]. True, it sometimes changes – in both the first and second parts of the above formula (6+6) appears occasionally instead of (8+6) – and sometimes the two sections are divided by one four- or three-foot trochee. But this makes no significant difference. Any discussion of whether Shevchenko took the fourteen-syllable metre from western Ukrainian versions of 'The Three-Leaved Herb' is unnecessary, for this metre is in any case usual for Shevchenko; it is found in more than half of his poems.

Shevchenko uses no specific metre in his poetry. 'At Catherine's,' for example, is written in folk metre and occasionally uses the seven-syllable trochee with a caesura following the fourth foot; however, it contains few 'pure' trochees, and iambs appear as well as trochees.

In the first verse, for instance, the first two lines exhibit a trochaic tendency, but in the last two lines iambs appear along with trochees:

$$\smile\smile\overset{\shortmid}{\smile}\smile\smile\,\cancel{\smash{\overset{\shortmid}{\smile}}\,\smile}\,\big|$$
$$\overset{\shortmid}{\smile}\smile\smile\smile\overset{\shortmid}{\smile}\smile$$
$$\smile\overset{\shortmid}{\smile}\smile\smile\smile\smile\overset{\shortmid}{\smile}\smile$$
$$\smile\overset{\shortmid}{\smile}\smile\smile\overset{\shortmid}{\smile}\smile$$

This violation of the fundamental rules of versification is closely bound up with the poet's artistic undertaking. This method has its roots in folk art. We can say of 'At Catherine's' that along with the majority of Ukrainian folk songs, it is rhythmical, but not metrical.

In his poems using folk metre Shevchenko usually rhymes the second and fourth lines. This rhyme scheme is also found in 'At Catherine's.' Contiguous rhymes appear along with interrupted feminine rhymes. Exact rhymes are rare; they are generally replaced by assonances (which are also characteristic of folk songs). There are no internal rhymes in this poem. Shevchenko took certain rhymes from 'The Three-Leaved Herb' (pomosti-hosti, dostane-stane). Alliteration appears as an aid to rhyme

('Druhyi kazhe: "Druzhe!"'; 'zaskrypily rano dveri,' 'Katerynu chornobryvu,' etc.).

Shevchenko's poem contains fifteen stanzas. Most of these are four-line stanzas; a few are five-line. This kind of strophic construction is found in other poems by Shevchenko written in free folk metre. Shevchenko borrowed this as well from folk verse.

As for certain expressions and figures of speech that appear very frequently in 'The Three-Leaved Herb,' Shevchenko borrowed very few, rejecting the rest as needless ballast which would only slow down his scenario and slacken its tension. Not a single epithet from 'The Three-Leaved Herb' can be found in Shevchenko's poem, yet it contains many epithets that characterize Shevchenko's earlier work. The epithet 'black-browed' (chornobryva) is especially noteworthy; it modifies the name 'Kateryna' several times in the poems 'Kateryna' and 'The Soldier's Well.' There are no similes in 'At Catherine's.'

We have already quoted an example of parallelism that occurs both in the first stanza of Shevchenko's poem and in 'The Three-Leaved Herb.' As an example of repetition, we can point to 'Arise, arise, Catherine' (vstavai, vstavai, Kateryno). There is no parallel example in 'The Three-Leaved Herb,' but there are many analogous examples where the imperative verb is repeated, for example, 'Cease, cease digging up the three-leaved herb' (Kydai, kydai trokh-zilia kopaty). There are many similar instances in other folk songs, for example, in 'The Cooper's Daughter' (Bondarivna): 'Flee, flee, cooper's daughter, misfortune will befall you' (Tikai, tikai, Bondarivno, bude tobi lykho). The words 'the first,' 'the second,' and 'the third' appear three times in Shevchenko's poem. The same words are also repeated two or three times in many versions of 'The Three-Leaved Herb.' Other repetitions occur as well.

As to diminutives, only one occurs in Shevchenko's poem, but it is a genuine folk diminutive: 'little head' (holovonka). It also occurs in 'The Three-Leaved Herb'; however, in the folk versions the form 'head' (holova or holivka) is more common. The diminutive form 'holovonka' is on the whole peculiar to folk poetry. This form was used by Shevchenko in other works, among them the poem 'I don't feel like drinking either' (Oi ne piutsia pyva-medy), written in Kos-Aral.

(1930)

Troizilie

Oi ikhaly kozaky z obozu,
Staly sobi blyzko perevozu,
Staly sobi hadonku hadaty:
'Dezh my budem nichku nochuvaty?'
Ieden kazhe: 'Oi temnaia nichka!'
Druhyi kazhe: 'Oi bystraia richka!'
Tretii kazhe: 'Khot sia konia zbudu,
A v divchyny na vecheriu budu.'
Pryikhaly tai staly na dvori, –
Shche sia svityt v Marusi v komori.
'Chy ne vyide Marusyna mama –
Ne tak mama, iak Marusia sama?'
Oi ne vyishla Marusenka z khaty,
Ino vyishla Marusyna maty.
'Ne nochuite, kozaky, na dvori,
Ne zbudite Marusi v komori.
Bo Marusia neduzha lezhala,
Chornym shovkom holovku zviazala,
Iz za moria zilia zabazhala.
Kotryi kozak troizilia distane,
Toi z Marusev do shliubonku stane.'
Pershyi kozak na te zasmiiav sia,
Druhyi kozak za holovu vziav sia,
A ostatnii otak obizvav sia:
'Oi ie v mene try koni na stani,
Ieden konyk iak sokil syvenkyi,
Druhyi konyk iak lebid bilenkyi,
Tretii konyk iak voron chornenkyi.
Oi tym syvym do moria doidu,
A tym bilym more pereidu,
A tym chornym troizilia distanu,
Z Marusenkov do shiliubonku stanu.'
Oi stav kozak troizilia kopaty,
Vziala nad nym zazulia kuvaty:
'Tiazhko tobi troizilia vkopaty,

A shche tiazhshe do shliubonku staty.
Oi ne kopai, kozache, troizilie,
Bo v Marusi vzhe z ynshym vesilie.'
Taky kozak troizilie kopaie,
Nakopavshy na konia sidaie.
Ukhvatylo ioho za serdenko,
Stav na dvori v Marusi zhyvenko.
Prybih kozak, z konyka zlizaie,
A Marusi vzhe i doma nemaie.
Ide kozak iz domu z troiziliem,
A Marusia vzhe z tserkvy z vesiliem.
'Ty, Marusiu, nepravdu skazala,
Svoho slova tai ne doderzhala.'
'Oi ia tebe odnoho liubyla,
Stara maty use narobyla.
Bulab rada, kozachenky, zhdaty,
Ne zvelila starenkaia maty.'
'Oi zahraite, muzyky-organtsi,
Nekhai pidu z Maruseiu v tantsi.'
To ne khmara v hori zashumila,
To v kozaka shablia zadzvenila;
Na horodi makivka brenila,
To Marusi holovka zletila.
'Otozh tobi, Marusiu, troizilie,
Ne zachynai bez mene vesilie!
I vsim bude takaia zaplata,
Kotri zvodiat virnoho kozaka.'

The Three-Leaved Herb

Three Cossacks riding from camp
Stopped near a river crossing
And began to wonder:
'Where shall we stay the night?'
The first said, 'Oh, the night is dark!'
The second said, 'Oh, the river is swift!'
The third said, 'My horse may give out

But I shall be at the maiden's for
      my evening meal.'
They rode up and stopped in the yard,
The light in Marusia's room was still burning.
'Will Marusia's mother not come out –
Or better yet, Marusia herself?'
Marusia did not leave the house
But her mother came out.
'Cossacks, do not spend the night
      in the yard,
Do not awaken Marusia in her room.
For Marusia lies ill,
She has bound her head with black silk,
She asks for an herb from across the sea.
Whichever Cossack brings back the three-
      leaved herb
Shall stand at the altar with Marusia.'
At this the first Cossack laughed,
The second took his head in his hands,
But the third Cossack said,
'I have three horses at camp.
The first is grey as a falcon,
The second white as a swan,
The third black as a raven.
I shall ride to the sea on the grey horse,
The white one will take me across it,
And upon the black one I shall fetch
      the three-leaved herb,
And with Marusia I shall stand at the altar.'
Oh the Cossack began to dig up the three-
      leaved herb
And a cuckoo began to sing above him:
'It is hard for you to dig up the three-
      leaved herb,
But even harder will it be to wed.
Cossack, do not dig up the three-leaved herb
For Marusia is already marrying another.'

But the Cossack dug up the three-leaved herb
And having dug it up, mounted his horse.
His heart had been captured.
Blithely he stood in Marusia's courtyard.
He ran up, and was getting down from his horse
But Marusia was already gone.
As he left the house with the three-leaved herb
Marusia came out of the church with the wedding
       party.
'You, Marusia, told a lie
And you failed to keep your word.'
'Oh it was you alone that I loved,
All this is my old mother's doing.
Cossack, I would gladly have waited
But my aged mother did not wish it.'
'Play, musicians, organ-grinders,
So that I can dance with Marusia.'
It was not a cloud that passed overhead
It was the Cossack's sword ringing.
The poppies rustled in the garden,
And Marusia's little head fell off.
'There is your three-leaved herb, Marusia,
Do not start the wedding without me!
And every one will be thus repaid
Who deceives the faithful Cossack.'

[Ivan Franko, 'Studii nad ukrainskymy narodnymy pisniamy,' *Zapysky naukovoho tovarystva im. Shevchenka* LXXXIII, 3 (1908) 18.]

NOTES

1 Translation of 'Geneza Shevchenkovoi poemy "U tiiei Kateryny khata na pomosti"' in *Shevchenko, Richnyk druhyi* (Kharkiv 1930). For a different approach to the same poem see Rylsky's article in this volume.
2 A. Konissky, *Zhizn ukrainskogo poeta T.G. Shevchenko* (Odessa 1898) 336-7.
3 M. Storozhenko, 'Dvi zapysni knyzhky Shevchenka,' *Nova Rada*, ukrainskyi literaturnyi almanakh (Kiev 1908) 32.

4 N. Sumtsov, 'Liubimye narodnye pesni Shevchenka,' *Ukrainskaia zhizn*, II (1914) 21.

5 *Ibid.* 23

6 T. Shevchenko, *Dnevnik* (Kharkiv 1925) 39.

7 I. Franko, 'Studii nad ukrainskymy narodnimy pisniamy,' *Zapysky naukovoho tovarystva im. Shevchenka*, LXXXVIII, 3 (1908) 18.

8 Ia. Holovatsky, *Narodnie pesni Halytskoi i Uhorskoi Rusy*, 24, I (Moscow 1878) 112-13. B. Grinchenko, *Etnograficheskie materialy*, III (Chernihiv 1899) 234-8.

9 N. Sumtsov, 'Liubimye narodnye pesni Shevchenka,' 23.

10 Drai-Khmara's references to different sources for these variants have been omitted in the rest of the article. Instead, a text and translation of 'Troizillia' has been added (ed.).

15

'O, Why Have You Darkened?'

STEPAN SMAL-STOTSKY

I have already turned my attention to an elucidation of the meaning of the poem 'Oi, choho ty pochornilo' (O, why have you darkened).[1] But as I now consider some of the points made in that study, which I do not have at hand, unfortunately, not to be completely accurate and since I do not find Vasyl Simovych's explanations satisfying, I must return to it again.[2]

In the interpretation of any work, I assume that the usual meanings of words should form the basis for the elucidation of the kernel of the idea contained in them. A more complete explication is possible only in the context of the poet's overall world view as embodied in his works. We should never ascribe to the poet our own ideas, ideas alien to him.

We cite the text of the poem:

Oi, choho ty pochornilo, zeleneie pole?
– Pochornilo ia od krovy za volnuiu voliu.
Kruh mistechka Berestechka na chotyry myli
Mene slavni Zaporozhtsi svoim trupom vkryly.
Ta shche mene haivorony ukryly z pivnochi –
Kliuiut ochi kozatskii, a trupu ne khochut ...
Pochornilo ia, zelene, ta za vashu voliu!...
Ia znovu budu zelenity, a vy vzhe nikoly
Ne vernetesia na voliu! – Budete oraty
Mene ztykha, ta, oriuchy, doliu proklynaty ...

O, why have you darkened, verdant field? / I have darkened from the blood shed for liberty free. / Near the town of Berestechko for four miles around / The famed Zaporozhians with their corpses covered me. / And the ravens from the north, they cover me too – / They are plucking out Cossack eyes but leave the corpse untouched. ... / My greenery has darkened too for the sake of your liberty! ... / I will grow green again but never again / Will you return to freedom! – You will plow me / In silence and, plowing, curse your fate ...

In distant Kos-Aral in 1848, Shevchenko, himself deprived of liberty, reflected upon his entire life and his ideas, and most persistently upon the misfortune and bondage of Ukraine. He recalled everything that he had experienced in 'three years' in Ukraine, his conversations with the people and in particular, their views on the bondage of Ukraine.[3] All this also appeared in his poem 'Oi, choho ty pochornilo, zeleneie pole?'

For he perceived that here on the field near Berestechko, which he once saw, Ukrainian history took that onerous turn in the direction which led to all Ukraine's misfortunes.[4] There 'the famed Zaporozhians with their corpses' ('slavni Zaporozhtsi svoim trupom') covered the field of battle, which forced Bohdan Khmelnytsky to seek protection for Ukraine from the Muscovite tsar, a step which Shevchenko never excused, a step for which he never forgave Khmelnytsky (cf. Rozryta Mohyla / The Ransacked Grave; Velykyi lokh / The Great Vault; Subotiv; Iak by to ty, Bohdane, pianyi / If, drunk, Bohdan, you were to), while at the same time always recognizing the great service Khmelnytsky rendered to Ukraine.

It was thoughts like these that he poured into his short, meditative poem 'Oi, choho ty pochornilo, zeleneie pole?' He tries here from yet another angle to set to rest those 'accursed thoughts' (prokliatii dumy) which so fiercely and constantly 'choked, tore at' (davyly, rozdyraly) his heart and the evidently stupid views of that 'brotherhood' which in the presence of evil 'keeps silent, standing goggle-eyed like lambs: let it be so – it says – perhaps this is how it should be' (movchyt sobi, vytrishchyvshy ochi, mov iahniata: nekhai – kazhe – mozhe, tak i treba).

The simple intention of the poet is to present a conversation between the darkened, verdant field and those who are anxious to know *why* it had turned dark. The field gives the reasons for this turn of events and at the same time asserts with absolute conviction that it will once again be green, but that those to whom it speaks will plow it and curse their fate, for they will never again have liberty.

This is clearly a poetic image. Let us examine it in detail. That the 'verdant field' (zeleneie pole) to which the question is addressed is not merely the actual 'field near Berestechko' (Near the town of Berestechko for four miles around / Kruh mistechka Berestechka na chotyry myli), but that it must also be understood as signifying Ukraine as a whole is shown by the fact that the field 'darkened with blood shed *for liberty free*' (pochornilo ... od krovy za volnuiu voliu), clearly not for the liberty of the field near Berestechko alone but for that of Ukraine as a whole. In addition, the field darkened 'for the sake of your liberty' (za vashu voliu), that is, for the liberty of those who pose the question. These questioners, then, can only be those who perceive or sense the desperate situation in which Ukraine finds herself but cannot accurately describe the causes that gave rise to this situation. This sad situation arose because the field was overrun by 'ravens from the north' (haivorony ... z pivnochi), that is, by Russian soldiers, and this historical event does not only relate to the field near Berestechko. Quite the opposite. From this very fact it becomes apparent that the image of the verdant field encompasses not only all of Ukraine as a country, as a land, but also her history.

Ukraine, then, is viewed here as a verdant field with her physical and moral might in full flower, as in the spring of her autonomous existence as a free nation, a vision of Ukraine which enchants the poet with its freshness and arouses hope for an auspicious future. Simovych sees the verdancy of the field as signifying happiness and nothing more; yet, at best, the idea of happiness has only a tenuous association with verdancy and, as a result, his interpretation is distorted, and even further distorted because from Simovych's explanation it would appear that Ukraine seemingly darkened solely 'from the blood' (od krovy), 'so much of it was spilled there for liberty.' ...

This image of the luxuriant verdancy of Ukraine flickers before the poet's inner eye only for a moment, for in the real world around him is a different image, obscuring the first. Around him he sees the vigour of Ukraine in terrible decline and in the image of the 'darkened' field he paints this state in dark tones (cf. 'chornishe chornoi zemli blukaiut liudy' / 'Darker than the dark earth the people wander' in the poem 'I vyris ia na chuzhyni' / 'In foreign parts I grew up'). Standing as it does in conflict with the usual, natural development of a country, this discordant image touches the poet's soul deeply and prompts him to consider solemnly the causes of such a state (that the verdant field had darkened). In the reply to the initial question he completes his depiction of this decline. Ukraine fell into decline (darkened) (a) 'from the blood' (od krovy), that is, grew physically weak as a result of her wars with Poland for the sake of 'liberty free' (za volnuiu voliu); (b) because her 'famed Zaporozhians with their corpses covered' her (slavni Zaporozhtsi svoim trupom vkryly), that is, because those who were always ready even 'to put their own child to the sword' (svoiu ridnu dytynu zarizaty) 'for honour and glory, for brotherhood, for the country's freedom' (za chest, slavu, za braterstvo, za voliu krainy) were no more (see 'Za dumoiu duma roiem vylitaie' / 'Thought upon thought wing past in swarms); because those who would 'proffer all their paltry belongings and their three sons to wretched Ukraine' (vsiu mizeriiu oddaty svoii Ukraini nebozi i trokh syniv svoikh) were no longer to be found (see 'Buvaie, v nevoli inodi zhadaiu' / 'It often happens that in exile I recall') and instead a degenerate generation had appeared, a generation which was giving its children to 'Muscovite slaughter-houses' (v riznytsi moskalevi), thereby bringing about not only the physical but also the moral decline of Ukraine; and, finally, (c) because of what else occurs – and this lies at the root of Ukraine's misfortune – because 'the ravens from the north covered' her (haivorony ukryly z pivnochi), that is, after the union with Russia, Russian soldiers beset Ukraine like ravens (cf. iak ta halych pole kryie / Like crows they cover the field in Tarasova Nich / Night of Taras) and 'are plucking out Cossack eyes' (kliuiut ochi kozatskii).

Here we must pause to consider the imagery contained in the line 'they are plucking out Cossack eyes but leave the corpse untouched' (Kliuiut ochi kozatskii, a trupu ne khochut). Simovych writes: 'In general these two phrases must be understood in a very broad sense. Where Poland did not deal the final blow (the defeat suffered at Berestechko was very great), then Russia comes in to pluck out the rest, collecting all the glittering remains (the Cossack eyes), all that is still of value, and corpses alone are left in Ukraine.' The misconception here lies at the very surface.

(a) For the antithesis 'where Poland did not deal the final blow ... then Russia comes in to pluck out the rest' does not find even the slightest justification in the text. Even if it is granted that historically 'the defeat suffered at Berestechko was very great,' nonetheless, in Shevchenko's conception, in Shevchenko's world view, in Shevchenko's understanding of the history of Ukraine as a whole, this is not how this event is interpreted. Quite the opposite. In his 'Poslaniie' (I mertvym, i zhyvym, i nenarodzhennym zemliakam moim v Ukraini i ne v Ukraini moie druzhnieie poslanie / To My Dead and Living and Yet Unborn Countrymen in Ukraine and not in Ukraine My Friendly Epistle) Shevchenko clearly agrees that those who boast 'that once we brought Poland down' (shcho my Polshchu kolys zavalyly) do so with justification when he says: 'You are right!' (Pravda vasha!) 'I have burned down Poland with all her kings' (Ia spalyla Polshchu z koroliamy), the Ukrainian raven boasts in 'The Great Vault.' The phrase 'Bohdan stole goods' (Krav Bohdan kram) can also be cited. Furthermore, even in the poem being considered here, it is stated that the field 'darkened from the blood shed for *liberty free*' (Pochornilo ... od krovy za volnuiu voliu) and 'for *the sake of your liberty*' (za vashu voliu), that is, that as a result of the battle of Berestechko, Ukraine gained her liberty. This interpretation of the battle of Berestechko that Shevchenko held is to a certain extent borne out by the facts of history. For subsequently there was the hetman state in which Shevchenko, although only in his poems 'Son' (The Dream, 1847) or 'Nevolnyk' (The Convict, 1848), so delighted; there was 'God's paradise' (bozhyi rai), which the 'half-witted hetmans caused to perish' (nedoumy hetmany zanapastyly), a deed for which Shevchenko reproaches them. It is thus impossible to say 'where Poland did not deal the final blow' for, as has been demonstrated, Shevchenko in fact supports the idea that 'once we brought Poland down' (my Polshchu kolys zavalyly) and this 'once' can only refer to Bohdan and to the battle of Berestechko. As Shevchenko understands these events, in the war of liberation against Poland much Ukrainian blood flowed, many of the famed Zaporozhians fell, but all the same Ukraine acquired that 'liberty free' (volnuiu voliu), that 'your liberty' (vashu voliu) of which the verdant field speaks. Nonetheless, Shevchenko cannot forgive even the 'famed' Bohdan for that union with Russia, and it is to this that the following lines refer: 'And the ravens from the north they cover me too – they are plucking out the Cossack eyes but leave the corpse untouched' (Ta shche mene haivorony ukryly z pivnochi / Kliuiut ochi kozatskii, a trupu ne khochut). It is this union which Shevchenko regards as the source of all Ukraine's misery, as the poems 'The Ransacked Grave,' 'Chyhyryn,' 'The Convict,' 'A Dream,' 'The Great Vault,' 'Subotiv,' etc. testify. Hence, the bleak situation in which Ukraine finds herself is of Russian rule.

(b) Of the 'ravens from the north' (haivorony ... z pivnochi) it is said that they 'are plucking out' (kliuiut), not that they 'have plucked out' (doklovuiut) Cossack eyes and further that they 'are plucking out Cossack *eyes*' (kliuiut ochi kozatskii) and not some other part of their bodies, for this, first of all, is what ravens do and, secondly, it conveys the desired meaning – that the ravens make living, sighted Cossacks, Ukrainians with Cossack eyes, into unseeing, blind men so that they will be unable to perceive that truly sad and 'dark' situation in which Ukraine finds herself (cf. the very similar reflections in the poems 'The Ransacked Grave,' 'Za dumoiu duma roiem vylitaie,' 'Epistle,' 'The Great Vault,' etc.). The phrase 'they are plucking out Cossack eyes' thus cannot be taken to mean that Russia collects 'all the glittering remains ... all that is still of value ...'

In this context, then, what is the import of the concluding phrase 'but leave the corpse untouched' (a trupu ne khochut)? Initially, it should be noted that this cannot refer to the corpses of the famed Zaporozhians which covered the field near Berestechko for four miles around, since here there was not a single raven from the north. Hence, Shevchenko must have had other corpses in mind. But which ones exactly? Who in Ukraine did he regard as a corpse? The answer to this question is provided by Shevchenko himself in the following passages from his epistle 'Shafarykovi' (To Šafařik):

Vyrostaly v kaidanakh slavianskii dity
I zabuly, nevolnyky, shcho vony na sviti. (italics mine)

In shackles were our Slavic children nurtured / *And forgot, these slaves, that they exist on this earth.*

I slavian semiu velyku vo tmi nevoli
Perelichyv do odnoho, perelichyv *trupy*,
A ne slavian ...(italics mine)

And in the darkness of bondage did you count to a man / The numbers of the great family of Slavs, count *corpses* / Not Slavs ...

Trupy vstaly i *ochi rozkryly*.
I brat z bratom obnialysia ...(italics mine)

The *corpses* rose and *opened their eyes*. And brother embraced brother ...

In this case Shevchenko's corpses are those who 'forgot, these slaves, *that they exist on this earth*' (zabuly, nevolnyky, shcho vony na sviti). This applies especially to those Ukrainians whom Shevchenko had to remind of their origins and circumstances by inquiring: 'shcho my? chyi dity? iakykh

batkiv? kym, za shcho zakuti?' (who are we? whose children? of what
fathers? by whom, for what enslaved?)

In his 'Epistle,' Shevchenko writes:

Okh, iak by to stalos, shchob vy ne vertalys,
Shchob tam i *zdykhaly*, de vy porosly!
Ne plakaly b dity, maty b ne rydala,
Ne chuly b u Boha vashoi khuly,
I sontse b ne hrilo *smerdiachoho hnoiu*
Na chystii, shyrokii, na volnii zemli. (italics mine)

Oh, if it could be that you would not return, / That you would croak where you
prospered! / Children would not cry, mother would not sob, / Your blasphemy in
the heavenly domain would not be heard / And in a land unsoiled, broad and free,
no *stinking dung* / Would be warmed by the sun.

Here 'stinking dung' (smerdiachoho hnoiu) taken in conjunction with the
verb 'croak' (zdykhaly) reveals that Shevchenko intended the decom-
posing, stinking dung, that is, the corpses, to signify those Ukrainians
who go eagerly to foreign lands, returning to Ukraine with a wealth of
big words and nothing else, who kowtow as they did before, skin their
unseeing peasant brothers alive, and once more eagerly turn to German
lands, to foreign (i.e., Russian) lands, to contemplate the luminous
truth.

In another instance he also characterized as corpses ('Buvaly voiny i
viiskovii svary' / 'There were wars and military feuds') 'the nursemaids
and servants of a foreign [Russian] homeland' (nianky, diadky otechestva
chuzhoho). After all that has been said it should be clear to everyone what
sort of corpses the ravens from the north *leave untouched*....Thus the results
of Russian rule in Ukraine are explained and the image of Ukraine as a
darkened field justified.

Simovych explains the phrase 'but never again will you return to freedom' (a vy vzhe nikoly ne vernetesia na voliu) in the following terms: 'This
is the most sombre expression of the view to be found anywhere in *Kobzar*
that Ukraine will never again know liberty. Elsewhere (Night of Taras, Do
Osnovianenka / To Osnovianenko; Haidamaky / The Haidamaks) the poet
says that 'the era of the Cossacks will not return' (ne vernetsia kozachchyna), that is 'has passed' (mynulos), etc. – but a sense of hope can be

felt throughout, while in 'Chernets' (The Monk) the poet expresses it clearly, as if weighing it down with a stone! Does this explanation not follow Jensen?[5] We cannot agree with it. For if we are never to have liberty again, what, then, is the meaning of the phrase 'I will grow green again' (ia znovu budu zeleniy)? Quite the reverse of what Simovych suggests is actually the case. In fact, Shevchenko rarely expressed his conviction more clearly that Ukraine would be green once again and, thus would be able to boast of the greatest development of all its physical, spiritual, and moral powers. In this Shevchenko always had an unshakable faith; in this he always placed all his hopes. To these convictions he dedicated all his energies throughout his life, even dedicated his very life. And he never lost faith. Here he also expresses his deep conviction and very forthrightly at that. Furthermore, the statement 'never again will you return to freedom! – You will plow me in silence and, plowing, your fate curse' (... a vy vzhe nikoly / Ne vernetesia na voliu! – Budete oraty / Mene ztykha ta, oriuchy, doliu proklynaty) does not contradict this. For this statement cannot be taken to have a general but only a specific meaning. It is addressed only to some Ukrainians. Thus, only this category of Ukrainians need be precisely identified, this 'you' clearly defined.

It was noted earlier that the 'your' as well as the 'you' encountered in this short meditative poem can only refer to those who ask the field why it has darkened and, hence, to those who perceive the true facts of the situation in Ukraine, but who see poorly enough, are blind enough, still insufficiently acquainted with the reasons for this to need to be told the source of all Ukraine's misfortunes, which is her domination by Russia, by those ravens from the north, Ukraine's executioners. With this in mind, we can identify this group of Ukrainians more precisely. They are those to whom the field says that 'my greenery has darkened too, for the sake of your liberty' (Pochornilo ia, zelene, ta za vashu voliu), that is, 'I darkened from the blood of the famed Zaporozhians so that you too ('ta' in the original) may have liberty!' This was unquestionably the motivation behind the wars of liberation fought against Poland. And not only the motivation. Ukraine actually did acquire her freedom then. But where is it? What happened to this freedom? Why did the verdant field darken? Hence, the 'we' in question here are those who did not know how to protect this liberty and are even amazed that it no longer exists. They are those who 'allowed the heart in them to decay in a puddle, in the mud and into a cold hollow,' that is, 'each into his own heart' (and not into a dead tree as

Simovych believes; cf. Simovych's observations) into a heart from which all genuine love for Ukraine had vanished is thus compared to a cold hollow, 'released serpents' (v kaliuzhi v boloti sertse prohnoily i v duplo kholodne hadiuk napustyly – 'Chyhyryn'). They are those in whose hearts 'living Cossack blood, pure and sacred' (zhyva kozatska krov, chystaia, sviataia – 'Chyhyryn') has ceased to flow. All other considerations aside, they are those to whom the poet addresses his 'Epistle' and 'Kholodnyi Iar,' the two poems most notable in this connection. They are those who *Cossack eyes* have already been plucked out by the ravens from the north so that they cannot even vaguely perceive the true cause of their misery – they are those corpses with their *Cossack* eyes plucked out which the ravens *leave untouched*, etc. And it goes without saying that these 'blind men' will never return to freedom – only those with Cossack eyes, those whose eyes were not plucked out by the ravens from the north, those who recognize the source of their misery – only the *Cossacks* will regain freedom.

Hence Shevchenko's conviction that Ukraine will once again be green. Her verdancy will be restored because of those Cossack eyes which the ravens from the north lacked the strength to pluck out, those Cossack eyes which clearly perceive the cause of all Ukraine's misfortunes. Her verdancy will return because of those green shoots upon the old oak which sprout and develop and then

> ... i bez sokyry
> Azh zareve ta zahude,
> Kozak bezverkhyi upade,
> Roztroshchyt tron, porve porfyru,
> Rozdavyt vashoho kumyra,
> Liudskii shasheli. Nianky,
> Diadky otechestva chuzhoho! ('Buvaly voiny i viiskovii svary')

... and without an axe, / With a roar and a rumble, / The headless Cossack will fall and will shatter the throne, / Tear purple robes to tatters and crush your idol, / O you human woodworms. / Nursemaids and servants of a foreign homeland!

Her verdancy will return, then, because those who fully realize the causes of Ukraine's misfortune are mindful of her liberation from Russian rule *in the Cossack fashion*. It should always be borne in mind that Shevchenko says 'are plucking out' (kliuiut) and this does not mean that the ravens have already plucked out all Cossack eyes: they are still plucking out eyes when the opportunity presents itself. In addition, it should be stressed that the word 'Cossack' (kozatskii) is not superfluous, here not simply the usual epithet, but has a very concrete meaning whose richness derives from Shevchenko's conception of those Cossack ideals which it brings to mind.

The Zaporozhians are always portrayed by Shevchenko as the most idealistic representatives of the chivalric spirit in Ukraine, the most determined defenders of the liberty, honour, and glory of Ukraine, the defenders of truth in general, whose social ideal was equality and fraternal brotherhood. In a word, Shevchenko's Zaporozhians and his Cossacks as a whole embody all the highest and finest accomplishments of the Ukrainian national spirit, all the Cossack ideals, to the realization of which every Ukrainian ought to dedicate his life. The Zaporozhians are Ukraine's glory; their most famed deed was their struggle to liberate Ukraine from Polish domination, the final act of which took place near Berestechko.

As we know, historically this is not totally accurate. Yet such a consideration is beside the point. What is important here is not history but *Shevchenko's ideology* and only from the perspective of this ideology can we correctly understand his poetry.

Still, how are we to explain that 'you will never again return' (ne vernetesia) when only he who has had freedom can regain it? Quite so! Indeed, this is precisely the case with those who converse with the field. Ukraine had liberty and will have it again but only Ukrainians *with Cossack eyes* will regain freedom – those with their eyes plucked out or those who are corpses will *never again* regain liberty!

(1934)

NOTES

1 Stepan Smal-Stotsky, 'Iak chytaty tvory Shevchenka,' *Nasha shkola* (Lviv 1914). This selection is a translation of 'Oi choho ty pochornilo,' by Stepan Smal-Stotsky, in *T. Shevchenko: Interpretatsii* (Warsaw 1934) (ed.).

2 See Taras Shevchenko, *Kobzar*, with commentary and annotations by Vasyl Simovych (Katerynoslav 1921) 302-3.

3 Poems written between 1843 and 1845 (ed.).

4 Berestechko is a town in Volynia, where in 1651 the Cossacks were defeated by the Poles and some 40,000 Ukrainians died.

5 A. Jensen, *Taras Schewtschenko: Ein ukrainisches Dichterleben* (Vienna 1916).

16

Shevchenko and Religion

DMYTRO CHYZHEVSKY

Shevchenko's attitude towards religion is one of the obscure, or rather, one of the most widely debated aspects of his personality.[1] This debate began during Shevchenko's lifetime. In the final years of his life there was even a police investigation of 'blasphemies' which members of the poet's small merry company heard issue from his lips during his final Ukrainian journey. Moreover, the then aging Mykhailo Maksymovych claimed that he parted company with Shevchenko because of these 'blasphemies' and 'impieties.' There are, of course, instances in the life of every person of expansive personality when, carelessly and unexpectedly even for himself, he blurts out something unpleasant and 'impolite' about the things he holds most sacred. But when the poet's entire literary legacy, including his letters and diary, gradually became available, it was no longer possible for later generations of Ukrainians to regard the 'blasphemous' passages in Shevchenko's works as simply 'random occurrences.' It became evident that there were indeed quite a few remarks on religious themes which might offend the devout church-going reader. This explains the attacks on Shevchenko, if not for outright atheism, at least for an 'unhealthy' religious scepticism, alien, as it were, to the very essence of faith and morality (for example, the attack by the Catholic priest, H. Kostelnyk). For their part, militant atheists recently have frequently used the poet's works to prove that he belonged to their camp. However, it has not been difficult for literary historians (mainly S. Smal-Stotsky) to demonstrate that Shevchenko's feelings about religion were not totally negative. Still, many readers were left with a negative impression, especially after reading some of Shevchenko's poems, and thus attempts have been made to 'reinterpret' all the 'negative' aspects of Shevchenko's works; to this end some authors have even employed falsifications. Conversely, individuals within Orthodox and Catholic circles have raised their voices in defence of the poet's religious point of view. Representatives of the relatively small Ukrainian Protestant community (such as Mykhailo Drahomanov) have attempted to portray Shevchenko as a 'precursor of the Ukrainian evangelical movement,' explaining away the negative elements in the poet's attitude towards religion by asserting that they were directed solely against the Catholic and Orthodox churches, and not against Christianity in general.

This dispute over Shevchenko's attitude towards religion is the result of a basic misunderstanding of major proportions. In the words of the greatest of poets, even one whom we recognize as the spiritual leader of an entire nation, we have no right to seek the answers to all our questions, questions which partially derive from a completely different set of historical circumstances with their own completely different set of problems. And we have still less right when it comes to a poet, living as he does not so much by the truth of the intellect and consequential thought as by that of the heart and emotional sequence, two distinct modes of knowledge which, taken together, can lead him to very simple and clearly apparent internal contradictions.

Yet, in the religious sphere no such sharp contradictions are to be found in Shevchenko's works! A rereading of his poetry, letters, and diary reveals that there is no one integral 'religion' or 'religious faith' informing his works, no one 'Christianity,' no straightforward Greek Orthodox faith. Rather, one is faced with a complex personality affected by historical, national, and cultural phenomena and diverse individual experiences.

Shevchenko experienced two types of religion – the religion of the common people and that of the official Russian Church. In Shevchenko's understanding, the folk religion was the living faith of the people, as well as the Church in the Ukrainian village. There are grounds to assume that the priests in and around Shevchenko's village, about whom he had heard a great deal, were at that time not yet completely removed from the religious life of the common people and had not become alien to the people as was later the case. (Not without cause, Shevchenko enjoyed spending time with the clergy, as A. Tatarchuk attests.)[2] Moreover, there is irrefutable evidence about Shevchenko's encounter, though much later in his life, with the priest Teofan Lebedyntsev, who sought to revitalize the spiritual life of the common people by delivering sermons in Ukrainian and Ukrainianizing the church functions; in Lebedyntsev's letters to Shevchenko the image of this priest, this Ukrainophile and populist, emerges clearly. Ukrainian church traditions which were consolidated by the religious strife of the seventeenth century could not be destroyed so easily.

A child of the village, Shevchenko always retained warm feelings for the religion of the common people and undoubtedly for this reason responded favourably to Lebedyntsev's ideas. This is why, when preparing his *Bukvar Iuzhnorusskii* (South Russian Primer, 1861), Shevchenko includes religious materials – prayers and brief articles. Clearly, neither censorship nor official requirements could have induced him to do so, especially since the materials which he includes exhibit his own understanding of Christianity (of which more later). In his poetry, too, Shevchenko speaks most warmly about the religion of the common people, of the Ukrainian village, which was bound up with every aspect of the folk way of life (*pobut*), having become part of it over the centuries. The religion of the witch or the servant girl (in the poems of the same name) with all its external manifestations – the candles placed before icons, the requiems celebrated on the fortieth day after a person's death (*sorokousty*), and the pilgrimmages to Kiev – is affectionately described (not merely indirectly endorsed through the poet's emotional identification with his heroines). Shevchenko acknowledges this naïve faith together with the folk *pobut* in its entirety. Characteristically, he does not present the common people and the Church as opposing forces; it will be remembered that, in accordance with oral tradition, Shevchenko has priests with censers and crosses (popy z kadylamy, z khrestamy) consecrate the weapons of the participants in popular uprisings.

In his stories, too, where the characters come not only from the peasantry but also, to a significant extent, from among the Ukrainian landowning gentry, Shevchenko depicts a *pobut* permeated by the Church, complete with priests, churches, chants, services, etc., as, for example, in 'Blyzniata' (The Twins), 'Mandrivka' (The Wandering), 'Naimychka' (The Servant Girl), and 'Varnak' (The Convict). These elements of life associated with the Church are sympathetically portrayed. The significance of religion for man is stressed in various instances: the blind Kolia from 'Neshchasnyi' (The Unfortunate One) matures spiritually under religious influence: 'For Kolia's soul, the Church became the one refuge which he sought out like a most beloved friend, a most tender mother. The simple, majestic motifs of our church life moved and permeated his entire being; the heavenly melody and the ecstatic lyricism of the Psalms of David raised his undefiled soul above the heavens themselves'; 'this chance occurrence wed his innocent, impressionable soul to the holy words and sounds and, cherishing in his heart this heavenly harmony, he was a thousand times more fortunate than a thousand sighted people.'

Describing old Sokyra in 'The Twins,' Shevchenko sympathetically emphasizes that 'he was very religious' and that this was 'the most attractive attribute of his nature ... most of all he liked to read the New Testament ... deeply understood and experienced the sacred truths of the Gospels.' The religious side of the convict's life in exile is depicted with the same warmth of feeling; the convict even confesses that his spiritual rebirth resulted, in the first instance, from his religious experiences: 'After going to confession and accepting the sacrament, I felt a sense of relief. A sacred, a mighty thing is religion for men, especially for such a sinner as I.' Shevchenko not only acknowledges but stresses the positive value of religious experience, while occasionally complaining that religion plays too small a role in certain circles: 'The majority of our land-owners,' Shevchenko asserts, 'keep the village clergy at a distance; this is an inexpressibly *sad* truth' (italics mine). Shevchenko does not speak only of the Orthodox Ukrainian clergy in this tone; the various priests encountered in his poetry are depicted either with sympathy or, in a few scenes, with only mild irony (the clergy in the apiary in the story 'The Servant Girl'). Also characteristic is the episode with the Polish Catholic priest M. Zielonka, whose hand Shevchenko kissed – undoubtedly because he respected Zielonka as a true Christian and a servant of God who was bound to his people and felt a responsibility for their fate.

It is quite another matter, however, when it comes to his contacts with the official Church, the church as an institution in its concrete manifestations. These contacts were either abroad (during the journey from exile to St Petersburg as recorded in Shevchenko's diary) or with foreigners, that is, with those representatives of the Russian Church in Ukraine who were cut off from the people (cf. the description of these types in Lebedyntsev's letter to Shevchenko cited above). The old style of Russian church painting seemed aesthetically unacceptable to Shevchenko (see his diary, 'Zhurnal,' for 16 February 1858 and 22 March 1858). Perhaps he felt like this because here no simple Ukrainian people surrounded him. That these negative feelings were directed not against religion or Christianity in general but against what Shevchenko regarded as its false and distorted external forms is affirmed by numerous passages in his diary and his creative works.

Such opposite responses to the Christian church and Orthodox faith are characteristic of Shevchenko. In all his experiences, emotions, and thoughts associated with religion, Shevchenko sees some kernel of genuine, 'natural,' pure religious faith in those external forms which conceal, obscure, and mar the genuine, deep, and sacred content of religious experience. If all those passages which offend or could offend the religious reader are examined, it will be found that they all have the same dual attitude – *negation of form* and, stemming from this, *affirmation of content*. The worship of images as form disassociated from content is in Shevchenko's view 'paganism': hence, 'where are the Christians?' ('Zhurnal,' 27 September 1857). His religious sensibility is affronted by the fact that the scriptures are read in a theatrical setting; the poet is incensed by this contradiction between the sacred content of the holy scriptures, on the one hand, and the external pomp and superficial circumstance of the episcopal church service, on the other ('Zhurnal,' 16 February 1858). Shevchenko is incensed by the 'drunkenness and gluttony' that occurs at Easter and on the feast day 'honouring the memory of the two heralds of love and peace,' Saints Peter and Paul, 'the great apostles' and 'teachers' (29 June 1857, 23 March 1858). While viewing a painting on a historical theme at an exhibition, Shevchenko was seized by the thought that 'in the name of Christ tears and blood had been spilled.' that 'Christians engage in mutual self-destruction' and 'spurn the Lord.' Similar themes typically run through the seemingly 'blasphemous' passages in Shevchenko's poetry.

Za koho zh Ty rozipiavsia,
Khryste, Syne Bozhyi?
Za nas dobrykh, chy za slovo
Istyny? Chy, mozhe,
Shchob my z Tebe nasmiialys?
Vono tak i stalos! (Kavkaz / The Caucasus)

For whom did You allow Yourself to be crucified, / Christ, Son of God? / For the likes of good people like us or for the word of truth? / Or, perhaps, so that we might laugh at You? / That is just what happened!

How far removed this is in tone from that 'atheism' and godlessness of which Shevchenko has been accused by some and for which he has been praised by others!

Whatever Shevchenko sees in religious faith, whether Christian or of other times and peoples, is tightly bound up with one of the essential sources of his world view – his *anthropocentrism*. With unusual emphasis Shevchenko always locates man at the centre of the world, the world of nature and of history. The reason for this may be sought in the nature of Shevchenko's poetic calling, for it could legitimately be argued that poetry is always 'subjective' and hence quite naturally places man at the centre of the world; yet, there are also many 'objective' poets and Shevchenko's own individuality is not so prominent in his works as always to be the leading component. Or it may be sought in the influence of romantic poetry on Shevchenko; however, for the romantic poets 'man' is often an abstract notion worthy of admiration while the individual is submerged, lost sight of, within the general categories of nation or cosmos. This conception is clearly alien to an anthropocentric poet like Shevchenko, especially since his anthropocentrism also extends to his social and historical views. Shevchenko sees in history not ideas, forces, and events but *people*, who 'groan in shackles' like the people of his own time, or struggle against injustice and bondage. The 'injustice and bondage' which he saw around him and fought with the fiery sword of his poetic word are not ethical concepts for him but concrete problems: *human* bondage (the bondage of the Ukrainian nation, the Ukrainian peasant, occasionally – of other peoples and other times) and *human* injustice (the injustice of the nobility, the tsars, the popes, etc.). The ancient Jewish kings, Ivan Hus, the 'neophytes' of early Christianity appear in his works because he sees in their fates the *typical human* fate, real human problems of his own time. Be it for social, political, or ethical problems, Shevchenko knows only the language of living human images and never – as happens with other poets – does he substitute the language of philosophy and philosophical symbols. This is the most characteristic difference between Shevchenko and the Polish messianists, with whom he shared an affinity in certain respects. In this connection the study of a work such as 'Velykyi Lokh' (The Great Vault) would be most revealing. In Shevchenko's poetry entire peoples are presented in human images – as Prometheus (The Caucasus), as mother, 'old mother,' 'tear-stained mother' ('Do mertvykh i zhyvykh ...' / To My Dead and Living ... Countrymen ...).

Shevchenko's historical anthropocentrism also informs his vision of sacred and church history. The religious past is viewed in the same light as the past of humanity as a whole. It is not merely accidental that in his imitations of the prophets Shevchenko replaces 'Israel' by 'Ukraine' ('Osia. Hlava XIV' / 'Hosea 14'). He sees in past religious movements stages of that same struggle for human freedom which was occurring in his own time (see 'Neofity' / 'The Neophytes,' 'Ivan Hus'). Sacred history is directly linked to the problems of his day ('Tsari' / 'Kings,' 'Saul'). This is also the case in *Knyhy Bytiia Ukrainskoho Narodu* (Books of Genesis of the Ukrainian People), the famous document outlining the aims of the Brotherhood of Saints Cyril and Methodius.

While the depiction of certain events, phenomena, and people from sacred history in Shevchenko's works may have the character of a pamphlet or caricature (the Roman Catholic Church and the clergy in 'Ivan Hus,' the ancient Israelite kings in 'Kings' and 'Saul'), this stems from the same source already discussed above. Here too Shevchenko juxtaposes genuine religion, a religion oriented towards man, with what he regarded as 'deviations' from genuine faith, arising at particular historical moments and in particular social conditions. Genuine religion, the enduring content of Christianity, the essence of Christ's teachings were essentially human for him. Shevchenko rejects all aspects of religion, past or present, that transform it into an abstract force indifferent to the actual living individual, occasionally assuming a position hostile to man, hindering his free development, and fettering his individuality with all its needs and aspirations.

When, characterizing the Orthodox hierarchy of his time, Lebedyntsev writes that 'no one utters a word to the people, no one will tell them how one is to live on God's earth, how to please God and bring well-being to the soul,' he expresses Shevchenko's feelings; it was precisely of this that Shevchenko felt compelled to accuse the church hierarchy – neglect of the religious needs of the people. Shevchenko opposed those aspects of established church practice that conflicted with man's aesthetic needs (hence his opposition to traditional church painting), that were contrary to human nature as a whole (asceticism), or that went beyond the powers of human reason (The Apocalypse; Zhurnal, 16, 18 December 1857). For the same reason he was against 'superstition,' against the abuse of religion for political purposes, against the 'spilling of blood and tears' in the name of religion, against religious wars, against 'the Inquisition and the auto-da-fé,' against the Church's attitude towards specific 'sins' which are incompatible with a natural human response (the prohibition of church burials for suicides).[3] In this Shevchenko sees a perversion of the 'genuine' religious idea, the decline of true religious faith which in its essence is a universal human truth. It should be noted that truth for Shevchenko was not merely theoretical, that is, cognitive truth, but also practical truth, that is, concrete justice, a just social order in the human domain; hence, the word has both ethical and ontological meaning. Truth is to be found in all spontaneous, simple, and naïve folk beliefs, perhaps even in the pagan beliefs of the savage (Shevchenko speaks of the 'wordless poetic prayer of the savage' 'Zhurnal,' 15 July 1857) which have been corrupted over time, partly with evil intent. This latter view Shevchenko simply took over from eighteenth-century philosophical thought, still alive in nineteenth-century Russia.

Shevchenko's ideas on the subject of religion not only have an obvious aspect but a second, deeper one as well. Shevchenko was far from outright rejection of Christian religion: Christ remained for him the central figure in human history and in the individual's life. He believed, however, that Christianity in the form it had assumed in his time, had to be cleansed of alien elements. For Shevchenko, as for the author of *The Books of Genesis of the Ukrainian People*, this cleansing process consisted of establishing an unmediated relationship between the individual and God. God alone was to be the object of faith and worship: 'I Tobi odnomu pokloniatsia vsi iazyky u viky i viky' (And to You alone will men of all tongues bow down for all time to come; 'The Caucasus'). Shevchenko cannot conceive of God in the image of a king, an image that is common both to Judaism and Christianity. For Shevchenko, the following is characteristic:

... karat i myluvat ne bude,
My ne raby ioho, my liudy ...

... He will not punish or forgive, / We are not His slaves, we are people ...

For precisely this reason Shevchenko does not see God as 'the Byzantine Lord of Sabaoth,' cut off from man by His unlimited majesty. In fact, the opposition God-Lord of Sabaoth captures the quintessence of that dualism in Shevchenko's attitude towards religion.

For Shevchenko, Christ is the central figure in world history; in Him the main issue of human life, the issue of freedom, is resolved; after Christ we no longer 'die as slaves.' Christ assumes this central position because, as well as being divine, He embodied in ideal form the acme of that which is human. When one critic wrote that Shevchenko expressed the idea that 'Christ is not God but a man who, through his power of reasoning, earned the eternal esteem of humanity,' this was, needless to say, an exaggeration. Yet, the idea has a basis in fact in connection with this characteristic linkage of 'the divine' with the human, a linkage which may at first sight seem a 'debasement' of the divine. It is, in fact, in order to establish this linkage that Shevchenko 'anthropologizes' Christ (and, indeed, all sacred history). Almost imperceptibly but persistently do notes with such an anthropologizing tone resound in the few lines about Christ in Shevchenko's *South Russian Primer*: 'Jesus Christ, the Son of God in the Holy Spirit, flesh of the Immaculate and Most Pure Blessed Virgin, taught godless people the word of truth and love, the only sacred law. The godless people did not believe His sacred, fiery word and crucified Him as a rebel and blasphemer along with the thieves on the Cross. The Apostles, his holy pupils, carried His word of truth and love and His Holy Prayer throughout the land.' Here the human elements of Jesus' life are stressed – the 'fieriness' of his words, his conflict with the 'godless people,' his crucifixion 'along with the thieves,' the conviction of Christ as a revolutionary ('rebel').

The most outstanding example of Shevchenko's 'secularization' of sacred history, however, may be found in the poem 'Mariia.' The poet's intention here is known from his letters. Shevchenko is making ready 'to analyse the heart of the mother as manifested in the life of the Blessed Mary ... to portray the heart of the mother as manifested in the life of the Immaculate Virgin, the Mother of the Saviour' (letters to Varvara Repnina, 1 January, 7 March 1850). As the dates of these letters indicate, Shevchenko was making plans as early as 1848-50. The plot of this poem is linked to other poems in which Shevchenko celebrates the girl-mother, this seemingly central image in his poetry. As to the religious aspect of the poem, here we have, to some extent, the same mood that in the West led to the numerous 'secularized' depictions of 'the life of Jesus.' An outstanding representative of this current in the West, David Strauss (*Leben Jesu*, 1835-6), by his own admission set himself the task of portraying 'the life of the historical Jesus on a simple human level,' a task which, in the opinion of one of Strauss's critics, Bruno Bauer, was equivalent 'to depicting *human nature* in its generalized form' (*Allgemeinheit*). And this corresponds to the views of the author of 'Mariia.' At the same time it points to that which all readers of 'Mariia' sense with certainty, even those who are touched to the quick by the 'debasement' of the life of the Blessed Virgin to the level of an ordinary, personal, romantic, human tragedy.

Shevchenko was not writing 'an epic about Gabriel,' as Pushkin had; his poem is not an act of blasphemy but a 'poem-psalm.' In the figure of Mary he perceives the universal tragedy of the mother. It is quite possible that in creating his poem Shevchenko made use of accounts from Strauss's book, for it is precisely this book that seems to provide the easiest explanations of certain details in 'Mariia'; for example, the 'herald of good tidings' who is sent to Mary by Elizabeth (why? in Shevchenko's poem no motivation is provided, while in Strauss's book it is noted as a significant moment in Heinrich Paulus's 1828 'Life of Christ') or Mary's role in the life and teachings of Jesus. Shevchenko could not have read Strauss's book because of the language barrier but could easily have remembered some details in it from accounts of its content. He also quite 'uncritically' employs apocryphal motifs from the legends about Mary known to him from both the oral and the iconographic traditions. In any case, Shevchenko combines hymns to Mary, such as the following, with a 'secularized' depiction of her life:

Vse upovaniie moie
Na Tebe, mii presvitlyi raiu,

...

Sviataia sylo vsikh sviatykh,
Preneporochnaia, Blahaia! ('Mariia')

...

Blahoslovennaia v zhenakh,
Sviataia Pravednaia Maty
Sviatoho Syna na zemli ... ('Neofity' / The Neophytes)

All my troth in you, / Most luminous Eden ... / Most holy of all holy ones, / Immaculate, Blessed! ... / Most blessed of women, / Saintly and heaven-born Mother / Of the heavenborn Son on earth ...

Such passages are characteristic of Shevchenko's works as a whole: in addition to the quoted segments from 'Mariia' see 'Molites, bratiia, molites' (Pray, my brothers, pray); 'Vidma' (The Witch) – 'Moliusia znovu, upovaiu' (I pray again and once again I hope); in his imitations of Psalm 11 and Isaiah 35, respectively – 'Mii Bozhe Mylyi' (Dear Lord), 'Raduisia, nyvo nepolytaia' (Rejoice, unwatered field); 'Smyrites, molites Bohu' (Humble yourselves, pray to God), etc. This is apparently the opposite of that 'debasement' of the sacred to the level of the purely human, to that 'secularization' of things held sacred, to all that for which Shevchenko has been accused of 'blasphemy.'

Little wonder that a Russian critic (K. Chukovsky) marvelled at the number of prayers in Shevchenko's poetry. Yet in these prayers there is that same tendency to bring God closer to earth or, if you will, to see him in his earthly manifestation. The error Shevchenko makes in quoting Lermontov is very revealing. In Shevchenko we find:

I vidiat Boga na zemle!

And they see God on earth!

While the actual lines in Lermontov are

I shchaste ia mogu postignut na zemle,
I v nebesakh ia vizhu Boga ...

And happiness I can attain on earth, / In the heavens I see God ...

For this reason it is doubtful whether one can speak of 'mystical' elements in Shevchenko's poetry (as S. Balei has done), especially if the term 'mystical' is understood in the narrow theological sense in which 'mystical experiences' designate man's transcendence of the boundaries of human existence, leading to a union with or, in less intense form, an unusual closeness to the divine being. As encountered for the most part in Skovoroda, a man privy to a mystical experience is 'submerged' in God, disappears in Him, 'dissolves ... fuses with God ... experiences an apotheosis.' However, human existence is so central for Shevchenko that 'an other-worldly existence,' the sphere into which a person would depart from his 'humanity,' does not play a large role in his world. Yet, since the 'mystical' is not the sole or the main form of Christian religious experience, its absence in Shevchenko's works need have no bearing on our conclusions here. In fact, religious poetry the world over rarely depicts the mystical experience or, if it does, describes it in terms of something else.

Shevchenko testifies to his concern with religion not only through those writings which describe direct religious experience but also through his many imitations of holy scripture and his epigraphs from the Bible. In exile he read the gospels. 'My one comfort now is the gospels,' he writes to Varvara Repnina on 1 January 1858; 'I am reading the New Testament with awesome trepidation,' he tells her again on 7 March 1850, 'am completing my reading of the Bible,' he informs Arkadii Rodzianko on 23 October 1845. He requests (28 February 1848, 1 January 1850) and, according to K. Hern, reads Thomas Hemerken von Kempen, an interest in whom he derived perhaps from the circles of the Brotherhood of Saints Cyril and Methodius, where 'Imitations of the Life of Christ' were valued highly. Neither does Shevchenko disdain religious ritual; that he went to church we can gather from observations in his diary to the effect that on some particular day he *did not* go to church and from references in his stories (for example, 'The Convict') to church-going as something that goes without saying; to Repnina he writes (28 February 1848):

I was overwhelmed by an indistinct feeling ('come all you who labour and are heavy-burdened and I will give you rest'). Before the bell was rung to announce morning services, I recalled the words uttered by the Redeemer on our behalf and seemed to take on new life: I went to the morning services and prayed joyously, with such innocence as perhaps never before. I am now fasting and today took Holy Communion. Would that my entire life were as pure and beautiful as this day!

Relevant passages from 'Neshchasnyi' (The Unfortunate One) could also be cited. In any case, there is no evidence that from the time of his exile Shevchenko succumbed to the atheism that was widespread among the

Russian intelligentsia of the time (the infamous 1860s). He derived the substance of his faith from his early years, and it included not only the religion of his native village (which, as we have seen, he held in high esteem even later in life and towards which he harboured warm feelings), but also the profound faith shared by the members of the Brotherhood of Saints Cyril and Methodius. Shevchenko's disenchantment with the Russian Church may have signified an inner crisis. In any case, he learned to be sceptical, and the spiritual crisis resulting from his reflections over the fate of his nation led him to repeated outbursts of despair, beginning with passages such as the following:

> Ia tak ii, ia tak liubliu
> Moiu Ukrainu ubohu,
> Shcho proklianu sviatoho Boha,
> Za nei dushu pohubliu ...

So do I love her, / So do I love my impoverished Ukraine / That for her I would curse the holy name of God, / For her my soul forfeit ...

> ... a do toho
> Ia ne znaiu Boha! −

... and till then / I do not know God! −

and extending all the way to the lines about the 'all-seeing eye' ('vsevydiashcheie oko').

It must be remembered, however, that such passages are primarily connected with the traditional poetic themes of titanic-Byronic romanticism: in the poetics of this romantic current, by which Shevchenko was so obviously influenced, the theme of despair was expressed in such doubts about the existence of God, in such 'protests' or in such a 'rebellion' against God. Yet, even if these and similar passages are accepted as adequate revelations of Shevchenko's inner feelings, a detailed examination clearly reveals that they cannot be used as proof of Shevchenko's atheism. Nor can they be used as a basis for drawing conclusions about his world view. On the other hand, the orthodoxy of Shevchenko's views was also shaken to a certain extent by the influence of Protestant ideas with which he became familiar partly through his association with the Brotherhood of Saints Cyril and Methodius.

A deeper impact upon Shevchenko's religious consciousness was probably made by David Strauss, whose name Shevchenko must have encountered throughout his life. In Kiev he would have heard it from members of the Brotherhood of Saints Cyril and Methodius. Strauss's name was so popular at that time that it even became the subject of current anecdotes (for example, about the student Oleksander Tulub, who had links with the Cyril and Methodius circles and employed Strauss's theories to make fun of his professor of theology, I.M. Skvortsov; or about the professor of philosophy, P.S. Avsenev, regarded as an authority in the Cyril and Methodius circles, who was hostile to Strauss and supposedly burned Strauss's *Leben Jesu*). In St Petersburg, Shevchenko could have heard about Strauss from the members of the Petrashevsky Circle whom he knew. In exile he became friends with Bronisław Zaleski, a friend of Antoni Sowa (Edward Zeligowski), whom Shevchenko often mentions in his letters; and in Zeligowski's drama-fantasy *Jordan* (1845), with which Shevchenko by his own testimony was familiar ('like my own heart'), we encounter Strauss as an enemy of historical Christianity. And, finally, in St Petersburg, after his return from exile, Shevchenko became acquainted with the Russian painter Aleksandr Andreevich Ivanov, in whom he had earlier exhibited an interest and whose work showed the decisive influence of Strauss's theology; Shevchenko must also have seen Ivanov's paintings – sketches for the canvas which was to display Strauss's entire theology (the scene of the feast of the Annunciation is surrounded by mythological parallels collected by Strauss). Furthermore, after his return from exile Shevchenko could not help but encounter that atheism which at the end of the 1850s and the beginning of the 1860s was widespread in Russian society. Yet he never became an atheist and 'Mariia' was a defence of the biblical account and of the figure of the Holy Virgin rather than an attack on them.

Influences on Shevchenko from another quarter, Polish Christian radicalism, were also significant. Shevchenko's acquaintances and friendships among the Poles extend in a long series throughout his life, beginning from the time when, as a serf, he was taken to Vilno and Warsaw, through the years in St Petersburg and exile, to the post-exile period in St Petersburg. This explains his knowledge of Polish literature and spiritual life. In many instances, conspicuous similarities between certain ideas expressed by Shevchenko and the ideology of Polish political writers allow us to postulate a direct Polish influence on Shevchenko. Particularly worthy of note is the unique union, encountered in both Shevchenko and the Poles, of Christian faith with political radicalism and a revolutionary spirit which, incidentally, was also characteristic of the ideology of the Brotherhood of Saints Cyril and Methodius, but had practically no parallels in the Russian context. There is a profound similarity between Shevchenko's religious ideology and that of one of the most interesting Polish works of this movement, Karol Ludwik Królikowski's *Polska Chrystusowa* (Christ's Poland, 1842) where, as in Shevchenko, religious and socio-political truths are equated and an unjust socio-political order is repudiated in the name of religious truth. Królikowski believed, as Shevchenko would later, that God was Truth and that mankind ought to submit to God alone, bow down before, and serve only the Lord Himself. To be sure, the elements of purely Polish messianism found in this Polish author are totally absent in Shevchenko. Yet, for precisely this reason Shevchenko is closer to those early western works which gave rise to the Polish movement (Félicité-Robert Lamennais) and with which Shevchenko might have been familiar.

Finally, it should be noted that Shevchenko's religious views bear traces, in varying degrees, of several fundamental errors of religious thought to which man's religious quest has led quite often. They are the flaws of almost every religious anthropocentrism. First, a certain a-historicism, neglect of the fact that life and human perceptions – and hence religious consciousness – are limited by man's position in the historical process. Along with this goes a certain disdain for the fact that man's spiritual life (and the Church as a historical structure) is only possible in the form of a specific 'positive' religion, a specific confession and confessional Church organization. From his perspective of consistent and radical anthropocentrism, it seemed to Shevchenko that man stood above the historical process and above culturally determined forms and structures. Yet he arrived at his conception of absolute value, of man, through his own philosophically limited, subjective experience, creating an idealized religion from his own limited, subjective anthropocentric perspective. The one-sidedness of Shevchenko's views on religious questions was significantly modified by his love for his native land and his people, a love which enabled him to perceive the eternal in the historically and culturally limited phenomenon that was the living faith of the Ukrainian people.

(1936)

NOTES

1 Translation of 'Shevchenko i religiia,' *Povne vydannia tvoriv Tarasa Shevchenka* (Warsaw, Ukrainskyi Naukovyi Instytut 1936), X. The bibliography has been omitted.

2 'He preferred acquaintances with priests, who all loved and respected Shevchenko.' V. Berenshtam, 'T.G. Shevchenko v vospominaniakh prostoliudinov,' *Kievskaia starina*, II (1900) 252.

3 Cf. 'Ivan Hus,' 'The Caucasus,' 'Svite iasnyi! Svite tykhyi!'

17

Some Problems in the Study of the Formal Aspect of Schevchenko's Poetry

DMYTRO CHYZHEVSKY

The formal structure of a poem is not entirely the consequence of conscious creativity.[1] With the possible exception of cases of deliberate poetic experimentation, most poets do not compose their metre, rhythm, or rhyme according to some 'plan,' some previously conceived disposition of materials, or scheme. Normally, the poet's work consists of the composition of verses 'by ear.' Often the poet himself would be hard put to say why he used this or that rhythm, this or that word or form, any of those individual things upon which not only the content but the rhythmical structure of the poem, its melody and 'euphony,' depend.

Doubtless it was 'by ear' that Shevchenko selected his rhythms when he created those folk or, rather, 'semi-folk,' rhythms new to Ukrainian poetry – rhythms based on the *kolomyika* (a rhythmical dance tune):

> Plyvut sobi spivaiuchy;
> More viter chuie.
> Poperedu Hamaliia
> Baidakom keruie ...

They sail along, singing; / The sea feels the wind. / At their head Hamaliia / Directs the boat ...

and on the *koliadka* (Christmas carol):

> Z Trubailom Alta mizh osokoiu
> Ziishlys, ziednalys, mov brat z sestroiu.

I vse te, vse te raduie ochi,
A sertse plache, hlianut ne khoche ...

In among the reed-grass the rivers Alta and Trubailo came together, / Joined like brother and sister. / And all that, all that gladdens the eyes / But the heart weeps, does not wish to look ...

It was 'by ear' that Shevchenko created the many versions of folk rhythms chiefly encountered in his imitations of folk songs:

Oi odna ia, odna,
Iak bylynochka v poli,
Ta ne dav meni Boh
Ani shchastia, ni doli ... (6A, 7b, 6B, 7b)[2]

Alone am I, all alone, / Like a poor little blade of grass in a field, / For God gave me / Neither happiness nor good fortune ...

Porodyla mene maty
U vysokykh u palatakh,
    Shovkom povyla.
U zoloti, oksamyti,
Mov ta kvitochka ukryta,
    rosla ia, rosla ... (8a, 8a, 5B, 8c, 8c, 5B)

My mother bore me / In lofty chambers, / In silk she swaddled me. / Like a flower in gold, in velvet covered, / I grew and grew ...

    Ponad polem ide
    ne pokosy klade,
Ne pokosy klade – hory!
Stohne zemlia, stohne more,
    Stohne ta hude! (6A, 6A, 8b, 8b, 5A)

Over the fields he goes, / Not mere strips does he mow, / Not mere strips does he mow, but mountains! / The earth groans, the sea groans, / Groans, and rages!

Oi ne piutsia pyva, medy,
Ne pietsia voda;

Prykliuchylas z chumachenkom
U stepu bida ... (8A, 5B, 8c, 5B)

Alas, neither beer nor mead / Does he drink, no more water does he drink; / Misfortune befell the wagoner / In the steppes ...

Oi, strichechka do strichechky, –
Merezhaiu try nichenky,
Merezhaiu, vyshyvaiu, –
U nediliu pohuliaiu ... (8â, 8â, 8b, 8b)

O, row after row, / Three nights I make lace, / Embroider, make lace, – / but on Sunday will I make merry ...

Oi, pishla ia u iar za vodoiu,
Azh tam mylyi huliaie z druhoiu.
  A taia druhaia,
  Rozluchnytsia zlaia –
Bahataia susidonka,
  Vdova molodaia ... (10a, 10a, 6b, 6b, 8â, 6b)

O, into the ravine for water I went / And there my beloved with another was playing. / And that one / Was a wicked spoiler, / A wealthy neighbour, / A young widow ...

Iak by meni cherevychky,
To pishla b ia na muzyky, –
      horenko moie!
Cherevykiv nemaie,
A muzyka hraie, hraie,
Zhaliu zavdaie ... (8a, 8a, 5b, 7c, 8c, 5b)

If I had a pair of shoes, / Dancing would I go, – Woe is me! / No shoes have I / But the music plays and plays, / Causes me sorrow ...

U peretyku khodyla
    po horikhy,
Myroshnyka poliubyla
    dlia potikhy.
Melnyk mele, sheretuie,

Obernetsia, potsiluie –
> dlia potikhy ... (8a, 4b, 8a, 4b, 8c, 8c, 4b)

To the thicket I went for nuts, / With the miller fell in love for fun. / The miller grinds, husks, / Turns and kisses me – for fun ...

I bahata ia,
I vrodlyva ia,
Ta ne maiu sobi pary –
> beztalanna ia! (5a, 5a, 8b, 5a)

I am rich / And beautiful, / But I have no mate – / I am unfortunate.

But this rhythmical richness is still not everything. The inherent musicality of Shevchenko's poetry derives from other factors as well.

Shevchenko's rhymes depart radically from earlier traditions in Ukrainian poetry, the sole exception being Skovoroda's verse. For baroque, classical, and romantic Ukrainian versification, like Western verse and that of Ukraine's neighbours, demanded the complete correspondence of the endings in both words of a rhyme (kuniaie-spivaie, hroshi-mikhonoshi, pytyrobyty, maty-daty, lezhyt-sydyt, dolynoiu-rodynoiu). Shevchenko decisively breaks with this tradition and to a degree follows the patterns of the folk song, while simultaneously linking his versification to baroque traditions (at any rate the spiritual songs, and perhaps also to Skovoroda – 'and I would copy Skovoroda or the carol "Three Kings and Gifts"'). Instead he offers partial instead of complete correspondence in the endings. In many instances some of the sounds in the word-endings are only similar, not the same.

The great diversity of incomplete rhymes encountered in Shevchenko's poetry permits classification. In the scheme that follows each consonant will be designated by a capital 'T,' each vowel by a capital 'A.' The meaning of other letters will be discussed separately in each case. It should also be noted that, when unstressed, 'y' and 'e' are really the same sound.

Type 1: Rhymes of the type TA-TAI are employed in old Ukrainian literature; for example, in Shevchenko: brate-bahatyi, khymernyi-zverne, mohyly-malosylnyi, kaidany-pohanyi.
Type 2: Very rarely encountered in old Ukrainian literature and very often in Shevchenko are rhymes of the type TA-TAkh ('kh' representing

a variable consonant) or ATA-ATAkh; eg, vytaiut-kraiu, liudy-nudyt, liubyly-skhylyt, pidkralys-ukraly, ruinakh-Vkraina, rozruinuie-sumuiesh, triasylo-vkrylos.

Type 3: But Shevchenko also varies the vowels in this type of rhyme, so that we have TU-TY ('U,' 'Y' representing variable vowels). Hence also TU-TYI; for example, porodyla-zatopyly, movy-slovo, poli-doliu, ochi-khochu, brovy-movu, ostylo-mohyla, laskave-slavu, vika-kaliku, divchata-maty, kraini-domovynu, khati-brata, vdova-rozmovu, muka-ruky, pustynia-domovyny.

Type 4: Vowel variation is combined with a variation in consonants (hence Types 2 and 3 combined): TU-TYkh; for example, divchyna-zahynuv, syrotyna-tynom, litaie-spivaiut, neboraky-plakat, plache-kozachim, zaplachut-bachyt, vodoiu-zahoit, pid tynom-khatyny, Ukraino-hynesh, shukaie-pidrostaiut, prostovolose-holosyt, nevoli-polem.

Type 5: In Shevchenko's verse one 'extra' consonant is sometimes placed between other sounds, or at the end, after a vowel: TAT-TAkhT or TAT-TATkh; for example, zakhovav-rozmakhavs, sertsia-smiietsia (phonetically 'smiietstsia'), Husa-strepenuvsia.

Type 6: There are also variations of vowels as in Type 5: TAkhT-TApT; for example, vesnianku-shynkarku, shynka-horilku.

Type 7: Variations of consonants which are altered forms of the 'original' phoneme are also possible; thus, in Shevchenko's rhymes we encounter in the same function consonants that are voiced and unvoiced, unpalatalized and palatalized, short and long: TAT-TAT' or TATA-TAT'A, TAT-TAD, or TATA-TADA, TATTA-TATA; for example, poborius'-Hus (rare in Shevchenko's poetry), znaiesh-zamizh, ptashka-tiazhko, shukaite-naida, bulla-zdryhnuly, popidtynniu-khatyny.[3]

Type 8: Finally, there are very frequent variations of vowels and consonants which one might call assonances rather than rhymes; for example, klyche-lyshe, proshchi-ochi, robysh-khodysh, bude-liube, plata-plakat', ladu-lahod', vyshni-vyishla, kvatyrku-dytynu, kormylom-khvyliakh, stohne-prokholone.

As noted earlier, Shevchenko's precursor in rhyme was Skovoroda, the reformer of rhyme in Ukrainian baroque literature. We offer several examples of similar types of rhyme from the works of Skovoroda: *Type 1:* ubohyi-nemnoho, solodkyi-hlotka, tielo-netsieloi, prenebrehaty-prokliatii, mynut-liutii; *Type 2:* hradom-stado, priiemliut-zemliu, pomozhet-Bozhe, voskhodyt-pokhody, luchy-uluchyt, svobody-rodyt; *Type 3:* biela-tielo, holovoiu-pokoie, blahodatiu-khodataiu; *Type 4:* rare in Skovoroda: for example, ucheny-sovershennoi; *Type 5:* krest-voskres, mir-vykhr, adamant-hrad; *Type 6:* apparently not found in Skovoroda; *Type 7:* significantly more frequent in Skovoroda, especially in his final period, than in Shevchenko: hospod'-rod, orel-otsel', dukh-kruh, hlaz-nas, semna-uveselenna, okiiana-obaianna, etc.; *Type 8:* rare in Skovoroda: narod-hrob, verba-voda, and so on. Thus, Skovoroda was clearly Shevchenko's precursor in rhyme. However, in every case, Shevchenko took a significantly different direction from his precursor.

In another respect as well, Shevchenko took the same position on the question of rhyme as Skovoroda and that was on masculine and ungrammatical rhymes. As employed by Shevchenko, both these types of rhyme were not entirely new. Masculine rhymes were forbidden by the poetic tradition of the Ukrainian baroque (perhaps reflecting the Polish tradition): before Skovoroda they are only encountered occasionally. These rhymes usually occur in the works of less well-schooled, dilettante poets. Masculine rhymes occur in the following percentages:

Songs in honour of feasts and didactic songs (1219 lines) 13%
Priest-monk Klementii (638 lines) 19%
Priest-monk Onufrii (622 lines) 22%
Vintsi (Garlands, in Peretts; 310 lines)[4] 0%
Velychkovsky (132 lines) 3%
S. Todorsky (270 lines) 0%
Kanty (Panegyric Verses, in Vozniak; 800 lines)[5] 13%
Dramas (in Rezanov; 2,000 lines)[6] 7%
Verses ... for the Burial of Sahaidachny, 1622 (629 lines) 13%
Umnolohiia (Versified Quips, 1630) 5%
Ievkharystarion (Eucharisterion, 1632; 188 lines) 0%
Ifika ieropolitika (Ethica Hieropolitica, 1712; 268 lines) 0%
Slovo o zburenniu pekla (Tale about the Destruction of Hell; 518 lines) 23%

In Skovoroda's verse, on the other hand, masculine rhymes are not fortuitous, occurring in specific places as determined by the stanza form:

Raznye stykhotvoreniia (Various Verses; 352 lines) 14%
Sad bozhestvennykh pesen (Garden of Heavenly Songs) 45%

It is interesting to note that in those poets whom Skovoroda quotes or praises, or under whom he studied at the Academy, there is a very small percentage of masculine rhymes:

Prokopovych (verses, 312 lines) 3%
Lashevsky (drama, 317 lines) 1.3%
Konysky (drama, 639 lines) 5.6%
Tuptalo (drama, 2,837 lines) 1.8%

But in Kotliarevsky's *Eneida* the stanza form results in thirty per cent masculine rhymes. Clearly, Kotliarevsky fully 'canonized' masculine rhymes and Shevchenko admitted them on equal terms. In fact, there are fewer masculine rhymes in his poetry than feminine (and occasional dactylic) ones. In any case, it is evident that Skovoroda's creative work formed a watershed in the evolution of Ukrainian rhyme.

It is much the same with ungrammatical rhymes. Naturally grammatical rhymes, being the simplest, are found in greater numbers in the dilettante poets, while in the works of the more gifted poets there is a larger proportion of 'original' or 'striking' rhymes, that is to say, ungrammatical ones. It should be noted that in this area Shevchenko, like Skovoroda, leads the way. The percentages of ungrammatical rhymes encountered are as follows:

Songs in honour of feasts ... 17%
Klementii 10%
Onufrii 10%
Garlands 17%
Velychkovsky 39%
Todorsky 27%
Skovoroda – *Various Verses* 58%
Skovoroda – *Garden of Heavenly Songs* 38%
Kotliarevsky – *Eneida* I 30%
Shevchenko – 'Kateryna' (Catherine) 54%

Compared with earlier techniques in rhyme, Shevchenko's is always 'revolutionary'.[7] This is somewhat less so in the case of incomplete rhymes. Similar reforms in Polish and Slavic literatures in general – somewhat later in Russian (incomplete rhymes in Blok, Maiakovsky, and others) – met with great resistance. Insofar as Aleksei Tolstoi was the first to bring incomplete rhymes into Russian verse, it is possible that this occurred under the influence of Shevchenko; Tolstoi moved in Ukrainian circles and had an interest in Ukrainian literature.[8]

It might appear that incomplete rhymes weaken the effect of the stanzas. But this is not so: 'incompleteness' in rhyme allows Shevchenko to avoid that monotony arising from the frequent use of the same endings, and encourages an increase in grammatical rhymes (see, in Shevchenko: hulialy-spivaly, znaie-shkandybaie, mlila-nimila, torbyna-dytyna, starohotovstoho, nizheniata-divchata, etc.). Because they are incomplete, Shevchenko's rhymes seem 'more unexpected,' 'richer' (as they are described in rhyme theory), 'more original.'

But Shevchenko balances the excessive loss of sonority which results from the use of incomplete rhymes in a number of other ways. First, he employs an abundance of internal rhymes, that is, rhyming words located in the same line. Parenthetically, it is interesting that internal rhyme was used with enthusiasm in the romantic ballad (the Western, but in the Polish and Russian as well). Compare:

Hama*liia*, sertse m*liie* ...
Hamaliia, the heart grows faint ...[9]

Iest u mene *dity*, ta de ikh po*dity* ...
Children aplenty but what to do with them ...

Us*iudy*, de l*iudy* ...
Everywhere where there are people ...

Toi mur*uie*, toi ruin*uie* ...
One builds, another destroys ...

I tsar*iata*, i starch*ata* ...
And little lords and little elders ...

Mizh iar*amy*, nad stav*amy* ...
Amidst ravines, above ponds ...

Na dvi n*ochi* kari *ochi* ...
For two nights two dark eyes ...

Khto spyt*aie*, pryvit*aie* ...
Who will enquire, greet ...

A tym chasom sy*chi* v no*chi* ...
And the while screech owls in the night ...

Prylit*aiut*, zabyr*aiut*
Vse dobro z soboiu ...
They come, take back all the goods with them ...

I sviataia tvoia slava
Iak pyl*yna* l*yne* ...
And your sacred glory, / Like dust is carried off ...

Spy Chyhyr*yne*, nekhai h*ynut*
U voroha dity!
Spy hetm*ane*, poky vst*ane*
Pravda na sim sviti!
Sleep, Chyhyryn, let children die / In the hands of the enemy! / Sleep, Hetman,
until truth arises in this world!

Babusenko, holubonko,
Skazhy, bo ty znaiesh, −
Khoche d*aty* mene m*aty*
Za staroho zamizh ...

Grandma, dear, tell me for you know − / Mother wants to give me / To an old man
in marriage ...

These internal rhymes in Shevchenko's poetry are not random occurrences.
They are a device employed systematically and frequently to strengthen
that sonority which is partially lost because of the use of incomplete
rhymes. But Shevchenko also employs other devices to strengthen the
sonority, the melody of his verse.

Shevchenko's poetry is significantly more melodious than that of all the
Ukrainian writers before him and of his contemporaries, too. A language as
internally euphonic was produced by few poets of the worldwide romantic
movement, those few who in their poetry were strongly oriented towards
'musicality' (for example, Clemens Brentano). Shevchenko achieves this

rare sonority primarily by the simple repetition of the same or related words. In the spirit of the folk song Shevchenko repeats individual words:

> Ukraino, Ukraino,
> Nenko moia, nenko ...

Ukraine, Ukraine, dear mother mine, / Dear mother ...

> Im *dostalas* dobra slava,
> Mohyla *zostalas* ...

A good name they attained, / A grave remained ...

> *Mynuv* rik, *mynuv* druhyi ...

One year passed, another passed ...

or various forms of the same word:

> ... bo *spochynu*,
> Iak batko *spochynuv* ...

... for I will rest, / As my father rested ...

> I vsi *pochyly*. Syvyi v khatu
> I sam pishov *spochyvaty* ...

And all rested. Into the house / The old man himself went to rest ...

Occasionally exact repetitions of words or repetitions of various forms of the same words are clustered in one brief stanza:

> *Mynaiut* dni, *mynaiut* nochi,
> *Mynaie* lito ...
> ... i ne znaiu
> chy ia *zhyvu*, chy *dozhyvaiu* ...
> ...
> A dai *zhyty*, sertsem *zhyty*
> ...
> A shche hirshe *spaty*, *spaty*
> i *spaty* na voli ...

The days pass, the nights pass, / The summer passes ... / And I know not /
Whether I live or fade ... / But let me live, live with all my heart / ... But far worse
it is to sleep, / Sleep and sleep in liberty ...

Indirectly and imperceptibly entire poems are constructed around constant
repetitions:

> Sadok *vyshnevyi* kolo khaty,
> Khrushchi nad *vyshniamy* hudut,
> *Pluhatari* z *pluhamy* idut ...
> ...
> A materi *vecheriat* zhdut.
> Simia *vecheria* kolo khaty,
> *Vechirnia* zironka vstaie,
> Dochka *vecheriat* podaie ...
> ...
> *Zatykhlo* vse ... tilko divchata
> Ta soloveiko ne *zatykh*.

A cherry orchard stands beside the house, / Above the house May bugs hum, /
Plowmen walk along with their plows ... / And mothers wait supper for them. / The
family sups beside the house, / A little evening star rises, / The daughter tends to
the table ... / Everything has grown still ... / only the young girls / And the nightingale are not still.

> Izza *haiu* sontse *skhodyt*,
> Za *hai* i *zakhodyt*;
> Po dolyni uvecheri
> Kozak smutnyi *khodyt*.
> *Khodyt* vin hodynu,
> *Khodyt* vin i druhu, –
> Ne *vykhodyt* chornobryva
> Iz temnoho luhu,
> Ne *vykhodyt* zradlyvaia ...

From behind the grove the sun rises / And behind it sets; / Along the valley in the
evening / A sad Cossack walks. / He walks for an hour, / Walks for a second, – /

The dark-browed beauty / Does not come forth from the dark meadow, / The treacherous one does not come forth ...

By further enriching the consonance which results from the repetition of words with individual sound repetitions, Shevchenko achieves unusual effects. In order to make clear the extent and significance of these sound repetitions in Shevchenko's verse, of this 'instrumentation' (as some formalists would describe it), those sounds that are repeated in each line will be listed separately:

... Ni, Stepane,	
Moia ty dytyno.	ty dy ty
I Hospod tebe pokyne,	po te po ky
Iak ty nas pokynesh.	ty po ky

... No, Stepan, / Child of mine. / Even the Lord will abandon you, / If you abandon us.

Entire stanzas of his poems are constructed around sonorous repetitions in words that are totally different and unrelated to one another:

bez myloho skriz mohyla ...	myloh mohyl

without my beloved, everywhere is like a grave ...

Chy to nedolia ta nevolia,	chy to ne olia ta olia
Chy to lita ti letiachi ...	chy to lit ti let

Whether it be misfortune and bondage, / Whether it be the years that fly ...

Korovy pidut po dibrovi ...	rovy pi dut po dibro ovi

The cows will walk through the grove ...

... idut molytsia	sia
Chentsi za Husa. Z-za hory	che tsi za sa za hory
Chervone sontse azh horyt ...	che on on tse hory

... the monks go to pray for Hus. / From behind the hill / A red sun fairly blazes ...

Shchob ia postil veselo slala	s l se lo s la la
U moria sliz ne posylala ...	s sy la la

so that I may cheerfully make my bed, / Not drown it in a sea of tears ...

| Selo! selo, veseli khaty, | se lo se lo ve se li ty |
| Veseli zdaleka palaty ... | ve se li al al ty |

Village! village, cheerful houses, / At a distance, cheerful mansions ...

Shyroki sela;	se la
A u selakh u veselykh	u se la u ve se ly
I liudy veseli ...	ve se li

Broad villages; / And in the cheerful villages / The people are cheerful too ...

Po dibrovi viter vyie	po ro vi vi vy
Huliaie po poliu,	lia po po liu
Krai dorohy hne topoliu	ra do ro po liu
Do samoho dolu ...	do do lu

Through the grove the wind howls, / Cavorts around the field, / By the road it bends the poplar / To the very ground ...

Chyhryne, Chyhryne!	Chyh ry ne chyh ry ne
Vse na sviti hyne,	vse na svi hy ne
I sviataia tvoia slava,	svia s va
Iak pylyna lyne	ly na ly ne
Za vitramy kholodnymy ...	vi my ny my

Chyhryn, Chyhryn! / All things on earth perish, / Even your sacred glory / Like dust is carried off / By cold winds ...

As with a musical melody, Shevchenko was able to evoke a specific effect with the sounds of his lines alone. The following are examples of instrumentation in a sombre key where the sounds 'r,' 'u,' 'or,' and 'ol' are employed:

Vitre buinyi, vitre buinyi!	vit re bui nyi vit re bui nyi
Ty z morem hovorysh,	ty z ore ory
Zbudy ioho, zahrai ty z nym,	z dy z ty z nym
Spytai synie more ...	yt ne ore

Blustering wind, blustering wind! / You talk with the sea, / Arouse it, roar with it, / Ask the blue sea ...

U nediliu vrantsi rano	ra ra no
Pole krylosia tumanom;	po los tu ma nom
U tumani na mohyli,	tu man na mo li
Iak topolia pokhylylas	pol po ly las
Molodytsia molodaia.	mo lod mo lod
...	
Ta z tumanom rozmovliaie:	ta tu ma nom mo
'Oi, tumane, tumane!	tu ma ne tu ma ne
Mii latanyi talane!	ta ta ny ta la ne
Chomu mene ne skhovaiesh	mu me ne ne
Otut sered lanu?'	tu la

Upon a Sunday early in the morn / The field was covered in mist; / In the mist upon a burial mound / A girl bends like a poplar ... / And with the mist converses: 'O, mist, mist! / My miserable lot! / Why do you not conceal me here / In the midst of the meadow?'

Or there is the following sombre symphony of lines:

Niby sertse odpochyne,	ne
Z Bohom zahovoryt ...	oho aho vory
A tuman, nenache voroh,	tum an ne na voro
Zakryvaie more	za ry va ore
I khmaronku rozhevuiu,	aro ro
I tmu za soboiu	tmu oiu
Roztylaie tuman syvyi,	ro tum an
I tmoiu nimoiu	t moiu moiu
Opoviie tobi dushu ...	

As if at rest, the heart / With God converses ... / And the mist, like a foe, / Covers the sea / And a tiny pink cloud; / And the grey mist spreads darkness behind it / And in its dumb darkness / Enshrouds your soul ...

In some instances it even seems that words are chosen because of their sonority: 'na mohyli' – 'molodytsia molodaia,' 'latanyi' – 'talane,' 'nenache voroh' – 'zakryvaie more,' etc.

Numerous passages in the works from all periods of Shevchenko's creative career are orchestrated in this way. And while in certain instances this instrumentation assists the poet in evoking a definite mood, occasionally it is used onomatopoeically, that is, in such a way that the sounds alone paint a particular scene; for example, the rustle of reed grass in the wind:

Viter v hai ne huliaie,	
V nochi spochyvaie;	
Prokynetsia, tykhesenko	sia ke se
V osoky pytaie:	so
'Khto se, khto se po tsim botsi	khto se khto se tsi tsi
Cheshe kosu? Khto se?	che she su khto se
Khto se, khto se po tim botsi	khto se khto se tsi
Rve na sobi kosy?	so sy
Khto se? khto se?' – tykhesenko	khto se khto se khe se
Spytaie-poviie ...	

The wind in the grove does not play, / In the night it rests; / It awakens and quietly / Of the reed grass enquires: / 'Who is it, who is it that over here / Is combing her tresses? Who is it? / Who is it, who is it that over there / Is tearing her tresses? / Who is it? who is it?' / it enquires, wafting ...

or in the dry leaves:

... shelestyt	she le sty
Pozhovkle lystia; hasnut ochi,	zho le ly stia snu chi
Zasnuly dumy, sertse spyt	za snu ly se tse
I vse zasnulo ...	se za snu lo

... yellow leaves / Rustle; my eyes grow dim, / My thoughts doze, / My heart slumbers / And everything slumbers ...

Or there is the favourite phrase 'revnuly harmaty' (cannons roared) or 'revily harmaty' (cannons were roaring) taken from the *dumy* (historical songs) by Izmail Sreznevsky, perhaps chiefly because of their usefulness in 'sound painting.'

Shevchenko employs musical devices in extremely diverse ways. Typical of his poetry are verses suited to musical expression, song-like (most of his 'songs' and many passages in his longer poems); furthermore, there are declamatory, rhetorical verses (poetic passages in his longer poems, the poems dedicated to other poets, his 'Psalms,' 'Do mertvykh i zhyvykh ...' / 'To My Dead and Living ... Countrymen ...'). And in addition to these verses there are others. The musical structure of all the types of verses is various. In a number of them the euphonic instrumentation is not as abundant as in some of the poems cited here.

Perhaps because of its musicality, Shevchenko's language affects the reader in such a way that, in spite of the accumulation of identical sounds, an impression of artificiality is avoided. His language is tightly bound to the folk song, yet Shevchenko does not copy it slavishly but creatively reshapes it. The study of instrumentation in Shevchenko's language may be completed by an analysis of the folk sources of his creativity. Here is one example:

SHEVCHENKO:

Izza haiu *sontse skhodyt*
Za hai i *zakhodyt*;
Po dolyni uvechori
Kozak *smutnyi khodyt* ...

From behind the grove the sun rises, / Behind the grove sets; / Along the valley in the evening / A sad Cossack walks ...

WAGONER'S SONG (Pereshory, Kherson province):

Oi, vysoko iasne *sontse skhodyt*
nyzenko *zakhodyt*;
smutno, smutno chumatskyi otaman
po taboru *khodyt*.

O, high into the sky does the sun rise, / Low does it set; / Sadly, sadly the wagon master / Around the campsite walks.

(1946)

NOTES

1 Translation of 'Shevchenko ta ioho doba,' *Pratsi shevchenkivskoi konferentsii UVAN* (Augsburg 1946). A similar text appears in D. Cyzevs'kyj, *A History of Ukrainian Literature* (Littleton 1975).

2 The 'schemes' of the lines are provided here in order to reveal the diversity of Shevchenko's rhythms. The discovery of the folk character of Shevchenko's

rhythm, of course, was made mainly by S. Smal-Stotsky. See his *Rytmika Shevchenkovoi poezii* (Prague 1925). His theoretical formulations, however, are not, I believe, always correct, an issue that cannot be discussed in detail here.

3 An apostrophe is used, where necessary, to designate the soft sign, otherwise omitted in the transliteration scheme employed here (trans.).

4 V. Peretts, *Issledovania i materialy po istorii starinnoi ukrainskoi literatury*, I-III (Leningrad 1926-9).

5 M. Vozniak, *Materialy do istorii ukrainskoi pisni i virshi* (Lviv 1913-25).

6 V. Rezanov, *Drama ukrainska* (Kiev 1926-9).

7 For more detailed information on the history of Ukrainian rhyme, see my *Ukrainskyi Literaturnyi barok*, 2 vols (Prague 1941). More precise indications of the sources used are provided there.

8 Some examples from Tolstoi:

> Blagoslovliaiu vas, lesa,
> Doliny, nivy, gory, *vody.*
> *Blagos*lovliaiu ia *prirodu*
> I golubye nebesa.

My blessing I bestow, upon you, forests, / Dales, cornfields, hills, waters. / My blessing upon nature I bestow / And upon the azure heavens.

> Menia, vo mrake i v pyli
> Dosel vlachivshego *okovy,*
> Liubvi krylia voznesli
> V otchiznu plameni i *slova.*

> I prosvetlel moi temnyi vzor,
> I stal mne vidim mir *nezrimyi,*
> I slyshit ukho s etikh por,
> Chto dlia drugikh *neulovimo* ...

In the darkness and dust / Dragging my shackles until now, / I, on the wings of love, was raised / To the land of flame and word.
And my dim gaze grew brighter and / A world unknown became visible to me / And my ear from that time hears / That which to others is imperceptible ...

Other examples: Type 1: Otlogo-dorogoi, zhadno-otradnoi, okovy-ternovyi; Type 2: v tumane-tkani, iuno-struna, vzor-goria, chuia-vsue, tlene selenia, voda-svobodu, dostoino-voiny, stremitsia (phonetically 'stremitsa')-kolysnitsa, otradu-stado, odezhdy-nadezhdy, etc. Also: ponuria-buryi, podiatyi-mlata, resnitsa-verenitsei, zlato-bogatyi, etc.

Tolstoi also uses rhymes with consonants that are single or doubled, voiced or unvoiced, unpalatalized or palatalized. But in Russian (and in the final sound at that!) the difference here is often only in orthography. Cf. borolos'-golos, grud'-put', ver'te-smerti, vod-rastet, pobed-net, etc.

Tolstoi, however, avoids rhymes with extra consonants, the kind of rhymes that are very typical of Shevchenko's verse. (See types 2, 4, and 5, pp 269-70.) His reform in the area of rhyme is therefore significantly less 'radical.'

9 In addition, there is also consonance before the rhyme here: ma*liia*-m*liic*.

18

Shevchenko and Russian Revolutionary-Democratic Thought

MYKOLA HUDZII

From the beginning of his literary career the great Ukrainian poet T.H. Shevchenko was far in advance of contemporary Ukrainian writers, not only because of his artistic mastery, but because of his sophisticated social and political philosophy.[1] Even his earliest poems were a revelation not only for Ukrainian but also Russian readers. Shevchenko was the first Ukrainian artist and writer to come from the common people. At the age of seventeen, and still a serf, he began his career as a painter and writer in Petersburg, capital of the Russian empire. He had already experienced a life in semi-slavery, with all its drudgery, fear, and humiliation, but he also remembered his grandfather telling of the heroic struggles of the *haidamaky* in defence of the freedom and national interests of the Ukrainian people. He passionately loved Ukrainian folk songs and *dumy* that described the Cossacks' courageous exploits in their campaigns against the enemies of Ukraine. He arrived in Petersburg feeling grieved and wronged not only by his own fate but also by the fate of all the serfs, whose suffering moved him deeply.

The mood of protest and revolt against society's hypocrisy and the militaristic tsarist regime struck a responsive chord in Shevchenko. As a result of historical circumstances, literature and social thought in Ukraine before Shevchenko were not yet as highly developed as they were in Russia. The Ukrainian literary heritage that Shevchenko as a poet drew upon had no Radishchev with his revolutionary tradition, no poems in praise of freedom by a young Pushkin, and no revolutionary Decembrist poetry. Only a few years before Shevchenko's arrival, Petersburg had been the centre of the Decembrist uprising. There can be no doubt that the leading

literature and social philosophy of the Russian capital captured all Shevchenko's attention soon after he had settled there. Franko wrote: 'It is
impossible that Shevchenko, living in Petersburg at the time, should not
also have been transported by that great progressive movement, or that his
fiery young soul should not have turned towards it, especially because his
own sympathies for the common people drew him in that direction. ... From
the early 1840s, Shevchenko ever more boldly and decisively set out along
this new path. Almost every new work of his was a step forward' (Temne
tsarstvo).[2]

Shevchenko himself, imprisoned during the affair of the Brotherhood of
Saints Cyril and Methodius, stated during the inquiry: 'Living in Petersburg, on all sides I heard impudent remarks and censure of the tsar and
the government.' Shevchenko had always been fascinated by and full of
respect for the Decembrists and their social achievements and naturally
they played an important role in the development of his political views. He
was well acquainted with the work of Ryleev, the best-known poet-revolutionary in the Decembrist camp. Shevchenko especially loved his poems
'Voinarovsky' and 'Nalivaiko' because the theme of both poems is the
Ukrainian people's struggle for freedom. Shevchenko remembered Ryleev's
work in 1843 when he was visiting the estate of N.H. Repnin (brother of
the Decembrist S.G. Volkonsky, who had been exiled to Siberia) in Iahotyn, Ukraine. There Shevchenko wrote his poem 'Trizna' (in Russian),
which was clearly influenced by 'Voinarovsky.' The influence of 'Ispoved
Nalivaiki' can be seen in Shevchenko's earlier Russian-language drama
'Nikita Gaidai' (1841) and also in his poem 'Liakham' (To the Poles,
1847). In a letter of that date (1847) to V.N. Repnina, Shevchenko quoted
parts of 'Voinarovsky' from memory. On his way back to Petersburg from
exile, Shevchenko heard excerpts from both poems read aloud and praised
the readings highly.

In 'Son' (The Dream, 1844) Shevchenko described the lives of the
Decembrists in penal servitude in such a way that every word conveyed his
great sorrow at their martyrdom. In 'Velykyi lokh' (The Great Vault),
written a year later, the first raven says:

Ia otse litala
Azh u Sybir ta v odnoho

Dekabrysta vkrala
Trokhy zhovchi

Lately I flew
Far away to Siberia
And from a Decembrist I stole
Some bile.

On the journey to Petersburg Shevchenko stopped over in Nizhny Novgorod, and there, at the home of an acquaintance, he met the Decembrist I.A. Annenkov, who was also returning from exile. He wrote this affecting account of their meeting in his journal: 'At Jacobi's it was my great honour to make the acquaintance of the Decembrist Ivan Aleksandrovich Annenkov, who was returning from Siberia. In his speech this greying, grand, and gentle exile shows not a trace of bitterness towards his cruel judges; he even banters good-heartedly about Chernishev and Levashev, the presiding judges of the supreme court and favourites of the crowned sergeant-major. I venerate you, one of our first apostles.' They talked until one o'clock in the morning. They discussed Nikolai Turgenev, who was returning from exile, and his book, and much more besides. Three weeks later Shevchenko met Annenkov again and they spent an entire evening together.

In Nizhny Novgorod, Shevchenko obtained a copy of Herzen's journal 'Poliarnaia zvezda' (The Northern Star) for 1856. Its cover showed portraits of the five Decembrists who had been hanged. Shevchenko wrote in his journal:

The cover, that is, the portraits of our first apostles and martyrs, weighed upon my spirit so much that even now I cannot rid myself of that gloomy impression. How appropriate it would be to strike a medal to commemorate that infamous event. One side would show the portraits of the martyrs with the inscription 'the first Russian heralds of liberty' and the other side a portrait of the unforgettable hindrance [i.e., Nicholas I] with the inscription: 'Not the first of Russia's crowned executioners.'

Shevchenko's meeting with Annenkov and the impression made by the portraits of the hanged Decembrists evidently prompted him to write (while still in Nizhny Novgorod) the poem 'The Neophytes,' in which Nero and the Christians he persecuted represent Nicholas I and his victims, the Decembrists. The poem 'Iurodyvyi' (God's Fool), in which the poet describes the Decembrists with great lyric emotion, was also written in Nizhny Novgorod.

In Moscow, Shevchenko made the acquaintance of the Decembrist S.G. Volkonsky, and in Petersburg that of another Decembrist, V.I. Steingel. The Decembrists' influence on Shevchenko was kept up through his relations with the circle of Petrashevtsy, who had to a great extent inherited the ideological tradition of the Decembrists. In Petersburg, Shevchenko was personally acquainted with two of the most radical of the Petrashevtsy, Mombelli and Strandman, who doubtless informed him of the main ideas of the brotherhood. Shevchenko's poems 'Son' (The Dream), 'Kavkaz' (The Caucasus), and 'I mertvym, i zhyvym, i nenarodzhenym' (To my Dead and Living and Yet Unborn Countrymen ...) have many ideas in common with the sociopolitical platform of the Petrashevtsy.

The members of Petrashevsky's circle displayed great interest in Shevchenko's work. Petrashevsky himself followed Shevchenko's literary career and was especially interested in the trial of the Brotherhood of Saints Cyril and Methodius. Antonelli, an agent of the third section, recorded Petrashevsky's remarks on the Brotherhood's activities at a meeting of the Petrashevsky circle that he managed to infiltrate: 'In spite of the failure of the undertaking [said Petrashevsky], it nevertheless took hold in Little Russia, and the process was greatly facilitated by Shevchenko's writings, which were widely distributed in that country and were the cause of great intellectual unrest ... the results of which are even now in ferment.'

Shevchenko was well acquainted with Pleshcheev, a poet and member of Petrashevsky's circle. He was a soldier who had been exiled to Orenburg and had corresponded with Shevchenko during their years of exile. In Shevchenko's only surviving letter to Pleshcheev, he wrote: 'For me every line and every word of your writing is the word of a brother and a sincere friend.' Pleshcheev translated several of Shevchenko's poems into Russian.

For Shevchenko, Herzen and the Decembrists were very closely allied ideologically. Shevchenko called the hanged Decembrists our first apostles and martyrs. He called the Decembrist Annenkov one of our first apostles. In 'God's Fool,' the Decembrists are called 'saintly slaves.' Shevchenko called Herzen 'an apostle' and 'a holy man' (in his journal for 11 October and 10 December 1857). Upon first seeing Herzen's newspaper, 'Kolokol' (The Bell) Shevchenko 'kissed it reverently.' He read Herzen's 'Golosa iz

Rossii' (Voices from Russia) out of which he copied a long excerpt of P.L. Lavrov's poem, 'Russkomu narodu' (To the Russian People) into his journal. He also read 'Poliarnaia zvezda,' became familiar with *Byloe i dumy* (My Past and Thoughts) and copied Herzen's portrait into his journal. Using Herzen's terminology, Shevchenko called Nicholas I 'an obstruction,' 'an unforgettable hindrance,' a crowned executioner, and a sergeant-major.

The Russian-language stories Shevchenko wrote in exile are often similar in theme to Herzen's *belles-lettres*, which Shevchenko first read in exile.

Shevchenko knew Herzen when he had been, as Lenin described him, awakened by the Decembrists, but was still in a stage of transition from the gentry revolutionism of democrats of various social origins (the so-called 'raznochintsy'). This was evident from Herzen's relations with Alexander II and his positive attitude to the latter's reforms, which certainly did not satisfy Shevchenko, as we can see from his journal entry of 16 October 1857. In it he wrote that 'Kostomarov's letter addressed to the tsar is being circulated among the students.' Shevchenko described this letter, which had not in fact been written by Kostomarov, as 'containing many truths and [being] on the whole more extensive and wiser than Herzen's letter addressed to the same person.' However, this disagreement with Herzen did not change Shevchenko's attitude towards him or towards this matter. That very day, Shevchenko made an entry in his journal about a rumour he had heard (which turned out to be false) that a Russian journal, *Posrednik* (The Intermediary) had appeared in Paris. The aim of this journal was 'to be the mediator between the London publications and periodicals of Iskander (Herzen) on the one hand, and the Russian government, and to reveal the baseness of 'Pchela' (The Bee), *Nord*, and all the other filth of the regime.' (Here Shevchenko was thinking of *Severnaia pchela*, a reactionary newspaper published until 1859 by Bulgarin and Grech, and *Nord*, the official French-language organ of the Russian government that began to be published in Brussels in 1855.) Shevchenko believed the rumour and expressed his fear that 'the crowned Cartouche,' that is, Napoleon III, would 'suppress this newborn child of sacred truth.' In his journal for 10 December of that year Shevchenko as before calls Herzen 'an apostle' and a 'holy man.' In 1860 he asked one of his correspondents to give Herzen a copy of *Kobzar* with his 'reverent greetings.'

For his part, Herzen, because he was interested in the Ukrainian people's fate and their struggle for freedom against tsarism, paid close attention to Shevchenko as the first Ukrainian poet and warrior for the happiness of his people. In 1859 he published 'A letter to the publisher of *Kolokol*' in which the author, Kostomarov, gave a brief outline of Ukrainian history and the tsarist regime's oppression of Ukraine up to the destruction of the Brotherhood of Saints Cyril and Methodius. Kostomarov also gave an account of Shevchenko's arrest and the hardships of his life in exile. In *Kolokol* for 1861, Herzen published a moving notice of Shevchenko's death: 'The Little Russian minstrel, T. Shevchenko, died on 26 February [10 March] in Petersburg. How sad it is that this unfortunate martyr closed his eyes so shortly before the promised day of freedom. Who had more right than he to sing its praises? It is well that the rising star of that day illuminated his entire life and lighted up his last days.'

Regardless of the way we now judge Herzen's attitude towards the emancipation, the fact remains that in these lines he emphasized the especially close ties between Shevchenko and the vital interests of his unfortunate people. That same year, in an editorial note, Herzen wrote with biting irony about the sculpture to commemorate Russia's millenium. The bas-relief portraits of St Mitrofan of Voronezh, the actor Dmitrevsky, and the '*serf kobzar*' Shevchenko were to be replaced by portraits of Nicholas I and Derzhavin. 'We agree,' wrote Herzen, 'that the actor Dmitrevsky and almost the only (*narodnyi*) [In Ukrainian and in Russian *narodnyi* can mean both 'people's' and 'national.'] poet of the people, Shevchenko, are hardly in the right company beside Nicholas ...' Thus, in considering Shevchenko to be the only people's poet, Herzen and Dobroliubov are of one mind. Their accord is even more obvious in Herzen's riposte of 1861, cited in E.F. Iunge's memoirs: 'He is great because he is a supreme poet of the people like Koltsov, but he is far more significant than Koltsov, for Shevchenko was a political activist and fought for liberty.'

Herzen thought Shevchenko's philosophy so significant that in 1863 he described it as having replaced the pessimistic philosophy of Chaadaev and, along with the work of Belinsky, beginning a new chapter in Russian history. The painter N.G. Ge recalled that Herzen, after reading Shevchenko's poems in Gerbel's translation, remarked, 'Great God, what charm! This is like a fresh breeze from the steppes! This is the open air; it is freedom.'

The mutual attraction between Herzen and Shevchenko was owing to the similarity of their views on the tasks of the movement for the revolutionary rebirth of Russia. In time, Shevchenko's political views ought to have come closer to those of the revolutionary democrats Chernyshevsky, Nekrasov, and Saltykov-Shchedrin. Shevchenko himself was a revolutionary democrat and for that reason his inherent agreement with the views of the Russian revolutionary democrats is not explained so much by the influence of the Russians who shared his views as by the similarity of their political and social experiences. Of course this does not exclude the influence of Russian revolutionary thought upon Shevchenko to the extent that it gave him the opportunity to formulate and become more conscious of the ideas which on occasion quite spontaneously arose in his consciousness.

Shevchenko had a very high regard for the journal *Sovremennik* (The Contemporary), which was edited by Chernyshevsky and Nekrasov. He evidently began reading it while still in exile and was very eager to publish his novel *Varnak* (The Convict) in it.

Shevchenko's daily journal testified to his genuine admiration for Saltykov-Shchedrin, one of the revolutionary-democratic writers. He was transported by 'Gubernskie ocherki' (Provincial Sketches), apparently the only one of Shchedrin's books known to him. 'I venerate Saltykov,' he acknowledged. Shevchenko was enthralled by Shchedrin because he saw him as the talented student of 'the immortal Gogol.'

Shevchenko never mentioned Chernyshevsky, but there is no doubt that their views on politics and aesthetics were very similar. Like Chernyshevsky, Shevchenko was a consistent materialist in his esthetic views, which is very clear from his famous judgment on the Polish philosopher Libelt's idealist treatise on aesthetics. We know that after his return from exile to Petersburg, Shevchenko met Chernyshevsky and even visited him at home. After his return Shevchenko's poems became more revolutionary in tone than they had been before his exile. Like Chernyshevsky, he now called upon Rus' to take up the axe; he used biblical references in his unsparing and hostile attacks on tsarism and on every despotic system. The satirical sharpness of his accusations became truly unparalleled. Sreznevsky, describing this last stage of Shevchenko's life, wrote: 'his accusations now became unrestrained. He began to strike and beat. He spouted some mad and annihilating fire.'

In allying himself with the representatives of the Russian revolutionary-democratic movement in Petersburg, Shevchenko simultaneously drew away from his liberal-minded friends, Kostomarov and Kulish. He also refused to have anything to do with I. Aksakov's newspaper *Parus*, (The Sail) because the issue on the Slavic peoples, which should have been devoted to their interests, completely omitted to mention the Ukrainians and because Aksakov, the editor, defended Prince I.A. Cherkasky, who advocated the use of wooden canes to punish villagers who had committed crimes. Upon the publication of an anti-semitic attack in the journal *Illiustratsiia* in 1858, Shevchenko, along with Chernyshevsky and other writers, signed a protest against it.

In Chernyshevsky's view, Shevchenko was not only a poet of great authority but also a man with broad political horizons. In his own arguments he relied upon Shevchenko's judgment of the situation in Ukraine. Thus, in his article 'National Tactlessness,' Chernyshevsky, arguing against the nationalist position of the pro-Austrian Lviv newspaper *Slovo* (The Word), stated that Shevchenko had explained to him that truth which he had guessed at, namely that the Ukrainian peasants' enmity towards the Polish land-owners was not owing to national and religious factors but simply to the fact that most of the land-owners were Polish. Class differences lay at the root of this enmity and the Ukrainian as well as the Polish villager harboured a general hatred for his oppressors regardless of their nationality.

Chernyshevsky consistently and unreservedly maintained a very high regard for Shevchenko as a great verbal artist. In his review of the first issue of the journal *Osnova* Chernyshevsky singled out Shevchenko and Marko Vovchok from all the other Ukrainian writers and stated 'having such a poet as Shevchenko, Little Russian literature needs no one's favours.'

Dobroliubov also valued Shevchenko's talents very highly, holding that the appearance of Shevchenko's poems was significant not only for the violent opponents of Ukrainian literature but for all who appreciate poetry.

Like Chernyshevsky, Nekrasov thought highly of Shevchenko as a national poet. When Shevchenko died he wrote a sorrowful poem in which he described the great poet's lifelong suffering. On another occasion, in 1871, along with Pypin and Kostomarov, he appeared as an expert witness in the affair of the court summons of Shevchenko's publishers. During this appearance Nekrasov pointed out that 'Shevchenko was a deeply and exclusively national (*natsionalnyi*) poet, specializing in an area to which he devoted his entire life.'

Among Shevchenko's most famous admirers was the poet-revolutionary M.I. Mikhailov, a political ally of Chernyshevsky and Dobroliubov, and author of the article about *Kobzar*, in which Shevchenko is counted among the world's greatest writers. Like Dobroliubov, Mikhailov emphasized Shevchenko's intimate bond with the people. He also translated some of Shevchenko's poems into Russian.

The thrust of Shevchenko's ideological and artistic development brought him very close to the leading revolutionary traditions of Russian life and literature. This was a profoundly organic tie. It was conditioned primarily by the fact that everything in Shevchenko's world view and in his experience impelled him towards these traditions. Shevchenko's social and political views steadily and progressively developed along the lines of revolutionary-democratic ideology. He contributed a great deal to the development of this ideology. This accounts for the high opinion of his work and his person held by members of the first rank of Russian revolutionary-democratic thinkers.

(1951)

NOTES

1 A translation of M. Hudzii, 'Shevchenko i rosiiska revoliutsiino-demokratychna dumka,' in *Svitova velych Shevchenka*, II (Kiev 1964). This article originally was written in 1951.
2 Ivan Franko, 'Temne tsarstvo,' *Tvory*, XVII (Kiev 1955) 11.

19

Shevchenko's Ballad 'At Catherine's'

MAKSYM RYLSKY

'He was truly a poet of the people.¹ We have no one like him. Even Koltsov is not comparable, for sometimes in his thoughts and aspirations he is far removed from the people. But for Shevchenko, all thoughts and emotions are in harmony with the life of the people. He was a son of the people and lived with the people. The circumstances of his life bound him closely to them.'

Dobroliubov's description is often cited, and it is undoubtedly true that Shevchenko was always close to the hopes and ambitions of his people. His creativity was based upon and nurtured by folk traditions. Shevchenko loved and believed in his people and he was greatly concerned about their freedom and happiness. But in examining his poetry we must not overlook the individuality of his creative genius. He did not merely continue the beautiful but fixed tradition of anonymous composers of folk songs and *dumy*. The rigidity of this tradition is exemplified in the constant use of set epithets which at times lead to the absurdities common in folk art (eg, 'to mow the green rye' (zeleneie zhyto zhaty) in unvarying comparisons, in repetitive symbolism, epic retardation, verbal rhymes (especially in the *dumy*), etc. Shevchenko gradually abandoned set folkloric (and literary, romantic) epithets such as 'the wild wind' (buinyi viter), 'the blue sea' (synie more), 'the grey eagle' (syzyi orel), 'the white face' (bile lychko), 'the pale moon' (blidyi misiats), in favour of his own original expressions such as 'crowned executioners' (katy vinchanni), 'the unwashed sky' (nebo nevmyte), 'the drowsy waves' (zaspani khvyli), 'the mournful *duma*' (skorbna duma), 'like a drunken reed' (nenache pianyi ocheret), 'the broad-leaved poplars' (shyrokolysti topoli), 'the vile sea' (nikchemne more), the ironic 'gracious God' (laskavyi Boh), the 'dove-grey eyes, almost black' (ochi holubi azh chorni), 'the bright world without darkness' (svit iasnyi, nevechirnyi), the 'golden-winged muse' (zoloto-kryla muza), and so forth. This is also evident in his metaphors and similes: the river Alta, who 'brings the news' (nese visti) 'like a scarlet snake' (chervonoiu hadiukoiu); Ivan Hus, standing 'like a cedar in a field of Lebanon' (mov kedr sered polia Lyvanskoho); eyes that shine 'with the precious brilliance of a diamond' (almazom dobrym, dorohym); Judea that 'stirred and roared like a serpent in the slime' (zavorushylas, zarevla, nenache hadyna v boloti); palaces 'blazing with purple and gold' (horiat purpurom i zlatom); 'slaves with bows (in their hair), lackeys in golden finery' (raby z kokardoiu na lobi, lakei v zolotii ozdobi) – all these derive not from folk tradition but from the poet's creativity, from his perception of the world and his own bold aesthetic.

It is also interesting to examine Shevchenko's versification. Even his first poem, 'Prychynna' (The Bewitched Woman) begins in four-foot iambic. This versification was traditional in Russian and Ukrainian literary verse before Shevchenko (eg, Kotliarevsky), but was not used in folk poetry. The introduction is followed by the so-called eight-syllable *kolomyika* metre, which would long be Shevchenko's favourite verse form. This relatively short passage is followed by the so-called 12-11 syllabification which clearly tends towards the amphibrach. This syllabification, the *kolomyika* metre, and occasionally (as in 'Slipyi' [The Blind Man]) the use of versification found in the *dumy* all characterize Shevchenko's poetry up until the last period of his career (ie, until his imprisonment, exile, and the period following his exile). This same four-foot iambic occurs as early as 'Kateryna' (Catherine) (at the beginning of Part IV) and in two parts of 'Haidamaky' ('Tretii pivni' / 'The Third Cock-Crow' and 'Honta v Umani' / 'Honta in Uman'). It also occurs in the extraordinarily metrically and rhythmically varied 'Hamaliia,' with Shevchenko's unique metrical structure at the beginning of the poem ('Oi nema, nema, ni vitru, ni khvyli' / 'There is no wind, nor wave,' the song of the Zaporozhtsi – 'U turkeni po tim botsi' / 'At the Turkish lady's on the other side,' etc.).

During Shevchenko's most creative period the four-foot iambic, not excluding, of course, syllabification and traditional folk versification, clearly predominates. Beautiful lyric poems such as 'Buvaie inodi, staryi' (Sometimes the old man ...), 'Khiba samomu napysat' (Perhaps I myself should write ...), 'I zolotoi, i dorohoi' (The golden and the precious), 'Hotovo, parus rozpustyly' (The sails were already unfurled), 'Iakby vy znaly, panychi' (If you but knew, lordlings), 'Ohni horiat' (The fires are burning), 'I dosi snytsia' (And yet I dream), 'Dolia' (Fate), 'Muza' (The Muse) with *kolomyika* embellishment, 'Son' (The Dream ['She was reaping wheat in the master's field']), 'Ia ne nezduzhaiu, nivroku' (No, thank God, I am not ill), 'Sestri' (To my sister), 'Mynaiuchy ubohi sela' (Passing by the poor villages) are written in four-foot iambic. This is also the basic versification in the poems 'Neofity' and 'Mariia.' Naturally, Shevchenko's iambic verse with its unequalled rhythmic richness differs greatly from Kotliarevsky's, just as Pushkin's iambic verse differs from that of his predecessors. That the origin of Shevchenko's verse is to be found in the literary and not the folkloric tradition in no way contradicts the notion that Shevchenko was a poet of the people who declared that his life history was part of the history of his native land.

In Shevchenko's strophic art and metrical structure (whose variety is rivalled perhaps only by Lermontov's) and in his traditional songs, which shone 'with the precious brilliance of a diamond' during the most difficult years of the poet's life – those of detention and exile – folkloric style and ambience are preserved while the strophic and metrical structures differ greatly from the traditional. An examination of *Kobzar*, that crowning achievement of Ukrainian poetry, confirms that Shevchenko was a truly national poet and at the same time a unique creative individual who, drawing upon traditional poetry and world literature, produced unequalled and inimitable works of art.

I regard the ballad 'U tiiei Kateryny' (At Catherine's) as one of the greatest examples of Shevchenko's artistic mastery. The ballad is thoroughly romantic. That it was written when the poet had firmly established himself as a realist is not a contradiction. Many of his early works, such as 'Kateryna' and 'Haidamaky,' are in part realistic. But of Gorky's works, 'Starukha Izergil' (Old Izergil), 'Pesnia o burevesnike' (The Song of the Stormy Petrel), 'Chelkash,' 'Skazki ob Italii' (Italian Tales), and many pages in *Foma Gordeev* and *Mat* (Mother) are romantic. Beside the sternly realistic *Fata morgana* and 'Shcho napysano v knyhu zhyttia' (What is Written in the Book of Life) of Kotsiubynsky there occurs the wonderfully romantic *Tini zabutykh predkiv* (Shadows of Forgotten Ancestors). Ianovsky's cruelly, unsparingly realistic *Vershnyky* (The Horsemen), Dovzhenko's basically realistic *Zacharovana Desna* (The Enchanted Desna) and *Poema pro more* (A Poem about the Sea) must also be counted as romantic. Romanticism as a characteristic of the human spirit and as a way of looking at the world (not as an artistic style) is found in Greek tragedy, in Dante, Shakespeare, and Goethe, in 'Evgenii Onegin,' and in Lesia Ukrainka's dramatic works, and in Ivan Franko, who ironically (but in fact quite seriously) stated at the beginning of 'Lisova idyliia' (A Forest Idyll): 'I am mounting a romantic horse' – although in fact it was Pegasus, a classical horse.

The versification of 'U tiiei Kateryny' is unique. Seemingly, it uses the *kolomyika* metre found in most of the poem 'Kateryna,' but has a fanciful arrangement of rhyme (*abcb*, or *aabb*, or *aabcc*, etc.). It contains deviations from the eight-syllable scheme along with recitative intonations which have been well put across by Lysenko in his musical score for the ballad.

Odyn utopyvsia (6 syllables)
U Dniprovim hyrli (6)
Druhoho v Kozlovi (6)
Na kil posadyly (6) etc.

This uneven syllabification brings to mind traditional *dumy*, whose versification has certainly influenced such passages as Stepan's *Duma* in 'Slipyi' (The Blind Man), but also 'U nedilenku u sviatuiu' (On Holy Sunday), a poem written in the same year as 'U tiiei Kateryny' (1848).

The basic function of this unusual syllabification, however, is very different here than in the *dumy* with their slow tempo. In this case it helps to give a stormy, passionate character to the poem. Let us examine certain characteristics of the ballad's style within the development of the poem. It begins:

U tiiei Kateryny
Khata na pomosti,
Iz slavnoho Zaporozhzhia
Naikhaly hosti.
Odyn Semen Bosy
Druhii Ivan Holy

Tretii slavnyi vdovychenko
Ivan Iaroshenko.

Catherine's house has a wooden floor
Her guests are renowned Zaporozhtsi.
The first is Semen Bosy,
The second Ivan Holy,
The third, a widow's famous son,
Ivan Iaroshenko.

This unusually condensed beginning plunges us into a world of dreams and romantic hyperbole. This Catherine is, of course, unique in all Ukraine and perhaps even in the world. Her exceptional beauty defies description even in poetry and legend. The Cossacks' surnames (Bosy [Barefoot] and Holy [Naked]) might prompt us to look for a description of their social origins, but they are the guests of a woman who owns 'a house with a wooden floor,' therefore certainly a rich woman, and one of democratic bent. That she is indeed a fabled beauty is proved by the conversation of her guests, the last of whom, again, is obviously unique in the land and well known even though he (the 'widow's famous son, Ivan Iaroshenko') is the poet's creation.

Zizdyly my Polshchu
I vsiu Ukrainu,
A ne bachyly takoi
Iak se Kateryna.

Through Poland and Ukraine we came
But never did we see
A woman like Catherine.

Ukraine itself, it seems, is not large enough: 'We travelled through Poland.' This recalls Gogol's 'An unheard-of marvel appeared near Kiev. All the gentry and hetmans gathered to marvel at it.' We are in a world similar to Gogol's steppes and Gogol's Dnieper. It is a world of the unusual, the unheard-of, the unique and unrepeatable, a world of indescribable beauty and boundless passion.

The author's terseness is remarkable; he gives no description of Catherine other than to say that her house has a wooden floor and that her beauty is completely natural. There is no account of her black brows, hazel eyes, or her other charms. The enraptured conversation of the Cossacks serves as her description.

> Odyn kazhe: – Brate,
> Iakby ia bahatyi,
> To oddav by vse zoloto
> Otsii Kateryni
> Za odnu hodynu.

> The first says, 'Brother, if I were rich
> I would give all my gold
> For but one hour with Catherine.'

> Druhyi kazhe: – Druzhe,
> Iakby ia buv duzhyi,
> To oddav by ia vsiu sylu
> Za odnu hodynu
> Otsii Kateryni.

> The second says, 'Friend, if I were strong
> I would give all my strength
> For but one hour with Catherine.'

Here are two natures, two world views: one uses wealth, the other strength, as a universal measure. But there is a third perspective:

> Tretii kazhe: – Dity,
> Nema toho v sviti,
> Choho b meni ne zrobyty
> Dlia tsiiei Kateryny
> Za odnu hodynu.

> The third says, 'Children, there is nothing
> I would not do
> For but one hour with Catherine.'

This is a love 'as strong as death' that puts neither wealth nor strength, but life itself, in the balance.

Iaroshenko addresses his comrades as 'children,' not as 'friends' or 'brothers.' This shows that to him, their love for Catherine is insignificant. 'Children' was pronounced with ironic emphasis by an acquaintance of mine, a marvelous reader, who made it sound like 'You, kids!'

Kateryna zadumalas
I tretomu kazhe:
Iest u mene brat iedynyi
U nevoli vrazhii!
U Krymu des propadaie.
Khto ioho dostane,
To toi meni, zaporozhtsi,
Druzhynoiu stane.

Catherine pondered
And said to the third:
'I have an only brother
Who is in cruel bondage
Somewhere in Crimea.
Whoever rescues him, Zaporozhtsi,
Shall be my mate.'

It is evident why Catherine addresses Ivan Iaroshenko: she knows that he loves her most ardently and blindly and that he is ready to lay down his life for her.

However, all three, having declared their unshakeable resolve dictated by passion, 'get up and saddle their horses' in response to Catherine's cunning, seductive command to deliver her brother from 'cruel bondage.' All three are possessed by love as strong as death and two of them meet horrible deaths:

Odyn utopyvsia
U Dniprovim hyrli,
Druhoho v Kozlovi
Na kil posadyly.

One drowned
In the Dnieper's tide.
Another in Kozlov
Was impaled.

Along with romanticism there is a realistic, historic accuracy which has the effect of emphasizing the romanticism: one man drowned not in an unnamed river but in the estuary of the Dnieper and the other was impaled not in an unspecified place but in Kozlov. This echoes the exactness of traditional poetry with its 'hundred-*pood* rods,' its accurate dating of events ('Oh, in the year one thousand seven hundred and ninety-one'), the precision of the *duma* about Samiilo Kishka, in which 'three flowers were painted on the galley,' where the Pole Buturlak 'was thirty years in bondage, and twenty-four years a free man,' where the galley sails not from an unidentified city but from Trapezont, where Alkan-Pasha hastens to Kozlov to court 'the maiden Sandzhakivna' and not some anonymous beauty. This precision is close to symbolism. But in contrast to the *duma*, Shevchenko has a very condensed style. Neither the Turks, the Mohammedans, nor the infidels are accused of the impaling, but nevertheless the reader knows exactly who did it.

> Tretii, Ivan Iaroshenko,
> Slavnyi vdovychenko,
> Z liutoi nevoli,
> Iz Bakchysaraiu
> Brata vyzvoliaie.

> The third, Ivan Iaroshenko,
> The widow's famous son,
> From cruel bondage
> In Bakchysarai
> Delivers the brother.

How does he do it? What adventures does he have? What feats of valour does he accomplish? The author will not say, nor does the reader need to know. The narrative is oriented towards a single goal; it is as taut as a bow that looses a single arrow to hit its target.

> Zaskrypily rano dveri
> U velykii khati.

> At dawn
> In the great house
> The door creaked.

Again, a single phrase ('In the great house') depicts the scene. Like the previous 'with a wooden floor' it implies a complete picture of a wealthy household.

– Vstavai, vstavai, Kateryno
  Brata zustrichaty! –

  Arise, arise, Catherine
  To welcome your brother!

In the voice of the widow's son we hear not so much hope for the sweet reward promised him as happiness for Catherine and her brother and a justified pride in his exploit.

  Kateryna podyvylas
  Ta i zaholosyla:
– Tse ne brat mii, tse mii mylyi,
  Ia tebe duryla.

  Catherine looked on
  And despaired:
  'Not my brother is he, but my beloved.
  I deceived you.'

Catherine pronounces these words not mockingly or triumphantly but as a lament. Alas! The punishment for evil is imminent and unavoidable.

– Oduryla – I Katryna
  Dodolu skotylas
  Holovonka ...

  She had lied
  And off came
  Catherine's head.

We are not told who murders Catherine. Iaroshenko? Perhaps, for, as we now say, his noblest feelings had been offended. Perhaps it was Catherine's anonymous 'brother' – in fact either her husband or lover. He may have been disillusioned by his beloved, or he may have taken offence at her treatment of his brave rescuer. But the 'black-browed Catherine' (this epithet is used at the beginning and end of the ballad to describe her beauty) trampled his love in the mud by her treachery. This mysteriousness, the sense of something left unsaid, is characteristic of romanticism.

Further on, we find the apotheosis of friendship and brotherhood:

Katerynu chornobryvu
V poli pokhovaly,
A slavnii zaporozhtsi
V stepu pobratalys.

Black-browed Catherine
They buried in a field.
And the famous Zaporozhians
In the steppe swore brotherhood.

With an admirable economy of words, all is said.

Perhaps my colleagues will take exception to parts, or even all, of my interpretation of Shevchenko's *chef d'œuvre*. If so, I shall be glad to have stimulated discussion. But I shall be even more pleased if my attempt at an aesthetic analysis of a poem of Shevchenko's should encourage my colleagues to do the same. For not too much has been said about our greatest verbal artist as an artist in words.

(1958)

NOTES

1 A translation of 'Balada Shevchenka "U tiiei Kateryny"' M. Rylsky, *Nasha krovna sprava* (Kiev 1959). The words *narod, narodnyi*, in both Ukrainian and Russian, can mean both 'people' and 'nation'; 'people's' and 'national.'

20

Shevchenko and Belinsky

VICTOR SWOBODA

The nature of the relationship between the greatest Ukrainian poet, Taras Hryhorovych Shevchenko (1814-61), and the greatest Russian literary critic, Vissarion Grigorievich Belinsky (1811-48), has been the subject of conflicting statements, representing Shevchenko as a pupil and comrade-in-arms of Belinsky or asserting that Belinsky was deeply hostile to Shevchenko.[1] The controversy has become particularly pronounced in the last decade or so and shows the increasing attention now given to the problem of Shevchenko's ideological parentage, which is extremely important in view of his continued immense popularity and influence among Ukrainians.

One problem to be considered is that of the personal and social contacts between Shevchenko and Belinsky. Opportunities for these existed during the five years from November 1839[2] until March 1845[3] when both men were in St Petersburg. But the only known record of any personal and social contact between them is in A.N. Strugovshchikov's memoirs.[4] Parts of the relevant passage have been frequently quoted or referred to:[5] it describes a musical *soirée* at Strugovshchikov's on 27 April 1840, mentions some thirty guests (twenty-seven of them by name), and adds the names of nine absentees, together with whom 'the list of guests which has been preserved in my possession would have given the complete roll of our *kruzhok*, with the few exceptions of those who were grouped more around Count M. Iu. Vielgorsky and Prince V.F. Odoevsky.'[6] The inclusion of both Shevchenko and Belinsky in the list of guests and the indication that the list contains the names of those who belonged to Strugovshchikov's *kruzhok* might seem to justify the conclusion of many commentators that

Shevchenko and Belinsky must have met at Strugovshchikov's on other occasions also.[7] But such a conclusion would be correct only if it is accepted that Belinsky really belonged to Strugovshchikov's *kruzhok*. This is doubtful. According to I.I. Panaev, Belinsky went out of his own *kruzhok* rarely and reluctantly and called on Strugovshchikov only occasionally.[8] Though he valued Strugovshchikov highly as a translator of Goethe,[9] he apparently did not see eye to eye with him on certain, possibly ideological, matters[10] or rate him as a friend in the same way as he did Herzen.[11] On the other hand, from the beginning of his stay in St Petersburg and during 1840-1 he was a not infrequent guest at the literary Saturday *salons* of Prince V.F. Odoevsky, who took a great interest in him.[12] It would therefore seem right to conclude that Belinsky was not only the centre of attraction of his own (and Panaev's)[13] *kruzhok* but could also be said to have belonged to 'those grouped ... around ... Prince V.F. Odoevsky.'[14] This implies that he did not really belong to Strugovshchikov's *kruzhok*.

Shevchenko is not known to have visited Strugovshchikov's on any other occasion than the *soirée* already mentioned. But M.A. Markevych mentions two occasions when Shevchenko and Strugovshchikov were among the company assembled at his house and another occasion when they were both at N. Kukolnik's.[15] On the whole, it seems likely that Shevchenko visited Strugovshchikov's more than once in the company of his greatly admired teacher and friend, Professor K.P. Briullov.[16] But the only occasion when he and Belinsky are definitely said to have been present at the same time was on 27 April 1840, and no real evidence has yet been produced for the contention that they met repeatedly at Strugovshchikov's.

Even at the *soirée* on 27 April they seem unlikely to have had much opportunity for close personal contact. It is not unreasonable to suppose that in this gathering of about thirty people Belinsky may have kept to the circle of his close friends, I.I. Panaev and V.F. Odoevsky, and Shevchenko to his new friend Markevych, the 'triumvirate'[17] composed of Briullov, Glinka, and Kukolnik, several fellow students from the Academy and certain other artists.[18] Strugovshchikov's account of what took place at the *soirée* should also be borne in mind in this connection. What he has to say does not end as it is usually quoted.[19] It goes on:

Dreyschock [A.], who, in the words of Glinka, was 'cutting chops with his fingers,' during that evening smashed two grand pianos hired by me from Wirt and made some, including Belinsky, leave before supper; to make up for this, Markevych astounded everyone by his playing, eclipsing Dreyschock and Stör [K.]. Everyone was rather tired, but a jovial conversation at supper revived us. We started talking about Glinka's new opera; unable to restrain himself, he rose from the table and sat down at the piano. ... Glinka was inexhaustible. ... A warm morning dawned; the windows were open and it struck seven o'clock, when someone noticed that passers-by were stopping. My guests left.[20]

This makes it clear that Belinsky left Strugovshchikov's before the end of the Dreyschock and Stör recitals, which seem to have been given during the first part of the *soirée*, and while they were in progress he could hardly have talked much to anybody.[21] It is not known when Shevchenko left; probably he stayed on with his friend Markevych.[22]

Ie. P. Kyryliuk has recently asserted that Hrebinka's was another meeting place: 'Shevchenko used to go to Hrebinka's literary *soirées*, where a wide circle of writers and artists used to gather. I. Panaev mentions in his memoirs that Shevchenko and Belinsky used to go there.' But Panaev's memoirs by no means bracket the names of Shevchenko and Belinsky in the manner which Kyryliuk suggests. It is true that at one point they describe a literary gathering at Hrebinka's and mention that Shevchenko was present. But it is not until very much further on that they say that Belinsky 'usually visited Hrebinka once a year when the latter called on him to invite him to Little Russian pork fat and liqueurs. Here and evidently at other similar gatherings he met various famous literary personalities: Kukolnik and others. ... But he did not want to become friendly (sblizhatsia) with them.'[23] The most that this would seem to indicate is that Belinsky and Shevchenko may very occasionally have chanced to be at Hrebinka's on the same day. But it can scarcely be regarded as definite evidence of personal contact between them.

If any personal contact between Belinsky and Shevchenko had existed, they might have been expected to exchange letters during Shevchenko's absence from St Petersburg in 1843-4 and after 1845[24] until his arrest on 5 April 1847. But no personal correspondence between them is extant. The only known letter of either of them to any third party which mentions the other man's name is Belinsky's famous letter to P.V. Annenkov, written in December 1847 after Shevchenko's arrest; and this gives no grounds at all for assuming that Shevchenko was in any sense a friend or 'comrade-in-arms' of Belinsky.[25]

Thus, the frequent assertions that Shevchenko was personally friendly with Belinsky, or used to meet him, must be regarded as mere conjectures with no reliable foundation in known fact.

Another problem to be considered is the attitude of Belinsky as critic towards Shevchenko as creative artist. It is sometimes asserted that Belinsky's attitude was influenced by an irreconcilable personal hatred. But this is incorrect and takes no account of three favourable comments by Belinsky which are often overlooked. The first occurred in February 1842 in a review of *Nashi, spisannye s natury russkimi*,[26] where Belinsky commented that 'The illustrations by Messrs Tim, Shchedrovsky and Shevchenko are distinguished by their typical originality and faithfulness to reality....'[27] The two others were not explicit. When Belinsky reviewed No. 13 of *Nashi, spisannye s natury russkimi*[28] in December 1842 he said simply that 'The pictures and vignettes (13 in number) are excellent,'[29] without mentioning Shevchenko, who had done the chief illustration. The other favourable comment came in June 1845 in a review of *Russkie polkovodtsy*,[30] where Belinsky found that 'The portraits are very well finished and seem to be very much like those from which they are taken.'[31] At the same time he criticized certain of Shevchenko's illustrations. In July 1841 he called one of them bad,[32] while in January and November 1843 he summarily condemned all the pictures in two editions of a book, some of which had been done by Shevchenko.[33]

It was a remarkable achievement for Shevchenko to have risen within nine years from the status of a serf to a lectureship in drawing at Kiev university, and his record as an artist was far from insignificant. But as Belinsky was, after all, a literary critic, it was Shevchenko's work as a writer which should have mainly attracted his attention. The first of Shevchenko's writings to be published was a collection of poems called *Kobzar* (The Minstrel).[34] It was passed by the censor on 12 February 1840 and appeared in print shortly afterwards. The first reviews of *Kobzar* came out early in May. They all acknowledged and acclaimed Shevchenko's talent as a poet, but differed in their attitudes towards the Ukrainian language as a literary medium. Belinsky, who had been a regular contributor to *Otechestvennye zapiski* since August 1839, was apparently not given *Kobzar* to review. But he must have read the favourable anonymous review which *Otechestvennye zapiski* published and possibly some or all of the six reviews which appeared elsewhere.

Several of Shevchenko's poems,[35] apparently of an earlier date, were published in 1841 in Hrebinka's collection *Lastivka* which included works by more than a dozen authors.[36] This Belinsky reviewed in June 1841.[37] It is noteworthy that he did not praise or criticize by name any of the authors included in *Lastivka*. Instead he argued at length that a Ukrainian literature ought not to exist, and that writers of Ukrainian origin ought not to write in their native language. At the very end of his review he gave two random quotations which were obviously meant to be taken as typical of the book as a whole. At any rate he neither said nor implied that they were drawn from contributions which were better or worse than the rest.[38]

Shevchenko's next work to appear was the historical poem *Haidamaky*, which came out in full in April 1842.[39] Belinsky may have read its first chapter in 1841,[40] and he reviewed the full version in May 1842.[41] The tone of his review was such that when S.A. Vengerov reprinted it for the first time[42] in 1904 in his edition of Belinsky's collected works he felt driven to comment: 'In the present notice Belinsky does not have even the remotest idea of the fact that he is deriding one of the greatest poets of the whole of Slavdom.'[43] It is also described as 'erroneous' or 'unjust' by Belinsky scholars today.

In 1939 V.S. Spiridonov advanced the view that Belinsky was the author of the anonymous review of Shevchenko's *Kobzar* which appeared in *Otechestvennye zapiski* in May 1840. He based this opinion on an analysis of the language and style of the review.[44] As editor of the last two volumes of the Vengerov edition of Belinsky's collected works, Spiridonov wanted to include the review of *Kobzar* among the material published in volume XIII. But the appointed 'readers' (retsenzenty) of the proposed volume found that his arguments for Belinsky's authorship were not sufficiently convincing, and the review was omitted when volume XIII appeared in 1948.[45] But even before that, in 1947, H.O. Lazarevsky in his unpublished monograph 'Kultura rosiiskoho narodu v zhytti Shevchenka,' which is kept in the MS department of the Institute of Literature of the Ukrainian SSR Academy of Sciences (*fond* 1, *edinitsa khraneniia* 572, *l.* 40), disputed Spiridonov's theory, putting forward as his chief objection the fact that

less than a year later Belinsky wrote reviews of *Lastivka* and *Haidamaky* which had quite a different tenor and quite a different attitude to Ukrainian poetry [from that expressed in the anonymous *Kobzar* review], moreover stressing in the latter [viz. in the *Haidamaky* review] the very fact that 'The readers of *Otechestvennye zapiski* are familiar with our opinion regarding the works of the so-called Little Russian literature'; that is, he obviously expressed no other attitude in the journal.

Lazarevsky also conjectured that 'it is not impossible that Kireevsky himself wrote ... the *Kobzar* review in *Otechestvennye zapiski*.' Here, 'Kireevsky' is obviously a slip;[46] the intended name is A.A. Kraevsky (1810-89), the editor of *Otechestvennye zapiski* (hence 'himself'), connected with Shevchenko at various times.[47] Lazarevsky's work, a 'substantial' one,[48] remained unpublished, though it surely deserves better treatment, even if only because of the author's personality: H.O. Lazarevsky († c. 1948) was son of O.M. Lazarevsky (1834-1902), a historian and one of Shevchenko's closest friends. Meanwhile, Spiridonov's theory, after the latter's death, was supported by I.I. Pilhuk, D.V. Chaly, and I.I. Bass, and further developed by F. Ia. Priima who in 1953 read a paper on this subject at a conference in Kiev;[49] regrettably, none of them appear to have seen Lazarevsky's monograph. Priima was 'chief reader' of the new edition of Belinsky's works, which appeared in thirteen volumes between 1953 and 1959. He dealt with all the volumes except volumes VI,[50] IX, and XII and also supplied commentaries to some of the material in them. This probably explains why volume IV of the new edition included the review of *Kobzar* with Priima's own comments, which repeated the arguments expressed in his paper to the Kiev conference.[51] Priima similarly expounded his case for Belinsky's authorship of the review of *Kobzar* in an article published in 1954,[52] which year also saw the publication of volume IV of the new Belinsky edition. The Spiridonov theory, elaborated and expanded by Priima, triggered off a continuing controversy among Soviet scholars. Some, among them M.I. Marchenko,[53] were not convinced by the theory, while the prominent Belinsky scholar, Iu. Oksman, adduced a number of detailed counterarguments to it,[54] provoking Priima's equally detailed rejoinder in which he reinforced his old argumentation.[55] However, in order to form a considered opinion on the problem of the attribution or otherwise of the review to Belinsky it will be very useful at this point to compare the opinions which Belinsky expressed in his review of *Haidamaky* with those to be found in the anonymous review of *Kobzar* on the one hand and with those which he expressed in his review of *Lastivka* on the other.[56]

Belinsky began his review of *Haidamaky* with the following remark: 'The readers of *Otechestvennye zapiski* are familiar with our opinion regarding the works of the so-called Little Russian literature.' This can surely refer only to his review of *Lastivka* and not to the anonymous review of *Kobzar* which wholeheartedly supported Shevchenko's right to use Ukrainian.[57] The review of *Haidamaky* went on to assert that Ukrainian literature had no reading public except the authors who wrote in Ukrainian. The review of *Lastivka* had also taken the same line, while the review of *Kobzar* had said on the contrary that books in Ukrainian 'of the kind of [Kvitka-] Osnov'-ianenko's *Lysty do zemliakiv*, or Hrebinka's *Prykazky*, or Shevchenko's *Kateryna*,[58] which have a moral aim and are written in a language intelligible to every Little Russian, will no doubt bring the greatest benefit to South Russian readers from among the ordinary people.' Belinsky even seems to have intended to challenge this passage from the *Kobzar* review when he wrote in his review of *Haidamaky*: 'And if these Messrs "minstrels" (gospoda kobzari) think to bring benefit by their "poems" to the lowest class of their compatriots, they are greatly mistaken in this....' Such an obviously derisive mention of 'minstrels' by Belinsky is also inconsistent with the sympathetic attitude which the *Kobzar* review had taken towards them. In his review of *Haidamaky* Belinsky referred scornfully to 'the new attempt at "singings"[59] of Mr Shevchenko, an apparently privileged Little Russian poet,' and said that it 'convinces us still more that works of such a kind are published for their authors' own enjoyment and instruction: they seem to have no other public.' This can be interpreted in two different ways. On the one hand it might mean that Belinsky had originally based his opinion on his knowledge of other Ukrainian poets than Shevchenko and had now confirmed it from his reading of Shevchenko's *Haidamaky*. If so, he could not have read Shevchenko's *Kobzar* or written the anonymous review of it in *Otechestvennye zapiski*. On the other hand it might mean that it was Shevchenko's own earlier poetry on which Belinsky's opinion had first been based. If so, he could not have been responsible for the very different opinion expressed in the anonymous review of Shevchenko's *Kobzar* in *Otechestvennye zapiski*. What seems most likely is that Belinsky had never read Shevchenko's poems until he received *Lastivka* for review, and that his attitude towards them was negative and was shown by the 'emphatic silence'[60-2] with which his review passed them over.

As Belinsky's review of *Lastivka* ignored the five poems contributed by Shevchenko, the review which he wrote of *Haidamaky* must be accounted his first review of Shevchenko's poetic work. It also proved to be his last.

When he reviewed *Molodyk na 1843 god* in December 1843 he made no comment at all on the Ukrainian part, which included three of Shevchenko's poems.[63] The reason for his silence was that he now grudgingly admitted that Ukrainian literature was not merely a part of Russian literature. 'After this,' he wrote, 'follows the so-called "Little Russian section," which, as not belonging to Russian literature, we pass over in silence.'[64] Possibly for the same reason he never reviewed the two publications of Shevchenko which appeared in book form in 1844.[65] On the other hand he similarly ignored Shevchenko's poem in Russian, *Trizna*,[66] which also appeared in 1844.

No other works of Shevchenko appeared in book form between 1844 and Belinsky's death in 1848. But in 1844 and 1845 Shevchenko was already writing his greatest revolutionary poems such as 'Son,' 'Kavkaz,' 'Velykyi lokh,' 'I mertvym, i zhyvym,' and 'Zapovit.'[67] He collected most of them in a manuscript volume bearing the title *Try lita* (ie, the three years in 1843-5), which he had naturally no hope of publishing at the time. But they circulated in a considerable number of manuscript copies among the admirers of his poetry, who included his fellow-members of the Brotherhood of Saints Cyril and Methodius, personal friends and acquaintances, and many who had never met him. Shevchenko's passionate revolutionary invectives against the reality of Russian tsarist oppression in the 'prison of peoples' brought the following and final comment from Belinsky in a letter to Annenkov of December 1847: 'I have not read these lampoons, and no one of my acquaintance has (which fact, by the way, proves that they are by no means malicious but merely flat and stupid). ... Shevchenko has been banished to the Caucasus as a private. I am not sorry for him; if I had been his judge, I would not have done less.'[68]

As Belinsky is often said to have influenced Shevchenko, it is important to consider whether Shevchenko adopted Belinsky's views on any major issue. Not surprisingly, a basic issue for Shevchenko was the problem of language, on which Belinsky expressed himself very clearly and forcefully. As early as August 1835, soon after the start of his career as a critic, he had dealt with a book in Ukrainian and had noted that it was in 'the purest Little Russian language which is completely inaccessible to us Muscovites (moskalei) and therefore deprives us of the possibility of judging it on its merits.'[69] In March 1838 he referred even more pointedly to the 'Little

Russian dialect' (malorossiiskoe narechie) when he exhorted Kvitka-Osnov'ianenko to follow Gogol's example and write in Russian. He assured him that if he did he would enjoy much greater fame.[70]

Belinsky again expressed his views on Ukrainian on three occasions in 1841. The first occasion was in June when he reviewed *Lastivka*. The second was in August in his review of *Snip*,[71] where he wrote with obvious sarcasm of the 'pure' Little Russian language. He said that he was unable to understand what could be interesting and poetical in stories and poems whose only merit was that they were written in a language 'spoken by no one, except Little Russian plebs (chern), that is, *muzhiks*.' He was also unable to understand why anyone should even want to write for a public which was not literate enough to read books, and he denied that anything which could be called a literature existed.[72] The third occasion was in November, when Belinsky defined his general attitude towards the poetic achievements of the Slavs. He believed that it was only the Russians, and perhaps also the Czechs, who could boast of a few great and remarkable poets. The rest of the Slavs, such as Bulgars,[73] Serbs, Dalmatians, Illyrians, and others, had nothing except their folk poetry, which was incapable of rising to the level of artistic poetry. His views about Ukrainian were specific and categoric. 'The literary language of Little Russians,' he wrote, 'must be the language of their educated society, namely the Russian language. Even if a great poet should appear in Little Russia, this could only be subject to the condition of his being a Russian poet. ... A tribe (plemia) can only have folk songs, but it cannot have poets, and even less, great poets.' He concluded by saying that Ukrainian could never be a literary language.[74]

Shevchenko's whole career shows how completely he rejected Belinsky's pronouncements on the language question. He ignored the exhortation to Kvitka-Osnov'ianenko to follow Gogol's example and write in Russian for greater fame. Instead he continued to write in the language of 'the Little Russian plebs' however incomprehensible Belinsky may have found his wish to do so. More important still, he showed the error of Belinsky's views by the sheer genius of his Ukrainian poetry.

It remains to be considered whether Belinsky's views may still not have influenced the content of Shevchenko's poetry even if they failed to change its Ukrainian form. In this connection it will be useful to examine the attitude of the two writers towards various historical events on which they both commented. The turning point in the modern history of Ukraine had been its incorporation into the Muscovite state in 1654. Belinsky was full of praise for Bohdan Khmelnytsky, who had been instrumental in bringing it about and described him as 'a hero and a great man in the full meaning of the term,' and as 'a great warrior and a great politician' who 'understood that Little Russia was unable to exist as an independent state.' He also believed that as a result of the incorporation 'Little Russia opened her doors to civilization, enlightenment, the arts, the sciences.'[75] Shevchenko on the other hand always regarded Ukraine's incorporation into Russia as a disaster and condemned Khmelnytsky for the part which he had played in it. The earliest poem in his manuscript volume *Try lita*, which is entitled 'Rozryta mohyla' and is dated 9 October 1843, makes Ukraine call Bohdan her 'foolish son' whom she 'would have strangled in his cradle' if she had known the slavery into which his deed would lead her.[76] 'Velykyi lokh,' written in 1845, also condemns Khmelnytsky's oath of allegiance to Moscow at Pereiaslav.[77] In 'Stoit v seli Subotovi' of 21 October 1845, Shevchenko concedes that Khmelnytsky's intentions were directed towards the mutual good of both parties; yet 'It did not come about like this; the dear Muscovites (moskalyky) plundered whatever they caught sight of.'[78] When Shevchenko again visited his native land after ten years of exile and was passing through Pereiaslav, he bitterly addressed Khmelnytsky as follows in his 'Iakby to ty, Bohdane pianyi' dated 18 August 1859:

> Amen to thee, O great man!
> Great, glorious! but not very ...
> If you had not been born
> Or had drowned in drink in your cradle ...
> I would not have dragged you though the mud,
> You, the most glorious one. Amen.[79]

His attitude towards Khmelnytsky never changed from youth till the end of his life, and in 'Hosea, XIV. Podrazhaniie,' written on Christmas Day 1859, he said that God punished Ukraine first of all for Bohdan.[80]

Shevchenko also saw Russia's civilizing mission in a very different light from that in which Belinsky saw it. He had no illusions about the blessings of enlightenment which Russia was bringing to the peoples of the Caucasus, those 'blind children,' or about the arts and crafts they would be privileged to learn from her:

> We are enlightened! what's more, we want
> To enlighten others,
> To show the sun of truth
> To blind children, you know!
> We will show you everything (just put
> Yourselves in our hands):
> How to build prisons,
> How to forge fetters,
> And how to wear them! ... and how to plait
> Knotted knouts, –
> We will teach you everything; just give us
> Your blue mountains,
> The last ones ... for we have taken
> Both your plains and sea ... ('Kavkaz,' 18 November 1845)[81]

The period of Russian history which always attracted Belinsky most was the age of Peter the Great. He looked on Peter as 'the personified power, the personified ideal of the Russian people'[82] who 'pushed Russia into world history with his mighty hand.'[83] His creation of St Petersburg was a historical necessity, satisfying the need for 'a new capital on the sea coast which would give us a means of easy and convenient relations with Europe.'[84] Not surprisingly Belinsky also glorified Peter's victory over Charles XII at Poltava[85] and could even say: 'his equestrian statue on Isakievskaia Square is not enough: altars must be erected to him on all the squares and in all the streets of the great tsardom of Russia!'[86]

But Shevchenko took a very different attitude. In 'Son,' written in 1844, he reflected, as he looked at St Petersburg, on the rivers of human blood which had been spilled in the building of it, and he made the spirit of Hetman Polubotok accuse Peter of filling the marshes with the bones of Cossacks and building his capital on their tortured bodies. The souls of the Cossacks make even worse accusations. As Shevchenko contemplates the famous statue of Peter, he sees how the tsar 'stretches out his arm as if he wants to seize the whole world'; he reminds his readers that it is Peter 'who crucified our Ukraine' and tells them that he is accursed, an insatiable serpent, an evil hangman, a cannibal.[87] His attitude towards Peter never changed, and even in 1859 he still described him as 'the rabid Peter,'[88] He regarded Peter's victory at Poltava as Ukraine's disaster, which brought her even greater tribulations:[89]

> Minstrels told us
> Of wars and fighting,
> Of hard, evil times,
> Of cruel trials
> Inflicted upon us by the Poles, –
> They told us everything.
> But what happened after the Swede's time!
> Even they got frightened,
> Blind unfortunates.
> So much did the voivodes,
> Peter's hounds,
> Tear and worry her ... ('Irzhavets,' 1847-14 March 1858)

In Shevchenko's view the disaster would have been averted if only the Ukrainian leaders, Mazepa and Semen Palii, had been united.[90]

It is often said that it was Belinsky's ideas which inspired Shevchenko's revolutionary ardour. But *Haidamaky*, which was the first of Shevchenko's poems to express revolutionary ideas, met with Belinsky's open hostility. Shevchenko's subsequent views were always characterized by his condemnation of Russian conquest and subjugation of other peoples and by calls to revolutionary struggle for national liberation. Belinsky on the other hand always expressed his whole-hearted approval of Russia's imperial expansion.

From what has been said it seems clear that the reasons for Belinsky's hostility towards Shevchenko can hardly have been personal, since the two men were not closely acquainted with each other and Belinsky was fair to Shevchenko as an artist. At the same time it has to be remembered that Belinsky described Shevchenko as 'an ass, fool and *poshlets*, and a desperate drunkard into the bargain, a brandy lover out of *Khokhol* patriotism. This *Khokhol* radical....'[91] This repetition of the pejorative *Khokhol* seems significant. For all his intellectual considerations of 'humanity in general,' Belinsky appears to have had an instinctive dislike of foreign things, particularly of languages which he did not understand: for example he asked in a letter that Herzen 'should not use Latin proverbs any more, which I cannot tolerate, like anything in languages foreign to me.'[92] He was also greatly irritated when people who appeared to be perfectly capable of writing in good Russian stubbornly produced a 'non-existent literature' in a 'language that nobody spoke.' His disdain for Ukrainian was that of a member of a master race for the language of a subject people who had to be assimilated and whose language had to disappear: he maintained that Ukrainian was 'spoken by no one, except Little Russian plebs, that is, *muzhiks*.' 'Even less do we understand,' he continued in his review of *Snip*, 'your desire to write for a public which reads no books at all because it is hardly literate.' It does not seem ever to have occurred to him that the 'Little Russian plebs' might have had some desire for education. His attitude should not be misinterpreted as merely that of an aristocrat towards the plebs: when Gogol expressed similar views about the Russian *muzhik*,[93] Belinsky immediately and most severely lectured him on the striving of the Russian common people (now prostoi narod, not chern) towards, and their deep need for, literacy and learning.[94]

The information about Shevchenko which Belinsky supplied to Bakunin through Annenkov at Bakunin's request indicates the extent of his antipathy towards Shevchenko.[95] Oksman has found that almost the whole of it was derived from a secret report from Count A.F. Orlov to Nicholas I. He considers that the real author of the report was M.M. Popov, a former teacher of Belinsky, who had become a senior official for special duties in the Third Department and took an important part in the conduct of Shevchenko's case.[96] It seems very strange that Belinsky should not have turned for information to his own friends and those of Shevchenko, but should have relied instead on sources serving the Third Department,[97] especially as he himself was not in the department's good books. His flat had been searched for papers in his absence as early as 1836[98] and only two months after his letter to Annenkov, when he received an official note from Popov to say that Dubelt, the chief of the department, wished to meet him,[99] he excused himself on the grounds of ill health, expected a search and arrest, and immediately proceeded to burn everything which might be politically compromising.[100] In 1842 when Kukolnik, who was one of Belinsky's pet aversions, ran foul of the Third Department for one of his stories,[101] Belinsky sympathized with him and referred to the action of the department as 'the increase of the censorship terror.'[102] This makes it all the stranger that he should not only have uncritically accepted the Third Department's version of the Shevchenko case, but should have expressed whole-hearted approval of the verdict.

The explanation seems to lie in the differences in the literary and political views of the two men. Belinsky denied the possibility of the development of literatures among other Slavs, and he condemned Ukrainian in particular to total disappearance as a natural consequence of Ukraine's incorporation into the Russian empire, of whose expansion and growth he was always a most enthusiastic supporter. Shevchenko on the other hand successfully used in his poetry the language which Belinsky wished to see disappear and saw nothing but disaster for his native country as a result of her incorporation into, and continued retention within, the Russian empire. Belinsky had no first-hand knowledge of Shevchenko's revolutionary works, but he must have known about his ideas from hearsay since he classed Shevchenko with P. Kulish ('a *Khokhol* liberal'), to whom he attributed the opinion that 'Little Russia must either secede from Russia or perish.'[103] As Belinsky whole-heartedly approved of Russian imperial expansion, he was naturally on the side of the government in this matter and therefore supported the Third Department's efforts to suppress Ukrainian nationalism,[104] however disgusted he may have been by its activities in other directions.

(1961)[105]

NOTES

1 Reprinted from *The Slavonic and East European Review*, XL, 94 (December 1961) 168-83; revised by the author in 1980.
2 Belinsky arrived in St Petersburg probably on 24 October 1839 (all dates prior to 1917 are given in old style). Iu. Oksman, *Letopis' zhizni i tvorchestva V.G. Belinskogo* (Moscow 1958) 212.
3 Shevchenko left St Petersburg on 25 March 1845; he was also absent for eight months from 13 May 1843 till the end of February 1844.
4 A.N. Strugovshchikov, 'M.I. Glinka. Vospominaniia. 1839-1841,' *Russkaia*

starina, IX (St Petersburg 1874) 701-2. They were written not later than 1857 (*ibid*. 696).

5 The fullest quotation is in *Biohrafiia T.H. Shevchenka za spohadamy suchasnykiv*, AN URSR (Kiev 1958) 37.

6 Strugovshchikov, 'M.I. Glinka ...' 701-2.

7 Thus, Ie. P. Kyryliuk, *T.H. Shevchenko. Zhyttia i tvorchist* (Kiev 1959) 82, says: 'The fact that this was not merely a single simply fortuitous meeting is proved by the subsequent words in the memoirs. Having mentioned some persons absent that evening, A. Strugovshchikov added: "With them the list of guests which has been preserved in my possession would have given the complete roll of our *kruzhok*".' Kyryliuk stresses the word '*kruzhok*' and ends the quotation with it; he thus omits the final part of Strugovshchikov's remarks, which is clearly of great importance.

8 I.I. Panaev, *Literaturnye vospominaniia* ([Leningrad] 1950) 256. Strugovshchikov and Belinsky, however, were colleagues both on *Otechestvennye zapiski* and on *Sovremennik* and occasionally met elsewhere (Oksman, *Letopis zhizni* ... 225, 264, 460; A.I. Herzen, *Polnoe sobranie sochinenii i pisem*, II (Petrograd 1919) 415).

9 V.G. Belinsky, *Polnoe sobranie sochinenii*, 13 vols (Moscow 1953-9) (referred to hereafter as *B*), II, 361, III, 63-5, IV, 126, 175, V, 263, XI, 262, 362-3, XII, 83.

10 '... I [Herzen] and Belins[ky] routed Strugovshchikov and Neverov ...' (Herzen, *loc. cit.*).

11 In 1846 Belinsky could not think of Strugovshchikov 'without a sinking heart and irritation of every kind' (*B*, XII, 300).

12 *B*, XI, 418, 420, 428, 436, 446, XII, 10; I.I. Panaev, *Literaturnye vospominaniia*, 99, 137, 296-300, 415, 431; *Literaturnoe nasledstvo*, AN SSSR, LVI, 135-6, 314; Oksman, *Letopis zhizni* ..., 245; Herzen, *Polnoe sobranie* ..., XIII (Petersburg 1919) 23-4.

13 V.A. Panaev, 'Vospominaniia' (*Russkaia starina*, vol. 79, 1893, p. 478).

14 See note 6 above.

15 *Biohrafiia T.H. Shevchenka...* 37-8.

16 I.I. Panaev intended to describe in chapter IX 'friendly *soirées* at Strugovshchikov's,' with particular reference to 'Briullov and Kukolnik at these *soirées*' (*Literaturnye vospominaniia* 269), but his death in 1862 cut short the progress of his memoirs (*ibid*. 422). The close friendship between Strugovshchikov and Briullov can be gathered from the fact that the former used to call at the

Academy to take Briullov with him when driving out to Kukolnik's (Strugovshchikov, *op. cit.* 700).

17 So named by I.I. Panaev (*Literaturnye vospominaniia* 44).

18 M.A. Ramazanov, A.M. Goronevich, Ia. F. Ianenko, P.V. Basin, S.F. Shchedrin, M.A. and P.A. Stepanov (*Biohrafiia T.H. Shevchenka...* 376-8).

19 See note 5 above.

20 Strugovshchikov, 'M.I. Glinka' 702.

21 Incidentally, it is interesting to compare the way in which Strugovshchikov's description is mutilated and misinterpreted by many writers on Shevchenko with the procedure adopted by Ie. Kann-Novikova, who wishes to prove the existence of personal contact between Glinka and Belinsky and asserts (in her *M.I. Glinka*, III (Moscow 1955) 142-3): 'Finally, it is A.N. Strugovshchikov who with complete certainty establishes the fact of personal contact between Glinka and Belinsky.' She gives the usual quotation from Strugovshchikov but only down to and including the sentence 'With them the list of guests. ... V.F. Odoevsky.' From Strugovshchikov's account of what happened at the *soirée*, which she does not quote, she vaguely concludes: 'It transpires from the context of Strugovshchikov's memoirs that music was the chief point of that *soirée*, and, in particular, Glinka's music, performed by the composer himself. By these memoirs the fact of personal contact between Glinka and Belinsky is reliably documented, and the widest circle of their common acquaintances is established.' By withholding the mention of Belinsky's early departure, she implies that he listened to Glinka's music (which, as has been shown above, is not true); she is also obviously unaware that Belinsky did not belong to Strugovshchikov's *kruzhok*.

22 It is significant that Belinsky was not acquainted even with Briullov until two and a half years later (*B*, XII, 125).

23 Kyryliuk, *loc. cit.*; I.I. Panaev, *Literaturnye vospominaniia* 103-5, 256.

24 See note 3 above.

25 *B*, XII, 440.

26 A.P. Bashutsky, ed., *Nashi, spisannye s natury russkimi*, 1-5 (St Petersburg 1841).

27 *B*, V, 602.

28 Bashutsky, *Nashi, spisannye ...*, 13 [St Petersburg 1842?], consisting of H.F. Kvitka-Osnovianenko's story 'Znakhar.'

29 *B*, VI, 497.

30 N. Polevoi, *Russkie polkovodtsy, ili zhizn rossiiskikh polkovodtsev ...* (St Petersburg 1845). 'The portraits, drawn by the well-known artist, T.H.

Shevchenko ... were engraved on steel by the famous English engraver Robinson, and printed in London.' (*ibid.* x.). Some of the portraits are initialled 'H.R.' ie, John Henry Robinson, RA. (1796-1871), who gained eminence in his profession (W. Sandby, *The History of the Royal Academy of Arts*, II [London 1862] 356; S. Lee, ed, *Dictionary of National Biography*, XLIX [London 1897] 29-30).

31 *B*, IX, 131.

32 When reviewing *Sto russkikh literatorov*, II (publ. by A. Smirdin, St Petersburg 1841), Belinsky said of N.I. Nadezhdin's story: '"Sila voli" is told in a clever, but cold and colourless way,' and then mentioned that 'The picture accompanying Mr Nadezhdin's story is bad.' Shevchenko contributed to this volume only one illustration (facing p. 399), with which he is credited in the list preceding p. 1. Belinsky's comment on Shevchenko's illustration is thus distorted by D. Kosaryk: 'The critic expressed himself negatively about the work itself [ie, Nadezhdin's story], but he commended Shevchenko's illustration to it' (*Zhyttia i diialnist T. Shevchenka. Literaturna khronika* [Kiev 1955] 41).

33 Reviews of N. Polevoi, *Istoriia ... grafa Suvorova Rymnikskogo*, two editions (St Petersburg 1843), in *B*, VI, 562, and VIII, 18-19.

34 T. Shevchenko, *Kobzar* (St Petersburg 1840) 114 pp.

35 The earliest extant poems, 'Prychynna,' 'Vitre buynyi,' 'Na vichnu pamiat Kotliarevskomu,' 'Teche voda,' and the first chapter of *Haidamaky* ('Halaida').

36 Ie. Grebenka [Hrebinka], ed., *Lastivka. Sochinenia na malorossiiskom iazyke* (St Petersburg 1841) 382 pp.

37 *B*, V, 176-9.

38 F. Ia. Priima (*B*, V, 800) unconvincingly argues that Belinsky criticized just the two authors quoted (ie, Hrebinka and Kvitka-Osnovianenko).

39 Shevchenko, *Haidamaky. Poema* (St Petersburg 1841).

40 See note 35 above.

41 *B*, VI, 172-4.

42 Though it had been quoted and referred to more than once, eg, at length in A.N. Pypin, *Belinsky, iego zhizn' i perepiska*, II (St Petersburg 1876) 223-4, 2nd ed. (1908) 472-3.

43 Belinsky, *Polnoe sobranie sochinenii v dvenadtsati tomakh*, VII (St Petersburg 1904) 595, note 130. Among the recent commentators, Ie. I. Kiiko suggests that 'Belinsky's opinion of T.H. Shevchenko is unjust and is to a considerable degree explained by the fact that Belinsky was little acquainted with his works'

(B, VI, 731, note 172[3]). This can hardly be disputed; Belinsky apparently did not read *Kobzar* and probably did not pay much attention to Shevchenko's poems in *Lastivka* (in the review of which he implied that nobody 'will have enough patience to read through the whole book ...' [B, V, 178]; however, he later implied in a letter [B, XII, 62] that he had read through it).

44 V.S. Spiridonov, 'Neizvestnaia retsenziia Belinskogo o "Kobzare"' (*Literaturnaia gazeta*, Moscow, 5 March 1939, no. 13).

45 *B*, IV, 625-6, note 171[1]

46 Either in the monograph itself or in Iu. D. Margolis, *Istoricheskie vzgliady T.H. Shevchenka* (Leningrad 1964) 123, whence Lazarevsky's comments are quoted.

47 For details of these connections, see V. Swoboda and Richard Martin, 'Shevchenko and Belinsky Revisited,' *Slavonic and East European Review*, LVI, 4 (October 1978) 550 n27.

48 In the opinion of Iu. Margolis, *loc. cit.*

49 F. Ia. Priima, 'Retsenziia V.G. Belinskoho na "Kobzar" 1840 r.' (*Zbirnyk prats pershoi i druhoi naukovykh shevchenkivskykh konferentsii* [Kiev 1954] 61-76); for bibliographical details of Pilhuk's and Bass's relevant writings, see Swoboda and Martin, 'Shevchenko and Belinsky Revisited' 548-9, nn17-19, where one can also find some examples of Bass's (who is more prolific of the two) method which was, on a later occasion, justly described by another Soviet scholar as 'patent falsification.'

50 In this volume, Kiiko's comment, though manifestly at variance with Priima's views, was allowed to pass unchallenged (see note 43 above).

51 *B*, IV, 171-2, 606, 625-7, note 171[1].

52 Priima, 'T.H. Shevchenko i russkaia literatura' (*Izvestiia AN SSSR, Otdelenie literatury i iazyka*, XIII, 3 [May-June 1954] 221-3).

53 In his *Istorychne mynule v tvorchosti Shevchenka* (Kiev 1957) 6, 8.

54 Iu. Oksman, *Letopis zhizni ...* 250, 567-8.

55 His 'K sporam o podlinnykh i mnimykh statiakh i retsenziiakh V.G. Belinskogo,' *Russkaia literatura*, I (1960) 113-30; partly repeated in his monograph, *Shevchenko i russkaia literatura XIX veka* (Moscow-Leningrad 1961) 69-75.

56 *B*, IV, 170-2, V, 176-9, VI, 172-4.

57 Kiiko (*B*, VI, 731, note 172[2]) also agrees that the reference is to the review of *Lastivka*.

58 First published in *Kobzar*, 1840, and again as a separate book in the same year; the latter was also never reviewed by Belinsky.

59 'Spivanii,' a possible mock formation.

60-2 Iu. Oksman's comment, *Letopis zhizni* ... 568.

63 I. Betsky (ed.), *Molodyk na 1843 god. Ukrainskii literaturnyi sbornik*, II, Kharkiv, 1843. Shevchenko's poems included here were: 'Utoplena,' 'Dumka' ('Tiazhko, vazhko ...'), and 'N. Markevychu.'

64 *B*, VIII, 34.

65 Shevchenko, *Chigirinskii Kobzar i Haidamaky. Dve poemy na malorossiiskom iazyke* (St Petersburg 1844) and *Hamaliia* (St Petersburg 1844).

66 *Trizna* [St Petersburg] 1844.

67 Cf. M. Ohloblyn-Hlobenko, '1845 rik u tvorchosti Shevchenka' in his *Istoryko-literaturni statti* (*Zapysky N.T. Sh.*, vol. 167), (New York, Paris, Munich 1858) 32-44.

68 *B*, XII, 440. This letter to P.V. Annenkov in Paris was apparently written between 1 and 10 December 1847 in St Petersburg and sent privately by way of Berlin (probably through A.A. Tuchkov) (Oksman, *Letopis zhizni* ... 535). Oksman believes that the letter was meant chiefly for his other Paris friends: Herzen, Bakunin, and N.I. Sazonov (*Literaturnoe nasledstvo*, LVI [Moscow 1950] 217); and that it was Bakunin (referred to in the letter as 'my believing friend') who was interested in Shevchenko's fate (Oksman, *Letopis zhizni* ... 515; cf. also *B*, XII, 571, note 20).

69 Review of I. Matyrenko (pseud. of O.M. Bodiansky), *Naski ukrainski kazky* (Moscow 1835) (*B*, I, 239).

70 *B*, II, 355-6.

71 A. Korsun, ed., *Snip, ukrainskyi novorichnyk* (Kharkiv 1841).

72 *B*, V, 287-8.

73 It seems that a month earlier he had given the reason for Turkish domination over the Bulgars as 'the historic right, which is might' (*B*, VI, 343, 749, note 343[2]), while in September 1842 he addressed the Bulgars in a very patronizing and condescending way: 'enlighten yourselves, good Bulgars! Good luck to you! Even write verses, if you cannot help it ...' (*B*, VI, 343).

74 *B*, V, 330-1.

75 *B*, VII, 63-4.

76 T. Shevchenko, *Povne zibrannia tvoriv v desiaty tomakh*, I (Kiev 1939) 225-6.

77 *Ibid.*, 294-5, lines 54-69.

78 *Ibid.*, 308.

79 *Povne zibrannia ...* II (Kiev 1939) 283.

80 *Ibid.*, 308.

81 *Povne zibrannia ...* I, 328-9.

82 *B*, I, p. 38.

83 *B*, III, p. 500.

84 *B*, X, p. 14.

85 *B*, V, p. 150, VII, p. 418, IX, p. 441.

86 *B*, V, p. 137.

87 Shevchenko, *Povne zibrannia ...* I, 249-51.

88 'Hosea, XIV. Podrazhaniie' (*Povne zibrannia ...* II, 308). A contemporary attests Shevchenko's violent outbursts, clad in poetic form, against Peter I, addressed to his immense clay statue in the Academy's casting yard (about 1858) (M. Mikeshyn, 'Spomynky pro Shevchenka' in Shevchenko, *Kobzar*, I [Prague 1876] xx, as quoted in *Biohrafiia Shevchenka ...* 228); cf. also J. Bojko, 'Taras Shevchenko' (*Slavonic and East European Review*, XXXIV, 82 [London 1955] 77-98).

89 'Velykyi lokh,' lines 70-133, 252-72 (Shevchenko, *Povne zibrannia ...*, I, 295-6, 300-1).

90 'Irzhavets,' lines 6-14, 51-74 (II, 25-7).

91 See note 25 above.

92 *B*, XI, 517.

93 'It is really nonsense to teach the *muzhik* to read and write in order to enable him to read stupid brochures published for the people by European philanthropists ... Actually, he has no need to know whether any other books exist apart from the sacred ones' (N. Gogol, *Vybrannye mesta iz perepiski s druziami* [St Petersburg 1847] 161-2.)

94 *B*, X, 69-70, 216.

95 See note 68 above.

96 *Literaturnoe nasledstvo*, LVI (Moscow 1950) 245, 249, notes 60, 110.

97 Oksman, *Letopis zhizni ...* 523; *B*, XII, 571, note 21.

98 M. Lemke, *Nikolaevskie zhandarmy i literatura, 1826-1855 gg.* (Moscow 1908) 416, 423; V.S. Nechaeva, *V.G. Belinsky (1829-1836)* ([Leningrad] 1954) 399-400, 482; *Literaturnoe nasledstvo, vol. cit.*, 202.

99 *Russkaia starina*, XXIV (1882) 434; *Byloe*, 10, I (St Petersburg 1906) 285.

100 *B*, XII, 469; N.A. Nekrasov, *Polnoe sobranie sochinenii i pisem*, X (Moscow 1952) 124.

101 *Russkaia starina*, III (1871) 793-4.

102 *B*, XII, 103.

103 *Ibid.*, 441.

104 'How can one complain about the government? What government will permit the preaching in print of the secession of a region from it?' (*loc. cit.*).

105 After the original 1961 publication of this article (see note 1 above), Priima entered into polemics with it in his paper 'Belinsky and Shevchenko,' read in March 1963 and published in *Zbirnyk prats dvanadtsiatoi naukovoi shevchenkivskoi konferentsii* (Kiev 1964) 190-209, where he largely repeated, and sometimes slightly modified, his old argumentation. A number of other Soviet scholars have been taking sides in the controversy after 1961; the most prominent one to accept Priima's theory is Professor Dr Ie. Kyryliuk, a corresponding member of the Ukrainian SSR Academy of Sciences. While admitting in his review of Priima's 1961 monograph (cf. note 55 above) in *Vitchyzna*, 11 (November 1962) 210-11 that there are 'certain scholars,' including such an eminent one as Academician M.K. Hudzii, who oppose Priima's theory, and that 'there is room for debate here,' he ominously warned his colleagues: 'But we, Soviet scholars, must not forget that this essentially academic problem also possesses a current political aspect,' clearly implying which answer to the problem is the politically acceptable one. And yet a number of Soviet scholars continued to reject Priima's theory, among them V. Shubravsky, who introduced new arguments against it and conjectured that Strugovshchikov could have been the initiator of the publication of the anonymous review. He accused Priima of not always facing up 'to the interests of scholarship and truth' and *inter alia* of intentionally concealing, in order to buttress his theory, the fact that as early as in March 1838 (and not only from 1841) Belinsky saw no future for literature in Ukrainian. Fuller details of the controversy during 1947-76, as well as the examination of certain pivotal points where Priima's argumentation is unsatisfactory or false, can be found in Swoboda and Martin, 'Shevchenko and Belinsky Revisited' 547-55 (cf. note 47 above). Since Priima's chief criteria for attribution are those of phraseology, vocabulary and style, and since he accuses his opponents of ignoring them, a stylometric investigation was undertaken, the conclusion from which was that the hypothesis that Belinsky was the author of the anonymous review of *Kobzar* had to be rejected also on stylometric grounds (for details see *ibid.* 555-62).

21

The Year 1860 in Shevchenko's Work

GEORGE Y. SHEVELOV

Striking reversals of fortune cut Shevchenko's life into clearly demarcated periods: serfdom, liberty, arrest and exile, liberty again.[1] This periodization has been applied to his work mechanically, without deeper analysis and without marshalling sufficient evidence. Too few works have been preserved from the years of serfdom – perhaps none, for dating 'Prychynna' in 1837 is controversial. Universally acknowledged, however, is the breakdown of Shevchenko's work into three periods: before his exile, during exile, and after his release.

In reality the situation is more complex. Shevchenko always remained himself. The unity of his work is striking: in the author of 'Mariia' one immediately recognizes the author of 'Prychynna' and 'Kateryna.' But at the same time there is a veritable gulf between the first and last of the poet's works in regard to style, *Weltanschauung*, mood, and philosophy. The changes in the poet's mind and the development of his creative style proceeded in steep ascents and abrupt falls, and to try to accommodate it in three periods is to oversimplify reality. No adequate periodization of Shevchenko's poetry has yet been devised, and one can trace many misunderstandings in interpretation to the tendency to give one period undue prominence while neglecting others. A complete picture of Shevchenko can be recreated only after scholars have worked out the particular periods in Shevchenko's poetry and have gleaned the common element from their differences and contradictions.

After six years' involuntary silence during exile, Shevchenko resumed his work by radically revising his 'Moskaleva krynytsia' (the first version had appeared in 1847, the second in 1857). In both topic and style, this work is more closely connected with the preceding years than with the following. This is Shevchenko's last epic poem drawn from Ukrainian life and filled with details of folk customs. The new period starts not with 'Moskaleva krynytsia' but with 'Neofity,' which is dated December 1857.

On the other hand, there is a clear division between the works written prior to 1860 and the works that originated between January 1860 and February 1861, the last year of the poet's life. In order to grasp the essential details of that last, brief period in Shevchenko's life one must at least glance at the characteristic features of his work from 1857 to 1859.

Here we find works of different genres and with different stylistic peculiarities. But what gives this period its imprint are Shevchenko's typical 'imitations' of biblical prophets and psalms (Psalm II, Isaiah 35, Ezekiel 19, Hosea 14) and two poems from the time of the beginning of Christianity: 'Neofity' (The Neophytes) and 'Mariia' (Holy Virgin Mary). Of the seventy-two printed pages filled by the works of that period, fifty-two are taken up by the above works. The particular style and mood of these poems, however, characterizes the majority of the other works of those years as well. They were years full of biblical visions portending a bloody retribution, a revenge which was to strike the sinners and exploiters, when 'Evil tyranny / Will bathe itself, itself / In its own blood' (Imitation of Ezekiel), (Zlaia svoievolia / Sama skupaietsia, sama / V svoii krovi / 'Podrazhaniie Iezekiilu'), when the poet hurled into the face of the sinners and the non-repentant:

> vsiudy
> Vas naide pravda-msta, a liudy
> Pidsterezhut vas na totezh,
> Ulovliat i sudyt ne budut,
> V kaidany tuho okuiut,
> V selo na zryshche pryvedut,
> I na khresti otim bez kata
> I bez tsaria vas, bisnuvatykh,
> Rozpnut, rozirvut, roznesut
> I vashei kroviiu, sobaky,
> Sobak napoiat ... ('Osii. Hlava XIV')

Anywhere / Justice-Revenge will find you, and the people / Will seek you out, / Will capture you and will not bring you to trial, / But will put you in tight chains, / Will lead you into the village to be stared at, / And on that cross, without an executioner / And without a tsar they will crucify you, Devil's kin, / Will tear you to pieces, will scatter your remains all around / And with your blood, you dogs, / Will feed the dogs. (Hosea, Chapter XIV)

Everything in this excerpt is characteristic – the identification of revenge with justice, the rejection of judicial trial in the name of mob law, the apotheosis of cruelty, the blind and bloodthirsty rebellion, the inebriation with the blood of one's victims, and the vision of a paradise to come after the triumph of the people's revenge. This is a poetry of apocalypse which, however, does not lead to the end of the world but to an idyllic future realm of justice; a poetry of hatred which flows from an overabundance of love; a poetry of martyrdom that one voluntarily accepts on behalf of others and which one tries to compensate for by torturing others. The entire poem is built upon contrasts, upon frequent and deliberate departures from logic, upon a morbid enjoyment of one's own and other people's suffering, and upon the dream of forever liberating oneself and all others from that suffering.

In style, this is above all a poetry of hyperbole and metaphor, which are piled on top of each other, which grow into odd clusters, now mutually contradictory, now frighteningly coherent in their visionary quality. The verse is constructed in such a way that the meter is constantly broken by pauses in the middle of the line, by tearing the phrases asunder by verses. The construction of the phrase would have been rhetorical, with a series of anaphoras and epistrophes, appeals and curses, if the rhetorical line itself had not been broken by 'side jumps' and deviations from that very same rhetorical structure. This is not simple rhetoric, it is a perverted rhetoric struggling with chaos and anarchy. The principle on which the style of the poems from those years is based is to let the reader perceive a certain scheme, a certain line – be it in the structure of the verse, in the arrangement of images, or in the pattern of the sentence – yet at the same time never to allow the scheme to materialize itself. It is the principle of the permanent conflict between the literary form and the self-will of the poetic genius.

From the viewpoint of poetical masterliness, Shevchenko's works of this period reach the pinnacle of his poetical achievements, and a more careful analysis will reveal behind the ostensible chaos an unusual command of the material, a hidden consequentiality and system.

This can be proved by analysing the particular logic in the development of images, by an analysis of the enjambements, and by an examination of the euphony of Shevchenko's poems. This is easiest to do and the results can be verified most readily if one examines the language of the poetry from this period. Already in 'Neofity,' a poem which opens the period, one is struck by the unprecedented combination of Church Slavonicisms, which are usually associated with the Church or with classical poetry; of vulgarisms, which had scarcely ever been admitted in serious poetry before; and of a few word structures typical of folk songs. If one tries to present this statistically, one receives the impression of a disorganized piling up of heterogeneous and mutually exclusive elements. If one adds to this the great number of Greek and Roman words (according to Ievhen Pelensky's calculations,[2] there are 80 words which are used 180 times to designate the *realia* of Roman life, but used in a capricious sequence, alternating with modern words with a trite everyday meaning) one can comprehend much better the feeling of utter stupefaction and confusion which the poem evoked in Shevchenko's generation and among his immediate successors....

The abundance of contrasts in the language of 'Neofity' affects both the meaning and the emotions. In terms of meaning, it lifts the subject out of the context of one epoch. By constantly shuttling the reader back and forth, from ancient Rome to contemporary St Petersburg, it finally creates the illusion that he is nowhere and yet everywhere; it renders the conflict universal. Emotionally, it unbalances the reader, chafes his nerves, tells him not to accept what he is reading as simply another literary work. The poet does not want to present the reader with just another literary piece, but with an outcry of pain, a piercing scream of raw nerves.

The union of contrasting elements in 'Neofity' has the character of a challenge, and its effect is of stupefaction. In 'Mariia' the same technique is used with less insistence and far more balance. The result is, therefore, a great deal milder although the means employed are none the less revolutionary, especially for its time. Vulgarisms have been excluded almost entirely from the poem. Its text is clearly divided into prayer-like sections distinctly orchestrated with Church Slavonicisms and sections in the vernacular. This is an approximate scheme of the division: lines 1-25 are in the Church Slavonic stylistic key; lines 26-91 in the vernacular; 92-117 in the Church Slavonic; lines 118-92 in the vernacular, with a gradual shift to a rhetorical, exalted presentation; lines 192-206 in Church Slavonic; lines 207-18 in the vernacular; lines 219-32 in Church Slavonic; lines 233-8 in the vernacular; 239-54 in Church Slavonic; lines 255-83 a peculiar synthesis of both styles; lines 284-366 in the vernacular; lines 367-86 in a specific archaic rhetorical key; lines 387-620 in the vernacular; lines 621-40 a synthesis of both styles; lines 641-55 in the vernacular; lines 656-743 a synthesis again....

The effect of this union of styles is one of an extraordinary wealth of associations. Things and events in daily life are transposed to the abstract religious plane, the prosaic becomes poetic, the remote and abstractly religious – close and intimate. Ivan Franko, sending Uliana Kravchenko a copy of 'Mariia,' wrote: 'This is, in my opinion, the most beautiful pearl of our poetry. Read it and keep reading yourself into it and pay close attention to how one can raise ostensibly prosaic things to [the level of] high poetry.'[3]

The effect of both 'Mariia' and 'Neofity' is that of universality. The action takes place in Galilee and concurrently in Ukraine, far away yet near, in the past and everyday. But in 'Neofity' this is achieved by emphasizing the incompatibility of the combined elements, in 'Mariia,' by their mutual interpenetration. The impression one receives from the style of 'Neofity' is of a sudden blow, the impression from the style of 'Mariia' is of caress, the soft, loving stroking of one's head. The contrasts in 'Mariia' are almost indiscernible. Nevertheless, the poem is built upon contrasts in everything, from the vocabulary to the verse torn apart by enjambements; it is built upon that which Drahomanov labelled the mixture of the Bible with Petersburg affairs. 'Mariia' has the elements of an idyll, which were almost absent from 'Neofity,' with its white anger and indignation, but the former poem includes no less tragedy and protest than the latter. It, too, belongs to the revolutionary and prophetic period in Shevchenko's poetry.

The situation changes noticeably in the beginning of 1860. Only one work from that period resembles 'Neofity.' It is 'Saul,' dated 13 October 1860: It is perhaps not accidental that this work remained unfinished or, to be more precise, was only begun. So far as we know, Shevchenko did not even try to take it up again. We would also look in vain in this period for imitations of the prophets or other parts of the Bible. They have disappeared.

An external indication of the change in style, tone, atmosphere is a distinct limitation in the number and role of Church Slavonicisms in the language of the poems. They can be found in greater concentration only in humorous, satirical poems, such as 'Velykomuchenytse kumo!,' 'Kuma moia i ia,' 'Umre muzh velii,' where their role is distinctly that of parody and they are directed against the Church. Apart from them, even in the lyric of political invective, which in Shevchenko's work earlier had constituted a veritable concentration of Church Slavonicisms in conjunction with vulgarisms, Church Slavonic words are hardly ever used. In 'Khocha lezhachoho ne biut' there are at most three Church Slavonicisms (*skorb, pechal, psy*; the latter two need not necessarily be considered as such), in 'O liudy! liudy neboraky!' there is one (*oskvernennyi*), in 'I tut i vsiudy – skriz pohano' there is none.

In place of the stylistic experiments of the preceding years when Shevchenko boldly introduced into poetry expressions which had never been used in it before, when he united words which, it seemed, belonged to incompatible stylistic areas, there now appears as a cardinal rule the law of wise economy. From a seething, expansive style the poet proceeds to the self-limitation of the mature artist. Work in breadth is replaced by intensive polishing of the given material. Semantic contrasts become more important than stylistic ones. The effect is calculated to invite the reader to deep thought, not to deal him a blow which will throw him off balance.

Significant from this viewpoint is Shevchenko's persistent work on the translation of excerpts from the 'Ihor Tale,' several versions of which are available. It is easy to note how much terser and more concentrated is the variant of 14 September than the version of 4 June. In other poems, too, the most general concepts and images of historical events and epochs are as if coded in brief symbols. Such is, for instance, the poem

I Arkhimed i Galilei
Vyna ne bachyly. Ielei
Potik u cherevo cherneche!
A vy, sviatii predotechi,
Po vsomu sviti roziishlys

I krykhtu khliba ponesly
Tsariam ubohym. Bude byto
Tsariamy siianeie zhyto!
A liudy vyrostut. Umrut
Shche nezachatii tsariata ...
I na onovlenii zemli
Vraha ne bude, supostata,
A bude syn, i bude maty,
I budut liudy na zemli.

Archimedes and Galileo / Did not even see the wine. The unction / Flowed into
the monks' big bellies. / And you, holy forerunners / Have spread yourselves
throughout the world / And have carried a morsel of bread / To the wretched tsars.
Perish / will the grain sown by the tsars! / But the people will grow up. Die / will
the not yet conceived princes ... / And on the renewed earth / There will be no foe
and adversary / But there will be a son, and there will be a mother, / And there
will be people on the earth.

In its composition the entire poem is built upon alternating contrasting
images of those who seek truth and justice and those who try to destroy
both of them. Archimedes and Galileo is the first image of the seekers of
truth; it is replaced by the image of the apostles, the holy forerunners, only
to expand into the image of harmonious people who will grow up in the
near future, and ends with the image of a harmonious community founded
upon the principles of the Christian family – the son, the mother, and the
people as such. With these are contrasted the images of the pot-bellied
leaders of the Church ('the monks' big bellies'), of the tsars and princes,
which are generalized in the image of the foe and adversary. As a composition the entire poem constitutes an interweaving of these two series of
images, in which now one, now the other series emerges in plain view as if
in a rope tied of two different strands, one black and one white. Furthermore, each series moves from the particular (Archimedes and Galileo are
lonely seekers of truth, on the one hand; on the other we find the well-
nourished princes of the Church) to the utmost generalization at the end of
the work: 'the people,' as such, are contrasted with 'the foe' as such.

A third series of images pertaining to food runs parallel. It is first introduced by the images of wine and unction which flow into the belly, it is

replaced by the image of bread, a staple food and not an expression of luxury and surplus, of bread which as yet exists only in wretchedly small, counted morsels, and is then generalized in the image of grain sown by the tsars and subject to destruction.

At first sight this poem consists of pithy, abrupt maxims. Actually its composition is extraordinarily consequential and severe in its juxtaposition of 'the people' and 'the tsars,' both words being used in a symbolic, generalized sense, which becomes clear after the poem moves through a series of partial images. The poet's judgment is rendered not by invective but by the oxymoron of wretched tsars who need 'a morsel of bread,' the slightest possible understanding of truth and justice.

The exposure of hidden semantic nuances of the word by means of antitheses, by the unfolding and the gradation of symbolic images, and the use of oxymorons becomes the chief technique of Shevchenko's poetry. Each poem seems to become an exploratory journey down into the deep mine of verbal meanings, an uncovering of the semantic wealth of the language....

The tendency to use semantic resources more deeply and more intesively to some extent determines the composition of the poems. One of Shevchenko's characteristic techniques is the insistent accumulation of words that have been taken from the same semantic field but are now used with different connotations and often in a metaphorical sense. This is a peculiar system of leitmotifs which occur over and over again, but each time in a different association. Such is, for example, the image or rather the semantic field of winter in the poem 'Mynuly lita molodii.'

> Mynuly lita molodii,
> Kholodnym vitrom od nadii
> Uzhe poviialo. Zyma!

The years of youth have passed, / A cold wind has already started blowing / [Away] from hope. It's winter!

The metaphor of cold wind, not too original by itself, first alludes to the semantic field of winter. The image of winter is introduced by a separate sentence. The metaphorical cold wind prepares the reader to understand winter as a metaphorical expression of old age. Later this image is made more concrete:

Sydy odyn v kholodnii khati

Stay by yourself in a cold house

– but only for the purpose of emphasizing the motif of loneliness:

Nema z kym tykho rozmovliaty,
Ani poradytys. Nema
Anikohisinko. – Nema!
Sydy zh odyn, poky nadiia
Oduryt durnia, osmiie ...
Morozom ochi okuie, –

There is no one with whom one could have a quiet talk, / Nor is there anybody to ask for advice. – There is not / A single soul. – There is no one! / Stay there alone until hope / Fools the fool, mocks him ... / Fetters your eyes with frost, –

This is a new stage in the exploration of the semantic field of winter, namely, frost, which now leads the poem to the theme of death. We continue to read:

A dumy hordii rozviie,
Iak tu snizhynu po stepu!

And the proud thoughts will be blown in all directions, / Like that snowflake in the steppe.

Another word from the same semantic field, the snowflake, this time is introduced not in the direct unfolding of the poem's theme but in a comparison. Thus the leitmotif of winter is again emphasized but in a particularly delicate way.

Sydy zh odyn sobi v kutku.
Ne zhdy vesny – sviatoi doli!
Vona ne ziide vzhe nikoly
Sadochok tvii pozelenyt,

Tvoiu nadiiu onovyt!
I dumu volnuiu na voliu
Ne pryide vypustyt ... Sydy
I nichohisinko ne zhdy! ...

Stay by yourself in the corner, / Do not wait for spring – the holy fate! / She will never descend again / To make your little garden green, / To renew your hope! / And to set the free thought free / She will not come ... Stay / And do not expect the slightest thing.

The theme of winter is here emphasized and denied by the antithetical image of the forever unattainable spring.

Other series of images which are repeated and further developed run parallel in the poem: the image of the deserted house which is later narrowed down to one corner and contrasted on the one hand with the cold snow-covered steppe, where powerless man seems to be dissolved in the cosmic elements, and on the other hand – but only in thought – with the green garden in springtime that had been cultivated near the house, the world which man would have liked to create for himself. Against the background of these unfolded images one is struck with particular force by the implicit, thrice-repeated image of hope – the waiting without hope. The culmination comes finally in the oxymoron of the enslaved free thought, which is expressed not directly, but by means of an allusion (the free thought which no one is able to set free!).

The verbal resources of the poem are unusually modest. No word that would have sounded out of place in colloquial language has been used – there are no Church Slavonicisms, no foreignisms, no vulgarisms. The lexical material is clearly neutral. The theme of loneliness, old age, and expectation of death, which is introduced as a meditation of a subjective, lyrical character, grows into a philosophical generalization about the pettiness and wretchedness of man thrown into this world. This is accomplished exclusively by a technique of probing more deeply into the semantics of a given word, a complete, radical exploitation of the possibilities of meaning inherent in a word....

The extreme simplification of language in an external sense coupled with an unusual condensation in utilizing the semantic nuances of words, which characterized Shevchenko's poems of that period, left its imprint upon the unexpected growth of a special poetic genre which one might call a poem condensed into a miniature. Along with the lyrical philosophical meditation and satire linked with invective this genre became basic in Shevchenko's poetry. Out of thirty-one poems of this period at least seven belong to this genre: 'Divcha liube, chornobryve,' 'Oi dibrovo – temnyi haiu,' 'Pod-razhaniie serbskomu,' 'N. Ia. Makarovu,' 'Tytarivna-Nemyrivna,' 'I den ide, i nich ide,' and 'Ziishlys, pobralys, poiednalys.'

Characteristic of Shevchenko's new, 'condensed' style is his 'Tytarivna – Nemyrivna' (The Sexton's Daughter from Nemyriv). This is the last in a long series of his poems about fallen girls, which starts as early as 1838 with 'Kateryna' and through a long chain of variants and variations in 1859 leads to 'Mariia.' Now Shevchenko takes up the theme again. But now he works it out in twelve lines:

Tytarivna-Nemyrivna
Haptuie khustynu ...
Ta kolyshe moskovshchenia,
Maluiu dytynu.
Tytarivna-Nemyrivna
Liudmy horduvala ...
A moskalia-proidysvita
Nyshchechkom vitala!
Tytarivna-Nemyrivna
Pochesnoho rodu ...
Vyhliadaie proidysvita
Moskalia z pokhodu.

The sexton's daughter from Nemyriv / Is embroidering a kerchief ... / And is rocking the Russian soldier's child in its cradle, / The little baby. / The sexton's daughter from Nemyriv / Would look down upon people ... / But secretly welcome / That rake of a Russian soldier! / The sexton's daughter from Nemyriv / Is from an honourable family ... / And now she is looking out for the Russian soldier, / That rake, to return from the campaign.

But this does not yet constitute the final achievement of condensation. A subsequent version reduces the theme to a single line. Here is the poem:

Ziishlys, pobralys, poiednalys,
Pomolodily, pidrosly.
Haiok, sadochok rozvely
Kruhom khatyny. I pyshalys,
Nenache kniazi. Dity hralys,
Rosly sobi ta vyrostaly ...
Divchatok moskali ukraly,
A khloptsiv v moskali zabraly,
A my nenache roziishlys,
Nenache bralys – ne iednalys.

We came together, married, became one, / Grew young and grew up. / We planted a little grove and a little orchard / Around the cottage. And we walked proudly, / As if we were princes. The children played, / They grew and by and by they became adults ... / The girls were stolen by the soldiers, / The boys were recruited into the army, / And we drew apart, it seems / As if we had wed, but never become one.[4]

The line which I have in mind is 'Divchatok moskali ukraly' (The girls were stolen by the soldiers). This theme can 'sing' (that is, can be made out distinctly) only because it has been included as a part of the broader context of the image of a family's disintegration. The motif of the boys who had been recruited into the Russian army and thus lost to the family and the country is almost as typical of Shevchenko's poetry as the motif of the fallen girl.

There is a poetry for poets. Shevchenko's miniatures of the type cited here are poetry for the readers of Shevchenko. If one reads 'Tytarivna-Nemyrivna' without being familiar with Shevchenko's entire preceding work it will be only a vignette, interesting because of its union of ironic notes with notes of sympathy, but nothing more. The stupendous wealth of muted themes, moods, and motifs will reveal itself only to him who knows the poems that Shevchenko had written on that theme. One may assume that the poet knew that his works as a whole would become the possession of millions of people and that each of his millions of readers would be sensitive to each allusion, each hint of his earlier works. In the poem 'Dolia' [Fate], of 1858, the poet had addressed his fate as follows:

Khodimo dalshe: dalshe slava,
A slava – zapovid moia!

Let us go forth: for fame beckons us forth, / And fame is my command-
ment.

The miniatures of 1860 are a poetry for the dedicated, esoteric poetry in
a certain sense, inaccessible to the uninitiated, to the casual passer-by.
Implicitness and deliberate abandonment of logic are no longer drawbacks.
Such are the departures from logic in the poem 'Ziishlys, pobralys' cited
above. It begins with five verbs. 'Married' logically follows 'came together.'
'Became one' only reinforces 'married.' But why does 'grew young' come
after that? Should one understand it as a metaphor, namely, they grew
young in spirit? This would have been a rather banal interpretation. But
even assuming this for a moment, one cannot justify the following 'grew
up.' Grew up after the wedding? Where is the subject for these verbs?
According to the logic of the Ukrainian syntax it would have been natural
in such a case to assume that the subject is one of third person plural, an
indefinite 'they.' But in the penultimate line of the poem there suddenly
and unexpectedly appears the subject 'we.' But who are 'we'? The poem
cannot be autobiographical because Shevchenko had not been married and
had no children. But one cannot judge Shevchenko's poems of this period
according to the criteria of a court of inquiry or those of a realistic work.
In them the planes of time and space have been either suspended or inter-
mingled. The action in the poems takes place nowhere and yet everywhere,
now and at the same time in the past and beyond the limits of time. What
matters is the union of images and motifs and the allusiveness of those
images and motifs and of their union. It is the children who grew young
and then grew up, but this refers to the parents as well, this also refers to
the childless Shevchenko. It is he who has been recruited into the army,
but it is also in himself that the image of the fallen girl is embodied. He
accepts and absorbs in himself all images of his poetry and all images of
reality. The poem becomes panchronical and pantopical, the dividing line
between lyric and epic poetry disappears, melts away.
     Implicitness is the principle which underlies the composition of this
eight-line poem:

Divcha liube, chornobryve
Neslo z lokhu pyvo.
A ia hlianuv, podyvyvsia –
Ta azh pokhylyvsia ...
Komu vono pyvo nosyt?
Chomu bose khodyt?
Bozhe sylnyi! Tvoia syla
Ta Tobi zh i shkodyt.

A sweet girl with black eyebrows / Was carrying beer up from the cellar. / I glanced, looked at her – / And bent my head ... / To whom is she carrying the beer? / Why is she walking with bare feet? ... / O mighty God! Your might / Is harming You Yourself.

No one has yet dared to give an exhaustive commentary on this poem. One can hardly provide one which would be adequate. Why is the image of the barefoot girl carrying beer from the cellar so tragic that the inference from it is the denial of the principle underlying the structure of the universe, in which beauty and goodness inevitably engender evil so that the point of challenging God becomes inevitable? What is hidden behind the image of the barefoot girl: the theme of a future prostitute? of a girl thrown out into the streets of St Petersburg? simply that of an insurmountable and persistent human loneliness which is also the theme of the poem 'Mynuly lita molodii'? One could write pages about this miniature, collect all those motifs in Shevchenko's poetry with which it can be linked by allusions but, at best, they would only be hypothetical, only possibilities. The point and sense of the poem is precisely that none of those possibilities excludes any of the others.

In the poems of 1860 the connection between Shevchenko's style and that of the folk songs becomes more and more pronounced. It will be remembered that the latter to a large extent characterized Shevchenko's lyric poems at the beginning of his literary career and then receded into the background during the period of the 'three years' (1843-5) and again during the first years after returning from exile (1857-9). But now the use of folklore style is subordinated to the new principles of Shevchenko's poetics....

From the motifs and the poetic resources of folk songs the poem 'Nad Dniprovoiu sahoiu' (On the Cove of the Dnieper) is composed. It starts out with the image of a sycamore among the bushes of osier, guelder rose, and fir. (In order to understand the poem it has to be kept in mind that in the Ukrainian language sycamore is masculine, and osier, fir, and guelder rose – feminine.)

Nad Dniprovoiu sahoiu
Stoit iavir mizh lozoiu,
Mizh lozoiu z ialynoiu,
Z chervonoiu kalynoiu.

On the cove of the Dnieper / There stands a sycamore among the osier, / Among the osier with the fir, / With the red guelder rose.

The vocabulary, the images, and repetition of the preposition *mizh* (among) – all this and the very measure of the verse, too – are completely in the spirit of the folk song. In the following quatrain this style is maintained, only the comparison of the sycamore tree with the unhappy Cossack is added:

Dnipro bereh ryie-ryie,
Iavorovi korin myie.
Stoit staryi, pokhylyvsia,
Mov kozak toi zazhuryvsia, –

The Dnieper is digging, digging, / Is washing the root of the sycamore. / The old one stands bent down / Like a Cossack in grief, –.

On the whole, this, too, is a comparison out of folklore, but in folklore man is compared to a tree rather than vice versa. This is thus the first departure from the style of folk songs (within this very style!), but it is as yet hardly noticeable.

In the following quatrain, however, the comparison is continued and almost becomes independent:

[Kozak] shcho bez doli, bez rodyny
Ta bez virnoi druzhyny,

I druzhyny i nadii
V samotyni posyviie!

[A Cossack] who is without fortune, without family / And without a faithful wife, /
A wife and hope / Will become grey in the solitude.

Obviously, there are too many details for a mere comparison. The motif of
the absence of a wife and growing grey sever the connection with the sycamore tree. But the image of the sycamore appears again in the following
semiquatrain.

Iavor kazhe: − Pokhyliusia
Ta v Dniprovi skupaiusia. −

Says the sycamore: 'I shall bend down / And bathe in the Dnieper.'

After this comes a radical break. The Cossack, who seemed to have figured
only in the comparison, is suddenly introduced into the main part of the
poem as an equal to the sycamore:

Kozak kazhe: − Pohuliaiu
Ta liubuiu poshukaiu.

Says the Cossack: 'I shall roam around / And look for my beloved.'

But the image of the beloved which the reader is now expecting does not
materialize. It appears to be true, but only in a comparison:

A kalyna z ialynoiu
Ta hnuchkoiu lozynoiu,
Mov divchatochka iz haiu
Vykhodzhaiuchy spivaiut,
Povbyrani, zakvitchani
Ta z talanom zarucheni,
Dumky-hadonky ne maiut,
Viutsia-hnutsia ta spivaiut.

But the guelder rose with the fir / And the supple osier, / Like girls who sing /
Coming from the grove / Dressing up in flowers / And, being engaged to fortune, /
Need not think [sad] thoughts / Wind and bend and sing.

Must one add that the last line again increases the ambiguity? For 'wind and bend' refers to the bushes only, 'sing' only to the girls.

Thus the resources of the folk song have been used very similarly to the original model, but by means of consequent, gradual shifts in the imagery the dividing line between the seemingly real Dnieper landscape and the comparison, between the images of nature and of people, between the always generalized and somewhat abstract folk song and the subjective lyrical poetry with 'I' as its hero, has been expunged. A multiplicity of planes and a removal from the context of a photographic reproduction of reality, the transformation of the objective into the subjective and vice versa – these are the main characteristics of Shevchenko's treatment of folklore in 1860.

I shall not analyse the poem 'Teche voda z-pid iavora' (Water Flows from under the Sycamore Tree). It, too, has been composed by giving the resources and images of the folk song different meanings, though here the shift is achieved not by switching from the plane of 'reality' to the plane of comparisons, but by a parallelism of three images that seem to be in no way connected among themselves, namely, the guelder rose and the syca-more, a duck with her ducklings, a girl who is not yet engaged promenad-ing in the garden. The poem breaks off on a most significant detail, without there being any clear indication what its 'meaning' is.

It is not difficult to guess why in the poems of 1860 Shevchenko turned again to the resources of folklore. Folklore now attracted Shevchenko with the universal character of its images and the simplicity of its language, a simplicity, however, which to a large extent was symbolic. The poetics of folklore suited the new concern of the poet, his transition from expansion to intensification, to introspection, to his search for the essential while accepting the transitory.

As if symbolic in this respect is Shevchenko's last poem 'Chy ne pokynut nam, neboho' (Should we not leave, my dear poor thing), which he wrote some ten days before his death, which does not exclude love of life and of this world. Stylistically speaking, this tragically serene idyll passes from one of Shevchenko's styles to another: it consists of a colloquial dialogue, of humorous elements almost in the fashion of Ivan Kotliarevsky, of passages modelled on folk songs, which are, of course, again personal-ized and arranged according to a scheme of multiple planes, when for example, the image of Ukraine simultaneously serves as the image of the otherworldly Paradise.

This is not the first time the theme of death has appeared in Shevchenko's work. It is one of the most constantly recurring themes, along with the liberation of Ukraine, the longing for a harmonious social order, the fallen girl, exile, the idyll of the family and the countryside. Nobody has yet analysed the direct and indirect ramifications of this theme in the poet's works, the evolution of his attitude towards death, although this would have been a fascinating and important aspect of Shevchenko's work. We have no space to enter into this question here. It suffices, however, to compare the poem of 1847, 'Kosar' (The Reaper), with the poem written shortly before his death to perceive the difference. The image of death in the poem of 1847 is the image of the inexorable reaper who

Ponad polem ide,
Ne pokosy klade,
Ne pokosy klade – hory.

Walks along the field, / Mows down not strips, / Mows down not strips – but mountains.

In anticipating his own death –

I mene ne myne,
Na chuzhyni zotne,
Za reshotkoiu zadavyt,
Khresta nikhto ne postavyt
I ne pomiane

And he will not pass me by, / Will cut me down far from my homeland, / Will strangle me behind the bars, / Nobody will put up a cross for me / And remember me

– there is a consciousness of inevitability but there is no acceptance of this inevitability. The atmosphere of the poem is one of terror and nightmares. It has determined both the brutally terse images of the poem and its staccato rhythm.

The tone of the poem 'Chy ne pokynut nam, neboho' is jocularly sad. However much the poet may love this world –

> Bach, iakyi shyrokyi,
> Ta vysokyi ta veselyi,
> Iasnyi ta hlybokyi

Look, how wide, / And high and gay, / Light and deep [it is]

– he himself requests his companion, the Muse, to leave this world together with him:

> ... khodimo spat,
> Khodimo v khatu spochyvat.
> Vesela khata, shchob ty znala.

... Let's go to sleep. / Let's go and rest in the cottage. / The cottage is gay, don't you know?

And again:

> Poky vohon ne zakholonuv,
> Khodimo luchche do Kharona –
> Cherez Letu bezdonnuiu
> Ta kalamutnuiu
> Pereplyvem, perenesem
> I Slavu sviatuiu –
> Moloduiu, bezvichnuiu.

While the fire is still warm, / Let us rather go to Charon – / Across the bottomless / And muddy Lethe / Shall we go and shall carry over / The holy Glory, too, / Young and ageless.

The *danse macabre* of 'The Reaper' has yielded to an idyll, the protest – to acceptance, the horror – to quiet sadness. Death now comes as a simple, logical, and lawful end of one stage in life. The other part of life – glory, fame, that is, his poetry, his accomplishments – remains to live. All aspects of life and death form a single harmony.

This evolution in the attitude towards death, this perception of the harmony in life and man is not only a key to this poem. It is the key to the entire last year in Shevchenko's work. The stylistic evolution which we have traced, the transition from the destructive seething style to a concentrated, monolithic, and harmonious one, was not a transition in form only. It was connected and went hand in hand with a change in the poet's mood and *Weltanschauung*. One after another, the themes and problems of the preceding years were reviewed and rethought, given a different meaning in the works of Shevchenko's last year. And everywhere the review and the rethinking proceeded in the same direction of renouncing external effect, of concentrating upon the inner world and the spiritual values of man, of a peculiar universal acceptance, balance, of merging with the universe in an ideal harmony.

The preceding years, after the return from exile, had been years in which the poet became inebriated on ideas of revolt and punishment, when he called upon everybody to rise to a blind and implacable rebellion:

> A shchob zbudyt
> Khyrennu voliu, treba myrom,
> Hromadoiu obukh stalyt,
> Ta dobre vyhostryt sokyru –
> Ta i zakhodytsia vzhe budyt. ('Ia ne nezduzhaiu, nivroku,' 22 November 1858)

In order to wake up / Wretched liberty one must together with all others / In the community sharpen the axe, / Make it like steel – / Then one can awaken her. – ('I am not ill ...').

The last vision of the inexorable national and social punishment was contained in the poem 'Osii. Hlava XIV' (Hosea, Ch. XIV), written 25 December 1859, with its bloody image of revolt and mob law, unparalleled in its cruelty:

> Ne vtechete
> I ne skhovaietesia, vsiudy
> Vas naide pravda-msta.

You will not be able to flee / Nor to hide, anywhere / Justice-Revenge will find you.

It is characteristic that the apocalyptic quality of Shevchenko's 'Imitation' stands almost wholly by itself, without much support from the original text. In the Bible the images of horror and punishment take only two verses: 'Assyria shall not save us, we will not ride upon horses: and we will no more say, "Our God," to the work of our hands.' The entire remaining portion of the chapter is devoted to an idyll of God's grace: 'I will be as the dew to Israel: he shall blossom as the lily,' etc. In Shevchenko the proportion of the parts is exactly reversed: out of the seventy lines of the poem only five mention the bright future.

This mood, these images are not recreated in any of the poems of 1860. One can trace the gradual reappraisal of revolt in the four versions of the poem 'Molytva' (Prayer), all of which were written at the end of May 1860. First, the poet's wrath is now directed exclusively against the 'tsars.' But even for them the poet no longer desires bloody punishment. In the version of 25 May he asks God:

Tsariv, kryvavykh shynkariv,
U puta kutii okui,
V sklepu hlybokim zamurui.

The tsars, the bloody tavern-keepers, / Put them into forged chains / And inter them in a deep dungeon.

The poet is not concerned with revenge and not so much with punishment as with simply rendering them harmless. But even this seems to him to be too strong now. In the version of 27 May he actually retracts his original wish that those who are responsible for social injustice should be put in chains. Now he writes:

Zlonachynaiushchykh spyny,
U puta kutii ne kui,
V sklepy hlyboki ne murui.

Stop those who conceive evil, / Do not put them in forged chains, / Do not inter them in deep dungeons.

And finally, in the version of 31 May the poet is even prepared to leave to the tsars all the goods of this world –

Tym nesytym ocham,
Zemnym boham-tsariam,
I pluhy, i korabli,
I vsi dobra zemli ...

To these greedy eyes, / The gods and tsars of this world, / [Leave] ploughs,
ships, / And all the goods of the earth ...

– thus leaving to humankind the happiness of work and the happiness of
inner concentration, shifting the entire conflict from the plane of social
action to the plane of the human soul, faith, and feeling.

Now his positive hero is not a revenger or an executioner but the man
he calls a 'peace-loving man ... with a good heart' (*dobroserdyi ... tykholiubets
sviatyi*) ('Molytva,' final version), his ideal is 'ageless, inseparable love'
(*liubov bezvichnaia, suhuba*) ('Rosly ukupochtsi, zrosly'), and his main
wish and prayer that God might help 'those whose hands create good' and
'those who are pure in heart,' (*dobrozyzhdushchym rukam, chystym sertsem*)
that He might send all – I emphasize: all – 'sense of unity and fraternal
love' (*jedynomysliie i bratoliubiie*)....

Shevchenko did not become unctuous and sanctimonious. The evil
reigning in the world continued to hurt him and to evoke his indignation.
From time to time invective breaks out in his work. But it is no longer
directed to incite the people to a social revolt which would drown the world
in a sea of blood. In the poem 'O liudy! liudy neboraky!' (O people,
wretched people) of 3 November 1860 the poet exclaims:

Chy bude kara
Tsariam, tsariatam na zemli?

Will there be punishment / For the tsars and princes on earth?

But he expects that it will be God who will punish them and not the
confused and blind mob:

Povynna but, bo sontse stane
I oskvernenu zemliu spalyt.

[Punishment] there must be, otherwise the sun would stop / And burn the defiled
earth.

If in 'Osii. Hlava XIV' he envisaged and desired that the evil would be punished according to mob law, now he sees how

> Liudy *tykho*,
> *Bez vsiakoho lykhoho lykha*,
> Tsaria do kata povedut. ('Khocha lezhachoho i ne biut,' 20 October 1860)

The people will *quietly* / *Without any evil spite* / Lead the tsar to the executioner. ('Though One Does not Kick a Man Who is Lying Down'; italics mine)

This is not bloody revenge, but the inevitable and deserved elimination of one who is responsible for the social evil.

Instead of the leader of a rebellious mob the poet now envisages in his dreams and aspirations an apostle of Justice and Reason:

> I den ide, i nich ide.
> I, holovu skhopyvshy v ruky,
> Dyvuieshsia, chomu ne ide
> Apostol pravdy i nauky! (5 November 1860)

The day goes by, the night goes by. / And grasping your head with your hands / You keep wondering why the apostle / Of Justice and Reason does not come.

The last months and literally the last days of Shevchenko's life were filled with his worries about the typesetting, the printing, and later the distribution of his *Bukvar* (Primer). The censor's permission was obtained 21 November 1860, and it was published in January 1861. The poet's letters in January and February are full of expressions of concern about the distribution of the *Bukvar*. There is, of course, such a big difference between the mission of the apostle of Justice and Reason, the reformer of the social order, and the publication of the primer that these things seem incompatible and their juxtaposition ridiculous. But the *Bukvar* was only the first stage in Shevchenko's plans, perhaps even a stage that was to some degree symbolic. In the letter to Mykhailo Chaly of 4 January 1861, Shevchenko told him about his further plans: 'There is an idea to print after the primer a textbook of arithmetic, at the same price and of the same size as the primer; after the textbook of arithmetic one of geography, at 5 kopecks; and one of history, but only of our [Ukrainian] history, I could perhaps squeeze into 10 kopecks. If God would help to do this small deed, the big one would take care of itself.'[5] Here one finds a clear underlining of the connection between the small deed – popular education – and the big: the emergence of a new and harmonious social order. Not the axe, but the book is to be found at the basis of the conception of the apostle of Justice and Reason. With the smallest book, the primer, Shevchenko began his activity as an apostle of Justice and Reason.

Ievhen Kyryliuk has carefully traced the use of the image of the axe as a symbol of revolt in Shevchenko's poetry. He has demonstrated how this image echoed the very same image in the revolutionary proclamation of Herzen, in Herzen's brochure *Kreshchenaia sobstvennost*, in the articles of *Kolokol*, in the letter to Herzen (which, in his opinion, originated in the circle of Nikolai Chernyshevsky), in one poem by Nikolai Nekrasov.[6] This makes more noteworthy the fact that Shevchenko now explicitly rejected the use of the axe. In the poem 'Buvaly voiny i viiskovii svary' (There Had Been Wars and Military Feuds) of 26 November 1860 he seems to engage in direct polemic with himself from a year before, writing that the change of the social order would come about without the axe.

> I bez sokyry
> Azh zareve ta zahude,
> Kozak bezverkhyi upade.

And without the axe, / With a roar and a rumble, / The headless Cossack will fall.

Shevchenko was not a sociologist, nor did he care at all about the refinements of ideology. But if we wanted to bring his ideas of 1860 together in a coherent whole his ideas could have been expressed more or less as follows. He was expecting a change in the unjust order of life as the result of the appearance of the apostle of Justice and Reason. The latter, basing himself on all those whose hearts were pure and whose hands created good, would eliminate the 'tsar,' who was responsible for all the evil, and would establish a new order in which brotherly love and justice would triumph. In this order everybody who did honest work and was pure of heart could build his life in harmony with other men like him and in harmony with the universe, *svit-brat* (one's brother – the world), which had been established in accordance with God's laws....[7]

In the last period of his creative career Shevchenko perceives and de-
nounces two sins of mankind. These sins are extraordinarily characteristic
and show how consistent and sincere was Shevchenko's philosophy of
those years. One of the sins is covetousness arising from self-aggrandize-
ment, greed, and violence. This is a mortal sin because it violates the
very basis on which the structure of the universe rests, the harmony and
balance of man in himself, of man in relation to other men, and of man in
relation to God. The image which embodies that sin is the image of the
'tsars' and 'princes.' It has already been characterized above, the basic
references have been cited, and there is no need to dwell on it any longer
here.

The concept of the second sin is no less characteristic of the new moods
of Shevchenko. The poems 'Himn chernechyi' (Nuns' Hymn), of 20 June
1860, and 'Velykomuchenytse kumo!' (O You Saintly, Martyred Woman),
of 2 December 1860, are devoted to that concept. This is a sin against
oneself, against one's own body, and consequently, against one's soul. This
is the sin of the non-acceptance of life, of an incomplete enjoyment of all
that which is offered by life. This is the sin of denying oneself sexual life,
of celibacy, which the poet calls with an oxymoron appropriate to this
period of his work, *hrikh pravednyi* (the righteous sin). It makes man
blind, 'inert of heart.' In his new synthesis, in seeking and confirming the
universal harmony, Shevchenko accepted all aspects and expressions of life,
with the exception of evil. Nothing was so alien and remote to him as
asceticism. As one who eternally dreamt about family happiness, he nevertheless would rather have even debauchery than virginity and he ended his
poem 'Velykomuchenytse kumo!' with the advice:

Prokynsia, kumo, probudys,
Ta kruhom sebe podyvys,
Nachkhai na tu divochu slavu
Ta shchyrym sertsem, nelukavo,
Khoch raz, serdeho, sobludy![8]

Awake, my good woman, awake, / Take a look around yourself, / Don't give a
damn for your maidenhead / And sincerely, without evil, / Err, my dear woman, if
only once.

Having made a sharp break with the rebelliousness of the preceding period, with its stylistic destructiveness, and having affirmed a *Weltanschauung* of harmony in the universe and in the social order, and asserted the principle of balance in the very style of his poetry, Shevchenko in the last months of his life adopted a somewhat new approach to the problem of the national freedom of Ukraine. There is no change in his nostalgia and his deep affection for his country. The landscape of his idylls is always the landscape of the Dnieper region (for example, 'Nad Dniprovoiu sahoiu' of 24 June 1860), of the Ukrainian village (for instance, 'Teche voda z-pid iavora' of 7 November 1860). Conversely, the landscape of his nightmares is always the landscape of Russia, usually of St Petersburg, as in 'Iakos to iduchy unochi' (13 November 1860), 'O liudy! liudy neboraky!' (3 November 1860), to some extent in 'Kuma moia i ia' (1860). In Shevchenko's last poem the Ukrainian landscape is clearly identified with Paradise:

... nad Stiksom, u raiu,
Nenache nad Dniprom shyrokym,
V haiu – predvichnomu haiu,
Postavliu khatochku, sadochok
Kruhom khatyny nasadzhu. ('Chy ne pokynut nam, neboho,' 15 February 1861)

... on the Styx, in Paradise, / Which is as on the wide Dnieper, / In the grove – the grove existing from times immemorial, / I shall build a small cottage and will plant / A small garden around the cottage.

It is significant that the landscape of Ukraine is always a serene summer landscape, without a trace of the romantic atmosphere of storm and flood rains from Shevchenko's early romantic period; a landscape on which there constantly shines a mild sun which seems never to set or to hide behind the clouds. The Russian landscape, on the contrary, is a night landscape of fog and blizzards, of mist and ghostly lights which emerge from the darkness, from nowhere, like the eyes of Satan.

The deep affection of the poet for his native country thus persists. But from the poems of this period there disappear themes derived from the history of Ukraine, the themes of national oppression which had been so characteristic of the period of the 'three years' (1843-5). The reason for this is easy to grasp: not in the bloody skirmishes and battles of the past and not in blind revolt does Shevchenko now seek the liberation of man, but in the establishment of the inner harmony of the human soul, the harmony in relations between human souls. If this harmony is found and achieved the problem of Ukraine will solve itself. The problem of Ukraine and her liberation is now subordinated to another, larger problem.

This is explicitly shown by the only poem of this period which is devoted to a philosophical interpretation of Ukrainian history. This is the poem, cited above, 'Buvaly voiny i viiskovii svary' (There Had Been Wars and Military Feuds), which was written 26 November 1860. In it Shevchenko negates the Ukrainian past. The revolts and wars of the old Ukraine now appear to him to have been in vain:

Buvaly voiny i viiskovii svary:
Halahany, i Kyseli, i Kochubei-Nahai,
Bulo dobra toho chymalo.
Mynulo vse, ta ne propalo,
Ostalys shasheli: hryzut,
Zherut i tliat staroho duba ...

There had been wars and military feuds: / Halahans, and Kysils, and Kochubeis-Nahais, / There had been plenty of that stuff. / All has passed, but not perished, / Borers have remained: they are gnawing, / Eating and helping the old oak decay ...

The ruling classes of Ukraine have brought about this tragedy by linking their fate with Russia, becoming what the poet calls the nursemaids and servants of a foreign fatherland ('nianky, / Diadky otechestva chuzhoho'). But the oak itself, that is, Ukraine, is still full of life though it may be hidden in the roots:

A od korinnia tykho, liubo
Zeleni parosti rostut.

But from the roots quietly and pleasant to look at / Green offshoots are growing.

Those are the apostles of Justice and Reason, about whose coming the poet had written three weeks before composing this poem. The poet continues about the offshoots:

I vyrostut. I bez sokyry
Azh zareve ta zahude,
Kozak bezverkhyi upade.

And they will grow to maturity. And without the axe,
With a roar and a rumble,
The headless Cossack will fall.

It is in this very poem that Shevchenko states that the end of the old
history of Ukraine will come about without the axe, not through a revolution, but through the triumph of Justice and Truth. And he repeats the line
he has used before in order to reaffirm the immortality of Ukraine:

Mynulo vse, ta ne propalo,

All has passed but not perished

and after that he resumes the previously begun sentence about the fall of
old Ukraine, the headless Cossack (headless because he had lost the ruling
class), the old oak, whose crown has been gnawed out by borers but whose
roots (the peasantry, the hard-working people from 'Molytva') are still
alive and producing green offshoots. In his fall, the oak

Roztroshchyt tron, porve porfiru,
Rozdavyt vashoho kumyra,
Liudskii shasheli.

Will shatter the throne and tear the purple,
Will crush your idol,
You borers in the form of men.

When analysed against the background of the ideas and moods of the
1860s, however, this poem leaves nothing unclear. The concept of Ukrainian history in this poem has been reviewed and subordinated to a new
general conception of life, man, and God in Shevchenko's work. From the
old there have remained two elements: the boundless love of Ukraine and
the belief in her special mission as a pioneer of the new order, but this
time not one that is limited to the Slavs, but one extending to all mankind.

'It would be a great mistake to consider Shevchenko's work as static and not to take into account his ideological and artistic development,' O. Biletsky and A. Deich justly observed.[9] Shevchenko's works are characterized by the framework of several distinct periods. It is true that the periods are brief, mostly two or three years each. But his entire poetical career, as we know it, embraces at most some fifteen years, if one excludes those barren years of exile in which nothing was written. And the number of brief periods in his short career only proves with what speed Shevchenko grew and matured, which is not surprising if one considers the fantastic quality of his life, which had carried him up from the lowest depth of society to its very pinnacle, which hurled him to the bottom and exalted him again.

The division into periods does not mean, of course, that there is nothing in common between the works of the different periods. There is an undeniable continuity, a cyclical quality in Shevchenko's turning again to themes, motifs, images, ideas, and moods that he had already examined. Speaking about the last period in Shevchenko's work, I have occasionally pointed out the similarities to and differences from works of the preceding periods, referring, for example, to 'Kosar,' the 'Prychynna,' and so on. But this is only a small part of what could and should be done in this regard. There are many more threads which link the periods together into a living whole. One of the primary tasks of Shevchenko studies is thorough research of each particular period in the poet's work so that later the common and the divergent characteristics of the periods can be pointed out....

That which now can be called the second Petersburg period after exile was even shorter than the other periods, not much more than one year. But the cause of this brevity was the poet's death. It would be idle to predict how long that period would have lasted had Shevchenko been fated to live longer. It might have been the beginning of a period of a stable balance, something on the model of Goethe's mature old age, which in the case of the German poet had replaced the youthful *Sturm und Drang*. It might have been a passing mood. An early death resulting from the raptures and catastrophes of Shevchenko's life interrupted his growth long before he had reached the pinnacle....

After all, these ideas were not new to Shevchenko. They had been very clearly formulated in his 'Poslaniie' (Epistle) to his dead, living, and yet-

to-be-born fellow countrymen, that is, as early as 1845, with his concept of
national unity, not revolution:

> Obnimite zh, braty moi,
> Naimenshoho brata, –
> Nekhai maty usmikhnetsia,
> Zaplakana maty.

Embrace, my brethren, / The smallest brother, / So that your mother will smile, /
The mother who has been crying.

In the first years after exile these moods and ideas did not disappear from
Shevchenko's work. But they co-existed more than ever before with ideas
of implacable revenge, a covetous and bloody social revolution. It may be
assumed that in this were reflected the sentiments in Russia at the end of
the 1850s, before the promised but intentionally delayed reforms, the
influence of the radical revolutionaries of St Petersburg and in particular
the influence of Herzen's *Kolokol* that is cited so often in the poet's diary
in the years 1857-8.

Dissociating himself from this circle of ideas and sentiments in 1860 was
not, therefore, something completely new. To a large extent, it was Shevchenko's return to himself, his overcoming and rejection of influences that
were alien to him. As in the 1840s when he was confronted with the complex of the '*haidamachchyna*,' another version of blind and bloody revenge,
and overcame it in the poems of the 'three years,' he now overcame the
complex of the Russian revolutionary radicalism of Herzen and his followers. Now, as then, he emerged from this conflict enriched, with the
diction of his poetry more manly and balanced. In this, it seems, lies the
essence of the last Petersburg period in Shevchenko's work.

(1962)

NOTES

1 First published in *Taras Ševčenko, 1814-1861: A Symposium* (The Hague
1962), here abridged.
2 Ievhen Iulii Pelensky, *Shevchenko-kliasyk: 1855-1861* (Kraków-Lviv 1942) 99.

3 *Literatura i mystetstvo*, 5 (Lviv 1941) 35.

4 Although I have translated the subject of these verbs as *we*, Ukrainian syntax leads us to assume an indefinite *they* and it is not until the penultimate line that there appears the subject *we*.

5 T. Shevchenko, *Povne vydannia tvoriv*, ed. by P. Zaitsev (Warsaw 1935) XI, 269.

6 Ievhen Kyryliuk, *T.H. Shevchenko: Zhyttia i tvorchist* (Kiev 1959) 507 ff.

7 It is possibly to this time that the recollection by Ia. Polonsky refers. 'I remember that once at a *soirée* at Bilozersky's, the editor of the journal *Osnova*, Shevchenko supported the idea of a visiting Slav from Galicia [Galician Ukrainian? (ed.)] that any politics was amoral, that it was because of political considerations that all kinds of injustice had always been committed and that from them all the misfortunes of nations and peoples were derived and that it would have been best for a state, therefore, to have no politics at all' (A.I. Kostenko, ed., *Spohady pro Shevchenka*, [Kiev 1958] 433).

8 In the first version of the poem Shevchenko had been even blunter. The last line of the poem read: 'Khoch z psom, serdeho, sobludy' (Err, my dear woman, if need be, with a dog). See *Povne zibrannia tvoriv v desiaty tomakh*, II, 478.

9 A.I. Beletsky, A.I. Deich, *T.G. Shevchenko: Vvedenie v izuchenie poeta* (Moscow 1959) 141.

22

Shevchenko in the Brotherhood of Saints Cyril and Methodius

VOLODYMYR MIIAKOVSKY

There are a number of reasons for the attention given by scholars to the political organization of Ukrainian intellectuals in the 1840s known as the Brotherhood of Saints Cyril and Methodius.[1]

First, the Brotherhood arose against the background of the European movement of that period, a movement that found its way to all the countries of central Europe and culminated in the turbulent events of 1848. Second, the ideology of the Brotherhood had an undeniable connection with and, indeed, a striking resemblance to that of earlier Ukrainian, Russian, and Polish political associations active in Ukraine. There was also a close ideological relationship between the Brotherhood and the liberation movement of the sixties and later. Finally, the Brotherhood had in its ranks a number of the outstanding men of that era – scholars and writers such as Taras Shevchenko, Mykola Kostomarov, and Panteleimon Kulish, who soon became known far beyond the borders of their own country.

The Brotherhood of Saints Cyril and Methodius was liquidated at the very beginning of its formation and activity. The exact date of its inception is not known, but it is assumed that the Brotherhood was active for no more than a year and a half. In that short period the Brothers were unable to implement any of their objectives, such as the publication of a popular journal for peasants and of basic textbooks. They had no time even to complete the organizational and ideological structure of their association. Their inspiring and original thoughts were buried in the records of the investigative committee, without having produced any great resonance in Ukrainian society.

Nevertheless, news of the Brotherhood began to spread, and interest in its ideological premises began to grow.

The investigation of the Brotherhood's activities was conducted in 1847 by the Third Division of the Office of His Imperial Majesty. The records of the investigation include the statements of the accused and of witnesses as well as the correspondence and works of members of the Brotherhood, and therefore constitute the most valuable source of information for the study of the history of the association and of the relations among the individual members.[2] To this source material should be added the few later memoirs of Kostomarov and Kulish. Kostomarov in particular referred several times in his writings to the Brotherhood and to Shevchenko's activity in it.

For the past fifty years, aside from a few articles and other brief publications on the history of the association and the roles of individual members, the literature on the Brotherhood has been limited to the works of V. Semevsky, M. Vozniak, Z. Hurevych, J. Gołąbek, and P. Zaionchkovsky.[3] Shevchenko's role in the Brotherhood has been broadly discussed in general works and in special studies of the poet. However, M. Novytsky's work, 'Shevchenko in the Records of the Court Proceedings of 1847,' is the only study based on first-hand source materials.[4]

Membership in the Brotherhood was mainly made up of the eleven men who were brought before the judicial inquiry and who were more or less severely punished for their activities in the association.[5] Along with a few scholars and teachers, the Brotherhood consisted of Ukrainian university youth, coming from various social segments and from provinces of Ukraine. The Brothers also had a wider circle of sympathizers and close friends who, as far as ideology was concerned, were an integral part of the association. Here D. Pylchykov and P. Chuikevych, both teachers, may be mentioned. There were also a few persons included in the investigation by pure accident, such as the well-known Slavophile F. Chyzhov.

Although there was a great divergence of interests and views among the individual members, three main problems were fundamental in their ideology: the Slavic problem, which under contemporary conditions and according to current concepts was basically the national issue; the social problem, centred on the demand for abolition of serfdom and for general education; and the political problem, involving plans for creating a federation of republics out of the imperial powers. All the Brotherhood's ideas were based on Christian ethical principles. This was stipulated for all members, including Shevchenko. The very taking of Cyril and Methodius, the first enlighteners of the Slavs, as patron saints of the Brotherhood suggests that the Slavic question was uppermost in the ideology of the association.

The idea of unity among and union of all Slavs was entirely in accord with the prevailing concepts of that romantic period in all the civilized countries of Europe. Romanticism paid close attention to all expressions of national 'spirit' in folklore, religious belief, and the like. The idea of Slavic unity was sought in the ancient past of the Slavic tribes, and from that point of view also the history of each individual Slavic nationality, its language and literature, customs, habits, and religious concepts were studied. Czechs such as Jan Kollár, P. Šafařik, and Václav Hanka were founders of these Slavic studies, and their names were universally identified with the Slavic renaissance.

Such events as the publication of a grammar of the Slavonic language by Jernej Kopitar (1808), the publication of Serb folk songs by Vuk Karadžić (1814-15), Hanka's discovery of the Královédvorský manuscript (1817), the founding of the Czech Museum in Prague (1818), which became the centre for collecting Slavic literary and historical materials and relics were landmarks in the development of interest in Slavic studies and in awakening interest in Ukrainian problems as well. By the late eighteen-twenties, and particularly in the thirties, there was in Ukraine a literary renaissance which closely resembled that of the Western Slavs. Thus, the collection of Ukrainian folk songs published by Mykhailo Maksymovych in 1827 and 1834; the first attempt, by D. Bantysh-Kamensky, to write a Ukrainian history (three editions: 1822, 1830, 1842); the discoveries of new historical documents, Cossack chronicles, made by Bodiansky, Kulish, Kostomarov, and others, and the dissemination among Ukrainian intellectuals of the well-known manuscript of the so-called 'Istoriia Rusov' (History of the Russes) – these and similar events supplied more and more data for comparison with what was known about Western and Southern Slavs.

Certain aspects of the Russian imperial ideology contributed to these developments. The official Russian three-unitary formula covered not only the Orthodox religion and czarist absolutism, but the factor of 'nationality' as well. The government's interest in developing Slavic studies is evidenced in the work of two Russian ministers of national education: Admiral A. Shishkov (1824-28) and Count S. Uvarov (1833-49). Shishkov even championed a plan to invite Hanka, Čelakovský , and Šafařik to Russia as teachers and scholars. In fact, the introduction of Slavic studies in St Petersburg was a result of Shishkov's initiative, and the Uvarov University Statute of 1835 introduced systematic Slavic studies in four universities, including that of Kharkiv. The University of Kiev, founded in 1834 (after the liquidation of the Vilna institutions of graduate education and the College of Kremianets, as a result of the Polish uprising) was in a special situation. The Uvarov Statute was introduced there first in 1842, but the Chair of Slavic History and Literature remained vacant for some time thereafter.

The selection of Kharkiv as a centre for Slavic studies was fully justified, since it had been the centre of Ukrainian cultural life since the turn of the century. Such outstanding writers as Petro Hulak-Artemovsky (1791-1856) and Hryhorii Kvitka-Osnovianenko (1778-1843) were active there. There, too, the first literary journals were published, such as *Ukrainskii vestnik* (1816-21) and *Ukrainskii almanakh* (1831), as well as literary collections such as *Zaporozhskaia starina* by I. Sreznevsky (1834-8) and, later, *Snip* by O. Korsun (1841) and *Molodyk* by I. Betsky (1843-4).

The Pan-Slavic ideas which Kostomarov brought to Kiev and circulated in the Brotherhood were directly related to the ideas of Izmail Sreznevsky, who had spent three years in various Slavic countries. In the thirties Sreznevsky had been in the centre of the Kharkiv group of young writers, pioneers of the Ukrainian literary renaissance who comprised the so-called Kharkiv school of romantics, with Kostomarov, no doubt, first among them. Sreznevsky, at that time professor of statistics, was interested in history, ethnography, and folklore, and recorded folk songs and historical legends and tales for his *Zaporozhskaia starina*. Born in Russia, he spent his youth in Kharkiv and became a Ukrainian convert. In 1835 he published his 'Ukrainian Chronicle of 1640-1657,' as a separate issue of his *Zaporozhskaia starina*. It was devoted entirely to excerpts from chronicles and songs of the Khmelnytsky epoch.

Sreznevsky's works were of great interest to the young Kostomarov, who was about to graduate (1836) from the University of Kharkiv, where there were no professors in this field. It was natural, therefore, that Kostomarov, being only five years Sreznevsky's junior, and, like him, a Ukrainian convert, should have adapted himself to the romantic atmosphere and idealized the Ukrainian past. He accepted as reliable sources such works as *Istoriia Rusov* and *Zaporozhskaia starina*. He was struck by the similarities between Ukrainian folklore and anthropology and those of other Slavic civilizations. This led him directly to the problem of Slavic unity. From the foreword to *Zaporozhskaia starina* Kostomarov derived his views on the importance of tales and historical songs (*dumy*) for the study of the past, and in particular for the investigation of the life of the Zaporozhian Cossacks. Sreznevsky had written: 'The scarcity of historical records about the past of the Cossacks compels the interested student to look for other sources of information, and he finds for his study a rich, inexhaustible mine in the people's legends and historical songs.'[6] Nine years later, in 1843, this idea formed the basis of Kostomarov's master's thesis, entitled 'Ob istoricheskom znachenii russkoi narodnoi poezii' (On the Historical Significance of Russian Poetic Folklore). In the thesis defence, Sreznevsky was the principal official opponent.

Under Sreznevsky's influence and encouragement, Kostomarov began to study Polish and Czech, and attempted to translate into Ukrainian excerpts from the Královédvorský manuscript. Through the very close friendship which developed between them, Kostomarov learned directly about the great upsurge of the Slavic consciousness in Slavic lands, a great enthusiasm for Slavic unity, and a tireless zeal for the study of the national past and the collection and publication of folklore.

Not long before he moved from Kharkiv to Kiev in 1844, Kostomarov planned a periodical publication of *Zapiski o Iuzhnoi Rossii i Slavianakh* (Notes on Southern Russia and the Slavs) in co-operation with Sreznevsky and Amvrosii Metlynsky. In Kiev, Kostomarov introduced Kulish to these publishing plans, which, however, were never realized. Kulish, for his part, attempted to convince Shevchenko to join the group. The publication was supposed to contain not only articles from the field of Slavic studies, but also prose and poetry in Ukrainian.

The whole complex of the romantic ideas of the Sreznevsky group – ideas about the Slavic renaissance and unity in close connection with the rebirth of the Ukrainian people – was brought to Kiev by Kostomarov, together with his own essentially historical interests, which at that time were concentrated on the Khmelnytsky era.

Slavic studies, as noted above, had not yet been introduced at the University of Kiev. Now, from the official point of view, they were particularly welcome, because until recently the faculty and student body had been predominantly Polish. This preponderance had been partially weakened through the university reorganization which resulted from the uncovering of the so-called 'Konarski conspiracy' in 1838. (See below.) Uvarov, Imperial Minister of Education, forced upon the university 'special' measures to suppress the 'plague of hatred between the two Slavic nationalities.'[8] Here Uvarov meant only the Russian and Polish nationalities. Czech Slavic studies, with their pro-Russian character, suited his purposes at the time. Thus, without even awaiting the establishment of an official chair of Czech language, a course in the Czech language was introduced in the curriculum, to be taught by Kondrat Strashkevych, professor of classical languages.[9] These official plans did not foresee, however, the existence of a third Slavic nationality, namely the Ukrainian, the young representatives of which had just begun to relate to Slavic studies the idea of a national rebirth of their own people.

Kostomarov found in Kiev a group of Ukrainian university youth who had been prepared by the lectures of Mykhailo Maksymovych for the adoption of these new ideas. Kostomarov soon became a spiritual leader of this group, as Sreznevsky was in Kharkiv. These youths were ready to be standard-bearers for the Brotherhood of Saints Cyril and Methodius. They not only studied Slavic languages and literatures, but collected Ukrainian ethnographic and folkloric material for comparative analysis; they also wrote poetry in Ukrainian.

'The Ukrainian songs and the oral tradition of the Ukrainian people inspired the young minds in Kiev with the blessed idea of raising their nation from the darkness,' said Kulish later,[10] and Kulish's autobiography, published later in *Pravda* in Lviv, added: 'Christianity and the history of the Slavs were the light and the warmth they needed for the great undertaking.'[11]

This group of young people and their student colleagues attended the lectures on Slavic mythology which Kostomarov gave in 1846, at the beginning of his teaching career. In these lectures he presented a comparative analysis of the pagan religious beliefs of various Slavic tribes. He concluded that 'the foundations of the religious beliefs of all Slavs were the same; this is apparent in the similarities among current national customs and rites, feasts, divinations, popular beliefs. There were also, of course, national differentiations in the religion of the Slavs.'[12]

This was the year – 1846 – when Kostomarov compiled his *Knyhy bytiia ukrainskoho narodu* (Books of Genesis of the Ukrainian People), the work which was to express the fundamental ideas of the Brotherhood. There he paid much attention to the 'Slavic question,' devoting to it almost the entire second half of the work. Outlining the history of the Slavic race, Kostomarov idealized certain elements, considering the Slavs superior to the romance and Germanic nations. According to his scheme, all were equal among the Slavs; there were 'neither kings nor masters' and 'even before the acceptance of the faith ... the Slavs worshipped one God' (stanza 57). Later, however, because of their own faults and sins the Slavs were subjugated to the Germans, Turks, and Tatars (stanza 63). Regeneration of the divided Slavs came through the idea of brotherhood, with the Cossacks as standard-bearers (stanza 76). Ukraine had to carry out a unifying rescue mission among the Eastern Slavs. A messianic notion of Ukraine's historic mission was clearly expressed at the end of the book (stanza 108): 'And Ukraine will rise from her grave and again will call to her brother Slavs; and they will hear her call, and the Slavic peoples will rise ...'[13] Thus the essentially scholarly problems of broad Slavic studies were fused with poetic romanticism and colourful idealization of the past and the future, even by such outstanding scholars as Kostomarov.

Of all the Brothers, Panteleimon Kulish and Kostomarov were closest in scholarly interests. Kostomarov himself related that during his first meeting with Kulish in 1844 they both discovered with great satisfaction that they had been familiar with the same historical sources – unpublished at the time. When they started to talk about folk songs, Kulish showed Kostomarov a sheaf of recorded texts.[14] Both men intended to become scholars. In 1846 Kulish received a fellowship to visit various Slavic countries. (He was unable to go because he was arrested when the Brotherhood was uncovered.) Kulish was interested primarily in Ukrainian problems, and was thus less enthusiastic than the other members about the concept of Slavic unity. Nevertheless, he believed that his and Shevchenko's work would benefit the cause of 'Ukrainian and Slavic freedom,' as he put it in his *Khutorna poeziia* (Homestead Poetry).[15] His Ukrainian patriotism was strong and deep; when the Brotherhood was active he stated that 'Ukraine and the Ukrainian language had become sacred to him.'[16] Here Kulish was closer in feeling to Shevchenko, whom he met in 1843, than to the 'convert' Kostomarov, who even hesitated to call himself Ukrainian sometimes. Kulish actually had to convince him that he was![17]

Within the Brotherhood it was Mykola Hulak and, in particular, Vasyl Bilozersky, who most effectively supported Kostomarov's Slavic idea. Hulak came to Kiev in 1845, upon completion of his studies in Derpt (Tartu). A lawyer, Hulak became greatly interested in studying Czech law at Kiev. Together with Posiada, a student, he began to study the Czech, and with Kostomarov the Serbian, languages. Of all the Brothers, only Hulak and Kulish corresponded with Hanka, the Czech historian and philologist, who sent to Hulak in March 1846 a book of old Czech law and a letter outlining his plans for publishing old texts in the Czech law. Kulish had great hopes for Hulak as a prospective scholar and writer, and as an active member of the Brotherhood. He helped Hulak to go to St Petersburg, where, Kulish believed, working conditions were most favourable. Kostomarov also kept in close touch with Hulak. The available data indicate that all the organizing work in the Brotherhood was actually handled by Kostomarov and Hulak, with Vasyl Bilozersky. Shevchenko and Kulish were not actively engaged in the organizational work of the association.

Vasyl Bilozersky said during the investigation that at the university 'he had read with great interest everything that concerned the Slavs, and in this way had become gradually acquainted with the history, literature, and languages of the Slavic nationalities.'[18] In a letter to O. Markovych he expressed great satisfaction with the news that Kostomarov was to lecture on Slavic mythology, adding: 'He was good enough and gracious enough to open my eyes to the great truths.'[19]

While teaching in Poltava, Bilozersky was working on his dissertation on the history of Slavic literatures. Kostomarov and Navrotsky sent him books and journals on the subject from Kiev. He also managed to find some books in his field in the library of the Poltava Military School. In his letters to the Brothers there are many comments on his reading. He read with great enthusiasm Kollár's poem, 'Slávy Dcera' (Daughter of Glory) – a quintessential statement of belief in Slavic unity.[20] He also made extensive notes on an article by a French Slavist, Robert, on literary and political Pan-Slavism.[21] He sought to surround himself with 'people of noble ideas,' who 'could translate words into deeds.'[22] Bilozersky also attempted to propagate the ideas of the Brotherhood at literary evenings, arranged in

Poltava by Sophie Kapnist-Skalon (see below). There he read the Ukrainian literary works of Kulish, Ukrainian, Serbian, and Czech folk songs, and excerpts from 'Slávy Dcera.' 'I shall attempt,' he wrote to Opanas Markovych, 'to give these evenings a very serious character; I shall select for the readings works which convey Christian and national ideas. I made for myself a plan of action which will grow and bear fruit.'[23] He found a very attentive audience, particularly in Alexandra Kapnist, younger sister of the hostess. He wrote to Markovych: 'Mlle Kapnist supported my ideas and I was surprised to find that she agreed with me when I was discussing Slavic aspirations and Slavic literatures, and maintaining that they would be a guarantee for the existence of Ukraine.'[24]

There he also met a Czech composer, Alois Jedlička, who sang Czech songs. 'And in addition,' Bilozersky wrote, 'he is personally acquainted with Šafařik, Hanka, and others dear to my heart. This is a real find for me.'[25] During the hearings Bilozersky admitted that the Pan-Slavist idea had so captured his interest that he 'had made himself wholeheartedly [its] champion.'[26] By the term Pan-Slavism he understood the unification of all Slavic nationalities in a common family. This would be automatically accomplished when all Slavic peoples felt the need for such fraternal unity.[27] At the hearings he formulated the Christian, idealistic aspects of his naïve conception of Pan-Slavism very well, which he accepted most sincerely. At that time Bilozersky wrote about the future union of the Slavs as follows: 'Being inspired by love of humanity it must develop in itself the Christian rules of life; apply them in society; and in this way bring a new element, a new driving force, so to speak, to the action of mankind.'[28]

In Poltava, Bilozersky recalled with emotion the earnest conversations at the meetings of the association. In particular he remembered those with Hulak.[29] From the views expressed by the members, it is clear that Bilozersky had great moral authority among them, although he himself said that he never pretended to be the leader of the Slavophiles.[30] 'Thank God,' Markovych wrote to Hulak, 'for making him the star leading us to Bethlehem.'[31] And Kulish, in one of his letters, saw Bilozersky as 'that very vessel,' into which he poured all his secret and veiled feelings.[32] What Shevchenko thought about Bilozersky as a Brother is not known. It is known only that Kulish brought the two together, and that Bilozersky was thrilled by Shevchenko's poems, that he kept a notebook filled with them. On the occasion of the publication of Shevchenko's poem 'Ieretyk, abo

Ivan Hus,' Bilozersky gave it an interesting evaluation which deserves to be quoted here as an appraisal by one of the Brothers of Shevchenko's importance for the Brotherhood:

I found myself thinking with pleasure what a genius we have in Shevchenko. Only a genius can with one deep feeling understand the demands of a people, even the needs of the whole century. No science or learning can do this without the fire of poetry and religion. I ardently hope that his translations of the Psalms will reveal this minstrel's true and blessed spirit. Then a new and inexhaustible spring of life would renew our literature and set it on a sound foundation.[33]

Here only one aspect of Shevchenko's poetry has been discussed – its religious and moral effect on the Brotherhood. It could be a strictly subjective reflection of Bilozersky's feelings. Kulish, Kostomarov, and Markovych appreciated in Shevchenko's works whatever corresponded most closely with their own romantic seeking of the national spirit in poetry. They all, Shevchenko included, deeply loved folk poetry and were engaged in collecting and recording folklore. This was a general phenomenon of the romantic era in the second quarter of the nineteenth century. But it became specific with the Brotherhood in its relating of the problem of Slavic unity with the Ukrainian national point of view, as it was elaborated by Kostomarov, Hulak, and Bilozersky.

Shevchenko's attitude towards Kostomarov is seen in Kostomarov's autobiography and in a few of his literary sketches published during the twenty years he outlived Shevchenko. These give a view of Shevchenko's attitude towards the Slavic question as it was understood by the Brothers. Kostomarov described the first months of their friendship:

At that moment my whole being was taken up with the idea of Slavic unity, the spiritual community of all peoples of Slavic descent, and when I began to talk about it with Taras Hryhorovych, I found that he had the same enthusiastic feelings and thoughts, and this made me very close to him.[34]

Kostomarov mentioned that Shevchenko was present at the last meeting of the Brotherhood at Christmas in Hulak's home, where the central theme was the Slavic idea. During the investigation, however, neither Shevchenko nor any other member gave a clear account of the poet's attitude towards the Slavic question. We know, however, that Shevchenko did not learn of the idea from the Brotherhood, but had been acquainted with it before he joined the association. It is much more difficult with Shevchenko than with Kostomarov to trace the sources of his knowledge. Of the various Slavic languages, Shevchenko undoubtedly knew Polish, which would have helped him to understand Czech, which is closely related.

The first statement of Shevchenko's views on the fraternity of Slavs appears in 1841, in his foreword to 'Haidamaky,' where he states: 'We are all – Slavs ... children of one mother.' However, in the poem this idea is applied only to two Slavic nationalities: Polish and Ukrainian. Similarly in his drama *Nikita Gaidai* (1841), of which only fragments remain, the idea of Slavic unity is built into the framework of Polish-Ukrainian relations. The source of this notion of Polish-Ukrainian Brotherhood could have been from *belles-lettres*. The idea could be traced to the so-called Ukrainian school in Polish literature, but I cannot indicate any definite, immediate source. It is certain, however, that the foreword to 'Haidamaky,' which presents a clear position on the Slavic question, is not taken from any of the Czech scholarly works which had been a source for Kostomarov and other members of the Brotherhood. One could refer tentatively to the literary works of Bohdan Zaleski,[35] Michał Czajkowski,[36] and Seweryn Goszczyński.[37] Their influence on Shevchenko in the 1840s has been considered by historians of Ukrainian literature. Michał Grabowski, Kulish's friend, with whom Shevchenko had some connection in 1843 while publishing *Zhivopisnaia Ukraina* (Ukraine in Pictures) is another possible influence.[38] Whatever the sources, it is important to stress that Shevchenko's ideas about the Slavs had already been formed by the early forties.

Shevchenko's interest in Slavdom was intensified during the so-called 'three years' (1843-5). At that time the subjects and the ideas in his poetry showed a closeness to the ideological atmosphere of the Brotherhood. The first appearance in his poetry of a topic from Czech history, specifically from the history of religious conflict, of struggle for the 'Gospel of Truth and Justice,' was not accidental. Neither was the fact that Shevchenko at that time began to translate the Psalms, which he published in his *Bukvar* (Primer) in 1861, nor that he took as a motto for his poem 'Ieretyk abo Ivan Hus' (1845) the same quotation from Psalm 117 (118) which was used a year later by Kostomarov as a coda for his *Books of Genesis of the*

Ukrainian People: 'The stone which the builders rejected has become the chief cornerstone.'

The theme from Czech history in the poem 'Ieretyk abo Ivan Hus' was given to Shevchenko by his friend Osyp Bodiansky, a Slavist who was sent to various Slavic countries on scholarly missions which coincided with Sreznevsky's. Bodiansky's studies in Bohemia were directed by Šafařik, and from Bodiansky Shevchenko could have heard a great deal about this Czech scholar.[39] In the correspondence between Shevchenko and Bodiansky, however, there is no evidence that the latter gave Shevchenko any information needed to write his 'Ieretyk.' Oleksander Chuzhbynsky in his memoirs quotes Shevchenko as saying that he had read all the contemporary source material about Hus and his epoch, and had even interrogated the Czechs he knew about the details he needed.[40]

At that time, the most recent source available to him could have been the thesis written in 1845 by S. Palauzov, one of Bodiansky's students: *Ioann Gus i ego posledovateli* (John Hus and His Followers). This thesis was published in Moscow when Shevchenko was in Ukraine, about a month before the poem was completed. If there is a possibility that Shevchenko used data from Palauzov's book, it would mean that he had seen it during the writing. This could have been arranged with Bodiansky's assistance.[41] Pavlo Zaitsev, Shevchenko's biographer, surmises that Shevchenko could have derived some data about Hus from Jedlička, the Czech musician and composer whom Bilozersky had met in Poltava, and whom Shevchenko met in July 1845, in the home of the Rodzianko family.[42]

Hus was presented in Shevchenko's poem as a fighter for the national and religious liberation of the Czech people. The work itself does not bear any marks of the Brotherhood's idea of Slavic unity, but in the 'Epistle to the Glorious P.I. Šafařik,' written a month later and attached to the poem as a dedication, the idea found its most outspoken expression. The idea of Slavic unity is linked here with Šafařik, who brought 'all Slavic streams into one sea.' The captivity and disunity of the Slavs is blamed on the Germans, who 'set the big house afire.'

Shevchenko mentioned Šafařik and other enlighteners of the Slavs in his 'Epistle' ('To My Dead and Living and Yet Unborn Countrymen in Ukraine and Not in Ukraine My Friendly Epistle') in December 1845. Here the view of the Slavic problem is essentially different. He reproaches Ukrainian society:

I Kollara chytaiete
Z usiiei syly
I Shafaryka i Hanku
I v slovianofily
Tak i pretes, i vsi movy
Slovianskoho liudu,
Vsi znaiete, a svoieii
Dastbih

And you read Kollar / With all your might / And Šafařik and Hanka / And elbow your way / Into the ranks of the Slavophiles ... / And all the languages of the Slavic peoples, / All of them do you know. / As for your own – / Be it as God grants!

He expressed this thought even more clearly and forcefully in 1847, in the foreword to a projected new edition of his *Kobzar*. He reproaches those educated Ukrainians who 'bartered away their own good mother to a worthless drunkard, and what's more, added a "v" [to their names].'[43] He asked 'why V.S. Karadžić, Šafařik and others had not become German (although this would have been convenient for them), but had remained Slavic, true sons of their mothers and had kept their good name. Alas! Yet, Brothers, do not despair, but pray and work wisely for our unhappy Ukraine.'[44]

This kind of nationalist Ukrainian interpretation of the patriotic element in the ideology of the Brotherhood distinguished Shevchenko's work in the 1840s, although of course the nationalist trend of thought was accepted to some extent by all the Brothers. This was the basis, a natural foundation, for all the other elements of their social and political ideology.

The most extreme expression of the patriotic element in the ideology of the Brotherhood is found in the form of Ukrainian messianism in Kostomarov's *Books of Genesis of the Ukrainian People* and in his short story 'Panych Natalych' (Master Natalych).[45] The messianic idea, however, is not found in any of the Brotherhood's documents, nor in the private correspondence of the members. Kostomarov himself made no mention of it in his recollections of the Brotherhood.

One can doubt if the messianic idea was ever really characteristic of Kostomarov's views. This author would be inclined to explain it as a literary reflection of Mickiewicz's *Books of the Polish People*, with Ukraine plainly substituted for Poland.

The Slavic idea of the Kievan group arose primarily under the influence of the literary works of the romantic period. It also had its source in the accounts of those who travelled in Slavic countries in the thirties and forties. These people were moved by a general enthusiasm for the idea of a revival of the Slavs. They were excited about the common past of the Slavs, and about the possibilities for their common future. As for the social ideas of the Brotherhood, they were born in life itself, fostered by the striking contrast between the idealism of youth and contemporary conditions. Testimony to this was given by almost every single member.

Kostomarov wrote the following in his letter to K. Sementovsky 12 September 1844 on the situation of the peasants: 'They would be better off at hard labour. ... They are treated so awfully that it exceeds any idea of oppression, and it terrifies a friend of mankind.' The position of the peasantry had not changed since Beauplan, he wrote: 'In Russia there is a terrifying barbarity; in Russia when you travel from the Great Russian provinces towards the Western provinces you may follow the deterioration of the life of the common people in direct relation to the traces of the fallen Polish Republic.' 'Their "terrific" liberalism,' as Kostomarov put it, 'does not prevent the Polish nobles from abusing the serfs. They are true Lafayettes only in words.' Kostomarov's diatribes against the nobility in this letter have a strongly anti-Polish character. 'There are no restrictions for the noblemen [the Poles] here and this is very bad. They are allowed to eat and fatten in their palaces like swine, to go abroad, to spend their money lavishly, to live at the expense of the Russian homeland, to slander Russia.'[46] These words were written in 1844, before the Brotherhood was founded. During the life of the association, these words were echoed in some anti-Polish passages in *The Books of Genesis*.[47]

Ivan Posiada, a twenty-four-year-old student, wrote during the investigation that when traveling through Poltava Province he saw the precarious position of the peasants, 'who were suppressed by the landlords and estate managers.'[48] In papers confiscated during the hearings he wrote: 'Everything is taken away from the peasants by the arrogant landlord at the very moment the peasants have need of it.'[49]

Opanas Markovych commented during the hearings on the sad plight of the peasants in Poltava Province, which might bring 'humiliation and extermination of the whole population' and 'corruption and moral decay in the common people.'[50]

One V. Tarnovsky, a manorial land-owner, read an article on serfdom in Hulak's presence at Bilozersky's place in Kiev, in which he pictured a gradual process in Ukraine of the conversion of a free peasantry into a new slavery, and he gave a 'terrifying picture of the cruelty of our time.'[51] Hulak's own analysis of the problem was from a legal point of view. In a letter to Hanka in 1846 he wrote that 'the legal condition of the lower classes ... slaves, serfs, servants, peasants, subjects, and others ... because of its gravity and timeliness deserves consideration above all other matters.'[52]

There is no need to cite Shevchenko's works on the subject. His views are too well known. During the hearings he clearly stressed 'the destitution and horrifying oppression of the peasants, by their landlords, the lease-holders, and their managers in Ukraine.'[53] Shevchenko's works and letters from the period before the founding of the Brotherhood, and particularly those of the so-called 'three-year' period, were more violent in their anti-serfdom than those of any other member. As a former serf, he simply could not stand the contempt for a fellow human being which was directed against the serf. Such poems as 'Son' (The Dream, 1844), 'Velykii Lokh' (The Great Vault, 1845) and, in particular, 'The Epistle' condemned the subjugation of Ukraine and the injustices committed against the Ukrainian peasant. The fierce imagery of these poems imparted a new intensity to the arguments of the other Brothers. Many had handwritten copies of them. Some knew them by heart. When Posiada wanted to give a full picture of the peasants' plight, he did so by paraphrasing passages from Shevchenko's 'Son': 'Terrible conditions prevail in our country; the old mother is left alone and her only son, the only hope and support of her old age, is taken from her for the army. For years the peasant has had to sell his last cow to pay the exorbitant taxes.'[54]

The Brotherhood developed no definite plans for abolishing this bondage, although obviously they considered the issue. One of them, Iurii Andruzky, a student, drafted his own interesting plan, which provided for redemption of those peasants in estates which were under wardship. Money for this purpose would come from planned economies in the army and the higher levels of the national administration. All male serfs were to receive their freedom at the age of sixty, and all females at fifty, with the land-owner obligated to provide subsistence until their deaths. All children with at least one free parent were to be freed as well. To prevent abuses, manorial lords could take over their estates only upon taking an oath. Moreover, they were to maintain schools for their serf-peasants. Voluntary emancipation of the serfs was to be rewarded.[55]

In the by-laws of the Brotherhood, Glavnye pravila obshchestva, the association's social program in general was set forth: 'The Association will concern itself immediately with the abolition of bondage and the spread of general literacy.'[56] During the hearings, Vasyl Bilozersky said: 'Introduction of schools was desired by all those concerned with the general welfare.'[57] In the Brotherhood there were two education plans; one by Andruzky[58] and another, more detailed, by Bilozersky.[59] Both plans provided first for the education of the teacher, who would then return to his village and teach there for the rest of his life.

General education and the abolition of serfdom were the conditions for broad political changes, which were to be based on Christian ethics, Pan-Slavic ideas, and, most importantly, on the personal freedom of all men, whatever their social class. Under such conditions, there would be, according to the *Books of Genesis*, neither 'tsar ... nor prince ... nor lord nor boyar, nor serf nor slave.'[60]

Historians are right in deducing that this political aspect of the Brotherhood's ideology is related to the merging of Decembrist with Polish democratic ideas. The Decembrists were vividly remembered in Ukraine two decades after the armed uprising of the Chernihiv infantry regiment in the Province of Kiev and its liquidation by the imperial armed forces, along with the severe chastisement of clandestine organizations. Many friends and relatives of the punished Decembrists, and some who had been members of pre-Decembrist organizations, no longer active by the 1820s, remained in Ukraine. After the severe punishment of the Decembrists, their ideas were still very much alive, and inspired subsequent political movements and organizations. Immediately after the hanging of the five leading Decembrists and the deportation of hundreds of young, educated, active men whose only aim was 'the welfare of mankind' a cult of the Decembrists began to develop, which kept alive the interest in those first 'champions of freedom.' Members of the Brotherhood were among those who paid tribute to the Decembrists' memory.

The ideological link between the Brotherhood and the Decembrist Society of United Slavs was demonstrated conclusively half a century ago by Vasilii Semevsky, a Russian historian.[61] The Decembrist associations had a forerunner in the Masonic lodge, Jedność Słowiańska (Slavic Unity), which was founded in Kiev in 1818 and had a predominantly Polish membership. Among the founders of the Society of United Slavs (1823) was a young Pole, Julian Lublinski, a student from Warsaw, born in Volynia and a member of the Warsaw political organization known as Związek Wolnych Polaków (Association of Free Poles). In the course of a year the Society of United Slavs had spread throughout Volynia and other regions of Ukraine, and at the end of 1824, in order to unify its activities, it merged with the Southern Association of Decembrists.

It is apparent from the ideological documents of the United Slavs, such as *Pravyla* (Rules), *Katekhizis* (Catechism), and *Kliatva* (Oath), that the society had two principal goals: 'unification of all Slavic nationalities' and 'abolition of peasant bondage.'[62]

Kostomarov says in his memoirs that, during the search of his rooms, an [old] newspaper containing information on the Decembrists lay on a table. The paper was not used against Kostomarov during the hearings, however, and there is reason to believe that it was a copy of the official newspaper *Russkii invalid* (Russian Disabled Veteran) containing the report of the investigating commission, with ample, although biased, information about the activities of secret societies in the 1820s.[63]

From this publication, Kostomarov could have received some idea of the program of the Society of United Slavs, a program which was stated as follows: 'The aim of the society was to unite eight Slavic tribes in a common alliance and in a republican system of government, while preserving the independence of each. These were enumerated on an octagonal seal as Russia, Poland, Bohemia, Moravia, Dalmatia, Croatia, Hungary with Transylvania, and Serbia with Moldavia and Wallachia.'[64] Ukraine was not listed there as a separate nationality. This particular correction was made by the Brotherhood. Like the United Slavs, however, they did not recognize Belorussians as a separate national group.

Kostomarov mentions the Decembrists in *The Books of Genesis*: 'And the voice of Ukraine resounded in Muscovy' with the demand 'to banish the tsar and destroy the nobility, to found a republic and unite all the Slavs with it ... and this Ukraine had desired and striven for, for almost two hundred years before this' (stanza 105).

There was another circumstance in Kostomarov's life, which has not been noted, which might account for his personal interest in the Decembrist movement. He was a native of Ostrogozhsk in the Province of

Voronezh. It was there that Kondrat Ryleev, on his return from campaigns abroad, was stationed with his cavalry-artillery troop. There he married the daughter of the local land-owner, Teviashov.[65] Ryleev, although living in St Petersburg, often summered at his family estate. Kostomarov was only eight years old when Ryleev's tragic death by hanging deeply moved the young Decembrist poet's contemporaries. Ryleev was enshrined as a martyr and his writings on Ukraine were copied out by hand and widely read by the youth. There were many references to Ryleev's influence in the thirties,[66] and memories of him in the Ostrogozhsk area must have been still vivid when Kostomarov was living there.

In order to realize the extent of Decembrist influences in Ukraine it need only be mentioned that it was in Ukraine (and Belorussia) that the troops of the First and Second Russian armies were stationed after the termination of the European military operations of the Napoleonic Wars. After the disbanding of the Semenovsky regiment in St Petersburg following its revolt in 1820, many of its officers who belonged to still secret societies were sent to various military units throughout Ukraine. There they founded new clandestine organizations and became active members of the Southern Society of Decembrists. The memoirs of their contemporaries attest to their close relations with the local populations in Right-Bank Ukraine, with Polish groups which maintained the traditions and ideas of the Polish statehood movement,[67] and in the Left-Bank Ukraine, with the Ukrainian landed gentry, which fostered ideas of Ukrainian autonomy. In Poltava Province in particular, in the first half of the century, there were several families enthusiastically concerned with the political movements that had resulted from the great developments in Western Europe at the end of the eighteenth and the first decades of the nineteenth centuries. Such noble families as the Repnins in Iahotyn, the Kapnists in Obukhivka, the Muraviov-Apostols in Khomutets, the Lukashevyches in the district of Pereiaslav, and the Shershevytskys in Myrhorod were still imbued with the ideas of 1825. It is, therefore, most interesting, and certainly not accidental, that most of the members of the Brotherhood came from the Poltava area.

The pro-Decembrist sympathies of the opposition among the nobility are known from the memoirs of Sophie Kapnist-Skalon, the daughter of a Russian writer and Ukrainian autonomist, Vasyl Kapnist. Sophie Kapnist was a close friend of Sergei Muraviov-Apostol; the Decembrist N. Lorer was very much attached to the entire Kapnist family, virtually a member of it. The Decembrist M. Lunin was also intimately acquainted with the family. No wonder, then, that the year 1826 was a year of tragedy for the Kapnist family, and for Sophia personally.[68]

From 1833, she had lived in Poltava, where she had conducted a literary salon. There she was closely associated with Hulak and Navrotsky, of the Brotherhood, and we have already noted her relationship with Bilozersky, who taught with her husband at the Poltava Military School. His participation in her soirées led the editor of her memoirs to comment that 'close ties were established between the members of the Brotherhood of Saints Cyril and Methodius, on the one hand, and on the other with the standard-bearers of autonomist ideas from the beginning of the century (V. Kapnist) and the left wing of the Decembrists (S. Muraviov-Apostol).'[69] Bilozersky made use of the enthusiasm for the Decembrists in order to propagate his Pan-Slavism, and Kostomarov was interested in applying the federalist and republican ideas of the Decembrists to the Ukrainian political ideology of the forties.

However, Shevchenko, of all the Brothers, was best fitted by his experience for acquaintance with Decembrist ideas. All his life he was deeply interested in the bearers of that ideology. He constantly sought personal contact with surviving Decembrists. Shevchenko spent his youth (1833-43), when his own world view was being formed, in touch with literary and artistic circles in St Petersburg, where the memory of the events of December 1825 was still very vivid. Count Fedor Tolstoi, Vice-President of the Acàdemy of Arts, who was a great influence on Shevchenko in the fifties, was in his youth a member of the Soiuz Blagodenstviia (Society of Welfare) where such outstanding Decembrists as Prince Sergei Trubetskoi, Nikita Muraviov, Sergei Muraviov-Apostol, and Pavel Pestel began their political activity.[70]

Shevchenko's stay in Iahotyn in 1843 brought him into close contact with the family of Prince Nikolai Repnin, whose brother was Prince Sergei Volkonsky, an outstanding member of the Southern Society of Decembrists. There Shevchenko also met Oleksii Kapnist, Sophia's brother, who had been an active member of the pre-Decembrist secret societies.

In 1845 and 1846 the poet made his celebrated journeys of the 'three-year' period in Ukraine, particularly in the Poltava region, where he visited people and places with memories of the Decembrists. Then he read aloud his most revolutionary works, in which allusions to the Decembrists can be found. These works were written during this period in various parts of the Poltava region. It is evident that he felt deep admiration for the Decembrist movement as a precursor of liberation, and contributed this sense to the Brotherhood.

It remains to examine certain Polish sources as possible factors in the development of the Brotherhood's ideology. This problem has been discussed a number of times, particularly in connection with the similarity of *The Books of Genesis of the Ukrainian People* with Mickiewicz's *Books of the Polish People*. Mickiewicz wrote the book in 1832, immediately after the Polish uprising of 1831, to life the spirits of the disillusioned conspirators, and it was one of the first propaganda works to influence the assembling of the beaten Polish forces for new resistance. By the mid-thirties, in addition to the old Patriotic Society, which had been active during the Decembrist period in the twenties, a number of new groups arose, particularly in such Polish émigré centres as Paris, Kraków, and Poznań. Vasyl Shchurat accumulated vast quantities of material in his work, *Shevchenko i Poliaky* (Shevchenko and the Poles) about these secret Polish societies, which may be considered the ideological forerunners of the Brotherhood.[71] It should be emphasized that all these Polish conspiratorial societies, which Shchurat linked ideologically with the Brotherhood, operated at least five years after the Decembrists. Thus the Poles were closer in time to the Ukrainian conspirators. Relations between the Southern Decembrists and the Polish Patriotic Society of the twenties had continued for several years, long enough to account to some degree for the influence of the Decembrists' federal-republican ideas upon the principles of the secret Polish societies of the thirties.

In the very first issue of *Połnoc* (The North) the official publication of Młoda Polska (Young Poland) there began, on the occasion of the tenth anniversary (1835) of the St Petersburg uprising, a series of articles, 'Republikanie rosyjscy' (Russian Republicans). The articles included excerpts from the report of the commission which had investigated the Decembrist movement.[72]

With the collapse of the Polish uprising of 1831 the movement's major handicap – its aristocratic character and consequent lack of popular support – became evident. This deficiency was readily acknowledged by the initiators of the uprising themselves. In consequence, such new centres of Polish conspiracy as the Democratic Society in 1832 and Young Poland in 1834 began to propagate in their manifestoes principles almost identical with the ideas of the Ukrainian democrats of the forties. In its appeal to the peasant guerilla fighters not only in Poland, but in Ukraine as well, the Democratic Society solemnly proclaimed: 'God gave soil to all men in order that everyone be nourished by its fruits....' Addressing the Belorussian and the Ukrainian peasants, the appeal asked: 'Where did the nobles find the law which lets them idle, and orders only you to toil?' It pictured familiar scenes from Ukrainian life: 'He [the peasant], is not responsible for the fact that he was born of a toil-worm mother, on straw or the hard earth.'[73]

This appeal is also interesting because it advanced some positive demands, such as the peasant's right to own the soil, to acquire an education, and to participate in legislation. These demands were fully acceptable to the members of the Brotherhood.

Shchurat quotes widely from contemporary Polish propaganda literature and shows its affinity with the Brotherhood, not only in ideas, but even in phraseology. Thus the articles of Mickiewicz's Towarzystwo Braci Zjednoczonych (Society of United Brothers) began with an invocation from the Gospel according to St John: 'You will know the truth, and the truth will make you free.'[74] The same sentence was referred to on Kostomarov's Cyril-Methodius seal, and was used by him in his *Books of Genesis* (stanza 22). In the writings of Ludwik Kulikowski, a member of Zjednoczenie (Unity) in the early forties, the principle is set forth that the only law in Christian Poland should be the Divine Law.[75] The view of Divine Law as the foundation of human law is basic in Kostomarov's *Books of Genesis*. In the investigation record the *Books* themselves are referred to as 'Divine Law.' Shchurat found in the revolutionary writings of the Polish political emigration in the thirties and forties such ideas as unification of the Slavs, abolition of bondage, republicanism, and a constitution based on the principles of the Gospel.

The only link Shchurat failed to establish was a direct one between the members of the Brotherhood and the Polish conspiracy abroad. Yet such a connection was not only theoretically possible, it doubtless existed through the political movement known as Konarszczyzna, a name derived from Szymon Konarski, an Emissary for the Patriotic Society, who founded in Lithuania and Ukraine in the late thirties some truly democratic branches of the society Stowarzyszenie Ludu Polskiego (Association of the Polish

People). In 1838 an investigation was conducted which uncovered considerable participation by the student body of Kiev University in these associations. As a result of the investigation the University was closed for two years, and all students were expelled. The University was reopened in 1840, the year Kulish enrolled. A year later, Bilozersky enrolled. Thus the Brothers must have had knowledge of the widely discussed liquidation of the Konarski movement. Konarski had concentrated his activities in Lithuania, Volynia, and Kiev Province. His agents distributed propaganda literature, smuggled into Volynia from abroad. Mickiewicz's *Books* held an important place in this literature, and were well known in Right-Bank Ukraine, and particularly in Volynia, since it bordered on Poland, where the Konarski movement was strongest. The great demand for Mickiewicz's works may be seen in the fact that four editions came out in a three-year period (1832-4).

During the Third Division's Investigation, Kostomarov acknowledged that he had had in Kiev, with his marginal notes, a copy of Mickiewicz's *Books*, which he called *Pielgrzymka* (Pilgrimage). However, the copy was not included with his record, which was dispatched with him to St Petersburg, and the nature of his notations is not known. Among his papers there was also a copy, in longhand, of the third part of Mickiewicz's dramatic poem 'Dziady' (Forefathers). Most of its characters were Polish insurgents who had been banished to Siberia. During the police interrogation, Kostomarov explained that he had received this poem from a Polish student in the town of Rivne. It is fairly certain that he also brought the *Books* from Rivne. He had used his stay in Rivne for collecting various historical, ethnographic, and folklore materials. From there he wrote to K. Sementovsky that he had obtained these materials through his students.[76] Since almost all his students were Polish,[77] it had been easy for him to get materials in Polish.[78] Along with the *Books*, so extensively used for propaganda by Konarski, Kostomarov could have acquired information about the ends and ideological premises of the movement (Konarszczyzna); he could have read the appeals that the Polish democratic press had published abroad. He would have found that they had much in common with his own thinking on the plight of the peasant and on the problem of the Slavic peoples.

These guesses are based on facts referred to by V. Shchurat. But the question of direct contact between the members of the Brotherhood and the clandestine Polish groups still remained open. Shchurat's rather marginal assumptions on Shevchenko's probable connections with the Poles for the most part have been rejected as unfounded by his critics.[79] One fact, however, established incontrovertibly by Shchurat, seems significant. Shevchenko had some contact with the Polish democratic group of Romuald Podbereski in St Petersburg. This group published *Rocznik Literacki* (Literary Annual), among the subscribers to which in 1843 was 'Kobzar, Taras Shevchenko.'[80] However, this group was rather literary, with a democratic orientation, and the Brotherhood had not yet been founded. Similar connections between Shevchenko and Polish literary circles of democratic orientation in St Petersburg have been mentioned in the biography of Jan Barszczewski, a second-rate Polish poet who worked for *Rocznik Literacki* and who also published the yearly publication *Niezabudka* (Forget-me-not) in St Petersburg from 1840 to 1844.[81]

Very important data about the relations of Shevchenko and the other Brothers with the Poles were first made available a year after Shchurat's work was published. In 1918 the memoirs of Julian Bielina-Kędrzycki were posthumously published in a Polish newspaper. Part of them, referring directly to Shevchenko, was published in Ukrainian by Shchurat in 1927.[82] A former student at the University of Kiev, Bielina was the first to present information on attempts by Shevchenko and Kostomarov to initiate talks about a Polish-Ukrainian understanding based on the ideas of the Brotherhood. According to Bielina, these talks took place between the twentieth and thirtieth of July 1846, after Shevchenko's return from the expedition which was excavating the graves of Perepet and Perepetykha. Shevchenko and Bielina had known each other earlier. They lived across the street from each other on Kozyne Boloto (now Shevchenko Place) in Kiev. Shevchenko had moved there in late April. Thus their acquaintance prior to the political talks could have lasted only some three months. (In late June and early July Shevchenko was away from Kiev with the Archeological Commission working on the excavations.) Bielina stressed the cordiality of his meetings with Shevchenko, and spoke of their intimacy as if they had known each other for many years. That period, the summer of 1846, was also the time of Shevchenko's closest relations with Kostomarov, the time of the most candid discussions of the problems of the Brotherhood. It was then that Kostomarov's *Books of Genesis* were composed. The initiative for these Polish-Ukrainian talks was taken by Shevchenko, while the cautious

Kostomarov had some reservations. 'He was not happy with the talks,' Bielina noted, 'expressed himself reluctantly ... and was not sincere.'[83] Kostomarov told Bielina in Shevchenko's presence of the formation of the Brotherhood, about possible future work in common for Slavic unity, and about a future federation of the Slavs. Bielina recalled that Kostomarov, not trusting a stranger, spoke without conviction of unification 'under one orthodox tsar, and in one orthodox faith,' in effect what he was to say, also without sincerity, to his police interrogators later. Shevchenko, too, stressed Kostomarov's lack of sincerity during the discussions. He said that one could simply gather from Kostomarov's words that he wished 'to put all Slavs in the priest's house.'

Shevchenko's political views on the government of Russia and on Ukrainian independence were clearly expressed in his revolutionary poetry of the forties. Kostomarov's views were recorded in his *Books of Genesis.* Like Shevchenko, Kostomarov dreamed of a free Ukraine 'without the tsar and nobleman,' but he lacked Shevchenko's straightforwardness, courage, and integrity and consequently was not firm in his views.

The question as to why Shevchenko decided to reveal the affairs of the Brotherhood to the Polish student Bielina-Kędrzycki has been partially answered in the memoirs of Wacław Lasocki. These memoirs supply a great deal of new information about student and political movements in Kiev in the middle of the nineteenth century.[84]

Bielina-Kędrzycki attended the University of Kiev from 1846 to 1851. Lasocki called him 'the lutist and chronicler in song of those gloomy times.' According to Lasocki, his poems were never published, but were extremely popular in those years. They were often sung on various student occasions. His poems were sharply satirical, exposing with a great deal of humour various aspects of social, literary, and particularly student, life. In his songs he criticized the editors of the conservative weekly *Tygodnik Petersburgski* (Petersburg Weekly). These were the notorious 'Moscowphiles,' Ignacy Hołowiński, Count Henryk Rzewuski, and Alexander Przecławski. These criticisms mean that Bielina was associated with the editors of the Polish annual *Gwiazda* (The Star). To avoid arousing the suspicions of the Russian censors, the first issue of *Gwiazda* was published not in Kiev but in St Petersburg, in 1846, under the editorship of Zenon Fisch, who later under the pen-name Padalica participated in the Ukrainian-Polish discussions with Kostomarov and

Antonovych. *Gwiazda* was published for three more years after 1846, in Kiev, edited by Jakób Jurkiewicz, whose pen-name was Benedykt Dołęga.[85]

The political and polemical articles in *Gwiazda*, particularly those written by Albert Gryf (Antoni Marcinkowski) were directed against the group of Polish conservative writers. Members of the Brotherhood were well aware of the existence of the young Polish journalists of democratic orientation in Kiev, and probably sought direct contact with them.[86]

Bielina related his talks with Shevchenko and Kostomarov to two student friends, Antoni Pietkiewicz and Alexander Jabłonowski, who suggested that they be discontinued.[87] Pietkiewicz, later well known as the Polish poet Adam Pług, was closely connected with the *Gwiazda* group. Jabłonowski, who later became a celebrated historian, had had previous knowledge of the Brotherhood, Bielina said.

Shevchenko and Kostomarov approached the discussions with a view of Bielina as a representative of Polish democratic youth; Bielina himself spoke in the discussions as a member of the Polish underground movement as well. It is evident from Lasocki's memoirs that in the mid-forties Bielina joined the clandestine group led by Izydor Kopernicki,[88] to which Zygmunt Miłkowski, a writer later well known as T.T. Jeż, and Alexander Szumowski, then a teacher at the Chernihiv Gymnasium, also belonged. It seems, however, that the Brothers were not aware of this area of Bielina's secret activities.

The attempts to bring about an understanding between the Ukrainian and Polish democratic groups failed not only because Bielina's friends Pietkiewicz and Jabłonowski had reservations about the talks, but also because half a year later the activity of the Ukrainian democratic group was stopped by the imprisonment of its members. The objectives of the Brothers were recalled some ten years later, but only in part, in the social and educational areas of their program. The era of Pan-Slavic ideas had gone, and the time for republican principles among Ukrainian intellectuals had not yet come. In the sixties the older members of the Brotherhood – Shevchenko, Kostomarov, Kulish, and Bilozersky – again attempted to realize their programs. At that time, however, a younger generation took over the burden of the plans of the Brotherhood.

(1962)

NOTES

1 This article was first published in *Taras Ševčenko, 1814-1861: A Symposium* (The Hague 1962).

2 The records of the investigation of the Brotherhood of Saints Cyril and Methodius have not yet been published in the Soviet Union in the form used for publication of the Decembrist and Petrashevsky files. The bulk of the testimony by the Brothers was published by M. Hrushevsky, in *Zbirnyk pamiaty T. Shevchenka* (Kiev 1915) 101-256, and in a separate reprint, *Materiialy do Kyrylo-Metodiivskoho Bratstva*, prepared by Hrushevsky (Kiev 1915). This publication was based not on the original investigation records, but on office copies, not always complete or exact, sent to D. Bibikov, Governor-General in Kiev, for his own information. Henceforth these texts will be referred to as *Materiialy*.

3 V. Semevsky, 'Kirillo-Mefodievskoe obshchestvo, 1846-1847,' *Russkoe bogatstvo*, 5, 6 (1911); reprinted in *Golos minuvshego*, Moscow, 10-12 (1918); M. Vozniak, *Kyrylo-Mefodiivske Bratstvo* (Lviv 1921); Z. Hurevych, *Moloda Ukraina, do visimdesiatykh rokovyn Kyrylo-Metodiivskoho Bratstva*, ed. M. Iavorsky (Kharkiv 1928); Josef Gołąbek, *Bractwo Św. Cyryla i Metodego w Kijowie* (Warsaw 1936); P. Zaionchkovsky, *Kirillo-Mefodievskoe obshchestvo* (Moscow 1959). Only the works of Semevsky and Zaionchkovsky are based on materials from the original archives.

4 *Ukraina*, 1-2 (Kiev 1925) 51-99.

5 They were Mykola Kostomarov, Mykola Hulak, Vasyl Bilozersky, Taras Shevchenko, Panteleimon Kulish, Mykola Savych, and students at the University of Kiev: Iurii Andruzky, Opanas Markovych, Oleksander Navrotsky, Ivan Posiada, and Oleksander Tulub.

6 A. Grushevsky, *Rannie etnograficheskie raboty N.I. Kostomarova* (St Petersburg 1911) 16-17.

7 Kulish's letter to Shevchenko, 31 December 1844, *Ukraina*, 1-2 (1925) 79.

8 M.V. Vladimirsky-Budanov, *Istoriia Imp. Universiteta Sv. Vladimira* (Kiev 1884) I, 75.

9 *Biograficheskii slovar professorov Imp. Universiteta Sv. Vladimira* (Kiev 1884) 627.

10 P. Kulish, *Khutorna poeziia* (Lviv 1882) 7; quoted here from Z. Hurevych, *Moloda Ukraina* (Kharkiv 1928) 10.

11 'Zhyzn Kulisha,' *Pravda* (Lviv 1868); quoted here from A. Pypin and V. Spasovich, *Istoriia slavianskikh literatur*, 2nd edition (St Petersburg 1861) I, 376.

12 *Slavianskaia mifologiia*, Sochinenie Nikolaia Kostomarova, extracts of lectures, held at the University of St Vladimir in the second half of 1846 (Kiev 1847) 105.

13 M. Kostomarov, *Knyhy bytiia ukrainskoho narodu* (Augsburg 1947) 24. English translation taken from B. Ianivsky, *Kostomarov's 'Books of Genesis of the Ukrainian People'* (New York 1954) (Research Program on the USSR, mimeographed series no. 60). Stanza numbering is from the translation.

14 N.I. Kostomarov, *Literaturnoe nasledie* (St Petersburg 1890) 47.

15 Quoted in O. Hermaize, 'P. Kulish i M. Kostomarov iak chleny Kyrylo-Metodiivskoho Bratstva,' *Shevchenko ta ioho doba*, collection 1 (Kiev 1925) 54.

16 Letter of 14 March 1846 from P. Kulish to O. Markovych, *Za sto lit* (Kiev 1927) 1, 50.

17 Letter of 2 May 1846 from Kulish to Kostomarov. See my publications 'Liudy sorokovykh rokiv (Kyrylo-Metodiivtsi v ikh lystuvanni),' *Za sto lit*, 2 (Kiev 1928) 83. Henceforth cited as 'Lystuvannia.'

18 *Materiialy* 87.

19 'Lystuvannia' 56, letter of 30 August 1846.

20 Bilozersky could have had this work in its latest enlarged edition (Budapest 1845), which included in its two parts 622 sonnets.

21 Ciprien Robert, 'Les deux panslavismes,' *Revue des deux mondes*, 1846, 1er novembre.

22 'Lystuvannia' 59.

23 *Ibid*. 68.

24 *Ibid*. 67.

25 *Ibid*. 60.

26 *Materiialy* 88.

27 *Ibid*. 91.

28 *Ibid*. 88.

29 'Lystuvannia' 55 and 59.

30 *Materiialy* 101.

31 *Za sto lit*, 1, 40.

32 'Lystuvannia' 47.

33 Letter of 1 May 1846, from V. Bilozersky to M. Hulak, 'Lystuvannia' 52.

34 'Pismo k izdateliu-redaktoru Russkoi stariny,' by N. Kostomarov, *Russkaia starina*, XXVII (1880) 598.

35 It is a well-known fact that Bohdan Zaleski was interested in the Slavic question and that he was even a candidate to go to various Slavic lands to prepare himself for lecturing on Slavic languages and literatures in Warsaw (V.A.

Frantsev, *Polskoe slavianovedenie kontsa XVIII i pervoi chetverti XIX st.* [Prague 1906] 390, clx). Zaleski helped Mickiewicz by supplying him with essential literature on the Slavs and translating Serb songs from the collection of Vuk Karadžić for his lectures at the Collège de France in 1840 (H. Batowski, *Przyjaciele Słowianie* [Warsaw 1956] 43, 45, 51, 55). Later on, in his poem 'Gwar Słowiański,' Zaleski mentioned Šafařik, Kopitar, and Vuk Karadžić (*Pisma* by J.B. Zaleski, II [St Petersburg 1852] 201).

36 Czajkowski's novel *Wernyhora* (Paris 1838, 2nd edition, 1842) was known to young Shevchenko, and it was used by him while writing 'Haidamaky': P. Fylypovych, 'Shevchenko i Hrebinka,' *Ukraina*, 1-2 (Kiev 1925) 25. Later (1855), Czajkowski supported Mickiewicz in the latter's mission to the southern Slavs, who were dominated by the Turks. This mission was sponsored by France (Batowski 166-76).

37 M. Mochulsky, 'Goshchynsky, Slovatsky i Shevchenko,' *Nasha kultura*, 4, 7-12 (Warsaw 1936). Also B. Navrotsky, *'Haidamaky' T. Shevchenka* (Kiev 1928).

38 Reference to this instance in Shevchenko's letter to O. Bodiansky, 29 July 1844, in T. Shevchenko, *Povne vydannia tvoriv*, XI (Warsaw 1935) 31. M. Grabowski had planned in 1839 to publish in Kiev a literary journal under the title 'Przeglądnik literatur słowiańskich.' For that publication he attempted to contact, among others, Hanka (*Michala Grabowskiego listy literackie*, ed. Adam Bar [Kraków 1934] 73-4, 92). One year later, in 1843, at the time of Grabowski's personal contact with Kulish, the former applied for permission to publish the journal *Słowianin* in Kiev: *Pypin i Spasovich* 749.

39 Bodiansky translated some of Šafařik's works into Russian: *Slavianskie drevnosti* in 1837, and *Slavianskoe narodopisanie* in 1843.

40 A. Chuzhbinsky, *Vospominaniia o T.G. Shevchenke* (St Petersburg 1861) 12.

41 On the use of Palauzov's book by Shevchenko: Ivan Bryk, 'Shevchenkova poema "Ivan Hus",' *Zapysky* of Shevchenko Scientific Society, CXIX-CXX (Lviv 1917) 119-20, 126-7.

42 Pavlo Zaitsev, *Zhyttia Tarasa Shevchenka* (New York, Paris, Munich 1955) 141-2.

43 A reference to those Ukrainians who russianized their names by ending them with the letter 'v.'

44 M.M. Novytsky, *Ukraina*, 1-2 (1925) 73.

45 A fragment of that short story, preserved among Kostomarov's papers taken during his arrest, was published by me; see: *Ukraina*, 1-2 (1924) 131-3.

46 *Ukraina*, 3 (Kiev 1925) 48.

47 'and they ravaged Poland, as before they had ravaged Ukraine. And Poland deserved this because she had not heeded Ukraine, and had destroyed her own sister,' *Books of Genesis* (stanzas 102-3).

48 Quoted from the records of the Cyril-Methodius case of the Third Division of His Imperial Majesty's Office. 'On the Ukrainian-Slavonic Society,' 1847, no. 81, part 9, sheet 15. Henceforth referred to as 'Case,' with relevant sections identified.

49 *Ibid.*, sheet 4, Posiada file, no. 3.

50 Case, part 11, sheet 20.

51 *Za sto lit*, I 37.

52 *Shevchenko ta ioho doba*, 2 (Kiev 1926) 131-8.

53 *Ukraina*, 1-2 (1925) 94.

54 Case, no. 81, part 9, sheet 4, manuscript no. 3.

55 *Za sto lit*, 2, p 35.

56 *Knyhy bytiia* 32.

57 *Materiialy* 96.

58 *Ibid.* 33.

59 *Ukraina*, 1-2 (1924) 126-9.

60 *Knyhy bytiia*, stanza 103.

61 V. Semevsky 141. The most comprehensive works from the history of the Society of the United Slavs are: M. Nechkina, *Obshchestvo soedinennykh slavian* (Moscow 1927), and chapter 14 in her two-volume work entitled *Dvizhenie dekabristov*, II (Moscow 1955) 133-82.

62 *Vosstanie dekabristov* (Moscow, Leningrad 1926) V, 12-13, 17-18; also Nechkina 149, 152, 181.

63 *Donesenie sledstvennoi komissii* (Report of the Investigation Commission), published as appendix to *Russkii Invalid*, 12 July 1826; see *Gosudarstvennie prestupleniia v Rossii v XIX v.*, by V. Bazilevsky (V. Bogucharsky) (St Petersburg 1906) I.

64 *Ibid.* 29.

65 Kostomarov's estate, Iurasivka, was located some 40 miles from the village of Bilohiria, Teviashov's estate.

66 See V. Miiakovsky, 'Vidhuky v Kharkovi ta Kyievi na smert Ryleieva,' in *Ukraina*, 6 (Kiev 1925) 57-68.

67 Pelagia Rościszewska's diary depicts very close relations of the Polish nobility with the officers of the Russian armies stationed in Right-Bank Ukraine. A few passages of the diary discuss the two most outstanding Decembrists in the

South: Sergei Muraviov-Apostol and Mikhail Bestuzhev-Riumin. Alex. Trubetskoi, brother of a Decembrist, married Rościszewska's daughter. Pelagia's husband, Walenty Rościszewski, was among the founders of the Masonic Lodge of the United Slavs and its first Master of Chair; Prince Sergei Volkonsky, a Decembrist, joined that lodge, too. Besides the above, the diary referred also to other close friends from among the Decembrists and members of Polish underground associations, who were arrested later, after the Decembrist revolt. See 'Excerpt from the Diary of Pelagia Rościszewska,' *The Annals of the Ukrainian Academy of Arts and Sciences in the US*, I (1951) 29-35.

68 *Vospominaniia i rasskazy deiatelei tainykh obshchestv 1820-kh godov*, general eds Iu. G. Oksman and S.N. Chernov, I (Moscow 1931).

69 *Ibid*. 293: 'Vospominaniia S.V. Kapnist-Skalon,' introduction by Iu. G. Oksman.

70 N. Kovalenskaia, 'Khudozhnik-dekabrist F.P. Tolstoi (1783-1873),' in the collection *Ocherki iz istorii dvizheniia dekabristov*, ed. by N. Druzhinin and B. Syroechkovsky (Moscow 1954) 516-60.

71 Vasyl Shchurat, *Shevchenko i Poliaky: Osnovy Shevchenkovykh zviazkiv z poliakamy*, reprint from the *Zapysky* of the Shevchenko Scientific Society, CXIX-CXX (Lviv 1917) 217-347.

72 *Ibid*. 233. At that time, this report of the Investigation Commission was the only source of information about the 'Decembrist Case.' Pelagia Rościszewska writes in her diary about the great interest this report aroused in her contemporaries; see *The Annals* 32 (her notations for 4 and 20 July 1826).

73 Shchurat 228-30.

74 *Ibid*. 251.

75 *Ibid*. 265: in Mickiewicz's *Books* – 'Divine Law'; cf. 'the rule, according to the Divine Law' in the 'Pravoslavnyi katekhizis' by S. Muraviov-Apostol.

76 'I instructed all my pupils to supply me with songs, and I received quite a few,' letter of 16 December 1844, *Ukraina*, 3 (1925) 53.

77 'My pupils one and all are Polish,' *ibid*. 45.

78 A report in the files of the Governor-General of Kiev (1845, Second Secret Section, no. 26, sheet 9) gives some idea of the sentiments among the students at that time: 'Kostomarov, a teacher at the Gymnasium of Rivne, had a notebook containing the compositions of his pupils. In this book, there were two compositions, one about the musician Lipiński and another about the astronomer Copernicus. In the latter it was said Copernicus was of Russian descent.

Below that article was a notation, made by one of the students: "Do not be insulted, but Copernicus was a genuine Pole".'

79 See review by M. Novytsky, *Zapysky* of the Hist.-Phil. Division of the All-Ukrainian Academy of Sciences, II-III (1923) 220-30.

80 Shchurat 317.

81 Gabriel Korbut, *Literatura Polska*, III (Warsaw 1930) 495. It is stated here in a reference note that Barszczewski was acquainted with Shevchenko. Barszczewski died in 1851. Thus his friendship with Shevchenko must have been in the eighteen-forties. This fact has not yet been brought out in the literature.

82 Bielina-Kędrzycki's memoirs in Polish were published in *Gazeta lwowska*. See especially nos. 38, 42, 61. Shchurat's translations into Ukrainian were published in *Ukrainskyi holos* (Peremyshl 1927). Part of the memoirs concerning Shevchenko was translated anew for the publication *Spohady pro Shevchenka* (Kiev 1958) 199-207. Henceforth referred to as *Spohady*.

83 *Spohady* 204.

84 Wacław Lasocki, *Wspomnenia z mojego życia*, I, ed. by Michał Janik and Felix Kopera (Kraków 1933).

85 The censor's permit to publish *Gwiazda* was issued in Kiev, 10 December 1846.

86 Among the subscribers listed at the end of the first volume of *Gwiazda* are Shevchenko's friend, Mykhailo Lazarevsky, and Vasyl Bilozersky of the Brotherhood. Among *Gwiazda*'s collaborators, Jan Barszczewski, Shevchenko's acquaintance from St Petersburg, was mentioned. Barszczewski published two poems in the first volume of *Gwiazda*; he was also very active as a subscription collector for *Gwiazda* in St Petersburg.

87 *Spohady* 205.

88 V. Antonovych's friend, he was later prosector of the dissecting room of the University of Kiev.

23

The Archetype of the Bastard in Shevchenko's Poetry

GEORGE S.N. LUCKYJ

Three discoveries by Carl Jung have had a profound influence on literary criticism: the collective unconscious, the archetypes, and the *anima*. Apart from the personal unconscious, there is in everybody, according to Jung, a deeper layer of the collective unconscious, from which consciousness has developed. 'The contents of the collective unconscious are known as *archetypes*.'[1] Although these are unknown, they may be apprehended in our consciousness as 'primordial images' or 'inborn forms of intuition,' revealing certain typical symbols common to the human race or to a certain culture. Ancient as they are, they may be modified by the individual consciousness and by the era in which they happen to appear. Yet another discovery was that of the feminine element (*anima*) in the unconscious of a man and of a masculine element (*animus*) in a woman. These complementary elements in human personalities are at the same time archetypes. In a man 'the compelling power of the *anima* is due to her image being an archetype of the collective unconscious, which is projected onto any woman who offers the slightest hook on which her picture may be hung.'[2]

The effect of these revelations (clinical research has made it difficult to regard them as mere hypotheses) on our understanding of creative processes has been very far-reaching. An entire school of literary criticism in Western Europe and North America followed these Jungian precepts. From the pioneering work of the English critic Maud Bodkin, *Archetypal Patterns in Poetry*, first published in 1934, to the German Erich Neumann, the American Philip Wheelwright, and the Canadian Northrop Frye, to mention only a few, critics in the West have used new approaches to literary analysis based to a greater or lesser degree on Jung's original discoveries. Frequently they use psychology merely as a point of departure for literary theory, and their criticism cannot be described as psychological. They deal chiefly with the literature of the West, advancing a new concept of literature as a 'reconstructed mythology.'[3] In the Soviet Union, Jung's influence has been negligible because his theories are regarded as reactionary. From time to time literary studies have appeared in Russian and other languages of the USSR which have touched on some problems of interest to 'Jungian' criticism (folk motifs, recurrent themes, imagery). By and large, however, this new field has remained unexplored.

Jung himself was interested in literature and left some acute observations on the nature of literary creation, as, for example:

Art is a kind of innate drive that seizes a human being and makes him its instrument. The artist is not a person endowed with free will who seeks his own ends, but one who allows art to realize its purposes through him. As a human being he may have moods and a will and personal aims, but as an artist he is 'man' in a higher sense – he is 'collective man' – one who carries and shapes the unconscious, psychic life of mankind.[4]

Having thus rejected Freud's concept of the artist as deriving his art from his personal experience, Jung emphasized the impersonal and intuitive origin of art. The artist was to him a seer and a diviner, not only of universal human values, but also of his national culture, which represented a fragment of the racial heritage. 'A work of art is produced that contains what may truthfully be called a message to generations of men. So *Faust* touches something in the soul of every German.'[5] Still referring to Goethe, he emphasized:

Here it is something that lives in the soul of every German, and that Goethe has helped to bring to birth. Could we conceive of anyone but a German writing *Faust* or *Also sprach Zarathustra*? Both play upon something that reverberates in the German soul – a 'primordial image,' as Jacob Burckhardt once called it – the figure of a physician or teacher of mankind. The archetypal image of the wise man, the saviour or redeemer, lies buried and dormant in man's unconscious since the dawn of culture; it is awakened whenever the times are out of joint and a human society is committed to serious error.[6]

One does not have to agree with all of Jung's intricate arguments to see in his aesthetics a kernel of truth about art – that artists are but instruments of a great force beyond their control. They may live, in Northrop Frye's words, in a 'world of myth, an abstract or purely literary world of fictional and thematic design, unaffected by canons of plausible adaptation to familiar experience.'[7]

Long ago, critics of Taras Shevchenko's poetry noted the presence in his works of certain dominant themes which set him apart from his contemporaries. They ascribed this to Shevchenko's *narodnist*, his dependence on the folk motifs of Ukraine. Yet even early researchers detected more than mere dependence. Writing in 1898, Sumtsov argued:

Shevchenko's *narodnost*, like that of Pushkin and other great poets, consists of two related elements: (a) an external *narodnost*, borrowings and imitations, and (b) an inner *narodnost*, inherited psychically. It is not difficult to determine the external, borrowed elements; to do this it is sufficient to acquaint oneself with ethnography and to find direct sources in folk tales, beliefs, songs, and customs. It is very difficult, and to do it fully, impossible – to determine the inner psychological folk elements.[8]

Kolessa[9] and Komarynets quoted Sumtsov with approval, although both denied that there was a clear demarcation line between the inner and the outer elements. The latter contended that Shevchenko inherited his *narodnist* from the 'toiling masses.'[10] Yet Sumtsov unwittingly put his finger on the existence of archetypes in Shevchenko's poetry. Its 'external' *narodnist* is only a manifestation of a deeper layer of primordial images rooted in the collective unconscious.

Some of Shevchenko's archetypal motifs are very prominent, recurring constantly in his poems from 1839 to 1861, that is, throughout his writing career. The archetype of the mother is the most striking, and a complete study of it would easily fill a book. Today, interest in this archetype is very active among psychologists, anthropologists, and literary critics.[11] Many of them accept, with reservations, the importance for our culture of the matriarchy which predated our patriarchal society and which was first pointed out by Bachofen.[12] The remains of the matriarchal order may be seen today, not only in the great civilizations of the Mediterranean, but also in India and North America. Moreover, they act as sources of artistic creativity for modern man, who in defence of the mother, 'like the hero of myth stands in conflict with the world of the fathers, i.e. the dominant values.'[13]

Shevchenko's image of the mother is many-sided. She is good mother earth, the protectress of the family hearth, but above all the seduced girl, *pokrytka*.[14] In the latter role she is the heroine of his long poems 'Kateryna' (1838), 'Naimychka' (The Servant Girl, 1845), 'Tytarivna' (The Sexton's Daughter, 1848), 'Maryna' (1848), 'Vidma' (The Witch, 1847-58), and 'Mariia' (1859). Several other poems also touch directly on seductions. Customary explanations of these poems solely in terms of the influence of sentimentalism (Karamzin) and Shevchenko's preoccupation with the wretched social position of the woman serf are inadequate. A new approach is needed in order to explore these phenomena, which are unquestionably archetypes. For reasons of space, I will focus attention on the archetype of the bastard.

In literature the bastard, as a product of an illegitimate union, is an offshoot of the mother archetype. There is no doubt that Shevchenko's social conscience was troubled by the high incidence of illegitimacy among the Ukrainian peasantry. But to describe his depiction of the lot of the seduced girl merely as condemnation of the serfdom which had led to these abuses would be tantamount to the view that Milton's *Paradise Lost* is merely a picture of Puritan England. Similarly, one cannot forget that in Shevchenko's personal life seduction left a deep scar: his childhood sweetheart, Oksana Kovalenko, was seduced by a Russian soldier, a fact recorded by the poet several times, above all in his poem 'My vkupochtsi kolys rosly' (We Grew Up Together Once, 1849). Yet this alone cannot account for his involvement with the bastard theme. The reasons lie much deeper.

The nature of the archetypes is such that they overlap and interpenetrate.[15] Their secretions create a web of images, thoughts, and feelings ranging from good to evil, beautiful to ugly. The archetypal mother, according to Neumann, has three forms: the good, the terrible, and the good-bad mother.[16] The same is true of Shevchenko's bastard, *baistriuk*. Although most frequently he appears as a tragic and lost figure, there are many other roles for him.

In the first poem by Shevchenko, the ballad 'Prychynna' (The Bewitched Woman, 1837), a hint is given that the small children who come out to play at night on the banks of the Dnieper may be spirits of bastards. They are water sprites, former 'unbaptized children.' Such creatures are common in other folk legends connected with the mother archetype. 'In all of them,' writes Neumann, 'the character of enchantment leading to doom is dominant.'[17] In Shevchenko's poem they set the mood for tragedy. In another ballad, 'Utoplena' (The Drowned Maiden, 1841), there is no doubt that Hanna, the beautiful daughter of a widow, is a bastard. Her mother, who loved the Cossacks, cannot see her own daughter grow up to be a beautiful girl and a possible rival. In a fit of jealousy she drowns her and loses her own life as well. There are no social or moral overtones here. The entire poem reflects the spirit of many folk songs, which are quite detached in their attitude towards illegitimacy. They go back to pagan times, when the very concept of illegitimacy was absent. In the matriarchal society (in Ukraine strong traces of matriarchy date from the period of the so-called Trypillia culture, 3000-1700 BC), sexual relations made the father of the child unimportant. An 'illegitimate' child was fatherless, and therefore he belonged entirely to the mother. The role of the woman as the leading partner – and her relationship not to the husband but to the child – dominate much of Ukrainian folklore. Capturing and seducing girls at Easter rites and wedding ceremonies is amply recorded in folk songs.[18] There is no moral censure attached to these 'games,' and illegitimate children mentioned in this connection are mentioned vaguely but tenderly.[19]

Not all folklore is amoral. Many Ukrainian songs about the seduced girl (*pokrytka*) are permeated by Christian morality, though here and there pre-Christian traces may be seen. In his study of this theme, Volodymyr Hnatiuk concentrated on the song about a girl who drowned her child.[20] All fifty-one versions of the song depict the girl drowning her illegitimate child and being punished for her crime. Though sometimes defiant, the girl is inevitably found out and severely punished. Hnatiuk dates the song to the sixteenth century.

Shevchenko was influenced by the attitudes of songs such as these though he did not imitate them very closely. His most moving poem about a *pokrytka*, 'Kateryna,' is based on the suffering inflicted on the heroine by punishment. Her father and mother turn her out of their ancestral home because of the shame she brought on them. They are cruel but just in the eyes of society.[21] Not only is there no chance of reconciliation between Catherine and her parents, but there is no future for her child. She loves and protects him, but when his father refuses to recognize him, she abandons the child and drowns herself. The poignancy of the child's fate is underscored: 'Shcho zostalos baistriukovi? / Khto z nym zahovoryt? / Ni rodyny, ni khatyny; / Shliakhy, pisky, hore ...' (What is there left for the bastard? / Who will speak to him? / No family, no home; / Only roads, sands, and grief ...).[22]

In the poem 'Naimychka' the bastard finds his way back to society. His mother abandons him and becomes a maid to the old couple who adopt him. Hiding her identity, she in fact becomes his mother. Her penance is accepted, and Marko, her son, is redeemed. In most poems written between 1847 and 1858, however, the evil of illegitimacy is unrelieved. It is so in 'Osyka' (Aspen, 1847, rewritten as 'Vidma' [The Witch] in 1858), 'Tytarivna,' and 'Maryna,' where the girls are seduced by landlords. One may doubt that the observation expressed by a student of family archetypes in literature applies to Shevchenko. Sven Armens wrote: 'The symbolic rape leads, without doubt, only to social chaos, the destruction of the weak and innocent, but the latter motivation, with its implication of a more permanent union, suggests the possibility of some enduring fount of tenderness, a gift transmitted by human male and female to their offspring.'[23] This tenderness is lacking. On the contrary, an agony of cosmic proportions is symbolized by Shevchenko in the figure of the bastard.

Either the mother abandons her child or the bastard turns against his mother ('U nashim rai na zemli' [In Our Earthly Paradise], 1849). The most precious image of the 'young mother and her small baby' is destroyed, and the poet displays an almost masochistic delight in showing the horrors of the demolished family order. This mood of universal gloom touches at times on the national theme, for Shevchenko regarded Ukraine as a seduced woman and considered the Russian masters of Ukraine to be 'Catherine's [the Second] bastards,' who like locusts despoiled his country. The mother image of one's country is an echo of the matriarchal order. Perhaps Shevchenko was aware that 'agricultural countries do not make history' but rather 'suffer it (*Geschichte erleiden*).'[24]

Yet, deep as it is, the darkness is not total. In an early work by Shevchenko, *Haidamaky* (1841), the bastard Iarema Halaida finds freedom during the peasant uprising. Rebellion brings him out of the lower depths (as servant in a tavern) to the very top of the new revolutionary order. In a short time 'his wings grow,' and he becomes a bloodthirsty avenger of his people. His triumph is short-lived. The outburst of hate and violence, however justified, brings no solution.

The poem in which Shevchenko attempted a 'solution' to the bastard theme is 'Mariia.' Written after the poet's return from a ten-year exile, 'Mariia' is one of his finest works. Myopic critics have often ignored it and labelled it 'anti-religious.' It is nothing of the kind. There is a deep serenity and wisdom in this poem, which is a true apotheosis of motherhood. Yet the strangest twist in the retelling of the familiar biblical story is that Shevchenko rejects belief in the Immaculate Conception and makes Jesus the son of Mary and a young wandering prophet. The daring concept of making Jesus an illegitimate son of Mary[25] can be understood only within the archetypal framework. What had always been the fruit of the darkest evil has turned into the vessel of the greatest good. Divinity itself has sprung from human frailty. Human love has been vindicated. True, the Messiah suffers defeat and is crucified. But his message is invincible. The union of mother and child is not transcendental, but valid here on earth for all of us.

> Vse upovaniie moie
> Na tebe, mii prysvitlyi raiu,
> Na myloserdiie tvoie,
> Vse upovaniie moie
> Na tebe, maty, vozlahaiu.
> Sviataia sylo vsikh sviatykh,
> Pryneporochnaia, blahaia!
> Moliusia, plachu i rydaiu:
> Vozzry, prechystaia, na ikh,
> Otykh okradenykh, slipykh
> Nevolnykiv. Podai im sylu
> Tvoioho muchenyka syna,
> Shchob khrest-kaidany donesly
> Do samoho, samoho kraiu.[26]

All my hope in / You, my glorious Paradise, / In your mercy / All my hope I place / In you, Mother. / The holy power of all saints, / Immaculate and blessed, / I pray, I cry and weep: / Look on them, o purest, / On these wretched, blind slaves. / Give them the strength / Of your martyred son / So that they may carry their cross – their chains / To the very, very end.

The sacrifice of the hero's life, the proper centre of the tragic vision, is not in vain because it occurs against a background of reverberations of the most cherished and most frequently abused act of love between man and woman. The myth of man-God, a son of woman, has been recreated in a great poem.

Recently Orest Zilynsky remarked perceptively, though rather cryptically, that Shevchenko's world is 'anthropocentric.'[27] These qualities invite a new approach to a poet who for too long has been studied as a national bard and a peasant revolutionary. A new facet of his greatness will be revealed in the archetypal meaning of his poetry.

(1970)

NOTES

1 C.G. Jung, 'Archetypes of the Collective Unconscious,' *Collected Works* IX, Pt I (New York 1959) 4. (The present article is reprinted from *Slavic and East European Journal* 14 (1970) 277-83.)
2 F. Fordham, *An Introduction to Jung's Psychology* (London 1966) 54.
3 Northrop Frye, *Fables of Identity* (New York 1963) 38.
4 C.G. Jung, *Modern Man in Search of a Soul* (London 1941) 195.
5 *Ibid.* 191.
6 *Ibid.* 197.
7 N. Frye, *Anatomy of Criticism* (New York 1967) 136.
8 N.F. Sumtsov, 'Glavnye motivy poezii T.G. Shevchenko,' *Iz ukrainskoi stariny* (Kharkov 1905) 85. First printed in *Kievskaia starina*, LX, 2 (1898).
9 F. Kolessa, *Folklornyi element v poezii Shevchenka* (Lviv 1939) 89.
10 T. Komarynets, *Shevchenko i narodna tvorchist* (Kiev 1963) 76.
11 Erich Neumann, *The Great Mother* (New York 1963); R.N. Anshen, ed., *The Family: Its Function and Destiny* (New York 1959); Sven Armens, *Archetypes of the Family in Literature* (Seattle 1966); Erich Fromm, *The Forgotten Language* (New York 1951).

12 J.J. Bachofen, *Das Mutterrecht* (1891).

13 E. Neumann, *Art and the Creative Unconscious* (New York 1959) 185.

14 *Pokrytka*, literally 'the covered one,' derives from the custom of covering the head of an unwed mother with a kerchief so as to remove her from the status of a girl to that of a married woman.

15 C.G. Jung, *Collected Works* (New York 1963) XIV, 103.

16 Neumann, *The Great Mother* 21.

17 *Ibid*. 81.

18 M. Hrushevsky, *Istoriia ukrainskoi literatury* (Kiev 1923) I, 254-70.

19 O. Kolberg, *Wołyń* (Kraków 1907).

20 Volodymyr Hnatiuk, 'Pisnia pro pokrytku shcho vtopyla dytynu,' *Materiialy do ukrainskoi etnolohii* (Lviv 1919) 249-389.

21 For an illuminating analysis of this and other poems by Shevchenko which centre on woman, see M. Shlemkevych, 'The Substratum of Shevchenko's View of Life,' in V. Mijakovskyi and G.Y. Shevelov, eds, *Taras Ševčenko, 1814-1861: A Symposium* (The Hague 1962). Shlemkevych was aware of Jung's theories and applied them to some extent in his study. See also A.V. Kultschytskyj, 'Ševčenko-Kult in tiefenpsychologischer Sicht,' *Taras Ševčenko* (Munich 1964).

22 Taras Shevchenko, *Povne zibrannia tvoriv u shesty tomakh* (Kiev 1963) I, 39.

23 Armens, *Archetypes of the Family in Literature* 44.

24 F.R. Schroder, 'Die Welt der Mutter und die Welt des Vaters,' *Germanisch-Romanische Monatsschrift*, XXXVIII (1957) 183.

25 Shevchenko is here anticipating what some modern scholars think about Jesus' birth: 'The nature of the historical Jesus has always been a problem for scholars and theologians (see A. Schweitzer, *The Quest for the Historical Jesus* [New York 1961]). In the gospel accounts, personal fact and archetypal image are so closely intermixed that it is almost impossible to distinguish them. However, although details remain uncertain, a definite historical personality with astonishing psychological insight is revealed in the gospels. Jesus was probably an illegitimate child. Certainly he demonstrates some characteristic features of the individual who has had no personal father.' (Edward F. Edinger, *Ego and Archetype* [Baltimore 1973] 132).

26 Shevchenko, II, 353.

27 Orest Zilynsky, 'Kilka aktualnykh dumok pro Shevchenka,' *Dukila*, II (1968) 141. Shevchenko's anthropocentric philosophy has been well discussed by Chyzhevsky in his article D. Chyzhevsky, 'Shevchenko i relihiia,' T. Shevchenko, *Povne vydannia tvoriv* X (Warsaw, Lviv 1936) 329-47 [translated in this volume].

24

Shevchenko's Profiles and Masks:
The Ironic Roles of the Self
in the Poetry of *Kobzar*

BOHDAN RUBCHAK

Much has been written on Shevchenko's use of irony as the literary expression of the ironical stance inherent in the folk culture of the Ukrainian people.[1] Although I have no intention of attempting to disprove that obvious fact, I should like to discuss Shevchenko's use of irony against the background of the Western romantic and post-romantic tradition. I should like to show that the dialectical movement of the poet's self which we observe in his work is energized by romantic irony as defined by Friedrich Schlegel and 'Socratic' irony as developed by Søren Kierkegaard.

Schlegel holds that in the 'new' (that is, romantic) irony all is exposed in heartfelt sincerity, while at the same time being hidden. The reason for this is that irony embodies, and hence awakens in our consciousness, the feeling of the insoluble conflict of limitation and infinity, the impossibility and yet necessity of unity of the inside and the outside. Such a seemingly paradoxical view of the world enables the ironist, particularly the poet, to stand outside his self and thus to transcend it. The external point of view upon himself, in turn, permits the poet to control his daydreams by the actuality of his life, while simultaneously enriching his daily existence with the poetry of his dreams of infinity. A reader who is 'tone deaf' to such matters does not know how to take the 'self-parody' of the poet, in which the latter expresses his desire for total unity through self-transcendence, while at the same time realizing its impossibility. Such a reader is forced to believe the poet and yet not to believe him, to take a joke seriously and a serious statement as a joke, until 'he becomes dizzy.'[2]

Kierkegaard's definition of 'Socratic irony' centres on the purgative chastisement of the hypocrite in ourselves by deliberate self-distancing through sustained games with masks. He begins by defining poetic irony as a liberating agent:

If I am conscious when I speak that what I say is my meaning ... and I assume that the person with whom I am speaking comprehends perfectly the meaning in what is said., then I am bound by what is said ... Furthermore, I am bound in relation to myself and cannot detach myself whenever I choose. If, on the other hand, what is said is not my meaning, I am free both in relation to my meaning and in relation to myself.[3]

Although such seemingly anarchic and 'insincere' jeopardizing of 'literal seriousness' and the resulting distancing of one's point of view on existence in total freedom (which Kierkegaard calls 'absolute negativity') is an indispensable condition of authentic poetry, Kierkegaard assures us that it should be considered only as the initial step to crucial ethical self-discoveries. The 'absolute negativity' of irony, while preserving its quality of negativity, must leave the vague metaphysical realms in which the German romantics put it and become a gesture towards actuality. Such a gesture will be significant only when the poet himself can find a sustained point of view on life, 'and in his own individual existence ... be master over irony.'[4] In other words, if the poet wants his poem to be an integral moment in his sustained view on life, rather than merely an isolated demonstration of his cleverness, wit, or even 'genius,' he should 'live poetically,' by which Kierkegaard means the poet's steady struggle for the discovery and preservation of his authentic self.[5] No matter how many masks the poet will then play with, the reader will immediately *feel* that the ironic device of negative distancing is meant not to be the final result but a way towards a synthesis and revelation of his authentic self and hence of his positive sense of authentic existence. It follows that the poet, upon his self-discovery, will use the ironic dissemination of his self not to hide it from others but to reassemble a sense of the totality of his being on a more authentic level. Deliberate poses of 'confessional sincerity,' therefore, are valuable only if they themselves are distanced by 'mastered irony,' as in Shevchenko's poetry.

It is not easy to find a poet more filled with his own self than Taras Shevchenko. The 'confessional' tone of his lyrical works seems to be so 'sincere' that it causes discomfort in his more reserved readers. Even in his dramatic and historical poems, from which genre one expects at least some distancing of the narrative voice, the 'I' intrudes in the obligatory introductions, the frequent lyrical interludes, and the unfolding of the narrative itself. On the other hand, the poet's self is never hermetically sealed: it eagerly meets not only the world engendered and controlled by the premises of the given work but the far less predictable world of the reader. Indeed, as opposed to the introverted lyrical poetry of many late romantics, the reader's presence is constant in *Kobzar*. Shevchenko frequently addresses his reader with informal directness, as if the reader were facing the poet and listening to his words. Shevchenko, in fact, often addresses *himself* thus: by the pronoun 'thou' and in the conversational expressions presumably directed by the poet to himself, the Other as interlocutor is invariably implied. Even when the pronoun 'I' is used in the numerous *Ich-Gedichte*, the poet's lyrical voice frequently is speaking for the reader.

The presence of the reader is evident with particular immediacy when the poet tells us that he has grown tired of his audience and now will write only for himself. In the following stanza, even while pretending to renounce his audience, he addresses it:

Ne dlia liudei, tiiei slavy,
Merezhani ta kucheriavi
Otsi virshi virshuiu ia –
Dlia sebe, bratiia moia!

Not for people who would bring me fame / Do I verse these embroidered and curly-haired verses, / But only for myself, my dear friends!

An actual threat of losing his audience, on the other hand, seems to throw him into a virtual state of panic:

Mabut meni ne vernutys
Nikoly dodomu;
Mabut meni dovedetsia
Chytaty samomu
Otsi dumy!

It seems that I am fated
Never to return home;

It seems that I am destined
To read these poems
By myself.

The irony is that Shevchenko's situation, like that of many emigré writers, led him to imagine his readers not only within his work (which is normal) but also in actuality (which is dangerous). He did not really know his Ukrainian audience when he lived in Petersburg and subsequently in exile, relying on memories of his childhood and of his brief sojourns in Ukraine to recreate his readers for himself.

No matter how vague or distant Shevchenko's readers may have appeared to him, he constructed vivid images of them by the force of his direct addresses to them: 'confessing' to them, haranguing them, exorting them, flirting with them. For such unabashed theatrical attitudes towards his imagined readers, Shevchenko developed a complex dramatic self, which I will call his *expressed self*. This expressed self is not constant (as it is with many lyrical poets), but performs a set of distinctly different gestures which develop through *Kobzar* in a loosely patterned alternating progression.

Behind such patterning of divergent attitudes – all, paradoxically, as 'sincere' as possible – a totalizing conceptualization of Shevchenko's 'real' self seems to elude our grasp. There are several reasons for this. To begin with, Shevchenko rarely explores his unconscious, most frequently making only indirect use of it, to mine material for his deliberately constructed metaphors. It is plain that all his 'dreams,' 'visions,' catalogues of feelings, and the like, are simply devices, sanctified by the romantic tradition, for the embodiment of almost philosophical ways of contemplating the world. This, of course, does not conflict with his romantic attacks upon the intellect and his hymns to the power of the heart: such passages, too, are embodied in lucid images. Another reason for our failure to conceptualize the 'person of the poet' in Shevchenko's work is that the ultimate privacy of the author's 'personality' is protected not so much by a dearth of autobiographical information within his poems (as, for instance, in the case of Shakespeare) as by its apparent surfeit. Shevchenko releases series upon series of quasi-facts about himself: while we supposedly 'weep and laugh' over them, however, we are gently stopped at certain thresholds and not invited inside. An obvious example of this is the frequency of statements on the pattern of: 'I would tell you the truth but what good would come of it?'; they effectively dramatize his control of the role that he has chosen to assume at a given moment. Another example is his rather formal portraiture of his friends, surrounded by warm protestations of friendship, in numerous epistles addressed to them. This reticence, embodied in too exuberant speech, becomes much profounder in Shevchenko's treatment of the objects of his love poetry, particularly the ever-present but elusive Oksana Kovalenko, who hovers in his verse as a figure shadowy to the point of transparency.

The reader's failure to *conceptualize* Shevchenko's 'personality' does not mean a failure to *intuit* the strong and constant presence of the poet's self in his work. Underlying the various roles of his expressed self and linking them in the continuous process of the poetical *œuvre* is a unique way of perceiving and expressing reality, and thus of appropriating it. We have here an example of the embodiment in language of an authentic style which begins on a deep level of the self, beneath the expressly conceived and deliberately formulated interests of a 'finished personality.'[6] No matter how assiduously a poet gifted with such an authentic style attempts to manipulate the manner of his writing for the purpose of distancing, it constantly shines through his text. And if the poet, as Kierkegaard advised, performs such displacements not in a desultory fashion but with existential lucidity, reflections of this style in his work will imply his authentic self that much more forcefully. Although Shevchenko deliberately hides his personality, while pretending to reveal it, an aware reader cannot help sensing in his style a particularly strong unifying current of a deep identity, from which the poet's various roles emerge to the surface of the text. I shall call this energy Shevchenko's *prepersonal self.*[7]

On the surface of the text (and supported by the deep style of the prepersonal self), the obvious unity of Shevchenko's poetical *œuvre* is achieved primarily by repetition or variation in different works of autonomous groups of lines of greater or lesser number, characterized by sharply-defined thematic motifs and stylistic features. I shall refer to such building blocks as *monads*. Occasionally the monads in *Kobzar*, particularly when they are brief and almost identical, seem to fulfil the function of medieval 'commonplaces,' or perhaps mnemonic 'control points' of Ukrainian oral poetry. As a rule, however, they are more loosely structured units, echoing each other by similarity, rather than by identity. Such similarities become apparent only when the monads forming a single series are lifted out of their varying contexts (which they reflect and which are reflected in them) and placed next to each other; it goes without saying, nevertheless, that this does not diminish their effect of providing continuity throughout the *oeuvre*. Isolating even a single series of monads and adequately describing the almost imperceptible transformations of the units within it – transformations conditioned by contexts – would require a lengthy study of its own. Here I merely want to show that the roles of Shevchenko's expressed self are frequently embodied in monads, and therefore the deliberate alternation of such roles is effected by the alternation of monads. This, in effect, implies a dialectical continuity of the roles throughout the *oeuvre*.

We notice that within the given frame of a short poem or section of a longer work the roles of the expressed self, embodied in monads, are frequently arranged in pairs: such bifurcation creates the tension needed for irony. Each pair constitutes, as it were, two 'profiles' of the 'face' that Shevchenko presents to his readers within a given frame. I shall call the one *the basic profile* and the other *the projected profile*. The basic profile is situated within 'actuality,' as such 'actuality' is constructed within the given frame. The projected profile embodies an act of desire, an imaginative flight out of the 'actual' situation towards the farthest horizons of existence. While one profile of the pair is forwarded and illuminated, the other is in shadow but remains potentially active under the featured profile, either implicitly questioning its assumptions or modifying it even more subtly: hence the shadowed profile becomes a point from which the illuminated profile is viewed ironically.

I shall use the term *mask* to designate those clearly delimited characters in *Kobzar* which externalize and hence distance an attitude or pair of attitudes of the poet's expressed self. Not all Shevchenko's characters serve such functions: his Saul and Amon, for instance, are not in such dialectical proximity to his expressed self. I suspect that a Freudian critic could make much of Shevchenko's evil Old Testament 'tsars,' as they embody some of the poet's 'obsessive' themes and images; this problem, however, has no bearing on either the expressed or the prepersonal self of the poet, as I have defined it in this article. Shevchenko's masks exist in ironical ambiguities similar to those of the profiles. Occasionally a single mask in a narrative poem reflects both the basic and the projected profile that we see in the *Ich-Gedichte* (Perebendia, Iarema, Mary, Christ). More frequently, however, it takes two masks to embody such a dialectic. Sometimes the required pair is found in a single narrative poem (Christ and Mary in 'Mariia'), and at other times we must search for it in different poems and even in different stages of the poet's career; in the latter case we establish it by finding dialectically related monads (Kateryna and Mary in the early poem 'Kateryna' and the late work 'Mariia'). More rarely, a single character develops such an ironical dialectic in various poems centred upon him (King David, Christ).

The most obvious connections between masks and profiles occur in 'personal' introductions to the narrative poems and in numerous lyrical interludes which interrupt and distance the narrative line by suddenly subjecting it to the scrutiny of the expressed self. It is within the masks themselves, however, that such links become most interesting: having projected himself into his mask, the poet ironically externalizes his point of view, which allows him to observe himself from the outside, in self-reflectivity even more radical than his expressed self. Such ambiguities occur particularly frequently in monads in which the mask employs the pronoun 'I' either in direct speech or in interior monologue. It is such monads (which certainly do not include all instances of the monologue in Shevchenko's narrative poems) that frequently echo monads found in the *Ich-Gedichte*. In the so-called third 'Son' (Dream), an old Cossack prays for a peaceful old age:

> Shchob dav meni dobru sylu
> Peresylyt hore
> I pryviv mene, staroho,
> Na si sviati hory
> Odynokyi vik dozhyty ...

Let Him grant me the good strength / To overcome my troubles, / And bring me – an old man – / To these holy mountains / Where I would end my lonely life.

And here is a 'personal' prayer from a lyrical poem:

> Dai, zhe, Bozhe, kolynebud,
> Khoch na starist staty

Na tykh horakh okradenykh
U malenkii khati.

Grant me, o Lord, to live sometime, / At least in my old age, / Upon those ravaged mountains, / In a small house.

The two monads just quoted are drawn even more closely together by the fact that the adjectives 'holy' and 'ravaged' are frequently used as epithets for mountains, supporting Shevchenko's important motif of ravaged holiness. In the poem 'Nevolnyk' (The Captive) and its original version 'Slipyi' (The Blind Man), the father of the hero, also an old Cossack, brings out his weapons to give them to his son. The veteran addresses his weapons:

     ... Zbroie moia,
Zbroie zolotaia,
Lita moi molodii,
Sylo molodaia!

My weapons, / My golden weapons, / My young years, / My young strength!

And here is a monad, one of a long series of its own, in which the poet expresses his longing for the powerful and joyful poetry of his youth – the symbol of his virility – now lost forever:

Ne vernutsia znovu
Lita moii molodii,
Veseleie slovo ...

My young years, / My happy word, / Will not return again.

In this pair of monads we have a particularly striking example of the distancing of the expressed self by a mask, since in many *Ich-Gedichte* Shevchenko compares his poetry to a weapon; hence the tension between an old warrior and an 'old' poet, underlying the motif of poetry as a battle for justice, becomes even more apparent.

Somewhere between the fully developed masks and the roles of the expressed self in the *Ich-Gedichte* we find a category of voice which may be called a *half mask*. Its externalization is made even more ambiguous by the use of the pronoun 'I' *throughout* the given poem; furthermore, it is not so much an individualized character (as, for instance, in Robert Browning) as a type. The most familiar half masks in *Kobzar* are those of the peasant girl, the old man, and the Old Testament prophet.

Although most of the poems spoken or sung by the peasant girl exhibit strong folkloristic stylization, deliberately creating the effect of 'entertainments,' such as Perebendia might have performed, nevertheless many monads within them are close to the more 'serious' tone of the *Ich-Gedichte*: frequently the difference between the voice of the expressed self and that of the girl is signalled solely by endings of verbs in the past tense, endings of modifiers of the given 'I,' and similar morphological designations of gender. And when the opposition between the song-like frivolity and the 'confessional' seriousness of tone becomes pronounced, this in itself creates an interesting ironical ambiguity, distancing by song the poet's desperate concerns: loneliness, unrequited love, injustices at the hands of the oppressors, even poses of pathetic dissipation as the only way out of an intolerable situation. In the following pair of examples, the first monad is sung by a servant girl, while the second is spoken by the poet's expressed self. The ironical tension created by the obvious difference in tone is enhanced by the feminine ambience in the first excerpt:

> Divchatochka na muzykakh
> U chervonykh cherevykakh, –
> Ia svitom nuzhu ...
> Bez roskoshi, bez liubovy,
> Znoshu svoi chorni brovy,
> U naimakh znoshu!..

All the young women / Have red shoes to wear to dances. / Only I am sad in this world. / Without pleasure, without love, / My black eyebrows shall fade in servitude.

> Ohni horiat, muzyka hraie,
> Muzyka plache, zavyvaie ...
> ...
> I vsi rehochutsia, smiiutsia,
> I vsi tantsiuiut. Tilko ia,

Nenache zakliatyi, dyvliusia
I nyshkom plachu, plachu ia ...
Choho zh ia plachu? Mabut, shkoda,
Shcho bez pryhody, mov nehoda,
Mynula molodist moia.

The lamps are lit, the music sounds, / Weeping and wailing ... / And everyone is laughing, / Everyone is dancing. Only I, / Like a cursed outsider, look at them / And weep in secrecy. / Why do I weep so? Perhaps because I regret / That my youth has passed without passionate escapades, / Like a grey, rainy day.

Let me remark incidentally that while the half mask of the peasant girl is obviously close to the expressed self, it approximates such full masks as Kateryna or Naimychka.

Shevchenko often addresses the peasant girl as his favourite imaginary reader, his imaginary lover, and even his muse. When we consider such apostrophes together with the peasant girl as the half mask, we see hints of identification between her and the poet – a sort of spiritual androgyny, or the Jungian unity of *animus* and *anima*. The poet identifies himself still more closely with the half mask of the old man: here even grammatical gender fails to differentiate between the two voices. The thirty-year-old author refers to himself as an old man so often that his reader may indeed picture him as a greybeard, utterly ruined by a long life. We may speculate that the young girl and the old man became the poet's most intimate *alter egos*, embodying temporal projections of his self, respectively his past and his future. As I shall attempt to show below, this temporal sequence reverses itself in Shevchenko's later poetry: the young girl becomes a projection of the poet's future and the old man of his past.

The two sources of energy behind the ironical bifurcation and the potential synthesis of the profiles and masks of Shevchenko's expressed self are time and space. These modes are in dialectical opposition to each other, negating and yet underlying each other, and thus implying a potential synthesis of their own – the precisely imagined *future space* of desire (based on the dream-invested space of the past) for a timeless personal and national utopia, in which projected and basic profiles will become one, the expressed self will become *openly* steadfast to the prepersonal self, and hence ironical ambiguities will become superfluous.

In the mode of spatial directions, Shevchenko's expressed self is bifurcated by imaginary flights of the projected profile and the corresponding 'actuality' of the basic profile. Frequently, particularly in the early poetry, the projected profile takes a vertical direction into metaphysical reverie. Although such images of vertical flight never vanish altogether, they soon enter into an ironical dialectic with horizontal flights of the projected profile, supporting its public function of 'reporting' what is seen on earth, rather than 'beyond the clouds.' The tension between vertical and horizontal directions of flight thus embodies the ambiguity between the private and public functions of the expressed self.

Images of spatial directions are supplemented by images of open versus closed space. In Shevchenko's early work, limitless space opens up before the projected profile, while delimited space encloses the basic profile (the sky, the sea, the steppe, versus the humble hut). In later stages of *Kobzar*, vast expanses threaten the basic profile (the sandy steppes – death's domain – of the North), while the projected profile longs for a delimited and civilized space (reveries of a warm family home, surrounded by a cherry orchard): the outsider who sleeps under other people's fences (*popidtynniu*) now wants to be master of his own enclosed space. In an interesting ambiguity, the empty, lonely hut in Shevchenko's later poetry – the basic profile's 'actuality' – serves as the counterpoint to, or the negative reverse of, the projected profile's reveries of a civilized enclosure, filled with the presence of loving people.

Images of open spaces, particularly in the early poetry, imply wide, expansive gestures not only on the part of the projected profile but also of various personages (Cossacks, haidamaks); images of enclosed spaces, on the other hand, imply concentrated contemplation. I am even tempted to apply that scheme to the formal aspects of the poetry, although this cannot be done systematically: images of open spaces are frequently embodied in longer lines, restless changes of meter, informal syntax; images of enclosed spaces, on the other hand, often appear in compact 'well-made' lyrical poems or such passages in longer narrative works.

We observe in *Kobzar* a pervasive ironical tension between the cyclic and the linear temporal movements. In the introduction to the narrative poem *Haidamaky*, for example, the cyclic temporality of natural sequences, imagined in personal reverie, ironically offsets the historical, and therefore linear, temporality of the action of the poem, thus putting the failure of history into the stoic perspective of *sub specie aeternitatis*. Later in the *œuvre*, the cyclic temporality of nature distances and thus underscores the inexorable flight towards death of the poet's autobiographical (hence historical and linear) temporality: while seasons rotate in the unbearably slow monotony of exile, years fly by rapidly, taking with them the poet's hopes for the future. Again we see the perspective of *sub specie*, but now desperately fatalistic, rather than stoically reassuring.

The dialectic between linear and cyclic temporality becomes more pertinent when we consider *ek-static* displacements of time in the private history of the expressed self and in the public history of the Ukrainian people.[8] Here the promised synthesis of a timeless utopia causes the temporal direction to appear as a linear progression towards a personally or socially fulfilling resolution, and yet finally is a cyclic journey, returning to its origins. Generally speaking, in the early work the poet's personal future founds itself upon the dream-invested national past: the poet hopes to become not only the participant but also the progenitor of his people's future, founded on overdetermined (by the needs of that future) models of its history. In the later poetry, the future of the nation is predicated upon the personal and equally dream-invested past of the poet's own life.

As we have seen already, Shevchenko's expressed self divides its activity between private and public functions. Frequently, these functions exist in an ironical tension, and the bifurcation of the expressed self and of its masks adjusts itself to accommodate such dialectical ambiguities. In the dimension of temporality, the more frequently the projected profile *in its public functions* assumes the half mask of the prophet, in order to cast a desperate glance into the bleak future of Ukraine, the more often the projected profile *in its private functions* flies backward in time, towards the imagined warm enclosure of a peasant house. In the later poetry, such images of house and hearth become a model for the sacred institution of the state, according to which the social and even political future of the nation should be built. Hence, in temporal cyclicity, the future is forced to repeat the past and public history to become autobiography; the future is embodied in the image of the happy child that the poet presumably once was. It is that image, fostered by the projected profile, that the basic profile is called upon to attack.

Let me illustrate my models of the temporal/spatial movement of Shevchenko's expressed self, and the ironical tensions that such movement implies, by a few examples from the early poetry and the poetry of *Try litá* (Three Years), with relevant allusions to the prison poetry and the late poetry.

As early as 'Dumy moi' (My Thoughts-Poems) – the first poem of the established canon[9] – Shevchenko originates an ironical relationship between the basic and the projected profile of his expressed self which will continue, with some readjustments, until the last poem of the *oeuvre*. The basic profile in 'Dumy moi' is 'a poor orphan,' an outsider living in a foreign land, either ignored or despised by his environment. This profile soon engenders its own antithesis and projects it into desire, while at the same time preserving essential connections with it. The projected profile represents the romantic poet at the peak of his uncanny powers: the expressed self becomes a shaman-magician, capable of resurrecting warriors of past centuries, capable of exploding the confining walls of a tiny hut into vast spaces, in which long-silent battles ring again, capable of transforming, in an act of *fiat*, the dead snows of Russia into the fertile fields of Ukraine.

The most mysterious gift of the projected profile, from which all his powers stem, is the poet's secret of 'looking at people with his soul.' The source of such visionary power is the heart. A central symbol throughout *Kobzar*, the heart is constantly opposed to the circumspect intellect, which weighs, measures, apportions, and rigidly controls experience, and which intimidates men into betrayal. The poet's talent of looking with the eyes of the soul enables him not only to resurrect the past but to intuit the very essence of the present, and hence to divine the future, both personal and national: this will soon engender the half mask of the prophet, which dominates Shevchenko's subsequent periods.

As early as 'Dumy moi,' the expressed self plays complex games with the imagined reader; they are based, as elsewhere in *Kobzar*, on the bifurcation of the two profiles. Each profile deals with its own circle of readers. The basic profile imagines itself in the midst of indifferent, cruel 'people,' who will scoff at *Kobzar*, while the projected profile associates itself with an equally projected image of distant Ukrainian readers, led by a peasant girl – the poet's ideal reader – for whom he performs his miracles, in expectation of her imaginary favours ('lasky divochi').

It is not difficult to trace in all this a faithful example of romantic irony. The orphaned outsider, a nonentity in fact, has the secret power to transcend his 'basic' existence in the projection of the poet-magician. Although such a projection is real enough in the metaphysical sense, the very existence of the basic profile implies that the projected profile is, after all, *created* and ephemeral. The poet knows, moreover, that the desire for the ultimate horizons of existence, invested in the projected profile, will bring him nothing but disappointment: the basic profile implies that the poet might be happier living the calm, anonymous life of a peasant on his land. As the *œuvre* progresses, that implication becomes increasingly overt (suggesting at times and with appropriate adjustments a model for the future of all Ukrainians), and enters into an ironical conflict not only with the elated activities of the projected profile but also, within the framework of the basic profile itself, with the poet's freely admitted desire for the mundane comforts that literary fame brings. In the 'vicious circle' of romantic irony, the projected profile opposes, by its implied example and overt sneers, such craving for the comforts of anonymity on the one hand and, on the other, for the comforts of fame. Hence the projected profile implies the inevitability of the curse of selfless sacrifice to the unattainable Ideal, whether private or public.

The mask whose own bifurcation corresponds to that of the expressed self in 'Dumy moi' is at the centre of the early poem 'Perebendia.' In the eyes of society Perebendia is an 'orphan,' an outsider without a home or family of his own. In contrast to the basic profile of 'Dumy moi,' however, he is far from anonymous: he is a clever professional entertainer who plays and sings what his public demands. His 'professionalism' is enhanced by a characterization which rests on the sentimental conception of a clown 'laughing on the outside, crying on the inside,' and which thus prefigures the ironic bifurcation of his profiles:

Vin im tuhu rozhaniaie
Khoch sam svitom nudyt.

He diverts them, / Although he himself is weary of the world.

Perebendia is an essentially romantic poet whose only 'public' is nature and God. In that profile, Perebendia not only addresses *essential*, alchemical questions to natural phenomena but is even capable of flying up into the sky and perching upon the sun:

> Spochyne na sontsi, ioho zapytaie,
> De vono nochuie? Iak vono vstaie?
> Poslukhaie moria, shcho vono hovoryt?
> Spyta chornu khmaru: Choho ty nima?

He rests upon the sun and asks it / Where it spends the night and how it rises. / He listens to the sea, to what it says. / He asks the black cloud: Why are you mute?

Hence the functions of the profiles of 'Dumy moi' and 'Perebendia' are reversed, prefiguring the important dialectic of the public and private functions of the expressed self. While the basic profile of 'Dumy moi' is resigned to anonymity, the projected profile longs for imaginary readers. In 'Perebendia,' on the other hand, the basic profile is known to the people, while the projected profile of the knower is utterly unknown; the poet, moreover, advises his hero to preserve his mystical anonymity at all costs. The poet, in fact, approves both Perebendia's basic, public profile and his projected, private one: here we see an ironical distancing of the self by the mask, since there is little doubt that the author addresses his advice primarily to himself.

An important development in the ironical relationship between the basic and the projected profiles of the expressed self, and of the parallel dialectical movement within the corresponding mask, occurs in Shevchenko's early quasihistorical poem 'Haidamaky' (The Haidamaks). In the introduction, the expressed self becomes bifurcated in a pattern very close to that of 'Dumy moi.' In his projected profile, the poet calls himself father of the rebels of some eighty years earlier (addressing them as he addressed his poems – his children – in 'Dumy moi'), whom he has resurrected in his hut and for whose enlightenment he has opened a vista upon a still earlier century, so that they might learn bravery and grandeur of demeanour from the glorious Cossacks. He ironically implies that such proceedings are predominantly literary, particularly when he complains that he has trouble 'finding' a leader for his boys within his poem.

In the polemical part of the introduction, where he sneers at his Russian critics, the poet complicates his basic profile by the pose of a naïve rustic (this ironical device appears in eighteenth-century Western satire as the 'naïve innocent,' usually a provincial or a traveler), whose down-to-earth sarcasm unmasks the 'refined' hypocrisy of the 'learned Russian gentlemen' hiding behind their fake liberalism:

> Teplyi kozhukh, tilko shkoda,
> Ne na mene shytyi,
> A rozumne vashe slovo
> Brekhneiu pidbyte.

The sheepskin coat [of a profitable literary career that you offer me] is warm / But unfortunately not cut for me, / And your wise words / Are lined with lies.

This elaborate pose, with its appropriate 'peasant' expressions, will be developed in the second part of 'Son' (The Dream). Incidentally, it exists in its own right in an ironical relationship with the poet's 'serious' dreams of rustic anonymity.

The mask, bifurcated to correspond to the two profiles in the introduction, is embodied in the hero of the poem itself. The action is reminiscent of a *Bildungsroman*, based as it is upon the 'discovery' and the moral education of a leader, a romantic hero, with whom Shevchenko identifies openly:

> Otakyi to mii Iarema,
> Syrota bahatyi.
> Takym i ia kolys to buv ...

Such is my Iarema, / A rich orphan. / Once upon a time I was like him ...

Iarema, a poor orphan (and yet, paradoxically, a 'rich' one) begins at the lowest level of his society, as a meek servant of a tyrannical taverner. But even in the initial stages of the action that basic profile of the mask implies its own projected profile, characteristically embodied in images of flight which in turn are offset by the opposite direction – the basic profile's lot – of bending to the ground:

Ne znav, siromakha, shcho vyrosly kryla,
Shcho neba dostane, koly poletyt,
Ne znav, nahynavsia ...

He did not know, the poor wretch, that he was growing wings, / That he will reach the sky once he begins to fly; / He did not know, he bent his back ...

Iarema joins the haidamak rebellion for the sake of booty, so that he can afford to marry his beloved Oksana, whose name immediately reminds us of Oksana Kovalenko (indeed, Iarema's initial motive can be compared to the poet's own dreams of personal happiness, expressed in the *Ich-Gedichte*). Later on, the hero's decision to go on fighting is motivated by his desire for military glory (which, in turn, reminds us of Shevchenko's own hankering after literary fame). It is only in the final stages of the action that Iarema recognizes his destiny: he is even willing to abandon his beloved, who now has become his wife, for a while longer – or perhaps forever – in order to win freedom for his people (we may read this as a parallel to Shevchenko's own awareness of his mission as a political poet). Hence it follows that not only in the introduction and the lyrical interludes but in the development of the action itself the poet constructs a network of systematic parallels between the mask and the expressed self.

I have alluded earlier to the most important ambiguity between the introduction and the main part of *Haidamaky*, generated by the two directions of time. The Introduction contains a hymn to cyclic temporality; mighty empires emerge only to vanish, and petty human strivings and failures dissolve in the light of the indifferent moon. This seems like a strange prelude to a poem in which the linear temporality of history dominates the action. One may speculate that with the help of such ironical distancing of linear temporality Shevchenko wishes to examine Ukraine's own moment under the sun. We know that later he will similarly examine the time of his own life by looking at it not only from the standpoint of the cyclicity of nature but from the distanced point of view of the historical time of his nation. More important, in some later works he ironically questions the morality of cyclic time from the standpoint of historical temporality. In a late lyrical poem, for example, Shevchenko speaks of the wealthy father who yearly clothes the grove – his daughter – in the sumptuous garments appropriate to each season. This seemingly innocent and even playful occupation, however, leads to a surprising conclusion. The mysterious father:

> Spat liazhe, vtomyvshysia
> Turboiu takoiu.

Will lie down to sleep, exhausted / By such troubles.

Judging by the numerous monads and more extensive passages throughout *Kobzar*, in which the indifferent God sleeps, while innocent people suffer and die – even while his own Son is hanging on the cross – we may read these lines as charged with profound irony: instead of undertaking the demanding 'troubles' of caring for humanity, the 'wealthy father' indulges in the gratuitous supervision of the seasons, and thus condemns the downtrodden to the injustices of their national and personal situation.

The second stage of Shevchenko's *oeuvre*, constituted by the group of poems under the heading of *Try lita* (Three Years), is dominated by desperate searching and painful doubt. Such tortuous internal quests continued until his last poem, although in later works they occasionally were mellowed by more mature scepticism. Hence from the second period on the projected profile will not emanate from the basic profile in a harmonious gesture, with the former always superior to the latter, although implicitly challenged by it: the two profiles will now be in open conflict, cuttingly interrogating each other. One may say that here Shevchenko leaves the 'romantic irony' of Schlegel and approaches the 'Socratic irony' of Kierkegaard.

The 'crisis' of the second period is evident as early as 'Try lita,' which introduces the group under the same title. (Such introductory poems, which appear at intervals throughout the *oeuvre*, frequently feature similar monads and thus dialectically develop the first introductory poem, 'Dumy moi'; indeed, 'Try lita' may be read as an anthitesis to that poem.) The ironical tension in 'Try lita' is energized by clashing images of temporality. Personal time now heads forward in a destructive stream, without the implied foundation of 'the eternal return.' The cyclicity of time, in fact, is now embodied in negative imagery; it becomes the tedium of days that repeat each other with unbearable monotony and *over* which the years gallop forward, towards the dangerous abyss of the future:

I kydaiut na rozputti
Slipoho kaliku ...

And [the years] abandon a blind cripple / At a crossroads ...

Note that here blindness symbolizes not Perebendia's role as a mystical visionary but the expressed self's role as a helpless beggar, standing bewildered at the crossroads of national and personal history.

Embittered by personal and political disappointments, and threatened by an uncertain future, the expressed self in 'Try lita' directs its projected profile neither into verticality nor into the dream-invested *national* past of Ukraine, but into its own imagined *personal* past. This vision includes Shevchenko's own early poetry and the process of its creation; it is as if the projected profile now identified itself with the basic profile embodied in the youthful poems as an innocent, happy, anonymous singer. Obviously, all we have to do is turn quickly to the beginning of *Kobzar* to see that not all is so cheerful there. At a time of crisis, even the memories of the beginning of the poet's career must be altered by desire.

The regression of the projected profile beyond the dream-invested vision of the poet's early work and into an idealized pastoral childhood, shared by an imagined female playmate, reinforces the longing for the closed space of a peaceful, anonymous familial existence, which will soon enter into ironical conflict with the longing for personal fame. The important moment here is that such longing culminates in the intense desire *to repeat* the anonymity of a dream-invested pastoral childhood *in the future*. 'Postavliu khatu i kimnatu' (I shall build a house with a parlour), the poet promises himself. That house will be populated by a family, patterned after his reverie of the past family that presumably blessed his childhood and after his desire for a future family, born out of the dream of an innocent relationship between himself as a child and his little female friend. Hence we notice, from 'Try lita' on, that the movement of personal time of the expressed self forms a circle, in which the past is perpetually transformed into the future; that cyclic direction is meant to supplant the now lost belief in the metaphysical validity of nature's cyclic temporality for individual or national destiny.

Throughout the later sections of *Kobzar*, the basic profile will ironically check the pastoral dreams of the projected profile, while the projected profile will mitigate such sarcasm of embittered experience by its own 'songs of innocence.' The basic profile, for example, will view the illusions of the projected profile as they are shattered by the social conditions of the Russian Empire, idiomatically expressing those illusions as the void of absence:

I vyris ia na chuzhyni,
I syviiu v chuzhomu krai,
Ta odynokomu meni
Zdaietsia – krashchoho nemaie
Nichoho v Boha, iak Dnipro
Ta nasha slavnaia kraina ...
Azh bachu, tam tilko dobro,
De nas nema ...

And I grew up in exile, / And I am going grey in a foreign land. / So, it seems to me / That even God's paradise is no better than our Dnipro / And our glorious land ... / But suddenly I see that goodness exists / Only where we don't live [an idiom paralleling the English 'the grass is greener ...']

As for the temporal regression of the projected profile into childhood, the basic profile will sneer at its potential infantilism. The original of the following example is expressed in an ironically informal, bantering tone:

Na batka bisovoho trachu
I dni i pera i papir!
A inodi to shche i zaplachu,
Taky azh nadto. Ne na myr
I na dila ioho dyvyvshys,
A tak – mov inodi upyvshys,
Didus syvesenkyi ryda
Toho, bachte, shcho syrota.

Only the devil's father knows why / I am wasting my days, pens, and paper! / And on top of it, once in a while / I break out in tears, and quite copiously at that. / Not because I contemplate the world and its affairs, / But just so, for no reason at all. / As if a drunken greybeard started / Bawling because, you see he is an orphan.

In the following excerpt, we find an ironic blending of the basic profile (in the role of an old man) and the projected profile (in the role of a child). Fate has abandoned the poet, and he again finds himself at a crossroads:

> ... kynula maloho
> Na rozputti, ta i baiduzhe ...
> A vono, ubohe,
> Molodeie, syvouse,
> Zvychaine, dytyna!
> I podybalo tykhenko
> Popid samym tynom
> Azh za Ural ...

[Fate] left the little boy / At the crossroads, and didn't care ... / And he, so poor, / So young, so greybearded – / A child, you understand – / Toddled off quietly, / Along the fence, / Way beyond the Ural Mountains ...

The mask paralleling 'Try lita' can be traced in the narrative poem 'Slipyi' (The Blind Man), from the same second period. As in *Haidamaky*, the connections between the mask and the expressed self are implied in the introduction. Also, the introduction is again in ironical opposition to the narrative, inasmuch as in it the poet vainly longs for the fulfilment of love which his hero, no matter how battered, finally finds. The hero sets off to battle not as the outcast Iarema but from the midst of a warm familial environment: his past thus corresponds to the dream-invested past of the poet's expressed self. Conversely, the hero does not end his exploits as a leader but as a broken cripple and a minstrel, as if here Shevchenko took up and developed his own 'self-portrait' from 'Try lita.' In spite of his handicap, however, the hero returns to his village, marries his sweetheart (who, almost incestuously, comes from his own family), and settles down to a peaceful rural existence. In the conclusion of the poem, the poet repeats the cyclic direction of human life, reminiscent not only of his reveries of a calm termination of his own broken life but also of his hopes for the future of his nation, as expressed in his late poetry.

The projected profile of the hero, in contrast to that of Iarema, turns out to be a rather passive participant in the military exploits of the Cossacks. Moreover, the hero relates his adventures first in a *duma* and then in a narrative for the benefit of his family, rather than directly taking part in the action, as Iarema does. Such deflection of direct action into relation, and the resulting removal of the sphere of the projected profile into the background, supports my supposition that in the second period of Shevchenko's *œuvre* the closed domestic space begins to take precedence over the open space of battle. Neither does this blind minstrel share the gift of mystical insight with blind Perebendia. 'Slipyi,' then, is in ironical opposition to the body of *Haidamaky* on the one hand and to 'Perebendia' on the other, as 'Try lita' is in opposition to 'Dumy moi.'

In the second period of his development, Shevchenko fortifies the framework of the public functions of his expressed self, which henceforth will be ironically opposed to his private hopes and reveries. The poem that establishes those functions is 'Son' (The Dream). Here the basic profile of the orphan pretends to be cynically embittered, striking the pose of a desperately profligate underground man who dissipates his life in protest not only against social injustices but also against the universal Absurd, of which the grievous social conditions are merely evidence. Corresponding changes occur in the projected profile of the poet-magician: its public functions force it to assume an ironical relationship not only to its own basic profile but also to the projected profiles in 'Dumy moi' and 'Perebendia.' To begin with, its flight is now not vertical (like Perebendia's) but horizontal, although vertical flight still tempts the poet, and he has a conversation with his soul about its possibility:

> Choho tobi shkoda? Khiba ty ne bachysh?
> Khiba ty ne chuiesh liudskoho plachu?
> To hlian, podyvysia! A ia polechu
> Vysoko-vysoko za synii khmary.
> Nemaie tam vlasty, nemaie tam kary,
> Tam smikhu liudskoho i plachu ne chut.

What are you sorry for? Do you not see? / Do you not hear human weeping? / So look, see! And I shall fly high up, / Beyond the blue clouds. / There is no mighty rule nor punishment there, / There neither human laughter nor weeping are heard.

The possibility of vertical flight is now considered from the standpoint of ethics, which was certainly not true of the alchemical inquiries into the secrets of nature by Perebendia's projected profile, echoing as they did the aesthetic interests of the early romantics. Hence such 'pure' views on nature in Shevchenko's youthful poetry are now 'marred' by ethics: the earth is now wounded by the ugly holes of silver mines in which people suffer, and the mountains are contaminated by blood. In short, magical inquiries into the secrets of nature, although still a cherished possibility, have become morally unaffordable. The poet's very soul has become the instrument of ethical questioning, and consequently 'looking at people with the soul' has turned into a source of unavoidable suffering. Hence various emphases must be reversed: Perebendia's projected *private* profile (which he hides from the people) has to recede, and the new magician's *public* profile (which will instruct the people) must take the centre and be projected. It follows that, as far as the public functions of the expressed self are concerned, the dream of Ukraine as an idyllic paradise must also be revised for the sake of ethical considerations. The poet's ironic debate with his soul continues:

On hlian: u tim rai, shcho ty pokydaiesh,
Latanu svytynu z kaliky znimaiut,
Z shkuroiu znimaiut ...

Look! In this paradise which you are leaving, / They strip a patched shirt off a cripple, / Together with his skin.

The direction of flight *must be forced* into uncompromising horizontality; the 'double standard' applied to Perebendia, allowing him to masquerade as a humble entertainer, would now be in bad faith. A different kind of 'masquerade' is called for, since the flight of the projected profile is not that of a blind seer anymore, but that of a mercilessly wide-eyed, lucid 'spy' of the human conscience. Hence the bird that symbolizes this new direction is neither the high-hovering eagle nor the nightingale, which we saw in the early poetry, but the repulsive owl. The poet resents the owl's kinship to his inspiration in several instances ('I vyiu sovoiu' / 'And I howl like an owl'), but he nevertheless needs such an unclean Muse because its eyes pierce the darkness of human duplicity and hypocrisy. And yet, while the

poet perceives the shoddy prospects of social injustice, his sight is ironically 'covered up' by the pretence that such painfully etched visions are
nothing but vapid emanations of a drunken dream (as opposed to Perebendia's pure ecstasy). However, the poet assures us that the ink-stained
'sober' Ukrainians in Petersburg, busy aspiring to clerical careers, cannot
hope to realize such 'drunken' dreams. The political vision of the projected
profile as an angry poet is thus 'masked' by an alcoholic hallucination of
the basic profile which masquerades as an anonymous drunk. The projected profile itself, moreover, must also be anonymous and *invisible* in
order to *see* better, to fulfil more efficiently its task of *spying*. The purpose
of such anonymity is the opposite from that of Perebendia's projected
profile, what with his hiding behind clouds to get a better view of the roots
of universal existence. As we see, the magic of a poem dealing with the
social conditions in the Russian Empire has to become black; this, I suppose, is the central cause of Shevchenko's frequent evocations of the myth
of his 'innocent' and 'pure' past, beginning with the second period of his
oeuvre.

'Son' is the grotesque embodiment of the poet's lucid vision of the public
present and its public space. In later poems the expressed self in its public
function begins to assume the half mask of the prophet, in order to
examine not only the present but also the future. The temporal orientation
correspondingly becomes the apocalyptic direction *forward*, as opposed to
the apparently *backward* pastoral glance of the poet's private reveries. The
half mask of Jeremiah, weeping at the crossroads of history, sees the future
space of the Ukrainian nation as a wasteland; such passive visions are
ironically counterbalanced by the half mask of Isaiah, who castigates his
people for their past mistakes and calls them to future conquests. Both
these prophets' half masks parallel the half mask and the full mask of
iurodyvyi (the holy fool), which symbolizes the 'irrational' hope against all
reasonable odds.

While the expressed self in its *private* functions regresses into the myth
of a 'pure' childhood, that self in its *public* functions repudiates the myth of
colourful – as aesthetically imagined – Cossacks and hetmans, whom Shevchenko delighted in resurrecting only a few years before. The prophet's
inexorable vision, as it unveils the future, pierces the theatrical trappings of
romantic historiography (in which Shevchenko's contemporary Ukrainian
historians had indulged with such abandon, and which the young poet him-

self adopted so uncritically), to expose the fatal errors of Ukrainian leaders of the seventeenth and the eighteenth centuries, such as their naïve trust in the honesty of their Russian 'Orthodox brothers' or their frequent disregard of the needs of their own dispossessed peasants. Shevchenko's condemnation of his nation's past in the name of the future on the one hand, and, on the other, his idealization of his personal past in view of the bleak future ahead of him as an individual, strengthen the temporal ambiguities which pervade his later work.

In the late poem 'Iurodyvyi,' Shevchenko sketches a skeletal plot, based on an actual episode, dealing with a young rebel – a 'holy fool' – who slaps the face of a high Russian official in a church.[10] Although such an incident did happen, a parallel with Christ's banishment of the money-changers from the temple immediately suggests itself. This parallel is supported by the poet's apostrophe to God the Father, which boldly identifies Him with a 'napping' despot:

A ty, Vsevydiashcheie oko!
Chy ty dyvylosia zvysoka,
Iak sotniamy v kaidanakh hnaly
V Sybir nevolnykiv sviatykh,
Iak morduvaly, rozpynaly
I vishaly. A ty ne znalo?
I ty dyvylosia na nykh
I ne osliplo? Oko, oko!
Ne duzhe bachysh ty hlyboko!
Ty spysh v kioti ...

And you, O all-seeing Eye! / Did you not see from above, / How hundreds of holy prisoners / Were being driven in chains to Siberia? / How they were being tortured, crucified, / And hanged? And you did not know? / And you looked at them / And did not go blind? Oh, Eye! Eye! / You do not see very deeply! / You sleep behind your ciborium.

Upon pronouncing this harsh judgment of the obtuse, indifferent God, the poet declares that he himself will fly to Siberia, in order to undertake, in the *human* way, the task of the ineffectual all-seeing Eye: he will look in order to witness and to speak.

A ia polynu na Sybir,
Azh za Baikal; zahlianu v hory,
V vertepy temnii i v nory,
Bez dna hlybokii, i vas —
Spobornyky sviatoii voli —
Iz tmy, iz smrada i z nevoli,
Tsariam i ludiam na pokaz,
Na svit vas vyvedu ...

But I shall fly to Siberia, / All the way beyond the Baikal; I shall look / Into the mountains, the dark caverns, and bottomless holes, / And I shall lead you into the light, / Out of the darkness and stench of your dungeons, / O defenders of holy liberty, to show you to the tsars and to the people.

The similarity of this monad to central monads in 'Son,' written thirteen years earlier, is immediately apparent: the horizontal flight, the look of an inexorable witness, the holy prisoners in caverns and holes (in 'Son' they include Christ Himself).[11] Nevertheless, in 'Iurodyvyi' the projected profile surrenders its role of a sarcastic but essentially passive observer; instead, it dares to act: to lead out into the light, to resurrect. That activity, in turn, is reminiscent of 'Dumy moi,' with the crucial difference that now the poetic logos resurrects not the aesthetically imagined past glory of the Cossacks but the ethically interiorized present misery of their 'grandchildren': the roles of prophet and magician are united by the energy of a temporal orientation towards the future as political and spiritual liberation.

In Shevchenko's later poetry the projected profile as prophet-magician frequently assumes the mask of Christ as rebel, martyr, defender of the meek, advocate of universal love, suffering son of an institutionalized father, and finally as supreme prophet, master of the logos. The functions of the Christ mask suggest the obligatory ironical bifurcation of profiles. Christ's basic profile is of an illegitimate child;[12] it is characteristic of Shevchenko's development, incidentally, that while Kateryna's illegitimate son is destined to become a minstrel ('Kateryna'), the illegitimate Son of Mary is destined to become the most exalted fighter for freedom. Christ, in his basic profile, is also a martyr: he appears thus in 'Son' and in a number of subsequent works. The following lines from 'Son' embody this basic profile as martyr, with his projected profile implied in a complex ironical move by the designation 'tsar':

> V kaidany ubranyi
> Tsar vsesvitnii! Tsar voli, tsar
> ˏShtempom uvinchanyi.

Chained in fetters is the universal tsar! / The tsar of liberty, the tsar / Crowned by a prisoner's brand.

The following quotation from 'Neofity' (The Neophytes), written thirteen years later, begins with a similar monad. The quotation includes a startling comment on God's and his 'helpers'' attitude to Christ's sacrifice:

> ... I za shcho
> Ioho, sviatoho, morduvaly,
> Vo uzly kuvaly;
> I hlavu ioho chestnuiu
> Ternom uvinchaly?
> I vyvely z zlodiiamy
> Na Holhofu horu;
> I povisyly mizh nymy –
> Za shcho? Ne hovoryt
> Ni sam syvyi Verhhotvorets,
> Ni ioho sviatii –
> Pomoshchnyky, pobornyky,
> Kastraty nimii!

Why did they torture and enchain Him in fetters – / Him, Who is Holy – / And crown His noble head with thorns? / Why did they lead Him together with some thieves / Onto the hill of Golgotha, / To hang Him among them? / For what purpose? The grey-haired Supreme Creator does not answer, / Nor do his saints – / The confessors, the defenders of the faith – / The mute *castrati*!

When we read such passages alongside reveries of Christ's pastoral childhood ('Mariia'), parallels between Christ's destiny and that of the poet himself become quite plain. Even Shevchenko's doubts as to the ultimate purpose of his own sufferings, particularly their historical justification, are implied in the disturbingly irreverent but wholly sympathetic interrogation of the Son of God:

> Narobyv ty, Khryste, lykha!
> A pereinachyv
> Liudei Bozhykh? Kotylysia
> I nashi kozachi
> Durni holovy za pravdu,
> Za viru Khrystovu,
> Upyvalys i chuzhoi,
> I svoiei krovy!
> A poluchshaly? Ba, de to!

You have really started some trouble, Christ! / But have you changed the Christian folk? / Our Cossack heads, too, / Rolled for Christ's truth and the Christian faith, / Having gotten drunk on foreign blood / And on our own! / And did we improve by it? In no way!

The projected profile of Christ's mask is the master of the logos in His final victory, resurrected from the dead to wield His Word on the side of the downtrodden. It is easy to see here parallels to the poet's own attempts to rise above the lethargic scepticism of his basic profile and to consecrate his own word as a weapon in the service of the future. For example, Ukrainians invariably quote the following lines as from Shevchenko's 'I,' although the context quickly shows that they are really spoken by Christ. Hence this excerpt puts the power of poetry and prophecy – the magic of the poet's and of Christ's projected profile – into a particularly acute ambiguity:

> ... vozvelychu
> Malykh otykh rabiv nimykh!
> Ia na storozhi kolo ikh
> Postavliu slovo!

I shall raise / And ennoble these mute, petty slaves! / And I shall place the Word / To guard them.

The mask of Mary exists in an interesting dialectical relationship to Christ on the one hand and, on the other, to the poet's own expressed self. Although we see instances of this in several moments of the *oeuvre*, it is in 'Mariia' that they stand out most plainly. In her basic profile, Mary is a simple, innocent, and rather earthy village maiden; the reader cannot help comparing her to the peasant girl who so frequently plays the role of the poet's ideal reader, muse, and lover, finally becoming a half mask of his expressed self. After Mary, because of her childlike trust in the power of the heart (which likens her to Kateryna), is seduced by an 'institutionalized' prophet, she lovingly rears her son in pastoral surroundings that remind us of the poet's myth of his own childhood. But when she is condemned to witness His execution – the more horrible betrayal of her trust in love, since it ends not in birth but in death – she cannot afford to continue to preserve her rustic anonymity, and her projected profile comes into play: she becomes a public person, gathering together her son's rather shiftless apostles (Ukrainian intellectuals from Shevchenko's environment?), and vigorously disseminating His logos. Parallelling the poet's dismal view of his own future, she finally dies as a forgotten beggar. Mary's public life suggests that she becomes Christ's projected profile, more publicly active than He himself. Shevchenko makes it quite plain, moreover, that without her, Christ's word would have remained unheard: here he reiterates his high regard for the symbol of the mother, and, more important for us, assigns a cardinal role to the feminine principle of spiritual existence, to the *anima* of Christ's and of his own genius.

Earlier in this article I attempted to show how the basic profile ironically 'checks' the projected profile of the poet's expressed self within its private functions. After the above discussion of half masks and full masks of the self in its *public* activity, it will be easier to establish how in that public sphere the basic profile as the martyred poet interrogates the projected profile as the revolutionary prophet. I have already suggested that the scepticism of the basic profile is frequently based on a dim view of Ukraine's historical past and its possible uses in the future. Here is an example of such self-interrogation, which is a part of a long series of monads:

Za shcho zh borolys my z liakhamy?
Za shcho zh my rizalys z ordamy?

Za shcho skorodyly spysamy
Moskovski rebra?

Why did we fight the Poles? / Why did we battle the Tatar hordes? / Why did we
rake / Russian ribs with lances?

Time and again the poet wonders if it would not have made more sense
to have *whole-heartedly* embraced the private sphere of existence, with its
promise of a future in the dream-invested pastoral past, instead of yielding
to the temptation of being witness and ultimately prophet. The nadir of
such disillusionment occurs in passages in which the poet curses those
older friends who have abducted him from the imagined paradise of innocence by teaching him to write poetry; one may compare this to the seduction of Mary by the 'institutionalized' prophet in 'Mariia.' In such passages
we perceive an ironical ambiguity between personal and national freedom,
which will ultimately resolve itself in the poet's realization that the one
cannot exist without the other. Bewailing his lost childlike purity, the poet
curses those who 'besmirched' him by artistic and intellectual encouragement, and now accuse him of 'wavering':

Bo vy mene z sviatoho neba
Vzialy mizh sebe i pysat
Pohani virshi nauchyly!
Vy tiazhkyi kamin polozhyly
Posered shliakhu ...

...

Teper idu ia bez dorohy,
Bez shliakhu bytoho ... A vy!
Dyvuietes, shcho spotykaius,
Shcho vas i doliu proklynaiu.

Because you brought me down from holy heaven / Among yourselves and taught
me to write bad verses! / You put a heavy rock in my path ... / Now I wander
without a way, / Without a high road. ... And you! / You wonder that I stumble, /
That I curse you and my fate.

Note, incidentally, that in the image 'holy heaven' the vertical flight of
Perebendia is directly substituted by reveries of an idealized purity of

childhood and youth. In an epistle to his fellow prisoners, on the other hand, the poet's projected profile in its public functions makes an ironical comment on 'irresponsible' reveries of an anonymous country life:

> Roziidemos, roznesemo
> V stepy, v lisy svoiu nedoliu,
> Poviruiem shche trokhy v voliu,
> A potim zhyty pochnemo
> > Mizh liudmy iak ludy.

We shall go our separate ways and / Carry our common grief into the steppes and into the forests. / For a while we shall go on believing in freedom, / And then we shall begin to live / Like people among people.

In 'Saul,' the public self seems to remind the private self that *it is too late*, and therefore immoral, to dream of such rural anonymity:

> ... A teper
> Pluhamy, ralom ne rozorem
> Prokliatu nyvu: prorosla
> Koluchym ternom ...

Now we are unable to plow the accursed field / Either with wooden or iron plows. / It is overgrown with prickly thistles.

The obvious implication is that plows must be hammered back into swords.

The ironical bifurcation of the expressed self between its public and private spheres of activity, together with the corresponding bifurcation of its profiles, continues until the last poem of *Kobzar*. In that poem, the private sphere – with the projected profile unhesitatingly entering the reverie of a pastoral childhood – is ultimately victorious. After a moving attempt to forestall death, the poet finally declines the kind of old age that literary fame, once so fervently desired, now has to offer: the writing of vapid odes to the throne, probably in the manner of old Derzhavin, or the churning out of honeyed sentimentalist prose. Shevchenko is surprisingly silent on the possibility of a future as prophet, if even an accursed one, implying perhaps that 'prophetic fire' would eventually burn out, leaving only the ashes of hackneyed 'literary production.' Instead, the poet wishes to build a model of his dream-invested past in the absolute futurity of death; he dreams of the intimate space of a small house, transcending and yet implying the grave, on the shores of his beloved Dnipro. It becomes plain that the synthesis of the public and private spheres of activity of the expressed self, let alone the synthesis of its profiles, never occurs.

There is, nevertheless, an implication of such a synthesis, a parched desire for it, on the philosophical level of *Kobzar*. The future of humanity in general and of Ukraine in particular, envisioned by the poet as prophet and as Christ, is based on the model of a village family, particularly mother and son, as epitomized by Mary and Christ. Here is an example of that wish, expressed in words of monumental simplicity:

> I na onovlenii zemli
> Vraha ne bude, supostata,
> A bude syn i bude maty,
> I budut liudy na zemli.

And there will be no enemy on the renewed earth; / There will be the son and the mother, / And people will live on the earth.

Even the angry words of the half mask of Isaiah imply a similar vista of transfigured peasant huts, when the prophet transforms, in the future tense, the harsh hills of Judea into a bucolic Ukrainian landscape:

> I pustyniu opanuiut
> Veselii sela

And the desert will be mastered / By happy villages.

The potential unification of personal past and national future, suggested by the potential unification of the poet's private and the public spheres, implies a unification of linear and cyclic temporality. We may think of it as an arrest of historical time or a utopian transcendence of temporality. On such an ideal level of temporality (or atemporality) history itself will atrophy, stifling the violence and the hatred that it itself necessarily generates: only in such a dream-invested, myth of the national future – as in the dream-invested myth of the personal past – will violence be replaced by universal love.

In the meantime, one is condemned to live among other people, condemned to strive, to suffer, and to die. This in *Kobzar* is the final ironical check of heedless utopian temptations of timelessness. In the early poetry the cyclicity of nature had been translated, provisionally, into the stream of human time by the projected profile of poet-as-magician. But soon that safe framework was shattered by the projected profile's sense of responsibility towards society, which old Perebendia could dispense with but which the young poet could not afford to dismiss. Hence it follows that he could not allow himself the bad faith of total immersion in the past (be it the imagined national past or the equally passionately imagined personal past), since his commitment to his imagined and real readers – to living among people which means caring for them – was much too tenacious for such escape.

Although the synthesis of the expressed self could not be completed for such demanding moral reasons, another and more authentic synthesis calms us by a sense of completion as we close Shevchenko's *Kobzar*. It is founded upon our intuition of the poet's strong prepersonal self, whose energy constantly flows in the various binary oppositions of profiles, masks, temporal dimensions, spatial directions, and spheres of activity. While the bifurcations of the poet's expressed self ironically distance the submerged energy of the prepersonal self, this energy gives the totality of his work a more authentic cohesion than any ideological or formal syntheses could do, embodied as it is in the unity of the writing – the unity of poetic utterance – which makes it possible to treat his entire *oeuvre* as a single poem. But such a unity of expression is not sufficient by itself. The relentless interrogation of the 'sincerity' of the various poses by each other – a 'sincerity' posited only in order to be questioned in the mode of romantic irony which here is a tool and nothing more – is a quest of the prepersonal self for itself as it is progressively unconcealed in language. It is this quest that not only founds but finally transcends the unity of *the book* into the unity of *an authentic life*, as Kierkegaard defined it.

(1974, 1979)

NOTES

1 This is a revised and expanded version of a paper presented at the Ukrainian Academy of Arts and Sciences in New York on 7 April 1974 and at the Uni-

versity of Michigan in Ann Arbor on 17 March 1979. The Ukrainian texts of quotations are taken from the first four volumes of *Povne vydannia tvoriv Tarasa Shevchenka*, 14 vols, eds Pavlo Zaitsev and Bohdan Kravtsiv (Chicago: Mykola Denysiuk 1962-4). All English paraphrases are my own, with the exception of three expressions borrowed from Watson Kirkconnell's translations in *The Collected Works of Taras Shevchenko*, ed. C.H. Andrusyshen (Toronto: University of Toronto Press 1963).

2 Friedrich Schlegel, *Kritische Schriften*, ed. Wolfdietrich Rasch (Munich: Carl Hanser Verlag 1971) 21.

3 Soren Kierkegaard, *The Concept of Irony, with Constant Reference to Socrates*, trans. Lee M. Capel (Bloomington and London: Indiana University Press 1968) 264-5. Although Shevchenko and Kierkegaard, who were contemporaries, could not possibly have known each others' work, the similarity of their thought in many instances is astonishing, and a comparative study of those two minds is sorely needed. Readers familiar with Kierkegaard will recognize several important parallels, outside the sphere of irony, implied in this article.

4 *Ibid.*, 337.

5 *Ibid.*, 338.

6 According to Merleau-Ponty, who based this observation on the thought of Gabriel Marcel, style is the uninterrupted connection between my body and the world: the unity of the body-subject, expressing itself and thus communicating itself to the world by the unity of its habits, manifests a common style of action. From this basis arises the style of my life in which there is expressed a continuous motif. Style both borrows from environment and shapes it. Merleau-Ponty is convinced that the style of a painter's, a poet's, even a philosopher's work is based directly on the style of the life of the body-subject: we 'recognize' his or her style by opening ourselves to those primary levels of experience on which our own deep self can meet his or hers. This conception of style goes directly against the accepted definition of style as a surface assembling and ordering of aesthetic values and devices. See Maurice Merleau-Ponty, *Phenomenology of Perception*, trans. Colin Smith, International Library of Philosophy and the Scientific Method, 144-5, 168-9, 327, *et passim*.

7 Ortega y Gasset is one among many (for example, Marcel, Merleau-Ponty) who define the 'deep' self on the basis of interest or desire. 'Pressing interest,' he claims, is the product of reflective consciousness and hence exists on the surface of 'personality.' The interests of the self *before* personality and its deliberate characteristics, dictated by situations, on the other hand, create a

field of *primal vision*, upon which reflective or thetic consciousness can rest. Fortifying Ortega y Gasset by existentialist thought, we may say that to live authentically, avoiding the self-delusion and bad faith that victimize our 'personality,' means to open ourselves as widely as possible to the influence of our 'deep' self, which never deceives. Needless to say, such a 'prepersonal' level of the self should not be confused with the Freudian subconscious or any of the numerous psychological categories related to it. See Jose Ortega y Gasset, *The Dehumanization of Art, and Other Essays on Culture and Literature* (Princeton: Princeton University Press 1968) 84 *et passim*. Also see note 6 above.

8 According to Heidegger's complex notion of temporal *ek-stase*, man is capable of standing outside his own present, while at the same time remaining in it – at a distance from himself and yet being himself – in order to experience care (*Sorge*) for the time of others. The human being, in other words, transcends his own present, reaching out beyond himself into his own future, which must be the future of others and which comes towards him already charged with his own past, which he shared with others. Hence an individual's present, future, and past create a dynamic system of references and forms, in which a single form implies all the others, thus bracketing the 'chronological sequence' of past, present, and future. Even such a simplified report as mine shows that Heidegger's concept of temporality is closely related to ironic distancing. For the central definition of *ek-static* temporality, see Martin Heidegger, *Being and Time*, trans. John Macquarrie and Edward Robinson (New York: Harper Brothers 1962) 377-8.

9 Shevchenko placed 'Dumy moi' as the opening piece of his first published collection, obviously intending it as a prologue. It is not the first poem written by him, however: dated 1839, it follows such poems as 'Perebendia,' 'Kateryna,' and other important early works.

10 The incident is somewhat changed in 'Iurodyvyi.' A young revolutionary did indeed slap a high official in a church. The 'victim,' however, was not the governor of Ukraine, Dimitrii Gavrilovich Bibikov, as the poem has it, but his secretary, Nikolai Erastovich Pisarev. The event occurred not in Kiev, as Shevchenko claims, but in Petrozavodsk.

11 The fact that commentators have attempted to identify the several appearances of Christ throughout the *oeuvre* with various actual dissenters of Shevchenko's time does not invalidate my argument but, in fact, strengthens it, sharpening as it does the ironical ambiguities between the human and the divine.

12 See Luckyj's article in this volume.

25

An Examination of Shevchenko's Romanticism

LISA EFIMOV SCHNEIDER

Since Fylypovych's article on 'Shevchenko and Romanticism' appeared in the twenties,[1] scholars have been concerned with the term 'romanticism' in analysis of Shevchenko's poetry and the identification of both 'realistic' and 'romantic' qualities, particularly in Shevchenko's early works. These two adjectives are used conventionally to describe literary movements that are historically consecutive and, to an extent, ideologically opposed; thus the appropriateness of their application to Shevchenko's first *Kobzar* has been a problem for critics. The following argument suggests that the 'realistic' elements in Shevchenko's earliest work represent his conscious effort to qualify the meaning of romanticism to his contemporary readers. In doing so, Shevchenko established a culturally responsible Ukrainian romanticism that contrasted greatly with the gaps between western romantic literary theory and poetic practice.

Ukrainian literary historians generally assign to Shevchenko a role analogous to that which Russian critics perceive for Pushkin – that of a bridge between the romantic and realistic periods.[2] Within such a framework, Shevchenko's early poems – especially those in the first *Kobzar* (1840) – are considered to represent his romantic idiom. Nonetheless, this particular critical pigeon-hole, which at first seems to clarify the general qualities of these poems, actually brings definitions and implications into the critical analysis which ultimately make the significance of Shevchenko's work harder to explain.[3]

M.K. Kotsiubynska has done more than merely justify the inclusion of Shevchenko among the romantics. She also has discerned many important features of Shevchenko's poems – qualities of realism, humanism, and simplicity – that set his work apart from the romantic norm.[4] In her view, Shevchenko understood the broad trends in European literature and, more important, was able to distil their intricacies into poetry that remains uniquely Ukrainian.

Although some scholars believe it is important to distinguish among national romanticisms,[5] others regard the term 'European romanticism' as an accepted critical category.[6] In Western Europe, romanticism represented a critical change in a long-established artistic tradition. If we use romanticism as a critical category in our discussion of Ukrainian literature, however, we must keep in mind that Ukrainian culture lacked such a tradition.[7] Shevchenko's early works cannot be described as embodying a literary metamorphosis of the European kind because the literary environments preceding romanticism in Western Europe and in Ukraine were quite different. Western European romanticism was based, in part, on opposition to the rational and ordered classical school; Ukrainian classicism had roots mainly in the burlesque travesty, in 'low' genres, and in the use of the vernacular and the mock epic style.[8] The popularity of such literature in Ukraine contrasts starkly with Western European attitudes towards such elements.

Hence it could be argued that Ukrainian romanticism was a less radical, more logical sequel to its particular brand of classicism than was Western romanticism, which overturned previous notions of aesthetics and form. Among the strikingly 'new' interests of European romantics were concern with the vernacular, irony, use of folk life and customs for literary content, and allusions to historic events and personalities, but these very features were already prominent in Ukrainian classicism.[9] The passion and emotional excess that characterizes Western romanticism is like the mock heroic style typical of Ukrainian classicism.

The difference between these two classicisms is significant for the literary history of the following generation. Western European romantic writers fought for freedom in both a formal and psychological sense; their new recognition of the value of the individual personality, based on philosophical and political experience, in turn demanded changes in form and aesthetics. However radical these demands became, they never threatened the very existence of literature, since respect for the ordered creativity of man's intellect was part of the heritage of European classicism. The upheavals that took place in all facets of early nineteenth-century European life were so fruitful in artistic terms precisely because of this tradition of artistic self-respect, which becomes (albeit in a different form) the central philosophy of romanticism.

The situation was quite different in Ukraine; confidence in and serious respect for artists or art had not been established. The burlesque tradition generated mockery of national customs and history.[10] The primitive language of the travesties revealed a painful lack of linguistic sophistication and a seemingly narrow scope of literary endeavour that such a language could sustain. While Western European romantic writers tried to make the literary language from the classical period closer to that of the common people, Shevchenko and his contemporaries struggled in the opposite direction; that is, they sought to create a new language from the 'base materials' of the travesties and folk speech. The Ukrainians were not simply trying to adapt literature to new philosophical exigencies, but to prevent literature from dying altogether.

The struggle of Ukrainian romantic writers against the lack of respect which the travesties show for the language and life of the people was a matter of greater political and social significance than anywhere else in Europe. Herder's work and the writings of the brothers Grimm enhanced the political strength and national potential already existing in Germany. In Ukraine, however, the romantics' interest in folk culture and folk literature represented a frustrating attempt to nurture and develop the most substantive as well as the most fragile and vulnerable elements of life.

Thus the tasks demanded of Ukrainian romantic writers by their own literary history were far different from those which their Western European counterparts confronted. Ukrainian writers of this period were not engaged in the happy uncovering of their heritage – as were writers in Germany, Scotland, and France – but were trying to wrest artistic life from its cultural subservience to Western Europe and, more significantly, to Russia. Russia's political domination of Ukraine and its success in tempting away Ukrainian intellectuals further endangered Ukrainian literary life.

From this point of view, the realism (or what has been seen by critics as romanticism imbued with startling realism) in Shevchenko's early work can be more easily understood.[11] He did not aim to emulate Western European romantics, to revel in idiosyncratic psychological probings or extol excesses of feeling as the hallmark of the new sensitive man; such concerns were entirely inappropriate for the situation in Ukraine, where neither the philosophical nor the sociopolitical basis for such writings existed. Shevchenko was faced instead with the task of making the language and life of Ukraine viable in literary terms and worthy of interest. His first *Kobzar* indicates that he realized this necessity and began with a romanticism attuned to reality.[12] He did not have to strive for contact with his own folk culture, nor was the history of this culture a new or adopted concern for him. Both the past and present realities of Ukrainian life were living experiences for Shevchenko; thus his poetry reflects the fertile imagination and talent of an individual whose life was defined by this greater national life.

The 'boudoir and salon' were as foreign to Shevchenko as the 'field and hillside' must have been to the first sentimental writers, and in reality he was at home with the 'simple uneducated rustic' who, despite Wordsworth's attention and interest, remained for Western romantics largely a highly malleable ideal. Many other strictly biographical elements establish Shevchenko as the ideal romantic artist, in contrast to his Western contemporaries for whom the romantic quest began as a search for the real world, in place of the artificial classical salon. Shevchenko's actual experiences of imprisonment, exile, solitude, and suffering again place him at the heart of romanticism's concerns. Such experiences, for most Western romantics, were felt only in the life of the mind. (Real as this mental and emotional realm may be, it is nonetheless one that may be altered and moulded, taking its shape by the free force of the imagination. I do not wish to imply that experience in the imagination is less meaningful than real physical events, but to suggest that the quality of purposeful choice is significant for distinguishing the two spheres of experience.) One of Shevchenko's refrains is that of both personal and national *dolia*, that is, the fate or destiny that brings about events that cannot be imagined away. His own isolation and pain did not stem from a particular *Weltanschauung*, but from the political and social situation in which he found himself; the immediacy of these experiences is evident in the unflinching honesty of his poetic treatment of suffering.

Wordsworth's seclusion at Grasmere and Byron's exploits in Greece show that these great romantic figures embraced their philosophies so closely that they chose to live in accordance with their inner spiritual priorities. The particular power of Shevchenko's personal situation, however, is that there was no such choice to make. Western romantics had the luxury of seeking alternative kinds of expression for their inner feelings and were encouraged by a relatively educated and tolerant public, while Shevchenko represents a literary voice fighting for its right to speak in a largely unreceptive environment.

The poems of the first *Kobzar* seek what is of value in the life of the world; moreover, they are comprehensible and accessible in a manner that contrasts sharply with the self-centred nature of Western European romantic lyricism. A great factor in Shevchenko's accessibility is undoubtedly his language, which possesses 'simplicity, not as the opposite of complexity, but as limpid and crystallized complexity.'[13] This crystallization works on a linguistic and symbolic level. In addition to suffering, the *Kobzar* treats a range of emotions and abstractions – sorrow, motherhood, sin, isolation, freedom, fate, and the past – through symbols whose metaphoric force is not diminished or confused by elaborate or artificial qualification. At the same time, the poems never become 'everyman' types of allegory, because the symbols are used in a specific situation, thus giving them immediacy and strength.[14]

For the reasons stated in these introductory remarks, I use in a qualified sense the literary categories romantic and realistic. I will show that the poems in Shevchenko's early *Kobzar* reflect the most basic tenets of the romantic movement – the importance of love, emotionalism, national consciousness, folk speech and culture, and attention to history – but in a manner that is rooted in real experience, because Shevchenko's social responsibility as a writer was the most vital aspect of his creation of literature. Since their culture was already firmly literary, Western romantic writers were free to translate private experience into art. They became idiosyncratic and extreme with regard to those aspects of style that cause Shevchenko to appear as a romantic realist on account of his sensitivity to his own milieu. In short, Western European romantic literature can be thought of as personal experience universalized, while Shevchenko's poetry represents universal experience made personal, and, thus, made real.

The most striking example of this personalization is the character of the kobzar, the blind folk minstrel who is both an orphan – that is, a social outcast – and a social necessity. Luckyj describes this dual function by pointing to a change evident in Shevchenko's presentation: 'What only a decade earlier was considered by Ukrainian intellectuals to be the prerogative of folk poetry in which the blind kobzar was the "father of poetry," became in Shevchenko's poem a new form – the minstrel turned into an archetypal figure of wise man and teacher.'[15] The figure of the wise blind man is at least as old as that of Tiresias, who spoke truth to Oedipus, but Shevchenko's kobzar is not absolute truth incarnate, to be feared as a supernatural being. The kobzar retains his humanness and is an integral part of everyday life. His songs and stories do not shock or paralyse; they merge subtly into the consciousness of his audience more like a Christian parable than a sudden revelation.

It is, in fact, the kobzar's constant communication with the common people which sets him apart from the romantic image of the poet as one whose revelations are incomprehensible to the mob and whose sensibility cannot bear the crudity of the social audience. This Western image of the artist emerges, I think, from a failure to distinguish romanticism as aesthetic theory and romanticism as a philosophy of life. Such confusion results in a suspension of life somewhere between the real world and the artistic ideal. The romantic poet has access to truths which are above the common ability to comprehend, and his social responsibility must be sacrificed in deference to the elevated romantic world.

In Western romantic literature, the image of the wandering poet is a more complex version of this idea; the wanderer does not sacrifice his social role even though he feels uncomfortable in it. Hugo identifies Goethe's Torquato Tasso as the first modern reincarnation of this ancient literary type, describing him as 'the creative individual who finds himself a marked man. Genius is his, as well as the respect of his benefactors; and they gladly bestow the laurel crown upon his brow. But he feels an apartness from them that they cannot be expected to understand.'[16] This 'apartness' is unlike the proud superiority of the antisocial poet; it is spiritual rather than intellectual or ideological. Moreover, there is a distance not only between the poet and his patrons or society but also between the poet as social servant and as private creative personality. According to Hartman, the healing of this split in the poet's sense of self is one of the chief motivating forces in romantic poetry; it is in the search for 'unity of being' that the poet becomes a wanderer.[17] This split is also felt in the identification of the poetic 'I.' 'In a lyric poem,' writes Hartman,

it is not the first person that moves us, but rather the 'I' to which that 'I' reaches. The very confusion in modern literary theory concerning the fictive 'I' whether it represents the writer as person or as persona, may reflect a dialectic inherent in poetry between the relatively self-conscious self and that self within the self which resembles Blake's 'emanation' and Shelley's 'epipsyche.'[18]

The poem 'Dumy moi,' which begins Shevchenko's first collection, is an exploration of these problems of identity and the relationship between identity and creativity. From the outset we hear a voice so different from that of a Western romantic poet; there is no musing on the experience of inspiration, nor complaint about the fickle nature of insight. The attention is not entirely on the poet as potential creator – the poetry is already written, almost self-created, and stands as a character in its own right, listening, as it were, to the poet's lament. There is another distancing of the poetic 'I' from his work, since it is not the poet but misfortune or affliction (*lykho*) which gave birth to his lines. The poet is simply their caretaker, the one who weeps over them. It would have been better, he says, if the poems had been destroyed, because then his sorrow would not be public, and no one could accuse him of burdening others. Despite the disarming simplicity of these lines, complex internal struggles are introduced in this first section. The 'I' of the poem is ambivalent about his creations: they are children of misfortune, but they are also his own; he wishes they had been drowned by tears or swept away by the wind, but he also cared for and nurtured them with tears. He wants his anguish to be private, but this very plea on paper makes it public. The effect of this ambivalence is to make the reader feel that he is somehow an interloper and privy to the poet's secrets, although his access to them is through the public medium of the printed page. Herein lies the poetic split: the poet who records this outpouring is clearly not the same as the 'I' in the poem who does not want the record to exist. As a result of the relationship between the two, the poet's dilemma is powerfully expressed, more so than in the standard romantic literary form, through which intimate emotions are meant to be public because their expression is unmediated by any other persona.

This split continues in the following section of the poem. The lines are both the poet's own work, set down in finished and ordered form, and also something separate and impressionistic – a collection of thoughts and memories about dark eyes, dark nights, the caresses of a young girl, a green cherry orchard, Cossack history, burial mounds, and the black eagle of Russia watching overhead – motifs which appear in the other poems of the collection. The poetic 'I' of the poem, however, continues to stress his distance from the poetry itself by claiming that he can only weep, that he has no words for any other kind of expression of his sorrow, and that no one will notice or ridicule him if his thoughts take the form of birds. Finally, a kind of resolution of the divided 'I' occurs when the poet sends his thoughts home to Ukraine, where they will be received not with mockery but with love and tenderness. Even so, an element of separation remains; the poems go on alone, while the poet stays in exile. Their future may be fortunate, but he awaits only death.

Thus, in this poem we encounter the poet as a double – there exists an 'I' that records, orders, and forms what the other 'I' feels and experiences. This split is resolved in the contrasting images of the people who ridicule the poet and the homeland where his words are cherished. This is a statement about national loyalty and the loneliness of exile that hints of a theme recurring in the other poems: the ideal society is characterized by sympathy and love, and the ideal homeland is the place where one's sorrows, rather than isolate, bind one more closely with others who are able to offer comfort. This homeland is the place where the poet becomes whole again, the place towards which the poet-wanderer is headed. The poet's temporary 'apartness' is necessary in the process because there are words and truths which must be left unsaid.

The poem 'Perebendia' presents the same split with a more narrow point of view. A narrator-poet who is free from the double situation structures the two visions of Perebendia so that the character's social and private natures are distinguished clearly. His social responsibility is to entertain and to teach the past. He does this in specific social settings – on the street, under a tree, at a banquet or bazaar – but even in these places, singing his familiar songs, he is not entirely at home. The question posed in the second line – 'Khto ioho ne znaie?' (Who does not know him?) – is, therefore, not simply a way of describing his familiarity. It suggests that although everyone recognizes his function, no one is privy to the poetic experiences which inspire his song. In the centre of the social world, where he is thanked for his role, he is, nonetheless, a homeless orphan. In addition to his historic folk songs, he also sings about Lazarus. This alludes to his loneliness and homelessness and also imbues his teaching with a prophetic quality. Rather than convey a specifically Christian message, these allusions indicate that his singing about the past is subtly identified with a sense of new life and truth.

These references also link with the second section of the poem in which Perebendia, free from the confines of his social role, is able to communicate with the universe. Only at this point in the poem does the reader realize how static and uneventful the initial section is, despite the crowds of people and the many songs. Shevchenko's mastery in effecting this change is evident in the longer, more free-flowing lines and in the greater concentration of active verbs in the second section. Even more striking is the description of the wild setting – the boundless ocean of steppe with its infinite succession of burial mounds, where the kobzar sits and sings his solitary song – that gives a feeling of the real Ukrainian land and also creates an otherworldly sense of a total wilderness, where nature and God are no longer mysteries. Amid such surroundings, the kobzar does not essentially change; he retains his laughter and tears that symbolise the dual nature of human experience. He sings on the steppe because he has the unique gift of divine communication, and, on a more realistic level, because he can sing in isolation without fear of social intrusion. In this isolation, Perebendia becomes privy to nature's intimate secrets and speaks with divine words. But the poetic narrator, who initially seemed impersonal, then intervenes and declares that our insensitivity is so complete that we would laugh even at this holy and liberated song. Thus, we are again reminded of our ambivalent relationship to the poet: we recognize him only insofar as he lives among us and assumes a pleasing and comfortable role in our lives, while we prefer not to hear his other song.

Perebendia's essence – and, indeed, the meaning of his social role – is in his isolated, divinely inspired song and in the strength he derives from singing it alone. Perebendia is so profound an image precisely because Shevchenko avoids the standard romantic convention of portraying a poet who is completely antisocial as a result of a unique vision, or is, like Walter Scott's Last Minstrel, a wanderer whose role is solely to relate historical events. Perebendia is clearly archetypal, and the structure of the poem indicates that the significance of the archetype must not be narrowed: the poet is both profound and simple, inspired and mundane, known and unknown. Although the crowd cannot understand poetic creativity, Perebendia respects his social role and continues to sing among the people.

Returning to the idea of resolution in Shevchenko's poetry, we see that, since this resolution is both social and poetic, it must take place within the world, among people, and not through any intervention of the supernatural. This is why the humanizing of Shevchenko's archetypal kobzar is so significant.

The essentially human kobzar figure is a powerful image that permits more than a social or psychological resolution. A comparison with Scott's *The Lay of the Last Minstrel* shows that Shevchenko's creation of a socially bound kobzar also affects the view of history expressed in the poems and indicates a particular poetic technique. The opening lines of Scott's work suggest a great similarity between Shevchenko's image of the wandering poet and the Western one:

> The way was long, the wind was cold,
> The Minstrel was infirm and old;
> His withered cheek, and tresses gray,
> Seemed to have known a better day;
> The harp, his sole remaining joy,
> Was carried by an orphan boy.
> The last of all the bards was he,
> Who sung of border chivalry;
> A wandering harper, scorned and poor,
> He begged his bread from door to door;
> And tuned, to please a peasant's ear,
> The harp a king had loved to hear.[19]

Differences, however, soon become apparent. Scott's Minstrel says that the experience of the past can be had only at night, if one takes a solitary path leading to old ruined buildings and gazes on them by moonlight. In other words, the historical events which the Minstrel is about to relate live on only in the dark, sepulchral, and mysterious world of dreams and spirits. In contrast, Shevchenko's kobzar tells his tales by day in the most bustling and energetic situations. There is nothing mysterious or unreal about the history the kobzar sings, so that, for him and for his audience, history is an appropriate part of life. Like the kobzar, Scott's Minstrel is sad, but largely for himself and for the loss of his past glory. The Minstrel is an unusual character, the last representative of the minstrels who frequented the courts of kings, while the kobzar represents a completely natural and familiar element in Ukrainian life. He has always been part of the scene and has not undergone the personal turn of fortune of Scott's character; he is a real social constant. Scott's figure stands for the unusual and, therefore, for the 'romantic,' but also for a kind of history that is timebound; an episode from the past serves simply as an evening's entertainment for a noble lady.

Scott's introductory comments to the *Lay* express his intention to describe 'scenery and manners'; he concludes with a statement about the poetic medium that seemed most suitable: 'the Poem was put into the mouth of an ancient Minstrel, the last of his race, who, as he is supposed to have survived the Revolution, might have caught somewhat of the refinement of modern poetry without losing the simplicity of his original model.'[20] Clearly, the Minstrel is a device whose purpose is to justify certain formal and linguistic innovations, and Scott's explanations emphasize the experimental nature of romantic poetry.

The poet's extreme consciousness of his craft often interferes with appreciation of the poem, since it is difficult for the reader to forget the technical reasoning behind the work; the new poetic territory explored by romanticism does not justify such authorial intervention. Shevchenko was as radical and exploratory as his Western counterparts, but he never attempts in the *Kobzar* to mediate between his readers and his poems. Perebendia is presented without explanation or interpretation, and this enhances greatly the symbolism and spontaneity of Shevchenko's work.

The differences between Scott's Minstrel and Shevchenko's kobzar are evident in the kind of history they sing. It is well known that Scott was the most important proponent of the idea, exemplified in his historical novels, that national history is a proper literary concern. (Of course, European classicism used historical themes, but had presented mythologized history, that is, personalities and events were exaggerated according to the prevailing hyperbolic style.) The main point of Scott's treatment of historical themes was to relate past events in a less stylized and freer form, as well as to recreate past experience by careful attention to details of local description, to linguistic accuracy, and to the depiction of ordinary behaviour and manners.

The *Lay* is almost a catalogue of such details: names of people and places and descriptions of ambience and action are connected by a narrative so long and complex that one must, in the end, question the success of the device – the Minstrel and the noble Lady (his audience) as a narrative frame. In the preface Scott provided the rationale for such a device, but it must be stressed that knowledge of the poet's purpose may elicit an intellectual curiosity in readers at the same time as it creates a barrier between the reader and the poetic work. The qualities most readily associated with a minstrel's lay – spontaneity, simplicity, and laconism – are nearly destroyed by such formal and contextual incongruities.

Finally, the Minstrel's audience – a noble Lady and her household – indicates the focus of such historical writing: it is for the refined and the educated, for those who have the leisure to listen; in short, for those who are happily removed from everyday cares and direct social involvement. And, judging from his lament that he must now sing 'to please a peasant's ear,' the Minstrel prefers the courts of kings, where he formerly gave his performances. Thus the history he sings has little social import; its purpose is to entertain with recollections of the past.

In Shevchenko's poetry, history has a much broader social significance. The historical poems in the first *Kobzar* – 'Tarasova nich,' 'Ivan Pidkova,' and 'Do Osnovianenka' – differ radically from Scott's, yet they reflect Herder's belief that the relationship between the history of a culture and its identity can be fully experienced only through authentic folk speech. The importance in Shevchenko's poems of folk cultural experience for validating individual feeling[21] is equalled by the importance of historical experience, which validates and illuminates communal or social feelings.[22] In 'Tarasova nich,' for example, we see the kobzar seated at a crossroads – a familiar setting. The timeless image of youth at a crossroads listening to the song of a wise old man makes a dynamic scene that increases the reader's expectation of an imminent truth.[23]

Shevchenko uses couplets when the kobzar actually narrates, each alluding very broadly to the battle against the Poles. This gives the impression that the audience is intimately familiar with these events and that no more than a hint is necessary to evoke the historic image. (Scott, on the other hand, provides historically arcane details.) The poem then describes not the details of battle but the spirit of the Cossacks' fight against oppression. In this description also, the connection with the audience is illustrated by a kind of code-word system derived from the folk song: the personification of Ukraine; the evocation of the sea, wind, and hills; and the repetition of lines beginning with 'Obizvavsia' that indicate the response of the heroes. Finally, the imagery of burial mounds stained with Cossack blood frame the historic event in verbal structures that are instantly recognizable and thus personally meaningful. In contrast to Scott's Minstrel, who says that history must be encountered in the mystery of night and ruins, the kobzar's song is immediately and vividly active in the life of the day. It is accessible and meaningful to anyone who passes the crossroads and is, in fact, meant for the 'peasant's ear' which, for the Minstrel, is a symbol of degeneration.[24]

In 'Do Osnovianenka,' Shevchenko appeals to his friend and contemporary Kvitka to write about Ukrainian history because, as an exile, he claims to be too helpless and too open to scorn to accomplish the task himself. Preceding this appeal, however, Shevchenko offers a personal lament for the past, which is similar to 'Ivan Pidkova' and 'Tarasova nich' in its use of the standard folk imagery and vocabulary described above. This imagery is used consistently and much like a formula, while the non-historical poems in the collection are, by contrast, free from this idiom. A few lines at the end of Shevchenko's lament reveal that this kind of writing is iconic in nature, deriving its power from the immediate recognisability of its form and features. The functional pronoun is not the poetic 'ia' but the collective 'my': 'nasha duma, nasha pisnia / I chyi my dity.' The historic song, therefore, is the expression of a communal consciousness and thus eternal.

The final four lines of the song are unadorned, simple, yet truthful; here the significant words are that the song is 'bez khytroi movy' (without cunning language). The linguistic contrivance and striving for effect – with which Scott and Wordsworth are most concerned in their theoretical writings – seem undesirable in light of Shevchenko's use of the adjective 'khytra' in this most important song. By rejecting this kind of intellectual concern, Shevchenko illustrates Herder's claim – that the truth of a culture lies in the merging of its historical experience with the ordinary language of the people.[25]

For this reason, Shevchenko's symbols need no further explication by the poet. In the poem 'Topolia,' for instance, we encounter the archetypal kobzar who, in speaking about love, tells his story in terms of a folk symbol – that of a poplar tree standing alone in a field and saddening every passerby because it is isolated. On closer examination, we see that, on another level, the poetic treatment of this simple folk tale actually concerns the distinction between rational and social knowledge and inner spiritual knowledge. This dilemma is first put in terms of foreknowledge: the kobzar suggests that if the girl had known what would happen she would never have fallen in love. Then the kobzar tells her it is best not to question fate, because the heart knows who to love no matter what else follows; it is better to do the heart's bidding than to try to avoid sorrow. Just as the girl's heart told her to love, so too it continued to 'know' that grief would come even when the lovers were happiest.

After the inevitable separation, the girl stops singing and is 'orphaned' although she is still with her family. This idea recurs in Shevchenko's poetry and is linked closely with the vision of the ideal society discussed above: one is an orphan when one is removed from real love. All too often the so-called love of family members for each other is no more than the rational relationship between members of society rather than a genuine spiritual affinity. Thus, the mother does not ask why her daughter is unhappy; she instead 'does what she knows,' which is to plan another advantageous marriage for her daughter. Because her own mother does not show true concern, the witch to whom the girl goes for help becomes a more natural mother who understands the girl's grief, since her own youthful experiences have not been forgotten. In this way, standard romantic imagery is overturned: the witch's advice cannot be interpreted as evil or destructive because it is motivated by real concern. The potion she gives to the girl crystallizes her into the fulness of her experience, so that she becomes the symbol of tragic love, graceful, isolated, yet one with nature.

Here Shevchenko also inverts the standard literary device of pathetic fallacy: nature does not mirror mood, but mood becomes a part, a fact of nature. Romantic pathetic fallacy was ambiguous on account of its complex attitude towards nature. On the one hand, nature became mightier and grander than man, diminishing his significance, and, on the other hand, nature involved itself in the expression of individual temperament and events. In Shevchenko's poem, nature is no longer a metaphor; it is a new incarnation of the human spirit in its most tragic situation – that of lost love.[26]

Most critics point out that Shevchenko's symbolism is drawn largely from folklore. He does not, however, rely wholly on the folkloric meaning; he constantly restructures and reclarifies each symbol in various poetic

contexts. For instance, 'Topolia' illustrates how Shevchenko creates a
meaningful and original ambience for the symbol so that its connotation is
clear without dissection.[27] By this process, the symbols are demythologized
and made real, and each new use of a particular symbol continues the
clarifying process.

This poem also shows how different Shevchenko's ideas about love are
from those typical of Western European romanticism. In the Western
literature of the period, love is almost entirely on a personal level – between man and woman – rather than familial or social; moreover, it frequently has sadistic, vengeful, or pathological results.[28] Although there is
little happy love in Shevchenko's poetry (except, perhaps, between mother
and child), he always examines the meaning of love within the bounds of
its social ramifications; romantic love therefore cannot be separated from
other kinds of love relationship. For example, in 'Topolia' and 'Kateryna,'
the tragic conclusion is precipitated by the insensitivity of the heroine's
family, not by the ill-fated love affair. Kateryna's parents cause her to be
an orphan because they are unable to withstand social censure, and they in
turn are orphaned by casting her out. Once lack of love breaks up a
family, all its members suffer.

In Western European romantic literature, the idea of good and evil is
usually presented in extreme terms that mirror the characters' extreme
emotional states. This approach tends to produce either Byronic shock
literature, in which the primary characters are ruled by a single passion, or
allegorical works or typological writing such as Wordsworth's *Lucy*
poems and Mary Shelley's *Frankenstein*, in which the characters give stock
responses to their situation. Since Shevchenko used elemental symbols in
specific socially oriented situations, judgments about responsibility, guilt,
and good and evil are less appropriate to his poetry than to the works of
these Western writers. In 'Kateryna' the parents are not condemned outright or made to appear evil for their harshness. The mother's speech as
she rejects her daughter does show some tenderness and love. This inten-
sifies the tragedy, however; if a mother can subject herself and her daughter to such pain, it is not surprising that Kateryna's Russian lover should
be capable of similar cruelty. Thus, it may be concluded that Shevchenko
rejects the romantic notion that the only love worthy of poetic or literary
attention is an unhappy affair between a man and a woman; that he believes the truth of love to be in the social structure as a whole, whose rules

of what is acceptable or desirable work, unfortunately, to destroy the very relationships it is its duty to support.

In 'Kateryna' we see how Shevchenko avoids certain romantic conventions, especially as practised by Russian writers. From the Russian point of view, romantic heroism means that Byronic types like Lermontov's Pechorin stand by unmoved while the young native girls they have seduced suffer and are destroyed. In Shevchenko's poem the artificiality and, indeed, the immorality of this kind of posture becomes apparent. The actions of the Russian soldier, stripped of all Byronic psychological and emotional trappings, are shown to be cruel and abhorrent. Readers must make a leap from reality before they can find such a character interesting or attractive.

With regard to 'Kateryna,' one more point must be made that again emphasizes the spontaneous quality of Shevchenko's work, in contrast to the self-consciousness of his European counterparts. Wordsworth is the European poet most akin to Shevchenko, at least in his intentions. In the famous *Preface to the Lyrical Ballads*, Wordsworth writes: 'the majority of the following poems are to be considered as experiments. They were written chiefly with a view to ascertain how far the language of conversation in the middle and lower classes of society is adapted to the purpose of poetic pleasure.'[29] He goes on to say that the language of the common people may be even more expressive of emotions and passions than literary language because it is used habitually to relate emotional experience and is unadulterated by an educated sensibility. Thus Wordsworth's and Shevchenko's positions are much the same: both exhibit an interest in writing in ordinary language about ordinary life, and both are concerned with using elements of realism to portray the ignored beauty of the life of the common folk.

The title of Wordsworth's 'The Emigrant Mother' suggests a Shevchenko-like theme, and the poem itself – a lonely Frenchwoman's song to a strange child about the separation from her own child – testifies to Wordsworth's genuine concern for expressing feelings and experiences more human and natural than those explored by Byronic verse. The impact of the poem, however, is entirely altered by the introductory stanzas describing the intention of the poet, who has seen the woman visit a neighbour's child:

Once having seen her clasp with fond embrace
This Child, I chanted to myself a lay,

> Endeavouring in our English tongue, to trace
> Such things as she unto the Babe might say ...

The emphasis here is on the poetic activity and not on the woman who is the central image of the poem. Guided by this emphasis, our reaction to the whole becomes a reaction to the experience of the poet rather than to his work, since the sensations described in the song are Wordsworth's and not the woman's. It could be argued that, on one level, Shevchenko's 'Topolia' works in the same way; that is, the poet (represented by the kobzar) tells his story of the poplar tree, or endows the central symbol with poetic meaning by making it the touchstone for his own imagined experience. But we must look for a deeper interpretation in order to account for the most important elements of 'Topolia.'

First, the distinction already described between the kobzar and the intellectual poet of the Western European romantic tradition indicates that the kobzar sings of real rather than imagined experience. Thus although the kobzar's introductory lines in 'Topolia' function as a statement of the emotional problem of love – the subject of the poem – the natural image of the tree in a familiar landscape immediately symbolizes the theme, and there is no sense in which the poet is felt to be manipulating the situation. He is simply recording what is there for all to see.

Second, since Shevchenko's, or rather, the kobzar's introduction fits formally and thematically into the rest of the text, the story of the young girl follows naturally and without a shift in point of view. Wordsworth's poem, in contrast, is not only disconnected from its introduction by the emphasis on poetic craft, but also by a change in form: the poem proper is a song,[30] an artificial form that curtails the spontaneity of language.

Third, there is nothing exotic about the young girl in 'Topolia,' nothing about her experience that is unnatural or intriguing in the romantic sense. By the inclusion of touchingly simple and human details, her encounter with the old witch (which approximates a stock romantic situation) does not become a venture into the supernatural. The lines 'Pishla b ia utopy-las – Zhal dushu zhubyty' (I would go and drown myself, but I don't want to lose my soul) are an excellent example of this control. The poignancy of the girl's naïve concern for her soul's immortality contrasts profoundly with the almost flippant romantic attitude towards suicide and death.

Wordsworth perhaps felt that a simple portrait of a mother singing to someone else's child might prove uninteresting. That his character is not simply French, but was 'driven from France' suggests political intrigue. She lives in 'a lonely hamlet,' and is further alienated in this romantically evocative setting.

Despite these differences, it can be said that Shevchenko's poem is romantic. The unusual use of nature symbolism, the central theme of tragic love, the isolated main character, and the seemingly supernatural conclusion all testify to Shevchenko's awareness of the literary power of such elements. At the same time, these elements could be called realistic and indicate that the poem does not depend entirely on a romantic formula. 'Topolia' retains the natural, real, and simple quality that Wordsworth sacrifices – despite his better intentions – for the sake of 'poetic pleasure'; moreover, Shevchenko's poem gains immediacy and power without the formal and thematic explanations of 'The Emigrant Mother.' The search for innovative forms and techniques, which often seems to be the primary reason Wordsworth wrote many of his poems, is apparent in Shevchenko's works only when the reader is aware of the poems' historical context.

Through comparison of Shevchenko's 'Kateryna' and Wordsworth's 'The Mad Mother,' we again see how different is the two poets' romanticism. In both poems a woman who has been rejected by her husband or lover wanders about talking to her child. As with 'The Emigrant Mother,' the Western writer feels that the basic situation does not provide enough viable poetic material. Hence Wordsworth uses madness as a device to heighten the drama of the woman's plight. Moreover, in the following lines it is suggested that the mother's insanity has been inherited by her child:

> Where art thou gone, my own dear child?
> What wicked looks are those I see?
> Alas! Alas! that look so wild,
> It never, never came from me.

In both Shevchenko's and Wordsworth's poems, the 'sins of the fathers are visited on the sons,' but Wordsworth also introduces madness in keeping with the romantic interest in the unusual, the mysterious, and the unnatural. Madness has no social significance in the poem; it functions as a purely poetic and richly connotative device suggesting genius or inspiration, or it functions as a shocking contrast with the normal serenity of motherhood.

Shevchenko, however, treats the same situation quite differently. Kateryna remains a social being; her sin is not peculiar or strange, nor is her response to the ensuing isolation. Indeed, the power of her story comes from her constant efforts to re-establish some sort of social normalcy by searching for another family – that of her lover. Even her parents tell her, when they banish her, that she should make a home with her mother-in-law. Thus she dies not because her emotional pain is unendurable, but because she is unable to find that home (see the foregoing discussion of 'Dumy moi') in which she would be accepted despite her social 'sin.' Kateryna's pleas to her lover are the outpourings of her panic in the most real sense and, even before the conclusion, they signify with great power that the fight she has sustained so long, through the strength of her love and trust, is hopeless.

That her son becomes the companion of an aged kobzar underlines both the social nature of Kateryna's tragedy and also the ambiguous relationship between the kobzar and his community. The child, like Kateryna, cannot find a place in society; he must remain an outcast and an 'orphan,' in all the senses which Shevchenko gives this word. At the same time, however, the child does share the social function of the poet, receives sustenance from the audience and is companion to the kobzar's sorrow. Thus, the poem's realistic elements make it a more truthful statement about human relationships. Shevchenko has offered insight into man's cruelty and suffering rather than mere description of emotions.

Although madness is an interesting theme, Wordsworth's 'Mad Mother' lies far from our experience and hence summons only an intellectual reaction. Shevchenko's 'Kateryna,' on the other hand, describes such an undeniable reality that an intellectual reaction is nearly impossible. To the extent that romanticism sought, in an authentic way, to penetrate the fundamental meaning of human emotion and spiritual experience by analysing man's internal state, we may regard 'Kateryna' as a successful romantic poem. 'Dumy moi,' 'Perebendia,' 'Topolia,' and 'Kateryna' express romanticism's concerns so well that, in comparison, a great discrepancy becomes evident between the stated intentions of Western European romantics and their final poetic product. Unfortunately, to bridge this gap, Western writers resorted to contrivance. Honest revelation, however, is the chief characteristic that we expect of the romantic movement, and it is the most outstanding feature of Shevchenko's poems in the early *Kobzar*.

(1978)

NOTES

1 This article was first published as 'Shevchenko i romantyzm,' in *Zapysky Istorychno-filolohichnoho viddilu VUAN*, kn. 4 (Kiev 1924) 3-18. (The present article was written for this volume [ed.].)

2 The leading works are Dmytro Čyževs'kyj, *A History of Ukrainian Literature*, trans. Dolly Ferguson *et al.*, ed. George Luckyj (Littleton, Colo. 1975), especially the chapter on 'The Significance of Ukrainian Romanticism' 578-84 and separate sections on Shevchenko; M.K. Kotsiubynska, 'Poetyka Shevchenka i ukrainskyi romantyzm,' in *Zbirnyk prats shestoi naukovoi Shevchenkivskoi konferentsii* (Kiev 1958) 49-124; S.I. Rodzevych, 'Romantyzm i realizm v rannikh poemakh Shevchenka,' in *Naukovi zapysky Kyivskoho Derzhavnoho Pedinstytutu*, I (Kiev 1939); M. Rylsky, 'Shevchenko poet-novator,' in *Shevchenko i mirovaia literatura* (Moscow 1964) and Z. Genyk-Berezovska, 'Shevchenko i ieuropeiskyi romantyzm,' *Radianske Literaturoznavstvo*, 1965, 3.

3 Without doubt, this approach – interpreting Shevchenko's early works in terms of the commonly accepted hallmarks of European romantic writing – was useful for the launching of Ukrainian literary scholarship, particularly during the initial stages of scholarly acquaintance with Shevchenko's work. Thus Čyževs'kyj, Volynsky, and others describe the fundamental role of literature in the development of national consciousness in the Slavic nations, which is a characteristic 'romantic' trait. Kotsiubynska's valuable article explained the vital role of Shevchenko's work in this process by indication of strong, multifaceted relationships between the poetry of the Ukrainian master and his European counterparts. Mykola Shlemkevych offers a good summary of this critical material; see his 'Substratum of Ševčenko's View of Life,' in V. Mijakovs'kyj and G.Y. Shevelov, eds, *Taras Ševčenko, 1814-1861: A Symposium* (The Hague 1962), 37-61, especially pp 37-9. Also see P.K. Volynsky, *Ukrainskyi romantyzm u zviazku z rozvytkom romantyzmu v slov'ianskykh literaturakh* (Kiev 1963).

4 Kotsiubynska, 'Poetyka Shevchenka' 75-9, 94-5.

5 A.O. Lovejoy, 'The Need to Distinguish Romanticisms,' in J.B. Halsted, ed.,
Romanticism: Problems of Definition, Explanation, and Evaluation (Boston
1965) 37-44; Oskar Walzel, *German Romanticism* (New York 1965). Halsted's
introduction to the aforementioned symposium is useful. See also Dmytro
Čyževs'kyj, *On Romanticism in Slavic Literatures* (The Hague 1957).

6 An outstanding example of a scholar who searches for signs of cohesion in the
period is Mario Praz; see *The Romantic Agony*, A. Davidson, trans., 2nd ed.
(1951, repr. 1956). Jacques Barzun has also written a 'non-nationalistic'
study of romanticism in 'Intrinsic and Historic Romanticism,' in Halsted,
Romanticism 18-29.

7 Čyževs'kyj's *History* points out the tenuous nature of Ukrainian literature as an
established artistic endeavour; the point is made passim.

8 See the chapter on 'Classicism' in Čyževs'kyj, *History* 370-434.

9 *Ibid.*

10 *Ibid.* 402: 'For Kulish, whose view was totally in accord with romantic ideology, the *Eneida* was nothing but a parody on the way of life and even the
language of the peasant, a parody showing "a lack of respect" for the
Ukrainian people.'

11 See note 1 and also Victor Petrov, 'Ševčenko's Aesthetic Theory: An Approach
to the Problem' in Mijakovs'kyj and Shevelov 62-7; Petrov admits to this
combination, but argues that the result should be viewed as a unique unity.

12 Shevchenko's biography illustrates well how natural and uncontrived this combination of seemingly contradictory notions was for him; while his life approximates in several instances the romantic desideratum, it none the less shows
crucial differences from the normal model of a romantic artist's situation.

13 Čyževs'kyj pays much attention to Shevchenko's poetic language and style in
the chapter on 'Romanticism' in his *History*; the quotation in the paper is from
George S.N. Luckyj, *Between Gogol' and Ševčenko: Polarity in the Literary
Ukraine, 1798-1847* (Munich 1971) 137.

14 For an illuminating study of Shevchenko's symbolism as archetypal, see George
S.N. Luckyj, 'The Archetype of the Bastard in Ševčenko's Poetry,' in this volume.
See also his 'Ševčenko and Blake,' *Harvard Ukrainian Studies* (March 1978).

15 Luckyj, *Between Gogol' and Ševčenko* 138.

16 Hugo, 'Components of Romanticism' in Halsted, *Romanticism* 36.

17 Geoffrey H. Hartman, 'Romanticism and Anti-Self-Consciousness,' in Harold
Bloom, ed., *Romanticism and Consciousness* (New York 1970) 49.

18 *Ibid.* 52.
19 Walter Scott, *The Lay of the Last Minstrel* (London 1806) ll. 1-12, p 1.
20 *Ibid.*
21 See especially the following discussion of 'Topolia.'
22 On the flourishing of interest in historical study at this time see Čyževs'kyj's chapter on 'Romanticism' in *History of Ukrainian Literature*, 437-584 and, in particular, the discussion of Kulish in which his historical novel *Chorna Rada* (1857) is compared to Scott's novels.
23 This example is just one (the most striking) among many that suggests that, in creating his kobzar spokesman attended by a young disciple, Shevchenko was in part influenced by the Harper and Mignon in Goethe's *Wilhelm Meisters Lehrjahre*; Goethe's Harper is also set to wandering by former sin. Goethe's figure is in striking contrast to the romantic examples from which Shevchenko differs. The Harper's songs are also all 'this-worldly' and concerned with a realistic view of suffering, pain, and expiation.
24 'Ivan Pidkova' offers perhaps an even better example of this intimate connection with the audience. Because there is little historical evidence that Pidkova actually made the voyage to Constantinople, the event described in the poem becomes more purely symbolic of the spirit of the past, created as a permanent present through the medium of poetry.
25 These short historical poems, however, only partially illustrate the inseparability of linguistic authenticity and cultural-historical experience because they do not, in fact, deal primarily with the relating of events. The long historical poem 'Haidamaky' (1841), published a year after the first *Kobzar*, offers a much more comprehensive application of this theory. Although a full analysis of 'Haidamaky' from this point of view is beyond the scope of this paper and warrants its own detailed study, a few comments may illuminate the point at hand. The poem has two major introductions; the first reiterates the poetic theory of the first *Kobzar* by repeating images from the early poems: The poetic lines are the poet's children, he is alone, his words are tears, he cannot bear the pain of public ridicule, etc. The iconic power of folk idiom is stressed here also – simple phrases about the sea and the steppe genuinely move the soul unlike the voguish subjects of popular writing. Because the poet is not willing to compromise this stance, he is visited by the shades of ancient heroes who discuss the past with him. In other words, it is his love of authentic folk language which allows him this vital connection with the past. The second preface, or introduction, is much simpler; it quickly and compactly sets

the scene in the past by listing place names and realistic historic details to explain the political situation surrounding the uprising of the Haidamaky. The most startling conclusion to be drawn here is that there is no difference in Shevchenko's work between 'romantic' fictional narrative like 'Topolia' or 'Kateryna' and historical account. Both kinds of writing are equally vessels of cultural truth because the power of folkloric idiom eliminates the distinction between historical truth and psychological truth. The narrative which follows these introductions presents a striking manifestation of the truth of this unity. There is no brooding over the scenes on the part of the poet, no interpretation, no further explanation; in short, no distancing of the poet or the reader from the events being described. Instead, the story is told episodically in terse, short lines, largely in broken and energetic dialogue, creating scenes of remarkable vividness and keen realism. Finally, in the mock preface at the end of the poem (in which Shevchenko claims that he cannot write a preface) the poet emphasizes once again the immediate and intimate nature of his relationship to the historical events he has just described. His inspiration was not intellectual curiosity, but rather the force of childhood memories of his grandfather, whose narration of these same stories made them a vital part of the poet's reality. Here again, the key to this intimacy is language which functions as a bridge across generations, and makes the past an integral part of the present.

26 The perfect unification in 'Topolia' of the dialectically opposed hurt of lost love and the perfection of the poplar is the best possible example of Hegel's maxim, 'The hand that inflicts the wound is also the hand that heals it,' quoted by Hartman 49. 'Topolia' thus becomes the outstanding example of what Brobert is describing in 'The Happy Prison' in Thorburn and G. Hartman, *Romanticism* (Ithaca, NY 1973) 62-79: 'For in its larger mythic dimension, the carceral imagery implies the presence of a threshold, the possibility of a passage, and initiation – a passage from the inside to the beyond, from isolation to communion, from punishment and suffering to redemption, from sadness to ... profound and mysterious joy....' (p 67). In the image of the topolia, Shevchenko has united all these opposites; the girl as the tree is not merely incarcerated but is at the threshold of her redemption.

27 Kotsiubynska contrasts Shevchenko with Kostomarov by saying that Kostomarov takes apart and explains his natural symbols (p 81).

28 The classical critical description of this phenomenon is in Mario Praz, *The Romantic Agony, passim.*

29 William Wordsworth, *The Lyrical Ballads with a Few Other Poems* (Bristol 1798) (repr. London 1926).
30 The terminology is important here. This is not the spontaneous lay of an authentic folk minstrel, but is rather a song, that is, a lyric which in Western romantic practice became the favourite vehicle for personal outpourings (see p 435 above).

26

'The Bewitched Woman' and
Some Problems of Shevchenko's Philosophy

LEONID PLIUSHCH

Shevchenko as philosopher is a topic that has scarcely been touched upon in the literature about the poet.[1] Now and again some comment of his, some thought on one subject or another, is noted. His overall world view, however, has not been examined. Perhaps the only exception is V. Barka's *Pravda Kobzaria* (The Kobzar's Truth),[2] but this study fails to subject the falsified, one-sided Soviet scholarship on the subject to critical scrutiny and hence, I believe, also is a somewhat one-sided interpretation of Shevchenko's poetry. This substantial gap in Shevchenko scholarship affects the resolution of other issues concerning his poetry, his poetics and the political, national, and social positions that he held.

It is true that poetic formulations of philosophical problems and their resolutions differ in substance from those of professional philosophical scholarship, differ to such a degree in fact that they elude precise definition and classification. Unlike Dostoevsky, for example, Shevchenko wrote no articles that would help to elucidate his world view.[3] Yet these facts alone do not explain the existence of this gap in published scholarly work.

When we turn to official Soviet scholarship, we are struck by the 'simplicity' of Shevchenko's ideology. In contemporary Soviet scholarship[4] Shevchenko is portrayed 'simply' as an atheist, a revolutionary democrat, an internationalist Russophile. Whatever does not fit into this scheme is either passed over in silence, interpreted, or falsified 'in the Party spirit,' indulgently overlooked as error deriving from the lack of education which he, a peasant, received or from his romantic idealization of the Ukrainian past, errors which, as it were, his nationalist friends inspired and his Russian friends of the revolutionary democratic persuasion helped him to overcome. When Iu. Ivakin, for example, comments upon the three-stanza poem 'Molytva' (A Prayer) in *Komentar do 'Kobzaria' Shevchenka* (Commentary upon Shevchenko's *Kobzar*),[5] he reduces it to a series of revolutionary democratic motifs à la Chernyshevsky and Dobroliubov – to revenge, punishment of the oppressors, and Shevchenko's call to armed insurrection against tsarism. The motifs of Christian mercy he dismisses, saying only that they were included for the censor, prompted by an attempt at self-censorship.

An examination of Shevchenko's vocabulary alone will suffice to shatter the myth of Shevchenko as atheist. If *buty* (to be) is excluded from consideration (verbs are indispensable in all but a few sentences), 'God' and 'Lord' are the most frequent words in Shevchenko's poetry. Hence, the discussion can only involve the specifics of his religious thought and world view, that is, his relationship with God, and not the absence of such a relationship.

It is precisely a discussion of this nature, a deep, all-embracing analysis, that is lacking even in non-Soviet scholarship about Shevchenko, where it is maintained, for example, that Shevchenko was a bard of Christian mercy.[6]

In the work of both Ukrainophobes and certain Ukrainophiles a 'counter-thesis' to the attestations of Shevchenko's Russophile internationalism is also to be found, notably the allegation that Shevchenko was a chauvinist who celebrated the slaughter of Ukraine's national enemies. (If one were so inclined, suitable quotations could indeed be taken from *Kobzar*.) In fact, almost irrespective of the issue, exegetists find in *Kobzar* whatever they wish, discover elements that conform to their own ideology.

It is precisely this – the diametrically opposed character of the interpretations which Shevchenko's works allow – that makes the problem of his world view, his religious, national, social, and political convictions, complex rather than 'simple.' Neither can this complexity be reduced to a question of the evolution of the poet's thought, his search for a ready-made, monolithic, and fixed ideology. One need only read *Kobzar* without ideological glasses to become convinced that an inconsistent and unstable world view was immanent in Shevchenko's poetry from the beginning, an inconsistency that is not the typical romantic leap from one point of view to another but is a specific, non-Euclidian, dynamic, and unstable harmony and hence permits us to speak about the kobzar's philosophy as something integral which – inconsistencies, self-contradictions, and variations notwith-standing – comprises the constant, invariable, unique, and essentially Shev-chenkian word for which none of the 'variations' alone can account. If this immanent inconsistency were not to be found throughout *Kobzar*, then the problem would be reduced to the study of the poet's creative development, which, when divided into periods on the basis of the evolution of his thought, would provide a foundation for the interpretation of a particular work.[7]

Shevchenko himself alludes to this peculiarity of his vision of the world and of the poetic structure of his works. His image of the ideal bard of the people, who converses with God and brings His word to the people is a kobzar who is characterized in 'Perebendia' as 'khymernyi' (chimerical, unpredictable):

> Staryi ta khymernyi!
> Zaspivaie, zasmiietsia,
> A na slozy zverne.

Old and chimerical! / He will sing and laugh, / But returns to tears.

Shevchenko likewise repeatedly describes himself as chimerical, that is, as a poet of the carnivalesque-tragic variety.[8] Further, he underscores the presence of this trait in the works of Gogol,[9] who brought carnivalesque Ukrainian folklore into Russian literature. In the poem 'Hoholiu' (To Gogol) we find the following characteristic words: 'Ty smiieshsia, a ia plachu' (You laugh but I weep). Yet, Shevchenko does not depict reality from a one-sided and fixed perspective and, thus, after the lines 'A shcho vrodyt z toho plachu? / Bohylova, brate' (And what will be the harvest from this weeping? / Weeds, my brother) which follow the scene describ-ing the ruin of Ukraine, he summarizes his approach to reality in the following words: 'Nekhai, brate. – A my budem / Smiiatsia ta plakat' (Let it be so, my brother. – And we will laugh and cry). Laughter through tears and tears through sarcastic or ironic laughter is one of Shevchenko's most pervasive, ambivalent images, the model for his poetic method of truth-seeking, for the carnivalesque structure of *Kobzar*.

One other aspect of this poem should be considered. Laughter and tears, in the images of Gogol and the narrator, constitute the two aspects of a single image. In the author's dialogue with Gogol, however, they themselves join in a dialogue, allowing for the creation of the dynamism inherent in the concept of 'laughter through tears.'

Yet another characteristic trait of a carnivalesque culture, dialogism – the second invariable feature of Shevchenko's unique word – in this way becomes the means of harmonizing his discordant world view. Throughout his *Kobzar*, Shevchenko participates in a dialogue with himself, his heroes, Ukraine, her past, present, and future, his friends and enemies, nature, and God. Philosophically, Shevchenko considers the main issues around which his poetic quest revolves in dialogue form, examining them from all sides, not only his own from his own point of view but also from others'. As the point of departure for my analysis of the set of philosophical problems arising in Shevchenko's poetry I take the poet's first published work, 'Prychynna' (The Bewitched Woman).

In this poem the features of Shevchenko's poetics mentioned earlier – inconsistency and dialogism – are already present. In this poem, too, Shevchenko poses questions of cardinal importance to himself and it is thus possible to analyse those elements which are found throughout *Kobzar* and unite them into a discrete 'word.'

Invariants make possible the examination of variants – the parameters of the word, that is, the analysis of the poet's evolution, the directions or tendencies defining his development. Subsequently, I will offer another reason for basing my analysis upon Shevchenko's first published work but for the moment I will turn my attention to the poem itself.

Critics commonly regard 'The Bewitched Woman' as the derivative work of a novice, a more or less traditional romantic ballad constructed upon folk motifs. Concealed in this thesis about 'The Bewitched Woman,' as in the more general interpretation which typifies Shevchenko as a folkloristic poet,[10] is one of the most interesting questions related to his poetry. In comparison with other 'founders' of national literatures, Shevchenko at first seems unusually uniform and 'clichéd,' with his fixed set (his own or derived from folklore) of images, epithets, themes, and poetic structures. Panteleimon Kulish took note of this many years ago: 'He wrote very little and what he did write reveals that his intellect failed to illuminate with sufficient breadth the life which he felt impelled to portray in his poems and poetic meditations. Had Shevchenko even possessed in his head all that Pushkin or Mickiewicz did, he would still not have become a poet like them, though it fell to him to plow virgin soil.'[11] If the crude criterion of 'quantity' (in the preceding segment Kulish accurately identifies the main reason for this – the misfortune which left Shevchenko little time and opportunity for creative activity) and the utter failure to comprehend the essence of poetic genius are set aside, then what Kulish describes as the 'narrowness' of the vision of life offered by *Kobzar* becomes a question of 'thematic narrowness.'

With respect to theme, *Kobzar* may indeed seem limited by the poet's largely 'childish' perceptions. So much of Shevchenko's poetry is devoted to 'sinful' romances, the punishment of them, and the tragedy of the mother and her orphan son that many scholars have felt compelled to look to the poet's biography for an explanation of the obtrusiveness in *Kobzar* and Shevchenko's stories of images of the *pokrytka* (unwed mother) and the bastard.

Explanations based on biographical information – the story of Oksana Kovalenko or even the fact that the theme of the *pokrytka* most clearly reflected the national and social oppression in Ukraine and expressed what was then a fairly typical human tragedy – are inadequate and, in fact, weaken the *pokrytka* image and its fundamental significance for Shevchenko's ethical-philosophical quest. To be sure, sin and its punishment and the senselessness of human suffering are most clearly expressed through the *pokrytka*. At the same time, however, it is broader, constituting a philosophical generalization of the narrower theme which enables the images of the *pokrytka* to assume a central position in Shevchenko's poetry. I have chosen to analyse 'The Bewitched Woman,' written before 'Kateryna,' Shevchenko's first poem about a *pokrytka*, in order to set forth this general, broader meaning of the image of the *pokrytka* and expand it beyond 'biographical' and 'psychological' interpretations. Only then can the paradoxical fact be explained that despite the 'thematic narrowness' and the clichéd, folkloristic character of his poetics, Shevchenko became an inexhaustible source of the diverse style and content of Ukrainian poetry and prose, which ranges from romanticism to the literature of contemporary surrealism and the absurd as well as other schools of poetic thought and technique. The same can be said of yet another paradox which Kulish did not perceive – the breadth of vision within the limited, uniform, and thematically 'narrow' confines of *Kobzar*.

'The Bewitched Woman' demonstrates how Shevchenko employs the clichés of both oral and written literature to create a new poetic form expressing the deepest and most intimate human experiences, ideas, and philosophical interpretations of life. Here is the traditional plot of a fantastic ballad (a bewitched maiden awaiting the return of her beloved, her death at the hands of the water nymphs, the young man's suicide upon learning of her death), a number of other traditional elements and clichés, a few devices for elevating the subject matter, and a generalization of the problems. Dostoevsky employed the traditional adventure novel form in order to go beyond the classical analyses of ethical, psychological, religious, and various other problems and developed a new mode for studying the human soul and human relationships. Breaking with the limited and hierarchical view which conceived human relations in terms of class and caste, he studied the universally human and the individual under stress. Similarly, Shevchenko employed the fantastic, irrational motifs of the ballad and its structure in order to pose the problems of greatest importance to him in the context of the most intense situations.

However, Shevchenko did not simply exploit the cliché. He modified it, making possible a more profound treatment of the problem and its resolution, for the very deformation of the cliché can transmit aesthetic information to the reader and be a device for penetrating to the deepest layers of his psyche.

As an established form, the romantic ballad has wide possibilities for combining an 'objective' representation of a human drama (story), the subjective experience of it by the heroes and the author (lyric), and its illumination from the point of view of various subjects (dialogue). But for that new word which Shevchenko brought to Ukrainian literature, for the revelation of the Ukrainian national spirit, the ballad, like the purely folkloristic forms, was too narrow. Even in his first work Shevchenko creates his own form, fusing the ballad and the folk song. He rejects the strict requirements of the ballad and its strophic form and consistently changes the rhythmic structure of his verse. This allows him to create a unique lyrical polyphony in which his own voice mingles with those of other characters and assumes an equal role in the various scenes of the drama, in the dialogue. The clichés derived from the ballad and folk song are as necessary to his vision of the world as the violation of the norms of these genres. A new poetic form and set of devices would distract the listener's attention from the philosophical content, the main concern of his poetry, while an established, fully conventional genre form would extinguish the new components.

Relying on thematic and stylistic clichés, Shevchenko elicits in the astute reader the most diverse conceptual and emotional associations, while by altering the cliché, he reaches beyond established thinking and convenient conclusions. Also, through his original synthesis of the folkloristic and the literary Shevchenko introduced peasant or folk (and thus for his time, also national) themes and language into 'enlightened' literature, for genuine folk themes played no part in the forms assumed by the aristocratic Russian literature of the period. Only by breaking free from the social and national narrowness of the literature of his time could Shevchenko portray what he saw as the universal human drama in a form whose intensity was only matched perhaps by Dostoevsky's novels. Through the author's participation in the drama's dialogue the reader is led beyond the given plot and the drama becomes a universal human one. The reader participates in the drama with the author.

Subsequently, Shevchenko incorporated the reader into his poems directly. Similarly, the national and social aspects which in 'The Bewitched Woman' occur in the drama through the setting alone (the Ukrainian landscape, the village) and the characterization of the heroes are in subsequent works more fully developed and intensified. It was these motifs which made Shevchenko a bard of Ukraine's national and social drama, a bard of the struggle against all human oppression.

The levels upon which the meaning and plot function and their various facets (conventionally rendered with the aid of well-chosen rhythmic and poetic devices) are unified by shared images, phrases, and ideas. Many recurrent phrases and elements in this ballad subsequently became standard features of his poetry, by the method of transformation. This method operates on levels of plot, situation, image, meaning, motif, and may even result in a complete inversion, a formal denial, of previously given elements or other works.

Transformation allows a problem to be broken down into its components and examined from differing points of view and various angles. It reveals the contradictory nature of the world and of solutions to problems. Moreover, it opens the way for the generalization and the probing into of the problems being examined and the discovery of the unchanging and permanent within the fluid and ever-changing.

'Kavkaz' (The Caucasus) offers examples of the simplest sort of transformation – instances where the sense in which words are used, their meanings, and the author's relationship to them change drastically. For example, the meaning of the word 'slava' (glory) changes from the sarcastic image of the *slava* of the tsars to a moving glorification of the heroism of the Caucasian hillsmen. This is indicated simply by a change in rhythm and image:

> Slava! Slava!
> Khortam, i honchym, i psariam.
> I nashym batiushkam-tsariam
> Slava.
> I vam slava, syni hory,
> Kryhoiu okuti.
> I vam, lytsari velyki,
> Bohom ne zabuti.

Glory! Glory! / To the hounds and harriers and their trainers / And our benevolent fathers, the tsars, glory. / Glory to you likewise, blue hills, / Fettered in ice, / And to you, might warriors, / By God not forgotten.

Slava, employed ironically and sarcastically as a substitute for blasphemy and curses, is transformed into *slava*-praise as Shevchenko 'glorifies' the warriors who battle against their 'glorious' executioners. Rather than avail himself of the clichéd transition from irony (or parody) to pathos, which automatically suggests itself here – 'Ni, vam slava, syni hory' (Nay, glory to you, blue hills) – Shevchenko employs that same 'i' (and), which linked all the glorious executioners to blasphemy and praise and thereby further stress the opposition of the glory of evil and the glory of good, the lie and the truth. This unexpected 'i' (and) instead of 'ni' (nay) shapes the clash of the hillsmen and the armies of Russian imperialism, their truth, honour, and glory. Yet, this is not simply the juxtaposition of two meanings of the word *slava*. It is rather a transformation which produces a discrete but ambivalent image of *slava* as blasphemy and praise, which Shevchenko subsequently developed in the poem 'Slava' (Glory) and to which he returned in his final poetry.

Even more complex is the transformation and resulting image encountered earlier in 'The Caucasus':

> A pravda nasha piana spyt.
> Koly vona prokynetsia?

Koly odpochyty
Liazhesh, Bozhe, utomlenyi?
I nam dasy zhyty!
My viruiem Tvoii syli
I dukhu zhyvomu.
Vstane pravda! vstane volia!

Our truth slumbers in a drunken stupor. / When will it awake? / When will you take your rest, / O weary God? / And let us live! / We believe in your might / And your living spirit. / Truth will rise! freedom will rise!

Here too the sudden change in Shevchenko's attitude to God is accompanied by a change in intonation. The various meanings and images are fused and the integrated image made all the more sharply discordant.

When the poet reproaches Truth for sleeping and wishes she would awaken, he links this with his desire that the 'ruler' of this world (and hence also all worldly evil) should fall asleep and let people live. God and Truth here are contradictory images and continue as such throughout the poem. Yet, later in the poem they also complement each other and together represent the one thing desired by the author – the living spirit of truth and freedom. This transformation of mutually exclusive concepts into a single emotionally positive image is prepared for in earlier lines by the author's ambivalent attitude towards truth. Although desired and regarded as necessary, it is portrayed in a drunken stupor.

These transformations in 'The Caucasus' reflect the nuances of the author's dialogue with God – prayer and entreaty, reproach, denial, petition, faith, scepticism. Closely allied with the ambivalence of his religious feelings, Shevchenko's ambivalent attitude towards 'truth' allows him to formulate the difficult problem posed in this poem in the sharpest and most complex form, that of the truth of man and the truth of God, their interrelationship in the canonical truths of the Church, which serve the interests of the tsars and the nobility who hide these truths from the people:

Za koho zh Ty rozipiavsia,
Khryste, syne Bozhyi?
Za nas, dobrykh, chy za slovo
Istyny ... chy mozhe,
Shchob my z tebe nasmiialys?

For whom did you allow yourself to be crucified, / Christ, Son of God? / For us, your good people, or for the word / Of truth ... or perhaps / So that we would have a good laugh at your expense?

The 'good people' transform love, brotherhood, and truth into an imperial, canonical prayer to Christ:

Shchob bratniu krov prolyty, prosiat
I potim v dar Tobi prynosiat
Z pozharu vkradenyi pokrov!

To be allowed to spill the blood of their brothers do they entreat / And then bring to you their offering / Of a shroud stolen from the conflagration!

The diabolical vaudeville, the historical drama of the conversion of good into evil, the clothing of evil in the vestments of good, the appropriation and falsification of Christ's law are all depicted by Shevchenko through the paradoxes linked by poetic transformation, disguised concepts, conversion of words into the masks of history and the removal of these masks – through words which rival each other in resonance and form but are opposite in meaning.

In 'The Bewitched Woman' the transformation has a somewhat different poetico-philosophic function. Its heroes are similarly described: dark-browed, dark-eyed orphans; they have a similar unfortunate lot ('taka ioho dolia' / 'such is his fate,' 'taka ii dolia' / 'such is her fate'); they both await the day when they will be reunited; they suffer the same 'sin' and 'punishment' – they are both 'killed' (vbyti); both are buried 'in the prescribed manner' (po zakonu), as suicides. The transition between her story and his is accomplished by the transferral of her characteristics to him. This transformation makes the drama of each character real and human.

Through transformation, the author's appeals to God ('O Bozhe mii mylyi! Za shcho Ty karaiesh ii, molodu' / 'O dear Lord! Why are you punishing her, this young maiden' and 'Prosty syrotu' / 'Spare this orphan') are carried over to the Cossack and the subsequent transformation of his query ('Za shcho vony rozluchyly mene iz toboiu?' / 'Why have they taken you from me?' which appears in another version as 'Za shcho vony tebe vbyly?' / 'Why have they killed you?') into the general, universally human question posed by the author, and through his mediation by the reader as well, to God and humanity: 'Za shcho ikh ubyto?' (Why were they killed?) This transformation and generalization are possible because the author is present in the ballad's drama and, like the Cossack youth and maiden, is a participant in the drama of life. (The same epithets can be applied to him, the hero's drama regarded as the author's own.)

While the introduction of the tragic image of the water nymphs carries the problem beyond everyday reality and emphasizes the eternal nature of these problems and their essential irrationality, the parallel between the human drama and the doves' drama carries it beyond human suffering to nature as a whole (in other poems Shevchenko uses a particular form of transformation – the anthropomorphizing of plants or animals; the fantastic water nymphs are also people metamorphosized) and expresses the problem of guilt and punishment even more poignantly:

> Chy vynna zh holubka, shcho holuba liubyt?
> Chy vynen toi holub, shcho sokil ubyv?

Is the dove to blame for loving her mate? / Is he to blame that he fell prey to the falcon?

Transformations allow problems to be generalized and examined from various perspectives and on various levels.

In 'Osiia. Hlava XIV' (Hosea 14) Shevchenko turns to God with the same question about the fate of Ukraine (the way is prepared by a series of descriptions of the common fate shared by the mother, the woman, and Ukraine):

> Pohybnesh, zhynesh Ukraino,
> Ne stane znaku na zemli.
> ...
> Mii liubyi kraiu nepovynnyi
> Za shcho tebe Hospod kara,
> Karaie tiazhko?

You will perish, cease to exist, Ukraine, / No trace of you will remain on the earth. ... / My beloved, guiltless land, / Why does God punish you, / Punish you so harshly?

In 'Mariia' Shevchenko asks this question in connection with Christ and Mary. Often he examines his own lot in these same terms of guilt, punishment, penitence, and destiny.

In this way the transformation of images, the transposition of fixed 'traits' from one image to another, becomes the device whereby Shevchenko poses problems central to his philosophy, of theodicy in the religious sphere and of social, national, and ethical justice in the extrareligious one. Why and to what end do people, nations, and all of humanity suffer? Who is to blame for this suffering? What will lead people into a 'new and free' world, of the good and the true?

This general question is posed in a narrower form in 'The Bewitched Woman': What is the reason, who was the cause, who killed the heroes of the ballad and why?

Throughout this ballad, Shevchenko offers various hypotheses concerning the cause of the drama. These possible explanations are given in ambiguous, and even implicit terms. The young Cossack promised the maiden he would return but did not return in time. This becomes one of the causes of her suffering and sin, that is, his 'guilt,' his 'sin.' Her fear that the Cossack has fallen in love with another – his sin in her eyes – is one cause of her death. But this is her sin, too – lack of faith in, suspicion of one's beloved is the more direct cause of her death.

Here Shevchenko poses the general problem of suffering for love, the responsibilities and consequences of love, that is, the question of the 'sinfulness' of love itself. Is the dove to blame for loving her mate? Sin imagined, and real sin, allow for the posing of the problem of real sin as it is defined in Church dogma.

During his journey home, the Cossack also sins by harbouring suspicions about his beloved:

Kolo sertsia kozatskoho
Iak hadyna vietsia ...

Around the Cossack's heart / It seems as if a serpent coils ...

This image of the serpent is the essence of sin imagined, that situation in which a person grows suspicious of a friend or loses faith in his own strength and gives in to a sinful, illusory thought.

In 'Petrus' such a serpentine thought leads to real sin – the murder of the general. Availing himself of the partial phonetic concurrence of the words *hadka* (thought) and *hadyna* (serpent), Shevchenko creates an image of abstractness, which exists on a higher level and partakes of a deeper content, expressing the concept of 'sin in thought,' which can occasion real sin, that is, contain evil. In this lies the justification for and explanation of punishment for a thought alone.

When the Cossack finds the girl dead, he takes his own life, that is, sins against God by not submitting to His will:

Ne tak sertse liubyt ...
Ne tak vono khoche, iak Boh nam daie:
Vono zhyt ne khoche, ne khoche zhurytsia.

Not thus does the heart love ... / Not thus, as God grants, does it wish things to be: / It does not wish to live, does not wish to grieve.

The Cossack's suicide is prepared for by the analogous sin committed in thought by the girl. She sins not only by suspecting her beloved's motives for failing to return but is also ready to strangle that imagined 'other woman' and, if the Cossack is dead, to take her place beside him in the grave. Her failure to submit to the will of God is already manifested in the fact that she seeks aid from a sorceress, who bewitches her to ease her suffering. There is an allusion to her desire to kill herself in the scene where she climbs to the top of a tree. Shevchenko does not explain her reason for doing so, leaving it to the water nymphs to transform the un-named desire into reality. The scene with the water nymphs can only be interpreted as a fantasy, an image signifying psychological self-destruction, as death stemming from a desire to die, as a substitute for the act of self-destruction that the girl wished to commit by throwing herself from the tree. That both were buried 'in the prescribed manner,' by the roadside, testifies to the fact that from the point of view of the community they both died sinfully.

Having examined these facets of the guilt of the Cossack youth and maiden, Shevchenko then strips them away, either denying the guilt of the lovers altogether or justifying their actions and defending them before God. He stresses that the girl 'wanders about in a daze' (sonna bludyt). The sorceress is the cause of her sin. The sorceress sins by tampering with the destiny of another, with the will of God. The Cossack's suicide is a consequence of the girl's death, which causes him to go mad. Hence, he commits this sin against God unconsciously. The sorceress's meddling is the cause of both his madness and his sin. There is also justification for the sorceress's actions; she wishes to help the girl. She contributes to the girl's death because she pities her.[12]

As to the sin of love, the entire *Kobzar* is an apology for it. As with sin in thought, Shevchenko justifies love that comes from the heart. For now it 'does not wish to live, does not wish to grieve,' now it 'does not wish things to be as God grants.' But the heart, like each thought, is God-given. (In 'Petrus,' the general's wife repeatedly prays to and entreats the Virgin Mary to help her to conquer her impure love, the serpent in her heart.)

The people in the drama who follow 'the prescribed codes' in all things are also sinful and guilty. Ridicule and the fear of it, the dread inspired by vicious mockery for violating prescribed codes are constant afflictions in Shevchenko's poetry.

Observing that 'there is no one to inquire why they were killed' (Nema komu zapytaty, / Za shcho ikh ubyto), Shevchenko not only repeats the Cossack's words but also alludes to a human sin related to the previous one. Man's interest in his fellows is restricted to passing judgment upon them in accordance with the prescribed codes, that is, to ridiculing them. Men are strangers to one another. They are cruel.

Yet, guilt is also stripped away from 'the people,' the community. Their lack of compassion towards the person who has sinned is explained in terms of the code. In some of Shevchenko's works these 'formal' codes are revealed to be just in that they protect the community from that which gives rise to sin – betrayal, murder, lawlessness.

All the possible offences presented either in clearly or vaguely defined terms, all the sins of real people, acquire philosophical depth through the clichés derived from the romantic ballad form, which are themselves based on various elements of folk mythology where various evil human traits or deeds have demonological images.

Even at the beginning of the ballad, when the poet is introducing the heroine, he links her with the water nymphs and hence also with the irrational character of sin. Scenes that include water nymphs, together with descriptions of nature, begin and conclude the ballad, emphasizing the unchanging backdrop against which this personal drama is played out. More particularly, if we consider that the water nymphs are the direct, ostensible cause of the girl's death, it is made eternal and universally human.

The opposition of evil (guilt) and good is introduced through colour symbolism, through the colours associated with nature, God's world, and the dramatis persona:

V taku dobu pid horoiu
Bilia toho haiu,
Shcho chorniie nad vodoiu,
Shchos bile blukaie.

At this hour along a hillside / Near that wood / Which gleams black above the water / Something white wanders.

The world of God in which 'something' wanders (the use of 'something,' 'shchos,' rather than 'the girl' suggests both the general nature of the problem posed and the general and irrational character of the drama); the woods are black, the 'something,' the girl, white. God's world is evil in some unspecified way, the person is innocent. In some of Shevchenko's poems this opposition is presented overtly, in others it is inverted: God's world, a garden paradise, is transformed into a hell by the people themselves. Through this opposition Shevchenko poses the problem of suffering, of the punishment of innocent sinners, at the very outset of his poem.

Shevchenko's most obscure work, the mystery play 'Velykyi lokh' (The Great Vault) also begins thus: 'Iak snih, try ptashechky letily' (Like snow, three little birds did fly). Peter does not allow them into Heaven – the first, because with full pails she crossed the path which Bohdan Khmelnytsky took when he went to sign the pact with the Muscovite tsar; the second, because, raped by the Muscovites, she obeyed Peter the First's orders and watered his horse; the third, because she silently smiled at another executioner – Catherine II.

Having identified the dramatis persona as an unspecified 'something,' Shevchenko then offers two versions of this 'something.' The first is the water nymph:

Mozhe vyishla rusalonka
Materi shukaty,
A mozhe, zhde kozachenka,
Shchob zaloskotaty.

Perhaps a water nymph has come forth / To seek her mother, / Or perhaps she awaits a young Cossack / To tickle and snare.

Although this image is later rejected, the water nymphs reappear in the ballad as dramatis personae. They are not supernatural causal agents and instruments of 'punishment,' but also are intimately connected with the sin, guilt, and innocence of the girl and the Cossack. They not only represent the world antagonistic to man, the world of the 'unclean,' anti-divine force, but also symbolize the hypostasis of the unjustly punished and the innocently guilty and are to a degree transformations of human beings.

Even in this image of the 'something,' the human sins of the water nymphs are introduced: the sins of their mothers, who drowned them, and the sins of the water nymphs themselves, which are rooted in their very natures, the enticing of young men to their deaths by tickling.

In the following lines the girl is contrasted to the water nymphs:

Ne rusalonka blukaie:
To divchyna khodyt.

It is not a water nymph who wanders here: / It is a girl who walks.

The water nymph-girl parallel is defined by their actions – *blukaie/khodyt* (wanders/walks). To wander is to walk aimlessly in no specific direction, without a goal in mind. Only when guilt arises, the problem of the girl's sin (her wish to die for love's sake), does Shevchenko return to the word *blukaty* (to wander) and in its most 'sinful' form at that – 'she goes astray' (bludyt) but 'in a daze' (sonna), that is, without being conscious of her actions. In this way he again draws the girl closer to the 'unconscious,' innocent water nymphs.

The irrational character of sin is most emphasized by the 'absurd,' surrealistic song of the water nymphs. The water nymph mother begins the song. She is a mother who drowns herself and becomes a water nymph[13] or a mother who drowns her child and is either herself drowned by someone else (perhaps her own child) or drowns herself.[14] She suffers either for the sin of suicide or of murder. In both instances she is guilty above all of turning her back on her child. This sin against the child to whom she gave life, but not a 'happy lot,' is related to the fact that she is usually a *pokrytka*-mother.

Through the water nymphs, who seek their mothers, and the water nymph mother, Shevchenko takes up what would become his most consistent theme – of the *pokrytka* and bastard, of unlawful, extramarital love, regarded as sinful in canon law. Here it is only vaguely formulated. Subsequently, however, Shevchenko examines this problem from divergent positions, either justifying the behaviour of the 'sinners' or blaming the will of God and the lot He bequeaths to man, upon the community, the people and their moral code or, conversely, demonstrating how sin as conceived by the Church is intimately bound up with real sin – with social or national betrayal, the suffering of a child, parent, or the mother herself, with suicide and other sins.

If the water nymph mother bears guilt, then the image of the water nymph children allows Shevchenko to pose a series of religious, mystical, and theological questions. In the song of the water nymphs the fact that the water nymphs are unbaptized is noted twice. They are thus innocent and guilty, sinful before sinning, bearing the hereditary sin of mankind. Yet it is the mother who is to blame for this, and so they endure punishment for and because of the sins of the person who has already punished them. The questions 'Why have they been killed?' 'Why have they been punished?' thus apply to the water nymphs as well.

In the ballad the water nymphs also do evil – they tickle a girl to death. But this is only because they are unbaptized, inheritors of a world of unclean, evil forces. Hence they turn to the moon so that with it they may nourish themselves upon the dead Cossack, whom they have doubtless tickled to death.

Necrophagia or vampirism is frequently (mostly inexplicitly) employed by Shevchenko to characterize the evil of the world. It is present even in such complex characters as Honta and Iarema, who are treated sympathetically, and accompanies such evil people as the tsars and the nobility. It is thus possible to juxtapose the destructive tsars and Honta with the poet's attitude towards the evil water nymphs.

Shevchenko increases the absurdity and irrational character of the scene with the water nymphs by having the water nymph mother (who, it is safe to assume, unlike the water nymph children, was baptized before her death by drowning and hence is the ambivalent baptized/unbaptized person typical of Shevchenko's later works) begin the song:

Mene maty porodyla,
Nekhreshchenu polozhyla.

My mother gave me birth, / Laid me unbaptized in the earth.

A sinful mother sings about a sinful mother and her sinful children. By not explaining the dual irrationality of the mother-water nymph image, Shevchenko amplifies the implicit issue of the absurdity of the endless circle of 'evil for evil,' 'punishment for punishment,' 'sin gives birth to sin' and thus leads up to the central question from the religious point of view, the question of original sin.

The water nymph children, like the Cossack and the girl, are orphans. They have already been punished in that they do evil because they are unbaptized. Being orphaned, someone else's previous sin, inspires the punishment suffered by the orphans, a punishment which conditions their sin and their very existence as bearers of God's punishment, itself again bringing about suffering and sin on someone else's part. The backdrop for this endless circle is immortal nature and the world of the innocently guilty.

The irrational character of the water nymphs, victims of this eternal 'circle of evil,' is perhaps even more striking in the champion from 'Tytarivna' (The Sexton's Daughter). The sexton's daughter mocked a person who was not her equal, a bastard, and was punished for this by conceiving an irrational love for him. Upon his return he leads her astray and makes of her a pokrytka who (in her thoughts) desires to drown her child in a well, but lacks the resolve. This intention is realized through the father (a poor orphan, a bastard), who peers out from behind a cranberry bush like a serpent and later casts his son – her bastard – into the well. For this deed the sexton's daughter is punished by being placed in the grave while still alive (the desire of the girl from 'The Bewitched Woman'). For the sin of 'derisive laughter' the innocent bastard child is punished and so is the mother herself, by dreadful means.

The Lord punished her with burdensome love for the bastard and thus caused her downfall (and that of the community). In an even more strange and terrible manner He punished the bastard father:

> Pokarav
> Ioho Hospod za hrikh velykyi
> Ne smertiiu! – vin bude zhyt,
> I satanoiu-cholovikom
> Vin bude po svitu khodyt
> I vas, divchatochka, duryt
> Voviky.

The Lord did not punish him / For his great sin / With death! – he will live and / As a human Satan / Walk the earth / And deceive you, my dear young maidens, / For all eternity.

Thus the punishment of sinners became the everlasting cause of new evil, new bastards, mothers, and fathers.

The theme of eternal evil runs through most of Shevchenko's poetry, assuming now more, now less, fantastic forms. In 'The Great Vault' the explanations of wrongdoing on the part of the bird souls, who are as white as snow, underline the incomprehensibility and irrationality of the evil and suffering. When Shevchenko speaks of the destruction of innocent Ukraine in 'Hosea 14,' he again stresses this irrationality:

> Za shcho tebe Hospod kara,
> Karaie tiazhko? Za Bohdana,
> Ta za skazhenoho Petra,
> Ta za paniv otykh pohanykh
> Do kraiu nyshchyt ...

Why does the Lord punish you, / Punish you so harshly? For Bohdan, / The rabid Peter / And those vile lords / He punishes you beyond measure ...

The fate of the unfortunate *pokrytka* becomes a symbol of Ukraine. The lords and tsars who scourge Ukraine represent her guilt, her sin (that for which she suffers – but in 'Hosea 14' God himself suffers, too).

In 'Haidamaky' (The Haidamaks), the absurdity of eternal evil is represented against the historical backdrop of the Haidamak uprising against the
Polish nobility, who in turn have risen against tsarism.

> Hliante, podyvitsia: to konfederaty,
> Liude, shcho zibralys voliu boronyt.
> Boroniat prokliati ... Bud prokliata maty,
> I den, i hodyna, koly ponesla,
> Koly porodyla, na svit prynesla.

Caste your gaze upon this, have a look: it's the Confederates, / People who have
gathered together to defend liberty. / They defend it, the accursed ones ... Accursed
be the mother, / The day and the hour that bore them, / Gave birth to them,
brought them into the world.

The Haidamaks rise up against the insurgent oppressors, spill oceans of
blood, the blood of their enemies, of their faithful followers and of the
innocently guilty. The leader of the uprising, Honta, repudiates his Catholic wife and with a 'consecrated blade' (sviachenym nozhem) slaughters his
own children (baptized-unbaptized) because they are Catholics, entreating
his victims:

> Ta blahaite, prosit Boha
> Nekhai na sim sviti
> Mene za vas pokaraie,
> Za hrikh sei velykyi

Entreat God, plead with him, / To punish me here in this world / For what I have
done to you, / For my great sin.

The tragedy of Honta, the circle of the sins of father-mother-child, here
is part of the universal human tragedy of fratricide and national antagonism.

> A za vishcho,
> Za shcho liudy hynut?
> Toho zh batka, taki zh dity ...

And why, for what, / Are the people perishing? / Of the same a father, the same children ...

Shevchenko blames the Catholic Church for the senseless endlessness of 'blood for blood,' 'grief for grief,' in its Polish-Ukrainian manifestation:

> Starykh slavian dity. A khto vynen?
> Ksondzy, iezuity.

Of the ancient Slavs the children. And who is to blame? / The Polish priests, the Jesuits.

But this is only within the context of 'The Haidamaks.' In his poetry as a whole, with the exception of 'Mariia' and 'The Neophytes,' there is no resolution of this problem of human suffering and evil. There is only a quest for a path leading out of it. Shevchenko returns to this tragic rift between fraternal peoples – Ukrainians and Poles – in 1847 and 1858:

> Pryishly ksondzy i zapalyly
> Nash tykhyi rai. I rozlyly
> Shyroke more sloz i krovi,
> A syrot imenem Khrystovym
> Zamorduvaly, rozpialy ...

The Polish priests came and set fire to our quiet paradise. / And unleashed a vast ocean of tears and blood, / Murdered and crucified orphans in the name of Christ ...

He entreats his Polish brothers:

> Podai zhe ruku kozakovi
> I sertse chystoie podai!
> ...
> I znovu imenem Khrystovym
> Vozobnovym nash tykhyi rai.

Give your hand to the Cossack / And your pure heart!... / And again, in the name of Christ / We shall renew our peaceful paradise.

The technique of transformation which Shevchenko employs to depict the eternal suffering and evil here is applied to the resolution of the problem posed in the poem. If orphans (personified by Christ) could be crucified 'in the name of Christ,' then in His name too, Shevchenko suggests, fraternal means can be employed to transform Hell into Paradise.

In glorifying the Haidamaks' heroic battle against their aristocratic foes, Shevchenko clearly depicts the inhuman cruelty of both sides and the futility of 'blood for blood':

Posiialy haidamaky
V Ukraini zhyto,
Ta ne vony ioho zhaly.

The Haidamaks sowed / Rye in Ukraine / But it was not they who reaped it.

To those who brag that 'we brought Poland down once' ('my – Polshchu kolys zavalyly') Shevchenko points out in 'I mertvym, i zhyvym, i nenarodzhdennym zemliakam moim v Ukraini i ne v Ukraini moie druzhnieie poslaniie' (To My Dead and Living and Yet Unborn Countrymen in Ukraine and not in Ukraine My Friendly Epistle)

Pravda vasha: Polshcha vpala,
Ta i vas rozdavyla!

You are right: Poland fell / But it also crushed you!

The technique of transformation of evil into good, of sin into worthiness, is a means of breaking the eternal circle of evil and realizing the hoped-for new world of truth and love. This technique Shevchenko also applies to resolving his most difficult problem, the problem of the sinful woman, the *pokrytka*.

The Virgin Mary expiates her canonical sin by nurturing and keeping safe the fruit of this sin – Jesus. The *pokrytka* Kateryna is transformed into the Mother of God, the Protectress of the sinner, of suffering humanity. She endured her lot, her suffering, was a *pokrytka* saved by Joseph and the shepherds, and herself saved the Saviour Who brought salvation and truth to humanity.

As in 'The Bewitched Woman,' Shevchenko regards every sin, every cause of evil, as an unconscious or semiconscious phenomenon and one that is occasioned by someone or something. But underlying all the secondary hypotheses is the central question addressed to God, who could cut off evil at its source: 'Why do you punish them? Why have they been killed?' He is the ruler of the world, of mankind, of human society. And because this is so, *Kobzar* is a continuous dialogue with God.

In 'The Bewitched Woman' Shevchenko entreats God to forgive the girl and grant her happiness. But although he defends her and her right to love, that is, the heart which does not submit even in the face of a God-given thought or destiny, yet he submits to God's incomprehensible will:

O Bozhe mii mylyi! Taka tvoia volia,
Take ii shchastia, taka ii dolia.

O dear Lord! Such is your will, / Such – her fate, such – her appointed lot.

But this act of submission also contains within it the reproach

Za shcho zh ty karaiesh ii molodu?

Why do you punish her, this young maiden?

and the question

Khto ii rozkazhe?

Who will tell her?

If each man's destiny derives from God, then no one is to blame. If God Himself will not help mankind, will not lead him to the path of righteousness, then how can His obstreperous children be held to account?

The two hypotheses – first, that the world of God as it has been created gives birth to suffering and sin and hence God is the ruler of evil; and second, that people have turned God's paradise into a hell on earth – are continuously juxtaposed in Shevchenko's poetry. In 'A Prayer,' Shevchenko associates the true character of God's world in his appeals for punishment of the executioners and for revolutionary change, and prayers to God to break the eternal circle of punishment by restraining the initiators of evil. In the third version of this poem the substitution of punishment of the destructive tsars as the prime social cause of evil is accompanied by a parallel substitution of an entreaty on behalf of the toilers of the world. Thus the tsars become the originators of evil, the toiling hands, the well-intentioned. And this is not accidental because Shevchenko does not make a cult of 'the worker' – he knows that he too can initiate a new cycle of evil. If he speaks of stolen land in the second poem, in the third he simply begs God 'to show' the well-intentioned hands how to do good and with His holy powers help them to resist evil.

Yet, there are no grounds for concluding that Shevchenko finally adopted the principle of forgiveness or an antirevolutionary stance. Until his final days he entreats, reproaches, and condemns God, submits to His will and, along with his heroes, rebels against it, scoffs at his faith and prayers and reproaches himself for his lack of faith. The three-stanza structure of 'A Prayer' brings Shevchenko's world view into bold relief.

Shevchenko's notebook contains the revised versions of what he regarded as his complete works. Included here are all three versions of 'A Prayer,' which indicates that these are not of one poem, but of the poet's own viewpoint. This can only be explained by the fact that his searches, his world view, do not fit into any definitive system. His was not only a never-ending movement towards truth but also a search for the path to truth itself and the criteria by which to find it.

Thus it does not seem accidental that in all Shevchenko's principal philosophical works (from 'Kateryna' to 'Mariia' and the Hebraic cycle of biblical 'imitations'), the images of road, crossroads, and quest are important. The main events in Shevchenko's poetry all occur on the road or by the roadside. Kateryna takes to the road in search of her beloved, Ivas's father; she meets him on the road, there entreats and curses him. Mariia-Mary gives birth to Jesus while on the road. A maiden is transformed into a poplar by the roadside. Brothers, sons, and betrothed young men who leave for the Sich say their farewells on the road. On the road beside a fence the oppressed rest, suffer, and die.

Kateryna's principal sin is her refusal to tread life's path. (On the religious level her 'aimless wandering,' her repudiation of life and her request that her son search for his father himself and thus expiate her sin, is a refusal to seek a path to God. Mariia becomes the protectress because she

expiates her human sin by submitting to her destiny and going with her
son to His Golgotha and further – to her own death.)

It is easy to follow the 'beaten path.' Yet, the road *will* persist in leading
to a crossroads. At the crossroads is the *kobzar*, the bard of truth and of
the past, of human sorrows and joys, of the future, the one who brings the
word of God to man because he himself communes with Him. At the
crossroads is Shevchenko, Šafařik, the prophets.

At the crossroads a path must be chosen. All men must choose, the
prophets, the bards of the law of truth, those who participate in a dialogue
with God. But Shevchenko knows that, even after choosing a path, we will
reach another crossroads and there will again be that despair that comes
when there is no known truth to guide us. The quest of truth is the eternal
quest for those paths which must be followed in order that good may be
confirmed.

The indeterminism that characterizes the crossroads of history, the
eternal mystery that is the truth of God and man, is characteristic of both
Shevchenko's perception of the world and of the structure of his poetry.
The two versions of Shevchenko's prayer – the revolutionary prayer (the
prayer-revanche) and the prayer for absolution – are two ways to truth: the
path of truth as vengeance, a truth in arms, a bloody truth (Chernyshevsky's 'Call upon Rus to take up the axe' and Shevchenko's 'to sharpen the
axe well' / 'dobre vyhostryt sokyru') and the path of truth as love, of
forgiveness, of Christ. These two paths contradict and yet complete one
another, co-existing in Shevchenko's world view. The three-stanza poem 'A
Prayer' is a model of Shevchenko's dialogue with the world, humanity, and
God, constructed upon complementary, if occasionally inconsistent, models
of the world and the path to its renewal. This model can be compared with
our current model of the world. The century-old discussion surrounding
the opposing wave and quantum hypotheses about the nature of light was
resolved in quantum mechanics, where both theories were incorporated into
a unified model in which light is seen both as the quanta or particles and
as waves in an electromagnetic field.

If even physical phenomena cannot be described by a single consistent
system or model, how can we expect this in modelling an infinite world?
The inconsistency of Shevchenko's poetry is the inconsistency of life
itself. Built into the very heart of Shevchenko's poetry is the indeterminism, the 'chaos,'[15] inherent in his models, which gives rise to dia-

logue, a complementary structure, the philosophical journey[16] rather than the philosophical system, the peculiarities of the style and structure of *Kobzar*.

Shevchenko's complex philosophy inevitably yields a wide variety of ideological interpretations of and speculations about his poetry. A multi-faceted study of the poetic and ideological structure of *Kobzar* is needed, one that would take account of the poet's evolution. The poetic and ideological structure must be studied from various points of view that would give due consideration to the biographical, psychological, and historical contexts of Shevchenko's poetry.

This article has simply identified the principal focus of Shevchenko's philosophical and poetic quest, the problem which he set himself from the beginning: of human suffering, theodicy, and communion with God. Each aspect of Shevchenko's quest discussed requires special study and should be supplemented by the study of other problems in much greater detail.

(1978)

NOTES

1 Written for this volume. The Ukrainian text has been published in *Suchasnist* (1979) III.

2 V. Barka, *Pravda Kobzaria* (New York 1961).

3 In spite of the universal interest it has attracted, Dostoevsky's philosophy remains subject to speculation and the basis for totally opposing currents of thought because Dostoevsky the publicist and Dostoevsky the artist are different. Russian messianism, even if fascist, and Russian humanism both draw support from Dostoevsky, while in the most recent decade even Russian 'communism' has begun to feed upon him.

4 I do not refer here to the unofficial scholarship, such as, for example, unpublished studies by Mykhailyna Kotsiubynska and the works of Ie. Sverstiuk and others that have appeared in *samovydav* publications. Unfortunately, almost none of this 'dissident' criticism has reached the West.

5 Iu. Ivakin, *Komentar do 'Kobzaria' Shevchenka* (Kiev 1964).

6 By S. Iefremov, Ie. Sverstiuk, and in certain measure V. Barka, although the latter examines Shevchenko's religious views in a more all-embracing manner.

7 There were such periods, but they are characterized by a deepening of the inconsistency of his world view rather than by a reduction of it to single, fixed ideology.

8 For a definition of 'carnivalesque' literature see M. Bakhtin, *Problemy poetiki Dostoevskogo* (Moscow 1972).

9 The influence of the Ukrainian carnivalesque tradition on the works of Gogol was established by Bakhtin some time ago.

10 M. Rylsky, not an untalented poet himself, challenges the validity of this thesis: 'Mariia,' 'Neofty' (The Neophytes), 'Sotnyk' (The Captain), 'Iurody-vyi' (God's Fool), such lyrical poems as 'I Arkhimed, i Halilei' (Archimedes and Galileo), 'Sontse zakhodyt, hory chorniiut' (The sun goes down, the hills grow black), 'Ohni horiat' (Fires blaze), the three-stanza poems 'Dolia' (Fate), 'Muza' (The Muse), 'Slava' (Glory), he says, are living proof that this is not so. By offering this list, Rylsky demonstrates that he does not understand the precise nature of Shevchenko's poetry which, availing itself widely of achievements in folklore, is an original and unique monument. If one were inclined to compile such a list, it would be more appropriate to rely upon the truly folkloristic poems: there are quite a few of them and they were necessary for Shevchenko precisely as a way to gain a deeper mastery of the potential and achievements of folklore.

11 P. Kulish, 'Kazky i baiky z susidovoi khaty,' *Vybrani tvory* (Kiev 1969) 526.

12 In 'Topolia' (The Poplar) this theme receives a fuller treatment.

13 This could be Kateryna from the poem of the same name.

14 This could be the mother from either 'Rusalka' (The Water Nymph) or 'Utoplena' (The Drowned Maiden).

15 We adopt this conception of philosophy, relying upon Professor Miall's analysis of the differences between the traditions of European philosophy and certain Eastern currents of thought.

16 This explains the prevalence in *Kobzar* of drunken and insane songs, songs of water nymphs, songs that are fantasies, absurdities. This is not merely the protest of rational thought against social chaos and absurdity, or a surrealist heightening of a real absurdity, but also a reflection of the essential omnipresence, uncertainty, and indeterminism of the crossroads, and of the entropy and despair encountered there.

27

A Consideration of the Deep Structures in Shevchenko's Works

GEORGE G. GRABOWICZ

Beginning with the first ambivalent reactions in the Russian press to the first edition of the *Kobzar* of 1840, and shortly thereafter with the more analytical studies of Kulish and Kostomarov, the critical genre now known as *Shevchenkoznavstvo* came to occupy an ever more prominent role in Ukrainian life. The critical, scholarly, panegyrical, ideological, and polemical attention devoted to Shevchenko and his writings has been immense – and immensely diverse. Some considerable results have been achieved, particularly in textual studies (including, of course, publication of the entire canon of Shevchenko's works and many facsimile editions), in historical and biographical documentation, in matters of prosody, poetic language, and some formal analyses. On the other hand, the meaning and the broader social, historical (and, need one add, political) implications of Shevchenko's work, specifically his poetry, have been and remain the source of intense and acrimonious differences. The ideologically polarized interpretations of the present day, with each side accusing the other of 'falsifying Shevchenko,' not only reflect the peculiarity of the Ukrainian political situation but in fact are also a logical culmination of the entire critical legacy. In a deeper sense, however, these divergences stem from the very nature of Shevchenko's poetry.

It is a poetry that touched the innermost core of the Ukrainian experience. In the words of Mykola Kostomarov, 'Shevchenko's muse sundered the veil of national life. It was terrifying and sweet and painful and fascinating to peer inside.'[1] Panteleimon Kulish, himself a tragic and fascinating individual, who was at once a continuator and exegete, rival and opponent of Shevchenko, put it even more directly in his eloquent funeral oration in

St Petersburg. 'None of us is worthy,' he said, 'to speak our native Ukrainian word over the grave of Schevchenko: all the power and all the beauty of our language were revealed only to him alone. And yet it is through him that we have the great and precious right to proclaim the native Ukrainian word in this distant land.'[2] It was Kulish who said that 'Shevchenko is our great poet and our first historian. It was Shevchenko who was the first to ask our mute burial mounds what they are, and it was only to him that they gave their answer, clear as God's word. Before all others Shevchenko realized what the glory of our antiquity is and what it will be cursed for by coming generations.'[3] As eloquent and true as these statements were, their implicit thesis – swelled in time by various less profound commentaries – soon gave rise to a mass of misconceptions. In a word, because of its unprecedented emotional directness and immediacy Shevchenko's poetry, his 'message,' was seen as essentially straightforward, indeed simple. Hand in hand with the growing cult of Shevchenko, his poetic *œuvre* came to be viewed as a convenient repository of handy bits of sentiment:

> Selo! i sertse odpochyne.
> Sela na nashii Ukraini –
> Nenache pysanka selo ...

A village! and the heart will rest / A village in our Ukraine / A village like an Easter egg ...

or of pious pedagogic injunctions:

> Uchites, chytaite,
> I chuzhomu nauchaites,
> I svoho ne tsuraites ...

Study, read, / Learn foreign subjects / But do not deny your own ...

or of political prescriptions:

>   ... Koly
> My dizhdemosia Vashingtona
> Z novym i pravednym zakonom?

When / Shall we see a Washington / With a new and just law?

or:

> V svoii khati svoia i pravda,
> I syla, i volia ...

In one's own house – one's own truth / And power and freedom ...

or finally of revolutionary calls to arms:

> Pokhovaite ta vstavaite,
> Kaidany porvite
> I vrazhoiu zloiu kroviu
> Voliu okropite.

Bury me and rise, / Break your chains / And with the enemy's evil blood / Sprinkle your freedom.

Most significantly, the practice of rifling the poetry for the appropriate sententia was not confined to propagandists, journalists, or school teachers – it also became the methodology for much of what passed as scholarship. By far the worst offenders were the engagé ideologues whose only method of discussing, for example, Shevchenko's alleged atheism or conversely his religiosity and piety, was simply the culling of citations to be interpreted by free association. In the absence of any rigorous and comprehensive method for dealing with the levels of meaning and symbolism in Shevchenko's works, the study of Shevchenko's writings became increasingly moribund – both in the Soviet Union and in the West. In fact, it was only the rare and outstanding scholar who ventured to remind his colleagues that the fundamental issues had still not been confronted. Such, for example, was the dean of Soviet Ukrainian literary scholars, Oleksander Biletsky, who at the ninth Shevchenko Conference held in 1960 in Leningrad, in a period of relative thaw, attempted to curb various endemic forms of vulgarization and inanity – and redirect the efforts of Soviet *Shevchenkoznavstvo*.[4] In the West, specifically in the emigration, the opportunity for free intellectual inquiry did not galvanize Ukrainian scholarship, and the Shevchenko scholarship that was undertaken was in its literary-critical conceptions and methods essentially parallel to, if not imitative of, what was being done in the Soviet Union; sadly, no new approaches were forthcoming. Perhaps the single exception was the *Symposium* published in 1962 under the editorship of Miiakovsky and Shevelov, which contained a number of fine articles. From our perspective the most provocative was the one by the late Mykola Shlemkevych which proposed to deal with 'The Substratum of Shevchenko's View of Life' through a kind of Jungian depth psychology.[5] The various insights presented here, however, were made rather on the basis of intuition than on scholarly method or mode of analysis; indeed – very revealingly – he doubted whether such investigations could readily be made the stuff of scholarship.

To sum up this brief summary, it is clear that there exists in modern Shevchenko scholarship (albeit still in a limited way) the understanding that Shevchenko's imaginative universe is highly symbolic and coded, and that beneath the surface structures – which I take to encompass not only such matters as ideology and in general the whole sphere of rational elaborations, programs, and so on, but also such things as conventions, that is literary romantic conventions – there are much more important deep structures. However, the deep structures and the symbolic code in which they are couched, have not been investigated at all. And it is to this that I wish to address myself.

The first issue to which we come, which is at the same time the most basic structure in Shevchenko's creativity, concerns the context, or rather the *placing in context* of the various forms and modes of his expression. It flows from the fundamental holistic premise that systematic analysis must deal with the whole of the phenomenon. Shevchenko, as everyone knows, *is* what he is by virtue of his poetic production, his Ukrainian poetry; but what many (including scholars) tend to gloss over, and many more probably indeed do not know, is that this is a segment – in quantitative terms a smaller segment – of his whole self-expression. In addition to the Ukrainian poetry, with which he is so often exclusively identified, Shevchenko also wrote some Russian poetry (two long poems), a considerable body of prose in Russian (by his own account about twenty novellas, of which nine have survived), a diary written in Russian that covers a crucial year of his life, a sizeable epistolary legacy in Ukrainian and Russian, a few prose fragments in Ukrainian, three or four dramas in Russian (of which two have survived, one in prose, in a Ukrainian translation probably made by

Kulish, and an unfinished one in verse), and a large body of pictorial art – paintings, drawings, and etchings, which while certainly pertinent to the overall question, will not concern us here.

One need not be a scholar and a specialist but only an informed and sensitive reader to see that there is a profound difference between the Ukrainian poetry on the one hand, and on the other all the other forms of expression. Let us provisionally call these the two basic categories in question. Leaving aside for the moment the obviously different mode of non-belletristic writings (letters, etc.) one could simply say that the difference between the two categories hinges on aesthetic and artistic quality – and the lack of it: where the Ukrainian poetry is powerful and moving and very often great, the other writings are often only good and frequently mediocre. While true, this does not suffice as an answer. For the task now is not to evaluate the works or categories in question but to determine their essential differences, their mode of existence, as it were. Ultimately, the aesthetic and artistic values are based on these differences.

One possible immediate answer is that the difference here is one of poetry and prose. Closer analysis, however, shows that while there is considerable consistency, this is not the basis for the fundamental divergences in question. One could show, for example, that various pieces of Shevchenko's Ukrainian prose, such as his postscript to the *Haidamaky*, or the preface to the unpublished second *Kobzar*, or fragments of various letters, are much closer to the spirit of his Ukrainian poetry than is the Russian poem *Trizna* (The Wake). This, of course, leads us to the most obvious and most frequently noted basis of differentiation, namely language. There is a whole critical legacy, going back to Kulish and still favoured by the nationalistically minded, that sees between Shevchenko's Ukrainian- and Russian-language works the basic division in his entire canon; it is, of course, explicitly evaluative (not to say biased), and, taking its cue from a statement made by Shevchenko himself in one of his letters where he castigated himself for confessing to the Russians in stale Russian ('spovidaiusia katsapam cherstvym katsapskym slovom ...'), it sees all of Shevchenko's Russian writings as inherently flawed (if not a betrayal of his Muse) by the very choice of linguistic medium.[6] Even more than the opposition of poetry and prose, this language criterion has validity: the Ukrainian works are strikingly different from, and as a rule greatly superior to the Russian ones. But this criterion as well does not provide the solution, for two reasons. One is the exceptions that undercut the whole equation: the Russian poem 'Slepaia' (The Blind Woman) or the fragments of 'Nikita Gaidai' are much closer to the spirit of the Ukrainian poetry than some of the Ukrainian letters. Similarly, we have the problem posed by the *Diary* – a work that is manifestly excellent and intimate – but is written in Russian. The other and much more important reason, however, is that merely stating (and then evaluating) the existence of these two classes of works leaves the entire question open: we are left no wiser as to what is and what can be said in the given medium, as to what is the structure of the respective contents of these two categories. This is precisely the task at hand.

Before turning to it I should like to adduce the following to illustrate my argument. As everyone who reads him knows, Shevchenko's poetry is highly personal, intimate, and autobiographical; if one deciphers the code of the narrative and 'political' poems, then, as we shall see, the autobiographical element appears to be virtually ever-present. But if we look at what is actually portrayed or alluded to, a most fascinating picture develops, for we see that whole segments of Shevchenko's life, indeed most of his mature life, remain outside the range of his poetry. There is, for example, no reference at all to his life in St Petersburg and the Academy of Arts (which as we know from his own novel *Khudozhnik* (The Artist) were so important to him), no reference to the time spent in Ukraine and his many contacts with the Ukrainians, especially the Brotherhood of Saints Cyril and Methodius, in fact no reference even to the momentous event of being freed from serfdom. The only apparent exceptions to this are the first years of exile and the last months of his life; on closer analysis, however, the exile poems are not an exception, and the very late poetry is also quite ambivalent in this regard. The issue is not even so much one of chronology, of time gaps, as of subject matter, of content. We know from Shevchenko's own writings – the autobiographical novels, the *Diary*, the letters – and from numerous other sources, such as the memoirs and letters of friends and acquaintances – of the kind of life he lived, not only in St Petersburg, in Kiev, in his travels in Ukraine, but indeed (and *mutatis mutandis*) at times even in exile, that is, in the first two years in Orenburg. It was the active, intense, and full life of a young artist and littérateur; it was full of social and intellectual contacts, of literary salons, theatres, and the opera. It was the life of an attractive young man accepted in the highest society, esteemed and in fact lionized by both Russians and Ukrainians. Given Shevchenko's origins this was, in a word, a remarkable success story. And yet literally none of this is reflected in his poetry. The only thing more remarkable than this massive 'blind spot' of his poetic creativity is the blindness of generations of Shevchenko scholars to this crucial situation.[7]

Now, I believe, we *can* define the basic duality in Shevchenko's creativity. It is a duality, an opposition, that rests on two very different creative stances, different self-perceptions and self-definitions, and entirely different intellectual and emotional modes of expression. In fact, one should not speak here of different stances, or styles, but of different personalities. Although I shall briefly refer to the psychoanalytic dimension in Shevchenko's creativity, I do not want this structure to be reduced solely to the psychoanalytic level, to an ego-split, or dissociation. For one, there is considerable interplay, in terms of common themes and values, as in *Naimychka* (The Servant Girl), the poem and the novella, or 'Kniazhna' (The Princess), and *Kniaginia* (The Princess); for another there are elements involved other than the purely psychological. The two entities are not hermetic, but they *are* radically different.

What are these two personalities? One, which is represented by the Russian prose, the *Diary*, the letters, and so on is what I would call the adjusted. Even while speaking out most forcefully against the inequities of the social order, above all the unspeakable outrage of serfdom, it manifestly sees itself as part of the imperial reality, and shares many of the civilized, progressive values of this society. The basic defining features of this mode are a sense of intellectual distance (for example, with respect to Ukrainian history), a sense of perspective on the role of Ukraine vis-à-vis the Russian Empire, and on the role and efficacy of the artist (for example, in the novels *Khudozhnik*, or *Muzykant* [The Musician]), a rational and basically measured perception of human behaviour, and, not least, the point of view of the mature self.

The other, represented primarily by the poetry, is what I would call, for want of a better term, the non-adjusted self. Shevchenko himself felt full well the power of this side of his ego, which in his *Diary* he saw as being animated by a 'strange and restless calling,' but he made no attempt to analyse it.[8] We, however, can do so. This personality is marked above all by an intense emotionality, and of the emotional perception of reality, which in consequence becomes totally or almost totally polarized into the sacred and the profane. In its sharpest form the world, mankind, is often divided into absolute good and absolute evil. But the poet himself is so polarized: he or his persona is either the victim, one of the lowly and despised – the bastard, the blind, vagabond minstrel, the fallen woman (the *pokrytka*) – or even the moral reprobate (see, for example, the poem 'Chy to nedolia ta nevolia ...' / 'Is it ill fate and captivity ...'), or he is the martyr and the prophet, the last hope of his nation. Significantly, there is hardly any middle ground: there is, rather, the apotheosis, again of the sacred and the profane. In contrast to the adjusted and the rational, this mode refuses to accept and abide by the truths and wisdoms of this world; it conjures up and revives the past that for everyone else is dead. But he wills it alive, as he says in the opening lines of 'Chernets' (The Monk):

U Kyievi na Podoli
Bulo kolys ... i nikoly
Ne vernetsia, shcho diialos
Ne vernetsia spodivane
Ne vernetsia ... A ia, brate,
Taky budu spodivatys,
Taky budu vyhliadaty,
Zhaliu sertsiu zavdavaty ...

In Kiev, in the Podil / There once was ... and what occurred / Will never return / What was hoped for will not return / Will not return ... and yet, brother, / I will continue to hope, / I will continue to expect, / To inflict sorrow on my heart ...

It is a mode that relies on visions to convey the past and the future, and when it turns to the present it does not present realia, but rather the depths of the whole collective soul, as he says,

... nevchene oko
Zahliane ... v samu dushu
Hlyboko! hlyboko!

... the untutored eye / Will look deep, deep into the very soul!

From the chronological or biographical point of view there is also a radical difference, for in contrast to the mature, man-of-the-world narrator and authorial ego of the novels, for example, the perspective of the authorial ego here is moulded – not equivalent to but moulded – by the child and the old man. Indeed, he at times explicitly conflates the two, as in the wonderful exile lyric 'A numo znovu virshuvat ...' / 'So let us versify again ...' where he conjures up the grey-whiskered child:

... bach, shcho [dolia] narobyla:
Kynula maloho
Na rozputti, ta i baiduzhe,
A vono ubohe,
Molodeie, syvouse, –
Zvychaine, dytyna –
I podybalo tykhenko
Popid chuzhym tynom
Azh za Ural. Opynylos
V pustyni, v nevoli ...

... see what [fate] has done: / She abandoned the little one / At the crossroads, and she doesn't care, / And it is poor, / Young, grey-whiskered, – / Just a child – / And quietly it dragged itself / Along someone's fence / Beyond the Urals. It arrived / In the desert, in captivity ...

In the sense that the world of the poetry is moulded primarily by the experiences and emotions of childhood (cf. for example, *Haidamaky*) (a childhood moreover that contains the principal narrative model of the minstrel-kobzar) we can speak of it – descriptively, not evaluatively – as regressed. This regression, however, is the source of the poetry's imaginative power and the foundation of its symbolic code. Again it is the power of this unadjusted, rebelling personality that must be stressed, for its effects are clearly visible to this day. For in contravention of the real state of affairs, and the large body of evidence that buttresses it, the picture now in the minds of millions of his countrymen, and indeed of many scholars, is that projected by Shevchenko's poetry: of Shevchenko the martyr and prophet living only in and for his *narod*. This has become the real Shevchenko. As the Parisian structuralists would say, he has become the product of his own myth.

My awareness of the fundamental dichotomy in Shevchenko's writings allows me to posit, perhaps for the first time with some rigour, a framework for dealing with the symbolic code of his poetry. Two basic lines of inquiry are possible, corresponding to the two basic levels of the code. One is the psychoanalytic, which deals above all with the author's symbolic autobiography. One can hardly offer conclusions or summaries without reconstructing a rather complex analysis, and for this reason I shall leave this for another occasion. Instead I propose to turn to the other level of the code, that of mythical structures. It must be stressed that the parallel existence of a psychoanalytic, that is, a personal – symbolically autobiographical – and a mythical, collective system of coding constitutes the second basic deep structure, which we now see as contained in the poetry itself.

Let me now summarize what I mean by mythical thinking, by the mythical organization of thought and experience. It is a mode that moves from structures to events: one starts with a structure, which in the case of Shevchenko is a sense, an understanding, a deeply felt 'truth' of, say, the nature of Ukrainian existence, and from this one creates or adapts various events or figures, for example an archetypal Cossack, or a purported historical event. Mythical thought is the opposite of rational, analytical, historical thought, which takes a discrete body of data, that is, events, and by analysis and deduction sees a pattern or meaning or structure in them. (Mythical and rational thought can co-exist, however, in the thinking of the individual and the group.) Moving as it does from structure to event, myth can generate any number of narratives, all of which convey the same basic structure or 'truth.' What in Shevchenko has traditionally been called history is in fact myth – the portrayal of the Ukrainian past – but with almost no regard for chronology, or dates, or concrete events or figures. Above all in myth, things are telescoped; we see this highlighted in a number of poems, in *Velykyi lokh* (The Great Vault), in *Chyhryne, Chyhryne*, and perhaps most strikingly in the poem *Slipyi (Nevolnyk)* (The Blind Man [The Captive]) which apparently in the lifetime of the title character encompasses the whole history of Cossackdom, from the sea raids against Turkey in the sixteenth century, to the destruction of the Sich and the creation of the Zadunaiska Sich in the late eighteenth century. A different kind of telescoping occurs in *Haidamaky*, where in contravention of historical fact, but because of the requirement of the structure, the haidamaks, the peasant rebels, are identified with Cossacks, which is a very different kind of thing.

Myth, and Shevchenko's is a quintessential example, operates on the emotional level; it is this which allows it to be understood by the mass of the audience – for it is geared to them, not the thoughtful or learned individual. Here is the very core of the difference between Shevchenko and Kulish, for the latter, in his novel *Chorna rada* (The Black Council), intended to present history rationally and even analytically; and it is not surprising that Kulish's work did not have even a fraction of the resonance of Shevchenko's so-called historical poems.

Shevchenko's poetry may be classified according to three different formal modes of presentation: (1) the tribunitial and prophetic poems, for example, 'Poslaniie' (I mertvym i zhyvym ...) (Epistle [To the Dead and the Living]), 'Kavkaz' (The Caucasus), 'Prorok' (The Prophet), the paraphrases of the Old Testament Prophets, and so on; (2) the intimate or 'purely lyrical' short poems, many written during exile, and (3) the longer narrative poems. The latter group, including such poems as 'Kateryna,' 'Haidamaky,' 'Vidma' (The Witch), 'Kniazhna' (The Princess), 'Slipyi' (The Blind Man), 'Moskaleva krynytsia' (The Soldier's Well) both versions), 'Tytarivna' (The Sexton's Daughter), 'Mariia,' and others, is by far more complex and in one sense more interesting, but, significantly, the least attention has been paid to it. Yet it is precisely here, with the almost obsessive repetition of motifs and patterns of movement and character, that we see the nature of Shevchenko's imaginative world at its best. For as in true myth (that is, primitive or classical), the essential unit is a narrative; and having established by comparison and superimposition the underlying structures in these 'versions' we can decode the whole. The redundancy, in fact, the repetition of patterns, the 'excess of information' (to which Shevchenko himself sometimes ironically refers: 'duzhe vzhe i meni samomu / Obrydly tii muzhyky, / Ta panychi, ta pokrytky' / 'I myself am very fed up / with these peasants, / and lordlings, and seduced girls'), is a sign of the mythical mode. The only means of 'defence' that myth has against deformation and against failure of memory is not the accuracy of the account – it is precisely the details that are first deformed and forgotten – but repetition through different versions. Ultimately, however, the first two categories as well, that is, the non-narrative poems, also express the same myth, though they tend to focus on one aspect of it.

At its most basic, Shevchenko's myth of Ukraine, like that of his countryman, Gogol, shows a world divided against itself; in more technical language, a situation of permanent asymmetry, with no hope of mediation.

As in Gogol, one side is the male, the Cossack, the mobile or nomadic, and the other the female, the peasant, and the settled world. (The similarity is to be fully expected, since both writers are expressing a common collective experience; on the other hand there will also be some significant differences.) The unresolved conflict between the two sides, their inability to develop and reproduce, is the curse of this world. Significantly (again as in Gogol), this is shown from both perspectives. From the perspective of the woman's world it is conveyed by the pattern of love (or sex), followed by desertion and then by transformation, either by death ('Kateryna') or transformation into the non-human, into nature, for example, in 'Topolia' (The Poplar). As part of nature this side survives, but neither is it capable of true, human life. The most revealing work in this category is 'Utoplena' (The Drowned Girl), which in the murder of the daughter by the mother to frustrate her union or symbolic marriage with the fisherman shows the working of the curse at its starkest.[9] In the present, all that remains of Ukraine is a suspended, helpless feminine world – the world of serfs tied to the land but with no memory of their glorious past, with no sense of identity, of descendants of Cossacks now willing slaves to tsarist despotism. It is a world of fallen women and illegitimate children; its cursed victimized state of being is stressed by the recurring motifs of incest and rape.

Once there was a golden age, not only of glory but also of harmonious existence; this is more alluded to than described, however. The great number of poems written from the male, Cossack perspective also show the workings of the curse – the impossibility of marrying, of vagabond wandering, and above all, insistently, of death. The image of the Cossack is invariably linked with the image of the grave, the burial mound, as in 'Ivan Pidkova':

> Bulo kolys – zaporozhtsi
> Vmily panuvaty.
> Panuvaly, dobuvaly
> I slavu i voliu, –
> Mynulosia: ostalysia
> Mohyly po poliu.

There was a time when the Zaporozhians / Knew how to rule. / They ruled and captured / Glory and freedom. / It has passed: there remain / Burial mounds in the fields.

The structure conveyed here, however, is not only that the Cossacks are now dead and in the past, but even more that they were precisely carriers of death, and they brought death to their people, the brother-peasants. And for this, as we see so vividly in 'Za bairakom bairak' (Beyond the Ravine, Another Ravine), in the words of the Cossack's song, they are cursed by a living death, by their descendants forgetting their memory, by the very earth refusing to accept them:

– Nanosyly zemli
Ta i dodomu pishly,
I nikhto ne zhadaie.
Nas tut trysta, iak sklo,
Tovarystva liahlo!
I zemlia ne pryimaie.
Iak zaprodav hetman
U iarmo khrystyian
Nas poslav pohaniaty.
Po svoii po zemli
Svoiu krov rozlyly
I zarizaly brata.
Krovy brata vpylys
I otut poliahly
U mohyli zakliatii.

They heaped up the earth / And went home, / And no one remembers. / Three hundred of us comrades, pure as glass, / Have perished here! / And the earth does not receive us. / When the hetman sold / The Christians into slavery / He sent us to drive them along. / On our soil / We shed our blood / And butchered our brothers. / Having drunk our brothers' blood / We have fallen here / In this cursed burial mound.

The most drastic instance of the destructiveness of the Cossack world comes in *Haidamaky* as Honta kills his children; as in its feminine counterpart, 'Utoplena,' this is also a symbolic killing of the mediating element, of any hope for reconciling opposites. And although it is given an 'ideological' elaboration, that is, that this is a form of holy vengeance against the Poles, the deep structure is unaffected by it.

There is also a third perspective. Where Gogol saw the Ukrainian curse as unresolved and unresolvable and fled to a different reality, Shevchenko does provide a resolution. It is a ritual mediation made by himself as the myth-carrier. The only resolution – and he is the only one to provide it – is to retell the past, to resurrect memory and identity, to open the eyes and ears of his debased countrymen to the great ruin that Ukraine has become. He does this in two ways: in the overt mode of the political poems where his impassioned appeals and invocations give a rational elaboration to what he had already presented in the structure of myth, and also on a more symbolic level where he becomes the martyr whose expiation will signal a new beginning. The images used to convey this are grandiose indeed: he is the martyr Hus and Prometheus, the holy tree (in 'U Boha za dvermy lezhala sokyra' / 'An Axe Lay behind God's Door') and the oak that represents Ukraine (in 'Buvaly voiny ...' / 'There had been wars ...'); he not only speaks *with* God as the sole representative of his people ('Zapovit' [Testament]) but in the very voice *of* God, in his paraphrase of *Hosea* Chap. 14. Yet this is precisely the domain of the myth-carrier, the shaman, to mediate for his people between the earth and the sky, the past and the future, to provide for their most fundamental spiritual needs. Shevchenko's claim to this role seems to have been substantiated by later history.

(1980)

NOTES

1 M. Kostomarov, 'Spohady pro dvokh maliariv,' in *Spohady pro Shevchenka* (Kiev 1958) 447.

2 P. Kulish, 'Slovo nad hrobom Shevchenka,' *Tvory Panteleimona Kulisha,* 6 (Lviv 1910) 495-6. See translation in this volume.

3 P. Kulish, 'Choho stoit Shevchenko iako poet narodnii,' *ibid.* 490. See translation in this volume.

4 O. Biletsky, 'Zavdannia i perspektyvy vyvchennia Shevchenka,' in *Zbirnyk prats deviatoi naukovoi shevchenkivskoi konferentsii* (Kiev 1961) 13-25.

5 M. Shlemkevych, 'The Substratum of Ševčenko's View of Life,' in *Taras Ševcenko 1814-1861: A Symposium* (The Hague 1962) 37-61. See also his 'Hlybynna verstva svitohliadu Shevchenka,' *Verkhy zhyttia i tvorchosty* (New York 1958) 61-108.

6 Cf. the letter to Ia. Kukharenko dated 30 September 1842. This problem, obviously, has not been given adequate attention. Some critics maintain that Shevchenko wrote in Russian to prove to the sceptics that he was proficient in the language, or, alternatively, because the addressee (in this case Princess Barbara Repnina, to whom Shevchenko dedicated his *Trizna*) did not know Ukrainian, or, finally, because he felt that by writing in Russian his opposition to serfdom would get the widest dissemination. In Soviet Shevchenko scholarship this question is also frequently answered by the assertion that Shevchenko wrote in Russian in order to demonstrate his progressive love for the great Russian people and to strengthen the friendship between the two brotherly peoples.

All these arguments are unpersuasive. They reduce a question of creativity to the level of pragmatism and to speculation about Shevchenko's extra-literary motivation. Such speculation is not only indeterminate, by the fact that it allows no verification, but also beside the point: the question that must be asked is not *why* Shevchenko wrote in Russian, but *what* and *how* he wrote in this language.

One may also mention here an interesting argument by one émigré critic, R. Bzhesky (cf. R. Zadnipriansky, *Chy Shevchenko buv 'malorosom'?* [np, 1946] and R. Zadesniansky, *Apostol ukrainskoi natsionalnoi revoliutsii* [Munich 1969]). He thinks that Shevchenko wrote in Russian, particularly his *Diary* and the novels, in order to mislead the gendarmes and various police spies into thinking that he was a loyal 'Little Russian.' The argument is interesting in that it is a classic example of the paranoid thinking so prevalent in the emigration.

7 To be sure, some of Shevchenko's poems do have a more or less clear relation to the current biographical or historical state of affairs. Above all, this is seen in the titles; for example: 'Na vichnu pamiat Kotliarevskomu,' 'Hoholiu,' 'Kostomarovu,' 'Kozachkovskomu,' 'Sestri,' 'Lykeri,' and so on, or in the dedications to the various poems, eg, to Balmen ('Kavkaz'), to Zhukovsky ('Kateryna'), to Shchepkin ('Neofity' and 'Zahovory meni volkhve'), to Šafařik ('Ieretyk'), to Chernenko, Makarov, and others. Even if in the broad sense these elements are part of the text, they are not part of the poetry. They are rather a unique frame for the work. In a sense they mediate between the world of Shevchenko's poetry and his everyday world. It is significant that for the most part the dedications (to Balmen, Zhukovsky, Kostomarov, and so on) and the dates – always! – are written in Russian, not Ukrainian.

The situation is similar in the physical context. Even when Shevchenko is in Ukraine, Subotiv, or Pereiaslav, for example, the Ukraine that he depicts in his poetry is different from the one everyone else sees, and in which he exists. We know, for example, that Shevchenko was a diligent and enthusiastic member of the Kievan Archeographic Commission and that he partook in the excavation of various burial mounds (eg, Perepiatykha, near Khvastiv), but we also see how he represents all this in his poetry, say in 'Velykyi lokh' or in 'Rozryta mohyla.'

Finally, this also has serious methodological implications. It shows that all attempts (which Soviet critics are so ready to undertake; see Ivakin) to understand Shevchenko's poetry through correlation with current events, acquaintances, possible reading material, and so on, are without any likelihood of success.

8 Cf. the entry for 1 July 1857.

9 The words of the young fisherman, his only words in the text, stress that the killing of the daughter also spells death for any continuity, normal life, hopes for the future:

– Nema v mene rodu,
 Nema doli na sim sviti, –
 Khodim zhyty v vodu!

I have no kin, / There is no luck in this world, / Come, let us live in the water!

Contributors

VOLODYMYR ANTONOVYCH (1834-1908). Historian and archaeologist, professor at Kiev University. Active in public life as head of the Kiev 'Old Hromada'

KORNEI CHUKOVSKY (1882-1969). Prominent Russian writer and critic. Chukovsky's mother came from Ukraine.

DMYTRO CHYZHEVSKY (1894-1977). Distinguished Slavist, professor at Marburg, Harvard, and Heidelberg universities. Author of many scholarly works, among them a history of Ukrainian literature.

MYKHAILO DRAHOMANOV (1841-95). Political thinker and scholar, father of Ukrainian socialism. After 1875 lived as an émigré in Switzerland and later in Bulgaria. Many of his works deal with Ukrainian literature.

MYKHAILO DRAI-KHMARA (1889-?). Poet and scholar. Member of the Neoclassicists, a literary group. Arrested in 1935, died in a concentration camp.

IVAN FRANKO (1856-1916). Writer, scholar, and social activist. Leading figure in the cultural and social life of Galicia.

PAVLO FYLYPOVYCH (1891-?). Poet and literary critic. Sentenced in 1936 to ten years' deportation. Died in a concentration camp.

GEORGE GRABOWICZ. Associate professor of Slavic literature at Harvard University.

BORYS HRINCHENKO (1863-1910). Novelist, critic, and lexicographer.

MYKOLA HUDZII (1887-1965). Ukrainian scholar who was for a long time professor of Old Rus literature at Moscow University. A leading historian of Russian literature.

SERHII IEFREMOV (1876-?). Literary historian and critic. Member of the Academy of Sciences. Arrested in 1929 as the alleged leader of the Union for the Liberation of Ukraine. Perished in a concentration camp.

MYKOLA IEVSHAN (1889-1919), pseudonym of M. Fediushka. Literary critic in the modernist circle around the journal *Ukrainska khata*.

PANTELEIMON KULISH (1819-97). Poet, novelist, and historian. A friend of Shevchenko, and one of his first critics. A complex and contradictory personality, Kulish played a prominent part in Ukrainian cultural life.

GEORGE LUCKYJ. Professor of Ukrainian and Russian literature at the University of Toronto.

VOLODYMYR MIIAKOVSKY (1888-1972). Archivist, librarian, and literary historian. Specialized in research into the Brotherhood of Saints Cyril and Methodius.

MYKHAILO MOHYLIANSKY (1873-1944). Publicist and literary critic. Because of his children's arrest in the 1930s he was forced to abandon scholarship. This article appeared under the pseudonym Chubsky.

LEONID PLIUSHCH. Mathematician, leading Soviet Ukrainian dissident. Emigrated to the West in 1976; now living in France.

ANDRII RICHYTSKY (1882-1937). Politician and literary critic of independent Marxist views. Executed on charges of Trotskyism and counter-revolution.

BOHDAN RUBCHAK. Associate Professor, University of Illinois, Chicago Circle, and a prominent poet.

MAKSYM RYLSKY (1895-1964). Poet, literary critic, and translator. An early Neoclassicist, he made his peace with the regime and on the whole maintained his artistic integrity.

LISA SCHNEIDER. PhD candidate in Russian and Ukrainian literature at the University of Toronto. Great-granddaughter of M. Mohyliansky.

GEORGE SHEVELOV. Linguist and occasional literary critic. Professor at Kharkiv, Lund, and Columbia universities.

STEPAN SMAL-STOTSKY (1859-1938). Linguist and writer. Before the First World War, professor at Chernivtsi University and a leader in the cultural life of Bukovyna.

VICTOR SWOBODA. Senior lecturer at the School of Slavonic Studies, University of London.

Glossary

Decembrists – members of a revolutionary movement in Russia and Ukraine after the Napoleonic wars. Led by officers, they carried out a revolt in St Petersburg in December 1825, which was crushed.

Dnieper (Ukr. Dnipró) – the main river of Ukraine, which divides it into Right-Bank and Left-Bank areas. The former was under Polish rule until 1793.

Dúmy – lyric-epic folk songs about the Cossacks (16th-17th cent.). Ukrainian romantics sometimes called their own poems dumy (thoughts, meditations).

Hetmanate (Hetmánshchyna) – an autonomous Cossack state (1648-1764). Centred on the Left Bank, it also encompassed the Right Bank.

Kobzár (The Minstrel) – the title of the first collection of Shevchenko's poetry (1840). Afterwards several expanded editions of his works were, rather illogically, also given this title.

Liakhý (pl.) – a pejorative name which the Cossacks gave to the Poles.

Moskál – in Shevchenko's poems the term denotes either a soldier or a Russian.

Muzhík (Ukr. muzhýk) – a peasant.

Naród – both in Russian and in Ukrainian it could mean 'the people,' 'the peasants,' or 'the nation.'

Naródnost (Ukr. naródnist) – it has been translated as 'national spirit,' 'national character,' 'national identity,' or simply 'nationality.' It can mean any of these, depending on the context.

Otáman – a military leader of the Zaporozhian Cossacks. The elected commander of the Zaporozhian Host was called Koshevýi otáman.

Póbut – the way of life (customs and mores) of the Ukrainian village.

Prosvíta (Enlightenment) – a popular educational organization, primarily in Western Ukraine, established in 1868.

Sich – the Zaporozhian stronghold on several islands on the Dnieper. Established in the first half of the sixteenth century, it was destroyed by order of Catherine II in 1775.

Szláchta – Polish for 'lesser nobility.' Also, the term was used in Poland and Ukraine for landed gentry.

Ukrainophiles – Ukrainians who, in the

second half of the nineteenth century devoted themselves to apolitical cultural activities for the Ukrainian cause.

Zaporozhians – name of the Cossacks associated with the *Sich*. The word means 'those who live beyond the [Dnieper] rapids.'

Index